Handbook

of
Thanatology

The essential body of knowledge for
the study of death, dying, and bereavement

David Balk, *Editor-in-Chief*

Carol Wogrin, Gordon Thornton, and David Meagher,
Associate Editors

Association for Death Education and Counseling
The Thanatology Association

www.adec.org

Routledge
Taylor & Francis Group

www.routledgementalhealth.com

New York • London

Handbook of Thanatology:
The Essential Body of Knowledge for the Study of Death, Dying,
and Bereavement

For information regarding further orders or customer service, please contact Routledge at:

United States
7625 Empire Drive
Florence, Kentucky 41042-2919, USA
1-800-634-7064
www.routledgementalhealth.com

Canada
800-665-1148 (Login Canada)
orders@lb.ca

International
+44 (0) 1264 343070
Book.orders@tandf.co.uk

For information regarding ADEC certification or membership, please contact:
Association for Death Education and Counseling, The Thanatology Association
60 Revere Drive, Suite 500
Northbrook, IL 60062, USA
847-509-0403
847-480-9282 (fax)
adec@adec.org
www.adec.org

ISBN: 978-0-415-98945-9

Book design by The Sherwood Group Inc., www.sherwood-group.com,
a full-service association management company.

Printed in the United States of America. 10 9 8 7 6 5 4 3 2 1 0

Disclaimer
This book is sold as is, without warranty of any kind, either express or implied. While every precaution has been taken in the preparation of this book, the authors, the publisher, and the Association for Death Education and Counseling, *The Thanatology Association*, assume no responsibility for errors or omissions. Neither is any liability assumed for damages resulting from the use of the information contained herein.

Handbook of Thanatology:
The Essential Body of Knowledge for the Study of Death, Dying, and Bereavement

Editor-in-Chief's Introduction to the *Handbook of Thanatology: Foundational Knowledge*

Thanatology — the study of death and dying — at its core centers on the whole person. Holistic knowledge and holistic practice intertwine in our interdisciplinary efforts. If ever there was an arena requiring that the research-practice gap be bridged, surely it occurs where thanatologists engage with persons dealing with human mortality. Mastering the complex, multidisciplinary arena that is thanatology is a task, however, beyond human capability.

As in all arenas of scholarship and practice, thanatology too has become more vast than any one individual can be expected reasonably to master. The Association for Death Education and Counseling (ADEC) — *The Thanatology Association* — sought to develop a comprehensive resource covering the fundamental and foundational knowledge in thanatology, while acknowledging that no one person can ever know all there is to know in this complex field. As one of the oldest interdisciplinary professional organizations in the field of dying, death and bereavement, ADEC is dedicated to promoting excellence and recognizing diversity in death education, care of the dying, grief counseling and research in thanatology. Based on quality research and theory, the association provides information, support and resources to its international, multicultural, multidisciplinary membership and through it, to the public. The *Handbook of Thanatology* is just one of these essential resources.

To find out more about the structure of the Handbook and how it came to be, see Certifications in Thanatology on page vii. This is not the be-all and end-all of thanatology resources; ADEC expects to release a revised edition of the *Handbook of Thanatology: The Essential Body of Knowledge for the Study of Death, Dying, and Bereavement* in years to come, as our vast field continues to grow.

David E. Balk

Editor-in-Chief, *Handbook of Thanatology*

Professor, Brooklyn College of the City University of New York

February 8, 2007

Certifications in Thanatology: How the *Handbook of Thanatology* Can Assist

The Association for Death Education and Counseling (ADEC) envisions a world in which dying, death, and bereavement are recognized as fundamental and significant aspects of the human experience. The Association, ever committed to being on the forefront of thanatology (the study of death and dying), provides a home for professionals from diverse backgrounds to advance the body of knowledge and to promote practical applications of research and theory. In addition, ADEC offers a two-level certification program for thanatology professionals. This program protects the public by creating a standard for thanatology practice while helping professionals develop and demonstrate their mastery of knowledge of thanatology and thanatology-related issues.

ADEC offers Certification in Thanatology (CT) and Fellow in Thanatology (FT), the details of which can be found at http://www.adec.org. *Certification in Thanatology* is a foundation certification that enhances the professional designation established by the academic discipline of each certificate holder. It recognizes the specific educational background in dying, death, and bereavement. Thus, a counselor/therapist or educator is defined by his/her education and work experience. The certification will note the special educational training in the field. The *Fellow in Thanatology* certification is an advanced professional certification for thanatology professionals. It recognizes practitioners and educators in the discipline of death, dying, and bereavement who have met specified knowledge requirements measured through a standardized testing process, and who demonstrate advanced levels of competency in teaching, research and/or clinical practice through a professional portfolio. Recipients of ADEC certification are required to undergo the recertification process every three years.

This *Handbook of Thanatology* emerged as ADEC members serving on the Credentialing Council, the Body of Knowledge Committee, and the Test Committee reflected on efforts to put into operation a reliable and valid exam measuring knowledge considered foundational to thanatology. The structure of this handbook comes directly from the inspired efforts of the Body of Knowledge Committee, chaired by Carol Wogrin, in a 2005 two-day winter meeting during which six categories considered fundamental to thanatology were identified. They are:

Dying: the physical, psychosocial, and spiritual experience of facing death, living with terminal illness, the dying process, and caring for the terminally ill

End-of-Life Decision Making: the aspects of life threatening illness/terminal illness that involve choices and decisions about actions to be taken, for individuals, families, and professional caregivers

Loss, Grief, and Mourning: the physical, behavioral, cognitive, and social experience of and reactions to loss, the grief process, and practices surrounding grief and commemoration.

Assessment and Intervention: information gathered, decisions that are made, and actions that are taken by professional caregivers to determine and/or provide for the needs of the dying, their loved ones, and the bereaved

Traumatic Death: sudden, violent, inflicted, and/or intentional death, shocking encounters with death

Death Education: Formal and informal methods for acquiring and disseminating knowledge about dying, death, and bereavement

Indicators

Several "indicators" applicable across categories formed the topics of the individual chapters in each category.

Cultural/Socialization: the influence of cultural/ethnic and social parameters on the experience of death and loss

Religious/Spiritual: the relationship between religious and spiritual belief systems and the reaction to and coping with death

Professional Issues: factors that affect professionals' training, abilities and responsibilities in providing care

Historical: the historical context and historical changes that played a role in the death experience, and the theoretical paradigms in the field of Thanatology up to 1980's

Contemporary: theoretical perspectives in death and dying and the factors that have influenced the perspectives from the 1980's to the present

Life Span: the consideration of death and dying and developmental perspectives from infancy to old age

Larger Systems: the social organizations beyond the individual and family that effect the experience of dying, death and grief

Family and Individual: Social, cognitive, and physical encounters and interpretations of dying, death, and loss from the standpoint of the person, and the group of people with a relational bond and long term commitment who define themselves as "family"

Resources: Involves materials, organizations and groups of individuals who facilitate knowledge acquisition. Ideas and materials are based upon the findings of empirical research and theoretical synthesis that add to the knowledge base.

Ethical/Legal: Aspects of dying, death and/or loss that pertain generally to determination of right from wrong, and specifically to the principles of medical ethics. Legal issues refer to the articulated laws of a society as they pertain to thanatology.

The six categories and twelve indicators form the Body of Knowledge (BOK) Matrix reproduced on the next two pages. The BOK Matrix is copyrighted by the Association for Death Education and Counseling. The examples in the various cells of the BOK Matrix are illustrative of topics considered probable when categories and indicators intersect. For instance, in the cell with the category Traumatic Death and the indicator Religion and Spirituality, you will see the illustrative examples of "meaning reconstruction" and "rituals." The topics in the BOK Matrix presented below are not considered exhaustive.

Body of Knowledge (BOK) Matrix

Indicators

Categories	Cultural/ Socialization	Religious/ Spiritual	Professional Issues	Historical Perspectives	Contemporary Perspectives	Life Span	Larger Systems	Family Individual	Resources & Research	Ethical/Legal
DYING	sociocultural perspectives on dying: health care/medical interactions, inhibitors to health care, death anxiety	facing death, rituals, meaning, suffering, treatment decisions, afterlife, symbolic imortality	self care, boundaries, compassion fatigue, burnout	hospice, demographics of death, Elizabeth Kubler-Ross	causes and patterns of death: US and international, inhibitors to health care, gender issues, hospice et. al., social constructions, coping theories, NDE, death anxiety	normative developmental issues, death anxiety, children and dying	hospice, palliative care, palliative medicine, biomedical model, institutions (prisons, nursing homes), dying trajectory, caregiver issues	hospice, palliative care, palliative medicine, dying trajectory, caregiver issues, gender roles, awareness context (Glazer & Strauss)	SUPPORT study, analysis of stage theories, organizations and journals, gender and medical research	allocation of resources, justice, truth telling – rights and responsibilities
END-OF-LIFE DECISION MAKING	advance care planning, euthanasia, organ donation, bioethical principles	advance care planning, euthanasia, organ donation, suffering	ethics of caring, rights and responsibilities, holistic		treatment options and choices, holistic	autonomy for special populations, developmental issues	advance care planning, assisted death, organ donation	advance care planning, treatment decisions, assisted death, gender differences in choices, organ donation, holistic	community organizations, professional organizations	bioethical principles, advance directives (proxy, living will), wills, trusts, DNR, euthanasia, assisted suicide, treatment decisions, termination of treatment, organ donation
LOSS, GRIEF, and MOURNING	factors affecting experience of grief and expression of grief, funeral rituals and body disposition, post death activities, mourning rituals, disenfranchisement, clash with legal system, stigmatization	meaning making, funeral rituals and body disposition, post death activities, suffering	burnout, compassion fatigue, knowledge of current research, translating research into practice – clinical competence	linear models; psychoanalytic perspective: Freud, Lindemann, attachment theory: Bowlby, Parkes task based: Worden, Rando, funeral practices, commemorative rituals	non-linear models; continuing bonds: Silverman/Klass, Dual Process Model: Stroebe & Schut, complicated grief, meaning reconstruction: Neimeyer, disenfranchised grief, grieving styles, funeral practice, commemorative rituals	developmental issues: children, adolescents, early adulthood, middle adulthood, later adulthood, parental loss, child loss, widowhood	rituals, body disposition, internet, stigmatization	rituals, coping styles, demands on family system – chronic illness, sudden death, anticipated death, normal grief reactions, expressions of grief anticipatory grief, changing family roles, gender differences in grieving, child loss, death of a parent, partner loss, sibling loss, disenfranchised grief, pet loss	empirical research on current theories: Bowlby, Parkes, Worden, Silverman, Stroebe, Neimeyer	workplace bereavement policies, body disposition, autopsy

ASSESSMENT and INTERVENTION	communication, cultural embeddedness, awareness context, truth telling, determination of death, multicultural counseling	team approach, predeath/post death rituals, suffering	communication, truth telling, identifying (wd?) risk factors, death anxiety, knowledge of current research, CISM, grief counseling vs. grief therapy	determination of death	complicated grief, life style, determination of death	life span grief counseling, grief therapy, death anxiety	after care, grief centers, support groups, self help groups, children's programs, assisted death	truth telling, awareness context, holistic, family meetings/functions, family functioning, complicated risk factors, bibliotherapy, expressive therapies, complementary therapies, gender styles and choices, special populations	criticisms of current practices, empirically based practice, community response – national and local, empirical research on support groups, self help groups, advocacy groups, gender issues regarding participation in research	determination of death, bioethical principles (autonomy, beneficence, nonmaleficence, justice), ethics of caring, body disposition, death certificate
TRAUMATIC DEATH	cause of death, rituals	meaning reconstruction, rituals	response considerations for public response (CISM, RC)	effects of war, famine	definition of traumatic death, terrorism, nuclear era, mass disasters, environmental destruction, war, prevention	demographics, suicide rate, developmental issues/stages- homicide, suicide,	public death, rituals, terrorism, homicide, suicide, horrendous death, natural disasters, man made disasters, role of the media	homicide, suicide, responses as a function of gender, rituals	major national organizations: NOVA, SIDSA, TAPS, MADD and AAOS	capital punishment, terror management, criminal justice system – impact on family
DEATH EDUCATION	cultural awareness, death anxiety, death system	clergy training, personhood, suffering	training and certification, health care professional/medical training, evaluation, qualifications	Aries, goals, prevention, denial of death	goals, promotion of life: health and well being	tailor education to children's conceptual development, death anxiety, death awareness	journalism, news reporting, TV, media (films, books, music), formal and informal, violence	family transition of knowledge, formal, informal, goals	resources for kids (literature), applying principles and standards, evaluative judgments	extension of life: issues surrounding treatment and decision making

© Association for Death Education and Counseling, *The Thanatology Association*

As early as July of 2003 the Test Committee floated a proposal that ADEC commission its own book on the material considered foundational knowledge in thanatology. After much discussion the current structure for the book got strong endorsement: to write separate chapters using a category-by-indicators focus. Thus, there would be a chapter on Culture, Socialization, and Dying; one on Religion, Spirituality, and Dying; and so forth through all the categories and indicators within the BOK Matrix. After some reflection, the editors decided two indicators (Professional Issues; Resources and Research) deserved more treatment that would cut across BOK categories (in contrast to the other chapters that focus on a BOK category by a specific indicator).

What you have in your hands is the product of those efforts. For those interested in thanatology certification, this definitive work and will continue to be a valuable resource for your practice.

List of Contributors

Arthur Zucker is Chair of Philosophy and Director of the Institute for Applied and Professional Ethics at Ohio University. He has taught medical ethics both in the Department of Philosophy and in the College of Osteopathic Medicine at OU. Before coming to Ohio University in 1985, Arthur Zucker taught medical ethics, philosophy of medicine and history of genetics in the Department of Humanities at the Pennsylvania State University, College of Medicine, Hershey, PA. Zucker has been an editor of the section "Law and Ethics" for the journal, *Death Studies* since 1984. He has published four textbooks, all with Prentice Hall. His most recent publications include: two entries, "Medical Ethics" and "Philosophy of Medicine," in the 2nd edition of *The Encyclopedia of Philosophy* (Macmillan, 2006); "Medical Ethics as Therapy," in *Medical Humanities*, June 2006 and "The Bearable Newness of Nanotechnology," forthcoming in an anthology on nanoethics with Springer Verlag.

Mary Lou Zanich, Ph.D., professor of psychology and chair of the Psychology Department at Indiana University of Pennsylvania, was a member of the board of directors and also staff support facilitator for the local hospice. She has co-instructed "Death in the Human Experience," published in *The Forum*, and presented at ADEC conferences.

Carol Wogrin, Psy.D., RN, a licensed psychologist and registered nurse with a background in acute care, home care, and hospice has been working with adults, children and families coping with life threatening illness and bereavement for over twenty five years. She is the Director of the National Center for Death Education, Mount Ida College, serves on the Board of Directors for the Association for Death Education and Counseling, is a member of the International Work Group on Death, Dying and Bereavement, and the author of *Matters of Life and Death: Finding the Words to Say Goodbye*. She has a private practice in Newton, MA.

James L. Werth, Jr. received his Ph.D. in Counseling Psychology from Auburn University in 1995 and his Masters of Legal Studies from the University of Nebraska—Lincoln in 1999. He was the 1999-2000 American Psychological

Association William A. Bailey AIDS Policy Congressional Fellow where he worked on aging and end-of-life issues in the office of United States Senator Ron Wyden (D - OR). He currently is an Associate Professor in the Department of Psychology at The University of Akron and is the pro bono psychologist for the local HIV services organization where he provides counseling and consults with a specialty medical clinic. He is on the APA Ad Hoc Committee on End-of-Life Issues and the APA Ad Hoc Committee on Legal Issues. He has authored/co-authored over 75 articles and book chapters, edited/co-edited seven special journal issues, and written/edited four books specifically on end-of-life matters and/or HIV disease.

Andrea C. Walker, Ph.D., completed her doctoral studies at Oklahoma State University in Human Development and Family Science, focusing on multicultural issues and grief within the family. She conducted an extensive study of the grieving behaviors and bereavement rituals of members of the Muscogee Creek Tribe, the headquarters of which are currently located in eastern Oklahoma and has published articles on this research. She has worked with adolescents and families of various cultures and places within the life span through the Oklahoma Association of Youth Services. Currently, she is Associate Professor of Psychology in the Department of Behavioral Sciences at Oral Roberts University in Tulsa, OK.

Gordon Thornton, Ph.D., FT, is a professor of psychology at Indiana University of Pennsylvania where he has taught a course in the Psychology of Death and Dying since 1975. He is a certified as a Fellow in Thanatology (FT) from the Association for Death Education and Counseling (ADEC). He is a former president of ADEC and chair of the Credentialing Council. He has given presentations on a variety of topics in the area of dying, death, and bereavement and has contributed articles to *Death Studies* and *The Forum*.

Albert Lee Strickland, CT, is a writer and musician. He is a past editor of ADEC's *Forum* Newsletter, received ADEC's Service Award in 1989, and was elected to two terms on ADEC's Leadership Recruitment and Development Committee. His musical presentations centering on themes of loss and death in American blues and gospel music include performances in Australia, Germany, Hong Kong, Canada, Italy, and the United States. Together with Lynne DeSpelder, he is coauthor of *The Last Dance: Encountering Death and Dying*, a college textbook first published in 1983 and currently in its seventh edition, and co-editors of *The Path Ahead: Readings in Death and Dying*. They were recipients of the ADEC Death Education Award in 2003 for contributions to the field. DeSpelder and Strickland are members of the International Work Group on Death, Dying, and Bereavement (IWG) and are life members of ADEC.

Robert G. Stevenson is currently a professor in the M.S. in Counseling program at Mercy College, NY. Two of his most recent publications are *Perspectives on Violence and Violent Death*, and *What Will We Do? Preparing A School Community to Cope With Crises*. His degrees include a B.A. (College of the Holy Cross), M.A. (Montclair State), and M.A.T. and Ed.D. from Fairleigh Dickinson University. He is a member of the International Work Group on Death, Dying and Bereavement and the Association for Death Education and Counseling. He has served ADEC on the board of directors, as chair of the Education Institute, and on the board of certification review. He received the 1997 Wendel Williams Outstanding Educator Award and the 1993 ADEC National Death Educator Award for his contributions to those fields. For service during the New York Guard activation in Manhattan after September 11, 2001, he was awarded the New York State Defense of Liberty medal.

Carla Sofka, Ph.D., MSW, is an Associate Professor of Social Work at Siena College in Loudonville, NY, and a fellow of the Alden March Bioethics Institute. Prior to her academic career as a social work educator and death educator, she was a clinical social worker in medical and psychiatric settings. She has published and presented on a variety of thanatology-related topics and is an associate editor of the journal *Death Studies*. Her section "News and Notes" appears in each issue of the journal. She has been an ADEC member for 20+ years and served the organization in various capacities, including the Board of Directors.

Ester R. Shapiro, Ph.D., is Associate Professor of Psychology, University of Massachusetts, Boston and Research Associate, Mauricio Gaston Latino Institute. Her work applies a cultural and developmental systems approach linking individual, family and social change. She wrote *Grief as a Family Process: A Developmental Approach to Clinical Practice* (Guilford, 1994; 2nd edition in preparation); was Coordinating Editor of *Nuestros Cuerpos Nuestras Vidas* (Seven Stories 2000), the Spanish transcultural adaptation of *Our Bodies, Ourselves*, and has published and presented extensively on a sociocultural model of interventions facilitating life cycle transitions and building resilience for diverse urban communities.

Paul C. Rosenblatt is Morse Alumni Distinguished Teaching Professor of Family Social Science at the University of Minnesota. Among his books dealing with death and grief are *Grief and Mourning in Cross Cultural Perspective; Bitter, Bitter Tears: Nineteenth Century Diaries and Twentieth Century Grief Theories; Parent Grief: Narratives of Loss and Relationship; Help Your Marriage Survive the Death of a Child;* and *African American Grief*. Among his current projects are a study of couple relationships following the death of a parent of one of the partners and also a theoretical work on family obliviousness.

Lillian M. Range, Ph.D., is Professor of Psychology, Our Lady of Holy Cross College, New Orleans, LA, and Professor Emeritus, the University of Southern Mississippi. Her research interests are suicide, bereavement, and health promotion. She is Associate Editor of *Death Studies* and editorial board member of several other scientific journals.

Jackson P. Rainer, Ph.D., is a psychologist licensed to practice in Georgia and North Carolina. He is currently in private practice with Midtown Psychological Associates in Valdosta, GA, specializing in psychotherapy work with children, adolescents, adults, couples, and families who are dealing with the crisis of loss due to catastrophic, chronic, and terminal illness. Dr. Rainer is known and respected in the professional community, having taught, researched, and supervised in the areas of counseling and psychotherapy, ethics, death and dying, bereavement, and crisis intervention. He is on the editorial board for seven psychotherapy journals and has written extensively on the topics of crisis intervention and systemic response to grief. He is a consultant to the American Academy of Bereavement and the CMI Education Institute.

Robin Paletti is a Master's candidate in Special Education at the City University of New York at Queens College. She currently teaches public school, and with special focus on crisis intervention and bereavement, has conducted extensive fieldwork among inner-city middle and high school students in the New York metropolitan area.

Kevin Ann Oltjenbruns, Ph.D., was a long-time faculty member in the Department of Human Development and Family Studies at Colorado State University where she served as Vice Provost for Undergraduate Studies for three years prior to her retirement in June 2005. She co-authored a textbook titled *Dying and Grieving: Lifespan and Family Perspectives* and also wrote numerous articles and chapters, focusing primarily on various issues related to developmental stage and grief. Dr. Oltjenbruns served a three-year term as editor for ADEC's newsletter (*The Forum*). In addition to many other community volunteer activities over the years, Dr. Oltjenbruns has been involved with Hospice of Larimer County in Northern Colorado and is a frequent guest speaker on topics related to grief. Currently, Dr. Oltjenbruns is serving as a Co-Director of the Osher Lifelong Learning Institute through the Division of Continuing Education at Colorado State University.

Illene C. Noppe, Ph.D., a graduate of Temple University, is a Professor of Human Development at the University of Wisconsin-Green Bay. Dr. Noppe developed the Dying, Death ans Loss course on her campus, and is the founder of the campus Death, Dying and Bereavement Institute, providing outreach education for professionals in Northeast Wisconsin. Dr. Noppe researches attachment and grief, death in child care centers, gender and death, and adolescent grief experiences. Three current projects involve an evidence-based model for death education, using the event sampling method to study adolescent grief, and assessing college student bereavement. She currently is the editor for *The Forum*, the newsletter/journalette of the Association for Death Education and Counseling. In addition to delivering numerous presentations and workshops on thanatology-related issues to the greater Green Bay community, Dr. Noppe founded Camp Lloyd (in partnership with a local hospice), a day camp for grieving children.

Robert A. Neimeyer, Ph.D., is Professor and Director of Psychotherapy Research in the Department of Psychology, University of Memphis, where he also maintains an active clinical practice. Dr. Neimeyer has published 20 books, including *Meaning Reconstruction and the Experience of Loss*, and serves as editor of the journal *Death Studies*. The author of nearly 300 articles and book chapters, and a frequent workshop presenter, he is currently working to advance a more adequate theory of grieving as a meaning-making process. Dr. Neimeyer served as President of the Association for Death Education and Counseling and Chair of the International Work Group for Death, Dying, & Bereavement. In recognition of his scholarly contributions, he has been granted the Eminent Faculty Award by the University of Memphis, and made a Fellow of the American Psychological Association.

Colleen I. Murray is Director of the Interdisciplinary Ph.D. Program in Social Psychology and Professor of Human Development and Family Studies at the University of Nevada, Reno. She received her doctorate from The Ohio State University and is an ADEC Fellow in Thanatology. Her research involves the application of theory to loss, grief of adolescents and families, cross-cultural media accounts and social construction of mass tragedies involving youth. She has over 60 publications in venues such as *Family Relations* and *Journal of Social and Personal Relationships*. Dr. Murray teaches courses in family relationships, research methods, adolescence, health, theories, and loss.

Robyn L. Mowery, Ph.D., LMFT, is Assistant Professor of Family Studies at the University of Kentucky. Dr. Mowery is a licensed marriage and family therapist, clinical member of AAMFT, and approved supervisor. Combining expertise in grief and loss, ethical decision making and clinical work with families, Dr. Mowery is currently establishing a program of research in medical family therapy specifically focused on family decision making regarding end-of-life and palliative care, and how professionals can facilitate this process. With grief and loss as a unifying theme, Dr. Mowery's 16+ years of professional experience specifically includes working with severely abused and neglected children and teens and their families, terminally ill hospice patients and their families, birth families, foster families, open adoption families, and patients and families shifting medical care from curative to palliative (i.e., comfort care). Additionally, she directed a teen pregnancy prevention program.

David K. Meagher, Ed.D., C.T., Professor Emeritus, Brooklyn College-CUNY, is the founder of the Thanatology Graduate Study Program at Brooklyn College. He has served on the advisory boards of two hospice programs in New York, and ElderPlans's Widowed Support Service. He is the recipient of ADEC's 2004 Death Educator Award. He has served as a special consultant to the Office of the Medical Examiner of Suffolk County, NY; the Floating Hospital of New York, the National Funeral Directors Association, and the New York City Department of Education. His publications include both journal articles and book chapters in over 20 edited publications.

Jennifer L. Matheson, Ph.D., is Assistant Professor of Human Development and Family Studies at Colorado State University. She is a faculty member in the Marriage & Family Therapy graduate program and is also the Director of the Center for Family & Couple Therapy at Colorado State University. She is trained in marriage and family therapy and has specific expertise working with adolescents and their families as well as general individual, couple and family issues. She teaches adolescent development at Colorado State and supervises marriage and family therapy students in their graduate clinical practice.

David Lester has doctorates from Brandeis University (in psychology) and Cambridge University (in social and political science) and is Professor of Psychology at the Richard Stockton College of New Jersey. He has written extensively on suicide, murder, life-after-death and the fear of death.

Marcia Lattanzi Licht is a psychotherapist and consultant, and co-founder of HospiceCare, Boulder, CO (1976). Marcia's numerous publications include *The Hospice Choice* as well as *Coping with Public Tragedy*. An internationally known educator, she was awarded an honorary doctorate in humane letters in recognition of her work in end-of-life care (University of Colorado, 2005), the 1984 Winston

Churchill Traveling Fellowship, the 2002 ADEC Educator Award, and NHPCO's 1995 Heart of Hospice. She received the Boulder County District Attorney's highest award in 1988, the Distinguished Service Award, for her work with victims of crime.

Dennis Klass, Ph.D., is a retired Religious Studies professor. His ethnographic study of a self help group of bereaved parents is reported in *The Spiritual Lives of Bereaved Parents* (Brunner/Mazel, 1999). He is co-editor of *Continuing Bonds: New Understandings of Grief* (Taylor & Francis, 1996), and co-author of *Dead but not Lost, Grief Narratives in Religious Traditions* (AltaMira, 2005). Klass lives on Cape Cod where he gardens, golfs, kayaks, and watches the trees grow.

Jeffrey Kauffman is a Licensed Clinical Social Worker in Pennsylvania. He maintains an active private psychotherapy practice in suburban Philadelphia, with a specialization in grief and trauma, including treatment of persons with mental retardation. He received certification from the American Academy of Experts in Traumatic Stress as a Board Certified Diplomate in Traumatic Stress. He is the author of more than 30 articles on death and dying and is editor of the book *Loss of the Assumptive World: A Theory of Traumatic Loss.*

Jack Jordan is a licensed psychologist who specializes in working with loss and bereavement. As an ADEC Fellow in Thanatology and the Director of the Family Loss Project, Jack maintains an active practice in grief counseling in the Boston area, with a specialization in work with suicide survivors. He is the Clinical Consultant for Survivor Services of the Samaritans in Boston, the Professional Advisor to the Survivor Council of the American Foundation for Suicide Prevention, and a member of the International Workgroup on Death, Dying, and Bereavement. He was the recipient of the ADEC 2006 Research Recognition Award for his work in bringing together researchers and practitioners in thanatology. Jack provides training nationally through the American Academy of Bereavement, the American Foundation for Suicide Prevention, and the Suicide Prevention Resource Center. He has published clinical and research articles in the areas of bereavement after suicide, support group models, the integration of research and practice in thanatology, and loss in family systems. He is also the co-author of *After Suicide Loss: Coping with Your Grief.*

Scarlett Jett, M.S., M.A., is a fourth year graduate student in the Psy.D. program at Indiana University of Pennsylvania. She is currently in the process of collecting data for her dissertation studying pro-eating disorder Web sites impact on body dissatisfaction and eating behavior in college women. She is also interested in other women's issues concerning sexual assault, and relationship violence.

Christine R. Harte received her Bachelor's in Psychology from The University of Akron in 2006. She has worked as a Nurses/Home Health Aide since 2001 in both nursing home settings and in home environments. She is currently a State Trained and Tested Nurses Assistant (STNA) working as a Home Health Aide for Hospice of Summa in Ohio. She has an interest in anticipatory grief.

The Rev. Richard B. Gilbert, Ph.D., CT, is executive director of The World Pastoral Care Center. A Certified Thanatologist and a member of the ADEC Board of Directors, Rev. Gilbert is a member of the adjunct faculty, The Graduate Theological Foundation and faculty advisor, The University of Texas Health Sciences Center: Teleconference Network of Texas. For further discussion or resource information you may contact him via e-mail, at dick.gilbert@yahoo.com.

Kathleen Gilbert is an Associate Professor of Applied Health Science where her work has focused on family and health issues. In this, she combines her interests in family and interpersonal dynamics with the long-term effects of loss on individuals and on families. Kathleen has identified a phenomenon in the family, "differential grief," which has a profound effect on the way in which a loss and resulting grief is processed in families. She has spoken extensively and authored books, book chapters, and articles on bereavement and grief in the family.

Kenneth J. Doka, Ph.D. is professor of Gerontology at the Graduate School of The College of New Rochelle and Senior Consultant to the Hospice Foundation of America. Dr. Doka has authored or edited over 20 books including *Disenfranchised Grief* and in excess of 70 journal articles and book chapters. He is editor of both *Omega: The Journal of Death and Dying* and *Journeys: A Newsletter for the Bereaved.* Dr. Doka has keynoted conferences in the United States, Australia, New Zealand, Asia, and Europe and appears annually on the Hospice Foundation of America Teleconference. He also is an ordained Lutheran minister.

Lynne Ann DeSpelder, M.A., an author, counselor, and a professor of psychology at Cabrillo College in Aptos, CA, holds a Fellow in Thanatology (FT) from ADEC. She conducts trainings and speaks about death, dying, and bereavement both nationally and internationally, recently in Italy, England and Japan. Lynne is on the international editorial board of the journal *Mortality*. Together with Al Strickland, she is coauthor of *The Last Dance: Encountering Death and Dying*, a college textbook first published in 1983 and currently in its seventh edition, and co-editors of *The Path Ahead: Readings in Death and Dying*. They were recipients of the ADEC Death Education Award in 2003 for contributions to the field. DeSpelder and

Strickland are members of the International Work Group on Death, Dying, and Bereavement (IWG) and are life members of ADEC.

David A. Crenshaw, Ph.D., is a licensed psychologist, Board Certified in Clinical Psychology by the American Board of Professional Psychology (ABPP), and Fellow of the Academy of Clinical Psychology. He is a Registered Play Therapist-Supervisor by the Association of Play Therapy and Co-Founder and current President of the New York Association for Play Therapy. He is author of *Bereavement* (now in its third printing), *A Guidebook for Engaging Resistant Children in Therapy: A Projective Drawing and Storytelling Series* (2004), and two books (he co-authored with John B. Mordock, Ph.D., ABPP published by Jason Aronson in 2005), *Understanding and Treating Aggressive Children: Fawns in Gorilla Suits* and *A Handbook of Play Therapy with Aggressive Children*. His newest book *Evocative Strategies in Child and Adolescent Psychotherapy* was published by Rowman & Littlefield Publishers in September, 2006.

Gerry R. Cox is a Professor of Sociology at University of Wisconsin– La Crosse. He is the Director of the Center for Death Education & Bioethics. His teaching focuses upon Theory/Theory Construction, Deviance and Criminology, Death and Dying, Social Psychology, and Minority Peoples. He has been publishing materials since 1973 in sociology and teaching-oriented professional journals. He is a member of the International Work Group on Dying, Death, and Bereavement, the Midwest Sociological Society, the American Sociological Association, The International Sociological Association, Phi Kappa Phi, and Great Plains Sociological Society, and the Association of Death Education and Counseling. He serves on the board of Directors of the National Prison Hospice Association.

Donna M. Corr, RN, MS in Nursing, took early retirement as Professor of Nursing, St. Louis Community College at Forest Park. With her husband Charles, the Corrs' publications include 30 books and booklets, along with more than 100 articles and chapters, in the field of death, dying, and bereavement. Their most recent publication is the fifth edition of *Death and Dying, Life and Living* (Belmont, CA: Thomson Wadsworth, 2006), co-authored with Clyde M. Nabe.

Charles A. Corr, Ph.D., CT, is a member of the Board of Directors, The Hospice Institute of the Florida Suncoast, the Executive Committee of the National Donor Family Council, the ChiPPS (Children's Project on Palliative/Hospice Services) Leadership Advisory Council of the National Hospice and Palliative Care Organization, the Association for Death Education and Counseling, and the

International Work Group on Death, Dying, and Bereavement (Chairperson, 1989-93). He is also Professor Emeritus, Southern Illinois University Edwardsville.

Alicia Skinner Cook, Ph.D., is a licensed psychologist and Professor Emeritus in the Department of Human Development and Family Studies at Colorado State University. Dr. Cook's scholarly work has focused on families and grief and on the ethics of bereavement research. She has published over 40 articles and four books, and has been a Visiting Scholar at the Hastings Center for Biomedical Ethics. She has developed and taught courses on death, dying, and grief and co-authored a book for grief counselors, *Helping the Bereaved: Therapeutic Interventions for Children, Adolescents, and Adults* (Basic Books, 1992).

Stephen R. Connor, Ph.D., is Vice President for Research and International Development at the National Hospice and Palliative Care Organization in Alexandria, VA. He has worked continuously in the hospice movement since 1976 and has been the CEO of four hospice programs. In addition to being a hospice and association executive, he is a researcher and psychotherapist, licensed as a clinical psychologist in California and Kentucky. Dr. Connor is a former JCAHO hospice surveyor and a board member of the International Work Group on Death, Dying, and Bereavement and the Association for Death Education and Counseling. He serves on the Editorial Board of the *Journal of Pain and Symptom Management.* Dr. Connor has published over 40 journal articles, reviews, and book chapters on issues related to the hospice movement and care of dying patients and their families. He is the author of *Hospice: Practice, Pitfalls, and Promise.*

David E. Balk, Professor of Health and Nutrition Sciences, directs Graduate Studies in Thanatology at Brooklyn College of the City University of New York. He graduated from the University of Illinois at Urbana-Champaign with a Ph.D. in Counseling Psychology. Dr. Balk is an Associate Editor of the journal *Death Studies*, and serves as that journal's Book Review Editor. He is a member of *Omega's* Editorial Board. His research has focused on adolescent bereavement; at first his work looked at adolescents' responses to sibling death, and now he is examining responses to bereavement while in college. For three years he chaired the Test Committee for the Association for Death Education and Counseling (ADEC) in its work to design and administer a national exam certifying foundational knowledge of thanatology.

Dying

Introduction to Part 1, Chapters 1-6

Chapters 1 through 6 focus on dying. The Body of Knowledge defined this major category of thanatology knowledge in this way: **the physical, psychosocial, and spiritual experience of facing death, living with terminal illness, the dying process, and caring for the terminally ill.**

The chapters in Part 1 focus on dying in terms of these indicators: culture and socialization, religion and spirituality, historical and contemporary perspectives, life span issues, the family and larger systems, and ethical and legal issues.

Chapter 1

Culture, Socialization, and Dying

Charles A. Corr & Donna M. Corr

The aim of this chapter is to examine some cultural and social aspects of the situation of those who are dying or closely approaching death, as well as the care they are offered. As we begin this examination, one important point to keep in mind is that *dying persons are living human beings*. Although individuals who are dying are often treated by others as if they were already dead, in fact those who are dying remain living persons as long as they are dying. Dying is a special situation in living, not the whole of life; death is the outcome of dying, not its equivalent.

Cultural Factors that Affect Dying

Every human being is born into and raised within a context in which cultural, social, religious, and ethnic factors influence his or her life. As such, these variables, which we subsume here under the broad heading of "cultural factors," affect each individual's views of and interactions with death and dying. This influence occurs whether the individual accepts or rejects the acculturation that he or she receives, since even in rejection these cultural factors provide a benchmark against which the individual defines and conducts his or her life.

One way to understand the various factors addressed in this section is to think of culture as "a unified set of values, ideas, beliefs, and standards of behavior shared by a group of people; it is the way a person accepts, orders, interprets, and understands experiences throughout the life course" (Thomas, 2001, p. 40). Clearly, in the United States and in many other countries, there are many, often quite diverse, cultural groups. Coming to know something about those cultural groups is a way of gaining a better appreciation of ourselves, other people, and our society as a whole.

If we think for a moment about what we know concerning religious differences in attitudes and practices, we can easily recognize differences between various

Christian sects, between orthodox and reform Jews, and between Sunni and Shia Islamic groups. At the same time, it is all too easy to develop stereotypes around religious and cultural differences. For example, we may think that members of one religious or cultural group are highly expressive and demonstrative in ways they face loss, while others may be thought to be much more reserved and even stoic. This perception may be true as a generalization about the group, but is it also true of every member of that group? In other words, are we settling for superficial stereotypes in what we think about cultural groups?

So our task is to be sensitive both to differences between cultural groups and to diversity within those groups. For this reason, it is notoriously difficult to speak in a general way about how cultural factors influence human beings and what results they produce. What is needed is an effort to enter into specific cultural groups and see how they address death-related issues, an effort like the one Morgan and Laungani (2002-2005) undertook when they set out to edit a series of volumes (not yet completed as this is written) about *Death and Bereavement around the World*. Our project, of course, will be on a much more limited scale.

In this chapter, we set aside issues related to death and the afterlife, as well as those involving post-death bereavement and mourning, in order to focus on selected examples of ways in which cultural factors bear on experiences of dying. Among many possible examples, we will consider here four prominent instances:

- Communication within family or cultural groups and between those groups and outsiders
- Decision making within some family and cultural groups
- Issues about who should be primarily responsible for care of a dying person
- Distrust by members of cultural groups with regard to the larger social system, its health care institutions, and some health care providers

Concerning *communication*, Thomas (2001, p. 42) has written that, "Communication about end-of-life issues is the key to understanding and making rational decisions." Nevertheless, several studies have reported that maintaining control over communication is an important issue for many Asian Americans (e.g., Tanner, 1995; Thomas, 2001; Tong & Spicer, 1994). Valuing control over communication may mean that members of such communities may be quite restrained in communicating to health care providers what they are experiencing when they are dying and in distress. Also, it may lead some family members to place a high priority on not telling dying persons that they are dying. Health care providers who do not share such values or who lack cultural sensitivity may become frustrated when they are caring for a dying person from such a cultural group.

Closely related to attitudes associated with communication are those related to *decision making*. Because patriarchal and hierarchical structures are prevalent in some cultural groups in our society, in such groups it is the oldest male or at least an older member of the family who is expected to make any decisions about the care of dying family members (Blackhall, Murphy, Frank, Michel, & Azen, 1995). To outsiders, this may appear to deny or at least infringe upon the autonomy of the ill person.

Another significant issue in which cultural factors play an important role has to do with *who should care for a dying person*. In contemporary American society, the provision of such care is often primarily assigned to outsiders—staff and volunteers in hospitals, long-term care facilities, and hospice programs. Studies of certain Hispanic cultural groups (e.g., Cox & Monk, 1993; Delgado & Tennstedt, 1997), however, have noted that this role is primarily and insistently held within the family and there most often assigned to female members.

Distrust has many causes and is often quite deep-seated. For example, among African Americans some have traced it back to the general implications of slavery and particularly to the Tuskegee study conducted by the United States Public Health Service. Begun in 1932, the study initially offered the only known treatments at the time to poor African-American sharecroppers in Alabama with syphilis. Tragically, participants were eventually allowed to go untreated to study the progress of the disease until they died. This research decision occurred even after penicillin became available in the mid-1940s and was shown to be effective in treating the disease. The study was not halted until it was exposed in the press in 1972 (Jones, 1992). More recent studies (e.g., Tschann, Kaufmann, and Micco, 2003) have reported that many African Americans believe the health care they receive is less adequate than that offered to Caucasian Americans and that they would not receive all of the appropriate health care they needed if they wrote a living will.

The issues noted here that affect dying persons and care of the dying are intertwined with the ways in which individuals and members of groups in our society view the importance of family, the role of religion, and the importance of being present at a death. They also carry over into other matters, such as whether or not persons are willing to making advance plans for treatment at the end of life, to consider opportunities for organ donation, or to take part in physician-assisted suicide.

Death Anxiety and Concerns that Affect Dying

Much attention in recent years has been given to the concept of death anxiety and its measurement (e.g., Neimeyer, 1994; Neimeyer, Wittkowski, & Moser, 2004). For example, many reports suggest that women report higher death anxiety than men in our society, while older adults appear to report less death anxiety than some younger persons. It has also been argued that death anxiety is a complex concept, one that varies with both demographic and personality factors, as well as with life accomplishments and past or future regrets (Tomer & Eliason, 1996).

Further, death-related attitudes may reflect very different concerns and responses such as those that are focused on:

My own dying: will it involve a long, difficult, painful, or undignified dying process, especially in an alien institution under the care of strangers who might not respect my personal needs or wishes—if so, perhaps I might wish that my dying would occur without any form of distress or prior knowledge, and in my sleep, or perhaps I might take deliberate action to prepare an advance directive, thereby hoping to insure that my dying will not be unduly or painfully prolonged; by contrast, concerns about my own dying might lead me to wish to avoid a sudden, unanticipated death, allowing time to address "unfinished business," bid farewell to loved ones (Byock, 2004), and "get ready to meet my Maker."

My own death: will it release me from hardships and suffering, or will it involve losing the life and all it involves that has been and is so important to me?

What will happen to me after my death: am I anxious about the unknown and fearful of judgment or punishment after death, or am I anticipating a heavenly reward, a passage to a better life, or a reunion with someone who had died earlier?

The bereavement of someone I love: am I mainly concerned about the burdens that my illness and dying are placing upon those whom I love and/or am I worried about what will happen to them after I am gone?

Dying in Our Social System: Once Upon a Time

In times past in the United States of America and in many other developed countries around the world, what Glaser and Strauss (1968) identified as *dying trajectories* were relatively brief and largely predictable experiences. Mainly caused by communicable diseases, dying typically involved clear and recognizable symptoms such as nausea, diarrhea, vomiting, headache, or muscle ache. Family members, friends, and those professionals who might have been available would have been able to recognize that these individuals were seriously ill. On the basis of past experiences with similar patterns of disease, it could often be predicted whether or not an individual afflicted in these ways would recover or would die and when the outcome would be known.

Care given to such individuals would largely have been supportive in nature, offered in the hope that the body would heal itself and concerned not to interfere in that process. This care would likely have focused on providing a place to rest, shelter from the elements, a cool cloth to wipe a feverish brow, and nourishing food ("chicken soup"). It would often have been accompanied by various forms of spiritual intercession. Many fortunate individuals would have been cared for at home and by family members. Hospitals likely would not have been available. Even when they were, they often took the form of charitable institutions (almshouses) with large, crowded wards that were typically dark, stuffy, unpleasant, and even life threatening since they threw together many different types of people with very different disabilities and often contagious conditions.

As Western culture became more urbanized, hospitals began to change. During the latter half of the 19th century, a biomedical model emerged that viewed disease as involving specific entities and predictable causes. Therapy became intended to "fix" malfunctioning parts of the human body. Specialization in carrying out therapeutic tasks became the norm. A division of labor came to characterize both health care providers and health care institutions. In particular, hospitals—now often called "medical centers" or "health centers"—came to focus on acute care in which scientific medicine sought to cure disease. A paradoxical result of this new focus on hospital-based, acute care is that within the very institutions in which nearly half of all Americans now die (Minino, 2005) death began to be perceived as involving a kind of failure.

Shift from support to "fixing" the disease.

Following passage of the Social Security Act of 1935, which added federal funding to the personal resources of individuals and their relatives, as well as health insurance and retirement packages, long-term care facilities began to be developed. These long-term care facilities (often called "nursing homes") filled the need for chronic care as families had often become small, nuclear groupings in which individuals frequently lived at a distance from their kin instead of extended clusters living in the same community. Chronic care became especially important as average life expectancy increased, individuals were no longer able to work or had decided to retire from work well before their deaths, and many required assistance in caring for themselves and in activities of daily living as they lived out the last years of their lives.

Many long-term care facilities in our society provide excellent services, but some have been hesitant when requirements for chronic care evolved into needs for end-of-life care. Some coped by transferring residents to acute care hospitals shortly before their deaths, while others tried to make do or develop their capacities to care for dying persons. However that may be, more that 22 percent of all Americans currently die in long-term care facilities (Minino, 2005).

Recent Efforts to Change Social Systems and Care for the Dying

During the early decades of the second half of the 20th century, new perspectives were advanced concerning the situation of those who were coping with dying (e.g., Noyes & Clancy, 1977), the nature of pain when one is dying (e.g., LeShan, 1964), and appropriate therapeutic regimes for such persons (e.g., Twycross, 1976). Above all, these new perspectives questioned how the social organization of programs serving those who are coping with dying affected the care provided, and they stressed the value of holistic, person-centered care and interdisciplinary teamwork. That led to the development of the hospice movement, heightened interest in palliative care, and efforts to apply hospice principles in hospitals, long-term care facilities, and other settings.

Unfortunately, there is evidence that these efforts have not benefited all who are dying in our society, especially those in the best of our acute-care institutions. For example, the research project called SUPPORT (Study to Understand Prognoses and Preferences for Outcomes and Risks of Treatments; SUPPORT Principal Investigators, 1995) examined end-of-life preferences, decision making, and interventions in a total of 9,105 adults hospitalized in five teaching hospitals in the United States with one or more of nine life-threatening diagnoses. The two-year first phase of the study observed 4,301 patients and documented substantial shortcomings in communication, overuse of aggressive cure-oriented treatment at the very end of life, and undue pain preceding death. The two-year second phase of the study compared the situations of 4,804 patients randomly assigned to intervention and control groups with each other and with baseline data from Phase 1. Physicians with the intervention group received improved, computer-based, prognostic information on their patients' status. In addition, a specially trained nurse was assigned to the intervention group in each hospital to carry out multiple contacts with patients, families, physicians, and hospital staff in order to elicit preferences, improve understanding of outcomes, encourage better attention to pain control, facilitate advance care planning, and enhance patient-physician communication.

The SUPPORT study used multiple criteria to evaluate outcomes, such as the timing of written "Do not resuscitate" (DNR) orders, patient and physician agreement (based on their first interview) on whether to withhold resuscitation, the number of days before death spent in an intensive care unit either receiving mechanical ventilation or comatose, the frequency and severity of pain, and the use of hospital resources. Results were discouraging. Phase 2 intervention "failed to improve care or patient outcomes" (p. 1591) and led to the conclusion that "we are left with a troubling situation. The picture we describe of the care of seriously ill or dying persons is not attractive" (p. 1597).

We are left to hope that the hospice movement—which cared for 1,060,000 dying persons in 2004, nearly half of whom were able to die at home (NHPCO, 2006)—and the related palliative care movement will eventually have a more favorable influence on care of the dying in hospitals and long-term care facilities.

Some Concluding Thoughts

Dying persons have always been members of the human community and responsibilities for their care have always been with us. In the Preface to her celebrated book, *On Death and Dying* (1969), Elisabeth Kübler-Ross reminded readers that we should pay attention to dying persons and to all who are coping with dying for three reasons (Corr, 1993):

1. They are *still alive* and often have "unfinished business" they want and need to address
2. We need to *listen actively* to them in order to identify with them their tasks and needs so that we can be effective providers of care;
3. They have *much to teach us* about our shared humanity and the final stages of life with all its anxieties, fears, and hopes.

To say this in another way, we pay attention to dying persons because they are living human beings, because we want to improve our society for all its members, and because we want to have better systems in place to care for us and for our loved ones when we face our own dying and death at the end of life.

LeARNIN3 Objective:
understand how CultuRAL + Social factors influence the experience of Dying, pARticularly in Contemporary United States. score

2-1-11   35/40 = 88% 0.875

40|35

Chapter 2

Religion, Spirituality, and Dying

Marcia Lattanzi-Licht

There are times in all of our lives when we are forced to reach deep into ourselves to feel the truth of our real nature. For each of us there comes a moment when we can no longer live our lives by accident. Life throws us into questions that some of us refuse to ask until we are confronted by death or some tragedy in our lives. (Wayne Muller, 1997)

Religion and spirituality are overlapping concepts, each with different significance. The focus for persons facing death includes addressing spiritual needs, both religious and non-religious. Religious needs center around one's relationship with God, and others, and possibly for preparing oneself for the afterlife. Religion for some people is the most important factor that keeps them going (Koenig, 1998). Religion may also contribute both to spiritual healing as well as spiritual pain.

Spirituality is associated with personal, transcendent meaning (Puchalski, 1999). For seriously ill persons, spirituality is often a bridge between feelings of hopelessness and a renewed sense of hope and meaning (Frankl, 1959). Spiritual needs are not limited to religion, and are often a thread that runs through physical, emotional/psychological and social needs and concerns. Persons facing the end of life acknowledge a greater spiritual perspective and orientation than non-terminally ill or healthy persons (Reed, 1987).

Facing Death

Recognizing that dying is more than a bio-psychosocial event, there have been human spiritual "tasks" identified for coping with dying. The work of these tasks centers around identifying, developing, or reaffirming sources of spiritual energy that can encourage faith and hope (Corr, 1992; Saunders, 1967). Those who care for people facing the end of life recognize and attend to a broad range of related spiritual needs:

- re-examining beliefs
- reconciling life choices
- exploring one's lifetime contribution
- examining loving relationships
- exploring beliefs about an afterlife
- discovering meaning.

Spiritual needs typically involve reflection and examination. Some people do the exploration in a solitary way, offering possibilities for understanding and healing that may never be communicated directly with another. Others find the reflection and feedback of another person helpful, and an aid in discovery. Active listening and being present promote the opportunity for persons who are seriously ill and dying to explore spiritual concerns. Weisman (1972) identified open communication and warm personal relationships as two of the important conditions that define an "appropriate death." In the unknown realm of sorrow and grief, caring human closeness is essential and can offer considerable spiritual strength (Lattanzi-Licht, Mahoney & Miller, 1998).

In 1997, a Gallup Poll commissioned by the Nathan Cummings and Fetzer Foundations examined spiritual concerns at the end of life (Gallup, 1997). The telephone interviews of 1,200 adults explored three areas:

1. How people find comfort in their dying days;
2. Things that worry people when they think about their own death;
3. How people plan for disability or death, including considering physician assisted suicide as a possibility.

Survey findings highlighted the importance of human contact as a source of both spiritual and emotional support at the time of death. Respondents reported looking to family (81%) and close friends (61%) to offer this support. Only 36% of people believed clergy could provide effective spiritual support and comfort.

The Gallup study (1997) showed 24 different matters that might cause concern for respondents as they consider their own deaths. Medical situations of suffering great pain or living in a vegetative state are at the forefront of worry for all age groups. Specific spiritual concerns move to the forefront for younger adults, and include worries about not being forgiven by God (72% of 18 to 24 year olds), and fear about death cutting them off from God or a higher power (63%). One explanation might be that younger people are still developing their personal spirituality and may feel less certain about facing ultimate questions.

In the realm of relationships and connections, the Gallup study (1997) found that those who responded equally feared "not being forgiven by God" (56%) and "not reconciling with others" (56%). Respondents also expressed significant concern about dying when feeling removed or cut off from God or a "Higher Power" (51%).

Faith has the potential to strengthen and comfort us in difficult times of our lives. It offers the possibility to transcend personal concerns and focus on a belief that is sustaining, including the belief in a caring or knowing presence. Spiritual well-being offers a measure of protection against end of life despair and depression in persons facing death (Mclain, Rosenfeld, Breitbart, 2003). In general, religious involvement and spirituality are associated with better health outcomes.

Meaning

While there is an ongoing interest in distinguishing religious and spiritual concerns, there is also an evolving understanding of the significance of "spirituality." In general, spiritual experiences can be seen as important opportunities for learning, growth, and meaning. Theologian John Shea (2000) presents the term *spiritualities* as the beliefs, stories, and practices that respond to a basic, shared human need to find an integrated meaning. These beliefs, stories, and practices are generated from our social actions and interactions and may or may not be linked to religious beliefs, practices, or communities.

Meaning can refer to a spiritual sense of purpose in life, which centers around the capacity of an individual to feel the worth of his or her individual life. Most major psychological and spiritual theorists, including Frankl, link meaning to one's contribution to the world through work, and to one's loving relationships. Meaning can also refer to the attempt to understand the personal significance of a loss of physical capacity or function, or physical pain, or the death of a loved one.

The question of meaning can be perplexing and insoluble. Meaning refers to a search for coherence or personal significance (Yalom, 1980). The challenging process of discovering meaning can help an individual grow spiritually. Frankl offers three avenues for discovering meaning: creating a work or doing a deed, experiencing something or encountering someone, and, the attitude we take toward unavoidable suffering (Frankl, 1959).

Exploring and attending to spiritual meaning is an essential focus for persons facing death. A growing body of research indicates that a sense of meaning in life is associated with improved psychological well-being, satisfaction with life, and overall quality of life (Fry, 2000, Fryback & Reinert, 1999; Rizzo, 1990). Spiritual individuals also tend to be more hopeful and to experience more meaning or purpose in life (Mahoney & Graci, 1999).

Treatment Decisions

Religious beliefs can be a significant influence upon ethics, and upon decision-making at the end of life. A person's beliefs and values can profoundly affect how a person copes with illness, and with the treatment of illness.

In health care, the most common end-of-life dilemmas that require "hard choices" can be influenced significantly by religious beliefs. These decisions center on attempting resuscitation, utilizing artificial nutrition and hydration, hospitalizing, and shifting from treatment goals to comfort goals (Dunn, 2001). Other areas that pose conflict are utilizing ventilators, antibiotic treatment, and pain control. As the entire country witnessed in the Terry Schiavo case, there can be great differences in religious beliefs and values among family members.

In a clear representation of choice and personal comfort, nearly 70% of people interviewed in the Gallup study wanted to die at "home" (1997). This decision, along with others about continuing futile treatment, are often not communicated to people, or are only offered in the final stage of an illness. By not giving people full information, their perceptions of time and opportunities can be distorted. The time people believe they have to spend meaningfully can be greatly diminished. Medical professionals have a sacred trust to offer seriously ill persons truthful information, balanced with realistic hope. Many people continue to hope for a miracle long after they know that the illness is rapidly progressing and treatment options are without reasonable promise. In a spiritual framework, the focus becomes healing in a symbolic, relational context, not from a physical standpoint.

Suffering

Suffering can be defined as "an actual" or perceived threat to the integrity or continued existence of the whole person (Cassell, 1982). Facing the end of life brings inevitable suffering, on physical, emotional, social, spiritual and existential dimensions. Dame Cicely Saunders (1967), founder of the modern day hospice movement, describes the realm of suffering by persons who are dying as "total pain," involving the interaction of physical, social, psychological and spiritual pain.

Beliefs can be enabling mechanisms for survival. They create a framework for us to live inside and find comfort and meaning. Cultural and religious beliefs influence personal ones in ways we may not recognize, and may complicate coping or increase efforts at discovering meaning. For example, Puritan beliefs center around a God that punishes people with illness based upon their actions or omissions. Questions of punishment, guilt, and "deserving" illness all create distress. Old Testament images of a god of retribution (Kushner, 1988) can create increasing feelings of isolation and abandonment. Protestant beliefs in predestination could engender a sense of powerlessness in some people. Even New Age beliefs can create a sense of failure or wrong living ("what goes around comes around"). And beliefs in Karma leave one wondering about past lives and past transgressions.

Frankl (1959) learned in his experience at Auschwitz that suffering itself is not destructive; suffering without meaning has the potential to destroy a person. It is possible to address physical suffering for a person facing the end of life. And, the possibility of continued emotional-spiritual suffering was a significant death-related concern for 51% of people in the Gallup study (1997). The intrinsic challenge of emotional or spiritual suffering is to engage in the discovery of personal meaning.

Quality of life, including an emphasis on addressing spiritual needs, has been a main focus for hospice and palliative care. By addressing the spiritual dimensions of personhood through care practices and research, it is possible to decrease suffering and enhance the quality of time remaining for individuals facing death (Chochinov & Cann, 2005).

Rituals

In a multicultural society, a person may express their spiritual nature in a variety of philosophical and religious beliefs and practices. These practices and rituals may differ greatly depending upon the person's religion, race, sex, class, ethnic heritage and experience (International Work Group, 1999).

Rituals are both religious and spiritual. They may follow prescribed religious formats, and they are markers to communicate meaning and to guide responses to loss (Irion, 1999).

Some people may express a longing for religious rituals or spiritual support at the end of life. Individuals can carry out specific practices (prayer, meditation, dietary practices, religious service attendance, etc.) as part of their religious or spiritual life. In settings where persons who are facing death are cared for, spiritual assessments look at ways to address the conditions or events that limit the ability to practice religious or spiritual rituals (e.g., weakness, immobility, hospitalization, depression).

Rituals are ways to address the great mystery of death and the profound questions it raises. Rituals related to dying are essential and offer three important elements of comfort to participants: They bring people together; they acknowledge a significant experience/event; and, they create opportunities for support. Religious rituals that recognize the profound human experience of death focus on the process of grief, including separation, transition and incorporation (van Gennep, 1960).

Religion and faith communities can contribute to spiritual healing or comfort in many ways, but particularly through rituals. Rituals can offer recognition of the finality of a life as well as a connection with transcendence, of the life to come. As rituals mark a turning point between an old reality and the new, they serve to help mourners find comfort and strength for the journey ahead.

Afterlife

Religious or spiritual ideas about immortality range from Christian beliefs about resurrection to the cycles of rebirth in Eastern faiths like Buddhism and Hinduism. Some who martyr themselves performing terrorist acts are assured by religious/political leaders that their sacrifice will earn them a place in heaven. Some religious practitioners sacrifice animals to gain protection from death. All of these beliefs imply freedom from one's biological finiteness, of living at a higher level of existence.

Beliefs in an afterlife can hold great comfort for persons facing death, as well as for their family members. Most religious beliefs in a future afterlife are predicated upon decent behavior in the present human existence. Notions of reward or punishment permeate conceptions of the afterlife. Some traditions believe that it is impossible to know whether life continues, but encourage ethical behavior as the key to any potential continuation of life.

Symbolic Immortality

Robert Jay Lifton (1979) shaped a comprehensive theory based upon the human need to symbolize continuity between death and life. Lifton defined a sense of "symbolic immortality," and believed that life is threatened when death is not transcended. The first of Lifton's five modes of immortality is "biological immortality," or the sense of living through and in one's children. Lifton also describes, as many great religions have maintained, a "theological immortality" that typically involves a form of personal afterlife and a type of reunion with the divine, or release to existence on a higher plane. The third mode of immortality is achieved through "works," or creating an enduring human impact, the sense that one's contribution will not die. "Natural immortality" diminishes the pain of death as a person's body returns to the earth where it is absorbed and utilized for new life, or survival by nature itself. And, finally, "experiential transcendence" involves a psychic state so intense that in it, time and death cease to exist, a continuous present. Adults can grow in their sense of symbolic immortality and purpose in life, and it acts to help them cope with the fear of death (Drolet, 1990).

Symbolic immortality, with its links to history and biology, can be seen as a way of trying to overcome the finality of death. Lifton made an important point about nuclear danger threatening cultural symbols of immortality while propagating haunting images of annihilation. The possibility that all means for transcendence will be destroyed creates fear that some believe has led to the growth of cults and religious fundamentalism, and to contemporary drug "epidemics."

In his writing on symbolic immortality, Lifton refers to Otto Rank who stressed humanity's need for reassurance about the eternal survival of the self. Rank held that "man creates culture by changing natural conditions in order to maintain his spiritual self" (Rank, 1958).

Conclusion

Religion and spirituality are important considerations for persons facing death, and for their family members. Understanding the influence of a person's religious or spiritual beliefs, practices and experiences can enhance care and comfort at the end of life.

Dying can be seen as a spiritual journey. Images of supporting people at the end of life often include journeying with them, following their direction. In addition to providing physical and emotional care and comfort, those who care for persons facing death join with them in exploring their beliefs and deepest life experiences, and sharing their questions about the mystery that mortality presents.

Another image that applies to people facing the end of life is that of a spiritual search. The search for meaning, connection, or hope does not involve an end or completion point, but rather is a continuing process, a process that engages one's spirit.

Learning Objective: 8 Questions 40/40
Identify how Religious & Spiritual beliefs affect Attitudes & behaviors in individuals who Are facing Death. (40/40)

Chapter 3

Historical and Contemporary Perspectives on Dying

Kenneth J. Doka

Early Efforts

While many people associate the historical roots of the study of dying with Kübler-Ross' epochal book *On Death and Dying* (1969), in fact, the roots of the field are earlier. In this section, I will explore some of the early and contemporary contributions to the study of the dying process. This chapter begins with a brief history of some of the early formative work, reviews the development of the concept of anticipatory grief, describes more contemporary efforts to develop task models of dying, and discusses theorists who have viewed dying as a developmental and transformative experience. This is, in no way, a comprehensive review of all the work that exists on the field. Rather, it represents the author's perspective of influential work that has contributed to the care of the dying. Persons who wish a more all-inclusive view may wish to consult varied social histories of the field (Pine, 1977; 1986; Corr, Doka, and Kastenbaum, 1999).

Perhaps one of the earliest efforts to understand some of the psychosocial processes of dying was Lindemann's (1944) study of grief reactions that introduced the concept of *anticipatory grief*—a topic that will be explored later in this section. Feifel's *The Meaning of Death* (1959) was one of the first publications and early efforts in the field. Though the book had a broad focus, some of the articles did address the dying process. In that same year, Cicely Saunders, who founded St. Christopher's Hospice published a series of articles focusing on nursing and the dying (Saunders, 1959). In 1962, Weisman and Hackett published a study on dying patients and the predilection to death.

Glaser and Strauss also published, in that era, two books that would contribute some enduring concepts to the study of the dying process. In *Awareness of Dying* (1965), Glaser and Strauss studied what dying people knew or suspected about their impending deaths. It is important to remember that in that period, general practice was not to discuss death with individuals who were dying. Nonetheless, Glaser and Strauss documented that dying individuals experienced four different awareness contexts. In *closed awareness*, the dying person had no inkling of his or her impending death. As Glaser and Strauss noted, this context was unstable and unlikely to last long as dying individuals began to respond to both external and internal cues. In *suspected awareness*, dying individuals expected their impending death — often trying to test their suspicions with medical staff or family. A third context — *mutual pretense* — was the most common. Here patients and family were aware of the impending death but to protect the other each person pretended that the patient would recover. As last context — *open awareness* — was where both patients and family were aware of and could discuss the possibility of death. Glaser and Strauss' (1965) work played a significant role in questioning the veil of silence that had surrounded the dying process.

Their second work, *Time for Dying* (Glaser and Strauss, 1968), focused on the temporal organization of death within the hospital. They noted that most deaths followed certain expected trajectories. "Badly timed" deaths where the death did not follow an expected trajectory often created great difficulty for staff.

Sudnow's *Passing On: The Social Organization of Dying* (1967) was an ethnographic account of dying in two hospitals. While Sudnow's work was wide-reaching and touched on numerous themes, one of his most enduring contributions was the introduction of the concept of *social death*. Social death referred to his observed phenomenon that family and staff often treated many comatose patients, though technically living, as if they were dead.

Hospice: A Way to Care for the Dying

In this early period, Cicely Saunders founded St. Christopher's Hospice, often credited as the first hospice, in the London area. Saunders emphasized that dying was not simply a bio-medical or physical event but also had psychosocial, familial, and spiritual implications. Care of the dying then needed to be holistic and centered on the ill person and his or her family as the unit of care. St. Christopher's tried to create a "home-like" atmosphere that sought a holistic, family centered way to allow dying persons to live life as fully as possible, free from debilitating pain and incapacitating symptoms. Both the hospice philosophy and the growth of hospice did much to improve the treatment of dying persons and to encourage the study of the dying process.

The hospice movement's remarkable history is well noted in other sources (see for example, Stoddard, 1978). It is, perhaps, one of the most successful grass roots movements in the last quarter of the 20th century. The holistic philosophy of hospice has permeated much of medicine now — at least in terms of a recognition that a patient's quality of life means meeting not only physical needs but psychological, social, and spiritual needs as well. Moreover, the success of hospice has led others to seriously question how well the medical system generally meets the needs of those who are dying as a result of multiple serious chronic illnesses (Myers & Lynn, 2001).

St. Christopher's became a beacon both of research and practice generating seeds that would grow throughout the world. Literally many of the pioneers who would influence the development of hospice and palliative care visited or trained there.

In the U.S. this resulted in the development of Hospice, Inc. outside of New Haven Connecticut in 1974. Branford also had a small home care unit. But it was Dr. William Lamers, a founder of a hospice in Marin County, CA, that viewed home care as both the heart and future of hospice. To Lamers, the idea of a "home-like" environment could best be offered within the patient's actual home. Lamers offered a model that freed interested individuals from fundraising for new facilities. This home care model of hospice quickly spread throughout the U.S. sponsored by a range of groups from churches and interfaith groups to junior leagues. Hospice, then took a very different cast in the United States compared to England in that in the U.S. hospices primarily offered home care, and heavily stressed psychosocial care and the use of volunteers (Connor, 1998).

Not everyone learned the same lesson at St. Christopher's. St. Christopher's impressed Dr. Balfour Mount, a Canadian physician. However, Mount was convinced that the lessons of St. Christopher's need not necessarily lead to a new form of care but cold be applied even in the high-technology environment of the modern hospital. When he returned to the Royal Victoria Hospital in Montreal, he pioneered the development of a hospital based palliative care model.

To Saunders and Kastenbaum (1999), the growth of hospice was a reaction to a number of trends. First, technology driven medicine focused on cure, seemingly abandoning those who were no longer responsive to treatment. Second, hospice resonated with two other themes of the era — "consumerism" and "return to nature." Both trends converged on the idea that individuals could create alternative, more natural organizations, where persons could take control of their lives — and their deaths.

Kübler-Ross and *On Death and Dying*

Few of these efforts, at least in the very beginning, captured as mush public attention as did the publication of Kübler-Ross' *On Death and Dying*. The book
appeared at the right moment. Kübler-Ross was a charismatic woman who spoke
of a "natural death" at a time when there was an increased aversion to technological and personal care (Klass & Hutton, 1985). Her message found a ready audience.

Kübler-Ross posited that dying persons went through a series of five (now
famous) stages — *denial, anger, bargaining, depression, and acceptance.*
Through her case vignettes, she made a powerful plea for the humanistic care of
the dying patient. In an excellent evaluation of Kübler-Ross' contributions, Corr
(1993) suggests that this call for humanistic care and her affirming message to talk
to dying persons, along with the heuristic value of the work, are the enduring legacies of the book.

The stages, though still popular in lay literature, are far more problematic.
Evaluations of her theory of stages (see, for example, Doka, 1993) note many problems. Some are methodological in nature. Kübler-Ross never really documented
her material. It is unclear how her data were collected or how many patients experienced what reactions. Nor has research supported the concept of stages (e.g.
Schulz & Aderman. 1974). There are other problems as well. While Kübler-Ross
insisted that the stage theory was not to be understood literally or linearly, the
book clearly offers an impression of linear stages. As such, individual differences
and the diverse ways that persons cope are often ignored. In addition, it is unclear
whether the stages represent a description of how persons cope with dying or a
prescriptive approach that stresses that dying individuals ought to be assisted to
move through the five stages and eventually embrace acceptance.

Weisman's (1972) work on denial suggests another difficulty — denial and
acceptance are far more complicated than Kübler-Ross perceived. In his work,
Weisman described orders of denial emphasizing that patients might deny symptoms, diagnosis, or impending death. Weisman notes that denial is not always negative. It allows patients to participate in therapy and sustain hope. Weisman introduces a very significant concept of *middle knowledge* — meaning that patients
drift in and out of denial; sometimes affirming, other times denying the closeness
of death. To Weisman the important question was not *"Does the patient accept or
deny death?"* but rather *"When, with whom, and under what circumstances does
the patient discuss the possibility of death?"*

In summary then, the 1960s and 1970s were a formative time for the study of
dying. In this period many of the classic works and key concepts were developed.
It also was a period when hospice continued to develop and began to expand.

The Evolution of the Concept Anticipatory Grief

In the closing section of study on acute grief, Lindemann (1944) noted that grief reactions could be in anticipation of loss. Fulton and associates (Fulton & Fulton, 1971; Fulton & Gottesman, 1980) attempted to develop this concept. Fulton's concern was that the term was easily misused. Fulton wrote at a time when many clinicians attempted to "encourage" family members to experience anticipatory grief under the assumption that the acknowledgement and processing of the grief prior to the loss would mitigate grief experienced after the death. He later described this as a "hydrostatic" perspective of grief — indicating a zero-sum notion of grief, that is, that there is just so much grief or tears that can be expended. Therefore whatever is experienced earlier on in the illness will not need to be encountered later (Fulton, 1987). Moreover, foreknowledge or forewarning of death does not seem necessarily to imply that anticipatory grief occurs. It is little wonder that research found little evidence that the anticipation of loss positively influenced later grief outcomes (see Rando, 2000, for an extensive review). Fulton has since re-evaluated the concept, stating, "I have serious reservations regarding the heuristic value—either theoretical or practical—of the concepts 'anticipatory grief' and 'anticipatory mourning'" (Fulton, 2003 p. 348).

Rando (2000), though has offered an extensive revision of the concept. Rando acknowledges that the term *anticipatory grief* is a misnomer. Yet, she still finds it useful. Rando redefines *anticipatory grief* referring to the phenomena as *anticipatory mourning*. This is a critical distinction. Anticipatory grief refers to a reaction while anticipatory mourning is a far more inclusive concept referring not only to reactions experienced but also the intrapsychic processes that one uses to adapt to and cope with life-limiting illness. Rando also redefines the concept as referring not only to the grief generated by the possibility of future loss but primarily as a reaction to the losses currently experienced in the course of the illness. The patient is not the only person to incur these losses. Family members and even professional caregivers may experience these losses as the patient continues to decline. Rando's reformulation then frees the concept from much of the earlier misconceptions that proved problematic.

Task and Phase Models of Coping with Life-Threatening Illness and Dying

Worden's publication of *Grief Counseling and Grief Therapy* (1982) represented a paradigm shift in the way we understand mourning — one that would contribute to the study of dying as well. While prior models offered a more linear stage or phase theory to explain the mourning process, Worden conceptualized mourning as a series of four tasks. As Corr (1992) noted, the use of tasks offered certain advantages. Implicit in the concept of tasks was an inherent assumption of individuality and autonomy not often seen in stage models. Bereaved individuals might find it easier to cope with some tasks than with others. They would complete tasks in their own unique ways. And grieving persons would complete these tasks on their own timetable or even choose not to address certain tasks. Also unlike stage theories, there was no assumption of linearity. Moreover a task model had clear clinical implications. A grief counselor could assist clients in understanding what tasks they were struggling with and facilitate these grieving clients as they sought to work on these difficult tasks.

Both Corr (1992) and Doka (1993, 1995) applied the concept of tasks to the dying process. To Corr, coping with dying involved four major tasks that correspond to the dimensions of human life — physical, psychological, social, and spiritual. The physical task was *to satisfy bodily needs and to minimize physical distress in ways that are consistent with other values.* Corr defined the psychological task as *to maximize psychological security, autonomy, and richness.* The social task was *to sustain and enhance those interpersonal attachments that are significant to the person concerned, and to sustain selected interactions with social groups within society or with society itself.* Corr's spiritual task was *to address issues of meaningfulness, connectedness, and transcendence and, in doing so, to foster hope.*

Doka (1993, 1995) building on the work of both Pattison (1978) and Weisman (1980) suggested that a life-threatening illness can be understood as a series of phases, noting that not all phases would appear in any given illness. The *prediagnostic phase* concerns itself with the process of health seeking. It refers to the time prior to the diagnosis. One of the most common, but not the only context, would be the time between when an individual notices a symptom and seeks medical assistance. The *acute phase* refers to the crisis period surrounding the diagnosis of life-threatening illness. The *chronic phase* refers to that period where the individual struggles with the disease and treatment. Many individuals may recover from the illness. However, Doka reminds that in the *recovery phase*, individuals do not simply go back to the life experienced before illness. They still have to adapt to the aftereffects, residues, and fears and anxieties aroused by the illness. The *terminal phase* revolves around adapting to the inevitability of impending death as treatment becomes palliative.

At each phase, individuals have to adapt to a series of tasks. These tasks derive from four general or global tasks — *to respond to the physical facts of disease; to take steps to cope with the reality of the disease; to preserve self-concept and relationships with others in the face of the disease, and to deal with affective and existential/spiritual issues created or reactivated by the disease.*

Though these models seem to have interesting implications for understanding the ways that individuals cope with dying and life-threatening illness, they have not been widely applied. Yet, they still represent a possible direction as we strive to develop new approaches and models of the dying process.

The Possibilities in Dying

In addition to coping with dying, there has been some work on possibilities for continued growth and development throughout the dying process. Kübler-Ross' (1975) in her edited book, *Death: The Final Stage of Growth*, suggested that by accepting the finiteness of life allows us to more fully live life — discarding the external roles and petty concerns that are essentially meaningless. Dying persons are our teachers, she asserts, since accepting the limited time left in their lives they can focus on what is truly important and meaningful.

Byock (1997) in his excellent book, *Dying Well: The Prospect for Growth at the End-of-Life* suggests that once a dying patient is freed from pain that person retains the human potential to grow and the possibility to use his or her remaining time to express love, finish significant and meaningful tasks, and reconcile with others.

The key caution is to remember that these are possibilities — possibilities that need to be embraced by the dying person. They become a danger when others, whether family members or health professionals, see it as their goals to induce the dying person to achieve such possibilities. Shneidman (1992) offers a fitting caution that no one has to die in a state of "psychoanalytical grace."

Conclusion

While the study of grief abounds with exciting ideas and the hospice movement has expanded exponentially, the study of the dying process has been relatively neglected. It can be hoped that the next decade will be one of increased attention to and development of new ways to conceptualize the ways that individuals experience dying and evidence-based interventive strategies to assist dying persons, their families, and their caregivers.

Learning Objective:

Explain how historical contexts influenced the experience of Dying and the theoretical models used to explain this process. (40/40)

Chapter 4

Life Span Issues and Dying

Robin Paletti

A central issue in thanatology research involves the physical, psychosocial, and spiritual experience of dying, and its implications across the human life span. For individuals facing death, negotiation of the dying process is often fraught with developmental challenges. It is the aim of this chapter to provide an exploration of these concerns, including such relevant factors as normative developmental task fulfillment, death attitudes across the life span, and palliative care issues. It should be noted that the varied experiences of dying—and indeed, human development itself—are shaped in large part by social, cultural, and historical factors (Morgan & Laungani, 2002; Parkes, 1996); a comprehensive examination of these influences, however, lies beyond the scope of this chapter, which instead offers a distinctly Western perspective, rooted theoretically in Erikson's (1963, 1968) widely recognized ideas concerning human life span development.

The term *life cycle* has been defined as the underlying order of the course of human life (Neugarten & Datan, 1973). The most generally accepted theories of human life span development describe a series of normative transitions through which individuals progress from infancy through adulthood (Erikson, 1963, Freud, 1917; Jung, 1933/1971). Among the most influential of these, Erikson's (1963) task-oriented model characterizes the human personality as evolved through social experience. During each of eight distinct stages of development, he asserts, a central psychosocial conflict presents itself, the resolution of which allows for the preservation of one's ego identity, and progression to the following stage. Failure to respond successfully to the task presented, according to Erikson, impedes the maturation process. For terminally ill individuals, confrontation with death poses significant barriers to normative task completion, giving rise to a number of urgent developmental concerns. As individuals across the life span strive towards personality fulfillment in the face of death, their experiences provide valuable insight into the dying process, and pave the way for the improved care of the terminally ill.

Infancy and Childhood

The term "childhood" generally refers to the first ten to twelve years of life, encompassing four basic developmental stages: infancy (birth through approximately 12-18 months), toddlerhood (infancy through approximately 3 years), early childhood (approximately 3 to 6 years), and middle childhood (6 years to puberty) (Erikson, 1963). While childhood deaths are relatively rare, according to the National Center for Health Statistics (NCHS, 2007), the largest number occurs during infancy. The overall infant mortality rate in the United States is approximately 690 deaths per 100,000 live births. Statistics, however, reveal discrepancies among racial groups; for African Americans, for instance, the mortality rate increases to 1,365 deaths per 100,000 live births, while rates among Hispanic and White Americans are 555 and 573, respectively. For older children, aged 1-4 years, the total number of deaths declines to approximately 32 deaths per 100,000 people. The majority of these deaths are accidental, with congenital malformations constituting the second leading cause. Among older children, the death rate decreases to approximately 15 children per 100,000, with the leading cause remaining accidents, followed by cancer (malignant neoplasms).

Developmental Issues

According to Erikson (1963, 1968) each of the four eras in childhood may be characterized in terms of a particular developmental task. Confrontation with death during any of these stages may hinder the maturation process. The developmental work of infants, for instance, involves the cultivation of trust versus mistrust, thus allowing children to develop a sense of hope, along with a perceived ability to rely on others to fulfill needs. For chronically ill infants, extended hospital stays, constantly changing environments, and painful and confusing medical procedures may interfere with the ability to develop a psychic bond with adults, and to develop the trust crucial to his or her development (Doka, 1996).

Later in childhood, according to Erikson (1963), an overriding tension emerges between a child's sense of autonomy and external control factors. The primary developmental task at this stage of development involves the establishment of a sense of independence; physical limitations, however, caused by illness and parental overprotectiveness may compromise toddlers' ability to develop a sense of self-control (Doka, 1996).

Terminal illness during early and middle childhood presents additional challenges. Between the ages of approximately 3 to 6 years, a child must begin to balance personal desires with moral responsibility (Erikson, 1963). For dying children, however, inconsistent discipline, coupled with parents' reluctance to set behavioral limits, may undermine the resolution of this conflict (Doka, 1996). In older children, the struggle to meet academic demands while coping with terminal illness may compromise the achievement of mastery and competence. Physical limitations, as well as parental safety concerns may also impede the development of children's industrial capacity.

Childhood Death Attitudes

Children's attitudes towards death are largely influenced by cognitive developmental levels, socialization, and prior experience with death and dying (Walker and Maiden, 1987). In general, research surrounding children's death concepts suggests three distinct developmental stages (Nagy, 1948). For children under five years of age, death may be perceived as reversible, or the result of magical or medical intervention (Speece & Brent, 1992). Among children aged 5-9, death is often personified, or perceived as a contingency, and beyond age 9 most children are able to recognize its universality (Nagy, 1948).

For children living with terminal illness, concepts of death and dying assume greater immediacy. As chronically ill children learn about their condition, they often develop heightened levels of anxiety (Corr, 1999). Perhaps unsurprisingly, studies suggest that death anxiety among dying children is greater than it is among healthy youth (Waechter, 1971). In early childhood, this anxiety arises from a fear of parental separation, while older children more often fear destruction and body mutilation following death (Corr, 1999).

Implications for Care

Consideration of developmental issues is key to effective care of terminally ill children. In addition to providing maximum physical relief of symptoms, caregivers may facilitate children's psychosocial development by encouraging active communication throughout the dying process (Adams & Deveau 1993). Corr (1999) cites music, art, or drama therapy as particularly helpful in this regard. Assigning children key roles in the management of illness and treatment decisions is also critical towards the development of mastery and the maintenance of a healthy self-esteem. Caregivers must allow children to function as active partners in treatment, allowing for the development of a crucial sense of autonomy, while supporting social interaction by facilitating access to peers.

Adolescence

Adolescence is generally understood as the period of life ranging from age 12 to approximately 18 years (Erikson, 1963); however, due to earlier onsets of puberty for the past several generations and to extended delays beyond the teen years in achieving autonomy, there is recognition of fluidity about the beginning and end of the adolescent years. The NCHS (2007) cites the number of deaths among younger teens at approximately 19 per 100,000 people, with accidents and cancer the two leading causes. For older adolescents, this rate increases to approximately 52 per 100,000 people, with accidents again the leading cause of death, followed by suicide. Normally a time of burgeoning possibilities, adolescence is a dynamic period in the human life span; when death occurs at this stage, it is accompanied by a number of complex psychosocial considerations.

Developmental Issues

Adolescents are confronted with a host of unique transitional issues. Along with profound physical changes, for instance, teenagers must also negotiate pressing psychosocial concerns surrounding the attainment of independence, peer acceptance, and self-esteem. Erikson (1968) describes the primary task of adolescence as identity formation, citing teenagers' struggle to formulate personal and occupational goals, and to address issues of sexuality and gender. Klopfenstein (1999) conceptualizes this period in terms of three substages: early adolescence, from age 10 to 14 years, involves a predominant shift in attachment from parents to peers, while middle adolescence, ranging from age 15 to 17 years, concerns the development of individual self-image, experimentation and the cultivation of abstract reasoning ability. Late adolescence, through approximately 20 years, describes a period of increased self-acceptance, concern for others, and an increasingly future-oriented view of the world.

Confrontation with death during adolescence frustrates normative developmental processes in several ways. Physically, changes associated with puberty may be delayed, replaced by unwelcome side effects of treatment, including hair loss, acne, weight fluctuations, or disfigurements (Freyer, 2004). Terminally ill teenagers' psychosocial development is also profoundly affected by the dying process. The crucial struggle for independence and mastery is often exacerbated, for instance, because physical and emotional dependence may increase as treatment progresses (Nannis, Susman, & Strope 1978; Freyer, 2004). Peer relations, critical to the development of adolescent identity, may also be hindered by chronic illness. Difficulty participating in social or athletic activities, a lack of sexual outlets, prolonged hospital stays, frequent outpatient visits, or home medication regimens may impede socialization, and lend themselves to a sense of isolation among terminally ill teens (Freyer, 2004).

Adolescent Death Attitudes

Research suggests that teenagers' conceptions of death evolve over the course of three stages of adolescence, and are intrinsically related to developmental issues (Noppe and Noppe, 1996). Concepts of death among younger teens most often involve parental separation, while individuals in mid-adolescence tend to focus on death's impact on others. For college-age youth, consideration of one's legacy supersedes concern with personal mortality. Teenagers' burgeoning abstract-thinking skills give rise to more fully developed concepts of death than those found in younger children, and by adolescence, most individuals understand death as universal and irreversible (Foley & Whittam, 1990). Still, the struggle to construct an identity may also impede a logical understanding of death, resulting in increased anxiety among adolescents (Noppe & Noppe, 2004). Death anxiety, in fact, is at its highest levels among teens at the peak of the identity formation struggle, who possess "less stable ego pictures" (Alexander & Alderstein, 1958, p. 175).

Implications for Care

Caring for dying adolescents is an interdisciplinary process involving physicians, nurses, social workers, therapists, and psychologists. Coordination among these practitioners is essential in addressing patients' physical, psychosocial, and spiritual concerns. Special consideration should be taken to support adolescents' unique developmental needs, including the application of treatment models which emphasize ego identity through acceptance of death (Nannis, 1978). In an effort to enhance teens' sense of autonomy and independence, caregivers might also allow for patients' graduated participation in treatment decisions, although such choices may be complicated by questions surrounding young people's cognitive capacities (Freyer, 2004). Schoeman (1980) also stresses the importance of family privacy, autonomy, and responsibility in end-of-life decision making among terminally ill adolescents.

Adulthood

Adulthood is a life stage that may also be conceptualized in three parts: young adulthood, extending throughout one's twenties and thirties; middle adulthood, including one's forties, fifties and early sixties; and late adulthood, or maturity, including the years beyond age 65 (Erikson, 1963; Cook & Oltjenbruns, 1998). Death rates among the latter group are the highest, at approximately 5,070 deaths per 100,000 people (NCHS, 2007). Among the elderly, heart disease is the primary cause of death, followed by cancer. In mid-adulthood, the death rate decreases to approximately 638 per 100,000 people, with cancer and heart disease again the two leading causes. Among younger adults, the death rate decreases further, to 140 deaths per 100,000 people, with accidents and cancer as the predominant causes. At each stage of adulthood, confrontation with the dying process demands negotiation of an array of pressing psychosocial issues.

Developmental Issues

The primary developmental tasks of adulthood involve the exercise of responsibility, and the expansion of competencies (Cook & Oltjenbruns, 1998). For young adults, love relationships are a principal focus, as individuals strive to achieve intimacy versus a sense of isolation (Erikson, 1963). At this stage of life, adults may commit to marriage, career, and parenthood. When terminal illness intrudes upon these developmental tasks, many young adults are fiercely resistant (Pattison, 1977). Intimate relationships may also be threatened by the onset of terminal illness, as partners become alienated by their own fears surrounding the dying process (Cook & Oltjenbruns, 1998). Nevertheless, close relationships often serve to allay fears of isolation, and aid the terminally ill in feeling valued as individuals.

As adults age, psychological emphasis shifts to contemplation of achievements and the process of stock taking (Butler & Lewis, 1982). Relationships remain important at this stage of life, along with a sense of individual and familial security (Pattison, 1977). Erikson (1968) describes middle adulthood in terms of generativity versus stagnation, as individuals focus increasingly on parenting and the next generation. Death at this stage usually follows considerable introspection, and a re-evaluation of one's accomplishments (Cook & Oltjenbruns, 1998).

By old age, death and dying emerge as more immediate concerns. Among the elderly, dying is often characterized by a process of life review (Butler, 1963), as individuals strive to maintain ego identity in the face of despair (Erikson, 1963). Successful resolution of this stage of development allows for the cultivation of wisdom, and a sense of acceptance and fulfillment. Failure to achieve these virtues results in a sense of hopelessness, derived from an individual's disappointment in a life perceived as poorly lived (Erikson & Erikson, 1982).

Adult Death Attitudes

Death attitudes in adulthood are influenced by a number of factors, including gender, environmental factors, generational differences, and experience with death and aging (Walker & Maiden, 1987). In general, studies have suggested that death anxiety decreases from mid-life to old age. Among older adults, for instance, Kalish (1989) reports greater levels of death acceptance, which he attributes to their having lived long lives and experienced the deaths of others. Abengozar, Bueno, and Vega (1999), however, have cited increased levels of despair, fear, loneliness and depression among older adults when confronting death.

Implications for Care

As in cases involving children and adolescents, key developmental issues must be addressed in caring for dying adults. As intimacy is a critical concern for individuals in this age group, its expression ought to be encouraged through open communication and, when applicable, marriage therapy. Modified continuation of occupational roles might also be encouraged for young adults with terminal illness (Cook & Oltjenbruns, 1998). At middle age, treatment choices ought to support generativity processes through the continued realization of social roles and relationships. Allowing individuals a prominent role in post-death arrangements is often helpful in this regard. Such participation in end-of-life decision making is also an important aspect of treatment for the elderly, for whom autonomy is vital to the maintenance of a positive self-concept (Corr, Nabe & Corr 2003). According to Corr, Nabe and Corr (2003), caregivers should encourage older adults to conduct life reviews, perhaps using photos as stimuli. Individualized care, they assert, either at home or within a personalized institution is also suggested, in order to help dying adults achieve maximum physical and psychic comfort levels.

Regardless of one's developmental level, confrontation with death is an experience described by intense psychological crisis. As situational challenges intensify developmental processes, individuals with terminal illness are faced with a multitude of complex concerns; ultimately, it is the struggle towards personality fulfillment in the face of death that characterizes the dying process across the human life span.

Learning Objective:
Recognize how the psychosocial tasks across the life span affect concepts of death and coping with dying. (35/40)

Chapter 5

The Family, Larger Systems, and Dying

Stephen R. Connor

Thirty years ago those working in the new field of death, dying and hospice believed that the need for specialists who cared for the dying would be obsolete in 20 years. Good care for the dying would become part of the larger health care system and separate organizations such as hospice would no longer be needed. While a laudable goal, it is now clear that the need for those who specialize in care of the dying will continue for the foreseeable future.

Improvements have been made in the way our health system provides care for the dying, and in this chapter we will explore the evolving structures that have emerged to deliver care, including: hospice care, palliative care, professional certification and hospice and palliative care as a new medical subspecialty, care of the dying in institutions, care for underserved populations such as prisoners, the disabled, minorities, those with uncertain prognoses or stigmatizing conditions, those in very rural areas, and the mentally ill. In addition the impact of death and dying on our evolving concept of family or attachment network will be examined including the biomedical-psychosocial-spiritual model, the stress of caregiving, and the current thinking on awareness of dying and the impact of differing trajectories of dying. Hospice care in the United States has been the most successful experiment at delivering palliative care to date despite a number of significant limitations.

Hospice Care

The National Hospice and Palliative Care Organization (National Hospice and Palliative Care Organization [NHPCO], 2000) definition of hospice states:

> Hospice provides support and care for persons in the last phases
> of an incurable disease so that they may live as fully and as comfort-

ably as possible. Hospice recognizes that the dying process is a part of the normal process of living and focuses on enhancing the quality of remaining life. Hospice affirms life and neither hastens nor postpones death. Hospice exists in the hope and belief that through appropriate care, and the promotion of a caring community sensitive to their needs that individuals and their families may be free to attain a degree of satisfaction in preparation for death. Hospice recognizes that human growth and development can be a lifelong process. Hospice seeks to preserve and promote the inherent potential for growth within individuals and families during the last phase of life. Hospice offers palliative care for all individuals and their families without regard to age, gender, nationality, race, creed, sexual orientation, disability, diagnosis, availability of a primary caregiver, or ability to pay.

Hospice programs provide state-of-the-art palliative care and supportive services to individuals at the end of their lives, their family members, and significant others, 24 hours a day, 7 days a week, in both the home and facility-based care settings. Physical, social, spiritual, and emotional care are provided by a clinically directed interdisciplinary team consisting of patients and their families, professionals, and volunteers during the:
1. Last stages of an illness;
2. Dying process; and
3. Bereavement period (NHPCO, 2000, p. ii).

Modern hospice care began with Cicely Saunders founding of St. Christopher's Hospice outside London in 1967. Today there are over 8,000 hospice or palliative care programs worldwide in 113 countries (Wright, Wood, Lynch, & Clark for The International Observatory, 2006). The first U.S. hospice began serving patients in 1973 (Stoddard, 1992; Connor, 1998). Today there are more than 3,000 U.S. companies that deliver hospice services at over 4,000 offices serving defined areas. In 2005 more than 1.2 million patients and families received services from a hospice provider (NHPCO, 2006). Of those served approximately 800,000 died, 200,000 were carried over into 2006, and 200,000 were discharged for a reason other than death, usually due to improved condition.

In 2005 there were an estimated 2.4 million deaths in the U.S. from all causes (Centers for Disease Control [CDC], 2006). Therefore, if 800,000 people died under hospice care in 2005 then one-third of all people who died that year had at least one day of hospice care before they died—a really remarkable feat for palliative care in the United States and a benchmark internationally. The true denominator for the need for hospice or palliative care is unknown but if we eliminate those who clearly would never access hospice or palliative care including those dying of sudden trauma, non-HIV infectious diseases, sudden heart attack or stroke, and those who become acutely ill and die but who were not dependent prior to their illness, we can eliminate almost one-third of all deaths from the denominator (Connor, 1999). Hospice in the United States may now be reaching half of those who need care.

However are people getting hospice care for a long enough period prior to death to benefit? In the early days of hospice care in the United States average length of service was about 70 days. For hospice to be maximally effective some (Iwashyna & Christakis, 1998) have suggested that 2-3 months of care are needed. This duration is to allow enough time to provide preparation and education for caregivers, to assist in getting affairs in order, to prevent anticipated and distressing symptom problems from occurring and to form a therapeutic relationship with the patient and family.

The length of service for hospice had dropped to a low of 48 days in 2001 and 2002 and has now rebounded to an average of 59 days. However a more accurate measure of the typical hospice patient's experience is the median length of service which was 26 days in 2005 and more troubling the percent of hospice patients on service seven days or less was over 30% (NHPCO, 2006). The number of hospice patients on service over six months has climbed to about 10%.

The length of service for hospice has been influenced by several factors. During the late 1990s hospices received increased government scrutiny focused on patients who were on hospice care for more than six months. In addition the Medicare Hospice Benefit prevents patients from receiving hospice care while currently receiving "curative" care. Each hospice provider is allowed to determine which treatments are curative and which are palliative. There is much disagreement over the definition of curative with many treatments aimed less at cure than prolongation of survival for usually short periods but at considerable expense. Many patients and families demand continuation of these treatments thus in some cases delaying hospice referral or admission.

Hospice payment under Medicare is governed by regulations referred to as Conditions of Participation or COP's (Centers for Medicaid and Medicare Services [CMS], 2006). These rules have been in place since enactment of the Medicare Hospice Benefit (MHB) in 1983 and specify how hospice care must be organized and delivered to qualify for payment. Key provisions of the *Conditions of Participation* require hospices to:

- admit eligible patients with a terminal illness with a prognosis of six months or less who agree not to continue curative treatment and agree to hospice care.

- re-certify surviving patients as being terminally ill at specified intervals (90 days, followed by another 90 days, followed by ongoing 60-day recertification periods).
- meet administrative requirements including a governing body, an interdisciplinary team, a plan of care for each patient, a medical record for each patient, a medical director, regular training, quality assurance, use of volunteers, and maintenance of professional management of the program.
- provide core services by hospice employees including a physician, nurse, counselor, and medical social worker; and provide other non-core services including physical, occupational, and speech therapy; home health aides/homemakers; medical equipment and supplies; medications, and short term inpatient care for symptom management and respite.

MHB payment is made for each day of hospice care on a per diem basis at one of four rates: routine home care; continuous home care for crisis periods in lieu of hospitalization; general inpatient care for severe symptom management, and inpatient respite care to give up to five days break for caregivers.

The COP's are being revised and the modified rules are expected to be released for implementation in 2008. Several organizations also provide voluntary accreditation for hospices including the Joint Commission on Accreditation of Health care Organizations (JCAHO), Community Health Accreditation Program (CHAP), and the Accreditation Commission for Health Care (ACHC). At present about 60% of hospices are accredited by one of these bodies (NHPCO, 2006).

Palliative Care

Palliative care is defined as "Patient and family-centered care that optimizes quality of life by anticipating, preventing, and treating suffering. Palliative care throughout the continuum of illness involves addressing physical, intellectual, emotional, social, and spiritual needs and to facilitate patient autonomy, access to information, and choice." (CMS, http://www.access.gpo.gov/nara/cfr/waisidx_04/42cfr418_04.html). That definition, recommended by CMS in the proposed Medicare Hospice Conditions of Participation, has been adopted by the National Quality Forum (NQF), with agreement by NHPCO and the Center to Advance Palliative Care (CAPC).

All of hospice care is palliative; however, not all palliative care is provided by hospices. In the last 10 years primarily hospital based palliative care has grown in the United States. The American Hospital Association and the Center to Advance Palliative Care report that there are now over 1,200 hospitals in the United States that provide palliative care services (CAPC, 2006). In addition many hospice programs are now adding palliative care programs and services for patients who do not qualify for reimbursement as hospice patients. (See Clinical Practice Guidelines or Quality Palliative Care at http://www.nationalconsensusproject.org/Guidelines_Download.asp)

Professional Certification

In September 2006 the American Board of Medical Specialties voted to approve Hospice and Palliative Medicine as a new sub-specialty. Any currently recognized specialty can add hospice and palliative medicine as a sub-specialty. So far 10 co-sponsoring boards have agreed to including Internal Medicine, Family Medicine, Surgery, Anesthesiology, Physical Medicine and Rehabilitation (PM&R), Obstetrics/Gynecology, Pediatrics, Neurology/Psychiatry, Radiology, and Emergency Medicine. This important achievement represents years of work mainly led by the American Academy of Hospice and Palliative Medicine and the American Board for Hospice and Palliative Medicine (ABHPM). The ABHPM will discontinue providing hospice physician certification, and beginning in 2008 physicians will be eligible to apply for recognition under their specialty board.

The National Board for Certification of Hospice and Palliative Nurses (NBCH-PN) continues to certify advanced practice nurses, registered nurses, licensed practical/vocational nurses and nursing assistants. As of 2006 there were 9,067 registered nurses, 271 advanced practice nurse, 578 LPN/LVNs, and 3,053 nursing assistants certified by the NBCHPN. There is currently no recognized certification for hospice or palliative care social workers, chaplains, or administrators. The Association for Death Education and Counseling (ADEC) Certification program is the only certification program for those practicing generally in the field of death, dying, and bereavement; note that the ADEC Certification in Thanatology (CT) certifies mastery of foundational knowledge, not of practice skills.

Care of the Dying in Institutions

The World Health Organization (WHO, 2006) estimates that there are 58 million deaths annually worldwide. In the developed world there is a much higher rate of death in institutions than in the developing world where death continues to come at earlier age and usually at home. Even in transitional countries like Romania home deaths are still over 80%. In the United States and generally in Europe hospital death rates are high. In 2005 U.S. hospital deaths were 50%, home deaths 24% and nursing home deaths 26% (Brown University, 2006).

Care of the dying in institutions continues to be a serious concern. A major study of dying in institutions was conducted by the SUPPORT Investigators (1995) with funding by the Robert Wood Johnson Foundation. The study looked primarily at teaching hospitals and found that overall pain control continued to be poor, patient's wishes for care were routinely ignored, and advance directives were often disregarded. In the first phase of this study only 47% of physicians knew when their patients preferred to avoid CPR, 38% of patients who died spent at least 10 days in an intensive care unit, and for 50% of conscious patients who died in the hospital, family members reported moderate to severe pain at least half the time.

More and more people are dying in nursing facilities annually. Average survival for chronically ill patients admitted to nursing homes is estimated to be 18 months (Rothera, Jones, Harwood, Avery & Waite, 2002). As such they are a natural population for palliative care. Hospice care to patients in nursing facilities has been shown to lead to a number of positive outcomes including: 1) hospice patients had superior pain assessments and hospice patients in daily pain are twice as likely to receive strong pain relievers than are non-hospice residents in daily pain, 2) a 93% increased likelihood that patients in daily pain will have at least some attempt made at managing their pain, 3) lower proportions of hospice patients compared to non-hospice patients had invasive procedures such as physical restraints, IV feeding, or feeding tubes, and 4) less likelihood of return to acute care facilities (Miller, Gozalo, & Mor, 2000).

In 2005 22% of hospice patients were admitted in nursing facilities and 23% died in nursing facilities (NHPCO, 2006). From this we can surmise that only about 1% of hospice patients are transferred from other settings to nursing homes before death. For the remaining 22% the nursing home was essentially the patient's home. For the hospice or palliative care provider the nursing home staff, along with any other family, becomes the patient's de facto family and a recipient of support from the hospice team.

Care for Underserved Populations

Palliative care has spread slowly for many underserved populations. Hospice care in the United States began mainly in more affluent areas where **minority populations** were less well represented. In the UK hospice has been criticized as deluxe dying for the few (Douglas, 1992). Over the last 30 years the proportion of minorities receiving hospice care has increased but is still not believed to be at par with the population. In 2005 less than 5% of hospice patients were Hispanic/Latino, about 8% were African American, and whites accounted for 82% of admissions.

The **prison population** is another disenfranchised population that has had limited access to hospice or palliative care. Since the early 1990s tougher sentencing laws resulting from the "Get Tough on Crime" campaign and the "Three Strikes and You're Out" law have increased the number of inmates housed in prisons. The number of inmates housed in federal, state and private correctional facilities has increased steadily. In midyear 2000, State, Federal, and private correctional facilities held 1,305,253 inmates, a 28% rise from the number of inmates held in 1995 (United States Department of Justice, 2003). Between July 1, 1999, and June 30, 2000, 3,175 inmates died in prison, with illness or natural cause accounting for 85% of deaths in federal prisons, 75% of deaths in state, and 66% of deaths in private facilities. AIDS was the second most common cause of death, accounting for 7% in federal, 10% in state, and 13% in private facilities (U.S. Department of Justice, 2003).

Although prisoners are entitled to health care that is commensurate with community standards, most inmates dying in prison do not have access to end-of-life care that meets these standards (Craig & Craig, 1999). Over the past decade efforts have been made to improve hospice and palliative care for inmates (Craig & Craig, 1999; Yampolskaya & Winston, 2003). However, several challenges remain such as reconciling incarceration practices with hospice practices; providing palliative care that complies with correctional goals; providing adequate pain management in an environment lacking of trust between inmate and staff members; and involving family within the confines of visitation restrictions.

Patients with developmental disabilities have also had limited access to hospice and palliative care. Many with **developmental disabilities** until recent years had lived in specialized inpatient facilities and died at relatively early ages. Today only those with the most profound disabilities are institutionalized and many are living to older age with the usual accompanying chronic diseases. One percent of the population is developmentally disabled and most now live independently or in group homes. Professionals working with the developmentally disabled have limited knowledge of palliative care principles and palliative professionals have limited knowledge of the special challenges of care for the developmentally disabled. For more resources on palliative care for this population see http://www.nhpco.org/i4a/pages/index.cfm?pageid=4733. Patients with **physical disabilities** also face added challenges receiving palliative care.

Dying Trajectories

It has been proposed that there are four primary trajectories to dying. They include 1) sudden death 2) death from predictable decline such as cancer 3) death from solid organ failure, and 4) death from old age including frailty and/or dementia (Lunney et al., 2003).

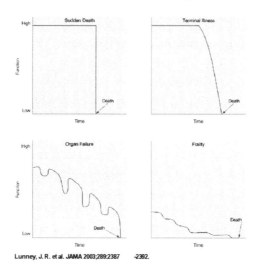

Lunney, J. R. et al. JAMA 2003;289:2387   -2392.

This categorization may oversimplify the variations in the way people die and certainly some of these trajectories will overlap, however it is a useful way to understand most common pathways to death. Obviously those dying suddenly will not be able to avail themselves of palliative care, except that families may benefit from bereavement support and some who sustain trauma will have a period of need for symptom control prior to their deaths.

Caregiver Issues/Gender Roles/Awareness of Dying

One of the factors that make hospice and palliative care so successful is a focus on empowerment of caregivers. At the time of admission to a hospice or palliative care service a thorough assessment of family and caregiver history, needs, and capacities is done. A defining characteristic of all palliative care is the idea that the patient and family are the unit of care, not just the patient. By family we mean those that are involved in the emotional life and care of the person dying, regardless of blood or marital ties.

In palliative care, families are taught to do almost anything a nursing professional can do, to the extent that the family member has the internal strength or ability to do this work. One of the reasons it is thought that families do better in bereavement after participating in hospice care (Christakis & Iwashyna, 2003; Connor & McMaster, 1996; Schulz, et al., 2001) is due to their effective involvement in caregiving. Post death, non-caregivers have been found to show more depression and weight loss.

To facilitate their involvement many families will need support. The International Work Group on Death, Dying, and Bereavement has published "Assumptions and Principles for Psychological Care of Dying Persons and Their Families" (Psychological Work Group of the International Work Group on Death, Dying, and Bereavement, 1993), which includes a statement on families need to be cared for in order to give care.

Find This

Caregiving can lead to positive outcomes as well as stressful negative outcomes. What determines positive or negative outcomes in caregiving depends largely on timing, circumstances, and perception of meaning (Folkman, 1997; Schulz et al., 2001). In general caregiving that is time limited in some way is easier to cope with, as in the case of hospice care. When caregivers perceive their job of caregiving as personally meaningful there is less stress and when the relationship to the person cared for is not an ambivalent one.

Caregiving in the United States is primarily done by women, who comprise 75% of caregivers. Two-thirds of caregivers are also employed and are between 35 and 64 years old (http://www.womenshealth.gov/faq/caregiver.htm). Numerous resources on caregiving can also be found on the Caring Connection Web site (http://www.caringinfo.org/i4a/pages/index.cfm?pageid=3279 including information on physical caregiving, comfort care, services available to assist caregivers, and caring for the caregiver.

Awareness of dying remains a difficult issue for dying persons and their caregivers. The term conspiracy of silence was used by Glaser & Strauss (1965) to describe the phenomena of physicians and families conspiring to keep information on the seriousness of a patient's condition from them. The underlying premise is that if you tell a patient they are dying it will result in the patient becoming depressed, giving up and dying sooner than they might otherwise have if they remained in blissful ignorance.

The problem with this premise is that patients usually know how serious their condition is even if not told directly. Instead of being protected from difficult information the patient is left in what Weisman (1972) refers to as a state of lonely apprehension. The more the conspiracy of silence is maintained the worse the situation gets. This example illustrates an instance where what one is trying to do to solve the problem actually makes the situation worse as honest communication becomes more difficult to convey over time. Most of what we perceive to be denial on the part of the patient or family is generally in the service of preserving interpersonal relationships. Avoiding discussion of the seriousness of the patients condition is due to fear that open communication will somehow harm the person or drive people away, when it is the lack of communication that is really creating discomfort.

What is known about the impact of truth telling on a dying person's emotional state is that after a sometimes strong emotional reaction to the bad news the patient usually adapts to the situation or chooses to ignore the information. No research has ever shown that telling a patient their accurate prognosis has any negative impact on survival. In fact some research has shown that truth telling can result in positive responses (Connor, 1992). And some research indicates that open family communication about dying can have a positive impact on the health and survival of widowed persons (Connor & McMaster, 1996; Christakis & Iwashyna, 2003).

Learning Objective:
Explain how hospice CARe reflects the way in which Social Organizations are designed to help individuals and their families through the dying process. (30/30)

Chapter 6

Ethical and Legal Issues and Dying

Arthur Zucker

Probably no one wants to die just to die — to see what it is like to die and then be dead and buried and/or cremated. Biology seems to teach that organisms will strive to live; strive against all odds. For many organisms, living seems to have as its goal, reproduction. But for people, there can be other important goals. Because of this human phenomenon, many codes of ethics will have as a rule, something like: Do Not Kill. Because of this ethical interpretation, we tend to think that people who want to kill themselves may not be thinking rationally. Consequently, we think of the health care professions as those whose end should be to help us to stay alive. In this chapter, we will see the roles that "Do not kill" and "the goal of health care should be to help us stay alive" play in issues revolving about the process of dying.

What precisely is—for our purposes—"the dying process"? There is a trite view that from the time of conception, we are all dying. This viewpoint may be true but not in any useful sense. To be dying, for our purposes, is to be terminal and to be terminal is to satisfy these two requirements: 1) a diagnosis of some condition where cure for that condition is very unlikely given (a) survival time for most patients from the time of diagnosis and given (b) the research state-of-the-art at the time and 2) there is a direct causal chain so that one can say that death was due to the condition and that it occurred sooner than one would have expected or predicted if the condition had not been present (Zucker, 1980). Thus, the question implicit in the topic for this chapter is what are the special legal and ethical issues that one finds with terminal patients.

Obviously, some terminal patients present no ethical or legal problems unique to their situation. There are, however, some special ethical and legal issues related to being terminal. Here are some:

1. what counts as therapy—is palliative intervention all that there is
2. can terminal patients enter into experimental protocols
3. is informed consent impossible with terminal patients
4. who decides/who should decide on care when the patient cannot
5. what is the status of living wills and advance directives
6. what counts as futile intervention
7. what is the role of the physician/health care team in decisions to end life
8. issues of allocation. (Callahan, 1987, 1990, 1993, 1998).

The easiest way to think about these issues is by looking at a case—a model case. Let us consider Mr. Thompson. He is 74 and has been diagnosed with terminal cancer. With the drug, dormativium, the cancer will take about five years to cause his death.

Suppose Mr. Thompson cannot afford dormativium. Should he get the treatment anyway and, if so, who will pay? If there is to be a health care system that pays for such treatments, should there be an age limit; should there be a limit based on how close to death someone is, i.e., how much they can profit from the drug? Who should judge "profit" in such a case? Suppose Mr. Thompson gets dormativium. As the years go by, as he approaches death, Mr. Thompson needs more and more care. Should he stay at home and try to tough it out; should he get nursing care; and, of course, who pays? At what point should he enter a hospice if at all?

Again, suppose Mr. Thompson gets dormativium. A drug company has a drug that promises to do a better job than dormativium. But it needs testing. Should Mr. Thompson be allowed into the protocol? Is it even fair to suggest entering the protocol to him? After all, what (real) choice does he have? This constraint is especially true as his five years run out. As his time does run out, he may get more and more upset with his quality of life. Mr. Thompson wants to die sooner than his five years. Is he *prima facie* competent or *prima facie* not quite competent? Who should decide this question and who should speak for him? He asks his physician for help in dying. Is physician assisted suicide ever acceptable? Is it acceptable in this kind of case? If it is never acceptable, should there be laws against it or is an addition to a professional code of ethics enough? Does "help in dying" cover only those cases that are classified as active euthanasia or does it extend to "passive euthanasia"? Is there a morally relevant difference between active and passive euthanasia?

The distinction active and passive euthanasia is contentious to say the least. The easiest way to think of the purported distinction is by example. If I push your head under water and keep it there until you drown, then I have actively killed you. If I see you drowning and walk away and do nothing at all to help you, then I have let you die—this is passive.

But now consider this possibility: As the cancer takes its toll on Mr. Thompson, he wants to fight to the very bitter end. He asks for all sorts of treatments including CPR should his heart stop. This treatment may count as futile to the health care team but may not seem that way to him. Should he get all the help that he wants or should he get only what the health care team decides he should get?

Now change the case a bit. Mr. Thompson is nearing death in a nursing home. He has an advance directive which states that in the situation he is now in he should not be given CPR; he should be given only palliative care. But his son tells the physician in charge, "You must do everything to keep my father alive for as long as possible." Does the son have more standing than the advance directive? Does his standing depend in any way on how often he visited his father; whether he was paying all or some of the bills? Legally, the advance directive trumps the son's request. But often, in practice, it will not. However, the question, "Does the son have more standing than the advance directive?" should be reframed as "Should the son have more moral standing than the advance directive?" This question has two sides to it that can be seen by imagining Mr. Thompson arguing with his son. The elder Thompson, about to enter the hospital for likely the last time before his death, wants to be identified in his chart as "do not resuscitate" (DNR). His son is adamantly opposed and tires to convince his father that making himself DNR is immoral. Should the son try to override his father's wishes? Should the father have put the son in this position by making an advance directive that he knew would fly in the face of his son's values? (One could imagine a similar argument over entering a hospice instead of a tertiary care hospital.)

Of course, it is not only men in their seventies who get sick and die. Women, children, infants, toddlers, adolescents and young adults are subject to the events listed in outline above. Do any of the answers for Mr. Thompson change if it is Ms. Thompson; if it is Baby Tom, infant Tom, etc? Clearly issues of consent will turn on age. But will other answers?

There is in the medical ethics literature a debate between the views of Tom Beauchamp and James Childress (2001), in shorthand known as the Georgetown Mantra, and the views of Bernard Gert and Charles Culver and K. D. Clouser (1997), who see the mantra as needing an overarching moral system. The mantra provides four principles, autonomy (sometimes put as "respect for others"), non-maleficence (basically, avoid harming others), beneficence (do good), and justice (treat equals as equals; sometimes thought of as fairness). Any case, they claim, can be handled by an appropriate juggling of these principles. Thus, in the case of Mr. Thompson's request for treatment that seems to the health care team as futile, we could say, using the mantra, that justice (a fair allocation of life saving treatments) demands that such treatments be denied Mr. Thompson. If we looked only at autonomy tinged with a bit of beneficence, we might grant his wish for 'futile' treatment. Thus, the need for the balancing act between the use of the principles.

The moral system proposed by Gert, Culver and Clouser (1997) lists ten rules:

1. Do not kill.
2. Do not cause pain.
3. Do not disable.
4. Do not deprive of freedom.
5. Do not deprive of pleasure.
6. Do not deceive.
7. Do not cheat.
8. Keep your promise.
9. Obey the law.
10. Do your duty.

The first five always lead directly to evils if violated. The second five, if violated, often lead to evils but not as directly as the first five. There are also moral ideals:

1. Prevent or reduce (risk of) death.
2. Prevent or reduce (risk of) pain.
3. Prevent or reduce (risk of) disability.
4. Prevent or reduce (risk of) loss of pleasure.
5. Prevent or reduce (risk of) loss of freedom.

Acting on a moral ideal is always right but never required unless such action is called for because of a special obligation that has been undertaken. Thus, if we promised as deliverers of health care, to perform CPR on Mr. T at the end of his five years, Gert's moral system might require that we perform the CPR. But there is a way out for those following the Gert-Culver-Clouser system. One is allowed to violate a rule if one is willing to advocate publicly (in principle) that the reason for violation would count for all people in similar circumstances and that a rational, impartial person would agree that this violation would be accepted under these circumstances for these reasons by all rational impartial persons. The two systems, which start out looking dissimilar, may in fact give the same answers. This is a hallmark of truly difficult ethical questions. Instead of one clear answer to which all agree, there is a range of acceptable answers. Choosing an answer within the range will turn on many other beliefs such as one's picture of the profession, what one takes to be the relevant facts of the case, and how one weights these factors in decision making.

Two cases recently discussed by ethicist Ezekiel J. Emanuel (2006) will illustrate both ethical, legal and allocation type issues that arise with the dying process.

Dr. Emanuel's patient was Virginia.

Her ankles were terribly swollen and her eyes were tinged with yellow. Five years earlier, she had been treated for a very small and early-stage breast cancer. For a while, she was fine—teaching third-graders, living with her husband and four children. Then, at age 56, her cancer came back. She began having difficulty breathing, and a CT scan revealed the cancer had metastasized to her lungs and liver. After a year and a half, the conventional drugs stopped working, but Virginia wanted to fight, and she opted for experimental drugs. The day she came to the office, Virginia had just completed a trial of a second experimental agent, but it had failed to halt the growth of the tumor in her liver.

Virginia wanted to continue her fight and asked if there weren't some other experimental drug she could try. But Dr. Emanuel thought that her battle was at an end. She was going to die from her disease and no experimental drug would help. It would only provide false hope. He says, "One of the hardest parts of being an oncologist is explaining to a patient that her battle has come to an end...While I began talking to Virginia about palliative care and hospice, all she wanted to know was if there was another experimental drug that she could take" (Emanuel, 2006).

His view is that allowing such patients the right to try these experimental drugs before they are proven effective is a mistake, not just because it provides false hope but because while these drugs are available, dying patients will shy away from entering randomized protocols to test the effectiveness of such drugs and thereby hurt all other dying patients. Moreover, as Dr. Emanuel correctly points out, the rest of us will have to bear the cost of letting patients use these drugs indiscriminately.

Emanuel points out that this set of possibilities came about because

...the District of Columbia Circuit Court ruled, in a 2-1 decision, that dying patients have a constitutional right to any experimental drug that has passed the safety phase of human testing—Phase I— even while the drug's effectiveness is still unproven and undergoing research. The case [is] *Abigail Alliance* v. *von Eschenbach*. The Court held that a "mentally competent, terminally ill adult patient [has a substantive due process right] to access potentially lifesaving post-Phase I investigational new drugs."

Emanuel thinks the decision a bad one for the reasons cited above. His arguments are reasonable but they can be countered. What follows is an argument meant to highlight another side of the issue that Emanuel presents so clearly. This other side will help fill out the issues, ethical and legal, that occur with the dying process.

Virginia's disease may be coming to an end. Her life may be coming to an end, but her battle need not, for those reasons alone, come to an end. It may just be beginning. This should be her choice not Dr. Emanuel's choice. This distinction raises a question of counseling ethics. Should the physician try to change a patient's mind about such issues or merely support a patient's decisions, within reason, no matter what those decisions are?

Does Virginia lose freedom here because of the probability that the drug will not help her or because she is dying. Or, is it some combination of both? One has to define "false hope." Hope is what the philosopher, John Searle (1995), would call an extrinsic feature of the world. It exists only because there are people and their properties. Molecules, Searle would say, are intrinsic features of the world. Even if there were no people, there would still be molecules. In everyday terms, "hope" is relative to a person's situation as that person is living through it. In other words, hope is subjective. The importance of informed consent may have been underestimated by Emanuel. If patients know just what they are getting into, then their choice is informed. If they are competent, as required by the Court decision, then they are *prima facie* free. At first face, At first view

Why should dying patients risk being randomized at all? Why should a dying patient be forced to take that risk? Shouldn't it be a choice freely made and not a sham choice? Taking a big risk is not necessarily folly. Again, what the risk is should be part of the consent to take the experimental drug. Asking dying patients, because they are dying, to be altruistic and risk placebo or old drugs is unfair.

The situation created by the Court's decision may have unfortunate consequences, although this outcome is yet to be determined. But it is not irrational and it is not unethical or immoral unless one assumes that the only way to make such judgments about treatment is by relatively simple utilitarian calculations. A simple utilitarian ethical principle holds that one should always do that action that creates the greatest good for the greatest number. Limiting the use of this principle to Virginia's case, the utilitarian would argue that more people are helped by not allowing Virginia (and patient's like her) to have more experimental drugs.

These sorts of calculations are always a part of ethics—but only a part. They need not tell the whole story. There are ways to justify making exceptions to utilitarian-decided outcomes. One way would be to exempt the dying from just this Emanuel-way of looking at the equation, which is what the Court, in effect, did in its decision.

Why shouldn't the healthy want to pay for peace of mind for some of the dying? Indeed, why shouldn't they be asked to pay some money when it is the dying who are paying the ultimate price? It is for the young and healthy to care for the elderly and the sick and, of course, the dying. It is in the young and healthy that we should expect and encourage altruism. Shouldn't I be willing to help you at least in part because I would want help if I were in your situation, the situation where I wanted to live a bit longer and were willing to risk my quality of life for that extra time?

These are just a few of the challenges to Emanuel that could be made. As noted above, these counter arguments exist within a range of acceptable arguments. It is important to develop the habit of ethical reflection: Thinking about these issues, getting clear on how you would address them, getting clear on your assumptions and being willing to evaluate and change your own positions.

LeARNiNg Objective: (35/40)
Consider the ethical And legAL issues Surrounding involved in the cARe + treatment of the dying.

End-of-Life Decision Making

Introduction to Part 2, Chapters 7-12

*Chapters 7 through 12 focus on end-of-life decision making. The Body of Knowledge Committee defined this major category of thanatology knowledge in this way: **the aspects of life threatening illness/terminal illness that involve choices and decisions about actions to be taken, for individuals, families, and professional caregivers.***

The chapters in Part 2 focus on end-of-life decision making in terms of these indicators: culture and socialization, religion and spirituality, historical and contemporary perspectives, life span issues, the family and larger systems, and ethical and legal issues.

Chapter 7

Culture, Socialization, and End-of-Life Decision Making

Andrea C. Walker

Culture is multi-faceted, multi-dimensional, and embedded in time and history. A complete definition is difficult to articulate, but culture involves a series of interactions and adjustments, negotiations and agreements of a person, or group of people, with her/their environment. Interwoven into culture is a series of expectations, perceptions of "rightness" regarding sources of power, values, social structures, religion, etc. Socialization involves learning the rules, beliefs, and expectations within a particular society, many of which are influenced and/or defined by culture.

Attributing a list of characteristics to particular groups is a tempting way to simplify culture, but the concept reaches beyond ethnic origin, race, or nationality to embrace heritage, family, experiences, and resulting belief systems. Kagawa-Singer and Blackhall (2001) recommended "finding a balance between cultural stereotyping and cultural empiricism...by neither disregarding culture nor assuming one is part of a list of stereotypical characteristics" (p. 2995). In sum, there may be much more variation within than between groups. Any terms used in this chapter referring to a particular group are used with the following assumptions: (a) there may be only a few commonalities among the group members, and (b) the group is likely to contain numerous subgroups.

The purpose of this chapter is to examine how culture and the socialization process affect the end-of-life decisions a person makes. I begin with a discussion of the dominant values of the U.S. health care system and move to a summary of the socio-historical context of five major cultural groups. I encourage independent study of additional groups or subgroups. Next, we review pertinent literature on specific end-of-life decisions and conclude with suggestions for practitioners.

Dominant U.S. Cultural Values

To understand cultural and social contributions to end-of-life decisions, one must be knowledgeable of related values in the dominant culture, as conflict between dominant and subculture can create misunderstandings and difficulties. Western medical ethical principles promote: (a) beneficence, honesty, respect, and all possible benefit to the patient, (b) non-maleficence, bringing no harm to the patient, (c) justice in matters of health care, and (d) patient autonomy. Such principles have been taken so seriously that they have been legislated into public policy with the Patient Self-Determination Act (Henig, Faul, & Raffin, 2001), which was passed as part of the Omnibus Budget Reconciliation Act of 1990 to increase patient autonomy regarding treatment options, advance directives, and when to discontinue treatment (Young & Jex, 1992). The passing of the Patient Self-Determination Act has brought up ethical issues revolving around withholding and/or withdrawing treatment, as well as more controversial issues of: (a) physician-assisted suicide, obtaining a physician's aid in committing suicide, (b) indirect euthanasia, the physician allowing a patient to die using more passive, less intrusive means, and (c) direct euthanasia, the physician's purposeful intervention to hasten death (Horacek, as cited by Marrone, 1997).

Cultural conflicts with the principles around the Patient Self-Determination Act have been explored in literature (Werth, Blevins, Toussaint, & Durham, 2002). A benefit to the dominant culture may be perceived differently in another culture. For instance, removal from tube feeding of a terminal, unconscious patient to minimize suffering may be perceived as "giving up" in an African American culture. As respect for the patient's value system and justice in treatment are likely to be important in all cultures, components of value systems and perceptions of justice may diverge. The idea of fidelity, forthright communication from the physician regarding the patient's diagnosis, prognosis, and treatment options, while important in the dominant culture, may seem cruel and inappropriate to some Chinese Americans (Yeo, 1995). Finally, the value of autonomy may not be seen as self-determination in many cultures, as it is in the U.S. (Winzelberg, Hanson, & Tulsky, 2005). Furthermore, some have challenged the idea that the western view of autonomy is always in the best interest of the patient. Hallenbeck, Goldstein, and Mebane (1996) described the ethical principles in the United States as having "sustained and reinforced a pervasive reductionism…and dominance of self-interest in decision making…" (p. 394). Quite simply, members of minority cultural backgrounds may not share dominant U.S. values of independence, self-reliance, and fear of being dependent on others as a result of lingering treatment (Kagawa-Singer & Blackhall, 2001).

Overview of Socio-historical Context

Each cultural group in the U.S. evolves from unique socio-historical context, enveloped in experiences encompassing country of origin, religious background, immigration to the U.S., and position in mainstream society. Psychosocial and demographic variables such as age, socio-economic status (SES) religion, education, perspective of health care, and meaning of death may account for the variation within cultural groups. For instance, in a study of older adults' personal preferences if faced with terminal illnesses and/or physical conditions (Cicirelli, 1997), many older adults were socialized to regard the physician as authority figure and, thus, themselves as having less decision making authority in their health care. Further, those who preferred to defer the decision to someone else tended to have external locus of control. In addition, Black participants' end-of-life decision preferences remained consistent across circumstances, SES, and religiosity, suggesting that the social history of African Americans may have helped form a strong sense of survival in the face of trauma unique to the culture (Cicirelli, 1997).

African Americans as a group tend to have a stronger focus on religiosity, believing that suffering is redemptive and that God has more authority over life and death than physicians (Kagawa-Singer & Blackhall, 2001). Another influence may unfortunately be a legitimate lack of trust by African Americans in the medical establishment (Bullock, 2006) based on experiences of injustice in health care, disregard for autonomy, and disproportionate involvement in research and experimentation. Several historical events, including but not limited to slavery, medical experimentation, the Tuskegee Syphilis Study, in which treatment was knowingly withheld from patients to track their digression, and lack of federal funding when AIDS spread to the African American community (Dula, 1994), along with social pressures of economic challenges and unequal rates of incarceration (Crawley et al., 2000), have resulted in some African Americans questioning whether or not they should trust the health care system (Amelle, Lawrence, & Gresle, 2005). Not all research has supported this notion of a lack of trust from African Americans, however, specifically among ambulatory cancer patients who reported trust in the health care system and feeling that physicians treated them equally well, regardless of race (McKinley, Garrett, Evans, & Danis, 1996). Still, the patients in this study did choose longevity significantly over White participants.

The term "American Indian" more than over five hundred tribes in the United States, each with their own cultural considerations. Much of the current culture within each tribe is influenced by the degree of acculturation and the influence of Christianity (McCabe, 1994). It is unfair to describe a socialization process generalized to all Native Americans, but some commonalities may exist. Very possibly, many tribes experience distrust in mainstream culture, resulting from a history of forced acculturation, relocation, and dishonored agreements with the U.S. government. In some tribes, particularly the Muscogee Creek, children attended boarding schools where they were not allowed to use their native language (Thompson, 2002, personal communications), accelerating their evolution away from their native culture. Also, many tribes were based on a communal structure though individuals were given responsibility and decisions. Navajos have a strong sense of autonomy, though decisions are rarely made without input from other tribal members, making the western ethic of confidentiality seem strange (McCabe, 1994). Finally, many tribes, traditionally responsible for harvesting or killing their own food, may have a particular disposition toward the natural flow of life and a more accepting position toward death, though grief may be strong.

Hispanic Americans are comprised of many diverse groups, including Mexicans, Cubans, Puerto Ricans, and Latin Americans with traditions influenced by both Spain and Africa. Representing a growing population in mainstream U.S., there may be a few similarities across groups despite the diversity. Many of these groups openly celebrate Day of the Dead to remember their loved ones, indicating a familiarity and acceptance of death, as well as emphasis on remembering family after death. Importance of family appears to be common across most groups and end-of-life decisions may be based on the family rather than the individual wishes. With the strong influence of Catholicism, religious beliefs are often intertwined with the view of death. Many Mexican Americans see health as a gift from God, and enduring the suffering of sickness may be a sign of strength (Klessig, 1992).

Asian Americans represent yet another vastly diverse category of minority cultures in the U.S., comprising Chinese, Japanese, Filipino, Vietnamese, Korean, Native Hawaiian, among numerous others. Many immigrated to the U.S. during several waves over the past 200 years, enduring some U.S. resistance evident in the Chinese Exclusion Act of 1882 and the Oriental Exclusion Act of 1924. Many Asian Americans, except Filipinos who are dominantly Catholic, originate from Buddhist and Taoist backgrounds, in which death is accepted, natural, and not final (Braun & Nichols, 1996). Chinese incorporate the Buddhist value of not causing suffering or burden on others (Bowman & Singer, 2001). Native Hawaiians experienced much loss of life upon their initial contact with the West when European missionaries arrived on their islands a few centuries ago. Influenced by a combination of Christianity and their Native religion, Native Hawaiians appear to accept death as a transition to the next life (Braun & Nichols, 1996). The value of filial piety, respect and care for one's parents and elders in the family, influences end-of-life decisions in Asian groups, particularly the Chinese, and precedence in decision making is given to the family over the individual (Bowman & Singer, 2001; Yeo, 1995).

End-of-Life Decisions

Typically, members of mainstream European-American culture are more likely to have knowledge and use of advance directives, withdraw life-sustaining treatments in futile conditions, and support physician-assisted suicide than those of minority cultures. As a whole, minority cultures tend to be less supportive of decisions that result in earlier death (Werth et al., 2002).

Advance Care Planning

Advance care planning provides family and health care practitioner with a person's treatment preferences prior to incapacitation through the living will, written specification regarding administration of life support due to terminal illness, and durable power of attorney, giving another person legal authority to make one's medical decisions when he/she is unable to do so (Doukas & McCullough, 1991). White Americans have shown to be the most likely group to have advance directives. Older Hispanics, Asians, and American Indians have lower rates unless enrolled in a special services program. African Americans were more likely to have negative attitudes toward advance directives due to distrust of the system, lack of access to health care, increased spirituality, a "survivalist" view of suffering and death, influence of social support systems, and other unknown reasons while controlling for SES (Bullock, 2006; King & Wolf, 1998; Kwak & Haley, 2005; McKinley et al., 1996). Because elderly Chinese rely on their children, they may see little value in advance care planning (Bowman & Singer, 2001). Braun and Nichols (1996) found that few Native Hawaiians had a living will, as property typically goes to the spouse and children, and family carried out the dying person's verbal wishes regarding death and/or funeral. Also, many Japanese participants actually had advance directives, Chinese believed in them but few had them, some Filipinos had them if they had been in the U.S. long, and Vietnamese participants were typically not familiar with advance directives (Braun & Nichols, 1996).

Life Support/Tube Feeding

Life support involves the use of mechanical devices such as intravenous tube feeding to sustain life when the patient would not otherwise remain alive. Repeatedly throughout literature, research indicates that African Americans, due to beliefs about death, remarkable familiarity with struggle, and increased use of spirituality to cope with life-threatening conditions, more strongly prefer the use of life support regardless of physical condition than other cultural groups (Amelle et al., 2005; Caralis, Davis, Wright, & Marcial, 1993; King & Wolf, 1998; Kwak & Haley, 2005; McKinley et al., 1996; True et al., 2005). Hispanics have also been found to prefer life-prolonging treatment regardless of condition (Caralis et al., 1993). To increase longevity, the likelihood of Chinese families to choose life support if the dying person is younger than expected also increases (Yeo, 1995). Elderly Chinese may actually prefer to not engage in life-sustaining treatments in futile conditions, even though their children may feel an obligation to do so (Bowman & Singer, 2001). When compared to White, non-Jewish participants, Chinese, Filipino, and Korean Americans were much more likely to agree to start, as well as less likely to terminate, life support, and Iranians, whose Muslim beliefs dictate that no one has the right to choose death, usually oppose terminating life support regardless of condition (Klessig, 1992). For Orthodox Jews, life support may be continued in any situation, but for non-Orthodox Jews the dying process should not be prolonged (Klessig, 1992).

Communication about Medical Condition

Many minority cultures in the U.S., including Chinese, Japanese, Korean, Ethiopian, Grecian, Italian, French, Eastern European, Mexican, Central and South American, and Native American believe that withholding the truth about a terminal medical condition from a person is more compassionate and ethical, and disclosure of information regarding diagnosis, prognosis, and treatment preferences is discouraged (Kagawa-Singer & Blackhall, 2001; Kwak & Haley, 2005). Japanese resident physicians are more likely than U.S. residents to discuss medical information with family before the patient (Gabbay et al., 2005). As full disclosure may be seen as distressing in some Latino families (Yeo, 1995), the value of filial piety may also make it difficult for some Chinese Americans to communicate bad news, as this may cause harm and discouragement to the dying person (Muller & Desmond, 1992; Orona, Koenig, & Davis, 1994; Yeo, 1995). Some studies have indicated that such communication is not discouraged among many African and White Americans (Kagawa-Singer & Blackhall, 2001), as well as some Hispanics (Caralis et al., 1993).

Locus of Decision Making

Whether a culture has a tendency toward individual or family/communal structure heavily influences who makes end-of-life decisions. Personal autonomy may be less important in many cultures than in the mainstream U.S. Asian and Hispanic Americans tend to prefer removing the burden of treatment decisions from the patient, while African American families tend to promote the individual person's wishes (Kwak & Haley; 2005). Chinese, Hispanic, Korean, Filipino, Mexican Americans are much more likely than European or African Americans to believe the family should be the primary decision maker (Kagawa-Singer, 2001; Klessig, 1992; Orona et al., 1994; Yeo, 1995), and Japanese resident physicians are more likely than U.S. residents to fulfill families' choices over individual patients' choices (Gabbay et al., 2005). Some Hispanics are more likely to refer to the physician's recommendation (Caralis et al., 1993). In a case study by Carter and Sadling (1992), an

American Indian mother deferred to the tribal elders her decision whether to allow her tragically deformed child to be kept alive by intravenous feeding, demonstrating the cultural tendency to consult group opinion when making individual choice.

Autopsy and Organ Donation

Evidence from empirical studies on cultural differences in choosing autopsies and organ donations was less plentiful. The dominant U.S. culture finds little ethical dilemma with either autopsies or organ donations, but some Asian groups have indicated otherwise. Chinese have divergent opinions of wanting to help others while not wanting to destroy their bodies, seen as gifts from parents; Japanese indicated hesitance to mutilate the body but acceptance, with Buddhist desire to help others, as long as the body appeared intact; Filipinos indicated a greater tendency to agree with the longer time spent in the United States; Vietnamese were generally against organ donation because of not wanting to be born into the next life missing an organ (Braun & Nichols, 1996). Mexican Americans, whose primary religion is Catholicism, tend to prefer not having autopsies or organ donations because of the beliefs that the soul remains with the body for some time after death, and that making such plans before death is equitable with giving up on treatment (Perkins, Supik, & Hazda, 1993). African Americans, on the other hand, tend to concur with the Protestant Christian belief that the soul leaves the body upon death and may be more likely to choose autopsies and to help others through organ donation (Perkins et al., 1993). Additional evidence indicates that willingness to donate organs is much lower in African than White Americans (Lichtenstein, Alcser, Corning, Bachman, & Doukas, 1997).

Suicide and Euthanasia

This controversial topic has received diverse opinions, even from members of mainstream U.S. society. In Lichtenstein et al.'s (1997) comparison study of African and White Americans, both supported legalizing voluntary and physician assisted suicide, but Whites were much more likely than African Americans to request it themselves (Caralis et al., 1993), possibly due to a stronger religious commitment and cultural condemnation of suicide among African Americans. On the other hand, this hesitance may again be attributed to distrust in the medical system, as some African Americans may fear legalization as formal permission to commit involuntary euthanasia (King & Wolf, 1998; Lichtenstein et al., 1997). Native Hawaiians are tolerant of suicide and in favor of passive euthanasia; Chinese tend to believe that suicide is wrong except in cases of rape and prisoners of war, and euthanasia is generally acceptable if it reflects the person's wishes and does not damage filial piety; Japanese are tolerant of suicide and support the family's decision in euthanasia; Filipinos are generally not supportive of suicide or euthanasia;

Vietnamese usually believe suicide is wrong and accept euthanasia only if family cannot afford continued health care (Braun & Nichols, 1996). These Asian group differences appeared to reflect education level and length of time in the U.S. (Braun & Nichols, 1996).

Conclusions and Recommendations for Practitioners

As seen in this chapter, most literature on culture and end-of-life decisions draws comparisons between groups. Some studies, however, indicate influence of other variables, such as age, cognitive capacity, degree of acculturation, etc. (Cicirelli, 1997; Kwak & Haley, 2005; Winzelbert et al., 2005), suggesting the additional importance of the socialization process. Hern, Koenig, Moore, & Marshall (1998) compared the choices of two Chinese women with terminal cancer, both immigrants to the U.S., and found notable differences in locus of decision making and methods of communication about the illness. These studies help to support my original hypothesis: There may be more within-group than between-group variance. Further, the socialization process itself may account for much of this variance. These types of studies focusing on within-group variance of minority cultures are underrepresented in literature, and future research is needed.

Literature provides us with specific suggestions in how to provide "culturally competent care," most of which target medical practitioners who are legally responsible for abiding by certain ethics, such as truth telling, which may be in direct conflict with a patient's cultural values (Hern et al., 1998; Klessig, 1992; Werth et al., 2002). Broadening these suggestions to include multiple disciplines, such as grief therapists, professional counselors, psychologists, etc., may be helpful. Laungani's (1992) model of understanding culture aids in the development of the following suggestions: (a) determine the locus of decision making in the family, whether patriarchal or matriarchal, individual, or family as a unit, (b) observe closely the communication styles and patterns within the family, including language used and whether unidirectional or bidirectional, (c) determine the family's locus of control, whether reality is perceived as deterministic or as a set of choices, (d) analyze how reality is perceived and expressed, whether through cognitive or emotional means, (e) understand how the family attributes causation of events, whether through scientific, material explanations or spiritual forces, and (f) adapt decision making processes to accommodate diverse perspectives toward end-of-life issues.

Doka (2005) recommends that practitioners consider all factors, complicating and facilitating, and realize that the process of providing appropriate care may take time and may not end at the family member's death. Ultimately, culturally responsible and effective practice will occur when a theme of sensitivity and respect is incorporated into interactions with each person. Doing so involves a reflexive evaluation of our own culture, socialization process, and values involved in our personal beliefs about end-of-life choices, a critical review of how our own personal biases might affect our interactions with those of other cultures and value systems, and finally, compartmentalization of our belief systems to objectively and compassionately embrace and respect perceptions of truth outside our own.

Learning Objective: (30/35)
understand how cultural and social factors influence end of life decision making in contemporary times in the U.S.

Chapter 8

Religion, Spirituality, and End-of-Life Decision Making

The Reverend Richard B. Gilbert

Introduction

Joyce Hutchinson and Joyce Rupp (1999) have a rich history of capturing the essence of the human experience and the spiritual implications within these experiences. They suggest that the two most vital moments, defining moments, in the human experience are birth and death. How a person approaches dying becomes the bulwark on which rests all that affords meaning and integrity for a person.

Rupp contends, with reference to the practices of her co-author, that caring for the dying is a privilege and is, indeed, a sacred time for the dying, their loved ones, and also for those who are beckoned to approach the bedside of the dying. She says, "Joyce [Hutchison] visualizes herself as accompanying each dying person to the door that opens to the other side. She walks them home with loving care, quiet joy, tenderness and compassion" (p. 19).

End-of-life care requires us to at least be available to the dying and their loved ones around the issues of meaning, beliefs, rituals and their longing for peace as they face whatever may be ahead for them. This accessibility means our willingness, with competence, to be available to others around spiritual concerns, wounds, religious issues, unresolved issues, guilt, "sin," fears about "tomorrow," a lack of certainty surrounding their faith and a sense of estrangement from God (or that which is their empowerment) or their religious connections. It requires us to stand firmly in their presence as guest, non-judgmentally, while also tracking our own spiritual/religious issues, challenges and shortcomings.

To assist our discussion we will follow this outline:

- Spirituality and religion: definitions
- Spiritual care: the invitation placed before all providers
- Spiritual assessment tools
- The place for ritual in tending to the dying (including diversity)
- "Managing" diversity within the family (especially points of dispute)
- When our spiritual/religious self feels inadequate or threatened as providers/caregivers
- Making better use of chaplains

Spirituality and Religion: Definitions

Three points are essential here. The first is that everyone has something that they express and experience as spiritual. This expression and experience takes on a new priority and intensity when a person is approaching the end of life. In the tension between "lasts" and "firsts" there may be an internal challenge or conflict previously unknown to the dying person and surrounding loved ones. Second, as caregivers (in whatever role) we must be particularly present and non-judgmental while monitoring and keeping watch over our own spiritual and religious beliefs and practices.

The third point is particularly important. While the murmurings of the dying and of the loved ones may seem almost profane in distancing from things spiritual, these longings and struggles for wholeness at the time of death's approach, paradoxically, serve as the ultimate fulfillment and the ultimate destruction. This longing isn't necessarily about heaven and hell, though it may be for some, but the reality that this is the final test of anyone's beliefs and practices. Even those who have experienced a profound spiritual sense throughout their life journey may feel their faith parched by the draining demands of unfamiliarity on the spiritual walk when dying. Said another way, this person has not faced death before, and this spiritual walk becomes the final stretch or wilderness. Gentle, non-judgmental, reassuring listening will be the mark for the providers so that the patient can be free to say, believe or search in any direction yet feel safe enough to risk moving onward to the tomorrow that awaits within the boundaries of their faith.

In their training manual for hospice physicians, The American Academy of Hospice and Palliative Medicine (1997) speaks of the search for meaning:

> The search for meaning is often characterized by a process that involves exploring questions of value and worth, letting go of former roles and expectations, and reframing events to support renewed hope and an enlarged sense of efficacy. When traumatic losses threaten or occur, patients and families begin the difficult process of adaptation by trying to make sense of what is happening to them. They search for meaning...(p. 17)

Then will unfold the questions of "Who, what, when, and why?" as we try to configure some pathway that we can follow that will make sense out of all of this. Seldom, of course, is it sensible. It is doable when we are enabled to make the right connections which, after all, is a person's expressed spirituality.

It is during this entanglement between life and death, doubt and belief, that some thread of hope is woven. Terminal illness is not necessarily the absence of hope. People can find a measure of hope, even confidence, as they again bringing together living/dying and their beliefs and practices.

The experience of dying and death is a first time experience for us, even if we had faced the deaths of many loved ones and friends. The spiritual framework, often felt to be crushed under the strong winds of death are the same reference points that, upon moving through the worst of death's storm may be the first familiar ground we recognize.

Awesome, So True,

A death is the interruption of a human relationship — whether through a sudden death in an emergency room, a lingering on through disease, perhaps in a nursing home or hospice; or the stealing away of the breath of life in pregnancy. Painful interruptions, wrong, by human standards, are a part of life, the created order. We grieve, we hurt, we lash out at the God we want to blame for all of this (Gilbert, 1995, p. 115).

In addressing the gay, lesbian, bisexual and transgendered community, a lifestyle so frequently immersed in isolation and abandonment, a strong religious criticism from many, it becomes clear why many in this community could suffer severe spiritual and/or religious doubts and wounds. Sweasey (1997), in citing spirituality as one coming to know the self, speaks of spirituality in this way. "Having a deeper sense of oneself, addressing the whole of life, and a connection with something bigger" (p. 12).

Religion often serves as the practical or structured (framing) around which we find a measure of community, familiarity and dependability (Corr, Nabe, Corr, 2006). "[Religious] experience, tradition, and shared attitudes had prepared individuals and the community as a whole to support each other and to contend with the cycles of life and death in their midst" (p. 45).

In his study on spirituality and aging, David Moberg (2001) reminds us that this separation between spirituality and religion has not been an easy separation, should not be seen as a divorce, and is relatively recent in its happening. He suggests that spirituality emerged as an "in" term, in part, because of a growing suspicion of, and separation from, religion. Spirituality became positive and religion was experienced as negative. Spirituality and religion share the common purpose of enhancing a person's self-worth, beliefs, coping with life and that which is eternal for them.

Spiritual Care: The Invitation Placed Before all Providers

Spiritual care is to remove our shoes, in a sense of humility and awe, as we tread upon the sacred ground that is defined and trusted by the dying patient. This intimate sharing is always scripted by the dying, and our ability to step into it is by invitation only. We bring our beliefs and practices and we have myriad spiritual assessment tools.

Sadly, some strong testimony suggests that spiritual care has been an area of some turf warring. Some hospices have not been honestly committed to professional standards for chaplains. Others have good chaplains who are blocked out by nurses and social workers "Who determine when the chaplains will visit," as one chaplain shared with me in a personal conversation.

Spiritual care is the work of all of us. If it rests with the patient primarily, and secondarily with the family, it is their right to extend the welcome mat to whom they wish. Obviously the team must build mutual trust and respect that replaces heroism with collaboration. The patient, for many reasons, may feel more comfortable with the doctor or the housekeeper, the nurse or the volunteer. Let it happen as it should happen, even when referrals come too late (to hospice) that the patient often has no opportunity to explore these important ingredients in their recipe for peace and wholeness.

Rachel Stanworth (2004), in remarks preceded by a strong case for chaplains and pastoral care, states, "The point I wish to make is that unless transparency to an ultimate horizon is valued in principle by employers, there is a danger that providers of palliative care will come to regard spiritual issues as a purely subsidiary interest of psychotherapeutic support, an impoverishment this book strongly resists" (p. 237).

Spiritual Assessment Tools

To assess is to value story, things said and unsaid, the collaborative viewpoints of the team, patient and family concerns, blending them together into, at least for palliative care, the medical model that then guides all team members in the care of the patient.

In part because of time constraints (staffing, late referrals, ability of patient to communicate when heavily medicated, no available family or family disruption that eliminates accurate reporting), along with our own comfort levels around spiritual and religious matters, spiritual assessment is frequently compromised. It has become easier to fit the person into the assessment tool, as one chaplain reminded me when visiting a patient in the hospital where I served. "I have no time to visit with you. I must complete the assessment form."

This practice is common and, equally common, is the risk for spiritual neglect and abuse. Once we have put processes first we have crossed a definitive boundary that, unless reclaimed, will confound despair and pain and further distress the person whose death approaches. It is about fitting who we are and what we offer into the story, the personhood, of the patient. To reverse that intention is to cross that boundary.

Several assessment questions are here offered as resources to guide you as the patient chooses to let you in. David Moberg (2001) suggests several approaches.

1. Questions for discussion and mapping the journey:
   - Do you feel that you have become more religious as you have grown older?
   - How would you describe your own spirituality and your own spiritual life?
   - What is your perception of death? Your attitudes toward death?
   - Are you afraid to die? Why or why not? (pp. 80-81)

2. Moberg shares these marking-points that allow patients to identify their spiritual health and need.
   - Assurance of God's continuing love
   - Certainty that life is protected
   - Relief from heightened emotions as of fear, guilt, grief
   - Relief from loneliness
   - A perspective for life that embraces time and eternity
   - Continue spiritual growth
   - A satisfying status in life as a person
   - The illusion of continued worth and usefulness (p. 93)

Gilbert (1996) offers these assessment questions that can work well when offered conversationally.

When you are discouraged or feeling despondent, what keeps you going? What are your sources of energy and courage?
   - Where have you found strength in past experiences of loss or struggle?
   - Where have you have found hope in the past? How do you define hope?
   - Who have you looked up to? Who inspires you?
   - What does dying mean to you?
   - What does suffering mean to you?
   - What does "religious community" mean to you?
   - What does "religious leader" mean to you?

Another approach is to consider, by observation, assessment and conversation, the signs or "symptoms" of spiritual wounds or crises. Donna O'Toole (1995) provides these statements as possible markers in the story.

- Feeling lost and empty
- Feeling forsaken, abandoned, criticized, or judged by God
- Questioning why to go on with life
- Extremes of pessimism or optimism
- Feeling or not feeling God (or other significant experiences) in life
- Needing to give or receive forgiveness
- Needing to give or receive punishment
- Feeling spiritually connected to what/who is lost.

Gilbert (1995) offers these approaches around feelings expressed, demonstrated or sensed as absent:

- I feel that I am letting God down..."
- "It's all my fault"
- "God will take care of me [often shield protecting further discussion or deeper examination]"
- "Why did this happen to me? Why now?"
- "My heart aches. Where are the pills?"
- "There is no hope"
- "Does God still love me?"
- "What if God knew this ...?"
- "I don't know how to pray any more."
- "Can you teach me how to pray?"
- "I am going home"
- "Will you pray with me?"
- "I want to see a priest"
- "I thought God promised..."
- "The Lord is my shepherd"
- "I prayed, and prayed, and prayed..."

The Place for Ritual in the Care of the Dying

Ritual is the marker, the "stamp of approval" that denotes where a person is on the journey, what is happening or has happened, and the spiritual significance of the moment. It can both comfort and clarify, and serves as a conduit to a person's faith, spiritual connections and religious sense. It is the anchor holding the person firmly in a most turbulent of seas.

It is important to bear in mind that, while rituals, especially sacramental ones, have a more universal definition and outcome, are important, they are still the product or choice of the patient and must not be imposed. This topic can be particularly tricky when the family is divided around spiritual and/or religious matters, each producing their own agenda. Questions like, "What rituals are important to you?" "What does a religious leader mean to you?" and that probe what keeps a person connected to God and religious community, may be your pathways for inquiring about patient wishes.

Any discussion about ritual needs to consider not only the diversity of religious expressions, even within a common group or denomination, but also the diversity of culture. It is imperative that providers keep clear in both thoughts and actions the differences between "diversity" and "different." Several extensive bibliographies on diversity and other related subjects are available free, by e-mail, from this author.

African Americans. As one minister noted, "We Blacks are very spiritual and we are very loud about it." African-Americans often speak about "passing" rather than dying. They generally reject organ donations, especially older generations, because they believe you must be whole to meet the Risen Christ. The religious leader often takes on a much larger role as minister, advocate, legal consultant, and ethicist.

Hispanics or Latinos. Do note carefully that we are speaking not only of diversity within families, communities and nation, but from one country to the next. What works with Mexicans, for example, may not be the approach of people from Argentina. "Death is different in Mexico (Irish et al. 1993, p. 69)." Death can be feared, and emotions and emotional needs run high. They are expressive, use art, religious objects, chants and prayers. The priest has a strong responsibility, both rooted in power and empowerment. Some providers may note, for the first time, something of the "magical use of religion." The line can blur. The rule of thumb is to follow the lead of patient and family.

In addition to the reminder of differences by families and countries, it is also a generational division. First generation Latinos, especially from Mexico, even those who are "legal," are so frightened of any authority (and thus place even more authority on the role of the priest) that they will say "Yes" to any statement by a professional, out of fear, often never understanding their right to say "No." Diversity, then, is not about translating words, but of helping people understand content (words), options (choices) and rights.

Even those who break away from Roman Catholicism and follow other denominations may still seek the rituals and sacraments that are more traditional. There can be variations from generation to generation, especially when moving from first to second generation. Providers must carefully facilitate both needs. Many Mexicans will need guidance around American funeral practices and also often need assistance when burial in Mexico is preferred.

Jews. There is variation, of course, by traditions: Hasidic, Orthodox, Conservative, Reformed, Reconstructionist. There can be language and cultural additions to the discussion. Some will pick and choose, preferring to see themselves as "cultural Jews." Many will require burial within 24 hours, and with specific preparations, including bathing and dressing. This requirement becomes a potential point of difficulty when an autopsy is requested or demanded, and, quite frankly, American society, especially around the logistics for death certificates and other vital statistics, is not a 24-7 operation. A Friday afternoon death might well, simply due to paper work, be delayed until Monday.

Roman Catholics. There is much diversity, including cultural, among Catholics. Some national groups will go back to old traditions, including Extreme Unction, refusing the strongest persuasion of the changes since Vatican II. They might seek both anointing (now stressing reconciliation) and Last Rites. The threefold burial rites of the Wake (often with the recitation of the Rosary), the funeral Mass and the burial is important. Some plans can be frustrated by the shortage of priests or the refusal of some priests or dioceses to facilitate options.

Hinduism, including the sect, *Jainism,* represents the oldest major world religion. It combines many religions and many beliefs. There also can be strong practices around caste and gender. This cultural influence has strong implications for providers. Organ donations generally are not opposed, and burial is within 24 hours, usually by cremation. The switch to crematories, now an American mainstay, is a significant cultural shift. Caskets are always open and sacred books and food play a significant part.

Buddhism stresses that the person passes through many reincarnations. This passage is imperiled when there are delays at the time of the death, including pronouncing the death, paper work, organ donation discussion and funeral arrangements. This aspect is well discussed by Donald Irish and his colleagues (1993).

Muslims, the Islamic faith, has become a contentious issue for many due to world events, politics and, at times, prejudice and fear. There is also variation due to country of origin, and frequently issues around gender and authority. Muslims view death as a universal reckoning, when people are called upon to account for their actions. They find their faith expressed in the *Five Pillars.* The casket is never open, there are readings from *The Qur'an,* prayers are recited and the deceased is buried (not cremated). Many times the graveside ceremonies are attended only by men.

Native Americans is a complex collection best described as diverse. There are strong tribal customs and differences, generally a profound sense of spirituality, and much that does not fit neatly into the American traditions. There are also generational differences. Oftentimes in communities with large Native American communities, one of the funeral homes is particularly expert in the needs of that community.

In all of these groupings, and there are many more, the key reminder is always that, while being informed about general practices and expectations, "Let the person tell you."

Managing Diversity within the Family

While there is no one way to do a burial (albeit while respecting state and community laws), there can be strong expressions around practices that are less acceptable for a particular family or family member. This conflict is often mirrored in issues surrounding religious diversity (Christian vs. non-Christian, religious vs. non-religious, "Born again" vs. those following a different definition or set of criteria). Some opinions or objections may be rooted in the nature of the relationship to the dying patient as well as in old wounds, bitterness or feuds. Sometimes there are secrets, others, as Ken Doka (1989) expresses so well, are "disenfranchised" and have a voice that is not heard. Remarriage and blended families, especially when there are adult children who have not "accepted" the new mom or dad, can be very conflictual. The patient's advance directives, even the fact that the family did not know there were any advance directives, may dictate things in ways unsuitable to the family or parts of the family.

These predicaments often create what feels like a conflictual role for providers. It is important that the team plans around these concerns and maintains a common approach. There may be necessary for one member of the team to be directive. While we stress that we follow the wishes of the patient, it is too easy to hide in that caveat and fail both to address the needs of the family (within reason) and how those needs, practices and memories help or hinder the patient as death approaches.

When Our Spiritual/Religious Beliefs Feel
Inadequate or Threatened

Even under the best of circumstances, the constant parade of dying patients brings significant challenges to providers. Various patients will "hook" you, snag you less in their "stuff" and more in yours. Sometimes it is the accumulation of deaths. For others it is the circumstances around the dying, the patient's age or gender, and the patient's family can contribute to this entanglement. These stressors are neutral unless they impact on the patient or compromise our ability as providers. For most of us it is missing the opportunity for us to explore our own beliefs and practices.

Sometimes our frustration is an invitation to learn, such as questions or a sense of inadequacy when responding to a person who represents different values, gender, beliefs, or lifestyle.

Just as we need to listen to patients intentionally, as a guest, and non-judgmentally, so we require that for ourselves. Many of us have trouble acknowledging and actualizing this fact. There must be a component of the team process that provides debriefing and the opportunity not only to "review the case," but to "review ourselves." Management must know how to discern team needs and when an intervention might be necessary, for the group (team) or for an individual. This discernment is also a good use of the chaplain's presence with team members.

Making Better Use of Chaplains

Chaplains have long served in the care of the dying. Even before the modern hospice movement there were various expressions of hospitality and care of the dying, often provided by monks and monastic communities.

Chaplains are specialists, usually with additional training and accountability, to work in a variety of traditional and non-traditional workplaces, including hospice. They need to be included as active members of the team, and it is important that they have full access to patients, families, staff, and charts. Chaplains have the responsibility of both being actively present while also standing at a distance, viewing the wider picture, including the needs of the staff.

In Conclusion

Few events in life both depend upon and stress a person's spiritual resources than to be approaching the end of their life. This ending is a time of profound, exaggerated experiences, feelings and needs, all of it at an intensity frequently unknown previously. For some, this new experience is more than their spirituality can bear. For others, things spiritual are the only things that will move them through it. Exploring the spiritual dimension is crucial for patients, families and providers when approaching end-of-life care.

LeARNiNg Objective: (35/35)
Identify the role of religious + Spiritual beliefs in end of life decision making.

Chapter 9

Historical and Contemporary Perspectives on End-of-Life Decision Making

James L. Werth, Jr. and Christine Harte

This chapter is intended to briefly review several areas that have implications for end-of-life decision making. To the degree possible, we have based our discussion on research and will provide both historical and contemporary perspectives on each area, although the length of time reviewed will vary by topic. We defined end-of-life decision making as choices made by dying individuals, their loved ones, or professional caregivers that take place during a person's dying process and/or have an effect on the manner and timing of death. Examples of end-of-life decisions include whether to create advance directives (i.e., a living will, a durable power of attorney for health care) and, if so, determining the specifics related to them; whether to continue, withhold, or withdraw life-sustaining treatment; whether to more actively hasten death such as by voluntarily stopping eating and drinking or requesting (or providing, in the case of personal and professional caregivers) assisted suicide or voluntary euthanasia (see also Kleespies, 2004). We will not deal with end-of-life decisions made and enforced by health care providers without the awareness of the dying person or loved ones (e.g., involuntary euthanasia) or over the protestations of the dying person/loved ones (e.g., futility determinations).

The chapter begins with a review of some demographics associated with people who have died, including both international and historical comparisons. Next is an overview of the causes and patterns of dying, such as causes of death, where death occurs, and how and when people actually die. This discussion is followed by sections on obstacles to health care and diversity issues in end-of-life decision making. Finally, there are sections on treatment options and holistic approaches to care near the end of life. This material is intended to highlight why end-of-life decision making has become an issue, including the challenges that have arisen and why: Basically, the changing patterns in the causes of death have, in general, led to people in the United States living longer with debilitating conditions, although there are still significant differences in the quality of care based on demographic variables such as ethnicity. These changes have led to more comprehensive approaches to care that allow the person near the end of life more control over the end of her or his dying process.

Demographics of Death

According to the National Center for Health Statistics (NCHS; 2005; see also Field, in press), in 2002 nearly 2.5 million people died in the United States. Approximately 75% of those who died were 65+ while less than 1% were under the age of 1. Because the majority of people who die are adults, as well as the fact that decision making for infants and children is complicated by a variety of factors, the focus on this chapter is on end-of-life decision making by and for adults.

In the U.S., currently, the average person can expect to live to be older than age 77 (NCHS, 2005; World Health Organization [WHO], 2004, Annex Table 1); in 1900 life expectancy was only 47 years (Field, in press). There are longevity differences based on sex and race/ethnicity (Field, in press; Kleespies, 2004; Stillion, 2006). Women can expect to live to be 80 while men can expect to live to be between 74 and 75. Thus, women are more likely to be single/widowed near the end of life and the current cohort of women is more likely to be poor because they did not work to the same extent as today's women (Stillion, 2006). Whites can expect to live to be nearly 78 while Blacks can expect to live to be just over 72. Combining these data, White women have the longest life expectancy, followed by African American women and White men who are nearly identical, and then African American men; other groups are harder to track.

In many other countries, life expectancy has also increased, but in some nations there has been little improvement. For example, Stillion (2006; see also WHO, 2004, Annex Table 1) noted that Japan (now, 82 years) and Sweden (now, 80.4 years) have also seen significant increases in longevity in the last century. Just as in the U.S. there are gender differences in longevity in most countries reporting mortality statistics, with women living longer (Stillion, 2006). On the other hand, reportedly primarily because of AIDS, life expectancy in some African countries has actually decreased (Kleespies, 2004). Thus, life expectancy of someone in many countries in Africa may be 45 or less (WHO, 2004, Annex Table 1).

Although not technically a death demographic, it is noteworthy that as people continue to live longer, the likelihood of some sort of cognitive decline increases, even without considering the people who develop dementia (Park, O'Connell, &

Thomson, 2003). Thus, there is the possibility that eventually any person may lose the capacity to make her or his own health care decisions, which has implications for the end-of-life decision making process.

Causes and Patterns of Dying

Just as longevity has changed in the past century, so too have the causes of death, the places where death occurs, and the ways that people die, all of which may impact decisions.

Causes of Death

During the early 1900s, the leading causes of death were diseases and conditions that led to death fairly certainly and rapidly (e.g., pneumonia); however, more recently, the primary causes of death are chronic conditions that often have an uncertain path and timeline (e.g., cancers, heart conditions; see Field, in press; Leming & Dickinson, 2007; Stillion, 2006).

The patterns of dying differ based on age group, sex, and race/ethnicity (Field, in press). For example, for people over 65, heart disease, cancer, and stroke are the three leading causes of death, while for those aged 15-24, unintentional injuries, homicide, and suicide are the top three. Alzheimer's disease and suicide are in the top ten list for Whites but not for Blacks whereas homicide and HIV disease are in the top ten for Blacks but not Whites.

Internationally, the causes and patterns of death look very different (WHO, 2004, Annex Table 2). For example, relatively few people in most of the Americas and all of Europe die from infectious and parasitic diseases but these are leading causes of death in Africa and in some places in Southeast Asia. Similarly, as alluded to above, the death rate related to AIDS is significantly higher across the African continent than anywhere else in the world. On the other hand, the death rates associated with malignant neoplasms (i.e., cancer) and cardiovascular diseases are much higher in the Americas and Europe than in Africa. The patterns of death underscore Ditto's (2006, footnote 1, p. 136) point that end-of-life decision making in the United States, much of Europe, and other industrialized and technologically advanced countries is very different from other parts of the world.

Where Death Occurs

Just as the causes of death have shifted over the last 100 years, the same is true of the places where death occurs, at least in the U.S. (Field, in press; Stillion, 2006). Although death used to take place in the home with the person surrounded by loved ones, current estimates are that approximately 80% of deaths will take place in institutions where people are likely to be surrounded by health care workers. More specifically, about 60% of people will die in hospitals (Faber-Langendoen & Lanken, 2000) and about 20% of older adults will die in a nursing home (Moss,

2001). Approximately 30% will die in hospice care, which may take place in a variety of settings including a personal home or an institution (Casarett, 2006; hospice will be discussed more fully below).

How and When People Actually Die

Given the information above — that people who die are primarily older adults who have chronic conditions (perhaps along with cognitive impairment) and are in institutions — it should not be surprising that the dying process and ways in which people die today reflect these changes. Instead of fading away at home as the body shuts down (i.e., "naturally"), the majority of people who die in the U.S. in modern times do so after a decision has been made to stop or not start treatment (Faber-Langendoen & Lanken, 2000). Thus, although technically people may die of an underlying condition, such as kidney failure, they actually typically die when treatment (e.g., dialysis) is withheld or withdrawn, so the timing and manner of their death is orchestrated or negotiated in some way by a combination of the dying person, loved ones, the health care team, and sometimes the courts. As with the other areas mentioned above, there are differences based on demographics, some of the possible reasons for this will be discussed in the next two sections.

Obstacles to Health Care

The issue of health care disparities has received significant attention in the last decade (e.g., Gamble & Stone, 2006; Satcher & Pamies, 2006). Given the history of exclusion of non-Whites from hospitals as well as the unethical medical experimentation on racial/ethnic minority individuals in the U.S., it is not surprising that there are sociocultural barriers to equal access and care that continue today (Shavers & Shavers, 2006). There are also differences in health related quality of life based on demographic factors (Lubetkin, Jia, Franks, & Gold, 2005), including treatment based on age (e.g., Schrag et al., 2001) and sex (Wizemann & Pardue, 2001). One of the major obstacles to health care is mistrust of the medical system, based on historical issues such as the Tuskegee Syphilis Study (Werth, Blevins, Toussaint, & Durham, 2002).

Pain management provides an example of how discrimination has continued into the present, can create obstacles to appropriate care, and therefore can have implications on decision making. A number of studies conducted in various settings and geographic locations have demonstrated that there are significant differences in the provision of pain medication across a variety of settings and for all types of pain (for a review see Green, Anderson, et al., 2003). For example, a recent study of patients who presented with musculoskeletal pain demonstrated that race (Black vs. White) and age (older vs. younger) were two factors leading to the number of prescriptions of opioids and pain medication in the emergency room and upon discharge (Heins et al., 2006); similarly, in another study, Blacks were less likely to receive opioids than Whites (Chen et al., 2005).

This lack of appropriate pain management has extended to chronic and terminal illness situations. Research has demonstrated that in such situations members of ethnic minority groups with cancer-related pain are less likely to receive the recommended amount of pain medication (and may even receive no medication) than European Americans (Werth et al., 2002). A related issue is that even if they receive prescriptions for the proper amount of pain medication, members of ethnic minority groups may not be able to get these prescriptions filled in pharmacies in their own neighborhoods because of insufficient supplies (Green, Ndao-Brumblay, West, & Washington, 2005; Morrison, Wallenstein, Natale, Senzel, & Huang, 2000). These problems with proper access and treatment have been linked to some of the decision making differences near the end of life attributed to ethnicity.

Diversity Issues in End-of-Life Decision Making

The literature on the apparent impact of cultural diversity on end-of-life decisions is fairly large and growing, thus we cannot cover all aspects of diversity and must rely on gross generalizations in the areas we do discuss (Blevins & Papadatou, 2006). We highlight some results related to age, ethnicity, and gender.

The impact of age on end-of-life decision making is difficult to identify because of confounding variables such as cohort effects (Blevins & Papadatou, 2006) and religiosity. This may explain the inconsistency in the literature regarding the beliefs of older adults about end-of-life decisions such as withholding or withdrawing treatment and having advance directives (i.e., living wills or durable powers of attorney; Werth et al., 2002).

On the other hand, research on the attitudes and actions of various ethnic groups has been fairly consistent (Werth et al., 2002). Given that they may be less likely to receive proper and timely care in the first place, it should not be surprising that members of ethnic minority groups appear to be less likely to make decisions that appear to limit care or potentially hasten death, such as requesting treatment be withheld or withdrawn (either in person, in a living will, or through a proxy). In addition, longevity may be perceived as an intrinsic good, either for the person himself or herself or in order to extend the length of relationships (Mutran, Danis, Bratton, Sudha, & Hanson, 1997; Werth et al., 2002). European Americans are more likely to have positive attitudes toward advance directives, assisted suicide, and euthanasia; to actually complete advance directives; and to request and receive assistance in dying, whether legally in Oregon or in unregulated fashion (see, e.g., Werth et al., 2002).

The literature on gender differences in end-of-life decision making seems to show some possible differences in a few studies on particular types of decisions, but overall the differences appear to cancel each other out (Werth et al., 2002). Yet, Kastenbaum (1995) noted that illness, debility, and death may have a different meaning for men and women, given cultural gender role expectations for women as caregivers of others and for men to be providers for their families. In addition, some research has shown that women are more concerned about having a "dignified death" than men (Bookwala et al., 2001).

Treatment Options

When diagnosed with a life-threatening condition, there are often many possible treatments, depending on the situation (Leming & Dickinson, 2007; Stillion, 2006). Some options may be physical or biological, such as medication, surgery, transplantation, chemotherapy, radiation, and/or complementary therapies; other possibilities include behavioral changes, psychosocial interventions, or spiritual activities. Different groups (e.g., immigrants) may be more or less likely to select a given treatment option based on cultural values, including religious beliefs (Juckett, 2005). For example, some cultures ascribe to a belief that there must be a balance between "hot" and "cold" and that imbalances cause disease, so if a person has a "hot" condition (e.g., a rash) and the physician prescribes a "hot" treatment (e.g., vitamins), an Asian or Latino person may disregard the advice and may have less confidence in the medical doctor (Juckett, 2005). Some cultures have their own diagnoses and treatments as well (Juckett, 2005). Further, in some groups, depending on the family relationships involved, the patient may not be the treatment decision-maker and in fact the family may not want the person told of her or his condition, especially if death may be involved (Werth et al., 2002).

Although many of the treatments for conditions that may lead to death are medical, the National Institutes of Health (NIH, 1997; NIH Technology Assessment Conference Statement, 1995) has acknowledged that psychological interventions are efficacious for some conditions and may be especially beneficial when used in concert with medical treatments. Psychosocial interventions may also be useful in dealing with the emotional reactions to the various medical treatments and the side effects of such approaches.

Kleespies (2004) stated that "conventional care" is focused on acute care and cure, especially in hospitals where advanced technology can be used, which works well for many people but not for those who are dying. Thus, another treatment option is palliative care, the goal of which is to alleviate or prevent symptoms and suffering that cause distress without striving for cure (Kleespies, 2004). Palliative care is often considered to be implemented when a person is dying, but actually can be offered in conjunction with other treatments (Stillion, 2006); however, it is true that hospice (see next section) is one particular type of palliative care that is reserved for people near the end of life.

Although some would not call them "treatment" options, withholding/withdrawing treatment, assisted suicide, and euthanasia are options for some people. These possibilities may get discussed in terms of "quality" vs. "quantity" of life, with different people having different goals (Rodriguez & Young, 2006). As noted earlier, most people in the U.S. die after a decision to withhold or withdraw treatment, but there is marked variation across countries (Sprung et al., 2003). Similarly, physician-assisted suicide is explicitly legal in Oregon but no other state has passed a law allowing it and euthanasia remains illegal in all states (Kleespies, 2004). Only a few other countries (e.g., The Netherlands, Belgium, Switzerland) have legalized assisted suicide and/or voluntary active euthanasia while others (e.g., Australia, England) have recently rejected efforts to allow either action (see Finlay, Wheatley, & Izdebski, 2005; Materstvedt et al., 2003).

Holistic Approaches

One treatment option that offers a holistic approach is hospice. Widely considered to offer the gold standard in care near the end of life (Casarett, 2006; Connor, Lycan, & Schumacher, 2006), the modern hospice began in England in 1967 when Dame Cicely Saunders started St. Christopher's (Stillion, 2006). The first modern hospice in the U.S. was established in New Haven, Connecticut in the early 1970s (Connor et al., 2006), and placed emphasis on home care as opposed to in-patient services. In 1982, the U.S. Congress added coverage for hospice through Medicare (Stillion, 2006). Today there are more than 3,600 hospices in the United States, most of which are nonprofit, and served more than 1,000,000 people in 2004 — nearly 80% of whom were European American, over 50% of whom had cancer, and over 60% of whom were 75+ years old (National Hospice and Palliative Care Organization [NHPCO], n.d.).

Hospices utilize a multidisciplinary team of nurses, aides, social workers, chaplains, and volunteers, under the direction of a physician, to provide biopsychosociospiritual care of the dying person and her or his family, often in the person's home (Connor et al., 2006; Kleespies, 2004; Leming & Dickinson, 2007). Hospice personnel excel at treating and alleviating pain and suffering. Once a person has been given a prognosis of six months or less to live, a person becomes eligible for hospice, although the median length of stay in hospice is only 22 days, with about 35% of people dying within a week of admission (NHPCO, n.d.). One potential reason for this short stay is that in order to access hospice care, the person must agree to forego any more attempts at curative treatment; thus some people (including physicians, patients, and caregivers) can interpret this as "giving up" and therefore resist enrolling in hospice (Casarett, 2006). Thus, the way hospice is explained to dying individuals and their loved ones can have a significant effect on the decisions of whether and when to enroll in hospice.

Conclusion

There have been many developments in the last century that have affected end-of-life decision making. We have mentioned a few, including technological advances and other changes in when, where, and how people die; obstacles to health care and related cultural diversity issues; and traditional and holistic treatment options.

LeARNING Objective: (30/35)

Explain how medical + technological developments over the last century affected end of life decision making.

Chapter 10

Life Span Issues and End-of-Life Decision Making

Andrea C. Walker

Consider the experience of a teenager with acute lymphoma that is unresponsive to any treatment, with a prognosis of death in the next two weeks, being approached by her staff nurse about where she would like to spend the rest of her days. On the other hand, imagine a healthy widower of ninety-four years with several children and numerous grandchildren and great-grandchildren, approached by his physician about end-of-life choices should an accident or unexpected illness occur, robbing him of his capacity to make decisions at that time. Finally, ponder the 40-year-old female diagnosed with level three breast cancer, recommended treatment of weekly chemotherapy, whose prognosis is unknown. The experiences of these individuals vary dramatically, as likely will their responses to end-of-life choices. A large part of the difference in responses relates to each individual's developmental "place" in the span of life.

Life span development is multi-dimensional, with cognitive, social, emotional, spiritual, physical, and behavioral elements, multi-directional, with increasing and decreasing capacities, based on context, subject to environmental and cultural changes, and ranging across the entire life, from infancy to the *oldest old* in scope. Erikson (1997) provided a noteworthy contribution to the life span perspective by explaining development in terms of psychosocial stages into late adulthood, rather than previous theorists who ignored development beyond adolescence, with each new stage presenting an opportunity to reach healthier development if "tasks" are resolved properly. The stage in which an individual is in his or her life largely influences how challenges are perceived and approached. The purpose of this chapter is to look at how life span issues affect the end-of-life decisions we make. We will begin with a discussion of theoretical perspectives of decision making, move to a literature review of end-of-life decisions at different life stages and with special populations, and conclude with implications for caregivers.

Decision Making Theories

Some theoretical perspectives have evolved to explain the processes of coping and decision making associated with dying. Gauthier and Swigart's (2003) theoretical model of the contextual nature of decision making in terminal illness views decision making in terms of personal understanding, values and beliefs, life context, and relationships. The model emphasizes the importance of a pivotal event triggering the realization of terminality, accommodating living with increased dependence and/or pain, and engaging uncertainty of the future. The sum of these variables totals Gauthier and Swigart's concept of embodied responding, action dependent on physiological, psycho-social, and spiritual issues. How a person might approach these issues, such as the realization of terminality, is likely to be subject to a person's place in the life span.

Another perspective, perhaps more appropriate for life span perspective in end-of-life decision making, is Corr's (1991) task-based approach to coping with dying. The model identifies (a) physical, (b) psychological, (c) social, and (d) spiritual dimensions of coping, each of which applies generally to humans and uniquely to each individual's specific experience. Corr proposed that each of the tasks inherent in the four dimensions are undertaken within the larger context of developmental tasks across the lifespan and must be resolved for effective coping to occur. This task-based model passed Corr's own criteria for robustness in models coping with dying, which included (a) facilitating understanding, (b) fostering empowerment, (c) including shared experience, and (d) providing guidance for practitioners. End-of-life decision making in this chapter is presented using a task-based approach.

End-of-Life Decisions Across the Life Span

Because end-of-life choices are usually made by those anticipating death, research typically involves older adults and terminally ill patients. Death occurs at all ages, however, and certain developmental tasks may characterize the experiences at different developmental stages.

Infancy and Young Childhood

The death of an infant or child is considered by most of society to be a non-normative event and looked upon as a tragedy. Health care thus tends to take on the role of "fixing the problem," doing whatever possible to prevent the tragedy from occurring. In such cases, it is necessary to weigh the consequences of decisions to reach the best possible outcome for the child and parents, who often need assurance that all treatments outside of futility have been tried. As infants and young children seek to develop trust, autonomy, initiative, and industry (Erikson, 1997), dealing with a traumatic illness, the treatment of which sometimes confines the child's activities and interactions, may leave them with unresolved tasks later in life. Should a life-threatening illness or death occur at this stage, much of the decision making responsibility falls to the parent or guardian.

Discussions about treatment and death, conducted according to the child's developmental level, provide more reassurance to the child than silence, and whenever possible the child's wishes about their treatment should be fulfilled (McConnell, Frager, & Levetown, 2004). As the perceived role of many parents is to protect their children, end-of-life decisions can be exceptionally stressful for them. Berg (2006) describes two mothers' experiences with critically ill young children, one a highly educated mother who lost a premature daughter after intensive struggle for life, the other a working mother who lost a toddler daughter to brain tumor. Both shared their experiences and needs for more engaged, sensitive health care staff. Many parents want to be fully informed of their child's condition and want their child's physician to understand their needs in making end-of-life decisions for their children (Wharton, Levin, Buka, & Emanuel, 1996). Parents are faced with serious decisions regarding do-not-resuscitate orders, artificial feeding, and terminal sedation to relieve symptoms, so information about the prognosis, treatment options, and the child's reaction to treatments must be communicated clearly.

Adolescence

Adolescence is characterized by pubertal and physical changes, increased emphasis on relationships with peers, increased need for autonomy and self-definition, and the beginning of separation from family (Erikson, 1997). Facing a terminal illness at such a critical life stage, during which the search for independence and identity heightens, can be especially challenging. Although adolescents may have cognitive capacity for abstract thought, they may regress to earlier concrete thinking and behavior when faced with crisis (Stevens & Dunsmore, 1996). This can result in family role alteration during illness, an experience described in a qualitative case study of a female adolescent dying of cancer (Penson et al., 2002), in which decision making began with the adolescent and, as her health regressed, transferred to the parent. Still, the health care system recognizes adolescents as having the capacity to participate in treatment choices (Children's Rights Task Force of the Midwest Bioethics Center, 1995) and generally encourages adolescents to participate in their end-of-life decisions.

Studies have confirmed adolescents' willingness and ability to participate in end-of-life decisions and have compared their choices with those of individuals much later in the life span. Both ill and healthy adolescents have been found to want to participate in decision making (Lyon, McCabe, Patel, & D'Angelo, 2004).

Participants in McAliley, Hudson-Barr, Gunning, and Rowbottom's (2000) study of mostly healthy adolescents were found to be competent enough to understand advance directives, to be comfortable discussing them, and to believe that it is important for people their age to have advance directives. Possibly due to less experience with death and less knowledge about outcomes of interventions, adolescents in this study chose medical and surgical interventions over choices to end life at a higher rate than have adults in past studies (McAliley et al., 2004). Ditto, Druley, Moore, and Danks (1996) compared end-of-life decisions of college students with adult seniors, age sixty-five and older, in terms of valued life activities (VLA). In both populations, the greater the condition interfered with VLA, the more negatively it was perceived and the more likely it was to exacerbate a choice to end life. Having a negative attitude toward death predicted higher likelihood to prolong life in college students, whereas belief in ability to perform VLA did so in older adults (Ditto, et al., 1996).

Young and Middle Adulthood

Young and middle adulthood is characterized by establishment of intimate relationships, family growth, and development of generativity (Erikson, 1997). Decisions of whether or not to terminate life-sustaining treatments in young and middle adults may be influenced by hope of recovery through treatment or medical discovery. When the prognosis of death is certain, whether a person has dependents and arranged provisional care of those dependents can influence decisions. In this complicated stage of life, as the chance of their own terminal illness increases, young and middle-aged adults are also more often faced with the possibility of end-of-life decisions of a terminally ill child or of their elderly or terminally ill parents. End-of-life decision making can touch individuals in this age range with more complexity than in others.

Current literature targeting young and middle adults is surprisingly limited, focusing mostly on special populations, such as persons with disabilities and mental illnesses, persons with HIV/AIDS, and lesbian and gay issues. Studies focusing on the end-of-life decisions of terminally ill individuals typically involve older adults, and more research on the decisions of terminally ill young and middle adults is needed.

Persons with disabilities and mental illnesses. End-of-life care for individuals with intellectual disabilities can take on a particularly complex situation involving interaction of medical staff, family caregivers, and patient wishes. Forbat and Service (2005) applied several case studies of end-of-life decision making to a hierarchy model utilized within the Coordinated Management of Meaning (CMM) approach (Cronen, Pearce, & Changsheng), emphasizing the contextual interaction of history, religion, culture, legal implications, financial status, and proposed patient's perspective to decisions such as tube feeding, do-not-resuscitate orders, and type or duration of home care.

Kingsbury (2005) suggested that improved person-centered planning be used to help developmentally disabled individuals communicate their end-of-life wishes. Despite the complexity of influencing factors, research emphasizes participation of intellectually disabled patients in this process. In particular, adults with Downs Syndrome have been found to need increased involvement in end-of-life treatment (Watchman, 2005). One parent of a Prader-Willi child indicated that though her child's disease is complex and will require assistance in end-of-life care decisions, she believes the best thing for her child is to remain as autonomous as possible (G. Hannefield, personal communications, August 20, 2006). [Prader-Willi is "a complex genetic disorder that includes short stature, mental retardation or learning disabilities, incomplete sexual development, characteristic behavior problems, low muscle tone, and an involuntary urge to eat constantly, which, coupled with a reduced need for calories, leads to obesity" (Retrieved January 29, 2007, from http://www.thearc.org/faqs/pwsynd.html).]

Whether persons with disabilities should be able to choose assisted death has been a highly controversial topic. Mayo and Gunderson (2002) present a compelling argument against disability advocates who want to eliminate the option of physician-assisted suicide for disabled persons. These authors argue that trying to prevent this option actually represents a return to medical vitalism and a shift away from the value of patient self-determination that currently dominates the medical system. Persons with serious mental illness have been found to be able to designate treatment preferences, with most participants choosing aggressive treatments against pain and most disagreeing with physician-assisted suicide (Foti, Bartels, Van Citters, Merriman, & Fletcher, 2005). As physician-assisted suicide in the United States is currently legal only in Oregon, the debate is still significant for persons without disabilities or mental illnesses, so the question regarding individuals with these issues is far from resolution.

Persons with HIV/AIDS. Although HIV/AIDS affects all age groups, its occurrence in young and middle adults is more frequent. The prognosis can be ambiguous at best, complicating questions regarding end-of-life treatment. Wenger et al. (2001) asserted that end-of-life planning is needed, and measured its occurrence among adults receiving care for HIV. Women and patients with children in the household were most likely to communicate with practitioners about end-of-life issues, and African Americans, Latinos, intravenous drug users, and less educated individuals were least likely to have had these discussions with physicians (Wenger et al., 2001). The prognosis of HIV infected individuals has improved with medical advances, likely influencing the choice for life-sustaining treatments in this population.

Lesbians and gay men. Negative societal attitudes, discrimination, and financial issues compound end-of-life issues for lesbians and gay men. The basic needs of lesbians and gay men dying of cancer are the same as those of heterosexual individuals (Smolinsky & Colon, 2006), however. Particularly effective intervention and communication from health practitioners is needed for these populations.

Elderly Adulthood

The majority of research on advance care planning focuses on elderly adults, who are often nearing retirement and needing to reassess priorities, values and hobbies, to ensure a sense of integrity over their lives (Erikson, 1997). A strong need at this stage involves maintaining social relationships (Ditto et al., 1996). In his book *The Virtues of Aging*, Jimmy Carter (1998) shared his experiences leaving the White House and makes recommendations for life after retirement. Carter discusses a need for information and end-of-life planning, emphasizing the importance of retaining one's lifelong character and personal dignity during dying. Lester (1996) also suggested that end-of-life choices relate to five concepts of an appropriate death, including (a) having a role in one's death, (b) maintaining integrity of the body, (c) consistency with lifestyle, (d) appropriate timing, and (e) different types of death (social, cognitive, biological, etc.) occurring simultaneously. These needs are likely to be common for most older adults.

Who completes advance directives? Research has tended to focus on separate issues of who completes advance care directives and what predicts the choices that are made. Surprisingly, health status may not be related to whether or not a person makes preparations, but discussions initiated by physicians are (Kahana, Dan, Kahana, & Kercher, 2004). In a study of 700 elderly New Yorkers, predictors of completing advance care planning were (a) having established primary care physicians, (b) personal experience with mechanical ventilation, (c) knowledge about the process of advance care planning, and (d) physicians' willingness to initiate discussions (Morrison & Meier, 2004). Interestingly, this study yielded no significant differences in rates of advance care planning across African Americans, Hispanics, and whites, a finding that conflicts with previous studies that found lower rates among African Americans (Cicirelli, 1997).

What choices are made? Researchers are somewhat divided in what predicts end-of-life decision making and/or advance planning, with social, religious, demographic, and psychological factors being considered. Older adults have been found to not necessarily want aggressive treatment interventions at the end-of-life but prefer those that will minimize their discomfort (Nahm & Resnick, 2001), a finding consistent with Ditto et al.'s (1996) finding that belief in one's ability to perform valued life activities predicts older adults' choices to prolong life. Elders with greater religiosity are more likely to extend their lives regardless of their condition, and

Surprising↑

those with lower religiosity and higher value of quality of life are more likely to hasten death (Cicirelli, MacLean, & Cox, 2000). Cicirelli (1997) suggested that choices may result from psychosocial and demographic factors rather than the cognitive weighing of consequences of a particular choice. In his study, those who preferred maintaining life regardless of conditions tended to be African American, of lower socio-economics status (SES) (less education and lower occupational status), and with greater subjective religiosity; they placed less value on the quality of life, had less fear of the dying process, and more fear of destruction of the body. Inversely, those who favored ending their lives regardless of conditions tended to be white, of higher SES, and with lower subjective religiosity; they placed higher value on the quality of life, and had more fear of the dying process. A surprising result of the study was that the majority of participants chose to continue living even with lower quality of life, which may indicate a survival instinct and/or socialized inhibitions against self-destruction.

Marital status, age, lack of psychological well-being, and gender has been found to have no influence on end-of-life decisions (Cicirelli, 1997). This conclusion was later challenged by Bookwala et al. (2001) who found that men prefer life-sustaining treatments more than women, and Kahana et al. (2004), who found that unmarried and younger individuals were more likely to have made end-of-life plans. Due to the heterogeneity of views, end-of-life decisions of older adults may not be predictable, and specific questions should be asked to consider each person's preferences individually (Vig, Davenport, & Pearlman, 2002).

The role of dementia. Older adults are living longer, and instances of end-of-life choices involving individuals with dementia are increasing. The existence or potential for dementia in an older adult with a progressive disease such as Alzheimer's underscores the importance of advance planning. Research has indicated that upon admittance to nursing homes, most patients are beyond the cognitive capacity to complete health care proxies, and many families are too emotionally distraught (Lacy, 2006). Further, though health care staff and family members of the patient are usually motivated by what is best for the patient, their opinions on end-of-life choices can diverge due to differences in religion and perspective (Rurup et al., 2006). Eggenberger and Nelms (as cited in Irwin, 2006) discussed the role of ethical principles of autonomy and beneficence in decisions regarding patients with advanced dementia, and Irwin expressed skepticism regarding tube feeding in particular based on the principles. Research supports this skepticism, indicating that predictors of satisfaction of end-of-life care for nursing home residents with advanced dementia include elimination of tube feeding, as well as specialized treatment for dementia, focus on patient comfort, and improved communication (Engel, Keily, & Mitchell, 2006). Much of the uncertainty, however, associated with end-of-life decisions of an older adult with dementia can be alleviated with completion of advance directives.

Implications for Care

Literature repetitively acknowledges a need for improvement in health care practices regarding end-of-life issues. The results of several of the studies referenced in this chapter have validated the importance of the physicians' role in advance care planning (McConnell et al., 2004; Morrison & Meier, 2004; Nahm & Resnick, 2001; Wenger et al., 2001). I will briefly highlight the implications for care at each life stage.

In the care of infants and young children, not only may the patient participate in part in decision making, but also parents and families also do, and their needs should be considered. Awareness of culture and family processes is important, and McConnell et al.'s (2004) cycle of pediatric palliative care decision making includes (a) assessing communication styles, culture, and beliefs, (b) assessing knowledge and perspectives, (c) assessing decision making capacity, (d) choosing the people and place for discussion, (e) opening discussions and framing decisions, (f) evaluating options and making informed choices, (g) preventing conflict and ensuring continuity, and (h) ongoing reassessment to ensure cultural and familial sensitivity. McConnell recommends following each step in this cycle when working with seriously ill children.

Terminally ill adolescents should be allowed to express their individuality as much as possible, particularly by ensuring their privacy, allowing them to "create their own space," and encouraging them to participate in their own end-of-life decisions to the degree with which they are comfortable (McConnell et al, 2004). Adolescents and their families benefit from working with a multi-disciplinary health care team. Parents report that stress associated with making end-of-life decisions for their children can be alleviated if they know everything has been tried and there are no other options (Penson et al., 2002). Adolescents have been found to be willing, capable, and interested in discussing end-of-life issues, and nurses should help assure parents of this while maintaining sensitivity to the family's interactive processes (McAliley et al., 2000).

Since adults tend to base their end-of-life decisions on "what it will be possible for them to do" with a given treatment, discussions about advance directives in terms of desired outcomes and valued behavioral functions might be a meaningful approach (Ditto et al., 1996). Caregivers must be self-aware and focused on not allowing their own needs to interfere with the medical system's ethical values of autonomy, beneficence, nonmaleficence, and justice for the patient. Six critical care nurses, who suffered from extreme physical, emotional, and psychological stress from their jobs, were interviewed regarding their role in the end-of-life decision making of their patients (Jezuit, 2000). These nurses routinely experienced conflict between meeting the patients' needs and their own moral beliefs. The nurses upheld ethical principles, as well as trustworthiness and compassion, and consistency in practice through embodiment of a deontological view of ethics, that is, a view stressing moral obligations and duties. Jezuit discussed a Theory of Duty, in which caregivers should act from the obligation of duty, which gives the action inherent moral worth. Using contributions from Kantian philosophy, Jezuit indicated that patients should be treated as "ends in and of themselves and not just as means to an end" (p. 49) and that any decision regarding patient treatment has morality if it can be generalized to other patients in similar situations.

Learning Objective: (35/35)
Recognize how the psychosocial tasks across the lifespan affect decisions that are made about end of life care.

Chapter 11

The Family, Larger Systems and End-of-Life Decision Making

Robyn L. Mowery

Historically families primarily shaped and were often shaped by the experience of death of a family member. In the United States as end-of-life care increasingly utilized advanced technological interventions that could delay death, the 'beneficent' and often 'paternalistic' voice of medicine—dedicated to the preservation of life at all costs—began to progressively drown out the voices of patients and families whose values suggested that there may be fates worse than death (Field & Cassel, 1997). Over the course of the last few decades, recognition of the interdependence and mutual influence between the patient and the family as a whole progressively disappeared in institutionalized medicine (Nelson & Nelson, 1995). This holistic perspective of the family's role at the end-of-life has been replaced, to a large extent, with an instrumental view of the family's sole purpose as service to the individual, rather than also bearing in mind the ways in which individuals within a family collectively contribute to the entire family system. The institution of the family has lost its decision making voice within the institution of medicine (a term used interchangeably with "the health care system"), and is now seen primarily as a substitute voice for a dying individual when the patient is unable to speak for him or herself (Nelson & Nelson, 1995; Winzelberg, Hanson, & Tulsky, 2005).

Such relations between the institutions of the family and medicine have been significantly shaped by the institution of law. In an attempt to have the values of family life heard, families turned to the legal system for support. Principally through the process of litigation of several landmark cases (e.g., Quinlan, Bouvia, Kevorkian, and Cruzan) as well as the enactment by Congress in 1990 of the Patient Self-Determination Act (PSDA), there emerged a legal consensus that amplified the voice of individual patients (Meisel, 2005; Werth & Blevins, 2002). The courts declared that end-of-life care decisions should be guided (either directly or through proxy methods) by the dying individual's wishes and the PSDA required health facilities to inform patients of their right to refuse medical treatment and formulate advance directives (Meisel, 2005). The legal system based its conclusions on an individual's right to privacy and self-determination (i.e., autonomy) without formally recognizing the moral or practical significance of other voices in the decision making process (Nelson & Nelson, 1995; Winzelberg, Hanson, & Tulsky, 2005). In this way, the legal system effectively reified the medical systems' modern tendency to focus on the individual patient without fully recognizing the significance of interrelated and interdependent family relationships.

This individualistic approach to end-of-life decision making, in which families are predominantly reduced to being extensions of the patient's voice at the end-of-life, has very recently begun to be challenged. Leading biomedical ethics scholars at the Hastings Center suggest that existing consensus thinking on end-of-life care is founded on several profound misconceptions and oversimplifications. Murray and Jennings (2005) assert that the current approach has been excessively rationalistic and individualistic. Hastings Center scholars further claim that problems with end-of-life decision making have been misdiagnosed as flawed practice at the individual patient and physician level when the shortcomings of end-of-life care may be more structural and institutional in nature (Lynn, 2000, 2005; Murray & Jennings, 2005). From this perspective, the excluded voice of the family system may have much more to do with differences between institutional cultures (Turner, 2005) and the contextual features that shape their practices than any intentional devaluing of family life. In short, the values and goals of one institution may make it deaf to the values and goals of another (Nelson and Nelson, 1995).

Using the practice of "institutional analysis," Palmer (2000) suggests looking across institutions and asking, which institutional processes are most likely to help (or hinder) society's optimal response to end-of-life care. The remainder of this chapter will employ the language of systems theory to explore the interrelated "voices" of medicine and law in the United States and the practical implications for how institutional factors may unwittingly constrain both the voice of the family and—ironically—the patient in end-of-life decision making.

Systemic Factors Influencing End-of-Life Decision Making

Systems theory posits that the whole is greater than the sum of its parts and, like a mobile in constant motion, each part simultaneously influences and is influenced by other parts. Families, therefore, are fundamentally more than simply a group of separate individuals, the institution of medicine is more than a compilation of discrete health care professionals or facilities, and the institution of law is more than a collection of attorneys and judges, independent court cases or acts of legislation.

Systems of people (including social institutions) develop idiosyncratic goals, beliefs, values, and ways of expressing themselves. They are governed by implicit and explicit roles, rules and procedures, and have boundaries which may be open or closed, rigid or flexible. Health care providers, family members, and attorneys are all socialized into the larger culture of their respective institutions as well as the particular versions of their immediate contexts (e.g., hospital or nursing home, nuclear or extended family, county or state legal system) (Turner, 2005). While all three institutions have overlapping aims, they each deploy different mechanisms for achieving their missions, which may or may not function harmoniously across institutional systems.

Institution of Medicine

Broadly considered, the primary end of medicine is the provision of health care, traditionally conceived as cure of acute illnesses and restoration of functioning (Preston & Kelly, 2006). Foundational to acute care is the idea that clear diagnosis leads to clear treatment protocols (Machado, 2005). With increased threat to life, comes escalated reliance on medical specialists and advanced technology for diagnosis and treatment. Roles for heath care professionals are often highly specific and organized according to types of disease and the degree and type of intervention needed (i.e., primary, secondary and tertiary care). Each of these types of care occurs in a specialized setting with its own implicit and explicit rules (e.g., limited visiting hours in Intensive Care Units) and norms (e.g., the expectation that life must be preserved at all costs). Thus, decision making within an acute care context tends to be focused on discrete issues and fragmented solutions. But this strategy for dealing with acute illness has created problems of its own.

As Joanne Lynn (2005) observed, "[The] great success of modern medicine has been to transform acute causes of death into chronic illnesses" (p. S14). This transformation has occurred precisely because mechanisms of modern medicine (e.g., advanced technologies and pharmaceuticals) have been so successful in achieving their purposes that living with and dying from chronic conditions have resulted in novel circumstances for which new mechanisms for making complex decisions have yet, or are only beginning, to appear. The role financial reimbursement mechanisms play in shaping end-of-life care within institutional medicine cannot be underestimated.

For example, nearly half of all Americans 65 years of age or older will enter a nursing home before they die and most of these will have incurable chronic illnesses (Zerzan, Stearns, & Hanson, 2000). Like acute care hospitals, however, policies governing nursing homes emphasize the goals of rehabilitation and the restoration of functioning (Johnson, 2005). Reimbursement mechanisms (i.e., Medicare, Medicaid, and private insurance) encourage the reliance on technological interventions to meet (often unrealistic) rehabilitation goals—even at the end of life—thereby limiting options during decision making for terminal care (Morrison, 2005; Zerzan, Stearns, & Hanson, 2000). Furthermore, funding mechanisms do not reimburse health care providers for the time it takes to invest in nurturing relationships even though research reinforces the importance of psychosocial support for health outcomes and quality of life (Morrison, 2005).

In addition to advanced physical care requirements, chronic terminal illness increases the need for enduring care relationships which can facilitate and sustain the slow transformation of one's identity and interactions with others over the course of the illness and dying process. From the perspective of institutional analysis (Palmer, 2000), the institution of medicine as it is currently organized is not well suited for this purpose. The institution of the family, however, has the development of individual and family identity and sustained intimate relationships as core to its mission.

Institution of the Family

The provision of health care in the context of the family is a secondary end, a derivative product of a shared identity forged by a moral commitment to the well-being of one another (Nelson & Nelson, 1995). This family reality is why death cannot be conceived of and dealt with solely in individual terms, and why dying patients frequently express more concerns about the suffering of their loved ones than their own physical status (Kogan, Blanchette, & Masaki, 2000; Murray & Jennings, 2005).

The role(s) the dying individual played in the family can affect the family decision making process. For instance, if the patient played the role of peace keeper or scapegoat within the family, his or her impending departure will likely destabilize relationships between other family members because there is no one now available to help manage or take the blame for conflict. Davies and her colleagues (1995) empirically delineated eight dimensions of family functioning, each representing a continuum of functionality, that affect the success or difficulty families face when confronted with the impending death of a loved one: integrating the past, dealing with feelings, solving problems, utilizing resources, considering others, portraying family identity, fulfilling roles, and tolerating differences. The more strengths families exhibit in each of these dimensions, the smoother (but not necessarily emotionally easier) the decision making process will be; while the opposite is also generally true. For example, families with rigid or closed boundaries are often suspicious of others, tend to function in isolation and have trouble collaborating with others during a time of need (Kristjanson & Aoun, 2004). Closed or rigid family systems may have difficulty adjusting to rapidly changing health conditions and treatment options and they may be resistant to new information or ideas, thereby struggling during the decision making process (Csikai & Chaitin, 2006).

The dimension of "considering others" (Davies, et al., 1995) is especially relevant from the perspective of institutional analysis. To be part of a family is to be morally required to make decisions on the basis of, not simply what is best for oneself, but based on thinking about what is best for all concerned (Hardwig, 1990). Ivan Boszormenyi-Nagy, a founding theorist in family therapy, argues that "relational ethics" is critical to healthy family functioning, such that failure of each family member to give 'due consideration' to the interests of other members is seen as the heart of family dysfunction (Boszormenyi-Nagy, 1987; Boszormenyi-Nagy, Grunebaum, & Ulrich, 1991). Boszormenyi-Nagy claims that family functioning is enhanced when members of the family can trust that the family system as a whole will facilitate the process of balancing considerations of the well-being of oneself with considerations of the well-being of others (Boszormenyi-Nagy, et al., 1991).

Indeed, clinical observation suggests that when healthy families are given permission to voice their own interests in the decision making process (i.e., when health professionals give due consideration to the family as moral stakeholders), they have an easier time giving due consideration to the patient's needs and wishes; such considerations often yield growth and development for all (see also Foster & McLellan, 2002). This is consistent with Panke and Ferrell (2005) who note that "opportunities for growth for both patient and family are tremendous even while they are coping with countless difficulties and sorrows as the patient's disease progresses" (p. 985).

Yet, relying on this model of shared decision making based on relational ethics within the family, stands in stark contrast to individually-focused biomedical ethics and a legal consensus about end-of-life decision making that is founded on the principle of an individual's right to privacy and autonomy. This difference is partially because the surrogate or proxy model of end-of-life decision making was initially forged in response to cases of extreme conflict between the institution of medicine and the institution of the family over the best interests of individual patients (Burt, 2005).

Institution of Law

While the institutional goal of medicine is protecting health and the institutional goal of the family is protecting development within a web of intimate relationships, the goal of the institution of law can be understood, at least in part, as protecting citizens' rights. Litigation and adjudication of narrowly defined questions and the legislation of broad socially sanctioned policies are the two primary mechanisms used by the institution of law to protect the rights of citizens. The courts protected individual rights of patients against 'paternalistic medicine' via landmark cases such as Quinlan, Bouvia, and Cruzan, which explicitly established the legal rights of patients to refuse medical treatments either directly or indirectly by designated health care surrogates. But just as medicine's solution to acute health crises created additional problems, the court's reliance on the language of individ- ual rights has created its own set of problems, especially for the family (Hardwig, 1990; Machado, 2005).

The legal consensus about end-of-life decision making assumes the existence of conflict whereby the rights of individuals to make their own decisions must be assiduously protected from either an over-zealous health care system or coercive family members (Nelson & Nelson, 1995). The Schiavo case highlighted the need for such protection in extreme circumstances; but the media attention the case received obscured the fact that it represented exceptions of family functioning rather than the rule. Further, the case illuminated the deleterious effects of policy decisions emphasizing the individual and stressing adversarial relationships within families and/or between family members and health care providers (Nelson & Nelson, 1995).

If Nelson and Nelson's (1995) and Boszormenyi-Nagy's (Boszormenyi-Nagy, et al., 1991) views of family functioning and relational ethics are correct, a purely indi- vidualized approach to ethical decision making at the end-of-life in the context of family dynamics may itself be a morally questionable activity that may increase the risk of harm to the family system (Mowery, 2005). Furthermore, it would suggest that being in intimate relationships with others changes the level of influence on ethical decision making considered to be appropriate, particularly in contrast to non-intimate relationships (Mowery, 2005).

Practical Implications

What have been the results of this individual emphasis during end-of-life decision making? During the last thirty years while the legal consensus was being devel- oped, home hospice care grew from a grass roots movement originating as a patient and family-friendly alternative to end-of-life care in institutional settings, to a federal and state subsidized (i.e., Medicare and Medicaid) form of health care. Despite these efforts, however, the vast majority of Americans still die in hospitals without having documented advance directives (Field & Cassel, 1997; Merrick, 2005), and with families having limited voice in the process.

Advance Care Planning and Treatment Decisions

Advance directives were designed to provide a means for people to retain autonomous control over their future medical care by documenting their treatment preferences in writing and designating someone who would make surrogate deci- sions on their behalf in the event that they no longer had the capacity to communi- cate their desires (Burt, 2005). Consistent with the types of carefully circumscribed questions posed in the court cases from which advance directives arose, and a medical system designed to apply curative treatments to clearly diagnosable acute conditions, these documents have tended to focus on narrowly defined treatment options (e.g., Do Not Resuscitate orders). Hickman, Hammes, Moss & Toole (2006) summarized numerous limitations of advance directives, while also reviewing recent alternatives. Newer approaches to advanced care planning emphasize articulating values and goals of care such as quality (i.e., freedom from pain and suffering) rather than quantity of life (e.g., Five Wishes) or increasing portability across treatment settings (i.e., Physicians Orders for Life Sustaining Treatments, POLST).

All of these approaches to advanced planning emphasize the need to discuss one's wishes with a designated health care surrogate as well as making them known to health care providers as a means of making sure one's autonomy is respected and advance decisions are carried out. Yet these improvements still fail to recognize that an autonomy driven approach to end-of-life decision making has not consistently served the interests of patients and families (Winzelberg, Hanson, & Tulsky, 2005). Recent attitudinal research suggests that most patients do not prefer a purely autonomy driven approach to end-of-life decision making (Nolan, Sood, Kub, & Sulmasy, 2005). These researchers found that while patients retain decision making capacity, most prefer to share decision making with physicians and/or loved ones (i.e., give due consideration to the medical expertise of the physician and the interdependent needs of the family), with additional weight given to the input (not necessarily substituted judgment) of loved ones once the patient loses decisional capacity.

Assisted Death

Current consensus that it is the individual patient's right to refuse medical treatment, even if doing so hastens one's death, has lead to controversy about whether the morally accepted view to permit 'nature to take its own course' (i.e., passive euthanasia) can and/or should be extended to permitting a terminally ill patient to 'direct nature's course' (i.e., active euthanasia or physician assisted suicide, PAS). The question is whether there is a moral distinction between intentionally *allowing* a disease process to result in death, or intentionally *causing* death (with or without the assistance of others) through the use of additional means (usually pharmaceuticals) to stop a disease process. Health care providers, bioethicists and families are divided in response to this question. The federal courts have said this extension of the principle of autonomy in end-of-life decision making is an issue that must be resolved through the legislative process in each state (Emanuel, Fairclough, & Emanuel, 2000). To date, though there have been numerous attempts to legalize PAS in various states in the U.S., only Oregon has legalized a process whereby patients can seek prescriptions from physicians for the express purpose of committing suicide (i.e., PAS).

Recent research with terminally ill patients and their patient-designated primary caregivers has suggested that there is broad support for euthanasia and PAS in hypothetical situations involving others in severe pain, but this support drops dramatically in scenarios where the imagined patient seeks termination of life due to the perception of being a burden on family (Emanuel, et al., 2000). However, only a small minority of sampled patients actively considered these options for themselves, with patient depression being the main motivating factor for interest in euthanasia and PAS. Furthermore, such personal interest in euthanasia or PAS appeared quite unstable with about half of those interested changing their minds over time (Emanuel, et al., 2000).

This research supports the provisions in Oregon's PAS law for multiple conversations between the patient and his or her physician over time. It is significant to note, however, that there is no mandated provision in the Oregon law to protect the family, to ensure that they are supportive of the idea of PAS over time, or that all other resources that could be brought to bear to help the family support the patient have been exhausted. The indictment of poor end-of-life care in the United States has been well documented (Field & Cassel, 1997). One must consider the degree to which euthanasia or physician-assisted suicide would still be considered if sufficient palliative care for the patient and the family had been in place throughout the *entire trajectory of the illness*, not just an option during the terminal phase.

New Directions in Palliative Care

Traditional medicine seeks to eliminate the underlying *cause(s)* of illness within an individual patient, while palliative care, utilizing a multidisciplinary approach, seeks to eliminate or minimize the physical, psychosocial, and spiritual *burden* of life limiting and terminal illnesses, recognizing that the *burden* is experienced and carried by both the patient and the family, albeit differently (National Consensus Project for Quality Palliative Care, 2004). Palliative care has long been the model for home-based hospice care. Its integration with inpatient care (i.e., hospitals and other assisted living facilities), however, has rapidly expanded in the last decade (Morrison, Maroney-Galin, Kralovec, & Meier, 2005, 2005). In the summer of 2006, both the American Medical Association and the Accreditation Council for Graduate Medical Education approved a new medical subspecialty in hospice and palliative medicine (see www.aahpm.org), thereby moving palliative care closer to its ideal of being integrated with curative treatment from the time of diagnosis of a life threatening condition (National Consensus Project, 2004). While the family's voice is more readily heard in the context of palliative care and this represents a significant advance over traditional medical care, the individualistic assumptions embedded in current models of surrogate decision making at the end-of-life still prevail in palliative care.

For instance, training for palliative medicine physicians emphasizes the importance of taking time to communicate with families during goals-of-care decision making meetings (Fineberg, 2005; Tulsky, 2005); but commonly does so with a view of the family as a collection of individuals. Communication training for physicians, therefore, has largely focused on dyadic communication skills between the physician and separate family members, with special attention given to the formal health care proxy. The clinical and research literature on palliative care has paid limited attention to the accumulated body of empirical data assessing dimensions of family systems functioning (e.g., cohesion, flexibility, and communication) (Olson, 2000). It has also not taken full advantage of the family therapy literature, which includes techniques for intervening in unhealthy family system dynamics (e.g., multi-directed partiality) (Boszormenyi-Nagy, et al., 1991) that are readily adaptable to facilitate family decision making during goals-of-care family conferences. Thus, while palliative care ostensibly does a better job than traditional medicine of including the voice of the family system in end-of-life decision making, until research, clinical practice, institutional policies, procedures and laws take full stock of the intricate web of interpersonal family dynamics in which end-of-life care decision making is embedded, the vision of the patient and the family as the true focus of palliative care will be stymied.

Learning Objective: (35/40)

Explain systemic factors influencing end of life decision making & their practical implications.

Chapter 12

Ethical and Legal Issues and End-of-Life Decision Making

Arthur Zucker

There are many reasons a patient might wish to die: terrible pain, pain that cannot be palliated; terrible emotional straits that make death seem preferable to life; knowledge of imminent death (after being told that one is terminal); most famously, being in a permanent vegetative state. Recently, the Terri Schiavo case captivated the public's eye (Sosa, Lin, DBarrett, et al., 2005; Werth, 2006). A good rundown of the Schiavo case can be found at http://www.cnn.com/2005/LAW/03/31/schiavo/index.html.

In the Schiavo case, which we will use as a brief introduction to advance directives, her parents wanted so much to keep her alive, despite her being in a persistent vegetative state, that they said that even if she had a living will, they would not have abided by it. In fact, her parents were so adamant on 'saving' her that they said that even if she had a living will, they would have tried to get it overturned (Wolfson, 2005). But she did not have any such document and this fact meant that her husband had the legal right to make her end-of-life decision, which in the eyes of her parents was based not on her best interests but rather on his best interests. There was no willingness to find a middle ground.

Advance Directives

The *Patient Self-Determination Act*, passed in 1991, mandates informing patients that they have a right to direct their own health care—especially through an advanced directive. There are two types of advance directives. One type is the living will, a document that makes it plain how a person would like to be treated under certain circumstances. The other type is a Durable Power of Attorney for

Health Care. In this type, the patient designates a surrogate decision maker, some-one to make decisions for the patient in the event that the patient can no longer do so.

Advance directives are documents representing the desires of a person regarding treatment and cessation of treatment in case of a loss of competence. They are meant to insure that patients who are unable, for any reason, to speak for themselves, will get the treatment that they would want.

The American Bar Association offers these comments on living wills and proxies:

A living will is your written expression of how you want to be treated in certain medical conditions. Depending on state law, this document may permit you to express whether or not you wish to be given life-sustaining treatments in the event you are terminally ill or injured, to decide in advance whether you wish to be provided food and water via intravenous devices ("tube feeding"), and to give other medical directions that impact the end of life. "Life-sustaining treatment" means the use of available medical machinery and techniques, such as heart-lung machines, ventilators, and other medical equipment and techniques that will sustain and possibly extend your life, but which will not by themselves cure your condition. In addition to terminal illness or injury situations, most states permit you to express your preferences as to treatment using life-sustaining equipment and/or tube feeding for medical conditions that leave you permanently unconscious and without detectable brain activity.

A living will applies in situations where the decision to use such treatments may prolong your life for a limited period of time and not obtaining such treatment would result in your death. It does not mean that medical professionals would deny you pain medications and other treatments that would relieve pain or otherwise make you more comfortable. Living wills do not determine your medical treatment in situations that do not affect your continued life, such as routine medical treatment and non life-threatening medical conditions. In all states the determination as to whether or not you are in such a medical condition is determined by medical professionals, usually your attending physician and at least one other medical doctor who has examined you and/or reviewed your medical situation. Most states permit you to include other medical directions that you wish your physicians to be aware of regarding the types of treatment you do or do not wish to receive.

A "health care proxy," sometimes called a "health care surrogate" or "durable medical power of attorney," is the appointment of a person to whom you grant authority to make medical decisions in the event you are unable to express your preferences. Most commonly, this situation occurs either because you are unconscious or because your mental state is such that you do not have the legal capacity to make your own decisions. Normally, a single individual is appointed as your health care proxy, though quite commonly one or more alternate persons are designated in the event your first choice proxy is unavailable. As with the living will, medical professionals will make the initial determination as to whether or not you have the capacity to make your own medical treatment decisions. The health care proxy is a durable power of attorney specifically designed to cover medical treatment. As with living wills, depending on your state of residence, it may be a state-determined form or may be drafted individually by your attorney (http://www.abanet.org/rppt/public/living-wills.html).

What follows is a boilerplate version of a living will.

This declaration is made on _____ [date]. I, _____, willfully and voluntarily make known my desire that my dying not be artificially prolonged under the circumstances set forth below, and I do declare:

If at any time I have a terminal condition and if my attending or treating physician and another consulting physician have determined that there is no medical probability of my recovery from that condition, I direct that life-prolonging procedures be withheld or withdrawn, when the application of the procedures would serve only to prolong, artificially, the process of dying, and that I be permitted to die naturally with only the administration of medication or the performance of any medical procedure deemed necessary to provide me with comfort or care or to alleviate pain.

It is my intention that this declaration be honored by my family and physician as the final expression of my legal right to refuse medical or surgical treatment and to accept the consequences for that refusal.

In the event that I have been determined to be unable to provide express and informed consent regarding the withholding, withdrawal, or continuation of life-prolonging procedures, I wish to designate, as my surrogate to carry out the provisions of this declaration:_____.

(http://estate.findlaw.com/estate-planning/living-wills/living-will-surrogate.html).

Clearly the idea is to protect the right of the signatory to determine her/his own fate at the end of life. This sample living will is an example of an advance care directive that appoints a proxy to enforce the already made health care decisions for a person in the event that that person can no longer do so. This document is to be distinguished from "substituted judgment," where one person tries to judge for another what that other would have wanted, given previous (reported) conversations and the apparent values of the person. Substituted judgment is always problematic, since what someone else would have wanted is a prediction that is very difficult to make, especially since there is no way to check to see which substituted judgments have been correct in the past. But even the legal documents are not free of problems. (1) What is to count as artificial and how does one judge prolongation? (2) What counts as, and who decides what is, "no medical probability"?

Of course, there are legal answers. But all sorts of unexpected contingencies can arise to muddy the waters—at least ethically. Suppose the technique being proposed is one that most physicians would now deem as artificial; but advanced specialists in the field know that the technique is in the process of being tweaked just a bit by biomedical engineers so that the technique will work much better and will soon become considered part of the usual intervention; indeed, so usual that prolongation will turn into decent odds for some degree of recovery. The temptation is to say, "All right. Go ahead and use the new, tweaked technique." But suppose that the surrogate refuses. Suppose the surrogate just cannot be made to understand the changes that are likely to occur? Should the new facts override the legality of the living will?

There is a much simpler non-technical version of this situation. Suppose I am your best friend and have been for years. You name me as your surrogate. We have a terrible falling out and now just hate each other—but being young and healthy, you never think to remove me as surrogate. Then, an automobile accident puts you in a vegetative state. I just can't wait to see you in the funeral home. Your brother knows this and tries to intervene. But he is the only one who knows (or perhaps no one else knows). This is not far-fetched. It is in fact a variation of the Schiavo case. Further complicating this whole area is this finding from the *New England Journal of Medicine*: "Rather than age or the severity of the illness and organ dysfunction, the strongest determinants of the withdrawal of ventilation in critically ill patients were the physician's perception that the patient preferred not to use life support, the physician's predictions of a low likelihood of survival in the intensive care unit and a high likelihood of poor cognitive function, and the use of inotropes or vaso-pressors" (http://content.nejm.org/cgi/content/abstract/349/12/1123). The compli-cation is the role of the physician as a decision-maker instead of a fact giver.

The usual terminology for end of life decisions revolve about quality of life. There is a traditional distinction: Quality of life (e.g., intellectual and bodily pleas-ures) is more important than quantity of life (how long one is alive). Usually there is an accompanying assumption that second parties looking in can never truly judge the quality of life for another. I may seem content to you but I may be in a horrible state, being able to trick you only because I am such a good actor (and per-haps) you are so naïve or do not know me very well.

The courts have held that a competent patient, or legally appointed or desig-nated advocate, can demand withdrawal of life sustaining treatment on the grounds that bodily integrity would otherwise be violated (Cruzan, 1990; In the matter of Karen Quinlan, 1976). The two central cases mentioned in the citation fol-low. Of the two, Quinlan is considered the case that addresses in a general way the legality of withdrawing treatment. Cruzan *qua* decision, is a much narrower deci-sion, focused only on whether the state of Missouri had the right to continue Nancy Cruzan's treatment. However, in Cruzan, the Court did speculate on when treat-ment could and should be withdrawn. It is this speculation that is important for any discussion of the ethics and legality of end-of-life decisions.

Quinlan and Cruzan

"Karen Quinlan collapsed at a party after swallowing alcohol and the tranquilizer Valium on 14 April 1975. Doctors saved her life, but she suffered brain damage and lapsed into a persistent vegetative state. Her family waged a much-publicized legal battle for the right to remove her life support machinery. They succeeded, but in a final twist, Quinlan kept breathing after the respirator was unplugged. She remained in a coma for almost 10 years in a New Jersey nursing home until her 1985 death" (http://www.who2.com/karenannquinlan.html). Ultimately, the deci-sion to let her die was made by the Supreme Court of New Jersey. The Court held that "no external compelling interest of the State could compel Karen to endure the unendurable, only to vegetate a few measurable months with no realistic possibil-ity of returning to any semblance of cognitive or sapient life" (In the matter of Karen Quinlan, 1976). The Court also said that she herself would have agreed with this decision even though there was no legal document signed by Karen to this effect. The case wound up argued back and forth in the media, and so it helped make the issue of letting a person die something that the public saw as important and inescapable. It also showed how necessary it was to have some sort of legally recognized documentation recording the wishes of a patient. The need for evidence was crucial in the next case.

An automobile accident left Nancy Cruzan in a persistent vegetative state beginning in 1983. Despite her parents request that the feeding tube be withdrawn, the state of Missouri refused saying that since there was no legally acceptable evidence concerning what Nancy Cruzan herself would have chosen, there was both a moral and legal obligation for the state to continue treatment. In 1990, the U.S. Supreme Court decided the case, holding that Missouri was correct in this instance, but that when there *is* clear evidence that a patient does not want or never wanted some treatment—life saving, life sustaining or otherwise—then that treatment may not be started or, if already begun, must be withdrawn. The Court cited liberties protected by the 14th Amendment in defense of their claim. They did not cite privacy, which in the minds of some legal scholars is not a constitutionally protected right (Cruzan, 1990). It is also notable, that the Cruzan Court did not limit what kind of treatment could be stopped or never started. The American Medical Association in its most recent Code of Medical Ethics lists as examples of life sustaining treatments: mechanical ventilation; renal dialysis; chemotherapy; antibiotics and artificial nutrition and hydration (Council on Ethical and Judicial Affairs, 2006-2007). In late 1990, her parents gave evidence to the state of Missouri that Nancy would not have wanted her life continued, and the Missouri courts ruled that Nancy's feeding tube could be removed. In December of 1990, her feeding was stopped. She died later that month.

Physician Assisted Suicide

Despite these court decisions, this ethical question for the health care profession, however, remains: If a patient can be kept alive, especially if there is—in the eyes of the health professionals involved—a chance for meaningful life, can it ever be ethical not to do so? At the very least, isn't there an obligation to try to get the patient (or the patient's advocate) to prefer life over death? This whole set of issues has been central to the legal and ethical challenges to the state of Oregon's Death With Dignity Act (Oregon Department of Health Services, 2005), which will be used here as a model for discussing many of the end-of-life issues relevant to this chapter.

To begin, Oregon allows physicians, under strict limitations, to prescribe a lethal dose of a drug with the knowledge that it will be used by the patient to commit suicide. This activity is considered physician assisted suicide (PAS). The ethics of PAS has always been debated, even in Oregon, where it has been legal since 1997. Administering such a dose, as opposed to merely prescribing it, is also ethically questionable. What makes either of these instances ethically questionable is a mix of law and the nature of the health care professions. Granted, the law often lags behind what is taken to be moral: slavery is a clear example; women's right to vote is another. In general, laws do reflect currently accepted morality. Thus, to break the law knowingly puts the burden of argument on the law breaker. The health care professions, as seen by many, should help to preserve health, and by implication, life. To use one's offices as a heath care professional to kill would seem to violate this major function of the health care professions. An oft-made *I would like to Argue this Point.* claim, one that trades on health care seen as aimed almost entirely at preserving life, is that if patients knew that sometimes doctors kill, trust in physicians, and in health care in general, would be undermined. Of course, the role of any profession can change. Ethically allowable surgery changed when anesthesia was introduced. Informed consent became a major part of nearly all doctor-patient interactions after the horrible excesses of Nazi 'medicine' were exposed. Even so, we may not want to change the life preserving goal at the center of health care. Moreover, even if the profession wants to stress patient desire over all else, if the law disallows PAS, asking practitioners to break the law may be impractical. It is odd to see an action as a professional or moral obligation when that action is forbidden by law. And, it would be odd to have a law allowing PAS if the profession as a whole con- *I disagree* siders PAS unethical. (It is a quirk of our country and legal system that PAS is allowed in one geographical location but not in another.)

Oregon's allowing PAS also raises the question of active versus passive euthanasia. Removing life sustaining means is usually considered passive and acceptable (if done with the patient's consent). But administering a lethal dose of morphine would be considered active and not acceptable. Thus the question is how close to injecting morphine is the act of writing a prescription for a lethal dose of a drug?

Oregon's Death with Dignity Act (voted in by a 51% margin) will show how ethical issues and the law mix. In 1997, Attorney General Janet Reno ruled that individual states are allowed to regulate their own doctors and by implication, can allow PAS. In 2001, Attorney General John Ashcroft threatened physicians with prosecution if they prescribed lethal drugs to their patients. He had wanted to use the Controlled Substances Act to block assisted suicide. His claim was that this use of the lethal drugs, which were almost always controlled substances, violated the Controlled Substances Act. But a Court of Appeals held that the Act was aimed instead at doctors who prescribe drugs for other than "legitimate medical purposes." Congress, it said, was trying to fight drug abuse, not regulate medicine.

In a dissent, Judge J. Clifford Wallace said, "There is simply no textual support for the majority's conclusion that 'the field of drug abuse,' as discussed in the Controlled Substances Act, does not encompass drug-induced, physician-assisted suicide" (Gonzales, 2006). More recently, the Supreme Court also upheld the

Oregon Act. In his dissent to this recent ruling, Justice Anton Scalia wrote, if the term "'legitimate medical purpose' has any meaning, it surely excludes the prescription of drugs to produce death" (Gonzales, 2006). Here we see, Justice Scalia appealing to the idea that preserving life is central to the purpose of medicine.

The rank order of reasons for choosing PAS as documented in Oregon is: loss of autonomy; life becoming a misery; loss of dignity; losing control of bodily functions; becoming a burden on friends and family and either inadequate, or fear of inadequate, pain control. Of these reasons, only inadequate pain control might be a purely medical indication. The others might be termed, psycho-social, and fall under quality of life judgments. One fear that some opponents of PAS have is that physicians (and perhaps all health care professionals) have a less sanguine picture of the quality of life of such patients than is necessary. According to opponents of PAS, what these patients need is appropriately sensitive counseling and not death.

Organs, Futility, and Counseling

Sensitivity is also needed when dealing with organ procurement. The withdrawal of life support has to be done only after carefully getting consent from the patient or the patient's designated surrogate. There is a question of when organ donation should be mentioned as a possibility. One can argue that mentioning the good done via an organ donation unfairly biases the decision of the patient or patient surrogate. However, one can also argue that in times of stress, neither the patient, nor patient's family and/or surrogate may be thinking of organ donation. Naturally, if it is clear that the patient desires donating his/her organs or raised the topic, then the issue is less pressing. Those who see saving lives through transplantation as their main obligation will have little trouble justifying the mention of organ donation if it will yield an organ that would otherwise not have been available for transplantation. Even so, to avoid any appearance of conflict of interest in the eyes of the patient or patient surrogate, there should be a clear line drawn between those who discuss end-of-life care and those who are members of a transplant team.

Appropriate counseling is also needed in cases of medical futility, where patients are in such bad condition that if they ask for more treatment, physicians feel it acceptable to say "No—it would be futile." But futility has another side, as illustrated by the following case.

> An 87-year-old woman refuses heart bypass surgery. Her daughter is distraught over her mother's decision and after pleading, her mother gives in and agrees to the surgery. During that surgery, she has a cardiac arrest and suffers some permanent brain damage. Once awake, she is aware of her situation and asks to be allowed to die. This request is relevant because she is on a ventilator because her lungs did not clear well after surgery. Weaning

her from the ventilator appears unlikely. She insists that the ventilator be disconnected. She is uncomfortable, sees no good future
for herself and considers that she is being demeaned by the treatment. Her daughter still wants everything done to keep her mother alive. The attending physician thinks she can be weaned and so
supports the daughter.

In this case, the patient wants to die—she sees her life as futile—but is forced to
live. In one case someone is seemingly forced to die and in the other someone is
seemingly forced to live.

The American Medical Association notes, "conflicts between the parties
[patient and/or surrogate] may interrupt satisfactory decision making close to and
adversely affect patient care, family satisfaction, and physician-clinical team functioning. To assist in fair and satisfactory decision making about what constitutes
futile intervention…All health care institutions, whether large or small, should
adopt a policy on medical futility" (Council on Ethical and Judicial Affairs, 2006).

The suggestion goes on to emphasize due process and focuses on the need for
characterizing futility for the patient at hand, decision making that reflects the
interests of all concerned, the use of an ethics committee if necessary, and referrals to other physicians or other institutions as needed. Interestingly, the guidelines
allow for no offered intervention if transfer to another physician's care or another
institution is not possible.

It is reasonable to depend on doctor-patient discussion to resolve conflict. But
there is an issue rarely mentioned when such discussions are mentioned as crucial.
Where is the boundary between not doing something callously and getting it done
so smoothly that no one recognizes that desires have been thwarted? We should
ask, "Is this talent for getting the 'right' thing done worth developing?" Do we want
our physicians to be so good at persuasion that we will never be quite sure when
we are deciding and when they have decided for us?

Moreover, as alluded to above, how is one to measure the fear of death, of
dying, of feeling that if only this or that had been asked for, had been tried, then the
outcome would have been better? These fears can cause suffering and the suffering is real. That they seem irrational to a clear-headed and healthy physician is
beside the point. Should health care professionals, by virtue of their profession,
have the authority to deny that a few more days or hours of any quality may mean
the world, actually be the world, to a dying patient? Why cannot it be the case that
sometimes *living* is just so important to a patient that even 'futile' measures, if
requested by that patient, should be taken. Doing otherwise may do violence to the
idea of medicine as a profession whose goal it is to ease suffering—not define suffering; and certainly not to choose death for patients who themselves choose life.

Of course, that was one edge of the two-sided sword of futility. Here is the more traditional side. Who are we to deny <u>fewer</u> hours to:

- Someone whose life at present is a misery?
- Someone for whom dying with control and with dignity outweighs all other factors?

Perhaps, we just have to help them, even if it means cutting some time off their lives.

Suffering

The role of suffering is the key to a full understanding of end-of-life decisions. Suffering is by its very nature personal. What will cause different degrees of suffering to be felt will vary from person to person. Thus, there is no way to generalize and say "When suffering is the justification, anything asked must be done." There is no easy way to draw the line between suffering that justifies extreme action (killing) and suffering that does not. But that does not mean that the line cannot and should not be drawn from case to case. (It is difficult to define "shoe" so that it covers slippers and galoshes but not socks or casts. Yet we can tell a loafer from a flip-flop.)

Some people feel that suffering is very human and makes us human or contributes to our being human; that suffering and enduring suffering is what creates moral fiber. We say things like: Grow up! No pain—no gain! If it doesn't kill you, it will make you stronger. But truly intense suffering makes for a feeling of isolation by, in effect, making us nothing more than our pain or fear. It makes us less than fully human. Why shouldn't the health professions see its major goal as release from suffering? This may mean that PAS is an obligation. But it may also mean that there is an obligation to extend life for a patient whose fear is death.

[handwritten notes:]

write a paper on this.
How can I relate this to the kids?

Learning Objective: (25/35)(35/35)
Consider the ethical + legal issues involved in end-of-life decision making and end-of-life care.

Smooth discussion

Loss, Grief, and Mourning

Introduction to Part 3, Chapters 13-18

Chapters 13 through 18 focus on loss, grief, and mourning. The Body of Knowledge Committee defined this major category of thanatology knowledge in this way: **the physical, behavioral, cognitive, and social experience of and reactions to loss, the grief process, and practices surrounding grief and commemoration.**

The chapters in Part 3 focus on loss, grief, and mourning in terms of these indicators: culture and socialization, religion and spirituality, historical and contemporary perspectives, life span issues, the family and larger systems, and ethical and legal issues.

Chapter 13

Culture, Socialization, and Loss, Grief, and Mourning

Paul C. Rosenblatt

There are thousands of cultures in the world that differ from one another in how loss is understood and how people are socialized and expected to grieve and mourn. "A culture" is a set of beliefs, values, ways of talking, rituals, ways of relating to other people, ways of organizing life, ways of defining self and others — all unique to a particular group. Everything arises from culture and is given meaning and form by it, including dying, death, and grief.

"Socialization" is embedded in culture and is both the process by which a person comes to fit her or his culture and the process by which others around a person shape the person to fit the culture. Socialization, development, and change go on throughout life, because they are constantly impacted by all that happens to them, the people around them, the mass media, and the culture(s) that surround them and that they travel through.

"Culture" and "socialization" are abstractions, concepts that help to focus our attention and summarize things we think we know. They can be useful terms for communicating and thinking, but they can also mislead us into believing we know more than we actually do. So even as this chapter offers ideas about how to think about people dealing with loss, the reader should not let the partial truths of this chapter erase personal curiosity, awareness, questioning, doubts, ongoing learning, and ways of thinking.

Examples of Culture and Socialization as They Relate to Loss

Culture and culture-based socialization are always at work in the areas of loss, grief, and mourning. When someone is dying, cultures differ in what is appropriate in the relationships of the person who is dying with those who are living. From

Korean culture, for example, there is evidence that while a mother is dying her children may not speak in her presence as though she is dying (Rosenblatt & Yang, 2004). But even though they may not talk about the mother's dying, they know she is dying and work to deal with the pending death. In particular, the mother and children work at carrying out intergenerational obligations that would be spread over many years if she were not going to die soon. For example, a dying mother may work hard to teach a young adult daughter to be a good cook, and adult children may move toward a higher level of achievement and respectability as a dying gift to their mother and as a token of their respect and obligation.

Following a death, cultures differ substantially in what expressions of emotion are appropriate. For example, some African Americans feel that, on the average, African Americans are more expressive at the moment of death and at the funeral than are Euro-Americans (Rosenblatt & Wallace, 2005b). There are cultures in which grieving people may become mute (e.g., Wikan, 1988, writing about women in Cairo, Egypt). There are cultures where bereaved people may injure themselves at the onset of bereavement or become so enraged as to be dangerous to others (Rosenblatt, Walsh, & Jackson, 1976). These culture-based emotional differences, in fact all culture-based matters discussed in this chapter, challenge simplistic, ethnocentric notions about grief pathology. If the concept of grief pathology means anything at all, it must be applied with awareness of the culture(s) involved. What is pathology in one culture is normal in another.

Often socialization has played a big part and continues to do so in shaping the genders in a culture to grieve in distinctively different gender patterns, for example, with women more expressive in grief, or women weeping more and men more often raging (Rosenblatt, Walsh, & Jackson, 1976).

Cultures differ widely in who the significant family and community members are who are likely to be present when a person is terminally ill or has died. In many cultures, the people likely to be present and to express feelings strongly include many more paternal kin than maternal kin. In some cultures those who would be most heavily involved would include a large extended family or even a clan (e.g., the Hmong, see Fadiman, 1997).

Cultures differ widely in the mourning activities people are expected to engage in. Many cultures have a mourning period that might last six months, a year, or longer, during which the principal mourners are limited in what they can do or what they can wear and in their affective expression (Rosenblatt, Walsh, & Jackson, 1976). For some people, not being able to engage in culturally appropriate mourning is very upsetting and may even be experienced as dangerous to themselves, their family, or the spirit of the deceased. In some cultures with extended mourning periods, the period of formal mourning is ended by a second funeral which may include ritual handling and disposal of the remains of the deceased (Rosenblatt, Walsh, & Jackson, 1976).

Cultures differ in how the deceased is thought of. A deceased family member may be understood to continue as an active and helpful presence in the lives of surviving family members. But in some cultures the deceased may be seen as dangerous to the living or dangerous if the proper rituals are not practiced. In some cultures these matters may change over the months following a death. For example, shortly after a death people may fear that the deceased will want other family members to die to keep him or her company, but years later the spirit of the deceased may be seen as no longer interested in the lives of the survivors.

Grieving people in many cultures develop stories (narratives) about the person who died, the dying, the death, and the consequences of the death (Rogers, 2004; Seale, 1998). These stories reflect culture. For example, African-American narratives about a deceased family member will often address how the deceased was affected by racism and resisted it (Rosenblatt & Wallace, 2005a), because African-American culture has had to develop to deal with a racist environment. Or, to take another kind of example, in some cultures most or all deaths are seen as caused by humans, even deaths that many in the U.S. would consider deaths by disease, natural causes, or accident. In such cultures, an important part of grief narratives is the identification of who was responsible for the death and why and how that person caused the death (for example, Brison, 1992, describing a culture in Papua New Guinea).

However, in some cultures, narratives are not an important part of grieving. In particular, there are cultures where people do not often talk with others about a death. For example, Turkish family members may not talk about a loss with each other and may expect visitors not to mention the loss (Cimete & Kuguoglu, 2006). This constraint minimizes the development of narratives.

Cultures are not monolithic, internally consistent, or unchanging. There could be quite a lot of diversity in a culture in, say, the meaning of dying in a certain way, ideas about how to grieve, or the importance of observing a particular mourning practice. For example, Israeli Jewish culture offers contradictory values about what a good death is (Leichtentritt, 2004). And cultures change. They may change in contact with other cultures or as their economic and political environment changes. But not everyone in a culture changes at the same time, so culture change increases a culture's diversity in how people deal with loss. Even within a family there may be substantial differences in views about how to deal with a death or how to grieve. Also, some families have members who come from more than one culture. When there is diversity within a culture or family, there may be interpersonal tension or conflict at the time of a death or afterward as the cultural differences in dealing with dying and death play out.

Some thanatologists emphasize the common humanity we all share with regard to dying and death, giving a sense that we are all in important ways the same. Perhaps there is similarity across cultures in certain matters. For most people around the world a death of somebody close has an emotional impact and causes sadness and personal disruption. But there is no good evidence supporting the notion that how people deal with loss is the same across cultures (Klass, 1999). In fact, it is appropriate to assume that there is substantial diversity of cultures in all matters dealing with dying, death, grief, and mourning.

Many cultures are minority cultures, surrounded by a dominant culture that may limit their culturally appropriate ways of dealing with death. According to Fadiman (1997), Hmong immigrants to the U.S. from Laos may, for example, find hospitals resistant to the large clan gathering when a person is dying that is very important in Hmong culture. The local community and police may try to stop them from carrying out important rituals that involve animal sacrifice or four days of drumming and chanting. But if these rituals are not carried out, Hmong grieving may be entangled in anxieties and fears about the spirit of the deceased, what other Hmong think, and a sense of having let down both living and dead. Moreover, the Hmong may be under enormous pressure from hospital authorities to autopsy a body of a deceased relative, but body mutilation has horrifying meanings in Hmong culture. Despite the demands of a surrounding culture, people in a minority culture need to grieve and dispose of a body their way. Anything less than that disenfranchises them ethically, violates thier human rights, and may have dire consequences for the course of their grieving and their spiritual well being.

So if we want to understand and help people we cannot make the assumption that they are like us or like people from our own culture(s) or that they grieve and mourn the way a textbook or a theory says people do or should. We also should not stereotype people based on our understanding of their culture, making simplistic assumptions that because they are a member of a specific culture we know how they will and should grieve. From that perspective, fact sheets or other materials that give a simple characterization of how the people in some culture deal with loss can be very misleading (Gunaratnam, 1997; Rosenblatt, 1993, 1997). We have to understand and respect cultural differences in the emotionality of bereavement and in how to understand and make sense of a death. And as part of that, we have to be open to the complexity, diversity, and changing qualities of how people within a culture deal with loss.

To be effective, those of us who work with the dying, the bereaved, and their families have to be knowledgeable about culture and ethnicity (Stroebe & Schut, 1998), at the very least because it makes us aware of possibilities. For example, knowing that in Zulu culture there is great stigma about HIV/AIDS and that widows traditionally do not look others in the eye (Rosenblatt & Nkosi, 2007), we will be prepared for that if we are working with a Zulu widow. But even more we have to develop good skills at understanding the beliefs and realities of people who we hope to help and accepting what they say as valid, important, and appropriate. At the very least that means we need to put aside our assumptions about how people do or should deal with loss and be ready to work comfortably and nonjudgmentally with people as they are.

Where appropriate, it is useful to be curious, to ask people what they understand to be true, what they think is appropriate for themselves and for us in relationship with them. If a person thinks and feels primarily in a language other than English, it can be helpful to realize that there are concepts, feelings, relationships, and much else that do not translate well, if at all, into your own language(s). Sometimes it is of great help to others if we make an effort to understand their terms and meanings in their own language. In fact, for a would-be helper even to try to learn what might be appropriate to say in another's language upon entering the presence of someone who is dying or grieving might be very helpful. But at the same time, people realize that there are cultural differences and may be tolerant of our attempts to understand and deal with them, even if what we do may be inappropriate or amateurish by their cultural standards.

From the perspective of socialization, a time of need or crisis may be a time when people most struggle to grow as individuals, whether they want to or not. For example, people who are dying or who are bereaved might hunger for a sense of what is normal and appropriate and how they can best deal with their difficulties, fears, and internal changes. This is a time when some turn to others. It may be a time when they try to learn more about their culture(s). It is also a time when they might be open to aspects of other cultures, even rather alien ones, that offer something that fits for them. However, it may be unhelpful, alienating, and harmful to try to change people from their socialized, culture-based actions, thoughts, beliefs, and rituals. It may be precisely when someone is dying or grieving that they most need to function as they think their culture and socialization tells them to function. In adhering to their own culture and socialization they may find a sense of security, of knowing what is right to do, of giving meaning to all that is going on, and of doing things right by the standards of God or the gods. From that perspective, the socialization that goes on at this time might as much socialization for the would-be helper from an outside culture as it is for the dying or the bereaved.

Learning Objective: (30/40) (35/40)
Acknowledge differences + Similarities in the ways
in which culture + Socialization frame grief
and mourning.

Chapter 14

Religion and Spirituality in Loss, Grief, and Mourning

Dennis Klass

Issues in religion and spirituality are inescapable when we grieve and when we try to help the bereaved because religion is about human limitations. To be sure, a great deal of what we call religion and spirituality is about claiming political power for one group and denying it to other groups, or about rules that keep the society orderly, or about maintaining ethnic heritage. Still, at their best, religions are about life on the boundaries: the boundaries between myself and others, between meaning and absurdity, between hope and despair, between life and death. Difficult bereavements bring us to the boundary of life and death, and so there the potential meaning of life and the potential meaningless of life becomes clear; the possibilities of both hope and despair are present; the boundary between me and the person that has died as well as the boundaries between me and other mourners become both defined and blurred.

Even though the religious issues might be at the heart of grief, religion may or may not be helpful to people as they try to come to terms with a significant death (Tedeschi and Calhoun, 2006). Grief tests the assumptions about how the universe works and our place and power in the universe (see Landsman, 2002). For some people, their prior religious life proves adequate to the task. They come out of their grief more secure in their faith than when they entered it. A man told me that as he stood in front of his mother's body in the casket asking "why" his father quoted scripture to him, "The Lord giveth and the Lord taketh away. Blessed be the name of the Lord." At that moment, he told me, he knew he was called to be a Christian minister. On the other hand for some people their prior religious life is not adequate to their grief. I remember sitting in a meeting of bereaved parents when the topic was "Where was God when my child died?" One woman said that after her child died she lost her faith. Then she added, "but I got a new one that's better." Testing, confirming, modifying, or abandoning prior religion or spirituality is not simply a matter of belief. "Coming to terms with the loss of our assumptive worlds is primarily about learning new ways of acting and being in the world" (Attig, 2002, p. 64; see Klass, 1999, chapter 5 for a fuller discussion of the vicissitudes of faith in individual grief).

The religious rituals, beliefs, and symbols that we find in grief are the same as those that offer guidelines in other aspects of life. A basic religious question, for example, is what is our relationship to our body? All religions offer guidelines on how to dispose of corpses as well as on the moral management of our sex drives. Should the body be preserved to await physical resurrection? Should the enduring bones be separated from the perishable flesh? Should the body be burned because the true self has no further need of it? To take another example, religions offer possible meanings for both physical and emotional suffering. Is suffering positive? Or is suffering negative because happiness is the normative or natural human state? Is it an occasion for participating in Christ's redemptive suffering or to realize Buddhism's First Noble Truth, or is suffering simply to be endured stoically or deadened as much as possible? When the bereaved tap into the rituals, symbols, and beliefs of religions, they do so within the whole context of the rituals, beliefs, and symbols that are woven into their lives and into the communities and cultures in which their lives are set.

There are, of course, many assumptions people make about how the universe works and about their place and power in that universe, and many, many ways by which religious meanings can be symbolized. We are at a very interesting time in human history right now. Most people in other times had access to only one or two religious traditions. If you were European, you were probably Christian. If you were Thai, you were probably Buddhist. With developments in technology of communications and travel, all the world's religious traditions have a voice in the modern world. There are many Pentecostal Christians in Mexico City and Tibetan Buddhists in New York City. We have Americans who have never been on a reservation, but for whom Native American rituals are meaningful, and Hindus who find French existentialism fits their life. Our age, then, is characterized by the meeting and mixing of religious traditions in a way that has few historical precedents.

In traditional societies with only one religious tradition, Tony Walter (1994) says, religious rituals, symbols, and teachings prescribed the inner experience of the mourner. Prescribe literally means pre-write, that is, the community rituals supplied the narrative that was the inner experience of the mourner. With the rise of modernity, however, the old rituals lost much of their power to order the mourners' inner worlds. People in grief today, therefore, have an incredible range of symbols available to them. That means their grief narratives are not pre-written, so they must engage in the difficult task of writing their narratives for themselves. There *Interesting* are, of course, many for whom the rituals still prescribe the inner narrative. For religious leaders, that is at it should be (Grassman and Whitaker, 2006). For others, however, their religious heritage is a grab bag of images from popular culture, a few texts and living examples from grandparents, and some symbols that have helped them make sense of their adolescent struggles, all integrated, more or less, into the radical individualism that permeates American culture (see Bellah, Madsen, Sullivan, & Tipton, 1985).

That means that if we are to take grief seriously, especially if we want to hold ourselves out as experts in helping the bereaved, we need to have a rather good grasp of the symbols by which people find meaning or lose meaning, and the religious traditions that supply those symbols. In this brief chapter we cannot give readers the advanced course in World Religions that would be helpful to them, nor can we reduce the world's religions to a few simple formulas. We can, however, think about some problems in the way religion and spirituality are presented in a great deal of the clinical lore about grief, and we can present a method that allows helpers to work with people from many religious traditions and at the same time give themselves a bottoms-up education in the world's religious traditions.

Is There "Spirituality" Without "Religion"?

We need to spend a few moments looking at the words "religion" and "spirituality." Spirituality and religion are often defined in opposition to one another, in the clinical lore and popular literature about grief. Religion is thus negatively associated with the external, authoritarian doctrines of Christianity while spirituality is positively associated with the individual search for truth, meaning, and authenticity (Garces-Foley, 2006). Thus we often hear, "I'm spiritual but not religious." This way of defining the terms, however, dates only from the mid-1980s and does not hold up to critical analysis. Lucy Bregman (2006), a scholar in the psychology of religion, says the term "spirituality" is a useful "glow word." She finds that not only has the term "spirituality" become fuzzier rather than clearer over time, but the by the beginning of the 21st century, it had been sprung free of any intellectual or cultural context. She notes Unruh, Versnel, and Kerr's survey (2002) of as many empirical and clinical studies as they could find which focused on "spirituality." They discovered 92 definitions of "spirituality," which they could sort, only with a great deal of effort, into six very disparate categories.

Human service professionals, especially those who base their practice in humanistic psychology, are more likely to distinguish between religion and spirituality than other people do. In both the United States and Ireland hospice personnel tend to be "spiritual" while the patients tend to be "religious" (MacConville, 2006;

Garces-Foley, 2006). Thus there may be a real disconnect between those who would help and those they would help.

The conclusion I would draw from this brief look at the claim that there is a "spirituality" separate from religion is that we need to recognize that "spirituality" is a religion too. If we use any of the 92 definitions as we work with the bereaved, we are missing most of what the bereaved are experiencing as they stand at the boundary of life and death, meaning and absurdity, hope and despair. Spirituality may be the religion that provides meaning to our lives, but the bereaved we seek to help very well might have religions with different symbols that give meaning to their lives.

Official Religion and Lived Religion

One of the difficulties we face as we try to help the bereaved from religious traditions which are different from our own is the gap between the official version of a religion and the same religion as we find it in bereaved individuals and communities. The problem is a practical one because as we look for the literature that will help us learn about bereavement in a religious tradition, we often find that it is written by religious leaders who are describing the official version or orthodox practice, not what people actually do. The official theology of a religion is only one element of the way grief is narrated or the way grief is expressed. In different cultural settings the same religion often provides very different styles of grief. Unni Wikan (1988), a Norwegian anthropologist, studied mothers whose children had died in Egypt and Bali, both Muslim cultures. Officially, Islam teaches that each death has been predetermined, even predestined, but the teaching is interpreted differently in different cultural settings. In Egypt, emotions are to be expressed, because mental health is damaged if they are held in. Egyptian village women beseech God

> to help them through the miseries they see as inescapably grounded in their own human lot.. . . . Theirs is a very close and present God, compassionate, just, and forgiving. Should not God not understand that sadness is one thing, subjugation to his will is another? (Wikan, 1988, p.459).

Wikan says that in Bali the family, including the mother, try to restrain their emotions and work to maintain a calm composure, especially to those outside he family. "But even among intimates, their reactions will be moderate, and laughter, joking, and cheerfulness mingle with mutely expressed sadness" (p.452). In Bali, she says, sad or negative emotions are not to be expressed because the emotions can spill from the individual to the community and thus cause the spirit of the individual and of the community to weaken. In the weakened state both the individual and the community would be vulnerable to black magic that causes up to 50% of deaths.

We find the same range of cultural differences within the official versions in all religious traditions. For example, the realization that all things are impermanent forms the basis of Buddhism. The suffering in grief is, for esoteric Buddhism, the beginning of the path that will lead to enlightenment. "All life is suffering" is the First Noble Truth. Yet in many Buddhist cultures, the religious rituals during the dying process and in bereavement are not to realize the Noble Truth. Rather the rituals are to build merit, often by devotion to a Bodhisattva, that can then be transferred to the deceased to help them toward a better rebirth. To achieve enlightenment, Buddhism officially teaches, we have as many lifetimes as we need. Reincarnation, rebirth to another lifetime, is a literal reality. Yet, in Japan, although the doctrine of rebirth remains in the tradition, in fact the dead, even the great founders of the various Buddhist sects, become ancestors and stay a part of the family and so are not reborn. For American converts to Tibetan Buddhism, reincarnation plays almost no part in their grief, and merit plays no role in in how they see themselves helping the bereaved or continuing their own bonds with the deceased (see Goss and Klass, 2005, chapter two; Goss & Klass, 2006).

The examples from Islam and Buddhism that we have given illustrate how the official teaching of a religion is not a good place to learn about how to help the bereaved from those traditions. We could, had we space, give further examples from all the world's religious traditions.

Beyond the gap between official religious teachings and the way the religion interacts with grief, we also see that there are major historical changes in all religious traditions in terms of some basic themes that come up in bereaved individuals and families. In some cases, when people immigrate from one culture to another, the religion changes in just a generation or two. Bereaved children or grandchildren in immigrant families may have very different religious frames than their bereaved parents or grandparents. There are also significant changes over the centuries. In the Western religious traditions, for example, continuing bonds with the dead are often described in terms of the dead appearing to the living as ghosts. When we look at those accounts over the last 2,500 years, we find an incredible diversity as well as a historical development (Finucane, 1996). We find great differences between individuals in any Western tradition, and between subcultures in how the appearances of the dead are described, what the dead expect, and how the living can respond to the dead. Heaven as a place the dead go has also undergone a lengthy historical development (McCannell & Lang, 1988). In clinical work, we often find any individual may hold simultaneously several ways of understanding the deceased's being in heaven, and experience their continuing bond with the deceased in ways that may or may not match their ways of understanding heaven. Unless we point it out, the bereaved may feel no contradictions between those views and experiences. When we investigate the official teachings of the religion about afterlife and continuing interactions with the dead, we are likely to find they bear little resemblance to the heaven in which the bereaved hope to rejoin their dead family members or to the active interaction with the dead that the bereaved maintain.

Learning World Religions from the Bottom Up

Amidst all this diversity, how are we to help the bereaved with the religious issues that are so central to grief? I would like to suggest a practical scheme that we can use to help the bereaved in religious/spiritual issues whether they be in our own cultural world or from cultural worlds very different from ours. First I will define the elements we find in religion as it is lived and show that each can be both problematic and helpful in grief. Second, I will look at the relationship of these elements that we can use to locate ourselves within the religious life of the bereaved.

Our definition must be useful in two ways: First, it must be applicable to all the world's religious traditions. Thus, an answer like, "Religion is beliefs about God" is wrong because not all religions have a God (and some have no God or gods). Further, in most religions, belief is not the most important part (see Smart, 1996). Second, to be useful we need a definition which will allow us better to understand the complexities of people living their everyday inner and interpersonal lives, not just the official teachings (see Chidester, 2002).

A useful definition of religion includes three elements. First, encounter or merger with transcendent reality, that is, the sense that there is something beyond our mundane existence that we can, at least for moments, experience as an inner reality. Second, a worldview, that is, a higher intelligence, purpose, or order that gives meaning to the events and relationships in our lives. Third, a community in which transcendent reality and worldview are validated. We can see this triune structure in many religious traditions. In Islam, for example, Allah is the God who can be found but who cannot be understood by human intelligence; the Prophet Mohammed was given the revelation to which humans should conform their lives; and the Ummah is the community of all those who submit to Allah. Buddhism has the three refuges: the Buddha, the Dharma, and the Sangha. Christianity affirms the trinity of God the father who is unknowable in Himself, God the son who is in human form, and God the holy spirit who is the giver of understanding and the under girder of the church. In Chinese religion, which is an amalgam of Taoism and Confucianism, Heaven or Ti is the unnamable reality; Tao is the ordering principle in nature and Li is the ordering principle by which humans can find harmony within society. In each of these traditions, the sense of the transcendent, finding purpose, and membership in community are all necessary elements of religious or spiritual life.

A significant death can reverberate in each of those elements in both helpful and unhelpful ways. In the first element: If when I pray, I feel close to god who feels like a protective father, who has blessed my marriage, I might very well feel abandoned by that father when the marriage was cut short because he did not answer my prayers that my husband recover from cancer. On the other hand, I might also trust that as god has protected me and my family on earth, he continues to protect my husband who is now with god in heaven.

In the second element: If I believe there is a divinely ordained plan for everything and that nothing happens without a reason, it may be difficult for me to understand any reason for a stray bullet from a fight among drug gangs going through the daycare window killing my preschooler. If, on the other hand, I believe that I have very little control over what happens to me, but I must control how I respond to events, then I might not wonder why my child died, but be very determined to make something good come from it.

In the third element: If I feel like I am alone in my grief, I will have a more difficult time. Crying alone is incredibly painful. Crying with others who are also sad over the death is painful, but also comforting. Communities that cry and remember together are helpful in grief. On the other hand, if members of my family or community keep my grief at a distance, and negatively judge my way of grieving, then the community is unhelpful. I remember a young woman whose child miscarried in the seventh month. Some older women in the church where she had been a very active member kept asking what she had done wrong to make the baby miscarry while the minister kept telling her that the baby's death was god's will and that her tears were a sign of her lack of faith. Needless to say, that community was not helpful to her.

In each element I have given positive and negative examples using only the Western religious traditions because I think those are the traditions with which most readers are most familiar. But as we learn how to include religious issues in our care of the grieving in a multi-cultural and multi-religious world, we will have to become acquainted with how these elements interact with grief in the many religions, even the secular religion that believes in "spirituality." We have very limited resources for working with multiple religious traditions. Kathleen Garces-Foley's *Death and Religion in a Changing World* (2006) is a good place to begin. The book *Dead but not Lost: Grief Narratives in Religious Traditions* (2005) that I wrote with Robert Goss is another.

These elements are not discrete. They work together. I have found that we can diagram the aspects as follows:

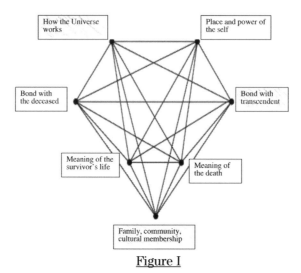

Figure I

The first element, encounter or merger with transcendent reality, is our bond with the transcendent reality (god in the Western traditions) that is often connected with our bond or continuing bond with the dead person. The second element, a worldview, that is, a higher intelligence, purpose, or order that gives meaning to the events and relationships in our lives, is expressed in our assumptions of how the world works and what place and power we have in the universe. The third element is our membership in a community.

My experience as a professional helping the bereaved is that as a statement in one of the boxes changes, all the others will change. For example, very often as the continuing bond with the deceased is established comfortably in the survivor's life, the bond with the transcendent becomes less troubling, the meaning of survivor's life becomes clearer, and troubled relationships in the community or family become less of a barrier. To take another example, when the bereaved person's relation to the community changes from alienated to integrated, the bond with the deceased and with transcendent reality feels surer as does the meaning of the survivor's live and we often see a development in the bereaved person's understanding of the meaning of the death as well as of the dead person's life (see Klass, 1999, chapter 6).

As we grieve or as we work with any bereaved person or group of bereaved people, we can listen closely and understand the content of each of the boxes as they are experiencing them. We can also listen for the content of each of the boxes to which their community's rituals, beliefs, and symbols are pointing them. From what I have said earlier, it should be clear that competent bereavement specialists will be especially attentive to disconnects or discrepancies between the experience of the bereaved person and the expectations of the community.

We do not have to know, then, "how Muslims grieve" to work with a Muslim individual or family, just as we do not have to know what the Christian, Jewish, Buddhist, Taoist, or whatever, way of grieving. We have already seen that the official guidelines and narrative for the bereaved often have little to do with what bereaved people actually do. All we have to do is to listen carefully and say as best we can how this individual or this family understands how the universe works and their place and power in the universe, the meaning of their lives and the meaning of the death, their bond with transcendent reality and their bond with the deceased, and the meaning for them of their family, cultural, and community memberships. We can learn our world religions, then, from the bottom up, not from the top down. Instead of beginning work with people from traditions different from our own with a stereotyped version of their religion in our mind, we can let the bereaved be our world religions teachers. If we are open and listen carefully we might find that people in our own religious tradition — even if it is "spirituality" — are quite different from us in how religion interacts with their grief. We might also find that in some significant ways, we and those we would help are alike, even if we are not the same.

Learning Objective: (35/40)
Understand how Religion + Spirituality intersect w/cultural practices involved in loss, grief and mourning.

Chapter 15

Historical and Contemporary Perspectives on Loss, Grief, and Mourning

Charles A. Corr and Donna M. Corr

This chapter explores some of the many ways in which clinicians, researchers, and scholars have tried to explicate the concepts of loss, grief, and mourning. It might seem a bit odd that there should be many different understandings and interpretations of experiences that are so basic and so familiar. After all, who among us has not encountered loss, grief, and mourning in his or her life? Perhaps, however, it is because these experiences are so fundamental in human life that they have been looked at from many different perspectives. In any event, our goal in this chapter is to try to throw light on some prominent accounts of these subjects.

Before we begin, it might be helpful to note some orienting thoughts. First, losses can take many forms, most of which do not involve death. In each case, primary losses are almost always accompanied by secondary losses, although those secondary losses may not be immediately evident. Second, "bereavement" is the term most often (although perhaps not always) applied to the situation of individuals who have experienced death-related losses. Third, "grief" is the term that applies to our reactions to loss, to all of those reactions whether they are physical, behavioral, psychological (cognitive or affective), social, or spiritual in nature. Fourth, "mourning" is the term used by some to designate all of the intrapsychic and interpsychic processes of coping or learning to live with loss and grief; by others it is restricted to social, public, or ritualized responses to loss. How one understands mourning is critical, but those understandings are complicated by writers who do not explain how they are using this term, who use it in different or inconsistent ways, or who do not clarify whether it is distinct from or equivalent to the term "grieving." Fifth, cultural, religious, spiritual, social, and individual factors may influence how grief and mourning are experienced and expressed. Sixth, outcomes of mourning have been described in many ways, such as regaining equilibrium or the ability to function in healthy ways in life, relearning the world, developing "new normals," or reconstructing meaning in life. Linear, fixed stages in mourning are not favored by contemporary scholars, nor is language such as "recovery," "completion," or "resolution" that may imply a misunderstanding of bereavement and grief or a fixed end point for mourning. Even metaphors such as "healing" or "getting through" should be used with caution since they may depict mourning in both helpful and unhelpful ways.

Mourning as Detachment

Sigmund Freud was among the first to address these subjects. He did so in many ways and contexts, but he is perhaps best known in relationship to these subjects for his paper, "Mourning and Melancholia" (1917/1961b). By "melancholia" Freud meant what would now be called clinical depression, a deviant, complicated, and unhealthy form of mourning. Freud's mature view of normal or uncomplicated mourning seems to have been that it involves a healthy, nonpathological response to the loss of a loved person or object (physical or symbolic). Because one has invested oneself in such a person or object, there is pain involved in its loss. According to Freud, mourning represents the work involved in uncoupling and achieving detachment or emancipation from the lost object, work that reflects both a desire to hold onto that object and a growing recognition that the object is no longer available to us as it once was. This work is complex and it can take a great deal of time and energy. For Freud, the goal is to withdraw libido (understood broadly as human energy) from the lost object and thereby free the ego for new and healthy attachments. As Freud wrote in "Totem and Taboo" (1912-1913/1961a, p. 65), "Mourning has a quite precise psychical task to perform: its function is to detach the survivor's memories and hopes from the dead." Many have taken the goal of detachment as Freud's last word on the subject, but both Siggins (1966) and Rando (1993) have suggested that may overstate or misstate his overall view of mourning.

Acute Grief

In his paper, "Symptomatology and Management of Acute Grief," Lindemann (1944) described typical characteristics of acute grief, including somatic distress, preoccupation with the image of the deceased, guilt, hostility, and alterations in usual patterns of conduct. Many bereaved individuals also adopt traits belonging to the deceased in their behavior. According to Lindemann, "grief work" involves efforts to emancipate oneself from bondage to the deceased, readjust to an environment in which the deceased is missing, and form new relationships. Individuals who try to avoid the intense distress involved in their experiences of grief may only inhibit and complicate their grief work. For Lindemann, delaying or distorting grief reactions leads to morbid or unhealthy forms of grief.

Attachment Theory and Stages of Grief

Drawing on a variety of perspectives and sources of evidence, attachment theory seeks to explain the development of affectional bonds or attachments between child and parent, and between one adult and another, in both human beings and higher order primates. Its principal proponent, John Bowlby, worked out this theory to revise some central tenets of psychoanalytic theory by showing that grief responses are instinctual, adaptational, and valuable for survival. That understanding of grief enabled him to explain processes of both normal and pathological mourning. His views on these subjects are set forth in an early series of articles (e.g., 1961) and in his three-volume work, *Attachment and Loss* (1969-1980).

Drawing in part on the work of Colin Murray Parkes (1972) with London widows, Bowlby described four general phases seen in the normal, uncomplicated responses of bereaved individuals to the loss of a loved one: (a) numbing; (b) yearning and searching; (c) disorganization and despair; and (d) reorganization. Complicated (that is, abnormal) responses are essentially distortions either in onset, degree, or duration. Urges to locate, recover, and reunite with a loved one, along with the anxiety, yearning, anger, protest, and searching that typically accompany them, are not pathological in themselves. They are part of a constructive process of making real ("realization") in one's inner world that which is already real in the objective world. Over time, however, healthy mourning leads to accepting the permanence of a death-related loss. If that is not so, something has gone wrong and grief becomes chronic or conflicted.

Tasks in Mourning

Worden (1982, 1991, 2002) recommended that we think of mourning as an active-process involving four tasks:

- *To accept the reality of the loss*: This task involves overcoming disbeliefand denial of death by acknowledging and accepting the reality of the death.
- *To experience or work through the pain of grief*: Productive mourning acknowledges that it is appropriate to experience pain during bereavement as long as the ways in which that pain is experienced are not overwhelming for the bereaved individual.

- *To adjust to an environment in which the deceased is missing*: In pursuing this task, bereaved individuals engage in a voyage of discovery to determine the significance of the now-severed relationship, to identify each of the various roles that the deceased played in the rela tionship, to adjust to the fact that the deceased is no longer available to fill those roles, and often to develop new skills to fulfill roles formerly satisfied by the deceased.

- Worden has described a fourth task in different ways: *To withdraw emotional energy and reinvest it in another relationship* (1982, p. 15); *To emotionally relocate the deceased and move on with life* (1991, p. 16; 2002, p. 35); and, in depicting mourning tasks for children: *To relocate the dead person within one's life and find ways to memorialize the person* (1996, p. 15). The main point of this fourth task is to call upon the bereaved person to modify or restructure his or her relationship with the deceased in ways that remain satisfying but that also reflect the changed circumstances of life and death. This task requires a bereaved person to reconceive his or her own personal identity, restructure his or her relationship with the deceased person in the light of the loss that has taken place, avoid becoming neurotically encumbered by the past in ways that diminish future quality in living, and remain open to new attachments and other relationships.

Worden's tasks reflect an interpretation of mourning as, in principle, a proac-tive way of striving to manage one's loss and grief. They depict mourning as involv-ing a set of interrelated tasks requiring effort intended to enable the bereaved per-son to regain some measure of control over his or her life. Worden (2002, p. 27) wrote that the tasks of mourning "do not necessarily follow a specific order," even though "there is some ordering suggested in the definitions." He believes that mourners must accomplish these tasks before mourning can be completed.

The Six "R" Processes of Mourning

Rando (1993) described mourning in terms of six "R" processes:
- Recognize the loss—acknowledge and understand the death
- React to the separation—experience the pain of the loss; feel, identify, accept, and give expression to all of the psychological reactions to the loss; and identify and mourn secondary losses
- Recollect and reexperience the deceased and the relationship— review and remember realistically; revive and reexperience one's feelings
- Relinquish old attachments to the deceased and the old assumptive world

- Readjust to move adaptively into the new world without forgetting the old—revise the assumptive world, develop a new relationship with the deceased, adopt new ways of being in the world, and form a new identity
- Reinvest

According to Rando, mourners need to acknowledge and gain insight into their losses, experience and express their reactions to those losses, connect with and restructure their former attachments, and find ways to move forward in new modes of living. Rando also draws attention to the many secondary or associated losses that are always involved in an important primary loss. Mention of an "assumptive world" reminds us that we all function within a set of assumptions concerning what we take to be real about ourselves and about the world around us. And the process of reinvestment involves using one's resources in appropriate and rewarding ways both to form a new relationship with the deceased loved one and to develop other or new sources of gratification.

Rando maintained that these six "R" processes must be undertaken for healthy mourning. They are, she wrote, "interrelated and tend to build upon one another, [although] a number of them may occur simultaneously" (1993, p. 44). Although they are set forth in a typical order, the sequence is not invariant: "Mourners may move back and forth among the processes, with such movement illustrating the nonlinear and fluctuating course of mourning" (p. 44).

The Dual Process Model

Stroebe and Schut's dual process model (1999) emphasizes an oscillation between two complementary sets of coping processes employed by bereaved persons: (1) one set of processes is loss oriented or concerned primarily in coping with loss; (2) the other is restoration oriented or concerned primarily in coping with "restoration." *Loss-oriented processes* involve the intrusion of grief into the life of the bereaved, grief work, and breaking bonds or ties to the deceased, as well as resistance to change in the form of denial or avoidance of restoration changes. *Restoration-oriented processes* include attending to life changes, doing new things, and denial, avoidance, or distraction from grief.

Note that the term "restoration" as it is used in this model is not about trying to make real once again the mourner's former world of lived experiences (which no longer exists) or the old assumptive world (which has also been shattered or at least rudely shaken by the loss). Rather, it has to do with efforts to adapt to the new world in which bereaved persons find themselves. What is restored, according to this model, is not a past mode of living, but the ability to live productively in the present and future. Thus, both loss-oriented and restoration-oriented processes address issues of coping; the difference between them is centered on their meaning or focus. The dual process model also suggests that emphases in coping with bereavement may differ from one cultural group to another, one individual to another, and one moment to another.

Meaning Making

Numerous authors have stressed in various ways the importance of "meaning making" for individuals who have suffered a significant loss in their lives. For example, Attig (1996, 2000) has written about "relearning the world" as a process that involves simultaneously finding and making meaning on many levels. According to Attig, relearning the world includes grieving individually, within our families, and within our communities and cultures, in ways that "engage with several of the great mysteries of life in the human tradition" and that allow us to "make a multifaceted transition from loving in presence to loving in absence" (2001, p. 34).

In a similar way, Neimeyer (e.g., 1998, 2000, 2001) has written extensively about the need for bereaved persons to engage in a process of reconstructing meaning in their lives and has asserted that "meaning reconstruction in response to a loss is the central process in grieving" (1998, p. 110). Any individual griever may engage in this process at different times, in different ways, and in different connections with his or her culture and community. Where a bereaved person finds it difficult to engage in meaning reconstruction or is not able to accomplish this project, as might most often be seen in violent or traumatic bereavements, it has been argued that harmful effects will likely follow.

According to Neimeyer (2000) meaning reconstruction includes:
The attempt to find or create new meaning in the life of the survivor, as well as in the death of the loved one.

- The integration of meaning, as well as its construction.
- The construction of meaning as an interpersonal, as well as personal, process.
- The anchoring of meaning making in cultural, as well as intimate, discursive contexts.
- Tacit and preverbal, as well as explicit and articulate meanings.
- The processes of meaning reconstruction, as well as its products.

In a recent article, Holland, Currier, and Neimeyer (2006) pointed to the distinction between "sense-making" and "benefit-finding" as two central forms of meaning making.

Sense-making denotes the comprehensibility of the loss or the survivor's capacity to find some sort of benign explanation for the seemingly inexplicable experience, often framed in philosophical or spiritual terms. Conversely, benefit-finding refers to the significance of the loss and entails the survivor's paradoxical ability to uncover a "silver lining" in the personal or social consequences of the loss, such as enhanced empathy, reordered life priorities, or a closer connection to other people within or beyond the family. (p. 176)

Among the conclusions drawn by these authors from their empirical study are the following: (1) "[I]n general, sense-making is a stronger predictor of grief outcomes compared to benefit-finding" (p. 183); (2) These findings "conform to a larger body of empirical and theoretical literature, which challenges the notion that grief unfolds in predictable patterns over time" (p. 183); and (3) "In summary, these results call for more research on the 'multiple meanings of meaning' . . . particularly around the way in which these interact in adaptation to loss" (pp. 185-186).

Continuing Bonds

Drawing on research with bereaved children, spouses, and parents, as well as other sources, Klass, Silverman, and Nickman (1996) noted the importance for many bereaved persons of efforts to maintain a connection to the individual who has died. By contrast with interpretations of mourning as involving "detachment from," "letting go of," or "forgetting" the deceased, this viewpoint reflects the active efforts of many bereaved persons to maintain a continuing bond, an internal representation of, or ongoing connection with that individual. This bond is not static but dynamic. It involves negotiating and renegotiating the meaning of the loss over time. It develops in ways that allow the deceased to remain a transformed or changed but ongoing presence in the inner lives of the bereaved. Connections of this type "provided solace, comfort and support, and eased the transition from the past to the future" (p. xviii).

According to these authors, although "the continuing bond has been overlooked or undervalued in most scholarly and clinical work" (p. xvii) and there has been "little social validation for the relationship people reported with the deceased or absent person" (p. xviii), continuing bonds involve new and altered relationships that reflect "the reality of how people experience and live their lives" (p. xix). They are aspects of normal mourning processes and do not represent psychopathology. Putting stress on continuing bonds in bereavement is, at least, an alternative to (if not a repudiation of) the view that mourning does or should lead to total disengagement from or severing bonds to the deceased.

Anticipatory Grief and Mourning

The concept of *anticipatory grief* was first introduced by Lindemann (1944) and has since been the subject of numerous inquiries (e.g., Fulton & Fulton, 1971;

Fulton & Gottesman, 1980). Broadly speaking, anticipatory grief refers to grief experiences that take place prior to but in connection with a significant loss, one that is expected to take place but has not yet occurred—for example, grief that occurs in advance of, but somehow still in relation to, impending death. A forewarning of death is a necessary condition for anticipatory grief, but the heart of the matter is the grief reaction to the anticipated, but not yet actually realized, loss.

Rando (1986, p. 24) originally defined anticipatory grief as, "the phenomenon encompassing the processes of mourning, coping, interaction, planning, and psychosocial reorganization that are stimulated and begun in part in response to the awareness of the impending loss of a loved one and the recognition of associated losses in the past, present, and future." This very broad definition of anticipatory grief includes both grief reactions and mourning processes. It refers equally to past, present, and future losses. It incorporates a shifting time frame as the dying person moves toward death, and it encompasses the perspectives of both the dying person and his or her survivors-to-be.

One problem with this definition is that the adjective "anticipatory" would seem to be incorrect since the grief in question is not limited solely to future or expected losses. A second problem is that the noun "grief" is inexact since the definition includes both grief and mourning. For those reasons, Rando (1988) first argued that although the phenomenon of anticipatory grief is real, the term itself is a misnomer. Subsequently, she decided to shift to the phrase *anticipatory mourning* in a later book, *Clinical Dimensions of Anticipatory Mourning* (Rando, 2000).

It seems clear, for example, that when a husband is dying, a wife may realize that she is already without the help he used to give her around the house (a past loss), that she is currently losing the vigorous ways in which he used to express his love for her (a present or ongoing loss), and that with his death she will lose the comfort of his presence (an expected or anticipated loss). Each of these losses may generate its own grief reaction, and each may stimulate a mourning process in which one tries to cope with that loss and its associated grief reactions. However, these experiences need not be inconsistent with maintaining the loving ties that characterize an attachment between two living people. After all, partners often experience other losses—a job, a beloved home, a loved parent or friend—but continue to love each other through those losses.

We might clarify the meaning of anticipatory grief by adopting a narrower definition, one that limits "anticipatory" grief (and mourning) to reactions to losses that have not yet occurred and are not yet in process—that is, to losses that have not yet moved from expectation to reality. If so, reacting to and coping with dying would become the master concepts in pre-death experiences of grief and mourning

(Corr & Corr, 2000). Prior to death, one might experience anticipatory grief and mourning related to losses that are expected to take place in the future, other (nonanticipatory) grief reactions and mourning processes that are associated with existing losses (past and present), and reactions to and coping with the new challenges that inevitably arise during dying. Anticipatory grief and mourning may affect the quality of post-death bereavement, but they need not be any more (or less) significant in this matter than all of the other aspects of coping with dying.

There is much that remains unclear about anticipatory grief and mourning. For example, Fulton (2003) has noted his "serious reservations regarding the heuristic value—either theoretical or practical—of the concepts, 'anticipatory grief' and 'anticipatory mourning'" (p. 350). These reservations arise from problems in conceptualizing, defining, measuring, and validating the key concepts. Fulton also argues that much research in this field has depended upon specific understandings of grief and mourning, notably psychoanalytic assumptions that cohorts of bereaved persons will experience a comparable volume of grief and will do so in a linear way. Conflating "forewarning of death" with "anticipatory grief" has led some to assume that the latter will inevitably follow the former and will, in turn, relieve the survivor of some share of post-death grief—when, as Fulton rightly insists, they differ in both duration and form.

Disenfranchised Grief and Mourning

According to Doka (1989, p. 4), *disenfranchised grief* is "the grief that persons experience when they incur a loss that is not or cannot be openly acknowledged, publicly mourned, or socially supported." To disenfranchise grief is to indicate that a particular individual does not have a right to be perceived or to function as a bereaved person. Thus disenfranchised grief is not merely unnoticed, forgotten, or hidden; it is socially disallowed and unsupported.

Doka (1989, 2002) argued that grief can be disenfranchised in three primary ways: the type of loss is not sanctioned, the type of relationship is not sanctioned, or the grievers themselves are not sanctioned. Some deaths, such as those involving suicide or AIDS, may be "disenfranchising deaths" in the sense that they either are not well recognized or are associated with a high degree of social stigma. In 2002, Doka recast this idea to speak of certain circumstances of death as disenfranchising and to note that ways in which individuals grieve or grieving styles can contribute to disenfranchisement.

Losses are disenfranchised when their significance is not recognized by society. These losses might include perinatal deaths, losses associated with elective abortion, or the loss of body parts. Such losses are often dismissed or minimized, as when one is simply told, "Be glad that you are still alive." Similarly, persons outside the relationship may not appreciate the death of a pet even though it may be an important source of grief for anyone, regardless of age. Also, society often fails to recognize losses that occur when dementia blots out an individual's personality in such a way that significant others perceive the person they loved to be psychosocially dead, even though biological life continues.

Relationships are disenfranchised when they are not granted social approval. For example, some unsuspected, past, or secret relationships might not be publicly recognized or socially sanctioned. These could include relationships between friends, co-workers, in-laws, or ex-spouses, all of which might be recognized in principle but not in connection with bereavement — as well as relationships that are often not recognized by others as significant or are judged illicit, such as those involving extramarital affairs or same-sex relationships.

Grievers are disenfranchised when they are not recognized by society as persons who are entitled to experience grief or who have a need to mourn. Young children and the very old are often disenfranchised in this way, as are mentally disabled persons.

Corr (1998, 2002) noted that these three factors (relationships, losses, and grievers) are the key *structural elements of bereavement*. In addition, Corr argued that the *dynamic or functional elements of bereavement* (grief and mourning) may also be disenfranchised. For example, a bereaved person might be told by society that the way he or she is experiencing or expressing grief is inappropriate, and/or that his or her ways of coping with the loss and the grief reactions are unacceptable. Some grief reactions and some ways of mourning are rejected because they are unfamiliar or make others in society uncomfortable.

However it occurs, "the problem of disenfranchised grief can be expressed in a paradox. The very nature of disenfranchised grief creates additional problems for grief, while removing or minimizing sources of support" (Doka, 1989, p. 7). Many situations of disenfranchised grief involve intensified emotional reactions (for example, anger, guilt, or powerlessness), ambivalent relationships (as in cases of abortion or between persons who were once but who no longer are lovers), and concurrent crises (such as those involving legal and financial problems). Disenfranchisement may remove the very factors that would otherwise facilitate mourning (such as a role in planning and participating in funeral rituals) or make it possible to obtain social support (for example, through time off from work, speaking about the loss, receiving expressions of sympathy, or finding solace within some religious tradition).

Grieving Styles

Many have claimed that patterns of grief and mourning are essentially related to gender, with men and women grieving (or mourning) in different and contrasting ways. Against this gender dichotomy, Martin and Doka (2000) argued that the issue is not really one of gender, but of style. Accordingly, they proposed a distinction between an "intuitive" grieving style that emphasizes experiencing and expressing emotion versus an "instrumental" grieving style that focuses on practical matters and problem solving. These contrasting styles are depicted as poles on a spectrum. Martin and Doka concede that in our society one of these styles may more often apply to women and the other to men. However, they caution that these applications are not universal, noting that they likely result from broad patterns of socialization that do not apply universally in rigid ways. Because individuals of both genders have different backgrounds, personalities, and ways of living out their lives, some women are instrumental grievers, some men are intuitive grievers, and perhaps many bereaved persons adopt some aspects of one or the other grieving style at different times and in different contexts. As a result, this analysis tends to legitimize individuality in coping with loss and grief, even as it identifies shared patterns among various groups of bereaved persons whose members may or may not be of a specific gender.

Complicated Grief Reactions

When contemporary writers speak of "complicated grief," they are using the adjective "complicated" to replace "pathological" (which has come into disfavor as too judgmental in tone), but their intention is still to refer to reactions and processes that are not only unusual but also abnormal in the sense of being mental disorders that are deviant and unhealthy. With this qualification in mind, we can turn to Parkes' statement (2006b, p. 2) that "numerous clinical studies have supported the existence of complicated grief, which is usually seen as taking two forms: an inhibited or delayed form and a chronic or persistent form." Parkes commented that, "Of the two, the chronic form is the most frequent."

> Nevertheless, Parkes added the following:
> Despite this evidence, the authors of the DSM [the *Diagnostic and Statistical Manual of Mental Disorders*] have consistently rejected including pathological or complicated grief as a psychiatric diagnosis on the grounds that it has not been clearly distinguished from, on the one hand, uncomplicated grief and, on the other, the other psychiatric disorders that can be triggered by bereavement, most notably Clinical Depression. (p. 2)

Not surprisingly, in recent years there have been several efforts to define the precise meaning of the phrase "complicated grief" and to provide empirical data that would establish it as a distinct clinical entity. Some of these efforts are reflected in a "Symposium on Complicated Grief" organized by Parkes (2006a), which also takes note of some contrarian views that the construct of "complicated grief" risks stigmatizing, pathologizing, and medicalizing a normal if difficult bereavement experience, thereby turning familiar supportive work on the part of family members and friends over to secularly trained professionals, and that complicated grief rather than being an internal reality is an externally imposed social role with cultural and historical origins.

LeARNiNg ObjEctive: (40/40)
Explicate Some of the WAYs in which
clinicians + Scholars have Conceptualized
loss, grief and mourning from historical
and Contemporary perspectives.

Chapter 16

Lifespan Issues and Loss, Grief, and Mourning

Part 1:
The Importance of a
Developmental Context:
Childhood and Adolescence as an Example

Kevin Ann Oltjenbruns

Research indicates that the experience of grief after a significant loss changes as life stages vary. Corr (1996) reminds us that developmental processes play an important role in determining how an individual deals with loss, as well as how one's bereavement experience may then influence subsequent development. Further, a person's understanding of the concept of death changes over time as does the use of particular coping strategies. A primary goal of part one of this chapter is to build an argument that, to be effective in helping the bereaved, we must use a developmental perspective. Examples relevant to childhood and adolescence will be used for illustration purposes.

Common Manifestations of Grief

Childhood. After studying even a small subset of articles written about grief experienced during the early years, it becomes clear that childhood bereavement is not "a different version of adult mourning but rather one unique to the child's capacities" (Sekaer & Katz, 1986, p. 292). Further, certain manifestations of grief are more likely to occur during various substages as compared to a later time frame. For example, regressive behaviors such as bedwetting or thumb sucking, separation anxiety, fear of abandonment, fear that others close to them will also die, guilt due to magical thinking are quite prevalent during early childhood. Manifestations of grief in later childhood are more likely to include learning difficulties, school phobia, and anger (Baker & Sedney, 1996; Birenbaum, 2000; Geis, Whittlesey, McDonald, Smith, Pfefferbaum, 1998; Silverman & Worden, 1992; Stahlman, 1996). As time since the death grows longer, particular manifestations shift over time; some are more common in the months immediately following the death and others may not appear until a couple of years later. Using data from the Harvard Childhood Bereavement Study, Worden and Silverman (1996) discovered that two years after a parent's death, there were increased levels of social withdrawal, anxiety, and social problems in the bereaved group of children compared to the non-bereaved control group. Given the power of the longitudinal design, the researchers involved in the Harvard study were the first to report a curvilinear relationship between the intensity of certain feelings and behaviors and the length of time since the death.

Adolescence. The grief of adolescents is multifaceted, as it is in other life stages. Common reactions include feeling different from one's peers; diminished social competency; loneliness, dysphoric mood, guilt, confusion, anger, sense of powerlessness, inability to concentrate, and acting out behaviors. Birenbaum (2000) studied the most frequently reported children's and teenagers responses (physical and psychosocial) in anticipation of and after the death of a sibling from cancer. They found differing responses among 3-5 year olds; 6-11 year olds; and 12-19 year olds at different points in time: two months prior to the death; 2 weeks, 4 months and 12 months after the death. Not only did responses change over time, but there were notable differences from one age group to the other.

When an adolescent's peer dies, many of the deaths are sudden and/or violent (suicides, accidents, homicides). Questions related to "why" are common given that these situations are regarded as unnecessary and possibly preventable. These types of deaths frequently exacerbate particular reactions such as fear or anger and may be further complicated by having had no time to prepare for the death. Death of an age-mate typically raises issues dealing with personal mortality — possibly for the first time. Even while engaging in certain dangerous behaviors (e.g., drinking and driving) because he or she feels protected by the "personal fable," some young persons begin to more fully understand that they too may die.

Understanding of the Concept of Death

Childhood. Cognitive capacity and understanding of the concept of death vary over time and influences how a child deals with the loss (Speece & Brent, 1996; Oltjenbruns, 2001). Within childhood, one discovers significant differences over time. The following list is not meant to engender a debate when one stage ends and another begins but is intended simply to encapsulate major shifts:

Early Childhood (2-4 Years)	Middle Childhood (4-6 years)	Late Childhood (7-11 years)
• is quite egocentric • thinks in concrete, literal terms • focuses on here and now • believes death is temporary, reversible • does not understand that death is universal • does not understand that dead persons are non-functional	• which diminishes over time • understands that death is irreversible • understands dead people are nonfunctional • begins to understand that death is universal (age 5—)	• understands death is final • understands that death is a natural part of life • has increased under standing of future with out person who has died • has more realistic under standing of causality of death

An understanding of a child's thought processes surrounding death provides important insight into how a child is responding to the loss and can also help guide appropriate support strategies. For example, since toddlers do not understand that death is final and irreversible, they may repeatedly engage in seeking behaviors for the deceased. Helpers, then, must explain numerous times that the loved one is not *ever* coming back. Since that same youngster thinks in concrete and literal terms, it is dangerous to use euphemisms that are confusing such as grandma is sleeping or your father has gone on a long trip. Indirect communication not only confuses the child but may ultimately undermine trust in persons around him or her, and/or trigger a fear response (Goldman, 2000; Goldman, 2004; Webb, 2002). Not fully understanding the nature of death, young children may conclude that they caused the death, simply by wishing someone would "go away." Caregivers must give con-crete explanations as to what really happened, at a level the child can understand, to let them know that he or she did not cause the other person's death.

Adolescence. Cognitive maturation during adolescence affects the individ-ual's ability to comprehend death and related concepts. Adolescents' increasing capacity to use abstract reasoning and understand symbolism allows them to more fully grasp the meanings of life, death, and time. With the ability to think in the abstract, adolescents become preoccupied with their own thought processes, as well as what others may think of them; as a result, teens often play to an imaginary audience. (Cook & Oltjenbruns, 1998). Young persons dealing with a significant loss, then, may camouflage feelings for fear of being regarded as different and then possibly ostracized by a peer group, thus working against a core age-appropriate issue of developing a sense of belongingness (Fleming & Balmer, 1996). Sadly, the more composed an adolescent may appear after a death, the greater may be their risk in experiencing unresolved grief (Lenhardt & McCourt, 2000).

Mastering Normal Developmental Tasks Within the Context of Bereavement

The classic work by Erik Erikson (1963) notes that within each normative crisis, there are related developmental tasks. Erikson believed that an individual deals with a series of psychosocial stages or crises during the course of his or her lifespan. During the life stages of childhood and adolescence, individuals are faced with challenges as they strive to develop what Erikson labels autonomy, initiative, industry (mastery of skill), a sense of identity. The outcome of each crisis is closely tied to the type of environment or social support that is available to an individual in that stage. Factors inherent to a loss experience may propel a person toward a negative or compromised resolution of a particular developmental challenge.

For example, the normative crisis of late childhood (initiative vs. guilt) involves attempts to develop numerous skills valued by one's own society, self-evaluation skills, self-confidence, and interdependence. Those giving grief support must also encourage success in each of these areas. Children should be allowed to continue to live their lives; continue with school, lessons, sports, peer interaction, etc. These activities should not be regarded as a distraction from grief, but rather as work towards accomplishing what needs to be mastered at a particular life stage. Failure to accomplish such developmental tasks may jeopardize mastery of subsequent tasks during later periods. This discussion brings to mind Stroebe and Schut's dual process model of coping. While we give support to children as they engage in the "loss orientation," we must also give support to them to continue with a "restoration orientation." This encouragement does not need to fall exclusively to parents but may also be provided by other caring adults.

The death of a loved one during adolescence is likely to add considerable upheaval to this time of life which is already characterized by ambivalence, struggle, and confusion, making it a different experience than that encountered by grieving children or adults (Meshot & Leitner, 1993). Erikson would define the key developmental task for adolescents as defining as sense of personal identity. Fleming and Adolph (1986) identify other "core issues" as being important focal points during this same stage, including: self-image, sense of belonging, sense of mastery and control, sense of fairness and justice. The need to focus on such developmental tasks and core issues influences various aspects of the loss experience. For example, the death of one's mother during adolescence can complicate defining a personal sense of self since a parent is often used as a mirror to help define either perceived positive or negative aspects of one's self. After the death of a parent, many adolescents feel pressured (by self or by others) to assume some of the responsibilities of the deceased; they may then struggle with accomplishing significant development tasks of individuation and separation from family.

Coping Strategies and the Need for Support

Each individual brings to a crisis situation a variety of coping mechanisms; these vary somewhat by life stage, personality, and previous experience. Although some adults would like to spare children the knowledge that a loved one has died and protect them from the ensuing grief, this protection is not helpful. Children need the opportunity to say good-bye, share feelings, and deal with emotions. Adults should be prepared to provide support to children who experience a loss in a developmentally appropriate fashion. Goldman (2000) recommends such "concrete" and active strategies as creating a worry box, engaging in dramatic play, and sharing memories through artwork. While children may be unable to find words to describe certain feelings and concerns, they can often express themselves through these types of modalities.

Coping strategies change as one matures. For example, children often try to derive comfort by seeking comfort from others; denying at times the impact of the loss; adherence to familiar activities and routines; using fantasy to ameliorate aspects of the loss (Baker & Sedney, 1996). As they enter adolescence, young persons begin to engage in more effective behavioral coping strategies (e.g., help seeking; problem solving; expressing feelings). Further, adolescents begin to engage in cognitive coping strategies (e.g., search for meaning; positive reappraisal; acceptance of the loss) (Schaefer & Moos, 2001).

There is growing body of research (Hurd, 2004) which delineates that the nature of support from caregivers is a key variable in regard to bereavement outcome for children and adolescents. Lin, Sandler, Ayers, Wolchik, and Luecken (2004) examined many variables that differentiate resilient children and adolescents from those with mental health problems following th⋯ a primary caregiver. They found that those survivors identifi⋯ ⋯rviving caregivers who provided greater warmth and more ⋯pared to those bereaved children and adolescents who experie⋯ ⋯ious mental health problems following the death. In a related study, Haine, Wolchik, Sandler, Millsap, and Ayers (2006) confirmed the power of positive parenting as a significant interpersonal resource which increased likelihood of dealing with the loss in a positive fashion. Another study concluded that children who are not supported in early phases of grief can develop serious emotional and behavioral problems. Providing education (and support) to surviving parents is important so that they might learn how to more effectively help their children (Kirwin & Hamrin, 2005).

Facing the death of a loved one may ultimately strengthen available strategies for coping with subsequent stressful events. Steen (1998) reminds us that dealing with a significant loss may ultimately result in negative emotional or physical consequences or, alternatively, lead to positive outcomes. Despite the many challenges faced as a result of the death of a loved one, many adolescents reported that grief experiences resulted in such positive outcomes a an increased sense of maturity, a willingness to deal with responsibility at a young age, an appreciation for life, an ability to cope with adversity, an increased sensitivity to others, an increase resilience, sense of optimism, and a desire to help others in need (Davies, 1991; Hogan & DeSantis, 1996; Walker, 1993).

Re-Grief Phenomenon

As years pass and the bereaved individual moves through later life stages, the context for understanding an earlier loss and adjusting to it changes. "Within this milieu of maturing developmental capacitates and shifting developmental tasks, an individual who experiences a significant loss … will often "re-grieve" the loss at a later time, from a different and more mature vantage point " (Oltjenbruns, 2001, pp.170 -171). Individuals may struggle repeatedly with a loss that occurred many years prior. While some persons never do resolve the loss and "get stuck" in their grief, the re-grief phenomenon is a developmentally appropriate processing of the experience from a different perspective than what was possible earlier. As one's cognitive capacity changes, a person often needs to add to what was understood earlier in order to create a fuller meaning of the loss which then supports one's continuing healing. Further, new issues may arise as an individual faces different developmental tasks as he/she progresses through more advanced life stages. For example, as a young woman struggles to refine her sense of identity (a normal developmental task of adolescence), she may need to re-grieve her father's death of many years prior. Newman and Newman (1999) stress that "one can review and reinterpret previous stages in the light of new insight and/or new experiences…themes of earlier stages may re-emerge at any point, bringing a new meaning or a new resolution to an earlier conflict" (p. 17).

Summary Remarks

One must wear a "developmental lens" in order to effectively help someone who is grieving. It is crucial to understand an individual's normal developmental capacities in various domains (e.g., psychosocial, emotional, physical, and cognitive) and to be aware of how those capacities interact with the need to accomplish certain "developmental tasks" at a particular life stage. This interplay has much to do with how the bereaved person defines the loss and how he or she uses both personal and interpersonal resources in the journey towards healing. Only with that insight can a family member, friend, or helper know the challenges faced by the grieving individual and only when that understanding is available can a person offer help that is meaningful.

The primary goal of this chapter was to illustrate, using examples from childhood and adolescence, the importance of becoming grounded in a developmental perspective. For those who would like to continue reading in this area, I would recommend Balk's (2007) new article entitled "Working with Children and Adolescents" which further synthesizes various theoretical and research perspectives.

Learning Objective: (35/40)
Explain how Children and Adolescents understand and experience grief and loss.

Chapter 16

Life Span Issues and Loss, Grief, and Mourning

Part 2: Adulthood

David E. Balk

The older a person, probabilities increase for the experience of loss, grief, and mourning. A scan of worldwide mortality statistics (http://www.who.int/whosis/mort/en/index.html) discloses that longevity of life brings with it greater likelihood of multiple losses such as the deaths of parents, siblings, children, grandchildren, and friends. For older adults, dealing with these losses becomes intertwined with problems endemic to aging: degradations in physiological operations, the onset of chronic and debilitating illnesses, and diminished functional performance.

Loss, grief, and mourning during adulthood is the focus for this part of the chapter. The topics covered are (a) various schema for understanding responses to adult bereavement and (b) the impacts of some deaths that adults grieve.

Overall Schema for Understanding Responses to Bereavement in Adulthood

Four schema will be presented about ways to understand responses to bereavement in adulthood: (a) a holistic appreciation of bereavement, (b) rhythms to the bereavement trajectories that adults report, (c) life span development concepts, and (d) cognitive-based coping models.

Schema 1: A holistic appreciation of bereavement

Bereavement affects people behaviorally, cognitively, interpersonally, emotionally, physically, and spiritually. Our understanding of life span issues and bereavement would be impoverished without this holistic template. Consider two examples: physical and interpersonal consequences. Clinical evidence (Goodkin, Baldewicz, Blaney, et. al., 2001; Hall & Irwin, 2001) indisputably demonstrates that a physical response to bereavement is a depressed immune system. Coupling immune system difficulties following bereavement to the normal degeneration of major human biological systems as one ages (Moss, Moss, & Hansson, 2001) makes clear the impact that bereavement increases older adults' vulnerability to opportunistic diseases. Another example comes from the interpersonal realm. In an increasingly mobile, secularized society with an aging population, adults face more and more the prospects of dealing with deaths less supported by loved ones than other generations have experienced (Benoliel & Degner, 1995).

Schema 2: Rhythms to the bereavement trajectories that adults report

Assertions that grieving occurs in psychological stages have been put to rest (Kastenbaum, 2001; Lund, Caserta, & Dimond, 1993). Bereavement trajectories form curvilinear paths, extend indeterminately (Lehman, Lang, Wortman, & Sorenson, 1989), and among adults involve basic groupings: a majority of persons who are resilient, a large plurality that struggles but recovers, and a small minority whose grief goes unabated without intervention (Bonanno, 2006; see also Bonanno, Wortman, Lehman, et. al., 2002; Bonanno, Wortman, & Neese, 2004).

While stages of grieving have fallen out of favor, phases ascribed to grieving, for instance, the phases that Bowlby (1980, pp. 85-96) identified, have retained considerable staying power in thanatology and have become a means for explicating changes over time in adult bereavement. Steeves (2002) noted that Bowlby's phases to grief readily demarcate the narratives whereby adult grievers describe their experiences: numbness characterized the initial few weeks, waves of sadness marked the next few months, and loneliness emerged about the sixth month and lasted thereafter. Reorganization and reorientation, the final phase in Bowlby's phases, could not be found in the narratives. As Steeves (2002) put it, "The loneliness did not disappear but seemed to become merely another 'fact of life'" (p. 7).

Using the idea of phases to understand the course of bereavement manifests the human intent to construe meaning out of the chaos of bereavement and to establish a rhythm to the temporal processes of grief. Applying the idea of phases to bereavement underscores that "bereavement is so obviously socially constructed" (Steeves, 2002, p. 5). What is clear is that an order can be applied to these narratives, one that disquietingly ends with an enduring loneliness. Steeves suggested that the course of bereavement typically lasts at most 9–12 months for elderly adults. Most persons I know dispute that the duration of bereavement is so short-lived. Perhaps Steeves followed his elderly research participants only into the diminishment of their acute grief and the onset of normal grief but did not interview them beyond the first year of their bereavement. Impressive national data indicate that many years after their spouses' deaths, widows commonly had memories of and conversations about their spouses and occasionally became sad and upset over reminders (Carnelley, Wortman, Bolger, & Burke, 2006); what these researchers discovered about the long-term process of grieving a spouse's death suggests the loneliness Steeves reported does extend well past the first two years of becoming a widow, but the national data also pointed to personal growth, such as, increases in self-confidence and personal strength, following spousal bereavement. These findings about personal growth are suggestive of reorganization and reorientation.

Schema 3: Life span development concepts

For several decades researchers have studied human development from a perspective that looks at how change over time describes the human life cycle (Baltes, Reese, & Nesselroade, 1977). One major contribution from the life span development perspective has been a template provided both for understanding critical life events and for designing interventions pertinent to them (Danish, 1977; Danish & D'Augelli, 1980). To wit, critical life events exhibit several properties, among them, probability of occurrence, sequence, and duration. To illustrate these life event properties, consider the death of a parent:

- there is high probability of the death for an aged parent, but low probability for a young parent;
- in countries with highly developed and accessible medical care, the death of a parent prior to the death of that parent's child is considered to occur in sequence, whereas the death of a child ahead of a parent's death is out of sequence;
- duration is much trickier as discrete events such as the death of a parent can have temporal repercussions that resonate for months and years. The notion of duration can be seen with these contrasting examples: the sudden death of a parent in a car accident versus the lingering death of a parent to cancer following several years of treatment, remission, and relapse.

Schema 4: Cognitive-based coping models

Coping is now understood from a cognitive-based perspective. "Cognitive-based" means that human coping involves comprehending implications, planning responses, and evaluating outcomes. Further, events that require coping do not occur in isolation. As Moos and Schaefer (1986) pointed out several years ago, life events are embedded in three sorts of factors: (a) personal and background factors (for instance, one's age, culture, religious beliefs, gender, and previous experiences with loss), (b) event-related factors (for instance, anticipated versus unexpected events, painful versus peaceful deaths), and (c) socioenvironmental factors (for instance, social support systems, accessible health care). Placed into the context of this chapter, consider young parents coping with the death of a toddler:

- Religious beliefs may help the parents find meaning in what seems so inexplicable.
- Preparing for a child's death due to an incurable terminal condition presents a different scenario than finding a child died in her sleep.
- Whereas some decades ago bereaved parents were basically overlooked, various support groups such as Compassionate Friends and the Candlelighters have emerged as the product of concerned parents.

Empirical evidence demonstrates that aging does not reduce the ability to use cognitive coping strategies but rather "older persons are increasingly effective in using cognitive strategies in regulating their emotions" (Moss, Moss, & Hansson, 2001, p. 243). The coping models that have gained currency (for instance, Folkman, 1991; 2001; Moos & Schaefer, 1986) emphasize adaptive tasks such as appraising the personal significance of the event, identifying what the event demands, preserving a sense of self-efficacy, reasonably maintaining emotional balance, and upholding interpersonal relations. Empirical research has found "older bereaved persons more likely than younger persons to have engaged in extensive account-making about their loss (searching for a private meaning in the loss) and more likely to have confided these accounts to others" (Moss, Moss, & Hansson, 2001, p. 243).

Impacts of Some Deaths Adults Grieve

In this section we will examine empirical evidence regarding three types of deaths that adults experience: (a) the death of an elderly parent, (b) the death of a child, and (c) the death of a spouse. While the death of an elderly sibling is one of the most likely bereavement experiences for an older adult, little research or clinical attention has been given to sibling bereavement during old age. Such a gap obviously needs to be filled.

The Death of an Elderly Parent

As adults see their elderly parents age and grow more frail, they naturally begin realizing their parents' deaths likely will happen, will occur in-sequence (that is, before the deaths of their children), and hopefully will take place without ongoing pain and suffering. Adult children begin to prepare for the deaths of elderly parents and to see these deaths as normative occurrences; it is disputed whether such anticipation mitigates the impact of the loss. Let us look at two issues that empirical research has uncovered about bereavement and the death of an elderly parent: (a) anticipating the death of an elderly parent and (b) the impact of an elderly parent's death upon the self of a middle-aged adult.

Anticipating the death of an elderly parent. The life span concept that events happen either in-sequence or out-of-sequence designates that in post-industrial societies children are expected to out live their parents. Anticipating the death of an elderly parent emerges as frailty becomes undeniable, as cognitive or physical functioning deteriorates, and/or as chronic and debilitating diseases become more pronounced. Two of the more harrowing deteriorations that persons witness as elderly parents age are the onset of senile dementia or the descent into Alzheimer's disease; the loss of the elderly parent under these conditions seems to occur before death itself and aptly has been called "ambiguous" (Boss, 1999). The #5 strains of taking care of a frail elderly parent suffering from senile dementia or Alzheimer's include financial, emotional, and physical strains (to mention three). For instance, emotional difficulties follow various paths for caregivers following the death of a parent afflicted with Alzheimer's — sorrow for some, clinical depression for others, numbness for others, to cite three examples — and emotional distress increases for caregivers who were already distressed prior to their parent's death (Aneshensel, Botticello, & Yamamoto-Mitani, 2004). Thankfully, senile dementia and Alzheimer's disease are not sure outcomes to aging.

As aging parents become old, their adult children begin to manifest "adaptation anxiety" (Moss, Moss & Hansson, 2001). Some manifestations of adaptation anxiety include worry over how to provide for parents at their very end-of-life, how to cope with their parents' actual dying, and how to manage life without their parents. Empirical evidence is mixed about whether anticipating a death proves helpful to grievers: some research concluded that following an elderly parent's death adult children who reported anticipatory grief were better adjusted than persons who did not experience anticipatory grief (Smith, 2005); other research indicated that adaptation anxiety did not make coping with an elderly parent's death any the less difficult (see Lund, 1989; Moss, Moss, & Hansson, 2001).

Clinical lore held for quite some time that anticipated deaths rather than sudden deaths were easier on the griever; part of the reasoning was that an anticipated death triggered a process called anticipatory mourning (Rando, 2000a; 2000b). The reality of anticipatory mourning is disputed (Fulton, 2003), and empirical evidence has shown that (a) over time spousal bereavement outcomes may be indistinguishable between sudden and anticipated deaths (Gilliland & Fleming, 1998) and (b) severe psychological costs may attach to an anticipated death that is difficult and drawn out over an extended time (Da Pena, 2002; Diwan, Hougham, & Sachs, 2004; Gibson, Breitbart, & Tomarken, 2006; Grunfeld, Coyle, Whelan, et. al., 2004).

Impact of an elderly parent's death on the self of a middle-aged adult. Event characteristics influence the impact on the self of an elderly parent's death. Typically these deaths are expected and considered normative. Acceptance of an elderly parent's death can be confounded if the death involved protracted suffering

(Moss, Moss, & Hansson, 2001). However, complicated grief following an elderly parent's death is rare and — as uncovered in other research about traumatizing bereavement (Prigerson, Shear, Bierhals, Pilkonis, Wolfson, Hall, Zonarich, & Reynolds, 1997) — has been associated with anxious attachment bonds. Vaillant (1985), who followed 268 males from adolescence into middle adulthood, concluded that long-term, deleterious effects following parental death were best explained by the ambivalence associated with having been raised by immature, conflicting, and mismatched parents. On the other hand, it needs to be noted that Scharlach (1991) tested for and found no evidence that anxious attachment accounted for unresolved adult grief following a parent's death. In short, links between attachment bonds, complicated grief, and bereavement over deaths of parents are not settled.

Empirical research on a middle-aged adult's sense of self-efficacy following bereavement over spousal death (Benight, Flores, & Tashiro, 2001; Ford, 2006; Solomon & Draine, 1995) has indicated that, as one would expect, positive adjustments are directly associated with greater awareness of self-efficacy; these findings align quite well with cognitive theories of coping discussed earlier (Folkman, 1991; 2001; Moos & Schaefer, 1986). Considerable reassessment of life, renewal of purpose, and extensive reflection on identity and human existence have been found in the lives of adult women following the deaths of their parents (Westbook, 2002). Several authors have noted that the death of an elderly parent accentuates for surviving children the sense of personal mortality (Doka, 1997; Douglas, 1990; Scharlach & Frediksen, 1993; Sherrell, Buckwalter, & Morhardt, 2001).

The Death of a Child

Through his in-depth ethnographic research Dennis Klass (1988) has disclosed in rich, intimate detail the phenomena of parental grief as manifested in the lives of bereaved parents who participated in self-help groups. A theme suffusing his research is that bereaved parents redefine their sense of identity and their relationship to others because of their experience of bereavement. For the majority if not all the parents Klass studied, their dead child was an ongoing presence in their lives. While the impressive longitudinal research that Silverman and Worden (1993; Worden & Silverman, 1996) conducted with bereaved children contributed to the acceptance of continuing bonds following bereavement, it was primarily Klass who noted that bereaved adult parents, defying judgments of clinical pathology, found solace in enduring attachments to their deceased children. Klass (1999) argues that enduring attachments with their dead children sensitized the adults to transcendence; the dead children served for the bereaved parents the same function that saints and bodhisattvas provide in Catholicism and Buddhism (see also Goss & Klass, 2005).

One thing we have learned from other research looking at bereavement involving children and parents is the central role that consistent parenting plays in the long-term adjustment of children following a death (Kirwin & Hamrin, 2005; Tein, Sandler, Ayers, & Wolchik, 2006; Worden, 1996). As noted earlier, Vaillant's (1985) extended longitudinal work with 268 males showed the impact on unresolved grief and difficult life adjustments for individuals raised by immature, conflicting, and mismatched parents.

An area of growing clinical and research interest involves the bereavement responses of grandparents (DeFrain, Jakub, & Mendoza, 1991-1992; Gardner, Scherman, Efthimiadis, & Shultz, 2004; Winston, 2006). Grandparents typically yield to the grief of others (Moss, Moss, & Hansson, 2001); further, whereas bereaved parents' attention centered on the dead child, bereaved grandparents' attention focused on the suffering of their own children — that is, on the parents of the dead child (Ponzetti, 1992). Grandparents' own grief typically gets overlooked. Overlooking grandparent grief illustrates a form of disenfranchisement (Doka, 1989). Ignoring the role of grandparents in the lives of families during bereavement does not match the cultural experiences of many groups of people — whether in the culturally rich amalgam that is the United States or in the rest of the world. For instance, African American grandmothers raising AIDS orphans do so often at great personal cost, and their coping strategies include reliance on deep religious faith (Winston, 2006).

Two forms of deaths of children are early pregnancy loss and Sudden Infant Death Syndrome. We look first at early pregnancy loss.

Early pregnancy loss is one form of bereavement over death of a child that has been overlooked on the whole. Epidemiologists report the rate of early pregnancy loss due to miscarriage ranges between 14-20% (Hutti, 1992; Kilier, Geller, & Ritsher, 2002; Klein, Stein, & Susser, 1989). The term *miscarriage* refers to the unintended, spontaneous end of a pregnancy resulting in fetal death. We use the terms *miscarriage* and *early pregnancy loss* interchangeably.

There is some variance in what clinicians and researchers accept as the duration of pregnancies that end in miscarriages: 14-16 weeks gestation to as high as 26+ weeks (Kilier, Geller, & Ritsher, 2002; Neugebauer, Kline, O'Connor, et. al., 1992; Shapiro, 1988). Time at which pregnancies end in recognized miscarriage is undergoing some downward shifts as medical technology enables awareness of fetal life to be gained earlier than previously possible (Cecil, 1994; Wilcox, Weinberg, O'Connor, et. al., 1988).

The medical literature is replete with understanding of the physical complications involved with miscarriage. These complications involve maternal and fetal risk factors (for instance, polycystic ovaries and embryonic chromosomal abnormalities) (Mishell, 1993; Rai, Backos, Rushworth, & Regan, 2000). Of singular importance for thanatologists is that "studies concerning psychological distress in the aftermath of (an early pregnancy) loss event are sparse" (Kilier, Geller, & Ritsher, 2002, p. 131).

Three categories of psychological distress following early pregnancy loss primarily have been noted: depression, trauma, and grief. Various researchers have emphasized the importance of depressive symptoms that fall below the level of clinical depression, or what is sometimes termed "psychiatric caseness." As Kilier, Geller, & Ritsher (2002, p. 133) wrote, "Failing to reach the threshold for caseness does not imply that an experience has had no significant impact on the person's subjective distress and social functioning." The prospect for major depressive disorder following miscarriage was found to be 2.5 times greater than a community control group exhibited (Neugebauer, Kline, O'Connor, et. al., 1997), and episodes of minor depressive disorder were found in 5.2% of women who had miscarried as compared to 1% in women in the community.

Anxiety is another psychological outcome noted less frequently but recently given more attention; intrusive thoughts and images as well as traumatizing flashbacks are major manifestations of anxiety and of yearning for what has been lost (Brier, 2004; Neugebauer, Kline, O'Connor, et. al., 1997). As Brier (2004, p. 14) noted, women whose pregnancies have ended in miscarriage will find that intrusive thoughts that defy control aggravate "the increased likelihood of reexperiencing symptoms of trauma (i.e., flashbacks, nightmares) which represent the person's attempt to 'take-in' the stressful elements of their pregnancy loss."

Outcomes for the majority of individuals and couples following early pregnancy loss involve recovery of a sense of purpose, of functional behavior, resourcefulness, and even renewed strength (Bennett, Litz, Lee, & Maguen, 2005; Conway & Russell, 2000; Swanson, 1999). The trajectory of bereavement following perinatal loss mirrors the findings of response over time of other bereaved persons: a majority (75-85%) who recover, and a minority (15-25%) whose ongoing adjustment difficulty requires professional help (see Bonanno, 2006; Bonannno, Wortman, & Neese, 2004; Bennett, Litz, Lee, & Maguen, 2005). Bereavement researchers and clinicians may note these parallel outcome findings and see here a call for collaborative work to develop, administer, and evaluate secondary prevention efforts aimed at assisting individuals and couples whose bereavement poses enduring problems with living.

Sudden Infant Death Syndrome (SIDS) is another form of death that claims the lives of young children. SIDS, the unexpected and abrupt death of an infant under one year of age, is also called by such terms as "cot death" in the United Kingdom and "crib death" in the United States (Deri-Bowen, 2001). The National SIDS/Infant Resource Center maintains that SIDS kills more infants between 1 and 12 months of age than any other cause (see http://www.sidscenter.org/SIDSFACT.HTM). The greatest incidence of such deaths occurs between the infants' second and fourth months of life, with very few SIDS death occurring in the first month of life. The death is associated with sleep and there are no signs that the infant had a medical disorder. However, as of yet no definitive cause for SIDS deaths as been determined. Medical researchers are focusing on central nervous system defects that control heart rate and breathing, on delayed brainstem maturation, on developmental changes during the first six months of life that destabilize infants' homeostatic controls, on outside stressors such as becoming overheated, and on brain irregularities that may make infants vulnerable to SIDS (http://www.sidscenter.org/SIDSFACT.HTM).

In the United States around 2,500 infants die from SIDS each year, a considerable decline from the prevalence rates of 5,000 to 6,000 annually during the 1980s and early 1990s (MacDorman & Atkinson, 1999; http://www.sidscenter.org/SIDSFACT.HTM); the decline is attributed to caregivers' following public education campaigns instructing them to put babies to sleep on their backs, not on their stomachs (National Institute of Child Health and Human Development, 2001). SIDS deaths in the United Kingdom during the 1970s and 1980s were approximately 1,600 per year, and due to health prevention campaigns giving the same advice as in United States campaigns, this number had been cut to 419 as of 1999 (Deri-Bowen, 2001).

The sudden, unexpected death of a healthy infant poses a very difficult bereavement for parents (as well as for siblings and grandparents). One of the first items noted in research literature is that such a death violates assumptions about the natural, expected order of events: children are supposed to outlive their parents (Rando, 1993; Raphael, 1983; http://www.sidscenter.org/SIDSFACT.HTM). Schiffman (2004) reported three prevalent emotional responses to a SIDS death were extreme guilt, anger, and blaming, and confirmed that spouses' communication and emotional support for one another decreased following a SIDS death.

While written more than years ago, Raphael's (1983) elegant synthesis of the grief reactions to a SIDS death remains an excellent source of information on parents' reactions. She notes mothers' and fathers' grief reactions show discrepant coping responses and dyssynchronous patterns of recovery. "The mother tends to be more depressed, withdrawn, more disrupted by her loss. The (father)....takes over protective, management functions, suppresses his feelings, deals with his distress more quickly and cannot understand his wife's continuing preoccupation with (the death)" (Raphael, 1983, p. 260). Citing a study from the late 1970s, Raphael wrote that it took on average a bit less than four months for the father to achieve normal functioning but more than 10 months for the mother. Here is another area for collaborative work between bereavement researchers and clinicians: do these differential time frames for fathers and mothers still hold?

Possible Research Topic

According to Raphael, fathers' responses to a SIDS death tend to be angrier and more aggressive than mothers'. She wondered if the fathers' apparently quick recovery of normal functioning actually masked or camouflaged their intense feelings which they feel very uneasy admitting or exploring. What may be occurring for fathers is what Judith Cook (1988) noted is the double-bind that grieving fathers experience when bereaved: men have been raised to understand that expressing strong negative emotions is to be kept in check; stemming from this socialization about expression of strong negative emotions is the dilemma in which grieving fathers find themselves: they are expected to comfort their wives and they are told healthy grieving requires disclosing the distress associated with grief.

Longitudinal research conducted in Australia (Vance, Boyle, Najman, & Thearle, 2002) examined responses over time to SIDS death. The study engaged couples bereaved over SIDS deaths and matched them carefully with couples who were not grieving. The researchers found clear differences in individual psychology and couple relations: two and one-half years from the start of the study, at least one of the partners in the bereaved couples (usually the wife) was much more likely to be psychologically distressed, whereas such distress was seldom found in the non-bereaved couples; of interest as well was the fact that very seldom were both partners in the bereaved couples distressed. It would seem researchers and clinicians would jump on this phenomenon as a promising arena for collaborative work that has both theoretical and pragmatic rewards.

Gender differences found in couples bereaved over SIDS deaths are commonly noted in research studies (Lang & Gottlieb, 1993; Wing, Burge-Callaway, Rose, & Armistead, 2001). These reactions run the holistic gamut: cognitive, somatic, emotional, interpersonal, behavioral, and spiritual. A very common response is to look for explanations, to attribute responsibility, and to find meaning.

A typical coping response to a life crisis (see Moos, 1986) is to seek information about what caused the calamity. "Parents try to find all the information they can about the syndrome" (Raphael, 1983, p. 256), and in this search they are aided by the autopsy and by the other procedures established to ascertain the facts in the case. The hunt for information about SIDS leads parents to the frightening realization that medical research does not know what causes infants to die from SIDS, and increases the parents' dread that they are powerless to prevent such a tragedy from happening again. It is as though caring for their infant was futile, but such a realization does not assuage "the overwhelming nature of parental guild and blame" (Raphael, 1983, p. 258). It is clear why a SIDS death would present a risk for complicated grief (Prigerson & Jacob, 2001).

While the great majority of wives and husbands bereaved over SIDS deaths came to accept the explanations that their physicians had given them, over one-quarter (26%) of mothers and more than one-tenth (13%) of fathers blamed the mother for the death. These gender differences in attribution, in meaning making, occurred despite medical evidence to the contrary (Wing, Burge-Callaway, Rose, & Armistead, 2001).

The search for a cause, coupled with the overwhelming parental sense of guilt, can militate against the parents being resources for one another as they cope with their loss. Wing and his colleagues wrote, perhaps with understatement, that "This unwarranted tendency to blame the mother is likely to cause unnecessary pain and difficulties, both in the marital relationship and in each partner's adjustment to the child's death" (2001, p. 65). As Moos and Schaefer (1986) noted, a key adaptive task in coping with a life crisis is to maintain interpersonal relationships. However, it would be wrong to leave the reader with the impression that marriages are doomed following a SIDS death. Longitudinal research with 220 parents bereaved following SIDS and other early childhood deaths learned that bereaved parents demonstrated positive signs of healthy adjustment over time to the deaths of their children (Vance, Najman, Thearle, Embelton, Foster, & Boyle, 1995). One can speculate that the same pattern found in bereavement recovery vs. enduring complications will be found in individuals and couples grieving a SIDS death. Here is an area worth exploration, and it holds forth both research and clinical implications.

The Death of a Spouse

Widows comprise the great numbers of persons who have participated in bereavement research and upon whom generalizations have been formed about loss, grief, and mourning. In longitudinal research with widows, Parkes and his colleagues (Glick, Weiss, & Parkes, 1974; Parkes, 1975; Parkes & Weiss, 1995) identified early signs of vulnerability to spousal bereavement. These signs included lower socioeconomic status, little time to prepare for a spouse's death, extensive and prolonged yearning for the dead husband, and the co-existence of other stressors, including marital difficulties.

Differences have been noted in the bereavement of younger versus older spouses. One difference involves autonomy and coping with the wider world. Due to feminism and other liberating processes in secular societies, younger widows have been educated and socialized to develop a repertoire of personal skills that succeed in the wider world; however, Moss, Moss, and Hansson (2001, p. 246) noted, "…many older widows (especially) who were raised in simpler times, in smaller and more tightly woven communities, were not encouraged to learn the skills that would assist them in accessing or developing new support relationships outside of the family."

Many researchers have concluded social support provides a major influence on adjustment to the death of a spouse (Impens, 2005; Larman, 2004; Silverman, 2004), although Wolfgang Stroebe and his colleagues (W. Stroebe, Zech, M. S. Stroebe, &

Abakoumkin, 2005; W. Stroebe, Stroebe, & Abakoumkin, 1999; W. Stroebe, Stroebe, Abakoumkin, & Schut, 1996) have raised several theoretical and empirical issues that question whether social support plays a singular role in bereavement recovery: for instance, social support was of greater benefit for widows when there were emotional attachments involved.

The intensity and duration of grief reactions of younger and older widows vary. For instance, widows under the age of 41 report more depression than do older widows (Larman, 2004). Applegate (1997) found younger widows more vulnerable to depression if they perceived little support from others following their husbands' deaths. Older widows report significantly less depression, less anxiety, and better adjustment over time than do younger widows (Zisook, Schuchter, Sledge, & Mulvihill, 1993).

The death of a spouse plunges many individuals, particularly females, into loneliness because friendships with married couples become awkward without the partner that death has taken (Lund, Caserta, & Dimond, 1993; Moss, Moss, & Hansson, 2001). However, Pinquart (2003) reported there are many more buffers against loneliness for widows than for widowers; one reason is contact bereaved women maintain with children, friends, and siblings. Financial stressors were found to impede widowers in seeking social support; widows with university education, particularly those women with a best female friend, coped well following their husbands' deaths (van Baarsen & van Grolmou, 2001).

Lindemann (1944) noted the physical symptoms of acute grief, among them chills, fatigue, diarrhea, and constrictions in the throat. Longer-term health issues following bereavement emerge directly from the suppression of the immune system, as mentioned earlier. The landmark Institute of Medicine volume examining bereavement considered bereavement poses a serious risk to physical health (Osterweis, Solomon, & Green, 1984). In his well-received book *Bereavement: Studies of Grief in Adult Life*, Parkes (1987) examined the increased risk for coronary thrombosis among the recently bereaved (spouses, parents, grandparents) and noted two significant points: (a) young widows were more susceptible than any other bereaved group and (b) it was not clearly understood what led to increased mortality among persons who were bereaved. However, dysfunctional behaviors used to deal with the distress of bereavement (for instance, smoking cigarettes, drinking alcohol, abusing prescription drugs) as well as intense emotional reactions (for instance, clinical depression and anxiety) place people at serious risk of physical health problems, including mortality, and are much more likely contributing factors than is bereavement by itself (see also Parkes & Brown, 1972).

Analysis of overall mortality statistics from numerous countries has confirmed that the bereaved are significantly more likely than married persons to die from cirrhosis of the liver, from suicide, from vehicular accidents, from diabetes, from lung cancer, from heart disease, and from leukemia (M. Stroebe & W. Stroebe, 1993). The Stroebes (1993) noted that mortality was highest among younger age bereaved groups and was more prevalent among widowers than widows. These gender differences do not match what Parkes (1987) found, but the age differences do fit his findings.

Endemic health problems of old age make bereavement one of many contributing stressors that characterize challenges to the elderly: examples include a series of chronic debilitating illnesses such as emphysema and arthritis and osteoporosis; forced relocation from one's home; and declining mental capabilities due to senile dementia or Alzheimer's. While severe reactions to the death of a spouse have been linked to younger adults and while the early response to spousal bereavement is more intense for younger adults, the duration of emotional, behavioral, and physical bereavement symptoms last longer among older adults (Moss, Moss, & Hansson, 2001). It is hypothesized that these age differences signal the fact that spousal death is much less a surprise to older adults but also that spousal death sets off an intertwined set of circumstances endemic to being old. As a team of gerontology scholars noted, becoming a widow signals to elderly persons that they have crossed the threshold into being old (Moss, Moss, & Hansson, 2001).

Summary Remarks

This part of the chapter on life span issues and loss, grief, and mourning examined bereavement during adulthood. Four schema were presented as ways to understand adult responses to bereavement: (a) a holistic appreciation of bereavement, (b) rhythms to the bereavement trajectories that adults report, (c) life span development concepts, and (d) cognitive-based coping. Empirical evidence was presented regarding three types of deaths that adults mourn: (a) the death of an elderly parent, (b) the death of a child, and (c) the death of a spouse. An important theme to remember is that bereavement in older adulthood is intertwined with problems characteristic of aging: degradations in physiological operations, the onset of chronic and debilitating illnesses, and diminished functional performance.

$(25/45)$ $(45/45)$

Learning Objective:
Explain how the life Span tasks and concerns of the Adult years affect the grief process.

Chapter 17

The Family, Larger Systems, and Loss, Grief, and Mourning

Alicia Skinner Cook

Death is a family event. It occurs within the context of existing relationships and family dynamics. While grief is often viewed as a personal experience, it is experienced in two realms simultaneously — the intrapsychic level and the interpersonal level. Grief occurs in a social context and is embedded in a web of complex relationships. In most societies, families are at the center of close relationships and attachments between and among individuals. In some cultural contexts the focus is on the nuclear family, while in other societies family is defined in broader terms and includes a large network of extended family members for whom there is much interdependence. In today's modern life, the definition of family has become increasingly complex and may include step-parents and other step relatives, both same-sex and opposite-sex relationships in which partners cohabit but are not married, single-parent and multigenerational households, and a wide range of other family structures. With changing demographics, families will increasingly represent four and five generations as the average life expectancy continues to increase (Galvin, Bylund, & Brommel, 2004).

Family Systems Theory

Each family is unique and is an entity that is greater than the sum of its individual family members. According to family systems theory, families are characterized by wholeness or unity. Central to this theory is the notion that one cannot understand individual behavior in isolation, emphasizing the importance of understanding one's responses in the context of the social group(s) to which one belongs. While the experience of grief is a personal event for individuals, it is also a "systems event" for families.

To understand any particular family system during the time of loss, one must look at individual family members, their relationships to each other, and their relationships and interactions with other individuals and systems outside the family. Family systems are made up of subsystems illustrated by marital, sibling, and parent-child relationships. The death of a family member can have a powerful impact not only on the family system but also on the subsystem(s) of which that individual was a part (Cook & Oltjenbruns, 1998). A death causes disequilibrium in the family system, often disrupting a family's functioning and affecting available emotional and physical resources. The death of a spouse may alter the extended kinship network, the death of a child may alter perceptions of the future, and the death of a parent or breadwinner can diminish a family's sense of security (Hansson, Berry, & Berry, 1999).

Grief and the Family Life Cycle

According to Shapiro (1994) "a systemic developmental perspective on the family life cycle crisis of bereavement suggests that the developmental course of all families is inevitably altered by the shattering blow of grief" (p. 278). The timing of a loss in the family life cycle can be a critical factor in adjustment. Deaths that are untimely in terms of chronological or social expectations are especially difficult. These include early widowhood, early parent loss, and death of a child. Surviving family members may know no individuals within their social networks who have coped with such untimely events and thus have few models for effective coping and support. The death of a child is one of the most painful losses a family can experience. Intense grief can extend over a long period of time as parents try to make sense of a senseless event that defies the natural order of life (McGoldrick & Walsh, 2005).

Timing of a loss can also coincide with other life cycle changes that pose unique challenges. For example, loss of a spouse can occur near the time of birth of the first child, which is a major transition in itself, or at the time a family is coping with the financial demands and launching issues of adolescents and college-age dependents. Multiple stressors, developmental demands, and related losses can result in overload and influence a family's ability to cope (McGoldrick & Walsh, 2005). Furthermore, these losses have the potential to affect both family relationships and individual development, particularly with regard to the processes of separation and individuation (Cook & Oltjenbruns, 1998).

The Cultural Context of Loss

The experience of grief is affected by the environment in which it takes place. In particular, the cultural milieu influences the manifestations of grief, opportunities for expression, and interpretation of the loss. The community and the larger society also provide the context in which family coping will occur. A family's ethnic and religious values and traditions influence the amount and type of support available to grieving families. Different cultures also have different norms regarding the appropriate length of mourning, beliefs about what happens after death, open displays of emotion and gender roles (Anderson & Sabatelli, 2007). For example, some traditions encourage outward display of emotion while others reflect the belief that feelings are private and are not to be shown in public.

Societal expectations can also affect who is expected to grieve a loss and under what circumstances. *Disenfranchised grief* is grief that exists even though society does not recognize one's need, right, or capacity to grieve (Doka, 2002). Pet loss is an example of a significant family loss that oftentimes is not acknowledged by the larger society. Cultures that are highly age-segregated may also deny children opportunities to grieve or say goodbye to a dying loved one. In some cultures, children are an integral part of all family rituals surrounding death and in others they are rarely included.

Healthy Family Processes Following Loss

Beavers and Hampson (2003) have concluded that the ability to accept loss is at the core of all processes in healthy family systems. Cook and Oltjenbruns (1998) along with other authors have documented the importance of families sharing their loss, maintaining open communication, reorganizing and regaining equilibrium, and effectively utilizing available support systems and external resources.

Sharing the Loss

Funerals, memorial services, and other post-death ceremonies can serve as meaningful times of coming together of family members to acknowledge and share the loss of a loved one. Imber-Black (2005) observes that every culture has rituals to mark profound losses, acknowledge the life of the deceased, provide support for survivors, and facilitate ongoing life after such loss. Following a loss, families begin a transition process as they cope with their loss. Whether formal or informal, rituals can have therapeutic value following a loss and facilitate emotional healing and family cohesion. Bosley and Cook's (1993) study of bereaved adults found that funeral rituals can be a tool to assist in accepting the reality of the loss; serve as an affirmation of faith, religious beliefs, and/or a philosophy of life; facilitate emotional expression and provide a context for emotional support from family, friends, and the larger community; and to reconnect to a greater sense of family and the integration of personal and family identity.

A ritual is a specific behavior or activity that gives symbolic expression to feelings and thoughts. Actions occurring many months or years after a funeral, such as going through the loved one's personal belongings and taking off a wedding ring, can be considered rituals and have important symbolic significance. Rituals following a loss also provide a context for reminiscence to occur. Rosenblatt and Elde (1990) view shared reminiscence about a deceased loved one as an important aspect of social support. They found in their interviews with adults who had lost a parent that shared reminiscence was common, particularly between siblings, and that it had positive implications for relationships with surviving family members.

Maintaining Open Communication

According to Galvin, Bylund, & Brommel (2004), communication may be viewed as a symbolic, transactional process of creating and sharing meaning. These symbols include words, verbal behavior, and the full range of nonverbal behavior as well as facial expressions, gestures, and spatial distance. The communications within the family are transactional in that family members have an impact on each other. Individual family members communicating within this interpersonal context often develop a shared reality or set of meanings. Open communication both before and after a death allows family members to share deep feelings and create stronger bonds, but family members must be accepting and supportive of the range of feelings that may be expressed. Some types of loss, such as death by suicide, may evoke strong feelings of anger and shame which may be particularly difficult to share with others. Lack of open communication has been shown to increase the possibility of blame, guilt, and conflict (Vess, Moreland, & Schwebel, 1985).

Reorganizing and Regaining Equilibrium

Death of a family member disrupts established patterns of interacting and requires an age-appropriate redistribution of roles and responsibilities. An unanticipated loss may require additional changes involved with relocation, changing jobs, or seeking additional employment. Open family systems in which information is freely exchanged with individuals both inside and outside of the system tend to cope better with change. These families have the adaptive capacity to reorganize in new and effective ways that support and acknowledge individual family members while maintaining the functioning of the system as a whole. In contract, closed family systems tend to be rigid and locked into strictly prescribed patterns. These families have difficulty accepting assistance from outside the system, have few skills or experience with adaptive change, and have difficulty responding to the demands following loss (Cook & Oltjenbruns, 1998).

Effectively Utilizing Support Systems and External Resources

Internal family resources are typically not enough to sustain a family following a traumatic loss, and external systems can offer valuable support to bereaved families. These external systems include extended family and friends, religious institutions, community and mental health services, and formal support groups such as

Compassionate Friends (for bereaved parents). Religion and spirituality play a major role in the lives of many families, and churches can often mobilize quickly after a death to offer assistance. Religious institutions also provide time-honored rituals surrounding death that can provide comfort for families and link them with others sharing their belief system (Cook & Dworkin, 1992).

Some families are more at risk than others for having inadequate external support. For example, geographically mobile families may lack strong social networks and links with their new communities and live considerable distance from close family and friends. Other families may have rigid unspoken rules about "dealing with our own problems" that prevent them from reaching out for additional support and professional assistance when it is needed.

Coping: Family-Level Variables

While the study of resilience among individuals has been a focus of research for quite some time, it has only recently been applied to the family as a system. Hawley and DeHaan (1996) support the notion that resilience can be conceptualized at the family level and reflects more than a collection of resiliencies of individual family members. Resilience is demonstrated in response to adversity and allows the family and its individual members to "bounce back," thus reaching or surpassing a precrisis level of functioning. Resilience is most likely to be found when protective factors are present and risk factors are minimized. Hawley (2000) cautions, however, that resilience is not a static characteristic in families, and can be conceptualized as "a pathway a family follows over time in response to a significant stressor or a series of stressors" (p. 106). Coming to terms with loss is a family process that has no timetable. As the process unfolds, new stressors may appear, internal and system strengths may be discovered, and thus the balance of protective and risk factors may be altered.

A number of protective factors within the context of family relationships have been examined by researchers. For example, Haine and her colleagues (2006) found that positive parenting served as a protective resource for bereaved children; other researchers' work agrees with these findings (Tein, Sandler, Ayers, & Wolchik, 2006; Worden, 1996; Worden & Silverman, 1996). Traylor, Hayslip, Kaminski, & York (2003) studied the association between adult grief and family system characteristics. Higher levels of family affect and family cohesion were predictors of fewer manifestations of grief over time.

Risk factors for poor outcomes after loss include internal family factors (e.g., poor communication, conflict in interpersonal relationships) as well as factors related to the loss itself. Sometimes other concurrent stresses are also present that are unrelated to the death such as loss of a job, caring for aging parents, or personal health problems.

Type of death also has implications for effective coping. Sudden, unexpected deaths can be particularly difficult for families because they have no time to prepare for the loss. Sudden deaths may also involve violence, such as in the case with homicide, and therefore involvement with the criminal justice system. Furthermore, individuals experiencing bereavement following violent death by accident, homicide or suicide have been shown to have difficulty making sense of the loss, and this failure to find meaning can lead to complicated grief symptomatology (Currier, Holland, & Neimeyer, 2006).

In the case of an anticipated death, the challenges are different as families adjust to the changing conditions associated with a particular illness. Families often spend extended periods of time at a medical facility prior to the death of a loved one, interact with a variety of health care providers, and may face complicated insurance and legal issues. The stresses associated with extended illness, such as financial expenses, can exacerbate already existing interpersonal issues within the family and accentuate tensions. From the time a life-threatening illness is diagnosed, the dying person, together with family members and friends, may begin to grieve. This *anticipatory grief* is related to the many losses associated with the dying process as well as the impending death itself. An anticipated death, however, does give loved ones the opportunity to say goodbye and to draw closure on a variety of concerns (Cook & Oltjenbruns, 1998).

Some illnesses, such as Alzheimer's disease, involve *ambiguous losses* in which the individual is physically present but perceived as psychologically absent during the later stages of the illness as the person experiences more dramatic intellectual and social decline (Boss, 1991). Watching these changes can be extremely painful for family members who often have a sense of helplessness. Kapust (1982) has described living with dementia as "an ongoing funeral" for the healthy spouse and other family members.

Negative Outcomes

The experience of illness or death can bring family members closer together but it can also cause significant discord. Each individual family member's grief is unique and based on relationship with the deceased, developmental level of the griever, personality and coping skills, prior losses, and a host of other factors discussed elsewhere in this volume. The manifestations and duration of grief of one family member may be quite different than that of another family member. This variability is referred to as *dissynchrony of grief.*

In a similar manner, family members may use different coping mechanisms or *discrepant coping styles* to deal with their loss. Some family members may prefer to grieve in private while others find solace in talking frequently about their loss and openly expressing their emotions. In particular, gender differences can influence the manifestations and style of grieving. Men are more likely than women to avoid grieving situations and use work as a distraction. Distraction can also take a form that is detrimental to the individual's health, such as excessive drinking (Umberson, Wortman, & Kessler, 1992). When grief is expressed, men tend to show anger more than do women (Gilbert & Smart, 1992). In studying couples who had experienced either a fetal or infant death, Kathleen Gilbert (1989) found that the majority of couples experienced marital discord following the loss. According to the researcher "inconsistencies in beliefs and expectations resulting in a perception of incongruent grieving served as the major contributors to most of these conflicts" (p. 609). These differences in grieving and ways of coping can result in a perceived *secondary loss* as a result of a change in the pre-death relationship.

Unhealthy patterns may also develop as the family reorganizes to meet roles and responsibilities involved in daily living. Parents may be so absorbed in their individual grief following loss of a child that they are unable to reach out to each other or to provide emotional support for their remaining children. In these instances, a surviving child may become "parentified" and be the one to attempt to care for all other family members, thus compromising his/her own development.

Positive Outcomes of Coping with Loss

Little attention has been given to the positive outcomes of grief. Despite the pain associated with loss, families often report finding meaning in their suffering. Many of these outcomes relate to changed self-perceptions of individual family members such as seeing oneself as stronger and more mature. Three-quarters of widowed persons in the Changing Lives of Older Couples study reported that they had become more self-confident as a result of having to manage on their own since losing a spouse (Utz, 2006). Other outcomes relate to changes in interactions with others such as more caring for others, enhanced communication skills, and more openness in sharing feelings (Calhoun & Tedeschi, 1990).

In their interviews with parents one to eight years after the death of a child, Brabant, Forsyth, and McFarlain (1997) found that the majority expressed a fundamental change in themselves, feeling more sensitive and more spiritual as a result of their loss, and also perceiving themselves to be better persons. Most also expressed a change in values, including a desire to help others more and placing a higher priority on family and less on money and work.

Klass (1986) has observed that death creates new bonds in some families as individual members pull together to cope with their shared loss. Surviving a common loss as a family can result in a renewed sense of closeness and cohesion, a better understanding of each other's strengths, and enhanced communication and flexibility.

LEARNING Objective:

Indicate the FACTORS that influence
families & family Relationships AS
they negotiate their way through loss.

Chapter 18

Ethical and Legal Issues and Loss, Grief, and Mourning

David K. Meagher

Advances in medicine and increased knowledge derived from research about the grief process have raised new ethical and legal issues about the consequences of losing a loved one to death. This chapter will briefly examine some of these issues: ownership of the remains of the deceased; the need for and practice of autopsies; limited options for disposition of the remains; and the inclusion of bereavement leaves within the structure of society. The first issue to be discussed in a logical ordering of the issues would seem to be at the moment death is declared.

Determination of Death

How do we know when a person is dead? Is it at that point when all the cells of the body have ceased to function (biological death) or when heart and lung function can no longer be detected (cardiac death) or when the person is said to be in a persistent vegetative state (psychological death)? Is a person dead when he/she meets the four criteria suggested by the Harvard Ad Hoc Committee on Brain Death Syndrome (unreceptivity and unresponsivity, no detectable movement or breathing, no reflex response, and a flat EEG) or when it has been judged that an individual has sustained either an irreversible cessation of circulatory and respiratory functions, or an irreversible cessation of all functions of the entire brain, including the brain stem (Uniform Determination of Death Act) (President's Commission, 1981). At this point, an individual may be declared dead, a determination that is made in accordance with accepted medical standards.

The criteria detailed in the Uniform Determination of Death Act are based on the certainty that the loss of function in the systems is independent of the use of any life-sustaining technology. It is important to note that the declaration that death has occurred is arrived at because a physician is not able to detect the signs of any body function. This declaration does not mean there are no bodily processes taking place. It means that, if any organ or system is functioning, current technologies are not sensitive enough to detect it.

Death by brain criteria is a clinical diagnosis that can be made when a decision has been reached that there is complete and irreversible cessation of all brain function. Since it is now technically possible to sustain cardiac, circulatory, respiratory and other organ function after the brain has ceased to be alive, a diagnosis of death by brain criteria can be made before the heart beat stops (Phillips, 2005).

How, then, may we be certain that a person has died? We accept the physician's decision as absolute and valid. The physician, in this case, is acting both as a medical practitioner and as an agent of the state. The declaration of death is first a medical decision. Even if a person, though appearing to be dead, was still alive, the decision that a patient has died will most likely be a valid one since all interventions cease at the moment a physician declares the person dead. Secondly, this declaration is also a legal one. Once a person is declared dead, a death certificate having been signed to validate the decision, the deceased no longer enjoys the rights and privileges enjoyed before death. The Declaration of Independence, the foundation of the laws of the United States, declared that all are endowed with certain unalienable rights which included the right to life. Each person has a right to his or her life. Each of us is given a life, and it is naturally our own. All legislation subsequent to the Declaration of Independence was enacted, at least in theory, to protect the rights of all members of society. Of course, the laws only protect those living members of a society. Do the deceased have any rights or protections under the law? If not, who, then, possesses the right to act in the name of the deceased? Who owns the body? What rights of the deceased, if any, may this person protect?

Many of the authors of the US Constitution believed that the "right to property" was a kind of summary right; in it were contained all the other rights (Randell, 2004). The remains of a decedent do not qualify in the ordinary sense as property. A surviving spouse or next of kin does not have a right of ownership over the corpse. However, in the absence of any contrary documents, a surviving spouse or next of kin does have the right to the possession of the body for the purpose of burial, or other lawful disposition which they may see fit. The questions of ownership and protection of rights to one's body are particularly important when it comes to the issue of organ and tissue donation.

Postmortem Organ and Tissue Donation

Within law and medical practice, organs mean a human organ whether whole or in sections, lobes, or parts. Organs that can be donated include heart, lungs, kidneys, pancreas, liver, and intestines. Blood vessels, bone, and the ossicles of the middle ear may also be donated for transplantation.

Tissue is defined as human tissue excluding the aforementioned organs. Tissues that can be donated include cornea, skin, bone marrow, heart valves, and connective tissue.

By some estimates, 92,000 Americans are waiting for an organ donation, with a name added to the list every 16 minutes. Twelve Americans die every day because a needed vital organ is not available (Harris & Alcorn, 2001). World wide numbers of persons waiting for an organ are difficult to ascertain, The Eurotransplant International Foundation (2004) reports approximately 16,000 potential recipients. The Wikipedia Encyclopedia (2006) reports there are more than 2 million patients in China, 50,000 in Latin American countries, and 2,000 in Australia and New Zealand on waiting lists for organs. The need is great; the resources to meet this need are extremely deficient. Individuals may indicate prior to their death their desire to be cadaver donors. In the absence of a pre-stated wish on the part of the deceased (signing one's name on a state donor registry or on line registry and/or indicate wishes on state driver's license), family members may be approached with a request that the deceased be an organ donor.

In the United States, the Uniform Anatomical Gift Act (UAGA) expressly grants the right to the next-of-kin to control disposal of the body, in conformity with the common law. The UAGA is a model set of laws regarding a person's gift of his/her body parts after death and has been adopted by most of the U.S. states. It includes provisions that govern how individuals can give their bodies to medical schools and hospitals for various purposes, and also has provisions that allow family members to make those decisions. The gift of body parts by an individual or next of kin may not be made if there are indications to the contrary within those who, by law, have a right to be involved in the decision.

Some general components of the UAGA are:

1. No witnesses are required on the document of gift, and consent of next of kin after death is not required if the donor has made an anatomical gift.
2. A gift of one organ does not mean there is a limitation on the gift of other organs after death if there has not been any contrary indication by the decedent.
3. An individual must be at least 18 years of age to be a donor.

4. For the wishes of a deceased to be a donor, document of gift signed by the donor is necessary. If the donor cannot sign, the document may be signed by another individual with two witnesses, all of whom have signed at the direction and in the presence of the donor.
5. If a document of gift is attached to or imprinted on a donor's motor vehicle operator's license, revocation, suspension, expiration, or cancellation of the license does not invalidate the anatomical gift.
6. A document of gift may designate a particular physician or surgeon to carry out the appropriate procedures.
7. Donation does not require waiting for a will to be probated.
8. A donor may amend or revoke an anatomical gift by: a signed statement; an oral statement made in the presence of two individuals; or any form of communication during a terminal illness or injury.
9. A stated wish to be a donor that is not revoked by the donor before death is irrevocable and does not require the consent or concurrence of any person after the donor's death.
10. In a priority listing, the spouse, adult child, either parent, adult sibling, a grandparent, guardian of the decedent, or any other person authorized or under obligation to dispose of the body may make an anatomical gift of all or a part of the decedent's body for an author-ized purpose, unless the decedent, at the time of death, has made an unrevoked refusal to make that anatomical gift.
11. If person proposing to make an anatomical gift knows of an objection to making an anatomical gift by any member of the above authorized list, the donation may not be made until the objection has been resolved.

In England and Canada, Human Tissue Gift Acts are common. In most situa-tions in both countries, any adult person can consent to be an organ or tissue donor in writing at any time, or orally if in the presence of at least two witnesses during the person's last illness. When a person has not given consent under these circum-stances, or in the opinion of a physician is incapable of giving a consent by reason of injury or disease and his/her death is imminent, the patient's next-of-kin or the person who is lawfully in possession of the body, may consent on his or her behalf. In any case, consent cannot be given if there is reason to believe that the deceased would have objected (Sperling, 2004).

In all cases, once a person is declared brain dead, families are not asked to "pull the plug" or to take someone "off of life support" because such actions would be impossible: the person has already died. Debates about whether to "pull the plug" or discontinue support on someone who is in a coma or in a persistent vegetative state have nothing to do with organ donation; such people still have brain function, and are not dead.

Organ and Tissue Donation after Cardiac Death

Typically when a person suffers a cardiac death, the heart stops beating. The vital organs quickly become unusable for transplantation. But their tissues — such as bone, skin, heart valves and corneas — can be donated within the first 24 hours of death.

However, in a return to where organ donation began 40 years ago, before the acceptance of brain death, some patients are becoming organ donors after suffering cardiac death. The medical community refers to this as non-heart beating donation (NHBD).

Some people with non-survivable injuries to the brain never become brain dead because they retain some minor brain stem function. If such individuals made the decision to be donors or their families are interested, organ donation may be an option. The option of donating organs after cardiac death or NHBD may be presented to these families after it is clear that their loved one cannot survive. Donation in such cases entails taking the patient off the ventilator, typically in the operating room. Once the patient's heart stops beating, the physician declares the patient dead and organs can be removed.

Today, organ donation after cardiac death has increased the donation of life-saving organs — mostly kidneys and livers — by as much as 25 percent in a few areas of the country. Some experts estimate that it could increase the number of deceased-donor organs in the United States by 30%.

Survivor-Family Response to Request

Family members or others responsible for making donation decisions have reported confusion and uncertainty around the moment of the request. Cleiren and VanZoelen (2002) report that many family members report not knowing or remembering what tests were used to declare their loved one dead. They seemed unaware what questions about brain death to ask a physician. Most did not know that, if the loved one was to be a donor, the body had to be artificially respirated. For some bereaved family members, they contend that no information about brain death was provided, and they cannot recall the moment when consent for donation was obtained. In only a small percentage of cases were donations discussed preceding the death. Family members felt superfluous and ignored afterward. The desire to be informed about the results of the transplanted organs was strong in almost all bereaved (Burroughs, Hong, Kappel, & Freedman, 1998). Some were frustrated that they did not receive information from the transplant coordinator, although this information had been promised. Sque, Long and Payne (2005) report that the perceived quality of hospital care affected families donation decision making and appeared to impact on their subsequent grief. Families needed 1) time to understand the information given, 2) care in the way and context that information was shared, and 3) attention to their emotional needs (Dinhofer, 2003).

The National Kidney Foundation (2002), along with a number of other professional organizations working with families of organ donors, has developed a set of care expectations these families have a right to expect. Known as the Bill of Rights of Donor Families, its purpose is to provide members of Organ Procurement Organizations (OPO) and other related associations with a list of services that they should be offering to donor families. Among other recommendations, included in this statement of rights are a number of actions which are designed to assist the family members with both their decisions and their grief. They are: 1) assuring that their loved one will be treated with respect throughout the process; 2) providing timely information regarding how any donated organs and/or tissues were used upon request and whenever possible; 3) if family members wish, giving an opportunity to exchange communications with individual recipients and/or recipient family members; 4) providing accurate updates on the condition of the recipients if families so request; and 5) providing ongoing bereavement follow-up support for a reasonable period of time. Included in such support are the provision of: the name, address, and telephone number of a knowledgeable and sensitive person with whom they can discuss the entire experience; free copies of literature about organ and tissue donation; free copies of literature about bereavement, grief, and mourning; opportunities for contact with another donor family; opportunities to take part in a donor or bereavement support group and/or the services of a skilled and sensitive support person (National Kidney Foundation, 2002).

Recipients of an organ or tissue donation should also be afforded rights. In addition, they should be willing to accept certain and specific responsibilities that are concomitant to the reception of their gift. The rights they should be entitled to include the right: to receive quality care, to be treated with respect and personal dignity, to have privacy and confidential handling of all medical records and communications; to have a voice in decision making; to have family members or significant others they designate be kept informed of their medical condition during hospitalizations; and to receive emotional support (Trasnsaction Council of the National Kidney Foundation, 1999-2000).

The recipients' responsibilities include: maintaining long-term health; committing to healthy living by making necessary lifestyle changes, informing the transplant team about any changes in health condition or any situation that may have an effect on emotional or physical well-being; and providing appropriate team members with a copy of an advanced directive, and/or medical power of attorney, if completed (Trasnsaction Council of the National Kidney Foundation, 1999-2000).

Autopsies

An autopsy may be required in deaths that have medical and legal issues and must be investigated by the medical examiner's or coroner's office. Deaths that must be reported to and investigated by these officials include those that have occurred:

1. Suddenly or unexpectedly, including sudden natural death, sudden infant death syndrome, or the death of a person who was not under the care of a doctor at the time of death.
2. As a result of any type of injury, including suicide, homicide, a motor vehicle accident, drug overdose, or poisoning.
3. Under suspicious circumstances.
4. Under other circumstances defined by law.

When an autopsy is required, the coroner or medical examiner has the legal authority to order an autopsy without the consent of the deceased person's family or next of kin. If an autopsy is not required by law, it cannot be performed until the deceased person's family provides permission.

The decision about an autopsy occurs at a difficult time for most families since they have just lost a loved one. Counselors or members of the clergy who specialize in bereavement services may be available to help families through the process. In cases in which an autopsy is not required by law, family members may consider requesting one:

1. When a medical condition has not been previously diagnosed.
2. If there are questions about an unexpected death that appears due to natural causes.
3. If there are genetic diseases or conditions that they also may be at risk for developing.
4. When the death occurs unexpectedly during medical, dental, surgical, or obstetric procedures.
5. When the cause of death could affect insurance settlements or legal matters.
6. When the death occurs during experimental treatment.

When the medical examiner or coroner decides there is a need for an autopsy to be performed and there is a cultural or religious tenet against autopsies, the law supersedes culture and religion. However, it should be expected that, in these cases, any invasion of the body be minimal and that all tissues and organs that have been removed for examination be replaced after the procedure is complete, thus maintaining the bodily integrity required by religious or cultural practice (Klaiman, 2005).

Other Legal Disposal Means

In addition to allowing the deceased's body to be harvested for useable tissue and organs in a transplantation program or for medical research, there are three other lawful means of disposing the remains of a loved one who has died: burial, cryonics, or cremation. The most common means of disposal is the burial of the body following a funeral or memorial service. Funerals provide an important rite of passage. Similar to rituals that mark other transitions in life, funerals provide a time for family and friends to celebrate the life of the loved one and share their feelings concerning the loss of this person in their lives. Coming together like this provides a satisfactory environment for mourning and expressing grief. In addition, funerals are important rituals for those the survivors. They affirm one's basic beliefs about life and death, and help one through the loss.

Funerary customs comprise the complex of beliefs and practices used by a culture to remember the dead, from the funeral itself, to various monuments, prayers, and rituals undertaken in their honor. These customs vary widely between cultures, and between religious affiliations within cultures. In most cultural groups and regions, funeral rituals can be divided into three parts:

A. **The visitation or wake**. During this part of the funeral process the body of the deceased is prepared for viewing. Depending on the religious affiliation of the deceased and/or family, there may be a ritual including the recitation of specific prayers. If there is going to be an open casket viewing, the body may be embalmed. There is no federal law that requires that a body be embalmed prior to burial. In fact, the Center for Disease Control (CDC) says no public health purpose is served by embalming (Hoyert, 2001). In addition, no state routinely requires embalming. A few states do have laws that require embalming generally:

1. when death occurs from a disease that may put funeral personnel at risk;
2. if the body will be transported by public transportation;
3. if the final disposition will not be accomplished within 72 hours after the death;
4. if the body will be publicly viewed; and
5. if so ordered by the commissioner of health for the protection of the public health (Funeral Consumer Alliance (FCA), 2006).

A supporting rationale for embalming states that it is primarily done to disinfect and preserve the remains. FCA (2006) counters this rationale with the policy that the process does not preserve the body forever; it merely delays the forces of nature. A second supporting position is that without embalming, an open casket viewing would be impossible. The body would become un-viewable within a short time. Refrigeration of the body during non-visitation periods would accomplish the same result as embalming if the viewing period is not too long. The United States is the only country in which embalming has been widely promoted by the funeral industry. It is rarely done in other countries, with no risk to public health. Even visitations are held in those countries without having the body embalmed first (FCA, 2006).

B. **The funeral service**. Funerals rank among the most expensive purchases many consumers will ever make. A traditional funeral, including a casket and vault, may cost $6,000 or more, not including the cemetery cost. Extras like flowers, obituary notices, acknowledgment cards or limousines can add thousands of dollars to the bottom line. The cost of many funerals is more than $10,000.

To protect the purchasers of funeral products and services, the U.S. Federal Trade Commission (FTC) (1994) enforces a set of regulations known as the Funeral Rule. According to the Funeral Rule:

1.   One has the right to choose the funeral goods and services he or she wants for themselves or for someone they represent.
2.   The funeral provider must state this right in writing on the general price list.
3.   If state or local law requires a person to buy any particular item, the funeral provider must disclose it on the price list, with a reference to the specific law.
4.   The funeral provider may not refuse, or charge a fee, to handle a casket someone has purchased elsewhere.
5.   A funeral provider that offers cremations must make alternative containers available.

Each year, Americans grapple with these and many other questions as they spend billions of dollars arranging more than 2 million funerals for family members and friends. The increasing trend toward pre-need planning — when people make funeral arrangements in advance — suggests that many consumers want to compare prices and services so that ultimately, the funeral reflects a wise and well-informed purchasing decision, as well as a meaningful one.

With the exclusion of Alabama, which is the only state without any pre-need laws, all states have some pre-need legislation. However, each and every state's pre-need laws are significantly different. Some states require 100% of pre-need funds to be placed in trust. Other states merely require the holder of funds to maintain a custodial relationship. Some states require an annual report to be prepared by a certified public accountant. Other states don't require any annual report (FTC, 1994).

C. **The burial service**. A burial service is generally conducted at the side of the grave, tomb, mausoleum or crematorium, at which the body of the decedent is buried or cremated at the conclusion. According to most religions, coffins are kept closed during the burial ceremony. In Eastern Orthodox funerals, the coffins are reopened just before burial to allow loved ones to look at the deceased one last time and give their final farewells.

In most areas of the country, state or local laws do not require the purchase of a container to surround the casket in the grave. However, many cemeteries require such a container so that the grave will not sink in. Either a grave liner or a burial vault will be required.

Cremation

Cremation is another method of disposing of the remains of a loved one. People choose cremation for a variety of reasons. Some do so based on environmental considerations. Others have philosophical or religious reasons. Still others choose cremation because they feel it is simpler and less complicated. There are a variety of options available with cremation. Most families hold services, which help the bereaved people find that opting for cremation gives them the opportunity to create and personalize the various service options for a more meaningful experience. Cremations offer families choices for final disposition of the cremation. One has the opportunity to select from a wide array of caskets and urns.

A service or ceremony can precede or follow the actual cremation. Prior to cremation, there may be a gathering, which can be either public or private, with an open or closed casket. Deciding what will be done with cremated remains will help determine what kind of urn to select. An urn can be buried in a family plot at a cemetery, placed in a niche at a columbarium, or kept in the home. Cremated remains may also be scattered over land or water.

The U.S. Environmental Protection Agency (EPA) allows for burial at sea of cremated remains. The burial may be by boat or plane and must occur at least three nautical miles from land and that each burial of cremated remains be reported to the EPA. "At sea" includes inland navigable water, but excludes lakes and streams. Scattering cremated remains from a bridge or pier is prohibited under federal law. Cremated remains must be removed form the container or urn before scattering.

Cremated remains may be scattered or placed on public or private property provided there is no local prohibition; the remains are not distinguishable to the public and not in a container; and the person with the control over the disposition has written permission of the property owner or governing agency.

Cryonics

Cryonics is the practice of preserving (freezing) humans or animals that can no longer be sustained by contemporary medicine until resuscitation may be possible in the future. The process is not currently reversible, and by law can only be performed on humans after legal death in anticipation that the early stages of clinical death may be reversible in the future. Clinical death occurs when a patient's heartbeat and breathing have stopped. Since breathing rarely continues when the heart is stopped, clinical death is synonymous with cardiac arrest or cardiac death. The reversal of clinical death is sometimes possible through CPR, defibrillation, epinephrine injection, and other treatments. Resuscitation after more than 4 to 6 minutes of clinical death at normal body temperature is difficult, and can result in brain damage or later brain death even if cardiac resuscitation is successful. Longer intervals of clinical death can be survived under conditions of hypothermia. Hypothermia also improves outcomes after resuscitation from clinical death even if body temperature is not lowered until after resuscitation.

Cryonics is based on a view of dying as a process that can be stopped in the minutes, and perhaps hours, following clinical death. If death is not an event that happens suddenly when the heart stops, we face philosophical questions about what exactly death is. Some have noted "…few if any patients pronounced dead by today's physicians are in fact truly dead by any scientifically rigorous criteria" (Whetstine, Streat, Darwin & Crippen, 2005). Donaldson (1988) has argued that "death" based on cardiac arrest or resuscitation failure is a purely social construction used to justify terminating care of dying patients.

Ethical and theological opinions of cryonics tend to pivot on the issue of whether cryonics is regarded as interment or medicine. If cryonics is interment, then religious beliefs about death and afterlife come into consideration. Resuscitation is generally deemed impossible because the soul is gone, and according to most religions only God can resurrect the dead. Expensive interment is seen as a waste of resources. If cryonics is regarded as medicine, with legal death as a mere enabling mechanism, then cryonics is a long-term coma with uncertain prognosis. It is continuing to care for sick people when others have given up, and a legitimate use of resources to sustain human life (Whetstine et al., 2005).

The costs of cryonics vary greatly, ranging from $28,000 to $150,000. What influences the differences in the fees is whether the final cost includes: a team standing by the bed of the patient to begin the process at the moment death has been declared; the particular service desired; transportation costs; or funeral director expenses. The expenses are comparable to major transplant surgeries. The largest single expense, especially for whole body cases, is the money that must be set aside to generate interest to pay for maintenance in perpetuity.

The Survivors and Grief

Wolfelt (2002) has created what he calls the Mourner's Bill of Rights, a list intended to assist in the healing process and the work of mourning. The list includes, but is not limited to, the following "rights":

1. The right to experience your own unique grief
2. The right to talk about your grief
3. The right to be tolerant of your physical and emotional limits
4. The right to make use of ritual
5. The right to search for meaning
6. The right to move toward your grief and heal

Often, the acuteness of the grief being experienced makes it very difficult for the bereft to fulfill normal daily activities, such as meeting one's occupational responsibilities (Rando, 1993). Having the opportunity to take a paid leave from work (bereavement leave) so that one would be able to focus on the felt grief and to help others in the family to cope would be a very positive support. However, there is no automatic right to time off with pay in instances of bereavement of a relative or friend. Any time off with pay is either stated in the company's terms and conditions of employment or decided by the employer at his/her discretion. The Employment Relations Act 1999, does give employees the right to time off without pay, in the event of the death of a dependent. In the legislation, a dependent is defined as, a spouse, child, parent, or a person who lives in the same household as the employee other than a tenant, lodger, or boarder.

The Financial Executives Institute's Committee on Employee Benefits conducted a survey of members to find out the kinds of benefits related to family needs that they are providing their employees. The survey found that larger firms generally offered the most benefits. Of the total number of companies surveyed, 80% reported that they provide paid bereavement leave (Deitsch, 1992).

Ethical-Legal Issue of Research

"The field of bereavement research has lagged behind the disciplines of medicine and clinical psychology in its consideration of ethical issues, and yet the researcher is confronted with unique and complex ethical challenges" (Stroebe, Hansson, Stroebe & Schut, 2001, p.12).

Some of the ethical issues are described by Cook (2001). They include issues of recruitment methods employed by the researcher, the timing of the recruitment, issues of informed consent, threats to confidentiality, increase in subject's distress induced by participation, a violation of cultural norms, and unethical application of study findings.

Several of the ethical concerns and responsibilities identified are particularly relevant to the question of how best to link research and practice. Intervention studies can be particularly ethically problematic because of the tension that exists between the need to generate data to inform clinical practice and the potential harm to the bereaved that may result through their participation in research (Genevro, Marshall, & Miller, 2003).

Summary

An examination of the ethical and legal issues of loss, grief, and mourning in a single chapter is a formidable task. There is not enough space within a single unit to completely address the issues presented. An attempt has been made to present the material in an organized manner so that the reader will find an easy transition form one issue to the next.

The topics examined focused primarily on postmortem issues. Almost immediately after a death has been declared, and often before the person has been so certified, issues of organ and tissue donation arise. The need for donors far exceeds the availability of organs and tissue necessary to save lives. The first concern is to be as certain as one can that a death has occurred. The declaration of death is both a medical and a legal decision. Not only does declaring a person dead bring a stop to all forms of aggressive intervention, but also removes any constitutional rights the deceased had.

We come to the next issue — who, if anyone, now owns the body. Not only does the answer to this question impact on whether an autopsy will be performed and on organ and tissue donor programs but also indicates who has the responsibility to dispose of the decedent's body. The subsequent issue is, once the determination of ownership or responsibility has been made, how might the body be disposed of?

Three additional issues related to the survivors are briefly discussed. These include the rights, if any, to a paid time off from one's job in what is popularly called bereavement leave. Lastly, since the research in bereavement requires subjects who have experienced a loss, what ethical practices should be followed to ensure the subjects are not caused any additional pain and suffering.

LeARNiNg Objective! (30/40)

Identify the ethical and legal issues involved in the determination of death, organ & tissue donation, and treatment of the body for disposal. (Section 250/280)

Assessment and Intervention

Introduction to Part 4, Chapters 19-24

Chapters 19 through 24 focus on assessment and intervention. The Body of Knowledge Committee defined this major category of thanatology knowledge in this way: **information gathered, decisions that are made, and actions that are taken by professional caregivers to determine and/or provide for the needs of the dying, their loved ones, and the bereaved.**

The chapters in Part 4 focus on assessment and intervention in terms of these indicators: culture and socialization, religion and spirituality, historical and contemporary perspectives, life span issues, the family and larger systems, and ethical and legal issues.

Chapter 19

Culture and Socialization in Assessment and Intervention

Ester R. Shapiro

Clinical Vignette: Carmen Ruiz was a 32-year-old single Puerto Rican woman and third of 11 siblings when her 50 year old mother Gloria died of breast cancer, leaving Carmen in charge of three younger siblings still at home, Mario, age 24, and a heroin addict, and two half siblings Roberto, age 16, and Luisa, age 11. Carmen had become her mother's co-parent from age 8, when her hard-drinking father died in a car accident in their home town in rural Puerto Rico, and her mother was pregnant with Mario. After her husband's death, Gloria Ruiz relocated her family to Boston where she remained single and had the two younger children. While older siblings married and had their own families, Carmen remained at home. She spoke little English, her world revolving around her intense loyalty to her mother and care of their household. With Gloria's diagnosis of Stage IV breast cancer Carmen became her mother's primary caretaker through the swift progression of devastating illness reducing her beautiful, sociable mother to agonized skin and bones. At her mother's request, Carmen became the children's primary parent. Carmen struggled to establish her parental authority but was thwarted by Roberto and Luisa's rebellion and rejection. She initially sought parenting help from a Child Guidance Center, but was referred to a new Family Bereavement Center where I worked. Respecting her request, initial interventions used behavioral parenting counseling techniques to help Carmen set consistent, age-appropriate limits with her half-siblings. As the climate in the household improved, Carmen requested help with her own overwhelming grief and conflicts within their immediate and extended family concerning the proper way to grieve. Carmen disclosed her continuing close yet conflicted relationship with her mother's spirit, who visited her nightly in "dreams" and scolded her for not taking proper care of the children. The children were especially spooked by Carmen's invocation of their mother's deceased spirit, intensified by preservation of their mother's bedroom precisely as it had been during her life.

In weekly individual meetings with Carmen conducted in Spanish, supplemented by family consultation sessions with the younger children and extended family, we explored Carmen's current grief in light of her history as designated family caretaker, framing her self-sacrifice as a generous contribution to the family's well-being. At the same time, we explored how Carmen might take up aspects of her own, interrupted development, enjoying the same independence she made possible for others. Carmen's experience as her mother's co-parent and continuing connection with her mother's spirit mirrored her great-aunt's relationship to her maternal grandmother, providing an intergenerational legacy consistent with cultural traditions. Respecting her own language for images of relationships in life, illness, and death, we revisited her relationship with her mother. Carmen requested help understanding her mother's illness and treatment, and we reviewed her thick medical chart, translating both the English and decoding the high-technology medical treatments. Carmen realized her mother had ignored the lump in her breast for some time, reluctant to face a diagnosis that would destroy her cherished feminine beauty and social life. As we turned to exploring their life-long relationship, Carmen grew more comfortable speaking about frustrations in their multi-faceted relationship, especially her thwarted needs for a life of her own. I coached her to respectfully speak out in her own defense to her mother's spirit, who became more supportive of Carmen and complemented her parenting. This transformed relationship with her mother's spirit freed Carmen to pursue her own life interests: she enrolled in English language classes at a local church, dated a family friend who had long expressed a romantic interest in her, and restructured relationships with her older and younger siblings so as to share household chores and caretaking more equitably.

When I met Carmen Ruiz in 1982, bereavement practice emphasized expressing distressing feelings and closure in relationship to the deceased, with little to offer in understanding culturally based experiences of death and grief for diverse U.S. communities. I was fortunate to work with colleagues exploring innovative approaches to race, culture, community, and bereavement who supported my application of an intergenerational family development approach to grief as a family process (Shapiro, 1994). I was helped by my own experience as member of an immigrant Cuban Eastern-European Jewish family whose family life cycle experiences of loss were shaped by political disruptions and diaspora; and by qualitative research on family life cycle transitions, both of which challenged my hospital-based psychopathology training.

In this chapter, I present a cultural and ecosystemic approach to thanatology practice designed to honor both the suffering and resilience of grieving families while promoting positive shared development under adversity. I selectively review current literatures on cultural competence in health care and multi-cultural counseling, including literature on culturally sensitive end-of-life and bereavement care. Cultural and multi-cultural counseling approaches view culture as dynamically constructed and emergent in specific intervention contexts, and as including the counselor's own culturally based beliefs and values, professional training and treatment setting. Culturally based care also has to connect to quality care initiatives in health care and community services, building bridges to consensus on "best practices" in bereavement care compatible with culturally meaningful assessment and intervention. To address these complexities in thanatology practice, this chapter integrates interdisciplinary, multi-cultural counseling, and cultural competence frameworks using ecosystemic models and collaborative approaches. We join families in creating a shared understanding and new "ecological niche" for facing death and grief, identifying and mobilizing positive coping resources while supporting attainment of desired goals for change and growth. This review emphasizes bridges to evidence-based or "best practice" in thanatology emphasizing meaning-making (Neimeyer, 2001), relationships as resources in coping with death (Silverman, 2000; Koenig and Davies, 2003), factors associated with resilience in bereavement responses (Bonnano, 2004), and intervention research applying family-centered multi-systemic approaches alleviating distress while mobilizing positive coping resources (Kissane & Bloch, 2002; Sandler & Ayers, 2001).

Cultural Complexity in Thanatology Practice: Understanding Death and its Impacts in Every-Day Life Contexts

Societies have traditionally taken tremendous care with the shared transformation of life into death, because of their responsibility to preserve everyday life's continuity and stability in the face of death's many disruptions. Cultural beliefs and practices concerning death and its aftermath emerge from a cosmology of shared world views incorporating death into interdependent, intergenerational life cycles under highly specific circumstances for every day survival. Who died, how they died, who remains to mourn and remember them, and what assistance they should expect from their community, are interpreted in light of cultural understandings of death, its timing and circumstances, and its place in connecting the arduous present to an ancestral past and a hoped for future. The United States is a pluralistic, diverse society, yet dominant assumptions supported by medical and mental health models emphasize private experience, individual autonomy, and capacity to overcome all challenges through problem-solving action. Culturally meaningful assessment and intervention in thanatology requires a shared journey of inquiry into the cultural complexity of death's place and its impacts in unique yet interdependent life pathways. Further, thanatologists train in multiple disciplines and work in diverse practice contexts. Each discipline and practice setting provides its own guidelines for culturally sensitive care within disciplinary and organizational guidelines for quality care. Culturally meaningful care cannot be conducted in a vacuum, but rather responds to changing health care and community service systems and current challenges to achieve greater efficacy and equity (Institute of Medicine, 2003).

Thanatology practice addressing the cultural complexity of encounters with death and grief can best be informed by **1. Ecosystemic models of human development in the context of culture**, locating individuals in specific multi-dimensional adaptive contexts which include the practitioner and treatment setting, and **2. Collaborative methods of communication, dialogue and goal-setting generating a culturally meaningful appreciative inquiry** exploring how individuals and their families experience the death, its circumstances and impacts, and define their own desired present and future goals. Interventions support these goals while also reducing ecosystemic stressors and increasing the resources reducing distressing symptoms while promoting recovery and resilience.

Ecosystemic approaches to practice (Becvar & Becvar, 2006; Boyd-Franklin, 2003; McDaniel et al, 2001) identify individual, family/relational, neighborhood/community, and sociocultural levels within which to assess relevant qualities of individuals, their relationships, formal and informal institutions, social practices or policies, and their interpretations or meanings contributing to particular adaptive outcomes of interest. **Collaborative practice models** are found in many disciplines, and draw from social constructionist views of change emphasizing the culturally and relationally based nature of subjective reality and the importance of power-sharing, especially in contexts of social inequality (Pare & Larner, 2004).

Ecosystemic models emphasize the dynamic complexity, interdependence and contingency/responsiveness to context of adaptive outcomes for any individual, while identifying risks and resources empirically associated with resilient, ordinary and expectable, or problematic adaptation, especially with exposure to adversity. Using a collaborative approach to ecosystemic practice, clinical assessment and intervention are understood as consultations, constructed through a compassionate, respectful dialogue using an individual and family's own language for their struggles, exploring culturally based assumptions and goals for interdependent development (Boyd-Franklin, 2003; Falicov, 1998; Shapiro, 1994, in preparation). This approach draws from relevant research literatures studying cultural protective factors in positive coping with the stresses of acculturation and racism (Boyd-Franklin, 2003); research on developmental pathways resulting in positive and symptomatic adaptive outcomes throughout the life span and emphasizing resilience in coping with adversities such as death, divorce, poverty, exposure to racism, or community violence (Luthar, 2006; Sandler, 2001); psychotherapy research on effective practice emphasizing patient-directed goals, mobilizing supportive relationships and resources within and outside therapy (Gibbs, 2002; Prochaska & DiClemente, 2005), and culturally meaningful adaptation of evidence based practice (Nagayama-Hall, 2001; Bernal & Saez-Santiago, 2006). It recognizes the scientifically demonstrated power of the sacred healing arts (Koenig, McCullough, & Larson, 2001), and conducts a culturally sensitive spiritual inquiry as part of a basic assessment.

Ecosystemic dimensions of culture relevant to thanatology must focus not only on death, its circumstances and meanings but also on the social resources available for rebuilding disrupted lives in the presence of death and grief. In every society, disparities in available resources due to race, ethnic minority status, gender inequality, or social class differences intersect uniquely to generate the circumstances, consequences, and meanings of death and grief. Culturally informed thanatology practice requires that we consider a society's distribution of stressors, risks, and protective resources exposing some individuals or communities to higher rates of mortality risk while depriving them of access to resources promoting recovery and resilience. Dimensions of culture relevant to thanatology practice include the cultural specificity of spiritual and religious beliefs and practices, an individual's location in immigration/acculturation processes; evaluation of individual's relationship to "dominant" cultural resources, beliefs and practices; and negotiation of individual differences in the interpretation of culture which may differ by personal style, gender and generation within the same family.

In conducting assessment and intervention from a cultural perspective, the thanatologist joins the ecosystem and has a responsibility to understand him/herself as a potential resource or barrier to successful adaptation, growth and change. Some authors argue that the medical and mental health fields have themselves become subcultures with their own beliefs and economic interests guiding their prescriptions for responding to death, dying and grief. An appreciative inquiry emphasizes the bereaved's own account of their experience and needs, highlighting culturally meaningful goals for life in the presence of grief. These approaches help us consider with each unique individual and family how cultural resources can help transform and repair altered landscapes, economics of survival, relationships and roles, and meanings shattered by a loved one's death and its circumstances.

Clinicians conduct a culturally meaningful appreciative inquiry into death and its impacts, creating a collaborative contract for interventions supporting person- and family-determined goals. Culturally meaningful thanatology practice:

- Recognizes the practitioner's own location in specific cultures of personal and professional experiences and practice settings: *When I first met Carmen Ruiz, I was secular Jew with hospital training in psychopathology and fluency in Spanish; I was able to work with Ms. Ruiz from a strengths-based cultural framework with the support of a multi-disciplinary team committed to emphasizing cultural and community resources in the face of social oppression.*
- Explores culturally mediated individual experience of death and its impacts using a multi-dimensional, dynamic understanding of culture as a force organizing roles, relationships, emotions and beliefs in every day life while connecting these to the flow of intergenerational time and to the wider society: *Carmen and her family found it helpful to understand differences in their grief responses as due to different ages and life experiences within the family. We framed Carmen's more extreme grief response as rooted in Puerto Rico's unique synthesis of Catholic, African, European spiritist, and indigenous beliefs in the enduring presence of spirits, as based in an intergenerational family legacy, and as reasonable given her assigned caretaker role after her father's death; these framings helped initiate a new conversation about how best to support Carmen in her grief and new roles while also addressing the needs of the younger siblings and extended family.*
- Conducts a culturally-informed appreciative inquiry into person and family experience and goals for life in the presence of death which is compassionate, strengths-based, and accountable to family-determined goals; *Carmen first requested help with more effective parenting. The success of structured behavioral interventions for setting limits at home made the next step possible, in which she requested help with her own deep bereavement and its discordance with that of other family members.*
- Creates a collaborative contract for interventions that closely follows the patient and family's stated goals, applying and adapting appropriate, effective clinical tools; *I followed Carmen's narrative lead in framing the visits from her mother's spirit as "dreams" and in hearing her distress at her mother's unfair criticisms. I appreciated Carmen's positive contribution as designated co-parent going back to her father's death, while using her mother as an example of how someone could grieve and also go on to enjoy a full life, to affirm that Carmen also had these rights. After a coaching session role-playing how Carmen could express her frustrations and needs to her mother's spirit, she was able to challenge her mother's criti-*

cism respectfully and constructively. Subsequently she reported that her mother's spirit had ceased criticizing and had instead complimented her, saying the children were looking well and "gorditos" or "plump," high praise in a culture concerned about economic survival associating plumpness with good health.

- Recognizes both individual uniqueness in death and grief responses and their interdependence based on gender, generation, and unique relationships to the dying and deceased: *While Carmen Ruiz felt a deep connection to an intergenerational legacy of continuing spiritual bonds to her deceased mother, her older, less acculturated siblings endorsed that tradition but felt she took it too far, while her younger, highly acculturated siblings found these traditions unfamiliar and frightening. Both individual sessions and family consultations were designed to increase positive family communication, mutual understanding, and resolution of conflicts in ways that negotiated differences while enhancing mutual affection and shared support.*

- Explores culturally meaningful resources for positive change, identifying "leverage points" helping reduce distressing symptoms while also mobilizing relationship and environmental factors associated with positive coping in responding to a loved one's death and coping with its aftermath. *In the Ruiz family, ecosystemic leverage points included:* **at the individual level,** *work with Carmen on her developmental history of grief as well as on making progress in adult skills and goals such as speaking out about her needs within the family, learning English, and exploring new intimacies outside the family;* **at the familial level,** *discussing differences in grief reactions made it possible for the family to negotiate differences and gain greater compassion for Carmen; behavioral interventions created a more stable home environment with age appropriate rules;* **extended family and community resources** *were mobilized to support Carmen in her new role as parent and in her new life goals.*

Culture, Socialization, and Human Development

The cultural dimension of death and grief has long been the province of anthropologists, who have appreciated the ways a community's rituals and beliefs facilitating the passage between life and death illuminate its beliefs and practices. Moments of social transition are valuable in understanding the workings of culture, because for most of us "culture" is part of the atmosphere or ethos of our every day lives, appearing as natural and unremarkable as the air we breathe or as the solid ground beneath our feet. We are socialized into culture from before birth, through the work of generations anticipating our futures. From birth, we are born neurologically incomplete, formed by relationships with caretakers whose talent for survival we depend on and from whom we learn our place in the world. Valsiner (2000) uses a cultural ecosystemic framework to articulate four interdependent dimensions of culture generating human development: landscape and the natural world, economic activities for survival, human roles and relationships, and cultural symbols and meanings. This experience of embeddedness in culture is reinforced by continuity in our social environments and by the neurocognitive schemas or "working models of relationships" we develop for making sense of the world. What appears to be a private, isolated self in Western psychology can best be understood as interdependent and contingent, organized by specific life circumstances, relationships and shared adaptive goals responsive to changing contexts for development. Our schemas or working models of relationships balance universal human needs for self-assertion and connection, responsive to cultural roles and meanings guiding gendered, intergenerational relationships as we confront specific problems of the family life cycle (Shapiro, 1996).

Throughout human development, both expected and unexpected life cycle transitions create disruptions and discontinuities which we bridge by drawing on the relationships, environments, private and shared meanings which offer stability and continuity, ways of making the new and unknown safe and familiar. Cultural anthropologists use the construct of "liminality" to describe rituals of transition as culturally sanctioned spaces of transformation bridging one state or stage and the next. Cultural death and grief rituals are designed first and foremost to reassure the broader society that a community's life goes on after a member's death. They may not necessarily fit an individual or family's unique needs in response to a very particular death, its circumstances and its cultural context. In culturally diverse societies, and in traditional societies changing through modernization, the relationship between culturally sanctioned death and bereavement rituals and an individual or family's grief experience may be discordant (Shapiro, 1996). For this reason, thanatologists conducting an assessment and planning an intervention with bereaved families need to understand cultural dimensions relevant to bereavement care as contextual, multidimensional and unfolding in specific contexts for shared development.

Models of Culturally Competent Practice: Implications for Thanatology

Clinical practice fields are currently developing guidelines for culturally informed practice that vary by discipline and by emphasis. Health care and medicine most often use the term **cultural competence**, while the fields of counseling and psychotherapy more often refer to **multi-cultural counseling competencies**. There is a great deal of debate in this field about use of the term "competence," as compared to "cultural humility," in capturing the complexity of culturally informed interventions and the clinician's stance as learner. Other current debates include:

1. The importance of ethnic-specific knowledge versus process approaches emphasizing universal principles for contextualizing care;

2. The value of ethnographic approaches in cultural anthropology or cross-cultural, comparative psychology versus multi-cultural counseling models emphasizing both diversity and power inequalities within a single social context; and

3. The relevance of research on effective practice, much of which has not included diverse patient populations nor culturally meaningful dimensions of treatment (Leong & Lopez, 2006; Nagayama-Hall, 2001).

In the field of cultural competence and health care, Arthur Kleinman's work on "illness narratives" as negotiated meanings has been especially influential (Kleinman, 1990; Fadiman, 1997), emphasizing the moral dimension of patient experiences of suffering, recommending that questions about the patient's own understanding of the illness and its cause also explore "what matters" to the patient within their specific social world. Carrillo et al. (1999) developed a framework for a patient-based approach to cross-cultural primary care incorporating Kleinman's questions into a culturally sensitive clinical interview emphasizing social contexts as well as private meanings. This model teaches skills for negotiation between clinician, patient's and family's explanatory models of illness and its impacts, and the patient's desired agenda for care. This model calls for a social context "review of systems" exploring economic burdens, migration history, social support, language literacy and health communication, doing so in ways that are patient-centered and problem-specific.

The most widely referenced models of multi-cultural counseling (Sue & Sue, 2003) argue for a process-oriented understanding of culture emphasizing clinician self-knowledge, respectful communication, and openness to learning even when one's own personal or professional assumptions are challenged by a unique individual or family. Sue and Sue (2003) present a multi-dimensional approach to developing cultural competence mapping three components of cultural competence: clinician awareness of attitudes and beliefs, knowledge about cultural groups and their complexity, and clinical intervention skills with knowledge of how to best adapt these to cultural beliefs and preferences. These components of cultural competence operate at multiple levels of individual, professional, organizational and societal, and require specific knowledge about racial and cultural groups. While these models often include major themes in world views of U.S. Latino-Americans, African Americans, Asian Americans, or Native Americans, they do so to heighten awareness of differences when compared to assumptions made by psychotherapy and counseling practice based on European Americans. These approaches caution clinicians to balance universalist (etic or "outsider's" view) and relativistic (emic or "insider's" view) methods by recognizing the ways both individual subjectivity and cultural socialization influence experience. Clinically, they require practicing what Sue and Sue (2003) call "dynamic sizing," assessing when to generalize and when to individualize interventions, depending on how well a particular group's cultural norms fit a specific individual. Further, different dimensions of culture become relevant in addressing specific challenges or problems. The specific challenges of death and its aftermath may call forth traditional ancestral beliefs in otherwise highly acculturated individuals, may bring deeply religious individuals into a crisis of faith, and may increase diversity within a single family whose members may mourn a death distinctly yet interdependently based on culturally meaningful differences in gender, generation and acculturation. In any treatment setting, the practitioner's socialization into cultural assumptions, the cultural beliefs and practices of a particular treatment setting, and the person in treatment will co-create a dynamic, multi-faceted cultural context for interventions.

Recent work on cultural competence and evidence based practice (Bernal & Saez-Santiago, 2006; Hwang, 2006; Nagayama-Hall, 2001) also emphasizes the importance of knowing empirically supported treatments relevant to a particular patient's care, while also adapting these in ways that are sensitive to culturally based values and experiences. Nagayama-Hall (2001) suggests that sensitivity to issues of interdependence, attention to religion and spirituality, and inquiry into experiences of discrimination are examples of culturally meaningful themes that can re-orient empirically supported treatments to increase their cultural competence.

Culturally Meaningful Care in Thanatology: Literature Review

Most of the published literature on assessment and intervention in culture, death, and grief uses an ethnographic cultural approach that considers cultural influences on behavior from a single cultural context, or a cross-cultural approach comparing cultural differences across different nationalities (Doka, 1998; Klass, 1999). Rosenblatt (2001) uses a social constructionist approach to culture, death and grief that emphasizes the dynamic, co-constructed nature of grief reactions. In the field of thanatology, the greatest progress in establishing guidelines for culturally sensitive care has been made in the field of end-of-life and palliative care. Jones (2005) reviews the qualitative research literature on diversity in end-of-life care, applying a view of culture as socially constructed which emphasizes philosophical differences with Western medicine and bioethics emphasizing patient privacy and autonomy. Jones suggests that family centered and meaning-making approaches in palliative and hospice care support the specific explorations into relationships, religious beliefs and spirituality, social roles and values needed in appreciating diversity in end-of-life care.

Barrett (2001) reviews the multi-cultural competency literature and its implications for end-of-life care. He highlights the need for self-knowledge of privilege on the part of clinicians, an attitude of respect and openness to learning about the role of cultural differences, their intersection with other factors such as social class or sexual orientation, and their relevance in a particular setting, sensitivity to histories of discrimination and their impact on cross-racial relationships, and willingness to consult with and refer to knowledgeable colleagues. He argues that culturally competent clinicians are sensitive to institutional barriers preventing minorities from accessing resources for end-of-life care, and to the need for ethnically and racially diverse practitioners offering consultation and care.

Searight and Gafford (2005) review cultural diversity issues in end of life care relevant for family physicians, identifying cultural differences in communication of "bad news," in who makes decisions concerning care, and in attitudes toward advance directives and end-of life care. They emphasize the greater diversity in preferences for end-of-life care among ethnic minority patients and their families, including sensitivity to cultures that see direct disclosure of terminal diagnoses as potentially disrespectful or harmful in eliminating hope and causing distress. Many immigrant groups, especially Asian American and Hispanics, place less emphasis on patient autonomy which they might see as isolating, instead valuing protection of patients from the burden of making treatment decisions which are handled by family members in positions of authority due to age or gender. Ethnic minority patients are less likely to sign advance directives, and family members may view advance directives or do not resuscitate orders as giving up on a patient's life, compounded by experiences of discrimination and barriers to access. Preferences for aggressive treatment at the end of life may also stem from different views of suffering and the value of life, or from emphasis on filial piety and the importance of elders to family life. Because of the complexity and sensitivity of these culturally based beliefs and communication processes, they stress the importance of asking direct questions concerning these preferences and using trained medical translators.

Koenig and Davies (2003) focus on culturally sensitive care for dying children and their families, identifying "differences that make a difference" including immigration status and different cultural beliefs about medical authority, disclosure of illness status, and ways that culture, ethnicity and race are distinct from social class. They emphasize the importance of communication and negotiation with families about appropriate care, use of medical interpreters when needed, and explaining medical decision making while taking into account cultural differences in attitudes towards palliative care vs. curative care or in declaration of death. They offer a template for assessing ethnocultural differences in care for children with life-limiting conditions and their families which includes: evaluating the actual language used by the child and family members and their openness to discussing diagnosis, prognosis, and death; determining the locus of decision making and their expectations concerning the child's involvement and the medical team's authority versus shared decision making; considering the relevance of religious beliefs concerning healing, death, and the afterlife; evaluating cultural attitudes toward suffering and expressions of pain; assessing how hope for recovery is regarded and discussed; evaluating desires for control of care and views of family involvement in nursing and supportive care; considering issues of gender, political, and historical considerations including immigration history, poverty, and histories with racism and discrimination, and using family and community resources in these evaluations. After the child's death, culturally sensitive assessments need to address expectations for how the body should be approached and handled and preferences for expression and duration of grief.

Summary: Challenges of Culturally Competent Thanatology Practice

In sum, culturally meaningful thanatology practice requires a commitment to personal and professional re-assessment in response to the challenges presented by cultural differences in death, dying and bereavement within a diverse society, for example:

- To appreciate the lived experiences of racism and grief described by African-Americans if we are protected by white-skin privilege (Barrett, 2001; Rosenblatt & Wallace, 2005).
- To understand intergenerational obligations constraining Japanese American bereaved adults, caught between elders expecting obedience and acculturated defiant teens, when we view mature independence as emphasizing individual rights (Hwang, 2006).
- To learn how Latino families bring indigenous and African beliefs into creative interpretations of Catholicism, when we have learned to label these practices as "primitive" (Falicov, 1996)

The great challenge for practitioners striving to understand another culture emerges both because we take our own cultural understandings for granted and because our power and authority makes it possible to inadvertently overlook or silence the experiences of more vulnerable others. For this reason, most guidelines for culturally informed practice emphasize the practitioner's rigorous self-questioning about their own cultural biases in every clinical encounter, because each creates a new unique configuration of clinician, patient, and clinical context. This relationally based self-knowledge is generated through respectful listening and willingness to leave the safe territory of expertise, in order to be educated, humbled, or surprised by what we learn from others about their culturally based experiences with dying, death, loss, grief, renewal, and growth. Families become the experts on their own experiences of death, dying, and grief within culture, and we gain enormously from these opportunities to leave our own cultural comfort zones. We learn how far we can go before we confront the limits of our expertise, and when we need to collaborate with or refer to practitioners with the appropriate linguistic and cultural background. We learn how to explore a bereaved family's own goals for grief, recovery, and growth and to help them mobilize the personal, family and community resources to do so. Clinical encounters with difference require that we carefully scrutinize our own assumptions in an ongoing conversation with colleagues and with the bereaved families we serve. Using terms such as collaboration and dialogue emphasize that communication across differences must be centered on knowing the lived experiences and desired goals of "others," especially when that knowledge will challenge our own personal and professional assumptions. Through the self-awareness generated by authentic dialogue, we can learn to appreciate how realities we confront in our lives and values we strive to live by shape distinctive pathways for new lives altered by death.

In ecosystemic, collaborative thanatology practice, the culturally meaningful appreciative inquiry initiating an assessment already incorporates important principles mobilizing positive growth, healing and wellness. Respectful listening sensitive to the ways death and its circumstances have impacted on family members, with an attitude of openness and curiosity about what a family might teach us about their understanding and traditions, creates a climate of relationship support honoring the family's narrative experience. This actively counters the experience of being treated in disrespectful or racist ways due to ethnic minority status, and of having relationships sidelined in the interest of high technology care in many settings. By conducting an appreciative inquiry, we have actively framed a way of listening, learning, goal setting and planning designed to reduce suffering and distress while also promoting positive developmental processes that mobilize positive adaptation and growth.

Culturally sensitive care requires a creative rethinking of our customary practice training, as we evaluate what we thought we knew for certain and discover the worlds of diverse patients we had little exposure to. It challenges us to learn new dimensions of our own cultural socialization in our own changing family life cycle, as we encounter diverse individuals struggling with illness mortality and loss. It rewards us with an extraordinary expansion of our world views and affirms the vast resources for replenishment available even in the midst of suffering and adversity.

Learning Objective: (35/40)

Learning Objective: (35/40)

Chapter 20

Religion, Spirituality, and Assessment and Intervention

Kenneth J. Doka

Introduction

One cannot understand life-threatening illness as only a medical crisis. It is a psychological, social, and family crisis as well. Yet, even more than that, it is a spiritual crisis — fraught with existential questions.

This chapter attempts to address, at least in part, those questions. The chapter begins by defining both spirituality and religion and exploring the ways that spirituality and religious faith influence the experience of life-threatening illness, death, and grief. It seeks to offer tools for assessing and utilizing the spiritual strengths of those who face illness and the prospect of death — recognizing that in this final encounter an individual needs to marshal all resources.

Religion and Spirituality: An Overview

Religion and spirituality are often elusive concepts that are difficult to define and differentiate. The International Workgroup on Dying, Death, and Bereavement defines spirituality as "concerned with the transcendental, inspirational, and existential way to live one's life" (1990, p.75). Miller's definition is more poetic:

Spirituality relates to our souls. It involves the deep inner essence of who we are. It is an openness to the possibility that the soul within each of us is somehow related to the Soul of all that is. Spirituality is what happens to us that is so memorable that we cannot forget it, and yet we find it hard to talk about because words fail to describe it. Spirituality is the act of looking for meaning in the very deepest sense; and looking for it in a way that is most authentically ours (1994).

To Miller, spirituality is inherently individual, personal, and eclectic. Religion, however, is more collective. Religion is a belief shared within a group of people.

Miller again offers a lyrical perspective:

Now religion works in a very different way. While spirituality is very personal, religion is more communal. In fact, if you take the words back to its origins, "religion means that which binds together," "that which ties things into a package." Religion has to do with collecting and consolidating and unifying. Religion says, "Here are special words that are meant to be passed on. Take them to heart." Religion says, "Here is a set of beliefs that form a coherent whole. Take them as your own." Religion says, "Here are people for you to revere and historical events for you to recall. Remember them." Religion says, "Here is a way for you to act when you come together as a group, and here's a way to behave when you're apart" (1994).

Thus while spirituality is very personal, a person's spirituality may very well be shaped by an individual's religious beliefs. Yet, because of the individual nature of spirituality, religious affiliation is not likely to be the sole determinant of spiritual beliefs. Often developmental outlooks, personal experiences, and cultural perspectives will join with religious beliefs in shaping an individual's spirituality.

However, whatever these beliefs are, they are likely to be challenged by life-threatening illness, dying, and death. As stated earlier, a life-threatening illness is an existential crisis. The encounter with the possibility or even the probability of death raises a series of questions. "Why do I have this diagnosis and why now?" "Is life worth this suffering, treatment, and uncertainty?" "Is it consistent with my belief system, my spirituality to cease treatment or forego certain types of treatment?" "If I recover what did I learn, what will I take, and what will I do with this experience?" "If I die, did my life have meaning, and how do I wish to die, and what will happen after?" Death brings similar questions: "Why did this person have to die — now or in this way?"

A life-threatening illness or death then is a reachable moment — a time where one's spirituality looms large. Because the assumptive world is now called into question a person is able to be reached — that is, to consider other ways to examine his/her spirituality. That spirituality may offer answers and reassurance, breeding resilience. Or that spirituality may seem empty now leading an existential despair or a new quest for a deeper spiritual sense that can sustain one in this crisis.

Religion and Spirituality: Complicating and Facilitating Factors

Research has indicated that religion and spirituality can both facilitate and complicate responses to life-threatening illness and grief. In reviewing this research, it is well to link both terms as the operational definitions of spirituality and religion vary considerably among the researchers. Nonetheless, this research has indicated that spirituality and religion can have positive roles in assisting individuals who struggle with life-threatening illness or grief.

For example, research has supported the fact that religion and spirituality can assist persons in finding a sense of meaning in the illness (Siegel & Schrimshaw, 2002). Often the diagnosis of a life-threatening illness challenges an individual's assumptive world as the person struggles with attempting to make sense of the illness. Later in the illness, individuals may seek to make sense of their suffering, their death, or their life.

Throughout this existential endeavor, religious and spiritual perspectives can offer meanings. Religious and spiritual perspectives may reassure persons with life-threatening illness that their illness is part of a larger plan or that the illness experience may offer lessons to self or others. Even with death, there is some evidence that religious and spiritual beliefs may minimize fear and uncertainty (Siegel & Schrimshaw, 2002). In short, spiritual and religious perspectives can assist individuals in making sense of the illness.

It may also allow a sense of a larger connection. Even in the inherent existential isolation of an illness, there may be a sense that a God or some Higher Power will sustain and protect. This connection may be more tangible as well. Many individuals may benefit from the social support available through the ministries of a chaplain, clergy, spiritual advisor, ministry team, or even within the larger faith community. The sense that one is not alone — others are caring, visiting, and praying seems to provide benefit (Siegel & Schrimshaw, 2002; Townsend, Kladder, & Mulligan, 2002).

Religious and spiritual practices and beliefs may even enhance health. Most spiritual belief systems suggest either abstinence or moderation in certain behaviors such as alcohol or tobacco use. Such practices and beliefs may discourage inappropriate coping techniques throughout the course of the illness or subsequent grief. Spiritual and religious beliefs also may enhance coping by encouraging self-esteem. Most religious and spiritual systems stress the inherent worth of the individual. Such beliefs may be especially important in a life-threatening illness or in grief where self-blame may loom large and self-acceptance is threatened. There is also some speculation that spiritual and religious beliefs may have physiological benefits such as lowering blood pressure or enhancing immune function through here the research has shown some inconsistency (Dane, 2000; Lin & Bauer-Wu, 2003; Miller & Thoresen, 2003; Olive, 2004; Sephton, Koopman, Shaal, Thoresen, & Spiegel 2001; Stefanek, McDonald & Hess, 2005).

Religious and spiritual beliefs also may influence an individual's sense of control. In a time of life-threatening illness, an individual may feel that they have little or no control. Religious and spiritual beliefs may reaffirm a sense of personal control. Self-efficacy can be expressed in a number of ways. Individuals may have a sense of interpretive control — that is the ability to find meaning or benefit from the experience. They may have a sense of vicarious control — leaving the illness in the hands of a Higher Power. In some cases, the control may be of a predictive nature, perhaps believing that God will cure them or be with them throughout this experience.

Yet, this discussion also demonstrates the ways that religious and spiritual beliefs may complicate the response to a life-threatening illness or grief. For example, a person with life-threatening illness may be convinced that he or she may be cured by a divine intervention. If death ensues such an individual or other family members may become immobilized, unrealistic in decisions, or even despondent.

Certain religious or spiritual beliefs may serve to increase rather than decrease death anxiety or complicate grief. For example, fears over divine judgment or uncertainty in an afterlife may not offer comfort to a dying person. The certainty with which religious and spiritual beliefs are held as well as the nature of such beliefs is a factor in the reasons that the relationship of religiosity and spirituality to death anxiety is inconsistent (Neimeyer, 1994). Moreover, religious and spiritual perspectives can sometimes conflict with medical practices and advice. For example, some spiritual systems such as Christian Science may eschew any medical treatment while others such as the Jehovah Witnesses may prohibit certain medical practices such as blood transfusions or blood-based therapies. In other cases, a fatalistic spirituality may inhibit health-seeking behaviors or adherence to a medical regimen. It is little wonder that Pargement, Koenig, Tarakeshwar, & Hahn (2004) found in a longitudinal study that certain types of religious coping such as seeking spiritual support or believing in a benevolent God were related with better health while other spiritual coping behaviors and beliefs such as a perspective of a punishing God or religious discontent were predictive of declines in health.

Religious and spiritual beliefs also may be evident in reactions to illness. For example, anger could be directed toward God. There may be anger that one has the disease or that the disease has come at an inopportune or unfair time. Guilt may be clouded by a moral guilt — a belief that this illness is a punishment for some transgression. Fear and anxiety, as mentioned earlier, can also have a religious or spiritual root, as one may fear the wrath of God in this world or the next. There may even be an existential sense of abandonment — a sense that one is facing the crisis alone, alienated from God. In all of these cases, religious and spiritual beliefs may intertwine with psychological and affective reactions to the illness.

Spiritual Task in Life-Threatening Illness

Throughout the illness, an individual may have to cope with distinctly spiritual tasks. In an earlier work (Doka, 1993b), I proposed, building on the work of both Weisman (1980) and Pattison (1978), that life-threatening illness can best be viewed as a series of phases. These phases are the prediagnostic, diagnostic, chronic, terminal, and recovery phases. In any particular disease, individuals may jump from one phase to another. For example, in some cases, a successful removal of a tumor may place an individual right into a recovery phase with virtually no chronic phase. In another disease, diagnosis may be immediately followed by a steep and inexorable decline toward death. In each phase, there were distinct medical, psychological, social, and spiritual tasks.

For example, with the first two phases, the prediagnostic and diagnostic phases, individuals had to deal with the diagnosis of a life-threatening illness. Weisman (1980) notes that even when the diagnosis is expected or feared, it still comes as a shock, creating a sense of "existential plight" where one's very existence is threatened. Often it is a life divide. Even if the person survives the encounter, it often will be seen as a turning point wrought with implications that follow for the rest of life.

Here the spiritual issue is incorporating the present reality of illness into one's sense of past and future. Questions such as: "Why did I get this disease, now?" loom large here. An individual now struggles to make sense of the disease and of the new reality of his or her life. Spiritual and religious beliefs may offer an answer to these questions or at least provide direction for further quest.

The chronic phase centers around the time of treatment. Here the individual must not only cope with the disease but also the burdens and side effects of treatment. Often as persons continue such treatment, they may resume some of their prior roles — returning to work or functioning within their families. Often, this time is lonely. The crisis of the diagnosis is now past, so family, friends, and other social support may not be as available. This phase can also be a time of great uncertainty as individuals cope with the ambiguities of both the disease and treatment. In the chronic phase, suffering may become a major spiritual issue. "Why am I suffering through this disease and treatment?" "Is it all worth it?" Persons will often look to their religious or spiritual beliefs to make sense of this suffering. Their beliefs may vary. Again some may see the suffering as retribution for sins in this or another life. Some may even find comfort, believing that suffering now may offer recompense or even purification that will mollify God or better prepare them for an afterlife. Others may see suffering as random. Still others may see their suffering as a learning experience allowing greater empathy. Others may see it as sacrifice, offering it as a way to gain a greater connection to God or others. Such beliefs can strongly influence patients' receptiveness to pain management (Doka, 2006).

Not everyone dies from life-threatening illness. Many individuals may fully recover, resuming their lives and others may face long, even permanent, periods of remission. Yet, the encounter with disease leaves all types of residues. Individuals may have an enhanced sense of their fragility, feeling that they are living under a sword that can strike at any time (Koocher & O'Malley, 1981).

There also are spiritual residues. Individuals may struggle with a sense of "the bargain." It is not unusual for persons to make spiritual commitments and promises in a cosmic deal to surmount the illness. Now that they have recovered from this threat, individuals may now feel they have to fulfill their promises. A failure to fulfill such commitments may loom large should a person experience a relapse or even encounter another disease.

There may be other spiritual changes as well. Some individuals may move closer to their religion or become more spiritually aware and active. Others may feel alienated either from their God or their spiritual community. Some may actively seek a new spirituality, perceiving that their past beliefs did not serve them well in this crisis.

During the course of a life-threatening illness, patients and their families will have to make critical ethical decisions about care. How long should active medical treatment persist even if it is perceived a futile? When should treatment cease and who should be empowered to make such determinations? Should the patient receive artificial hydration and nutrition? Can treatments be withheld, or if administered, withdrawn? Is assisted suicide ever a valid ethical choice in life-threatening illness?

Health professionals have long realized that religious and spiritual systems play a significant role in the ways that patients and their families make end-of-life decisions and resolve ethical dilemmas (Koenig, 2004). As patients and their families struggle with these decisions, they often turn to their religious and spiritual values, and even to their clergy or spiritual mentors, for guidance.

The terminal phase, the goals of treatment moves from extending life or curing the individual to a strictly palliative goal. In this phase, individuals often struggle with three spiritual needs (Doka, 1993a; 1993b). The first is to have lived a meaningful life. Individuals may assess their life to find a sense of meaning and purpose. Here individuals may struggle seeking forgiveness for tasks unaccomplished or for hurtful acts that they may have committed. Life Review and Reminiscence Therapy can assist individuals in achieving a sense of meaningfulness. Individuals may struggle with a second goal — to die an appropriate death, however that experience is individually defined. A final spiritual need is to find hope beyond the grave: the individual needs a sense that life will continue — in whatever appropriate way is supported by the person's spiritual understanding. This sense of continuity can include living on the memories of others, in the genes of family members, within one's community, in the creations and legacies left, in a sense of "eternal nature" (that is that one returns to the cycle of life), in some transcendental mode, or in an afterlife (Lifton & Olsen. 1974: Doka 1993b).

Spirituality and Grief: After the Death

Families, too, may cope with similar spiritual issues. Even after the individual dies, the family may still spiritually struggle, trying to reconstruct their own faith or spiritual system that may have been challenged by that loss (Doka, 1993a). There may be very significant spiritual issues as individuals experience grief. Bereaved individuals may experience a number of spiritual reactions. There may be a loss of faith. Individuals who are grieving may have a spiritual or cosmic anger — alienating them from sources of spiritual strengths such as their beliefs, rituals, faith practices, or their faith community. They may experience a sense of "moral guilt" — or a belief that the death of the deceased is due to some moral failing or sin that is now being punished.

As in illness, spirituality can be both facilitating and complicating. It may allow a sense of meaning — that this loss fulfills some purpose or is part of a cosmic plan. Spirituality can offer a sense of connection — a belief that the deceased is now safe or happy, or a belief that even entertains a possibility of future contact or reunion. Spiritual beliefs and practices can even allow a continuing connection — through, for example, prayer, veneration of ancestors, or other some other form of contact.

Yet, not all beliefs or practices are facilitating. Some beliefs may disallow or disenfranchise the normal feelings of grief as indicating a lack of faith. Other beliefs may trouble the bereaved. For example, a survivor of a committed suicide who feels that a person who commits suicide faces eternal damnation may find such a belief complicates grief.

Assisting Individuals and Families at the End-of-Life: Utilizing Spirituality

Since spirituality is so central as individuals and their families struggle with later life, it is important that holistic care includes spiritual assessment. While there are a variety of tools to assist assessment (Hodge, 2005; Ledger, 2005), the key really is to engage both the individual and family in an exploration of their individual and collective spiritual histories. The goal is to understand the collective and individual spiritual journeys. Do they identify with a particular faith? Do they actively practice that faith — engaging in public and private rituals and practices? Do they belong to a church, temple, synagogue, or mosque? How important is their faith system in making decisions?

Such an assessment should go beyond religious affiliation. It might be worthwhile to explore with individuals when and where they feel most spiritually connected. What practices they utilize when they're stressed, anxious or depressed? What are the stories, prayers, or songs that offer spiritual comfort? Such approaches may allow a larger exploration of the very distinct ways that individuals find meaning and hope. An assessment may yield information on spiritual strengths that an individual possesses, themes within an individual's spirituality (such as grace, karma, fate, or retribution etc.), and experiences that have tended to challenge that person's spirituality. Occasionally, such an assessment may uncover forms of spiritual abuse — spiritual beliefs or practices or behaviors of spiritual mentors that have resulted in a sense of spiritual alienation.

Once an assessment of spirituality is made, an individual can be encouraged to connect with their spiritual strengths. Often, this connection involves their clergy, chaplains, spiritual mentors, or members of their faith community. Clergy, chaplains, and other spiritual mentors can play an important supportive (and sometimes an unsupportive) role as an individual responds to a life-threatening illness, death, or grief. Their visits throughout the illness may be valued. Clergy, chaplains, and other spiritual advisors may be sought as an individual or family member responds to the spiritual questions inherent in the experiences of grief and illness. Despite the importance of ministry to the ill, the dying and bereaved, many clergy reported little formal seminary education on dealing with dying patients and their families (Doka &Jendreski, 1985; Abrams, Albury, Crandall, Doka, & Harris. 2005).

While clergy, chaplains, and other spiritual mentors play an important role, faith communities also can play a critical role. Often, such communities can offer spiritual comfort and connection; visits, calls, cards, and letters that show support and ease isolation; and assistance with tangible tasks such as cooking, home maintenance, transportation, and caregiving.

Spiritual beliefs and practices also may be sources of strength. A person's spiritual beliefs may be critical in making meaning throughout an illness and for family, after the death. Often a simple question such as, "How do your beliefs speak to you in this situation?" can engage the person in spiritual exploration. It may also be useful to investigate the ways that the individual's beliefs assisted and helped the person make sense of the experience in earlier crisis. There may be situations where the individual's beliefs seem inadequate or dysfunctional.

Spiritual practices such as prayer and meditation also may have a role in the illness. At the very least, intercessory prayer (that is the prayer of others), is a tangible sign that the individual is not facing this crisis alone. It offers family and friends a tangible thing to do — reaffirming a form of vicarious control in an unsettled time. Individuals who are struggling with physical illness often use prayer as a form of coping (Ribbentrop, Altmaier, Chen, Found, & Keffala, 2005). There is some evidence that prayer and meditation do affect physical health in a number of ways including lowering stress levels and blood pressure (Mayo Clinic Health Letter, 2005). Schroeder-Sheker (1994) has even pioneered the field of musical thanatology, using spiritual music as a way to ease the transition to death. T.Q. #7

Rituals also can be a source of comfort to both the ill or dying patient as well as family. Many faith traditions that have rituals for the sick and the dying, such as the Roman Catholic Rite for Anointing of the Sick (popularly known as "Last Rites") or rituals at the time of death such as washing or preparing the body.

Individuals who do not have distinctive rituals as part of their tradition may still be invited to create one at the time of death. Lighting a candle, anointing the dead person, and joining in prayer or meditation, singing a spiritual hymn or song, or in other, individual ways saying a final goodbye to mark the transition from life to death. Rituals work well in these liminal or transitional moments — offering participants a way to acknowledge loss and transition.

Certainly rituals after the death such as funerals can be critically important to families and others as they cope with loss. Funerals can allow mourners a sense of reality of death, a chance to ventilate feelings, meaningful actions in a disorganized time, opportunities to remember the deceased, bring together supportive others, and interpret the death according to their own philosophical or spiritual background (Rando, 1984). The value of funerals can be enhanced when mourners have opportunities to plan and participate in the ritual (Doka and Jendreski, 1985). Moreover rituals can be utilized therapeutically throughout the mourning process (Martin & Doka, 2000).

Conclusion: The Challenge of Spiritual Support

Spiritual support can be a challenge. Many health professionals have little specialized training in spirituality. Moreover, there may be concern lest one impose his or her own spirituality upon a patient or family member. Sometimes out of respect for the diversity and individuality of a person's spiritual beliefs, health professionals may be reluctant to enter into conversations involving religion or spirituality. Thus, there often is temptation to leave these issues to chaplains, clergy, or other spiritual mentors. Such delegation to spiritual mentors is unlikely to suffice. Spiritual concerns arise throughout the entire experience of the illness. Patients and families will choose when, where, and with whom they will share these spiritual concerns. These choices may not always fit into neat organizational charts or job descriptions. They are the responsibility of the team.

Nor can these spiritual concerns be neglected. Holistic care entails that spiritual concerns both are acknowledged and validated. A true respect for spirituality means that such concerns and struggles need by addressed by every professional. Spirituality therefore cannot be ignored. Death, after all, may be the ultimate spiritual journey.

LEARNING OBJECTIVE: (40/40)

Describe the role of religion and
Spirituality in Assessment and
intervention in end-of-life B'ment
CARE.

Chapter 21

Historical and Contemporary Perspectives on Assessment and Intervention

John R. Jordan & Robert A. Neimeyer

Historically, care for the dying and the bereaved has been the responsibility of family members and the larger community. People have traditionally sought comfort and support from those who knew the deceased and shared the loss. The development of organized professional caregiving systems to provide support and intervene with cases of problematic grief has been essentially a 20th century development, rooted in the rise of psychotherapy as a distinct intervention for mental distress of all types. The growth of organizations such as ADEC and the inclusion of mandated bereavement care in federally funded hospice services suggests that organized bereavement care systems are viewed as necessary and valuable adjuncts to informal community support in the face of loss. This chapter offers a brief review of these more formal caregiving systems, and the approaches that have developed to ameliorate problematic grief responses. It is divided into four sections: (1) historical perspectives, (2) contemporary methods of assessment, (3) interventions for grief, and (4) future directions for this area of thanatology. For reasons of space, we will focus primarily on problematic patterns of grief and on the responses of adults (rather than children) to the death of a loved one.

Historical Perspectives on Assessment and Intervention

Foundational Ideas about Normal and Complicated Grieving

Perhaps inevitably, efforts to understand problematic grief lead to questions about the boundary between "normal" and complicated responses. Indeed, the issue of what constitutes normal grief, and whether there is any form of grief response that should be "pathologized," is one that is still contested within thanatology (N. S. Hogan, Worden, & Schmidt, 2006; Neimeyer, 2006a; Prigerson & Maciejewski, 2006). While the potential for losses to be devastating has been the subject of human reflection for thousands of years, the scientific study of bereavement can be dated to the work of Sigmund Freud (Freud, 1957). His idea that healthy mourning involved decathexis (the withdrawal of emotional energy from the deceased), while pathological bereavement involved a failure to psychologically "let go" of the deceased, has profoundly influenced both professional and public views of what is to be expected in mourning. Subsequently, most of the major 20th century bereavement theorists have set forth variations on this theme of decathexis (Bowlby, 1980; Parkes, 1996).

Closely related is the conceptualization of the mourning process as psychological work that entails experiencing and expressing the difficult thoughts, emotions, and memories that have been triggered by the loss (Rando, 1995). Seen from this broad psychodynamic perspective, grieving has been viewed as a process of painfully reviewing or "working through" and then letting go of the attachment to the deceased by way of confrontation with the reality of the death and catharsis of the resulting emotions. This has been referred to as the "griefwork hypothesis" (Stroebe, Gergen, Gergen, & Stroebe, 1992). From this perspective, assessment of the grieving process involves judging the extent to which this griefwork has been accomplished (or avoided), and interventions are designed to facilitate the resolution of the attachment by assisting in this necessary labor. The failure to confront the reality of the loss, as well as the failure to perform the psychological work involved in letting go, have been viewed as the core of a pathological grief response. Note that this viewpoint is largely intrapsychic in nature, with pathological grief residing within the "psychological skin" of the mourner.

Building upon this foundation, the 20th century also saw the emergence of various stage and task models of bereavement. Beginning with the popularity of Kubler-Ross's book *On Death & Dying* (Kubler-Ross, 1969), stage and task theories have been widely accepted by the professional community as well as the public. Typically, these models suggest that mourners begin in a state of denial of the reality of the loss, and move through a series of unwelcome emotional phases of adaptation marked by anger, bargaining and depression before achieving some form of acceptance or resolution. Alternatively, other theorists emphasize the necessary activities of grieving, such as the need to accept the reality of the death, experience the pain of the grief, and adjust to an environment in which the deceased is missing (Worden, 2002) Correspondingly, the failure to progress through the stages or tasks implies unfinished griefwork, and interventions are presumably designed to facilitate this uncompleted activity.

Recent Challenges to the Traditional Griefwork Model

These traditional views of mourning are being challenged on many fronts in contemporary thanatology. For example, longitudinal studies of bereavement adaptation fail to provide any support for a model of stages of emotional response to grief (Zhang, Maciejewski, Block, Vanderwerker, & Prigerson, 2007). Furthermore, new research has called into question the necessity of confronting and working through a loss for all mourners. These researchers present compelling data that suggest that, at least after spousal loss, not everyone appears to go through a painful process of depression and mourning. They argue that traditional models of grief have underestimated the resilience of people's capacity to adapt to loss and trauma (Bonanno, 2004; Bonanno, Wortman, & Nesse, 2004; Wortman & Silver, 1987).

Likewise, the idea that decathexis is central to the process of grieving is being challenged by theorists who argue that the establishment of on-going bonds with the deceased is both healthier and more normative across human cultures than the notion of detachment from the deceased (Klass, Silverman, & Nickman, 1996; Rubin, 1999). While refinements are emerging in the types of continuing bond with the deceased that may be adaptive or pathological (Field, Gao, & Paderna, 2005), the field appears to be rapidly moving away from the earlier view that, successful mourning necessarily involves a relinquishment of the emotional attachment to the deceased. Instead, evidence suggests that maintaining an emotional bond with the loved one may be comforting or distressing, depending on such factors as how far along survivors are in their bereavement (Field & Friedrichs, 2004), whether they have been able to "make sense" of the loss (Neimeyer, Baldwin, & Gillies, 2006), and perhaps their level of security in important attachment relationships (Stroebe & Schut, 2005).

In the wake of growing skepticism about traditional models of mourning, new theories have been proposed. One such model is the Dual Process Model of coping with bereavement formulated by Stroebe and Schut (Stroebe & Schut, 1999), which argues that normal grief involves an oscillation between confronting the loss (Loss Orientation) and compartmentalizing it so that the mourner can attend to the life changes necessitated by the death (Restoration Orientation). This important departure from traditional thinking describes mourning as a cyclical rather than a linear and stage-like process, as the mourner repeatedly revisits the loss and its associated emotions, strives to reorganize the relationship to the deceased, and to take on new roles and responsibilities necessitated by a changed world. This formulation also extends our understanding of pathology by suggesting that the inability to distract oneself from or avoid grief may be as much a sign of pathology as the inability to confront it.

A second important development is the emergence of narrative or constructivist theories about the mourning process. In this view, bereavement is viewed as challenging the survivor's self-narrative, the basic organization of life events and themes that allows them to interpret the past, invest in the present, and anticipate the future (Neimeyer, 2001). When life events such as the death of a loved one disrupt the "assumptive world" (Janoff-Bulman & Berger, 2000) whereby a person maintains a sense of coherence, identity, and direction, a prolonged struggle to integrate the loss can result (Neimeyer, 2006b). Recent evidence demonstrates that such disruptions are especially profound in cases of suicide, homicide, and fatal accidents, where the inability to "make sense" of the death accounts for the more debilitating grief responses stemming from violent, as opposed to natural deaths (Currier, Holland, & Neimeyer, 2006), From this vantage point, griefwork is not simply a matter of emotional catharsis, but rather a process of meaning reconstruction whereby the mourner re-establishes the sense of coherence of their narrative structures after a loss (Neimeyer, 2002).

Lastly, although social support has generally been acknowledged as important by most grief theorists, the failure to grieve "successfully" has traditionally been understood as a problem contained within the individual mourner. Recent approaches, particularly those based in the "meaning reconstruction" view just mentioned, have begun to focus on the transactional nature of mourning (Nadeau, 1997; Neimeyer & Jordan, 2002). This view suggests that the meaning of the loss for an individual cannot be separated from the family, community, and societal meanings ascribed to death and loss and the resulting social responses to the mourner. This more social-psychological approach recognizes that the bereaved must adapt not only to a world where the deceased is no longer physically available, but where many other altered aspects of the post-loss interpersonal landscape must be confronted. While these changes have clear intrapsychic components, they also intimately involve the interactions that mourners have with other people, who provide approval and support for or disapproval and withdrawal from the bereaved based on the fit of the mourner's coping style with their altered social networks. Broadly sociological theories of grief (Walter, 1999) and data from family studies (Traylor, Hayslip, Kaminski, & York, 2003) reinforce this perspective.

Implications for Understanding Complicated Grief

All of these developments in bereavement theory are changing our understanding of what constitutes an expectable response to loss. These new ideas are also reshaping and expanding our view of what constitutes pathological grief. This shift can be summarized by noting that thanatology is developing a more complex and refined understanding of the heterogeneity of the grief response, rather than its uniformity. The implications of this shift are very important for intervention, since the general "one size fits all" approach of traditional bereavement services fails to take into account differences in mourner personality, culture, gender, life situation, and death circumstances. In the next section, we will focus on contemporary developments in the assessment of grief that flow from these emerging conceptualizations of the mourning process.

Contemporary Perspectives on the Assessment of Grief

The Development of a Complicated Grief Diagnosis

The mental health community, as represented by the current edition of the Diagnostic and Statistical Manual of the American Psychiatric Association (DSM IV-R), does not formally recognize any pattern of grief as pathological. Bereavement is a viewed as a life problem that may need clinical attention, but it is not, in and of itself, a mental disorder—instead difficulties adjusting to a loss must be diagnosed in terms of depression, anxiety, or other disorders, such as posttraumatic stress disorder (PTSD). This official position notwithstanding, there has been a movement over the last 15 years to create a new diagnostic category called Complicated Grief (CG). If the CG diagnosis is accepted, the particular pattern of grief response described in the proposed criteria (see Table 1) would officially become a psychiatric disorder in the next edition of the DSM.

Table 1. Criteria for Complicated Grief Proposed for DSM-V

Criterion A: Chronic and disruptive yearning, pining, longing for the deceased.

Criteria B: The person must have four of the following eight remaining symptoms at least several times a day or to a degree intense enough to be distressing and disruptive:
1. Trouble accepting the death
2. Inability to trust others
3. Excessive bitterness or anger related to the death
4. Uneasiness about moving on (for example, making new friends, pursuing new interests)
5. Numbness/Detachment (for example, feeling disconnected from others)
6. Feeling that life is empty or meaningless without deceased
7. Feeling bleak about the future
8. Agitation (for example, jumpiness or edginess)
Criterion C. The above symptom disturbance causes marked and persistent dysfunction in social, occupational or other important domains.
Criterion D. The above symptom disturbance must last at least 6 months.
Adapted from: Prigerson & Maciejewski (2006)

The criteria for CG essentially describe a combination of intense and prolonged yearning for the deceased, along with signs that the mourner's adaptation socially and psychologically has been compromised by the death. Note that the diagnosis refers to symptoms experienced by the mourner, regardless of the circumstances of the death, which may or may not be sudden or violent. A considerable amount of empirical research has demonstrated that the presence of CG is associated with elevated rates of psychological distress, physical illness, and social dysfunction (Ott, 2003; Prigerson & Jacobs, 2001). Moreover, the CG diagnosis has been shown to cohere as a predictive symptom cluster and to differ sufficiently from major depression and post-traumatic stress disorder to be legitimately considered a separate diagnostic category (Prigerson & Maciejewski, 2006).

The movement to develop the CG diagnosis has not been without its critics. Concerns about this work range from the potentially deleterious effects of "medicalizing" and pathologizing grief to the validity of the precise criteria being proposed (Hogan et al., 2006). Nonetheless, it appears that some version of the proposed criteria will find its way into the diagnostic nomenclature of DSM-V, and thus into the thinking of many medical and mental health professionals. Moreover, the acceptance of this diagnostic category will likely pave the way for new research into the causes and course of CG, methods for treating the syndrome, and insurance reimbursement for that treatment. While other patterns of problematic response have been described (such as avoided or inhibited grief, distorted grief, etc. (Rando, 1995), the outline of grief described in the proposed criteria for CG is rapidly becoming the *de facto* definition of a problematic grief response.

Risk Factors and Assessment Methods

Bereavement outcome research over the last 40 years has identified a number of factors that are associated with and predictive of the development of problematic grief responses, including CG. These include a lack of forewarning about the death, violence in the manner of death, the lack of perceived social support following the death, previous exposure to loss and trauma, a history of psychiatric disorder (particularly affective disorders such as depression), and an insecure attachment style (Parkes, 1990; Stroebe & Schut, 2001). Moreover, certain categories of mourners are more likely to experience elevated rates of problematic grief. The relevant variables appear to be close kinship relationship to the deceased (for example, bereaved mothers) and survivors of certain types of losses (for example, suicide) (Jordan, 2001).

A number of paper and pencil measures for the assessment of the grief response have been developed. Although widely used, early measures such as the Texas Revised Inventory of Grief (Faschingbauer, 1981) and the Grief Experience Inventory (Sanders, Mauger, & Strong, 1985) have a questionable psychometric

foundation (Neimeyer & Hogan, 2001). Several newer bereavement measures offer the promise of more psychometrically valid and clinically useful tools. These include the Hogan Grief Reaction Checklist (Hogan, Greenfield, & Schmidt, 2001), the Core Bereavement Items (Middleton, Burnett, Raphael, & Martinek, 1996), the Grief Evaluation Measure (GEM) (Jordan, Baker, Matteis, Rosenthal, & Ware, 2005), and the Inventory of Complicated Grief (ICG) (Prigerson & Jacobs, 2001). Of particular interest is the ICG, which has been developed as a measure that specifically taps into the symptoms of CG outlined in the proposed diagnostic criteria. Some specialized bereavement measures have also been created for specific types of losses, including suicide (Barrett & Scott, 1989), sibling loss (Hogan & De Santis, 1992), and perinatal loss (Toedter, Lasker, & Alhadeff, 1988). All of these measures show promise in helping the assessment process in bereavement care become more evidence based and effective in coming years.

Key Elements to Consider in Assessing the Grief Response

As a prelude to bereavement counseling, a thorough assessment of the mourner should cover a broad range of domains. These include:

1. *The mourner's narrative of the death and of their reactions to the loss.* This domain includes the trajectory of any illness and circumstances of the death, the mourner's participation (or lack of it) in the dying process, the funeral, and the subsequent experience of living without the deceased. Of particular relevance is the individual's perception of how prepared they were for the death, as well as any aspects of the death that were horrifying or terrifying for the survivor, since they are likely to indicate traumatic as well as grief responses.

2. *An exploration of the meaning of the loss for the mourner.* This domain is obviously a broad topic, and facilitating discovery of the meaning of the loss can be a central goal of grief counseling itself. Topics might include the role of the deceased in the mourner's life, the nature of the relationship with the deceased, the changes that the loss is bringing about in the mourner's psychological and interpersonal world, and the degree to which the coherence of the mourner's assumptive world has been challenged.

3. *The grieving person's own evaluation of his or her response to loss.* Asking, "Is there anything about the way that you are responding to this loss that especially concerns you?" can alert the clinician to a range of less obvious problems, such as his or her sensed failure to function in other important relationships (such as those with chil-

dren), as well as acute problems such as suicide ideation. It can also help bring to light aspects of grieving that might be disallowed and hard for the griever to acknowledge or accept, such as anger or guilt.

4. *An assessment of the ethnic, cultural, religious, gender based, and social class factors that affect the mourner's experience of the loss.* These aspects often give a sense of the implicit "grieving rules" to which the survivor is striving to conform.

5. *The quality of perceived social support from family and the larger community.* This domain includes the degree to which mourners feel understood by others in their grief and the amount of interpersonal strain or abandonment that has occurred around the loss. Also important is an assessment of the mourner's interpersonal skills and willingness to elicit social support from others in their network.

6. *The psychiatric history of the mourner.* Of particular relevance are major affective disorders (depression and bipolar disorder), post - traumatic stress disorder, and substance abuse problems. If the mourner has a positive history for psychiatric disorder, follow-up should investigate whether the person has received treatment, its success, and any signs of the disorder(s) reoccurring within the context of the grief

7. *The stability of the mourner's life situation*, including employment, marital and family relationships, and living arrangements.

8. *Additional stressors the mourner may be confronting*, such as health, financial, interpersonal, and work related difficulties.

9. *The quality of the mourner's past relationships*, both in their family of origin and in subsequent relationships. Of particular importance is the quality of close relationships with attachment figures, and of relationships that may have been abusive or traumatizing.

10. *The coping skills possessed by the mourner.* The mourner's ability to both confront the reality of the loss when necessary (Loss Orientation in the Dual Process model) and to avoid the grief to make necessary changes in their world (Restoration Orientation) is very pertinent. Also significant are the person's previous coping methods when faced with emotional injuries and losses, with particular attention paid to coping efforts that are self-defeating or self-destructive (for example, substance abuse, suicidal behavior, etc.). The manner in which the mourner has adapted to earlier life losses can also suggest personal, social, and spiritual resources that could be useful in dealing with the current loss.

11. *The mourner's expectations about counseling and how it might be of help.* Previous experiences with therapy (whether bereavement related or not), and their perceived helpfulness or unhelpfulness, will also be important to assess.

Interventions for Bereavement

Types of Interventions

There is simply no universally agreed upon intervention to assist with problematic grief, or even to facilitate the normal grieving process. There also is very little data on the numbers of people who actually receive some type of formal intervention after the death of a loved one. In the United States, hospices routinely provide some type of bereavement follow-up with families that have received services. Hospices are probably the largest providers of bereavement care in the U.S. The typical hospice offers some type of follow-up (phone call, home visit, etc.) with the bereaved over the first year. Hospices also may provide a general bereavement support group for adults, as well as specialized bereavement services for particular populations, such as summer camps for grieving children.

Other community organizations that provide bereavement care may include funeral homes, churches, hospitals, and social service agencies, with the great majority of these providing facilitated bereavement support groups. Likewise, there are "self-help" organizations, such as the Compassionate Friends (Klass, 1999) or Widow to Widow (Silverman, 2005), that offer "drop-in" type bereavement support groups or other forms of support. Most agency sponsored support groups are conducted by a mental health professional or clergyperson, while self-help groups are typically facilitated by a lay survivor(s). Researchers have conducted very few controlled studies of the effectiveness of the typical community-based grief support group. Nor has there been much standardization of the models used to guide these types of groups, although creative curricula to guide the conduct of such groups have been offered, incorporating not only emotional self-expression and group problem solving, but also a wide range of storytelling, expressive arts, music, meditation and body work procedures (Rogers, 2007).

A variant of the support group model is Critical Incident Stress Debriefing (CISD) or Management (CISM). This procedure employs a structured protocol for a group meeting (typically a single session) after a traumatic event, such as a natural disaster or a terrorist attack. Participants are encouraged to recount their experience with the distressing situation and are offered information about the nature of the post-traumatic response. Originally developed for emergency response workers such as police and fire personnel, this form of intervention has been widely adopted by organizations involved with disaster response, such as the American Red Cross. More recently, however, CISM has been criticized as lacking in empirical support, and possibly even harmful for some participants (Gist & Lubin, 1999; Litz, 2004).

Still another important variant of the support group model is the Dougy Center in Portland, OR (www.dougy.org). This pioneering children's bereavement service offers developmentally attuned play or discussion support groups for bereaved children of all ages, plus discussion/support groups for parents. The program has been extensively replicated in the United States and around the world, and is widely accepted as a valuable form of bereavement care for children, although again, formal studies of the efficacy of the program appear to be lacking at this time.

With regard to individual grief counseling, again, there is no one model that has been studied or universally accepted. Worden (2002) and Rando (1993) have authored the most widely used textbooks in grief counseling, and their published works have been extremely influential with bereavement care professionals. Generally speaking, the dominant psychodynamic view of mourning described earlier has meant that most interventions focus on providing support for the client to confront the reality of the loss, engage in emotional catharsis, and diminish the attachment to the deceased. Perhaps the best known technique of grief counseling is the "empty chair" (Worden, 2002), wherein the mourner is instructed to have an imaginal conversation with the deceased. This procedure can be viewed as an opportunity to deal with "unfinished business" and say goodbye, or as an occasion to develop and strengthen a continuing bond with the deceased. However, "chair work" can be quite evocative, and so is probably best undertaken by clinicians who are well grounded in emotion focused and experiential therapies (Greenberg, Watson, & Lietaer, 1998).

A small number of family oriented interventions for bereavement care have also been presented. Shapiro has described a model that draws on psychodynamic, family developmental, and cross-cultural perspectives to provide support for grieving families (Shapiro, 1994). Walsh and McGoldrick (Walsh and McGoldrick, 2004) and Nadeau (Nadeau, 1997) have also articulated principles that emerge from a systemically informed constructivist or meaning making point of view.

Research on Bereavement Interventions and Promising Evidence-Based Programs

While having intuitive appeal and face validity, most of the intervention services in bereavement care lack any empirical evaluation. The well known Institute of Medicine report in 1984 indicated that our research-based knowledge about bereavement interventions was quite limited (Osterweis, Solomon, & Green, 1984). A recent similar summary of the progress in the field reported that while there is considerably more data now about the nature of grief, there is still a relative lack of empirical evidence on which to base interventions (Center for the Advancement of Health, 2004). Jordan and Neimeyer (2003) have reviewed the empirical meta-analyses of grief counseling and concluded that there is relatively little evidence that grief interventions (whether group or individual) are effective or even necessary for uncomplicated grief reactions. However, they did suggest that for high risk mourners, interventions appear to be more efficacious, highlighting the need to identify and intervene with this population. Jordan and Neimeyer also found that the design of the research on bereavement interventions often lacks methodological rigor or sophistication, making it difficult to draw conclusions about the effectiveness of the services. A recent review of the outcome of controlled evaluations of grief therapy for children yields similar conclusions (Currier, Holland, & Neimeyer, 2007).

Despite the general lack of an empirical foundation for most bereavement care, there are some examples of promising programs that are derived from theory, clearly operationalized, and evidence-based in their evaluation. Sandler and his colleagues have developed the Family Bereavement Program, a well conceptualized group support program for parentally bereaved children and surviving caretakers that has shown long-term efficacy for helping parentally bereaved children (particularly girls) (Sandler et al., 2003). Likewise, Kissane and colleagues have reported on Family Focused Grief Therapy, a family oriented intervention for use in palliative care that shows evidence of effectiveness with certain types of family styles (Kissane et al., 2006). Goodkin and his colleagues have published studies on the effectiveness of bereavement support groups for people bereaved through the loss of a loved one to AIDS. Impressively, these groups have shown measures of not only psychological but physiological (for example, immune system) improvement in the participants (Goodkin et al., 1999). Shear and her associates have reported data on the first treatment protocol specifically developed for the treatment of complicated grief (Shear, Frank, Houch, & Reynolds, 2005). This treatment is a multi-faceted intervention that includes psychoeducation about the grieving process, cognitive restructuring of negative grief related thoughts, a social network intervention, homework assignments to engage in new activities, repeated review of the mourner's reactions to the death, and an "empty chair" dialogue with the deceased. This treatment was found to be superior to another treatment often employed in bereavement or depression situations called Interpersonal Therapy. Lastly, a German research group has recently reported impressive outcomes for an individualized Internet-based intervention for people with complicated grief, which like the Shear et al. intervention has a strong narrative component (Wagner, Knaevelsrud, & Maercker, 2006).

Future Trends in Assessment and Intervention

An organizing theme in this chapter has been the sweeping changes in theory and practice in bereavement care that thanatology is witnessing. We would like to conclude with some thoughts about the implications of these changes for the future of assessment and intervention in bereavement care. A fundamental conclusion of the research on bereavement outcome over the last 25 years is that most mourners probably do not need formal or professional intervention after the death of a loved one. Human resilience in the face of loss has been the subject of literature and the arts for many years. It appears now that social science is confirming that such resilience may be more the norm than the exception for most people after most losses.

In contrast, another important conclusion is the recognition that for a subset of mourners, the risks of an unfavorable bereavement trajectory may be high. Both clinical practice and empirical study are revealing that mourners with certain types of backgrounds (for example, a history of insecure attachments, abuse, trauma, or excessive loss), or who have endured certain types of death circumstances (for example, sudden, violent death), or for whom good social support is missing (for example, stigmatization for suicide survivors), the probability of developing a CG response is much higher. Thus, we believe that in the coming years bereavement care professionals will increase their focus on identifying these high-risk mourners and then designing services that address their often complex needs.

This fundamental observation about the differences between high-risk and low-risk mourners has additional implications. We believe that the effort to develop the new CG diagnosis, while not without its potential problems, is an impressive and empirically grounded effort to identify those at risk for a more problematic course of bereavement. If this new diagnostic category is adopted, we expect that it will lead to a valuable increase in research and clinical innovation in ways to provide help to high-risk survivors. Accompanying this activity will be an increase in more objective methods for assessing complicated bereavement reactions, and an increase in awareness by caregivers (medical, human service, and clerical) about the necessity of providing help for mourners who are not likely to recover on their own.

A second trend that seems likely to grow is the recognition that both assessment and intervention in thanatology must become more culturally sensitive. While this statement obviously refers to developing culturally competent responses to mourners of differing ethnic, racial, and religious heritages, it also applies to the other social differences that people bring to encounters with organized bereavement care systems. Differences that arise out of gender, sexual orientation, age, ability, social class, family style, and individual personality all need to be better studied and incorporated into the design of interventions for the bereaved. At the risk of over-generalizing, most bereavement care interventions have evolved to meet the needs of Caucasian, middle class, older female mourners. We hope and expect that over time, our ability to assess and offer assistance that is customized to the particular needs of a much wider range of mourners will increase, so that individuals and families seeking help will be able to comfortably utilize the resources provided, rather than struggling to adapt to services that may seem alien to those whose bereavement coping style does not fit the limited range of services currently offered.

Thirdly, we believe that there will be a growing interest in bridging the great gap that exists between bereavement caregivers who are "in the field" and researchers and academics "in the ivory tower" (Bridging Work Group, 2005; Jordan, 2000). Perhaps more than most human service areas, much of the assistance given to the bereaved in formal support programs is provided by "para-professionals" — clergy, hospice volunteers, lay leaders of self-help groups, etc. We believe that the findings of social science research should be made available to bereavement care providers at all levels of professional standing in all types of settings. Likewise, we hope that researchers and theoreticians will do more to study the grief support programs that are routinely delivered in the settings where the bereaved are being served. Researchers should look not only to caregivers, but also to "consumers" of bereavement care, that is, the bereaved themselves, for inspiration and support in developing studies that have more relevance in the "real world." We are encouraged by the growing efforts at bridging the gaps between caregivers and providers through organizations such as ADEC and its certification process for the field.

Finally, we believe that in the future the specialization of bereavement care will pay more attention to fostering growth and resilience after loss, not simply ameliorating psychopathology. The new research on resilience, the focus on the development of continuing bonds with the deceased, and the promising studies of post traumatic growth all suggest that loss can be a source of psychological maturation for human beings, not simply emotional injury. The field has just begun to consider how good bereavement care might foster this kind of growth in the bereaved. We look forward to the emergence of new approaches and techniques that invoke the potential inherent in all loss for the growth of self-awareness, interpersonal connection, and a deeper understanding of what it means to be alive.

LEARNING Objective: (35/35)
Describe the Major theoretical shifts in
thanatology over the last century and
the ways in which these have influenced
CARE.

Chapter 22

Life Span Issues and Assessment and Intervention

David A. Crenshaw

It is impossible to separate assessment from intervention because sound intervention strategies need to be based on a careful assessment of developmental and life
span issues in children and adults. In addition, for intervention to be effective it is
important to forego all preconceived notions of what the child or adult needs but
rather to assess the intervention needs of this particular child or adult at this specific point in time in the context of present life circumstances.

An important issue pervading assessment at all stages of the life cycle is
whether grief is proceeding along a healthy path or whether it is taking a pathological turn that requires professional assistance. In the former instance, professional
intervention is typically not needed as individuals and family turn to their friends,
relatives, and the community for support. In the latter case, one of the crucial
issues of assessment is whether the grief has developed into complicated bereavement or even traumatic grief or has led to clinical symptoms of depression or anxiety or perhaps post-traumatic stress syndrome (for a thorough discussion of
assessment issues in the case of traumatic grief in children see Brown & Goodman,
2005; Cohen, Goodman, Brown, & Mannarino, 2004; Cohen & Mannarino, 2004;
Cohen, Mannario, & Deblinger, 2006; McClatchey & Vonk, 2005; Melhem, Day,
Shear, Day, Reynolds, & Brent, 2004; Webb, 2002).

Assessment

A. Issues for Children

Children vary in their concepts of death and in their abilities to undertake grief
work. Recent research suggests that if children experience the death of a parent
prior to age 5, it is more likely to be traumatic due to their inadequate cognitive and

emotional resources to handle a loss of such magnitude (Freudenberger & Gallagher, 1995; Lieberman, Compton, Van Horn, & Ghosh Ippen, 2003). While such a statement is conceptually sound and supported by research, it should not be assumed that this outcome would always be the case, lest it become a self-fulfilling prophecy. Rather the assessment should be based on a thorough developmental evaluation of the child with generous input from parents, teachers, day care providers, or other caregivers.

A child whose developmental progress has been halted or derailed as a result of a death of a family member or other important person may require professional intervention. A starting point is to do a developmental history with input from family, school, and other caregivers. There are quite useful developmental questionnaires for preschool, school age, and adolescents developed by Melvine Levine, a pediatric neurologist (The ANSER System available from Educators Publishing Service, http://www.epsbooks.com/) that the author has found extremely helpful for an initial screening. The forms are available in both a parent and teacher version and there are self-report versions available for children ages 9+. After reviewing the questionnaires filled out by parents and teachers, the counselor can flag areas that need further inquiry and exploration.

Counselors who are trained in doing developmental play assessments with young children can gather important data regarding cognitive, as well as emotional and behavioral functioning by direct observation of the child's spontaneous play. The counselor can also direct the child to engage in structured play and drawing activities and observe carefully the child's responses and coping skills. The therapist might, for example, ask the child to use the puppets to create a story about a scared puppy and observe whether the puppy is all alone, or does someone come along to help or does the puppy seek out someone to help. A wide range of such structured tasks have been described by Gil (2006) and in previous writing (Crenshaw, 2006; Crenshaw & Mordock, 2005).

In all stages of the life span one of the key areas of focus will be the changes in the person's functioning following a death and to what extent in the case of children and adolescents has developmental progress been impeded. School age children will be able to collaborate more fully in the assessment process due to their greater verbal facility and cognitive skills but input from the family and school will still be critical since children may not be fully aware of some of the psychological and behavioral changes observed by adults after a death.

B. Issues for Adolescents

Teenagers typically have more cognitive and emotional resources than do children to understand death and to grieve the death of someone important to them, but they are also at a vulnerable age. If the life of someone important, particularly a peer, is snuffed out at the very time the adolescents are beginning to claim a life and identity of their own, the emotional impact can be devastating. It can cause enormous anxiety, insecurity, and fear of taking risks (Dowdney, 2000). Changes in adolescents following a death may take the form of acting-out behaviors such as increased alcohol or illicit drug use, reckless behavior such as unsafe driving, or engaging in unsafe sex (Dowdney, 2000; Crenshaw, 2002). This acting out is particularly likely with boys but occurs in girls as well (Azarian & Skriptchenko-Gregorian, 1998). Adolescent girls are at increased risk of symptoms of anxiety and depression or other symptoms of internalizing disorders such as eating disorders or self-harming behaviors (Martin and Doka, 1999). A sudden drop in academic grades in either gender may signal developmental impediment related to grief taking an unhealthy path.

C. Issues for Young and Middle Age Adults

In adult life significant changes or disruptions in the family and social relationships subsequent to the death of a relative or close friend would signal a need for further assessment and likely intervention. Increased alcohol use, abuse of prescription or illicit drugs, dramatic deterioration in professional or occupational performance would be important indicators of the need for more careful exploration along with the more obvious signs of clinically significant degrees of anxiety and depression.

D. Issues for the Elderly

The elderly command a special concern. Olga Silverstein, now retired from the faculty of the Ackerman Institute for the Family, in a presentation (1995) titled, "Inclusion/Exclusion" noted the irony that the elderly tend to lose their partners at the very point when they can least afford it, at a time of physical decline, and social as well as energy constraints, and increased illnesses leading finally to death. Erik Erikson (1959) identified the developmental crisis of this final stage of life as ego integrity versus despair and disgust. Erikson noted that ego integrity is manifested in "the acceptance of one's own and only life cycle and of the people who have become significant to it as something that had to be and that, by necessity, permitted of no substitutions. It thus means a new different love of one's parents, free of the wish that they should have been different, and an acceptance of the fact that one's life is one's responsibility" (1959, p. 98). In contrast, despair is revealed in the lack of acceptance of the one and only life cycle accompanied by the feeling that time is short and there is not time to start another life or seek alternative paths. Assessing this difference is crucial in grief work with the elderly. Those already suffering from ego despair will be further disturbed by the death of someone close to them.

Close and meaningful attachments are a crucial buffering and protective factor in the lives of people at any age but become especially critical in the elderly. When death disrupts important attachment bonds, other stressors such as economic strains, poor health, loneliness, or other prior losses compound the emotional devastation in an elderly person. The risk of suicide needs to be carefully considered at any stage of life in the face of a devastating loss, but it becomes especially important to evaluate in the case of the elderly, especially if they live alone, are in poor health, suffer from ego despair, or manifest other risk factors such as alcohol abuse (Hawton & Harriss, 2006; Osvath, Kovacs, Voros, & Fekete, 2005). The presence of clinical depression or any prior history of mood disorder or suicidal ideation or attempts would be further indicators of risk and need for careful assessment by a licensed mental health professional (Lyness, 2004). This indication is especially true for elderly males, because these individuals — particularly elderly Caucasian males — are at higher risk for suicide than any other age group (Garand, Mitchell, Dietrick, Hijjawi, & Pan, 2006). Bell (1970) observes that technology, by extending the human life span beyond the average person's usefulness in a youth-oriented culture, has had the effect of devaluing the aged and relegating their deaths to technologically advanced but depersonalized and dehumanizing medical procedures that prolong life. Important ethical issues arise if technological advancements allow us to extend life but in the process we strip the elderly of their humanity and dignity (see Fulton & Owen, 1987-1988; Kastenbaum, 2004a; and Kastenbaum, 2004b for a fuller discussion of these issues).

Interventions

Four forms of interventions will be described as they relate to life span issues: 1) death education; 2) bereavement support; 3) individual, family or group counseling; and 4) professional caregiver support.

1. Death Education

In societies where death is treated as a taboo or unmentionable topic, death education plays a crucial role in preparing children especially for the possible deaths they will face as they advance through childhood, the death of pets, perhaps grandparents, other relatives, in some cases a friend or perhaps a teacher. Becker (1973) delineated the many ways in which people avoid awareness of death. Becker viewed this denial as emotionally detrimental in that people unable to confront the fact of their own mortality are unable to appreciate life and live fully. Parents should be encouraged to fully utilize opportunities afforded to teach toddlers about death by capitalizing on their natural curiosity. They often ask questions about dead insects or birds and they can be helped to see that death is a natural part of life and as basic to all living things as birth and growing older. Toddlers should be given simple and direct explanations about questions they ask about death. The death of a family pet affords an opportunity, although painful, for children to learn in a natural way about death. Children in the age range of 3 to 6, in what Selma Fraiberg (1959) described as the "magic years," will need help to differentiate the true versus the fantasy causes of events, especially the painful ones in their lives.

School-aged children and adolescents should feel free to approach the trusted adults in their lives when they have questions about the mysteries of death. It is not uncommon that children go through phases of fear of death. As they continue to advance in their cognitive and emotional development they began at around age 9 to understand death in a more complex way. They begin to understand that death is not reversible, that it is inevitable and universal. These abstract concepts are hard for younger children to grasp because they have a limited capacity for abstract thought and concepts.

It is not just children and adolescents who shy away from discussing death. It is astounding that even in the current age when so many other taboos have vanished there are plenty of adults who do not feel comfortable talking about death. Death for many adults is a subject to be tucked away and visited only when forced to by circumstances beyond their control. There is still great potential for increasing the coping capacities of children and adults throughout the life span for handling death by expanding our educational efforts not only through formal death education courses but also in parent and teacher training.

2. Bereavement Support

Throughout the life span the primary intervention for most bereaved children, adults, and families is some form of bereavement support. The majority will receive this support from their families, church, synagogue, or mosque, their school, or the larger community. Young children will primarily receive it from their families although the parents may seek advice from their religious advisers or counselors how to help children through the grieving process. The Bramley Story Series was written with this objective in mind to guide parents in helping toddlers and pre-school children through the grieving process (Crenshaw, 2006). Older children and adolescents often receive support from school counselors and in the case of sudden or traumatic death many schools have organized crisis support teams to offer counseling immediately after the death to those who are affected. Resources for adults and the elderly are available often through support groups organized within the community by church organizations, hospice, or the local mental health association. Often support groups are available for children and adults of various ages and also by the type of death. Suicide survivor groups, and groups for parents who have lost children, or for surviving siblings are available depending on the size of the community.

A wide variety of bereavement support groups and self-help groups are typically to be found in communities sometimes sponsored by the local mental health association or the bereavement branch of hospice organizations throughout the country. In addition private and non-profit counseling organizations specializing in bereavement are often found in larger cities and surrounding suburbs. The self-help groups cover an immense range of bereavement conditions from death of a child, cancer support and bereavement groups, and suicide survivors groups as well as groups for widows and widowers.

The availability of social supports early in the bereavement process has been found to help reduce isolation and other negative effects of widowerhood (Balaswamy, Richardson, & Price, 2004). Vanderwerker and Prigerson (2004) found that overall social support was protective against major depression, PTSD, and complicated grief and associated with better quality of life. In this study they found that use of technological assisted communication by e-mail exerted a positive influence in terms of connectedness with others in the bereaved. This technology is not always familiar and comfortable for elderly people in today's world but that is changing rapidly as even the older generation is learning to use computers to stay in touch with distant relatives and friends.

3. Individual, Group, or Family Bereavement Counseling

While most bereaved do not need or seek professional counseling there are circumstances that may require such intervention which can take the form of either individual, group, or family counseling conducted by a mental health professional and/or certified grief counselor. Sudden and traumatic deaths are prime examples of the types of bereavement that may require professional intervention. While such an event would be stressful at any point in the life span they exert a particular toll on children, adolescents, and the elderly. Children are vulnerable because their development is still in progress and they may lack adequate cognitive, emotional, and social resources for coping with such a stressful event and may result in developmental arrest in one or more domains. Cohen and Mannarino (2004) define childhood traumatic grief as a condition in which the trauma symptoms interfere with the child's ability to undertake the normal grieving process. Recent work by Cohen and Mannarino (2004) had led to an empirically derived treatment model that addresses childhood traumatic grief (CTG). This treatment program addresses both trauma and grief symptoms and includes a parental treatment component. Bereaved children tend to be more amenable to less invasive treatment interventions that include therapeutic play, narratives, metaphors, symbol work, drawing and storytelling strategies (Dominquez, 1999; Crenshaw, 2002; Crenshaw, 2004; Crenshaw, 2005; Crenshaw, 2006).

As mentioned in the assessment section, adolescents may require professional intervention depending on the circumstances of the death and many other variables including their prior loss history, pre-existing psychiatric conditions, and their developmental vulnerability related to their need to move away emotionally from their families and begin the process of making a life and a separate identity.

Sudden death can shatter the life assumptions of the bereaved at any stage of the life cycle but the blow suffered to the adolescent's sense of omnipotence and invulnerability is particularly shocking.

Adults are not exempt from traumatic or complicated reactions to death that under such circumstances may require professional counseling intervention or treatment by a licensed mental health professional. Young adults who are most likely to be faced with the death of a young child are particularly at risk because this may be the most stressful bereavement of all. A child confronted with the death of a parent or a parent with the death of a young child represent some of the most anguishing and heartbreaking of all human experiences. Adult bereavement can be complicated in the case not only of traumatic death but when the relationship of the bereaved and deceased person was highly conflicted or highly dependent. In the later case, the bereaved adult may suffer a loss of identity as well as anxiety and depression. The concept of "complicated grief" and whether it should be incorporated into DSM-V as a diagnosis has been widely debated in the field (Goodkin, Lee, Molina, & Zheng, et al., 2006). The issue at the heart of the debate is whether "complicated grief" is a separate and distinct pathological condition separate from major depressive disorder, posttraumatic stress disorder, and "uncomplicated forms of grief." Complicated grief contains elements of grief, depression, and traumatic stress as well as a unique element of separation distress. Those who argue for complicated grief as a separate syndrome emphasize its distinction partly based on the intensity and duration of the symptoms shared with the other diagnostic syndromes and its significant disruption of daily life functioning.

The loss of loved ones, which is a universal human experience, increases in frequency as we age along with the decline in physical vigor and increased poor health. The incidence and prevalence of depressive symptoms increase, although duration decreases with advancing age (Blazer, 1982). Since social isolation is a concern for the elderly bereaved, group support is a helpful adjunct to any individual counseling. The involvement of other family members in the counseling may strengthen the social support network available to the griever.

In recent years there has been increasing emphasis on evidence-based treatments for bereavement. The review of carefully designed and conducted empirical studies on the efficacy and effectiveness of bereavement interventions has so far yielded the following preliminary conclusions: 1) Adults experiencing normal grief do not typically require intervention and such intervention is likely to be unproductive; 2) Adults at risk for developing complicated grief may benefit from therapeutic intervention; 3) Adults experiencing complicated grief are likely to benefit from psychotherapeutic interventions; and 4) Evidence-based treatment guidelines are available for adult who are experiencing bereavement-related depression (Center for the Advancement of Health, 2004).

Studies of bereavement interventions with children, adolescents, and families are notable largely by their absence. A review published in 1994 reviewed the literature over a 30-year period regarding bereavement programs with parents and children. Of the 53 studies reviewed only four utilized randomized controlled trials. Two of the studies show benefit of the bereavement interventions and two did not. All four studies were criticized in the review for methodological flaws (Schneiderman, Winders, Tallett, & Feldman, 1994).

4. Professional Caregiver Issues

Caregivers and professional counselors face their own inevitable losses and it is necessary that they adequately attend to their own grief issues in order to be effective in providing bereavement support and counseling to others. As caregivers and counselors go through life the number of losses in both their personal and professional lives accumulates and the distance to their own death diminishes. This personal history may make it hard to hear the continuing sad stories of the bereaved, especially the horror narratives of the traumatically bereaved. It is imperative that professional counselors and caregivers counterbalance the inherent stress of work with the bereaved by providing adequate care and consideration to themselves. The caring and support of family is a crucial balancing force, along with healthy lifestyle habits of regular exercise, adequate nutrition, engaging hobbies, as well as sufficient rest and relaxation. In addition both the support of colleagues and supervision or consultation with more experienced colleagues are essential. When counselors are working with families who have experienced the heartrending death of a child or traumatic death of any nature it may create anxiety in the counselors since it can heighten their own since of vulnerability. Trauma tends to shatter beliefs and assumptions that the world is a safe place, and counselors are not exempt from such assaults on assumptions about reality. In the wake of major disasters or terrorist attacks, counselors will be particularly challenged for they will have the same concerns for their own safety and the safety of their families at a time when they are attempting to make themselves emotionally available to their clients. It would be especially critical in disaster work for the counselors and caregivers to attend to their own sense of woundedness and to draw on the support of their team of colleagues (Kastenbaum, 2004b). No one should do this work as a "lone ranger."

4/4 Learning Objective: (20/35) (30/35) Explain how the life Span tasks and Concerns affect the Assessment and Intervention process in end of life be'ment Care.

Chapter 23

Assessment and Intervention in the Family and Larger Systems

Jennifer L. Matheson

Grief and loss can impact not only the individual but an entire family system as well as larger systems such as neighborhoods, communities, schools, businesses, and countries. Recent national and international disasters such as school shootings, war, and natural disasters like hurricanes, tsunamis, floods, and earthquakes have brought to light the importance of grief assessment and interventions on a larger scale.

The experience of family or group grief has similarities and differences to grief experienced by an individual. Clinicians have found that in some ways, group grief can create an environment for additional support and a sense of belonging but can also complicate the bereavement process as individuals grieve in different ways and go through different processes. Walsh and McGoldrick (2004) have endorsed a systemic approach to family grief which understands "the chain of influences that reverberate throughout the family network of relationships, including partners, parents, children, siblings, and extended kin" (p. 6). Others agree that grief occurs in two areas at the same time: the individual level and social or interpersonal level (Cook & Dworkin, 1992). Therapists may be called to help with families or larger systems such as communities who have experienced traumatic loss. Regardless, therapists who are comfortable using an eclectic approach to treatment and intervention will likely find the best results (Lattanzi-Licht & Doka, 2003). Increasingly in recent years, experts in the area of family bereavement have also depended on strength-based, competency-based, and resiliency approaches as a key element to effective intervention and treatment (Hemmings, 2005).

Research suggests that not all people and groups who have experienced significant grief pursue treatment for symptoms. Those with normative patterns of grief rarely feel the need for formalized treatment, though they may explore the types of support that is available in their communities. When grief is complicated by other stressors, however, it is often the job of clinicians to assess for grief-related problems and provide interventions to relieve chronic or acute symptoms. The needs of the family or the group are crucial, and interventions aimed at the whole family or larger system often depend on an accurate assessment of clinical need. While many assessments are available for individuals, few have been designed explicitly for families and large groups.

General Considerations of Assessing and Treating Families and Larger Systems

There are general, overarching issues that should be explored when planning or executing an intervention for families or larger systems dealing with grief and loss. The first key issue is the meaning a family or community makes of the loss event. Nadeau (1998) identified factors that can enhance or inhibit the process of family meaning-making. Some enhancers are family rituals, the frequency of contact among members, and openness of members to share their meaning. On the other hand, things that can inhibit the process include secrets, incompatible beliefs, and the level of fragility of relationships in the family. Regardless of the intervention, it is important to incorporate ways to help people explore meaning-making at different points in their coping process, and allow for wide variations in the meaning people make of a loss event.

In addition to meaning-making, those who assess for grief symptoms and provide interventions for families and larger systems should consider gender and cultural differences. While there is some evidence to suggest that, in general, men may cope with bereavement better than women, research suggests that gender differences in bereavement outcomes are few and small (Hayslip, Allen, & McCoy-Roberts, 2001). Of the few studies that show any differences, one study indicated that woman may prefer individual, couple, or family therapy or support groups, whereas men may benefit more from talking with friends and families (Rich, 2000). Women may be more confrontive and expressive in their grief than men (Stroebe, 2001). Another suggested that women's grief in general has more of an intuitive pattern where men's is instrumental, but that a better model is to weave both into a comprehensive model that addresses both types (Martin & Doka, 2000). Overall, having some sensitivity to the needs of clients based on individual gender differences may be helpful to improving assessment and treatment outcomes.

Finally, and equally important, the cultural and spiritual make up of a family or community should be considered when planning an intervention. While some elements of grief are nearly universal, people from different religions, ethnic, or cultural backgrounds may have different ways of experiencing, expressing, and ritualizing loss events. Developing sensitivity to these differences can help those who assess and treat loss symptoms. In addition, respecting the individuality of families and communities by including them in the planning of any interventions is a good way to ensure their particular religious or cultural needs will be met.

Theories That Guide the Assessment and Treatment of Grief in Families and Larger Systems

For individuals, families, and communities, the process of bereavement can be understood from a wide range of theories that incorporate issues of attachment, coping, and loss (Williams, Zinner, & Ellis, 1999). One theory that may help guide the assessment and treatment of grief symptoms in families and larger systems is Family Systems Theory. This theory encompasses a broad set of interventions used to treat families and larger systems in general, and can be applied to the assessment and treatment of groups of people experiencing significant loss and grief. According to Nichols & Schwartz (1998), "Working with the whole system means not only considering all the members of the family, but also taking into account the personal dimensions of their experience" (p. 8). Therapists who are trained in family systems theory are often trained to use an eclectic approach that may include a number of key models of therapy. These models include Cognitive-Behavioral Family Therapy, Structural Family Therapy, Narrative Therapy, Internal Family Systems, Solution-Focused Brief Therapy, Psychoanalytic Family Therapy, or Experiential Family Therapy. These models are often paired with the available models of treatment for bereavement to treat grief in families and groups. Regardless of the clinician's theory of choice, however, how a family or group experiences grief will depend on their individual, family, social, cultural, and spiritual context (Stokes, 2005). These contextual issues also must be included in any thorough assessment, and may serve as either resources or stressors that must be considered in treatment.

Most of the theories that address grief and loss at a larger systems level deal with tragic or traumatic losses that larger groups experience together. This larger systems level may be church communities, workplaces, neighborhoods, communities, states, or entire countries. Many of the theories on grief that exist for individuals can be applied to larger systems as well. In general, trauma theory is prevalent in helping people understand what happens when a community or larger system grieves, mostly because community grief usually follows a tragedy or traumatic event. Most people who experience a larger systems level loss are resilient, though many may have both acute and long-term stress reactions (Williams et al., 1999). Learned helplessness is often replaced by learned resourcefulness (i.e., Antonovsky, 1990). According to Antonovsky, the community has found a way to make sense of the event with the help of targeted interventions that help make the event manageable make resources available for recovery. The theory suggests that these communities heal also because they find meaning by reframing the event as a challenge. Regardless of the theory used, most use Miller's and Steinberg's (1975) long-standing notion of community grief that specifies, "having options, a plan of action, or a knowledge of how to cope gives strength to an otherwise traumatized community" (in Williams, et al., 1999. p. 14).

Assessment of Needs

Few formal assessment instruments exist to measure the severity of grief being experienced by families and larger systems. When families present with grief or bereavement, therapists can encourage parents to invite children to the session as long as the information will not be too sensitive or complex to discuss in front of children (Hemmings, 2005). According to Stokes (2005), assessment provides "clarity and an understanding of how individuals within the family are experiencing the bereavement" (p. 29). Stokes adds that the assessment should aim to establish the impact of the death for this family at this time living in this community. Other determinants of grief that should be assessed include: who the person was in relation to them; the nature of the attachment; strength of the attachment; security of the attachment; ambivalence of the relationship; conflicts with the deceased; mode of death; historical antecedents; personality variables; social variables; rituals; and concurrent stressors (Parkes & Weiss, 1983). Stokes also suggests beginning with a genogram that has a number of advantages in a bereavement assessment including recording who is in a family, previous losses, past coping strategies, and key family transitions that may have an impact on bereavement. Assessing both the risk factors of a family and the elements of resilience are important. It is important when children are present in a family to include them in the assessment, but to use activities and language at a level they can comprehend. After the assessment phase is complete, therapists should be prepared to recommend family work, individual work, or a combination of both. Being explicit with families about what the therapist notices as areas needing attention, and providing some information about what specific interventions may be used, can help families feel safer and more grounded in treatment.

For larger systems, a few key questions can help guide the assessment of need for grief and bereavement services (Williams et al., 1999). Those questions include:

- "What is the community's history of similar losses?"
- "What is the community history in general?"
- "What is the nature of the losses experienced by this community?"
- "To what extent was the event normalized?"
- "To what extent does the community have the support it needs?"

- "What are the cultural practices, beliefs, rituals, and customs that can help or interfere with healing?"
- "In what ways has the community found meaning in the event?"

These questions can help determine what interventions would be most effective in any given community at any given point in time.

Family Interventions

There is a wide range of interventions that can work with families who are grieving. These techniques come not only from the family therapy field but from psychology, social work, counseling, pastoral counseling, and other fields of mental and spiritual health disciplines. Some of these approaches would fall under the category of family support, especially in cases where the grief and loss issues are less complicated, whereas family therapy would be indicated in situations where the symptoms of grief are beyond what is usual and expected or when grief is complicated by other factors.

Family support from caring peers and professionals is undoubtedly an important part of healing from loss. Family support is indicated in cases when symptoms and experiences of grief and loss are considered within a normative range during assessment, or if families choose this form of intervention. National organizations have formed grief centers solely for the purpose of providing grief support and aftercare to individuals and families. Some of the most well known and national organizations include the Compassionate Friends and Partnership for Parents. In addition, other support groups are available through smaller organizations such as local hospice programs, the Dougy Center, Growth House, Inc., GriefShare, SHARE Organization, MISS Foundation, Rainbows, and UNITE. The Internet is an excellent resource to help families locate these organizations and groups near their homes.

Besides interventions that follow a family systems perspective, family support can come in the form of bibliotherapy (Cook & Dworkin, 1992; Hynes, & Hynes-Berry, 1986; Rubin, 1978). Bibliotherapy is the use of literature for therapeutic intervention and has been used for decades to help people identify with characters or situations in the hopes that it will lead to increased insight into their own situation. It can be used as a form of or in conjunction with family therapy, or it can be used in a family support role. Providing a list of books that are helpful for different types of families, a range of ages, and a range of issues can be helpful. For some, reading in itself can be calming, relaxing, and comforting. Fiction, non-fiction, plays, or poetry can be helpful and can be used individually, between couples, or by entire families to create an atmosphere of support and healing.

While family support is indicated for the majority of families who are coping with loss, family therapy may be indicated for families who experience unresolved or complicated grief. Experiential techniques have been combined with Family Systems Therapy by a number of scholars as a way to bring people together around a common, pleasurable task that has the capacity to increase enjoyment and decrease inhibitions (Gil, 1994). These interventions have been used with families and larger systems, partly to make the treatment of grief more relevant and inclusive of children (Hemmings, 2005). Treatment providers who offer these forms of intervention during times of bereavement "emphasize caring for all members of a family, including children" (DeSpelder & Strickland, 2005; p. 365). Children often have more limited ability and interest in communicating solely through verbal means. Besides providing a way to integrate children into the assessment and treatment of family grief, family play therapy can be highly effective as a way for individuals and groups to begin to heal from symptoms of grief.

Experiential Family Therapy is an eclectic grouping of theories and techniques that emphasizes the here-and-now experience of clients with an emphasis on increasing sensitivity and feeling-expression (Nichols & Schwartz, 1998). Many experiential family therapy techniques can be effectively applied to problems related to grief and bereavement in families. These techniques include activities such as psychodrama, role playing, play therapy, and dance, music, and art therapies. These techniques are useful because they access multiple parts of the human brain so that each individual can experience the intervention from their own set of skills and needs. They are flexible enough to be able to be used by multiple age groups or generations at the same time.

Family play therapy is a related theory that can be used with families and larger groups who are dealing with grief and loss issues. Eliana Gil has written extensively on the use of play therapy with families, extending the work of classical play therapy with children to the family and larger system. One example of a family play technique is the use of puppets to help families tell a story together, assessing their process, interactions, and the content of the stories to help them work through issues (Gil, 1994). The technique "stimulates communication and demonstrates how a family mobilizes toward a goal or task" (p. 46). It helps put families at ease, allows them to have fun, encourages them to be spontaneous, and can be used during the assessment phase to examine family functioning. This technique also encourages symbolic communication in that families can use it as a way to speak in code, especially about difficult, painful, and sensitive topics that often exist in times of grief and loss.

Various forms of art therapy such as drawing a family tree, family portrait, or self portrait are useful in treating families with complicated grief symptoms. Sand tray techniques where families can express their thoughts and feelings through the use of miniatures may also be effective. Therapists can also help families create a memory jar or box of items and stories that relate to their deceased loved one (Way

& Bremner, 2005). Games such as the Talking, Feeling, Doing Game as well as feeling cards (which clinicians can make themselves with basic paper and markers) can be a fun and engaging way to help families talk not only about their thoughts or behaviors, but their feelings as well. Finally, some techniques are not only effective, but they are also very inexpensive and require no specialized or costly materials and supplies. These may include story-telling activities and other drawing or writing tasks that only require paper, markers, or pencils.

Regardless of the intervention, it is always important to remind clients about the individual nature of grief and that family members can be both supportive during the grief process and also create challenges for one another when the processes do not match well in terms of type of things such as individual expressions of grief and length of time grieving.

Larger Systems Interventions

Community grief is a complex process that may take months or years to fully resolve (Williams et al., 1999). Community tragedies occur when one or more members of a group die unexpectedly. These losses can involve many or few, but the larger the number of people who die or are injured, the wider the impact on the community. Besides death and injury, these tragedies can also include destruction to property, relocation, unemployment, and short- and long-term health risks (Williams, et al., 1999). The more unexpected the loss, the more severe the grief and loss experience. These experiences can be an opportunity for growth and bonding or an ongoing crisis for a community. Swift, targeted, caring interventions are needed to help communities cope and recover.

The effective resolution of community grief is needed for the loss to become a reality within the identity of the community. While it would be normal for some residual pain to exist, the outcomes that come from effective community grief recovery can become a shared history that evokes enhanced feelings of closeness and pride. Support groups for communities and larger systems are available to help these large groups cope with losses. Children's programs are available through many of the above organizations, but also through individual communities and schools (discussed more below). These programs help children cope in a group setting in their own personal ways. Hospitals, churches, community mental health, and other community-oriented organizations also often develop grief support groups that are either ongoing or are developed in response to particular community crises. Support groups exist all over the world and are easier to find than ever, thanks to the Internet. Experts believe that in order for these types of centers and groups to be most effective when a community or larger system is coping with loss, these mechanisms should be in place prior to the loss event (Williams et al., 1999).

Procedures can be activated and followed-through more effectively so as to help restore community functioning as members heal.

In addition to group support, there has been a growing popularity of online Internet resources for bereaved families and individuals such as Bereaved Families Online, griefnet.org, caringinfo.org, Grief and Healing Discussion Page, Sidelines National Support Network, and Grief Watch. While most experts agree that face-to-face treatment is the foundation of grief therapy, the use of technology can decrease the literal space between service providers and clients when necessary (Stubbs, 2005). It also allows for interventions to occur on a larger scale when multiple lines are open and utilized at once. Phone and e-mail support for bereaved individuals and communities can be used from the very earliest points of an intervention when geography or other logistics make it impossible to be in the same location. When this service comes in the form of a phone help line, it affords the potential client anonymity, control, immediacy, and ease of contact, and accessibility. E-mail support has been used since the early 1990s, and offers many of the same benefits as phone contact. Of course, these methods that do not have the advantage of face-to-face contact have the obvious disadvantages of having neither nonverbal cues nor the ability to see the expressions and hear the finer nuances of a conversation.

Schools can be a crucial point of support for individual or groups of children who have been bereaved. Silverman and Worden (1992) reported that children who received support at home and at school following the death of a parent had fewer problems than children who did not have the school support. But staff and teachers often feel unprepared for how to respond to bereaved children (Rowling, 2005). Short- and long-term interventions both inside and outside of the classroom should be planned ahead of time. Schools should incorporate training for teachers and administrators as well as form partnerships with outside agencies and the families of the school's students to prepare for present and future needs in the area of grief and loss. Facilitators can be trained early in bereavement support so that short-term interventions can be provided on the school grounds as soon as they are needed. Schools may also benefit from asking the students for input on what they want or need in the short- and long-term. Schools must be prepared for the long-term needs of the students and staff, not only for the crisis intervention activities that are sometimes needed.

In cases of community mourning complicated by issues such as trauma, violent crime, and terrorism, there are a few models of intervention widely used with groups. The most widely used is called Critical Incident Stress Management (CISM) (Everly & Mitchell, 1999). CISM has been cited as the standard of care for intervention of crisis situations and originated as a treatment for police, paramedics, and firefighters who provide assistance in emergencies (Gamino, 2003). While this approach has been questioned for its lack of empirical evidence and for possible iatrogenic results (Gist & Lubin, 1999; Litz, 2004), CISM remains a widely accepted form of treatment for individuals and groups who have experienced a critical incident that overwhelms their "usual coping mechanisms resulting in psychological distress and a disruption in adaptive functioning" (Gamino, 2003, p. 125). CISM is a seven component program of stress management. Group members come together after a traumatic event and discuss what happened to them, the thoughts and reactions they have had, and the symptoms they are dealing with. Then they learn that many of their symptoms are normal and they are not alone in facing them, and finally are given time to wrap-up and develop a plan for any needed future action. CISM interventionists are trained in: pre-crisis preparation; individual crisis intervention; large group demobilizations or informational briefings; critical incident stress debriefing; family/organizational consultation; and follow-up referral. For a shorter-term intervention, one element of the CISM model is helpful. The Critical Incident Stress Debriefing (CISD) can also be used with groups after a traumatic event. CISD is a structured group discussion of a crisis that lasts somewhere between one and three hours and is implemented no less than 24 to 48 hours after the incident occurred. This model is not therapy but instead is meant to help achieve closure on the event, if possible. It also provides an opportunity to reach out to people who otherwise might not attend a longer-term intervention and to provide needed information and referral sources.

Another model that has emerged for the intervention of community grief is Everly's (1995) SAFE-R model. This model teaches community leaders to: S=Stabilize the situation, reduce stressors; A=Acknowledge the crisis by inquiring into facts and reactions of the crisis; F=Facilitate normalization by understanding; E=Encourage adaptive coping; and R=Restore homeostasis and referring out for aftercare where needed.

Finally, Kalayjian's (1996) seven-stage model of community healing may be helpful to community leaders. It begins with a preassessment before the intervention is implemented that includes exploring the dynamics of the community, to whom the event occurred, who are the survivors, community preparedness, and what is the overall civic climate of the community. They do an on-site assessment to determine community strengths and weaknesses, resources, and motivation for change. Next the community's response to the event is evaluated and a plan for services is developed. The plan is implemented; then an evaluation of the intervention is completed. To conclude, the community leaders modify and reevaluate the intervention for possible changes when it is implemented again in the future.

Conclusion

In the assessment and treatment of grief in families and larger systems, many techniques can be effective and used in multiple contexts that embrace and honor the cultural, spiritual, gender, and familial needs of the group and individual members. Regardless of the intervention and how eclectic a therapist is in her or his interventions, the relationship with the clinician continues to be thought to be one of the most important factors for short- and long-term positive outcomes. This relationship must be filled with a sense of trust and the notion that the therapist understands the individual's and group's issues in order for treatment to be effective.

One benefit to doing family or larger systems therapy on issues of grief is that it is less likely that the individuals will feel isolated and alone in their grief. Interventions that involve whole families or whole groups enable people to embrace the individual nature of grief and create a less isolated, lonely environment. On the other hand, the complication present in treating families or groups who are experiencing significant grief is that all members will grieve at their own pace and in their own way. Helping members to honor the ways in which others grieve can be therapeutic for families and larger groups.

4-5 Learning Objective: (30/35)
Describe the role of A Systems perspective on
grief and loss in Assessment and intervention
with families and larger Systems Coping with
grief & loss.

Chapter 24

Ethical and Legal Issues in Assessment and Intervention

Jackson P. Rainer

To effectively address death from the perspective of ethical and legal issues in assessment and intervention, attention must be given to end-of-life issues. As T. S. Eliot wrote, "...the mind of God in me shows what it is time to move on to and what it is time to let go of. What we call the beginning is often the end and to make an end is to make a beginning; the end is where we start from" (1936, p. 86). Advances in managing and treating acute, life-threatening illnesses have led to greater longevity and have brought a lengthening of the typical dying trajectory which gives the individual a prolonged period of disability. This prolonged disability causes ethical and humane concern about the prospect of longer, medicalized, and impersonal deaths. Individuals in our current day are progressively more interested in a greater degree of self-determination in the dying process. With the current health care crisis and the high cost of dying, economics further confounds the proposition of self-determination.

Seale (2000) notes that the average life expectancy worldwide has risen from 48 years in 1955 to 65 years in 1995. In developed countries, such as the United States, the average life expectancy has increased from 47 years in 1900 to a record high of 76.7 years in 1998 (National Center for Health Statistics, 2000). Gains continue to be made in the average life expectancy in this country, primarily because of the changes in the causes of death. Despite many problems with the health care system of the United States, advances in medicine and public health have led to the diminishment of infectious disease as a cause of death. Now, degenerative diseases that occur more frequently in adulthood, such as cancer, heart disease, and stroke, have emerged as the leading causes of death. Progress has been made at a slower rate in the treatment of these diseases, and current research involves more speculation about how the body may be able to repair the damage it does to itself through disease and aging. Molecular biology, genetics, and stem cell research hold great promise in significantly extending average life expectancy, which baby boomers heartily embrace.

Quality of life has emerged as important an issue as longevity. High profile cases, such as Karen Ann Quinlan (In *re Quinlan, 1976*) and Nancy Beth Cruzan (*Cruzan v. Director, Missouri Department of Health,* 1990) brought public attention to the fact that medical technology had advanced to the point where it could sustain life even when the individual was in a persistent state of unconsciousness with no hope of recovery. In the recent past, Floridian Terri Schiavo's case brought public attention to the private matter of extension of life and definition of death. In 2003, the relatives of Schiavo, a young woman who had suffered a brain injury in 1990 and exhibited no cognitive function, had a serious dispute about her treatment that triggered actions by officials of all three branches of Florida's state government (*Schindler v. Schiavo,* 2003).

The Quinlan case allowed parents to obtain court authority to refuse unwanted medical treatment, in this case mechanical ventilation, on their daughter's behalf. Even without this treatment, she lingered for another eight years while receiving artificial nutrition and hydration. Thirty years later, the wake of this court decision has helped the medical health care team to be forthright in the withdrawal or withholding of life sustaining treatments under similar circumstances where there is apparent meaninglessness of existence without consciousness. In the Cruzan case, it was established that an incompetent, terminally ill individual could forego life sustaining treatment (with the decision of a surrogate), but that the state had the right to set evidentiary requirements for surrogate decision makers. In Missouri, this court decision meant that the state could demand clear and convincing evidence regarding what the individual would have wanted if competent. The judgment has led to the use of advance directives to protect the self-determination of individuals who have reached a point in their illness when they are no longer about to make their own decision about their care (Wachter & Lo, 1993).

In these cases, there was an ethical dilemma regarding the definition of death. Historically, before the development of intensive care, an individual was declared dead when breathing and circulation stopped. However, such traditional concepts of deaths are now problematic because an individual's breathing and circulation can be sustained on life support after all cerebral functions are permanently lost, as occurred in the Quinlan and Cruzan cases. Criteria for brain death have been developed and are now widely accepted. It is defined as "irreversible loss of functioning in the entire brain, both cortex and brainstem" (Lo, 2000, p. 178). This condition is known as whole-brain death, also defined as "permanent cessation of the functioning of the organism as a whole" (Bernat, 1992, p. 21). Most states have adopted the Uniform Determination of Death Act as an effective ethical definition of death. It declares death occurs for "Any individual who has sustained either (1) irreversible cessation of circulatory and respiratory functions, or (2) irreversible cessations of all functions ~~of all functions~~ of the entire brain, including the brain stem. A determination of death must be made in accordance with accepted medical standards" (Meisel, 1995, p. 188)

Symbolically, the "moment of death" is no longer momentous. Deathbed scenes throughout history have held cosmic drama in the expunging of weakness and sin, purification of the soul, and redemption, all which occurred close to the moment of dying. This concern for dying in grace carried over to rites for disposition of the body and for religious customs that would protect the dead on their journey into the afterlife. While this tradition persists, there is less theatricality due to the blurring of the terms "brain death," "clinical death," and "persistent vegetative state." Population aging and slow decline from multiple chronic conditions now frequently result in cognitive and communicational impairments before death. Nevertheless, more people are now in a position to bring their own beliefs and values to the end-of-life situation.

Psychologists James and Elizabeth Bugental assert that in our humanity, we have two fundamental "givens." They write, "Humans have the capacity of acting or not acting, and humans have choice" (Bugental & Bugental, 1984, p. 543). It is out of our choices that meaning is created. Choice and control are vital to personal sanity, even in the presence of death. In contemporary society, families and patients must wrestle with medical advances and hard choices. The traditional understanding of the Hippocratic Oath acknowledges that in some circumstances medical treatment is futile, and has no reasonable possibility to "cure, ameliorate, improve, or restore a quality of life that would satisfactory to the patient" (Haley & Brody, 1996, p. 571). With the advent of medical technologies, however, it has become the slogan of many physicians and medical practitioners, as well in society at large, to "keep the patient alive at all costs." This stance is not necessarily the best decision or the only choice.

While the meta-ethical principles of beneficence, nonmaleficence, justice, and fidelity all apply as they might in any studied dilemma, the principle of autonomy has more weight during death assessment and intervention. Three terms must be defined. **Autonomy** is a fundamental concept in the law that proclaims the right of individuals to act on their own, to make decisions, and to determine their fate. **Consent** is a legal term indicating an agreement regarding something to be done. It is known to be an act of reason following deliberation. Consent offers an alternative to submission and is one of the derivatives of autonomy. An **advance directive** is a legal document consisting of two elements: a living will and a durable power of attorney for health care. A living will is an advance directive to the physician regarding the dying individual's feelings about the use of life-support equipment or other extraordinary measures to sustain life. It is recognized as a legal document in most states, though in some it may be known as a different document. For example, in Massachusetts, a living will is known as a health care proxy. The use of living wills is still not widespread and applies only to a narrowly defined range of circumstances. It is easily rescinded even though it indicates the individual's thoughts regarding heroic care. The Durable Power of Attorney is a document appointing a caregiver who is legally designated to make decisions about treatment and medical care. There are state-by-state restrictions on the enactment of the document, oftentimes requiring the aid of a notary or lawyer to draft and execute (Rainer & McMurry, 2002). A third type of directive is a "Do Not Resuscitate" (DNR Order), also known as a "no code." The DNR conveys a physician's order that a dying individual should not receive cardiopulmonary resuscitation if the patient stops breathing and/or the patient's heart stops beating. All three advance directives are based on the concept of autonomy, and ensure continuity of decisions made while the individual is competent in the event of later loss of decisional ability.

Autonomy affirms the right to make decisions, consent describes the process of making decisions, and advance directives ensure continuity of decisions across time. Advance directives take the elements of decision making from the presumed moral authority of the medical practitioner and place them into the consumer driven perspective of health care where the individual assumes the responsibility of choice. Dying is no longer a matter simply between a patient and a physician. It is expanded to include intimates, family, and community, all subsumed under the legal definition of "surrogate." Over time, the value laden concept of "quality of life" has replaced the more difficult to define phrase "death with dignity." However, the primary question revolves around constitutional guarantees of a right to life. At the same time it does not allow clinicians to end a sustained life, even by "artificial" means. The landmark Quinlan, Cruzan, and Schiavo cases are benchmarks of the great dissonance between the law and clinical practice.

Because it declares the right of an individual to act in personal "best" interest, autonomy is basic to health care decisions. An individual need not submit to treatment and can knowingly consent to or refuse treatment. It is a fundamental right that enables each person to be treated as an individual rather than as a part of a collective. The concept of autonomy and its practical translation allows the individual to make informed treatment decisions that are consistent with personal culture, values, and belief systems.

Consent is an autonomous act that gives permission for a specific therapy, treatment, or procedure to be performed. Included in consent must be information of the risk/benefit ratio of the treatment. Ideally, it is not a static event but an ongoing process that involves clear communication between the individual and the health care provider. "To perform a procedure or treatment on a patient in the absence of consent constitutes abuse and subjects the one who performs the procedure to charges of abuse or assault. Consent to perform procedures on patients who lack the ability to provide consent lies with a guardian appointed by the local court. Parental consent is required in order to treat children and juveniles" (Lamers, 2005, p. 111).

Informed consent is the voluntary decision made by a person with decisional capacity who is cognizant of all relevant facts. The phrase implies that the person who grants consent is truly informed about the subject and is capable of making a decision based on the facts. The individual must understand the problem, treatment alternatives, and possible outcomes, including side effects, costs, and timing. Veiled language, euphemisms, and poor vocabulary are clinically discouraged, though are actively practiced in many aspects of death-related care. Most informed consent is explicit, and includes a written legal document that is signed and dated. Implicit consent is inadequate in end-of-life and death-related care. Without a record that necessary facts were revealed and discussed, there is no sense that the individual was able to make critical decisions regarding the course of treatment or care.

Any discussion of the ethics of death care regarding assessment and intervention must consider those who will speak for the deceased, particularly when there is disagreement among those in the person's intimate system. Despite the growth of the hospice movement in the United States in the past 30 years, more than 50 percent of American die in hospitals and long-term care facilities (Beckwith, 2005). This mortality statistic implies a continuing cultural distance from death. As a result, the dying process of a loved one can be a difficult family experience that tests even the closest family relationships. Family caregivers provide more than 80 percent of all home care services, yet receive no formal training or support for their roles (Beckwith, 2005).

Such caring brings focus to the meta-ethical principles of beneficence and nonmaleficence. Beneficence refers to the notion of caring and "doing good," while nonmaleficence means "do no harm" in the process. To many families and health care teams, death still translates as failure. For family caregivers, this stance may lead to increased isolation, misunderstanding, and feelings of abandonment when their loved one dies. When family members are spread across the country and geographic dispersion is added to the multiple derivations of families, e.g., stepfamilies and civil unions, the intimate system often will delay and postpone decision making until an emergency forces the issue. Differing belief systems, interests, lifestyles, experiences, and codes of ethics come into play by the "committee" of family members obligated to make death-related decisions, potentially causing conflict.

Family members may disagree about the type of care that should be provided. There may be disagreement of the disposition of the body or of funeral rites.

However, the most common issue is related to the settlement of the deceased's estate.

It is well documented that most couples and families do not want to discuss death. Often, at the point where there is no avoiding the subject, the patient, too ill or sedated, is unable to participate in the conversation. Decision making then falls to the surrogate or to unprepared family members. The potential for strained communication is mitigated if clinicians provide timely clinical and prognostic information and offer continuous psychosocial support to all involved in the death discussions. Effective communication includes sharing the burden of decision making with other family members. The shift from individual responsibility to a patient-focused consensus permits the family to understand, even with great reluctance and sadness, how to proceed in the most caring and beneficent way.

Again, the notion of advance directives comes into play. These documents should be considered equally important to the dying person and to family members following the death. It should be noted by the clinician, though, that a complication of the advance directive process can add pressure to a family. Some individuals will indicate they want their family's wishes to take precedence over their own previously stated wishes, in the belief that the family will do what is best (Sehgal, Galbraith, Chesney, Schoenfield, & Lo, 1992).

A final advance directive to be discussed is the last will and testament, a legal document stating the individual's wishes for the settlement of her estate after death. A will is the best way to determine the distribution of personal belongings and assets, to provide for family needs regarding underage children, to plan wisely for taxes, and to make charitable contributions. Only by having a will can the individual be assured that personal wishes will be carried out after death.

There are legal and ethical issues to be addressed regarding the death certificate and body disposition. Although death is an individual event, it is also of great social significance. Like other significant life events, death is celebrated by rituals and is institutionalized through documentation. As an institutionalized entity, death entails a legal process of death registration that in turn generates mortality statistics. The death certificate represents one of the officially reported documents about the individual's death. This document includes a variety of information, the most important being cause and circumstances of death. The cause of death is the most important source of information for public health analysts, since it provides information for mortality statistics relevant to public discourse, including "estimating a component of population growth and preparing population projection; delineating health problems, planning public health programs, and accessing health progress, and studying the natural history of disease" (Hanzlick, 1997, p. 265).

Body disposition is a highly personal process. Memorial expressions and the symbolism found in body disposition reaffirm a social identity for the survivors, providing a place for grief and mourning in the context of the collective identity of the deceased's social network. As an individual dies and the survivor must dispose of remains, a sense of continuity between life and death is established, as is a relationship between the living and the dead. The relationship may be defined through any number of disposition rights, including burial and cremation as the most popular rites. In modern Western cultures, burial dictates placing a body (which may or may not be embalmed) in a wooden or metal casket, then placed either in the ground or entombed in a mausoleum crypt. During cremation, the body is subjected to extreme heat to reduce it to a mineralized skeleton, which is further reduced to a granular consistency known as cremains, or colloquially, ashes. These may be buried, scattered (according to state law), or kept by the family and memorialized in urns designed to hold cremated remains. Other body disposition possibilities are beyond the scope of this discussion. It is clear that upon death, practical decisions must be made concerning the final disposition of the physical body. These decisions are guided by religious tradition, social custom, and personal preference.

The fundamental meaning of the word 'care' is "to grieve, to experience sorrow, to cry out" (Rainer & McMurry, 2002). To care for another is an invitation to enter into that person's pain and suffering. There are few 'right answers' in the ethics of assessment and intervention at the time of death. The complexity of the time is marked by its fluidity and developmental nature. During impending and actual death, there is a progressive loss of social convention and a diminished expectation and capacity for efficiency. Clinicians are obligated to provide instrumental aid and psychosocial support through the significant, difficult, and intimate life transition. There is an ethic related to care: it is to assist dying persons and survivors of a death to maintain dignity with as much autonomy as might be mustered. Accepting help from another amounts to an admission of vulnerability, which should never be taken lightly. Such care is be delivered in non-judgmental, unconditional, and empowering ways. Ethical caring explicitly states that the individual and support network have the right to participate in decisions concerning their care, and that caregivers should not judge those decisions based on their own beliefs. The critical question regarding the ethics of care revolves around "What constitutes a good quality of life?" This is a highly personal question that presents multiple challenges in assessment and intervention, since it has such a subjective answer.

Death is a unique experience for each person, bringing multiple possibilities of ethical dilemmas. There is no substitute for the power of presence of the clinician. Professionals working to assess and intervene in this stage of grief will find a high degree of systemic confusion and must serve to balance fears with openness and anxieties with trust.

Learning Objective: 20/30 / 20/30?
Identify the ethical and legal
issues pertaining to the
provision of care of the dying
and the bereaved.

Traumatic Death

Introduction to Part 5,
Chapters 25-30

Chapters 25 through 30 focus on traumatic death. The Body of Knowledge Committee defined this major category of thanatology knowledge in this way: **sudden, violent, inflicted, and/or intentional death, shocking encounters with death.**

The chapters in Part 5 focus on traumatic death in terms of these indicators: culture and socialization, religion and spirituality, historical and contemporary perspectives, life span issues, the family and larger systems, and ethical and legal issues.

Chapter 25

Culture, Socialization, and Traumatic Death

Jeffrey Kauffman

Trauma uniquely resists formalization. This constraint is true of individual, cultural and social trauma. Caruth (1996) argues that traumatic events are inherently incomprehensible because at the core of trauma is forgetting. Blanchot (2000) and Krystal (2002) carry this issue further, suggesting that the most traumatic aspect could not be experienced, but is intensely dissociated, continuing to happen until it can, if possible, be remembered, or otherwise, lived with, in one way or another until one dies. One is frozen in the moment of traumatization. The disruption of memory in trauma is corollary to the disruption of self. The core of traumatic death remains dissociated and incomprehensible, but its consequences are life defining. Trauma is a remarkable response of the human organism, in which the cohesion of the self is shattered, producing a diversity of "symptoms" and other life re-defining consequences. Caruth argues that traumatization is being "possessed by an image or event." And, what the image or event means is "being *possessed* by the ravages of the self violated by or *exposed* to a traumatizing death." While trauma is outside the realm of meaning, persons who have been traumatized may present differently than the usual post-traumatic stress disorder (PTSD), with just about any of a wide spectrum of mental health disorders, such as bipolar disorder, major depression, addictive disorder, borderline personality disorder, somatic symptoms, phobias, dissociative disorder, schizoaffective disorder, and anxiety disorder. Traumatization releases a monstrous upheaval within. Trauma consequences vary widely or, as we say more technically, trauma is plastopatholic.

Plastopatholic designates that traumas do not result in a uniform symptomatology, but that the pathology is highly variable; the psychopathology of traumatic grief has a high level of plasticity to it. Disturbances of traumatic grief savage the soul in such a way that, while dissociation may be rampant, and self-loathing, shaming self-blame may be typical, the forms these symptoms take are molded around the history of life experiences in diverse ways. Traumatic grief disrupts the capacity to experience oneself. It disrupts the continuity of time, based in the continuity of one's experience of oneself. The power of trauma to cause fragmentation, and compromised self-healing efforts, leaves the traumatized griever unable to maintain the normalcy of self-experience, developing diverse disorder patterns. Plastopathic means the collapse of boundaries, or destabilization of boundaries between one pathology and another.

Human Relationships and Identity

Van der Kolk observes that traumatized persons "avoid intimate relationships" (1987, p.3). Relationships may be sought, but they tend to be turbulent, and emotional intimacy is usually not possible. The grief from a traumatic death is especially socially alienating. The sense of safety and self-belief are fragile, and, while the survivor of a traumatic experience of death may aggressively pursue goals in the social world, he or she lives on the thin ice of the vulnerability of the traumatized self to disintegrate, to be abandoned in extremis, to flee in terror, reliving being helpless to stop the catastrophe. The traumatized, in the extreme that characterizes the condition, "have no self, no 'me', no individuality" (van der Kolk, 1987). Young and Erickson (1989) see trauma as disrupting the sense of continuity, leaving one alienated and isolated. The trauma disturbs experience so severely that the pre- and post-traumatic self are discontinuous. The disruption of the temporal continuity of experience disrupts one's connection to oneself and to others. "Victims of extreme social violence often have difficulties relating to family members and to the community at large" (Suárez-Orozco and Robben, 2000, p. 43). Traumatic death may impair ones capacity to experience social support, where safety normally would be found.

Special Social and Cultural Concerns

Bioarchaeological research shows that throughout the history of our species, interpersonal violence, especially among men, has been prevalent. Cannibalism seems to have been widespread, and mass killings, homicides, and assault injuries are also well documented in both the Old and New Worlds. No form of social organization, mode of production, or environmental setting appears to have remained free from interpersonal violence for long (Walker, 2001).

Trauma and Modernity/Postmodernity

Bracken (2002) emphasizes the sociocultural context of traumatic death, with a special concern that those who work with victims of wars, mass violence, and natural disasters, put aside their culture-bound assumptions, and be open to the unique languages in which other cultures experience traumatic death. He writes, "the current discourse on trauma is simply inadequate to grasp the complexity of how different human beings living in different cultures respond to terrifying events" (Bracken, 2002, p.8). Bracken suggests that the psychological concept of trauma is culture-bound specifically by the postmodern occurrence of an "economic and cultural shift to an intense form of consumer capitalism" which defines our "contemporary experience of trauma, distress and alienation" (Bracken, 2002, p.14). This understanding may be too narrow a causal attribution, as economic influences are one of many key dimensions that define our culture.

Young takes a more radical approach, arguing that, "during the 19th century, a new kind of painful memory emerged. It was unlike the memories of earlier times in that it originated in a previously unidentified psychological state, called 'traumatic,' and was linked to previously unknown kinds of forgetting called 'repression' and 'dissociation'" (Young, 1995, p. 3). This argument takes trauma as a 'new kind of painful memory' that originates in our sociocultural world in the 19th century. His argument is basically that the emergence of this new psychological *language* signifies a new way of experiencing; but this approach seems to overstate the point, for a trauma by any other name is a trauma. Nonetheless, a new age of traumatic death with mass killings and savagery seems to have been repeatedly erupting since the French Revolution.

Young sees not just the concepts as new, but also the phenomena identified as sociocultural constructs. Trauma theory is, then, itself sociocultural evidence of the emergence of a new condition which Young traces to a new 19th century sensitivity to and perception of the suffering of traumatic grief, a sanctioning that comes to recognize a particular disruption of memory and identity on all levels of human organization. Trauma is not just culturally diverse; it is, according to Young, an historically bound phenomena of our culture.

Friedman and Marsella (1996, p.11) report that accounts of "emotional reactions to extreme stress have been noted by historians and literary authors for 4,000 years...," however pre-19th century reactions to devastating events may not have had the particular meaning that trauma-as-hysteria has in the work of the 19th century psychologist Janet. The difference between Janet's (1978) work on hysteria and the trauma theory that has emerged in the last quarter of the 20th century are late 19th and late 20th century reflections of trauma in an age which is particularly dissociative, and where the social and cultural symbolics in which traumatic death was assigned a meaning are not functioning very well. In this nineteenth and twentieth century phenomena called trauma there is a psychological sensitivity to and awareness of the disturbances in which a psychic injury is inflicted from outside.

We can look at trauma theory as itself a sociocultural reaction of modernity, to an urgency in a culture which, perhaps since the French Revolution. (Fritzsche, 2004), has been traumatized. This view of trauma as a sociocultural construct takes trauma to be a specific name for an experience that was emerging in the West in the 19th century, that is, that modernity and postmodernity are 'an age of trauma.' Bracken, echoing Janoff-Bulman (1992), argues that in the contemporary world, "the experience of horror calls into question the basic order of the world." (Bracken, 2002, p. 3)

The world of post traumatization, for Bracken, is the onset of a sociocultural world in which, while traumatic death narratives are more abundant than ever, traumatic death becomes socioculturally more pervasively alienated. Farrell (1998) makes the interesting argument that trauma is a "strategic fiction that a complex stressful society is using to account for a world that seems threateningly out of control" (as cited in Bracken, 2002, p. 3). The very conceptualization of trauma in modern times is, by this light, a self-expression of the traumatization of the social world, an assumption or construct intended to control a world whirling out of control, by recognizing it, and by way of the imagination, developing strategies intended to manage it. Suarez-Orozco and Robben write that "the 20th century brought us some of he most barbaric episodes of large-scale violence and trauma" (2000, p. 1). The 20th century was, globally, an age of traumatic death. This fact is highly consequential, as traumatic death becomes more intense at the beginning of the 21st century. In the 21st century death is traumatizing on a global scale, and Americans are notably fearful.

Collective Trauma

In *Everything In Its Path* Kia Erickson introduces a concept of collective trauma, describing how a traumatized community "gradually realizes that the community *no longer exists* as an effective source of support and that *an important part of the self has disappeared*" (Erickson, 1976). The loss of self may be a consequence of the loss of community. Davoine and Gaudilliere argue that "historical and social traumas" (2004, P. xxiii) have a pervasive affect on individuals, and on the culture or society as a whole. They also assert eccentrically, that historical-cultural trauma is the root of "madness." But, it may not be so eccentric. Traumatic disturbances embodied in a culture may instill psychological disorder in the culture. They suggest that madness is a consequence of sociocultural traumatic events.

Suarez-Orozco and Robben argue that collective trauma targets "the body, the psyche, as well as the social order." The socio-cultural context "intertwine[s] psychic, social, political, economic, and cultural dimensions" in an affliction of massive trauma (2000, p. 1) Cultural identity is shaped by traumatic death, as the trauma is encoded into cultural narratives which are transgenerationally transmitted

(Suarez-Orozco and Robben, 2000). A group subjected to traumatic deaths receives "an indelible mark upon their group consciousness, marking their memories forever and changing their future identity in fundamental and irrevocable ways" (Alexander, 2004, p. 1). In traditional societies traditional symbolics, practices, and rituals respond to collective trauma to secure collective identity and the stability of meaning (Alexander, 2004). These are, it is generally recognized, less available, less powerful and less consequential in the post-traditional world, and do not adequately serve the social re-integrative function of pre-modern post-traumatic sociocultural practices. Major traumatic deaths shape a deeply interior aspect of collective reality. Traumatic exposure violates the most private interior of psychic and sociocultural being.

Alexander, following Herman (1992) and many others, argues that the restoration of collective psychological health is in "lifting societal repression and restoring memory"(Alexander, 2004, P. 7). Remembering is only a starting place towards restoration, though, especially regarding collective death traumas, remembering is a defiance of sociocultural and political powers which ignore, disavow, or derealize historical collective traumatic deaths.

Trauma and Moral Responsibility

Alexander elaborates upon a social construct theory of trauma, by bringing in a very significant moral dimension. "By constructing cultural trauma... social groups, national societies, and sometimes even entire civilizations not only cognitively identify the existence and source of human suffering but 'take on board' some significant responsibility for it" (Alexander, 2004, p. 1). This responsiveness to trauma is not an American strong suit. Alexander's account of the genesis of cultural moral consciousness of trauma begins in the act of *recognizing* the occurrence or presence of trauma, and once recognized, it becomes the conscience of the culture, a moral call for a just healing. The concepts of justice and healing sometimes are, with regard to trauma, closely related.

Cultural Diversity

PTSD is a culture-bound concept; though aspects of it are found in non-Western cultures, these aspects are found through the eyes of Western cultural and psychological assumptions. If societies construct reality, traumatic death will have a different *meaning*, and will be a different *experience*, in different socially constructed realities. Below we say more about such difference, but at the outset note that this notion of cultural distinctions implies that our own social construct of traumatic grief expresses something specific about our own culture.

Friedman and Marsella summarize the basic question about the universality and cultural diversity of trauma by writing that "while a universal neurobiological response to traumatic events most likely does exist, there is room for considerable ethnocultural variation in the expressive and phenomenological dimensions of the experience, especially among comorbidity patterns and associated somatic, hysterical, and paranoid symptoms and experiences ... If more sensitive cross-cultural research and clinical methods are used in the study of PTSD, ethnocultural variations may emerge with greater regularity and clarity" (2004, p. 107). Notice that the explanatory categorization system used here is Western psychology. Friedman and Marsella say the universal response *most likely* exists. In this argument, a universal response is implied by the trauma reaction being basically neurobiological, and assuming that the neurobiological is not evolutionarily affected by cultural factors.. Also, we may infer from this account that variations between cultures are on the level of *experienced meaning*. There is not enough research that attempts to phenomenologically describe the experienced meaning of traumatic death cross-culturally. Most authors interpret non-Western behavioral languages of traumatic grief in Western psychopathological terms, and not in terms of experienced meaning.

Kirkmayer claims that the major difference in non-Western cultures are in the *somatic* and *dissociative* expressive languages of some cultures. He questions the accepted view that trauma is an anxiety disorder. He argues that "the symptomatology of PTSD overlaps with affective, somatoform, dissociative, and anxiety disorders" (Kirkmayer, 2001, p. 131), and suggests that trauma is closely associated with depression and "some degree of enduring loss," that is grief. He says that cross-national and cross-cultural studies of somatoform disorders indicate three problems for existing nosology. These are, "(a) the separation of somatoform disorders from anxiety and mood disorders reflects distinctions between physical and emotional distress that are not made in other cultures; (b) in many cultures, somatic symptoms and attributions commonly are used as idioms of distress to convey a wide range of personal and social concerns that may or may not indicate individual psychopathology; (c) the nature of physical symptoms varies cross-culturally with ethnophysiological theories, illness models, and previous illness experience" (Kirkmayer, 2001, p.132f).

Robben and Suarez-Orzco approach the problem of describing traditional cultures on their own terms, asserting, "traditional, non-industrial societies have often sought to collectivize the social injuries of massive trauma. They have created healing rituals, religious ceremonies, communal dances, and revitalization movements, and have restored symbolic places" (2000, p. 22). They argue that due to repeated exposure to trauma the Navajo developed a ritual. "The Navajo Enemy Way ceremony represents the culture's ritualized attempt to cleanse returning warriors from the deleterious impact of war trauma and to help... reintegration into peacetime Navajo society" (2000, p. 24). Friedman and Marsella claim that what one culture experiences to be traumatic, another may appraise to be a rite of passage, as in the case of the Navajo. Fairbank et al. (1995, p. 24) suggest that in societies that provide stable and safe social bondedness, vulnerability to traumatization is reduced. Such considerations as these need more study. Traumatic death in our culture may be on the rise, and our culture's rituals and norms may be hard pressed to integrate and symbolically transform traumatic death.

Learning Objective:
Recognize Socialization and cultural factors
that impact our understanding of traumatic
death.

Chapter 26

Religion, Spirituality, and Traumatic Death

Gerry R. Cox

Religion and Traumatic Death

Sociologists generally view religion as the way in which peoples put their beliefs into practice. Religion is something that people do. Death is not a private event, nor is it only a psychological event. The rituals of religion help us to recognize, understand, and process our beliefs about dying and death. The challenge of traumatic death often causes those providing social support to be even more involved in religious rituals. Those who provide social support do so by attending the wake or visitation, funeral, cemetery rituals, the meal afterwards, donating to favorite charity, bringing food for the grieving, visiting, or simply sending a personal sympathy note. For many religious organizations, death rituals are quite predictable. As an example, Roman Catholic practices are very similar from one church to another, from one region or nation to another, from one year to another year.

Using religion to manage traumatic death can produce both positive and negative outcomes. Positive religious outcomes would include feeling connected with God, finding comfort and assurance in God's love and care, seeking God's aid in overcoming anger and/or seeking forgiveness, perceiving God as a source of strength in time of need, and attempting to find control through God's grace and help. This positive religious outcome allows one to better accept and adjust to the traumatic loss. Negative religious outcomes would include questioning God's love and mercy, feeling abandoned by God, feeling punished by God, questioning what I did wrong to make God punish me, and feeling confused or dissatisfied with God. Those who experience positive religious outcomes will exhibit fewer negative symptoms and psychological stress. Negative religious outcomes could lead to depression, lowered quality of life, and other negative psychological symptoms. For the religious person, death can bring out the frailty of faith, and it can detach us from any promise or hope that can lead to despair, hopelessness, leaving a dark cloud on our remaining days (Aden, 2005). Koenig (1997) found that negative religious coping led to greater depression and lower quality of life. Death is both natural and mysterious that activates a complex of emotions, thoughts, behaviors, and changes like no other experience in life (Richards, 2001). Rituals/ceremonies evoke a cognitive means of making sense of our traumatic losses.

For the Australian Aboriginals, ceremonies are sacred and secret at the same time. Elders hold knowledge that is crucial for survival, and this knowledge is kept secret because it only has meaning when it is spoken by the ceremonial elder to an initiate in a way that affects every aspect of his being (Randall, 2003). As in Native American religion, the Aboriginal religion does not separate the spiritual from the practical. After a traumatic event, a Lakota might go to the hills for spiritual renewal. For the Hopi, their sacred place would be the land of the red rocks, a place with a deep, reverent connection to their ancestor spirits as well as those of animals and plants (Aitchison, 1992: 31). For the Australian Aboriginals, there are also many sacred sites. The Katatjuta, or Olgas, located in the Northern Territory; Uluru, or Ayers Rock, located in the center of Australia; and even Mother Earth in her entirety is sacred. Like Native Americans, the Aboriginals think that the destruction of sacred sites causes illness and even death among elders (Voigt and Drury, 1997). Native Americans and Aboriginal peoples both manage traumatic death through rituals and ceremonies. The destruction of culture, the loss of tradition, and the influence of modern society has made it much more difficult for these groups of people to manage traumatic deaths.

For all religions, ritual and ceremony are basic. Hindus use elaborate cremation ceremonies that involve the entire community, African villagers engage in a series of mourning rituals that often last for weeks, Jewish traditions require burial within 24 hours but require a seven day mourning vigil or Shiva, Irish-Catholics hold wakes that includes humor and sadness from stories about the deceased in a long practiced ritual (Biziou, 1999).

While the rituals and ceremonies vary immensely, all religions use them to help manage traumatic death. The Chinese both detach and maintain connections with the deceased. Traditional Chinese farewell rituals are designed to assist the deceased in terminating their relationship with this world and their passage to the next with spiritual guides offering prayers during the wake, the funeral, burial service, and every seventh day from the date of death times seven (Cheung, Chan, Fu, Li, & Cheung, 2006). Cheung and colleagues report that the Chinese, unlike those of a Judeo-Christian background, typically link death to ghostly actions, to painful death, and to judgment in hell as punishment for any wrongful act that the person may have committed during their lifetime (Cheung et. al., 2006). Buddhists suggest that death is inescapable, that life is short, that the young and healthy may die before the old and infirm, that as sheep are taken to slaughter one moves closer to death with each step, and that rebirth leads to suffering and death (Klein, 1998). Dying and death are viewed as a religious opportunity in the process of dying and rebirth while traumatic death, depression, suicide, desperation, or fear can put the person at risk in the process (Klein, 1998) For all groups, rituals aid those who are grieving. Christians, Buddhists, Native Americans, and many other groups after experiencing a traumatic loss engage in rituals such as creating a sacred place, journaling or story-telling, drawing or writing, humor, music, art, creative experiences, and ritualistic prayer to aid their coping with loss. For example, a Buddhist family might create a sacred place in a room or less often used portion of the home containing pictures, trophies, and other artifacts from the person's life, candles and other sacred items, and items from the deceased person's life. Christians might include icons, crucifixes, rosary beads, and other religious items as well as the other items used by Buddhists. Such ritualistic acts allow us to keep the deceased close and to allow us to remain spiritually with them.

Spirituality and Traumatic Death

In recent years, there has been a trend to speak of spirituality rather than religion. What might have been described a generation or so ago as a religious person is now described as a spiritual person. As science and secularism have grown in society, the use of the term *spiritual* has replaced the term *religious*. People who do not even attend church can now be considered to be spiritual.

Catholic theologian Matthew Fox describes spirituality as the search for one's roots (Fox, 1981). Rabbi and scholar Earl Grollman suggests that being embraced by a loving community is fundamental to Jewish spirituality (Grollman, 2000). John D. Morgan suggests that spirituality is the human quest for meaning (Morgan, 1993).

The role of spirituality in grief is to offer the grieving ways to express their grief, to share their grief, and to bring them back from the chaos of traumatic death. Rituals allow the expression of our spirituality and aid our grief. Tom Golden (1996) suggests that ritual provide a way to release the chaos (Golden, 1996). Golden suggest that ritual activity is intended to connect with our pain and grief and allows us to move out of ordinary awareness and into the experience of grief in a safe way for a period of time (Golden, 1996). Elisabeth Kubler-Ross argues that each human has four quadrants: physical, intellectual, emotional, and spiritual. (A quadrant is literally "each of four parts of a circle, plane, body, etc., divided by two lines or planes at right angles." See http://askoxford.com).

The spiritual quadrant, which is based upon love we receive from others, sustains us through time and helps us through the windstorms of life that are all of the tragedies of our lives (Kubler-Ross, 1991). Not only does spirituality allow us to express our grief, but it also allows us to grow through meditation, reflection, prayer, and ritual expression.

Rabbi Jack Spiro suggests that if there are no rituals or ceremonies to appease the dead, then the living can turn fear into anxiety, and the bereaved can come to feel or be the victim of overwhelming hostility (Spiro, 1967). He also says that Jewish culture reflects the same ambivalence as other cultures between the desire to hold onto the dead and the desire to get rid of them as soon as possible, and that while immediate burial gets rid of the body as soon as possible, mourning rites and ceremonies guarantee the perpetuation of the dead (Spiro, 1967). By contrast, Buddha preached a religion devoid of ritual and suggested that the intense self-effort required to manage the end of suffering was in our hands (Smith, 1994).

Death is considered a natural occurrence within life, something to be accepted rather than feared. Rather than disconnecting with the dead, Native American peoples continue to have a relationship with them. From the Native American perspective, death is not a defeat. It is not the result of an offense against God or some other deity but, rather, the common fate of all.

Almost universally, tribes make provisions for a spirit journey, whether for a single burial or for a group burial (Atkinson, 1935). Tribal groups did not abandon their dead but provided them with ceremonies and dignified disposal.

Many spiritual practices exist for all cultures. Disposing of the dead is a universal spiritual practice. No where are losses of tradition in cultural practices more evident than in the realm of funeral practices. The European immigrants to the United States, Australia, and elsewhere have lost their own traditions and have attempted to destroy the traditions and practices of those whom they conquered. (From the indigenous perspective, the people who invaded the Americas, Australia, New Zealand, etc., are immigrants who conquered native peoples and destroyed or at least tried to destroy their cultures and religions.)

Golden (1996) suggests that the rituals of Potlatch Ceremony of the Athabaskan tribes of the Northwest North America allow the entire community and not just the grieving family to move from grief into a more joyous ceremony. The dominant U.S. culture, lacking grief rituals like the Potlatch, makes grief to be private and, paradoxically, places obstacles to connect to the grief within (Golden, 1996). David Adams (2002) suggests that after traumatic death, the spiritual challenges are not given sufficient attention, but rather the clergy are given the job of attending to religious rituals at the time of the funeral, burial, or cremation and that spirituality is often a low priority in family life (Adams, 2002).

All cultural groups develop patterns to manage death as a community. People wash and prepare the body. Family and friends mourn the loss. Some wear mourn-

ing clothes. All cultures engage in mourning practices. Some cremate, some bury the deceased. The deceased is assisted on his or her journey by song, laments, eulogies, gossip, laughter, joking, conversing with the dead, appeal to spirits, appeals to God, dancing, prayer, and ritual. Some cultural groups drop tradition because they become too sophisticated, cultured, religious, or educated to follow the "old ways." Spirituality and rituals that are not used are soon forgotten. Generally, most immigrants to the U.S. have deliberately rejected and long since forgotten their traditional ways.

Native American Spirituality

The values of Native Americans are reflected in their spirituality. Although all individuals do not think alike (McMaster and Trafzer 2004), the sacred is an important part of this world. The sacred is reflected through symbols in music, dance, silence, meditation, rituals, and ceremony. Encounters with the sacred evoke deep emotions and behavioral transformations. Music, dance, drama, art, and sculpture inspire spiritual engagement while providing explanations for why things such as birth, existence, and death occur. Each of the hundreds of indigenous nations have a diverse, rich, heritage of forms of spirituality, expressions, and traditional narratives (Tinker, 2004).

Evil also is embellished with meaning. The ultimate evil is often portrayed as death. The world is a violent, dangerous place, and yet, spiritual worlds evoke images of peace and harmony. The sacred gives meaning and purpose to human existence.

Spiritual empowerment originates from ritual, sharing with family and community, and living according to the model of spirituality of the group. All cultures have rites of passage, marriage, adulthood, aging, and death. Stories are told of children dying, engaging mythic monsters in combat, and challenging spirits in battle. In funeral rites, the newly dead are often thought to be in an in-between state. The dead are respected as ancestors; such ancestors also are feared as a potential source of death for those who live. Rituals that manage dead spirits are developed to cope with grief and loss. Artistic expression is also used to aid with loss.

Spirituality and Native American Values

A single American Indian religion cannot be identified. Nonetheless all religions and spiritual orientations have similarities. Native Americans believe they dwell in a world filled with spirits; birds carry messages, animals tell tales, rocks speak, and spirits roam the earth. Communication with mysterious beings is available to all. Dreams and visions provide messages or instructions that all may receive as a gift from the spirits. The dead remain a part of our lives. As Attig (2001) suggested that we can continue to love in the absence of our loved ones, Dennis Klass views the continuing relationship with the deceased as a way not only to recognize their death and to mourn them, but also to continue the bond with the deceased and give meaning and validation to our relationship with them (Klass, 2001). All life has a purpose/meaning; each person exists for a reason, and they spend their lives trying to identify what that reason may be. Visions, dreams, rivers, rocks, animals, birds, and spirits can give messages to be listened to. Cultures with oral traditions can travel back as far as the chain of memory will allow. In a world filled with spirits, the past provides a guide to the present. Storyteller's tales of animals that talk, of spirits that roam the earth, of rocks that have messages both instruct and entertain those who listen. Storytellers play drum, sing, and dance as they weave their tales, while masks, costumes, regalia, and performance mark their stories. Such rituals serve a spiritual role of aiding us in our spiritual journey of grief (Richards, 2001).

All of us face losses. One's spirituality can be an important component in that learning process. Tom Attig suggests that intellectual/spiritual coping helps us through concepts and beliefs to orient us to reality (Attig, 1995). Death is natural and mysterious. Traumatic death is not natural, but it does create mystery. Why did it occur? How did the person die? While losses are constant in life, traumatic death is not.

The person who is grieving a loss may ask others questions that are painful and confronting when they are in pain. We need to listen to the pain of our loved ones without judging or lecturing on the rightness or wrongness of their reactions (McKissock, 1998). After suffering a loss to a violent act, we may suffer dramatically over the loss of a favorite toy, a pet, or the loss of our house to a fire or other disaster and show little emotion over the death of a loved one. Our public reaction to the loss does not necessarily reflect the magnitude of the loss. Our grief for the toy or pet or even our grief for a person who was distant from us may be an outlet for other losses that occurred long ago (Gilbert, 1999). When grieving the loss of a loved one to a violent death, the loss of a pet may be more than we can handle. Little losses become big losses. We may or may not understand this process, but we need to try to understand the process of loss and growth to be able to cope with violent death.

Learning Objective: (30/40) (35/40) Understand that traumatic death is influenced by religious and spiritual aspects in a persons life.

Chapter 27

Historical and Contemporary Perspectives on Traumatic Death

Lillian M. Range

Traumatic deaths may contain elements of (a) suddenness and lack of anticipation, (b) violence, mutilation, and destruction, (c) preventability and or randomness, (d) multiple deaths, and (e) the mourner's personal encounter with death (Rando, 1993). Examples of traumatic deaths include suicide, homicide, terrorism, pervasive epidemics, genocide, and natural disasters. This review covers early theories (psychodynamic, attachment, cognitive-behavioral, and systems) and contemporary theories (existential, terror management, and constructivist/narrative) of traumatic deaths.

As early as 1920, psychodynamic theory addressed the issue of traumatic death. In an essay entitled *Beyond the Pleasure Principle*, Sigmund Freud (1975) developed the psychodynamic idea that humans have two instincts, both derived from broad, all-pervading biological principles. One instinct, called eros or libido, involves sexuality or love. The other instinct, called thanatos or aggression, involves death or self destruction. Aggression turned outward would result in murder, war, etc.; and, aggression turned inward would result in melancholy, depression, suicide, and destructive habits such as smoking, alcoholism, and other drug abuse, etc. According to psychodynamic theory, traumatic deaths that have a human component (such as murder) are a manifestation of the aggressive instinct.

After an experience such as a traumatic death, a person may develop annihilation anxiety, which is an exaggerated fear of his or her own death, or a repetition compulsion, which would involve intrusive thoughts, images, nightmares, etc., about the death. According to psychodynamic theory, the annihilation anxiety represents an unconscious fear that the death resulted from personal wishes, for which the person feels guilty. The repetition compulsion is an attempt to attain a psychic state such as analgesia or excitement, which reduces emotional pain. These responses may occur because of the person's heightened feeling of personal vulnerability to suicidal and homicidal impulses.

Psychodynamic theory emphasizes the critical importance of childhood conflicts. Thus, traumatic death may correspond in its essential features to some early childhood trauma or conflict-laden fantasy. The individual would then misperceive current reality in terms of the childhood conflict, and respond as he or she did in childhood. Alternatively, traumatic death may lead an individual to turn away from current reality and unconsciously seek gratification in the world of fantasy. The individual would then develop psychological symptoms based on the childhood conflicts (Arlow, 2004). Psychodynamic theory would posit that traumatic death overwhelms the person's ability to handle instincts, particularly the aggressive instinct. Historically, psychodynamic theory was precursor to other theories that also addressed the issue of traumatic death.

An outgrowth of psychodynamic theory, attachment theory began with a monograph summary of a report for the World Health Organization in 1951. John Bowlby (1969, 1982) emphasized the importance of attachment to the mother, particularly during the second half of the first year of life, when the relationship is developing. After World War II, Bowlby studied children who were orphaned by the war, or hospitalized for long periods for such problems as infectious diseases that made visits with their caregiver impossible. According to Bowlby, the effects of these separations were disastrous: after an initial reaction of devastation, the child typically displayed boredom and indifference with substitute attachment figures. Further, the problem was not ameliorated by reuniting with the caregiver. Attachment behaviors are instinctive, and have as their goal maintaining contact with another individual, in children thereby insuring survival. Attachment theory posits that the relationship with the mother forms the basis for all other relationships.

When the attachment bond is broken, people experience grief. A normal and universal phenomenon, grief requires those who experience it to reevaluate and reorganize their attachments to significant others. Bowlby posited that death of a loved one requires reorganization of attachments, a process that progresses through four phases: experiencing and expressing outside of oneself the reality of the death, tolerating the emotional suffering inherent in the grief while physically and emotionally nurturing oneself, converting the relationship with the deceased to a memory, and developing a new sense of identity based on a life without the deceased. These phases are generic to all who experience disruption in attachment bonds, but the duration and/or intensity differs from person to person, depending on a number of influencing factors.

Three social conditions introduce complications into the grieving process: the loss is socially unspeakable, the loss is socially negated, and the loss occurs in the absence of a social support network (Worden, 1991). Traumatic deaths are often unspeakable (e.g., suicide), socially negated (e.g., homicide), or in the absence of a social network (e.g., aftermath of hurricane Katrina). Therefore, traumatic deaths can threaten the attachment bond even more than other losses, thereby damaging the person's ability to make subsequent secure attachments.

Bowlby further distinguished between secure and insecure attachment. Insecurely attached children doubt the mother's good feelings toward them, and easily misinterpret things. Bowlby would say that traumatic deaths violate the young child's expectation of the parent as protector, and are especially likely to result in insecure attachment. Psychodynamic and attachment theory emphasized early life events, and laid the groundwork for other ways to understand traumatic deaths.

In the late 1950s, behavior theory emerged as a reaction to the psychodynamic theory prevalent at the time. Associated with Russian scientist Ivan Pavlov and American scientists B. F. Skinner, Joseph Wolpe, and Albert Bandura, behavior theory approached assessment and treatment of psychological problems based on classical and operant conditioning, emphasizing the role of contingencies in shaping human responses and adaptation. Behavior theory stressed the importance of commitment to the scientific approach, including testable hypotheses, measurable outcomes, replication, and innovative research strategies that allow rigorous evaluation of specific methods (Wilson, 2005). Behaviorism initially focused solely on observable behavior, rejecting all cognitive mediating processes.

Scientific Approach

Newer revisions of behavior therapy, associated with scientists such as Aaron Beck and Albert Ellis, however, recognized the importance of cognitive mediating processes. Thus, cognitive/behavioral theory posits that environmental events influence behavior depending on how the individual perceives and interprets them. For cognitive/behavioral theorists, whether or not a death is traumatic depends on how the individual interprets it.

For example, a person might react with learned helplessness to the sudden, unexpected death of a loved one, and subsequently develop depression. In this case, cognitive/behaviorists would examine current determinants of the depression rather than possible historical antecedents. The cognitive behaviorist would attempt to modify faulty perceptions and interpretations of the death, and would collaborate with the individual in acquiring new coping skills, improving communication, or learning to break maladaptive habits and overcome self-defeating emotional conflicts. A cognitive/behavioral therapist would examine the person's beliefs about self, other people, and the world, and conduct behavioral experiments to examine alternative interpretations and generate contradictory evidence. Along with its predecessors psychodynamic and attachment theory, cognitive/behavioral theory stressed individual responses to traumatic death.

CBT Approach

In contrast, systems theory focused on the entire family unit. In the 1950s, Murray Bowen and others began focusing on the family when treating disorders such as schizophrenia, with the view that illness in the person is the product of a total family problem (see Bowen, 1985; Sagar, 1997). In the family systems view, death can disrupt the equilibrium of the family unit, particularly the death of the breadwinner, a parent in a young family, or the head of the clan. Such deaths send an emotional shock wave through all family members, even those who were not close to the deceased person. From a systems theoretical view, traumatic deaths are those that disrupt family equilibrium. However, one type of death commonly considered traumatic, suicide, would not necessarily be considered traumatic death from a systems view. Suicides are commonly followed by prolonged grief and mourning reactions, but not an emotional shock wave unless the person who died played an essential role in the family.

Because of this view of all psychological disorders, systems therapy sessions involve multiple family members, sometimes across more than one generation. The goal of family therapy is to modify the family relationship system. The therapist(s) encourages family members to talk to each other, and avoids taking sides. One overriding concern would be to increase communication. A family systems approach to traumatic death would involve helping the family to cope with the death, perhaps by helping parents share their thoughts and feelings and helping children speak and be heard.

Psychodynamic, attachment, cognitive/behavioral, and systems theories all addressed the issue of traumatic death, and laid the groundwork for contemporary theories. Newer theories addressing traumatic death arose out of existential theory, and include narrative/constructivism and terror management.

Existentialism arose in the minds and works of a number of psychologists and psychiatrists in Europe in the 1940s and 1950s as a way of understanding humans that was more reliable and more basic than the prevailing psychodynamic theory. Associated with Ludwig Binswanger and Medard Boss in Europe, existentialism was introduced to the United States in 1958 with the publication of *Existence: A new dimension in psychiatry and psychology*, edited by Rollo May, Ernest Angel, and Henri Ellenberger. Existentialism asks fundamental questions about the nature of being human, and identifies four ultimate concerns: death, freedom, isolation, and meaninglessness. Existentialists note that death is unavoidable, and at the deepest levels we respond to this knowledge with mortal terror. A core conflict is between awareness of inevitable death and the simultaneous wish to continue to live.

To existentialists, any death plays a major role in internal experience, haunting the individual as nothing else can (May & Yalom, 2005). To cope with this terror, individuals erect defenses against death awareness. These defenses are based in denial, and include an irrational belief in being personally special, and an irrational belief in the existence of an ultimate rescuer. Anything that reminds people of their own mortality, especially a traumatic death, fundamentally challenges their denial, reminding them of their own death, and causing them to be terrified.

To help people confronted with traumatic death, an existentialist would strive to understand their current life situation and fears. The therapist would focus on personal responsibility for their own lives, such as by saying "You mean you won't face the death instead of you can't." The therapist would emphasize life choices, helping persons recognize that they themselves must generate and choose among options. The goal would be to help persons who have experienced traumatic death live life authentically, being open to nature, others and self.

According to existentialists, human beings spend much energy trying to transcend personal experience. A confrontation with one's own mortality, as in traumatic death, may block transcendence efforts or may be an impetus to live life more completely and fully, with increased mindfulness. Thus, any reminder of their own mortality such as traumatic deaths may push survivors to anxiety or despair. Alternatively, traumatic deaths can also motivate survivors to choose how to bear the ensuing suffering and focus on the positive aspects of the experience. In this case, survivors might count their blessings, and let go of the petty concerns that previously held their attention.

One outgrowth of an existential understanding of traumatic death constructivistic/ narrative theory, stresses the basic assumptions people hold about the world and themselves. These assumptions typically include a belief that the world is predictable and controllable, that the world is meaningful and operates according to principles of fairness and justice, that individuals are basically safe and secure, that the world is benevolent, and that, generally speaking, other people can be trusted (Janoff-Bulman, 1992). Assumptions of a benevolent world and a worthy self provide tremendous comfort.

Assumptions of existentialism

Traumatic deaths are out of the ordinary, directly experienced, and perceived as threatening survival and self-preservation. In traumatic deaths, individuals confront their own mortality and recognize their fragility as physical creatures. They recognize that what has happened does not readily fit their long-standing, fundamental, comfortable, and comforting assumptions about themselves and the world (Corr, 2005). Traumatic deaths shatter the assumptive world.

An early proponent of constructivistic/narrative theory, Ronnie Janoff-Bulman, focused on grief, mourning, and bereavement following the traumatic loss of a loved one. Janoff-Bulman maintained that a person who is unable to reconstruct or reinvent a new assumptive world is vulnerable to pathological grief, mourning, and bereavement, and may manifest the dissociative symptoms characteristic of post-traumatic stress disorder.

Constructivistic/narrative theory notes that in the immediate aftermath of a traumatic death, survivors may be confused about what exactly happened. They ordinarily need to review of the sequence of events in some detail, and may be frustrated and dismayed that information is inadequate to formulate a coherent account of the experience. Nevertheless, a starting point in placing the experience in the context of one's life is developing a basic narrative that includes some plausible causal explanation. The person needs to achieve a sense of cognitive mastery and to reestablish a sense of safety and control for the future. The process of forming an account of a traumatic death includes the questions, "What happened?" and, "How did it happen?" (Landsman, 2002). Because traumatic deaths fall outside cognitive schemas, violate assumptions, or shatter illusions, they are especially likely to lead to a crisis of meaning.

Another outgrowth of existentialism, terror management theory, was inspired by the writings of cultural anthropologist Ernest Becker, who synthesized ideas from the natural sciences, social sciences, and humanities to formulate what he hoped would become a general science of man (Becker, 1971). Terror management theory (Greenberg, Solomon, & Pyszczynski, 1997) posits that because of their sophisticated cognitive capacity, humans experience self-consciousness. As a by-product of self-consciousness, people are burdened not only with the knowledge that their existence will inevitably end and but also the recognition that potentially lethal events can never be fully anticipated or controlled. This knowledge, juxtaposed with a predisposition for survival, creates the potential for debilitating terror.

To cope with the terror, people construct cultural worldviews, humanly created symbolic conceptions shared by members of a group, that present a credible and security-providing depiction of reality to the acculturated individual. Cultural worldviews give meaning, order, and permanence to existence; provide a set of standards for what is valuable; and, promise some form of either literal or symbolic immortality to those who believe in the cultural worldview and live up to its standards of value.

Cultural worldviews promise literal immortality in their explicitly religious aspects that directly address the problem of death and promise heaven, reincarnation, or other forms of afterlife to the faithful who live by the standards and teachings of the culture. Cultural worldviews promise symbolic immortality by enabling people to feel part of something larger, more significant, and more eternal than their own individual lives through connections and contributions to their families, nations, professions, and ideologies. Cultural worldviews emphasize the psychological separation between humans and nature through a wide variety of cultural practices, such as eating with utensils, avoiding public nudity, and creating cultural artifacts, like automobiles and plastic bags. Cultural worldviews serve an important anxiety-buffering function thereby facilitating day to day functioning.

According to terror management theory, people often turn to their cultural worldview when faced with the crisis of death. Different cultures mold their members' transient experiences quite differently, but all cultures provide order, stability, meaning, and personal enduring significance (Pyszczynski, Solomon, & Greenberg, 2003). Research supports the premise that making death momentarily salient increases liking for members of one's own cultural in-group, and increases hostility for one's own cultural out-group. Any threat to cultural worldview, such as the mere existence of people with different cultural beliefs, would make people especially likely to respond by derogation, attempts at assimilation, or annihilation. Traumatic deaths would be especially likely to have this effect.

A substantial proportion of human activity is devoted to maintaining faith in one's own cultural worldview and the belief that one is meeting or exceeding the standards of value derived from that worldview. By heightening the tendency to turn to their cultural worldview, traumatic deaths would greatly intensify efforts to maintain personal faith and self-esteem.

Different theories may define traumatic deaths differently, stress personal history or current circumstances, and focus on individual, family, or culture. All recognize, however, that individual reactions are unique and personal needs vary for individuals who lose a loved one to traumatic death.

Learning Objective: (35/40)
Identify historical and Contemporary perspectives about traumatic death.

Chapter 28

Life Span Issues and Traumatic Death

David Lester

The experience of death has changed dramatically over the centuries. Life expectancy has increased tremendously and this change, together with the decline in extended families sharing the same residence, has resulted in people today having less experience of death of any kind. For example, in one parish in London in the 1580s, for every 100 babies born, about 70 survived to their first birthday, 50 to their fifth, and only 30 to their fifteenth (Forbes, 1970). Life expectancy in the United States rose from the 40s in 1900 to the 70s in 2000 (Lamb, 2003).

In the United States, wars have not occurred on American soil since the Spanish-American War of 1898-1902. The Civil War in 1861-1965 resulted in roughly 215,000 battle deaths, and the Spanish-American War only 385 battle deaths. Of course, the attack on the World Trade Towers in New York City on September 11, 2001, resulted in 2,948 deaths. Natural disasters have continued to take lives, although not to the extent as those in the past. The most lethal earthquake (in San Francisco in 1906) resulted in about 500 deaths, the most lethal hurricane (in Galveston, Texas, in 1900) resulted in roughly 7,000 deaths, and the most lethal set of tornadoes (in the South in 1884) resulted in about 800 deaths (Lamb, 2003). More recent disasters have not come near to breaking these records, and so traumatic death from these sources has become less common over the years.

In other parts of the world, of course, wars and disasters still account for deaths in large numbers. In these traumatic deaths, those of all ages can be victims and, in wars, children can even be perpetrators. However, there are few statistics available on the involvement by age in these traumatic deaths, although www.child-soldiers.org reported (March 27, 2006) that there were up to 300,000 children actively involved in armed conflicts. Epidemics of disease such as AIDS have also had a disproportionate effect by age, in some countries leaving a large proportion of children orphaned, while other catastrophes (such as famines) can result in higher mortality in children than in adults. However, accurate numbers on the impact of these events are not obtainable.

Accurate data on the incidence and experience of traumatic death are available primarily for suicide and homicide.

Homicide

The Victims

The incidence of homicide shows interesting trends. Lester (1986) found that the peak rate for being a victim of murder was most often being an infant in the first year of life, closely followed by being a young adult (25-34 years of age). Those nations with a peak rate for infants were, surprisingly, primarily nations in Western Europe such as Austria, Denmark, England and Wales, Germany, Norway, and Switzerland.

Even in the United States, the distribution of the murder rate by age is bimodal, with a secondary mode for infants. For example, in the year 2000 (www.who.int), the highest rates for being a murder victim for men were 20.9 per 100,000 per year for men aged 15-24, 16.2 for men aged 25-34, 10.2 for men aged 35-44 and 9.8 for infants. For women, the highest rate of being murdered was for infants (7.4), followed by women aged 25-34 (4.1)

These data suggest that more modern nations manage to suppress the murderous impulses of adults toward one another, but are less successful in suppressing the murderous impulses of parents and other adults toward children. Since stepchildren are murdered at a higher rate than children in intact homes (Daly & Wilson, 1996), the high rates of divorce and remarriage may be responsible in part for the high risk of being murdered for infants.

The majority of victims of homicide are male. Lester (1986) found that this outcome was so in almost every nation. Interestingly, Lester and Frank (1987) found that in the United States, babies of both sexes are murdered at the same rate. The sex difference in victimization appears only after the age of one. For the first year of life, the sex of the baby does not affect its risk of being murdered.

The Murderers

Just as the risk of being murdered is greatest for those aged 15-24, so the rate of murdering is greatest in youths of that age. In the United States in 2002, the rates of being a murderer by age ranged from 26.8 per 100,000 per year for those aged 18-24 to 1.4 for those aged 50 and older (www.ojp.usdoj.gov/bjs). The high rate of murdering by youths accounts for the fact that the proportion of youths aged 15-24 in the population is a very good predictor of the nation's homicide rate (Holinger, 1987).

Suicide

Fuse (1980) described three patterns in the distribution of suicide rates by age: (1) in the Hungarian pattern, the suicide rate increases with age, (2), in the Japanese pattern, the major peak is in old age but there is a minor peak in young adulthood, and (3) in the Scandinavian pattern, the suicide rate is an inverted U-shape with a peak in middle age. These labels for the patterns are not the best (for example, the pattern in most nations varies by sex), but these patterns are the most common found.

Lester (1982) and Girard (1993) found that the level of economic development was critically associated with suicide. The suicide rates for men peak in old age for almost all nations. For women, the peak rises from 55-64 to 75+ as the economic development of the nations decreases until, for the poorest nations, the peak is found in women aged 15-24. In the United States in 2000 (the latest year with data available on www.who.int), the suicide rates peaked at 42.4 for men aged 75 and older and at 6.7 for women aged 45-54.

Rising Youth Suicide Rates

Recent years have witnessed several claims of rising suicide rates in the youth of the world, sometimes in particular ethnic groups such as African-Americans or the Maoris in New Zealand. This increasing youth suicide rate is found primarily in male youths and not in female youths (Eckersley & Dear, 2002). Furthermore, often other age groups have higher suicide rates than youths. For example, Lester (1998) noted that, although suicide rates had risen in black males aged 15-24 in the United States, their rates were still lower than the suicide rate of black males aged 25-34. Not all nations experienced this increase in youth suicide. For example, the suicide rate for men aged 15-24 in Japan dropped from 40.9 in 1960 to 15.8 in 2000, in contrast to the United States where the rate rose from 8.1 in 1960 to 17.0 in 2000.

To explain the rising youth suicide rates in some nations, many commentators claim that the lives of youths have become increasingly stressful and unpleasant (e.g., Eckersley, 1993). Eckersley and Dear (2002) saw the high rate of suicide in youths as "the tip of the iceberg of suffering," arguing that the majority of youths today have a harder time developing identity and attachments than they did in times past.

In contrast, Lester (1990) used Henry and Short's (1954) theory of suicide to argue that, as the quality of life improves, suicide becomes more common (since there are fewer external sources to blame for one's misery, and the responsibility is internalized). Thus, the rising youth suicide rate, Lester argued, was a result of the improving quality of life for the youth. Indeed, worldwide, suicide rates are strongly associated with the quality of life in nations — the higher the quality of life in a nation, the higher the suicide rate.

Differences in the Circumstances of Suicide by Age

The motives and circumstances for suicide differ for younger and older suicides (Leenaars, 1989). Younger suicides are often reacting to interpersonal conflicts, whereas elderly suicides are often reacting to personal problems. Maris (1985) found that younger suicides (in their teens and 20s) more often had experienced suicide in their families, more often had divorced parents, had lower self-esteem, and more often killed themselves out of revenge. Lester (1994a) noted that older suicides use guns and hanging more than younger suicides, more often have an affective disorder (whereas younger suicides more often have a personality disorder), have experienced less recent stress, and are less motivated by interpersonal conflicts.

Lester (1994b) found that the major theories of suicide differed in how appropriate they were for particular age groups. For example, Ludwig Binswanger's (1963) theory was more appropriate for the elderly suicides, while theories of Carl Jung (1974), Henry Murray (1981) and Harry Stack Sullivan (1956) were less appropriate.

Suicide in the Very Young

Traditionally, medical examiners and coroners did not classify deaths of those under the age of 15 as suicides, but this tendency has changed in recent years as clinicians have documented suicidal behavior in younger and younger children (Pfeffer, 1986). For example, Leenaars (1996) presented the case of a suicide attempt in a four-year-old boy who tried to hang himself.

The Impact of Suicide on Survivors

Those who experience the suicide of a loved-one are called "survivors," and the variation of suicide rates with age affects survivors of different ages. Countries that have a higher youth suicide will more often leave parents bereaved, while countries with a high suicide rate in the elderly will more often leave children bereaved. Since survivors are at increased risk of suicide, this has important implications for the suicide rate of later generations.

The Impact of Traumatic Death on Survivors

There has been virtually no research on the grief process and possible post-traumatic stress in those of different ages, primarily because the same psychological tests are not appropriate for those of varying ages. What little research exists suggests that the grief associated with trauma is similar in children and adults (Melhem, et al., 2004). Repeated exposure to traumatic experiences appears to protect children from adverse outcomes (Garbarino & Kostelny, 1996) but, again, comparative studies of children and adults have not appeared. A study by Pfefferbaum, et al. (2006) on the reactions of children in Kenya after the 1998 bombing of the American Embassy in that nation reported that post-traumatic stress was associated with physical exposure to the bombing, stress from other negative life events, the type of bomb-related loss, and subsequent losses, associations that would be expected in adults exposed to the same trauma.

Discussion

For suicide and homicide, causes of mortality for which many nations keep accurate statistics, it is easy to show variations in their rates over the life span. There is less information as to how the meanings, motives and circumstances of these acts change over the life span. Although a few trends were noted for the act of suicide, acts of murder have not been studied in depth. Future research should explore how the phenomenon of murder varies with age and, in addition, should endeavor to collect more accurate data on the experience of other forms of traumatic death by age. Comparative studies by age of grief and post-traumatic stress after traumatic loss are also scarce, and this is another area that needs to be explored in the future.

LeARNING Objective: (40/40)
Describe the occurance of traumatic
death Across the Life Span.

Chapter 29

The Family, Larger Systems, and Traumatic Death

David A. Crenshaw

The Impact on the Family System of Traumatic Death

The wake of traumatic loss can reverberate through a family system for multiple generations (Bradach & Jordan, 1995; Brave Heart, 2003; Freudenberger & Gallagher, 1995; Klein, 1974; Rynearson, 2005). In clinical work this bereavement legacy has been known for some time but independent validation has recently come from an unexpected source: attachment theory research. Attachment researchers have found that unresolved grief and trauma result in disjointed and incoherent life narratives for adults and reduce their ability as parents to raise securely attached children (Siegel, 1999). Trauma disrupts the emotional life of the family and in some respects may halt the family's life cycle progress. In a family, for example, whose mother died of a crack overdose the children may be acting like much younger children five years later as if they were trying to turn the clock back to the time before the trauma occurred.

While the effects of the trauma may be registered in each family member in different ways, typically no one completely escapes the impact. While the family system is deeply affected by the devastating blows of trauma events, it also contains the healing forces that potentially enable its members to resume full participation in life in due time.

The Family Systems Approach to Reconciling to a Traumatic Loss

Families who have suffered a traumatic loss cannot expect to return to the pre-loss state. A more reasonable expectation is that they can reconcile to the traumatic loss and gradually resume full participation in life, but such events cause families to be forever changed. We should not assume that the family will be changed in a pathological way. The process of reconciling to such a devastating loss may strengthen the family's ties and deepen the inner resources of the individual family members. The art of family systems work is to conceptualize and to intervene within a relational framework. Important relational questions are pursued such as "Who within the nuclear family and the extended family was most affected by the trauma events?" or "What changes have been observed by other family members as a result of the traumatic loss and who else in the family has been most affected by those changes?" Additional questions to pursue would include "Who is most worried about the most affected members in the family?" and "Who in the family is having the hardest time right now?" These relational questions stem from the assumption of family systems theory that changes in one or more family members will impact the homeostasis (stability) of the entire family unit and this issue needs to be carefully considered and sensitively understood in planning interventions in the family.

An example may be helpful in illustrating the ripple effect of change within the family. A family living in an economically deprived neighborhood suffers the trauma of their 17-year-old son dying in a drive-by shooting on his way to school, and his 13-year-old sister soon develops separation anxiety and refuses to leave the house even to go to school. It would be logical to assume that the younger sister fears leaving her house and going to school because of the murder of her brother while he was on his way to school. By asking relational questions, however, it is learned that while those fears are part of the explanation of her symptoms, it is only part of the story. It soon becomes apparent by exploring effects of the trauma on different family members, that the daughter's main worry is about her mother who has been clinically depressed since her brother's death. She is afraid to leave her mother alone in the house. Further exploration leads to the revelation that her worst fear is that her mother might commit suicide if she were left alone. If the daughter's symptoms had been viewed simply as part of a Post-Traumatic Stress Disorder without the relational component the main underpinning to her fears would not have been addressed.

Thus, the family systems approach to traumatic loss honors the centrality of relationships and attachments in our lives and the focus is on the family unit as a whole. The constant pursuit of the helper is to determine who else in the family is connected or affected by the traumatic event. A valuable resource for all who work with traumatic loss in the family context is *Living Beyond Loss: Death in the Family, Second Edition* (Walsh and McGoldrick, 2004). In understanding the impact of traumatic loss in general a helpful resource is *Loss of the Assumptive World* (Kauffman, 2002).

Families need education about trauma issues so they can be enlisted as an ally and a partner in trauma treatment rather than be viewed as a hindrance. Figley and

McCubbin (1983) identified some key family strategies for coping with trauma. They identified the following strategies as helpful: 1) taking a solution-focused approach and avoiding blaming; 2) respecting the right of each family member to grieve in their own ways;) clearly expressing affection and commitment for other members of the family; 3) maintaining open and clear communication within the family; 4) achieving a high degree of family cohesion; 5) manifesting considerable role flexibility within the family; 6) utilization of resources within and outside the family; and 7) avoiding physical violence and abuse of alcohol or drugs.

The Trauma-Focused Treatment Approach for Children and Families

An empirically derived treatment model for childhood traumatic grief (CTG) has been developed that includes a parental treatment and family sessions as well (Brown & Goodman, 2005; Brown, Pearlman, & Goodman, 2004; Cohen, Goodman, Brown. & Mannarino, 2004; Cohen & Mannario, 2004a; 2004b). Their work builds on the groundbreaking work of Pynoos and Nader (1990) in helping children and families exposed to traumatic death. Cohen and Mannarino (2004b) define child-hood traumatic grief (CTG) as "a condition in which trauma symptoms impinge on children's ability to negotiate the normal grieving process" (p. 819). Brown and Goodman (2005) add further clarification, "According to our current understanding of CTG and normal grief, thoughts and images of a traumatic nature are so terrify-ing, horrific, and anxiety-provoking that they cause the child to avoid and shut out these thoughts and images that would be comforting reminders of the person who died" (p. 255, 257). The treatment model includes addressing both grief and trauma components and involves separate sessions for the children and the parents but some family sessions as well to facilitate sharing of the trauma narrative within the potentially healing context of the family. The treatment protocol is relatively short-term (approximately 16 sessions). A recent attempt to build on the solid foundation of the work of Brown, Goodman, and Cohen and Mannarino to develop strategies for children and families who have suffered multiple traumas and losses and who may require both a more extended treatment intervention is described in previous writing (Crenshaw, 2005). The strategies consist of projective drawing and story-telling strategies that offer clinicians tools to deal with such seriously impacted youth and families. These techniques offer the advantage of approaching the trau-ma events gradually in the relative safety offered by symbolism and metaphor.

Mass Trauma and Death—When the Unthinkable Happens

The events of 9/11 and the more recent impact of hurricane Katrina reminds us in a shocking and horrifying way that trauma can occur on a massive scale even on our own soil, not necessarily in some distant part of the world. Such events are so horrifying they are unthinkable; it is hard to grasp the magnitude of the devastation entailed. In a lecture after 9/11, Bessel van der Kolk (2003) described how immediately after these horrifying events that New York City and Washington, D. C. were transformed from the hustle and bustle of major metropolitan areas into something you would expect to find in a small town in the Midwest. People were patient, kind, and helpful with one another. Van der Kolk noted that this change in behavior was absolutely necessary in order for people to survive after such a terrifying event. Otherwise persons would simply "lose their minds." It was also a time when we all learned how important home and family is to each of us. Van der kolk noted the almost universal wish of Americans on that day and the days that followed to find their way back to home and be reunited with family and loved ones.

Robert Kastenbaum (2004) notes that mainstream thanatology has focused its efforts on improving the understanding, care, and social integration of people who are exposed to life-threatening illness or bereavement, but that in light of the large-scale disasters the world has recently witnessed it may now be time to expand the vision, scope, and mission to include large-scale death. He discusses the 9/11 terrorist attacks as an example of mass death with complex correlates and consequences. A useful reference for counselors involved in mass disasters is a recent book, *Mass Trauma and Violence: Helping Families and Children Cope* (Webb, 2004). The book describes a range of effective interventions to help children and families cope with major traumatic experiences such as community violence, war, and terrorist attacks, and are based on the latest knowledge on stress and coping, bereavement, attachment, and risk and resilience.

Grief on a Large Scale and the Public Response

When major disasters or acts of terrorism occur resulting in large numbers of casualties, not only are there many bereaved survivors, but the larger community or even the nation may experience grief not only for those directly effected but it may trigger memories of traumatic losses in their personal histories. When the 9/11 attacks occurred, Lenore Terr (May, 2003) in a presentation to the New York Association for Play Therapy described how children and some adults as well who were thousands of miles from the Twin Towers or the Pentagon experienced what she called "distant trauma." This impact was heightened by the constant replay on television of the videos of the planes hitting the Towers and their subsequent collapse and the wreckage of the planes in Washington, D.C. and Pennsylvania.

When the public is impacted on such a dramatic and large scale, it is important as van der Kolk stated in a lecture at the 2003 (March) Psychotherapy Networking Conference in Washington, D.C. that a strong leader who is able to retain effective executive functioning (frontal lobe skills) emerge and take charge just as Mayor Rudy Giuliani did in New York City. The public felt reassured that someone had a grip on what steps to take and was exercising strong leadership. As Phillips (2005) observes, when death occurs on such a large scale not only are there many members of the public in need of bereavement support but many of the structures that would ordinarily provide support, such as schools and churches, may be disrupted and unable to carry out their usual role of providing stability and comfort to the community. Fortunately, national organizations like the American Red Cross and hospice programs have bereavement and trauma support services and provide invaluable support in the wake of such events. Bereavement support groups at times of great public grief offer additional support when major disaster relief organizations may be strained in terms of resources to meet the needs of so many. In addition many professional organizations, the American Psychological Association would be one example, have disaster response teams consisting of trained volunteers who work with Red Cross and other volunteer agencies to provide psychological and bereavement support.

At times of either traumatic grief within the family, or on a large scale within a community due to a natural disaster, or in the case of a nation in the event of a terrorist attack, the environment for recovery is bolstered when family members or the public at large can be reassured as to the restoration of stability and safety. While public rituals of grief and mourning can be enormously helpful in providing sanction and support for grieving and the reinforcement of the love and concern of others, the return to normal routines as soon as feasible can also bring significant comfort. Going to school for children, going back to work for adults, restores structure to one's life. Attending church or the synagogue or mosque is a source inspiration and strength to many, and these regular ways of functioning in life provide a secure and predictable framework in the lives of people at a time when their world appears to be crumbling. While it is difficult to find evidence-based bereavement support programs, it is noteworthy that the Family Bereavement Program, which has components that are both child focused and family focused, is currently studied in outcome studies to not only evaluate its overall effectiveness but how specific components of the program effect its outcome (Sandler, Ayers, Wolchik, Tein, et al. 2003; Tein, Sandler, Ayers, & Wolchik, 2006).

Issues Faced by Survivors

In a recent review of the literature Cohen (2005) concludes that while empirical knowledge regarding effective treatments for traumatized children increased in the past decade, there still remains much that is unknown. There has been increasing support for the efficacy of trauma-focused cognitive behavioral therapy (TF-CBT) for treating PTSD but few other psychosocial treatments have been adequately evaluated to date. Psychopharmacological studies have identified some promising medication treatments, but these are yet to be tested in randomized, placebo-controlled trials. No empirical studies have evaluated the efficacy of early interventions provided to children in the acute stages following mass disasters or terrorist attacks. Cohen identifies the need for more research to identify effective treatments for traumatized children and families and to identify effective methods for implementing evidence-based treatments to community practitioners. The same lack of solid empirical support for grief counseling in general was the focus of a recent review (Jordan & Neimeyer, 2003). The authors call for more focused research to answer the questions of when and for whom grief counseling is helpful. I would further add the question whether there might be circumstances when it is contraindicated or even harmful.

Dyregrov (2004), like Jordan and Neimeyer, as well as Cohen, raises the important question of when is professional assistance empowering or disempowering to survivors of traumatic deaths. Dyregrov at the Center for Crisis Psychology in Norway reviewed studies that indicated that bereaved families want to receive help after traumatic deaths from mainstream sources, but this help is not always available. She observes that families experiencing traumatic bereavement are not able to access appropriate services along the same lines as those suffering similar levels of somatic complaints. She argues that the key contributing factors for this disparity is lack of knowledge and inadequate organization of services and that somatic service issues take priority over psychosocial difficulties and suffering. The same lack of preparedness, disorganization, and frustration of survivors was seen in our own country after the hurricane Katrina disaster.

A public mental health approach to the postdisaster treatment needs of children and adolescents was detailed by Robert Pynoos and colleagues including recommendations for needed levels of organization, methods of screening and triage, training and supervision of mental health professionals, design and implementation of treatment approaches, and longitudinal monitoring of intervention outcomes (Pynoos, Goenjian, & Steinberg, 1998).

A study in Israel of two communities impacted by mass trauma identified certain factors that may help identify persons at greater risk for posttraumatic stress disorder (Shalev, Tuval-Mashiach, & Hadar, 2004). These investigators suggest that acute stress reactions and overall resilience in the victimized communities are the rule rather than the exception. Risk factors affecting long term outcome include the severity of the trauma, lack of sufficient and accessible support systems, and mass violence caused by malicious human intent more than natural disasters; persons at greater risk for PTSD include school-aged children, women, persons with existing psychiatric illness, and those who experienced significant losses or threats to life. Shalev, Tuval-Mashiach, and Hadar (2004) further recommended that early intervention in communities suffering mass trauma should consist of general support and bolstering of the recovery environment rather than psychological treatment; some forms of early psychological interventions may worsen outcome.

Issues faced by Rescue Workers

Those who courageously and selflessly rush to scenes of mass disasters or terrorist events to help others are faced not only with physical dangers but mental health risks as well. A recent study of disaster workers following 9/11 found that perceived safety is an important factor in health and the ability to work after traumatic exposure to disaster events (Fullerton, Ursano, Reeves, Shigemura, & Grieger, 2006). The study examined symptoms of PTSD, depression, and perceived safety in disaster workers two weeks after the 9/11 terrorist attacks. The findings indicate that perceived safety was lower in those workers with greater exposure and was associated with greater symptoms of intrusion and hyperarousal but not avoidance, depression and peritruamatic dissociation.

Another recent study suggests the advisability of assessing and following up the partners of rescue workers at the scenes of disasters (Pfefferbaum, Tucker, North, Jeon-Slaughter, Schorr, Wilson, & Bunch, 2006). They evaluate 24 female partners of firefighters who helped in recovery efforts with the terrorist bombing in Oklahoma City. The partners were assessed 43 to 44 months later. Most of the participants with post-bombing symptoms suffered from pre-existing conditions. 40% met both intrusive re-experiencing and hyperarousal criteria. More than half met the criteria for hyperarousal criteria on at least one measure. These researchers recommend that partners of disaster recovery workers be assessed for mental health and physiological consequences related to their indirect exposure since these outcomes may persist years after the event, even in the absence of a diagnosable psychiatric condition.

A significant portion of disaster workers will not utilize mental health services even when readily available (Jayasinghe, Spielman, Cancellare, Difede, Klausner, & Giosan, 2005). In a study of disaster workers assigned to the World Trade Center, among 174 workers given psychotherapy referrals following psychiatric screening for WTC-related symptoms, 42.5% attended at least one session, while 57.5% chose not to attend to all. Race/ethnicity and severity of symptoms as rated by clinicians distinguished workers who utilized treatment from those who did not. A study in Norway following a bus disaster in 1988 in which 12 Swedish children and three adults were killed and many were injured found that helpers experienced most reactions following disengagement from the disaster work (Dryregrov & Mitchell, 1992). Among the common reactions were helplessness; fear and anxiety; existential insecurity; rage; sorrow and grief; intrusive images; self-reproach, shame and guilt; and alterations in values. Clearly the suffering of heroic rescue workers and their families needs to be a major priority for disaster planning and intervention.

Issues Faced by Counselors

Counselors have their own histories of loss and perhaps experience trauma and concerns for their own safety and that of their families at the same time they strive to be fully emotionally available and responsive to the victims of disasters. This work-related reality presents both a unique challenge and an occupational hazard. Compassion fatigue is the term elaborated by Charles Figley (1995) as a variant of secondary trauma occurring in those helpers who become emotionally overwhelmed in their efforts to provide comfort, compassion, and support for others facing traumatic stress. Figley (1995) defined compassion fatigue (CF) "as the formal caregiver's reduced capacity or interest in being empathic or bearing the suffering of clients and is the natural consequent behaviors and emotions resulting from knowing about a traumatizing event experienced or suffered by a person"(p.7). Figley views CF as consisting of two components: secondary trauma and job burnout (Adams, Boscarino, & Figley, 2006).

A study of mental health clinicians working with traumatized victims of terrorism in New York City and Israel found that the strongest predictors of compassion satisfaction were 1) little attachment anxiety and 2) ample clinical experience treating trauma victims (Racanelli, 2005). She found that the strongest predictors of burnout were 1) negligible clinical experience, 2) nominal experience with trauma victims, and 3) avoidant attachment patterns. These findings are significant in the implications for selecting mental health workers to do disaster trauma work and the training and experience required to do this extremely emotionally taxing work.

We can ill afford to ignore the mental health needs and support that front line counselors require in order to be effective in their dedicated efforts to help traumatized survivors. It is crucial that those who do this heroic work make a priority of self-care. Resistance to deleterious effects of exposure to trauma victims includes maintaining relationships with family and friends that provide important nurture and support, engaging passionately hobbies and a variety of interests, providing adequate nutrition, getting enough rest, and engaging in regular exercise along with fun and relaxation (see Webb, 2004 for other self-care suggestions).

Learning Objective: (40/40)
Detail the family + public Responses
to traumatic death.

Chapter 30

Ethical and Legal Issues in Traumatic Death

David K. Meagher

Introduction

Events in the recent past have resulted in the need for grief counselors to become more knowledgeable of the impact of trauma on the grief process. The bombing of the federal building in Oklahoma, the terrorist attack on the World Trade Center in New York and the Pentagon building in Washington, D.C., on September 11, 2001, the train bombings in Madrid, Spain, on March 11, 2004, and the underground bombings in London, England on July 7, 2005, have demonstrated the need to prepare more effective trauma-grief support personnel.

The purpose of this chapter is to introduce the reader to a number of legal and ethical issues around the diagnoses of, treatment strategies for, and research into trauma and traumatic grief. In addition, a discussion of the rights of the victims of traumatic deaths will be presented. An awareness of the issues should provide sufficient motivation to those skilled in grief counseling but not in trauma support to further their studies and training prior to offering assistance to individuals who have experienced a traumatic event.

Definitions

A first step in a discussion of the ethical and legal issues in traumatic death must be the task of arriving at universal definitions of trauma, traumatic death, and traumatic grief. This agreement is necessary in order for there to be:

1. objective criteria for assessing a response to a loss;
2. reliable means of identifying needs of the affected individuals;
3. valid instruments for data collection; and
4. development of effective intervention techniques.

Trauma describes the exposure of an individual to an event that is, for that person, out of the ordinary – a traumatic event, if you will.

Traumatic event, then, is one that is beyond what could be expected to occur in the normal course of a person's life.

Traumatic grief is defined as the elements of sudden, perhaps horrific, shocking encounters in addition to a loss.

"When the circumstances of a loved one's death are traumatic (as in cases of death through homicide, suicide, or disfiguring accident) or when the loss itself violates the 'natural order' (as in the untimely death of children or young adults), then additional challenges to the survivor's adaptation arise beyond those associated with bereavement per se. As with the basic impact of bereavement, these (challenges) can be observed on both biophysical and psychosocial levels" (Neimeyer, 2002, p. 936).

Although virtually all death may be perceived as personally traumatic, five factors are usually considered necessary for the diagnosis of **traumatic death**:

1. suddenness and lack of anticipation
2. violence, mutilation, and destruction
3. preventability and/or randomness,
4. multiple deaths, and
5. the surviving mourner's personal encounter with death, where there is either a significant threat to personal survival or a massive and/or shocking confrontation with the death and mutilation of others.

In addition to the above definitions, the professional literature also includes other syndromes describing difficult responses to death loss. Often these terms are used synonymously with or are considered to be the same as traumatic grief syndrome. Two responses frequently described are pathological grief and complicated grief (Prigerson, 2005; Stroebe, Hansson, Stroebe, & Schut, 2001).

Pathological grief has been defined as a grief response that becomes a threat to the health and well-being of the person. It is seen as a detectable, harmful departure from what would be considered as a *normal grief response*. Within this model, inhibited grief, delayed grief, or chronic grief are the defining elements.

Complicated grief or **complicated bereavement** is often the term used to describe a person's failure to accept the fact of the loss (Rando, 1993). Complicated grief brought on by the death of a significant other may evoke a traumatic grief syndrome (TGS). TGS, according to Neria and Litz (2003), is a pathological response to the loss of a significant other. It is separate and distinct from states of depression and anxiety and posttraumatic stress disorder (PTSD). TGS, these authors posit, is comprised of two sets of symptoms: separation distress symptoms and traumatic distress symptoms.

T.Q. 5

The Diagnostic and Statistical Manual of Mental Disorders (DSM) IV (American Psychiatric Association (APA), 2000) lists five basic criteria for **Posttraumatic Stress Disorder**: the stressor event, a re-experiencing of symptoms, avoidance behavior, a numbing of general responsiveness, and arousal. The disturbance must cause clinically significant distress in significant areas of life (APA, 2000).

Although differences between PTSD and TGS have been reported in the literature (Courtois, 2004; Davis, 1998), these differences are more theoretical than empirical in nature. Clearly, "more exploration of the overlap between trauma and loss is needed, including the processes involved, the nature of the responses, and theoretical or conceptual notions that might link these two areas of study addressing some of the most difficult experiences that we, as humans, must endure" (Green, 2000, p. 14).

Legal Issues

The major legal problem inherent in the area of traumatic grief is a lack of agreed-upon definitions that permit the development of reliable and valid tools of diagnoses and assessment. Misdiagnosis and inappropriate techniques of intervention can cause harm to the grieving person. Incidents of harm are considered a major reason for the institution of malpractice suits against trauma specialists and grief counselors.

If there are not clear distinctions between traumatic grief syndrome and post-traumatic stress disorder, as inferred earlier, then the chances of a misdiagnosis and subsequent inappropriate intervention techniques are increased. Significant overlap in the signs and symptoms of normal grief, traumatic grief, and posttraumatic stress syndrome make it very difficult to arrive at a valid diagnosis.

Other legal issues that will be discussed with ethical concerns later in the chapter include:

1. diagnosis and treatment of children;
2. the rights of victims of traumatic deaths, including the rights of crime victims; and
3. informed consent issues in trauma research.

When Pitman and Sparr (1998) write that the use of PTSD as a diagnosis of a psychologic disorder has severe diagnostic reliability and validity, they might have also been describing issues of TGS. They identify common errors leading to both the over-diagnosis and under-diagnosis of PTSD. The following table outlines these errors.

PTSD DIAGNOSES ERRORS

OVER-DIAGNOSES ERRORS	UNDER-DIAGNOSES ERRORS
Failure to separate expectable emotional distress from the mental disorder.	Characterization of PTSD symptoms as normal reactions to a traumatic event.
Application of fewer criteria than are required for the proper diagnosis.	Basing opinion on inadequate, open-ended interviews without an adequate attempt to explore details of the traumatic event and subsequent symptomatology.
Failure to consider the contribution of earlier, unrelated traumatic events to the client's illness.	Idiosyncratic thresholds for diagnosis.
Failure to diagnose preexisting psychopathology.	Failure to acknowledge that the diagnosis of PTSD may be made despite the presence of major vulnerability factors.
Failure to identify a positive family history of mental disorder that may point to another etiology.	Mistaking predisposition for pre-existing psychopathology.
	False attribution of the client's symptoms to other life events.

(Pitman & Sparr, 1998, pp 2-3)

Diagnostic Issues

The need for valid, reliable instruments of assessment is substantial. Although Baldwin, Williams, and Houts (2004) support the use of current PTSD diagnostic tools, they do remind the diagnostician that the assessment scales are based primarily on subjective descriptions by the victim. Simon (1995) raises the legal issue of the objective validity of the instruments. It is his position that both the psychological and physiological scales designed to objectify the diagnosis of PTSD are based on subjective accounts. With regard to the physiological measures, the results may indicate the presence of a general stress response not connected to a traumatic experience (Simon, 1995).

Questions concerning the ability to distinguish among the varied responses to a loss need to be answered so that appropriate necessary forms of intervention may be utilized. The issue becomes more clouded when the concepts of complex posttraumatic stress disorder (CPTSD) and disorders of extreme stress not otherwise specified (DESNOS) symptoms not addressed by a PTSD diagnosis, is added to the mix of possible trauma responses. Instruments designed to diagnose PTSD may not reveal the complexities of CPTSD/DESNOS (Courtois, 2004).

A number of problem areas reducing the reliability of assessment instruments to diagnose CPTSD/DESNOS have been identified. They include:

1. difficulty in controlling affective impulses;
2. issues associated with maintaining attention;

3. changes in self-perception;
4. significant changes in a person's belief system;
5. inability to trust or feel close to others;
6. onset of medical problems affecting all major body systems; and
7. feelings of hopelessness and a lack of belief that others can understand them or their suffering (Courtois, 2004, p. 414).

Ethical Intervention Issues

Certain issues are both ethical and legal in nature. For example, confidentiality is both an ethical concept that often serves to protect the client or patient and a legal term that refers to a client's statutory right to have confidential information protected. National and state mental health associations have developed and continue to refine ethical standards in an attempt to create a model code of conduct to ensure the protection of patients' rights. These standards are also promulgated to provide guidance for the profession, and help prevent patient exploitation and impairment of therapists' judgment.

Two issues critics raise concerning the effectiveness and timing of trauma counseling (Dyregrov, 2004) are:

1. What determines the need for professional assistance? and
2. Does professional assistance help (empower) or do harm (disempower) a person experiencing a traumatic reaction to a loss?

There have been several strategies offered for defining the limits of professional assistance. They range from not intervening unless the affected individual requests help to offering immediate debriefing assistance with or without long-term follow-up. Any strategy of intervention must have, at a minimum, the following goals:

1. normalizing the situation,
2. minimizing recovery time,
3. reducing distress,
4. restoring functioning, and
5. mobilizing resources (Dyregrov, 2004).

When selecting a treatment strategy, issues of age, severity level, type of trauma response, and acuteness of the response must be taken into consideration. Overall, the most highly recommended techniques are anxiety management, cognitive therapy, exposure therapy, and psychoeducation (Dyregrov, 2004; Marotta, 2000).

Maguire (1997) suggests a recovery bill of rights for trauma survivors encompasses four major areas of legal and ethical concerns: (1) personal authority — the right to manage and direct one's recovery; (2) personal boundaries — the right to have one's person respected and to be permitted to accept or reject any and all suggestions for treatment; (3) communication — the right to clear explanations and respect for one's feelings; and (4) intervention — the right to choose one's own counselor, to expect that the counselor is trained in trauma treatment and he/she will abide by the laws and ethics of confidentiality. Clients should expect that they will be taught skills that lessen the risk of re-traumatization.

It is essential that grief counselors identify best practices for providing trauma loss services. The counselor must develop practice guidelines so as to demonstrate not only the effectiveness but also the ethics of the practice.

Intervention with Children

Children who have experienced a traumatic event present special legal and ethical issues and what little information is available is sometimes contradictory. For some, terrorism is not a discrete event for children. It is a continuous stressor. This position holds that children who develop PTSD after exposure to terrorism often continue to manifest symptoms of PTSD over time, even though the terrorist threats are no longer present (Street & Sibert, 1998). Fremont (2004) suggests using the term "continuous stress syndrome" for children. However, Henry, Tolan, and Gorman-Smith (2004) found no differences between pre- and post-September 11 in children in symptoms of traumatic grief or PTSD; specifically on measures of child anxiety, depression, and feelings of safety.

There are many serious methodological problems inherent in, and specific to, research on children and trauma: (1) current diagnostic formulations of PTSD may not be operationally sound when applied to children as they lack age-appropriate diagnostic sensitivity and specificity; (2) symptom characteristics unique to PTSD can affect reliability and validity estimates of trauma measures; (3) few studies of trauma and children have utilized control groups, and specific, trauma-related studies have assessed effects on small, unique samples making generalization difficult; and (4) few treatment outcome studies incorporate designs with adequate empirical rigor to explore effectively the respective influence of possible moderator variables (e.g., race, age, or gender) or mediator effects (e.g., treatment compliance or family support (Cook-Cottone, 2004).

The signs and symptoms of PTSD in children can vary dramatically with respect to the severity, chronicity, and number of symptoms (Chibbaro & Jackson, 2006; Faust & Katchen, 2004). Professional interveners must distinguish between an unanticipated single event and repeated exposure characterized by massive denial, psychic numbing, and personality problems. These manifestations may be consistent with classic PTSD symptoms (Cook-Cottone, 2004; Faust & Katchen, 2004). The professional caregiver/counselor must modify the treatment employed, especially with the child's grief reactions. Grief work must be conducted prior to addressing the PTSD reaction and the processing of grief should be revisited periodically.

When becoming involved with children who are experiencing signs of a traumatic response, or when designing studies to involve direct contact with children, consideration must be given to their attention span, level of development, and literacy skills. Of course, working with children requires consent of the child and informed consent of an adult caregiver. The child's consent is not sufficient to begin intervention or data collection but it should be necessary to begin the process. Even assuming that parents or guardians make decisions that are in the best interests of their children does not absolve counselors or researchers of their responsibility to ensure that no harm is caused by the intervention.

Cunningham (2003) cautions potential interveners not to ask children to participate in a trauma study that is not in the best interest of the child. Such studies should be used when the information cannot be gained in any other way. If a child is still at risk, the appropriate social services consistent with local ordinances should be notified.

Victim/Survivor Rights

Unlike many other countries, the United States does not have a national legislated set of legal rights for trauma or crime victims. A constitutional amendment to protect the rights of crime victims was introduced into Congress in 2003; however, the proposal was referred to committee and never returned for a vote.

Every state has a victims' bill of rights. These rights generally include the rights associated with criminal cases and deal with issues of protection, intimidation, notification, victim input at bail hearings, plea bargaining, sentencing, and parole, the use of victim trauma as evidence, and due process rights. What remains unaccomplished is any comprehensive cataloging or interpretation of these cases. As a result, it is unclear whether there can be any certain prediction about how victim rights will eventually be interpreted in the criminal justice system (Young, 1997).

A summary of rights that have been suggested include the rights to be:

- treated as human beings, not as evidence;
- provided with information about case status and what to expect at trial;
- evaluated as to the onset of any psychological trauma the victim may be experiencing;
- permitted to have someone present at the trial on whom the victim can count for emotional support;
- informed and consulted with about potential plea-bargain or diversion procedures; and
- given the opportunity for input into proceedings when possible, including the opportunity to make a victim impact statement (Kilpatrick, 1986; Jackson, 2003).

A few states have enacted measures allowing victims to recover damages resulting from acts of terror. These measures generally allow victims and their families to recover damages for emotional distress and any other relief that the local or state courts may deem necessary. Kilpatrick and Resnick (1993) suggested guidelines for criminal justice and victim service professionals that can increase their understanding of, and development of policies related to, the mental health treatment of crime victims include:

1. trauma victims and their family members may experience immediate, short-term, and long-term trauma-related mental health problems that require treatment;
2. considerable individual variation exists among trauma victims in the types of psychological injuries they are likely to sustain, and how long it will take them to reconstruct their lives, with or without treatment;
3. for many victims, elimination of trauma-related psychological injuries may not be a realistic treatment goal. Rather, helping victims to learn to cope is the main objective; and
4. at times of stress (including criminal justice system-induced stress), victims are likely to have exacerbations of psychological injuries.

Cultural Issues

Trauma must be viewed from the perspective of the culture. A Western perspective sees trauma as an individual phenomenon. Support strategies are created to address this individual response. This view is not universal, and it does not permit attention to a wider, social element of the traumatic situation. An emphasis on the trauma and intervention focused on the individual may be contrary to the culture in which the person resides.

While all recovery from trauma and loss requires: (1) the reconstruction of meaning; (2) the rebuilding of hope; and (3) the sense of empowerment needed to regain control of one's being and life; intervention, to be successful, must be provided within historic contexts (Valent, 1998). Stresses may be brought on by or exacerbated by such socio-cultural factors as armed conflicts, racism, economics, and politics. As such, it is imperative for the intervener to learn about and validate local cultural traditions.

Research Issues

A complete discussion of all the legal and ethical issues of trauma research is beyond the scope of this chapter, a brief look at some of the more prevalent issues will be presented.

Methodologies to help subjects tell their stories in a respectful manner need to be created. Instruments designed for a trauma study should be developed and

employed. Trauma research should be grounded in the needs of the study participants, to help them receive more effective service. Seven trauma research principles are outlined below:

1. the research must adhere to all standards for the ethical treatment of
   research subjects including informed consent, voluntary participation, confidentiality, and anonymity;
2. the research should be gender, culturally and developmentally sensitive in
   its design and conduct;
3. the researchers must be prepared to provide appropriate referral or treatment of participants who are identified as being in crisis or needing a mental health intervention;
4. the researchers must treat research subjects with respect, attend to their
   privacy interests and chose methodologies that are not unduly demanding of
   their time;
5. those conducting the study should communicate and distribute research
   results in language and formats that are accessible to practitioners, clients,
   policy makers, and legislators
6. in designing and conducting the study, the researchers need to identify the
   implications of their findings for legislative and policy reforms and work
   cooperatively with community partners to communicate those implications
   to relevant officials
7. the researchers should consider the potential for unintended consequences
   of laws, policies, and programs as well as the benefits (Cunningham, 2003,
   p. 3).

Summary

Before strategies of intervention or research of trauma response can begin, there
must be an agreement on what is being treated or studied. Clear distinctions must
be made among normal grief, complicated grief, traumatic grief syndrome, and
posttraumatic stress disorder. Many legal problems arising from trauma intervention programs evolve from what is sometimes perceived as the subjectivity of the
employed measures of diagnoses.

In addition to the need for agreed-upon bases for professional actions, there
are special areas of concern when children are the object of support and study.
Informed consent and privacy issues may be more problematic when children are
involved.

A number of factors influencing trauma response have not been addressed; i.e.,
the impact on victims when experiencing difficulties with such organizations as the
Federal Emergency Management Agency, Social Security Administration, insurance companies, and/or banks. In addition, studies of the grief responses of family

members who have lost a loved one in an act of capital punishment or other socially stigmatized ways may reveal unique legal and ethical considerations. While studies addressing these issues were not found in the literature, the professional caregiver must be cognizant of their potential influence on traumatic grief.

LEARNING ObjeCtive: (25/40)
List the ethical and legal issues
that are involved in traumatic
DeAth.

Death Education

Introduction to Part 6, Chapters 31-36

*Chapters 31 through 36 focus on death education. The Body of Knowledge Committee defined this major category of thanatology knowledge in this way: **formal and informal methods for acquiring and disseminating knowledge about dying, death, and bereavement.***

The chapters in Part 6 focus on death education in terms of these indicators: culture and socialization, religion and spirituality, historical and contemporary perspectives, life span issues, the family and larger systems, and ethical and legal issues.

Chapter 31

Culture, Socialization, and Death Education

Lynne Ann DeSpelder & Albert Lee Strickland

As the television camera was turned off, the interviewer turned and asked quietly, "Why are Anglo funerals so serious?" Answering this question requires "cultural competency," that is, the ability to explore, consider, and respond appropriately to cultural differences. Reading this chapter, you will have an opportunity to add to your knowledge and gain skills regarding culture, socialization, and systems for dealing with death that can be applied in understanding and working with people from diverse backgrounds. Take our television reporter. Notice that she used the word "Anglo." Considering her word choice, her name, and her appearance, you might guess that her background is Hispanic. Her use of the word "serious" also deserves attention.

Cultural competence requires the ability to listen and gather information. Recall the reporter's question. What kind of response might you give to gain a better understanding of her heritage? It is best to get information before framing a response. Thus, a useful question is: "What has been your experience with Anglo funerals?" It is doubtful that she is talking about a British Anglo-Saxon funeral. More likely, she is asking about Caucasian funerals as contrasted to rituals of her own family or ethnic group. By matching her language and using the term "Anglo" in response, she is likely to give you more specific information.

She describes two recent deaths, one of a Caucasian colleague and the other of a family member. The contrasts between the two funeral ceremonies were quite perplexing to this young woman. The Caucasian funeral was a Protestant service held at a mortuary. The young reporter described her experience at the visitation and funeral for her colleague. She arrived at the mortuary to find the deceased's body in a small, empty room. Walking through the door, she noticed a condolence book set out for her to sign. She did so, briefly viewed the body, and left. During the funeral, the family sat behind closed curtains, cut off from the view of the casket and the mourners sitting in the public portion of the funeral chapel.

The funeral for her uncle was held in his parish church (Catholic) in an area of Miami populated mostly by Cuban immigrants. The funeral itself was preceded by several days and nights of viewing at a funeral home where family members, including small children, visited. Cuban music played in the background, and central to the gathering were jokes, laughter, and stories about the deceased. Laughing and crying together, the family visited with other members of the community who came to pay their respects.

As she talks about the differences in the funeral rituals, her use of the word "serious" is placed in context. Now we have much more information about the cultural differences that spark her curiosity. As you imagine the contrast between these two gatherings, it makes sense that, to the reporter, one seemed to be more "serious" (solemn and staid) than the other. Attitudes that we bring from our cultural experiences reflect the practices that are a familiar part of our heritage. Paying attention to how people use language reveals a great deal about personal as well as cultural attitudes toward death. By becoming aware of the metaphors, euphemisms, slang, and other linguistic patterns that people use when talking about death, we can appreciate more fully the range of attitudes and responses elicited by encounters with death, dying, and bereavement (DeSpelder & Barrett, 1997). Understanding attitudes toward death, our own as well as others, is an essential component of death education (DeSpelder, 1998).

In Greek mythology, *Thanatos* was the personification of death, the twin brother of *Hypnos* (sleep). Over time, the ancient Greeks came to use *thanatos* as a generic word for "death." Our word "thanatology," which is defined as the study of death, is a linguistic heir of the Greek term. Progress in understanding cultural differences, language usage, and the manner in which children learn about death points us in a direction for improving our dealings with death, dying, and bereavement in our respective countries.

For example, consider terms used to describe thanatology in Japanese. Thanatology is usually translated as *shiseigaku*. *Shi* means death, *sei* means life, and *gaku* means learning or study. Thus, *shiseigaku* literally means the study of death and life. Many scholars prefer the word *shiseigaku*, and this word is often used in books and articles. Some people translate thanatology as *shigaku*. That means simply the study of death. The main death education organization in Japan is called *Seitoshi wo Kangaeru Kai*. That means the association for thinking about life and death. Thus, in this case, life comes first. The Japanese translation of the word "death education" has variety. Some translate it as *seitoshi no kyoiku*, meaning the education of life and death. The internationally known pioneering thanatologist, Dr. Alfons Deeken, who lives and works in Japan, uses the words *shi eno jyunbi kyouiku*, meaning "preparatory education" for death. Some use the words, *shi no kyoiku*, meaning the education of death. But, recently, especially school teachers prefer the words, *inochi no kyoiku*. This phrase translates to "the education of life." *Inochi* means life. *Inochi no kyoiku* includes not only topics about death and bereavement, but also topics about the birth of life, the preciousness of life, life stages, and so on. With this usage, the word death or *shi* is omitted from the description of life and death studies among school teachers at the elementary and secondary school levels (personal communication, K. Takeuchi, Reitaku University, Chiba, January, 2006). Does this change in phrasing make thanatology more acceptable to the Japanese school system?

One of our jobs as thanatologists is to provide our clients and students with materials to deepen their intellectual understandings about death. This responsibility means that we must continually educate ourselves about theory, research, and practice in thanatology. A second job is to stimulate thinking about attitudes concerning a range of issues in our field. These two tasks are designed to bring about a balance between the affective and the cognitive aspects of death education. Both the intellectual and emotional aspects of death education apply whether we are working with individuals and families or with a group of students (DeSpelder, 2006; DeSpelder & Strickland, 2004).

As pioneering Italian thanatologist Francesco Campione (2005) points out, death is not only a topic for reflection, study, and research; it is also an "existential problem," which touches every aspect of human existence and every field of knowledge. Robert Kastenbaum (1993) says that, although the term thanatology is usually defined as the "study of death," it is perhaps better defined as "the study of life with death left in.

Death is a universal human experience, yet our response to it is shaped by our cultural environment. Learning how people in different cultures relate to death in their lives can shed light on our own attitudes and behaviors. Various cultures can be thought of as occupying a continuum that ranges from "death-welcoming" to "death-denying" (Becker, 1973). As you reflect on the cultures you are familiar with, think about where you might place each of them on the welcoming-denying continuum. Consider, too, where your own "cultures"—the national, ethnic or subcultural, and family groups of which you are a member—might fit on such a continuum.

Remember our reporter? Her question about Anglo funerals is a part of the developmental process known as *socialization*. This process involves learning and internalizing the norms, rules, and values of society. Through socialization, younger members of a society acquire knowledge, behavior, and ideals from older generations. Socialization does not stop with childhood's end, but continues throughout life as people develop new social roles and values. Nor is it a one-way process whereby individuals simply learn to fit into society. Society's norms and values are modified as its members redefine their social roles and obligations.

Society can be defined as "a group of people who share a common culture, a common territory, and a common identity; and who feel themselves to constitute a unified and distinct entity which involves interacting in socially structured relationships" (Goodman, 1992, p. 42). The social systems and institutions of a society give it a distinctive flavor and set it apart from other societies. This sense of distinctiveness is captured in the term _culture_, which is a kind of shorthand for referring to the lifeways—that is, the ways of thinking, feeling, and acting—of a given group of people. We often refer to societies in ways that highlight this cultural distinctiveness—for example, Japanese culture, Western European culture, and so on.

Culture can be defined as "all that in human society which is socially rather than biologically transmitted" (Marshall, 1994, p. 104; see also Brenneis, 2002; Erickson, 2002). This definition encompasses both material and nonmaterial components. Material culture consists of "things"—that is, manufactured objects (for example, buildings and consumer goods) or physical manifestations of the life of a people. Nonmaterial aspects of culture lie in the realm of ideas, beliefs, values, and customs.

Socialization involves a variety of influences, beginning with the family and extending to the mass media and the global "transcultural" environment. Children today are exposed to a broader range of influences on their socialization than at any other time in history. As Hannelore Wass (2003, p. 27) says, "Children adopt many values and beliefs from significant adults in their world [including] parents, teachers, public figures, sports heroes, and famous entertainers."

Although the main phases of socialization occur during the years of childhood, the process continues lifelong. _Resocialization_, a term that refers to the "uprooting and restructuring of basic attitudes, values, or identities," occurs when adults take on new roles that require replacing their existing values and modes of behavior (Goodman, 1992, pp. 84-85; see also Etzioni, 2000). This process occurs, for example, with religious conversion, starting a new job, getting married, having children, or surviving the death of a mate. Widowhood involves changes in many areas of life, as new roles and activities are taken on (Silverman, 2004; see also Campbell & Silverman, 1987). Rapid social change also leads to resocialization, as in the case of women's roles in the United States in the recent past. Resocialization takes place as the norms and values we learn in childhood are modified later in life.

People tend to acquire their learning about dying and death on an _ad hoc_ basis; that is, in a disorganized and impromptu fashion. Formal education about death is offered through courses, seminars, and the like, but these avenues of socialization are not part of most people's experience. The term _tactical socialization_ refers to strategies that hospice caregivers, for example, use to informally teach people about death and dying (Mesler, 1995). It involves an active effort to change other people's perceptions and behaviors about some aspect of their social world. The founding in 1982 of the Japanese Association for Death Education and Grief Counseling is another example of tactical socialization. Prior to the Association's birth, prolongation of the physical life of a patient often had been the main concern of doctors, whereas the quality of life of the dying was largely neglected. Today, the association's founder considers the changes in interest and understanding of death and dying, hospice care, and grief to be substantial. There are currently chapters of the association in 50 Japanese cities (Deeken, 1999).

Culture is dynamic; that is, it changes as the members of a society reevaluate inherited beliefs, values, and customs in light of circumstances and experiences. In this sense, culture operates as a framing device that channels, rather than determines, attitudes and behaviors.

There is no formula or recipe for understanding a particular cultural group. While generalizations about beliefs and practices might be helpful guides, the map is not the territory. Do not assume that all individuals of a particular religion, race, cultural, or national group share the same beliefs. Each person is unique. Norms can be used only as a guide. They are not a substitute for individual assessment. Operating with a stereotype or generalization in mind can block an authentic understanding of a particular individual or family's attitudes, beliefs, and practices.

Stereotypes will trip you up every time. When you hear a generalization about a cultural group, ask yourself how this might help you understand a particular individual or family. Understanding culture requires knowledge of how an individual defines his or her heritage. The Barrett-Inferential Model points out that this heritage may be better understood by exploring factors such as cultural associations, spirituality, and social class (Barrett, 1998, pp. 88-91; DeSpelder & Barrett, 1997, p. 68). Research on African American death customs points out that, even within particular cultural groups, there is tremendous diversity. The African American experience is more heterogeneous than homogeneous. Thus, skin color is not the determining factor in matters of death, dying, and bereavement (Barrett, 1995a). Other factors include geographic location, rural or urban setting, family influences, and the number of generations from immigration to a particular country

Consider the power of social class. The celebrations for the living and the dead in Mexico, *el Día de los Muertos*, seem more fully embraced by the poor. The Mexican government has instituted a program in the city of Oaxaca to interest the middle and upper class in the traditions of their ancestors. As noted in the African American research, the affluent in a culture are more likely to move away from their communities of origin, thus becoming less traditional. The poor are more likely to follow traditional practices.

Different religions and religious affiliations shape spirituality in different ways. The more conservative the religious experience, the more conservative and traditional will be the attitudes, beliefs, and values that ultimately affect behavior. More conservative believers can be characterized as the "keepers of the tradition." They hold to old ways of relating to death, dying, and funeral rites. Some conservative believers, for example object to blood donations, autopsies, and tissue or organ donations.

In central California and other areas of the United States, where there is a large Hispanic population, the impact of the number of generations from immigration can be seen also in the celebration of *el Día de los Muertos* (Lomnitz, 2005, p. 467). Many second- and third-generation individuals and families are rediscovering the elements of the celebration that their parents and grandparents had left in the "old country."

The study of dying, death, and bereavement compels us to look at our own stories, as well as the stories of our neighbors, both locally and globally, with the aim of comprehending not only the diverse social and cultural influences on our understanding of death, but also our personal mortality. The decision to embark on such a study is usually made out of a variety of personal or professional reasons. Some come to this study with no prior direct experience with death; others with what feels like too much.

In cultures that maintain strong bonds between the living and the dead, "the land echoes with the voices of the ancestors" (Smart, 1977, p. 231). Together, the living and the dead comprise the clan, the tribe, and the people. The bond between living and dead is a sign that the community endures beyond the limits of death. In Balinese society, the village territory belongs to the ancestors, and the living members of the community maintain contact with them to ensure their livelihood and well-being (Warren, 1993). The community is a partnership of the living and the dead. This understanding is implicit when people refer to the "founding fathers" of a nation or college, who are spoken of metaphorically as "being with us in spirit" as living members of the group meet to celebrate their common purpose with those who preceded them.

If calling a person's name is a way of summoning the person, then refraining from using a name will presumably leave its bearer undisturbed. Hence, a practice related to the dead is name avoidance: The deceased is never again mentioned or is referred to only obliquely, never by name. For example, the deceased might be referred to as "that one," or allusions may be made to particular traits or special qualities a person was known for during his or her lifetime. Thus, "Uncle Joe," who gained renown as an expert fisherman, might be referred to after his death as "that relative who caught many fish." A woman who had displayed extraordinary bravery might be referred to as "that one who showed courage." In some cultures, the deceased is referred to by his or her relationship to the speaker.

Customs like these involving name avoidance continue into the modern era among indigenous people who value their traditional cultural practices. When a famous Aborigine painter died in 2002 at age 70 in the remote central Australian town of Alice Springs, family and friends asked the media not to publish his name out of respect for the Aborigine belief that the dead not be identified by name. Although he had achieved international fame during his lifetime for Dreamtime paintings depicting his homeland, he became anonymous in death because his people's beliefs forbid the mention of the deceased's name.

Name avoidance can be so complete that living people with the same name as the deceased must adopt new names. Among the Penan Geng of central Borneo, naming practices involving death are incorporated into all forms of social discourse (Brosius, 1995-1996). When a person dies, "death names" are given to closest kin. Thus, as a person goes through life, he or she may take on a series of names and titles that refer to different categories of relationship to the deceased.

Some cultures, rather than avoiding the deceased's name, give it special emphasis. For example, the name may be conferred on a newborn child. Such naming takes place out of a desire to honor the memory of a loved one or to ensure that the soul of the dead person is reincarnated. In some cases, when a woman nears the time of giving birth, she has a dream that reveals which of her ancestors is to be reborn, thus determining the name her new baby receives (Gaster, 1964, p. 241). Among Hawaiians, children may be named for ancestors or even named by the gods. Especially important are names bestowed by gods, which are communicated through dreams. The name of a child who died earlier is sometimes given to a child born later. Naming a child for a relative who has died allows the name to live again (Handy & Pukui, 1972, pp. 98-101).

People sometimes talk or write about "Death in the United States," but this phrase conceals what, in fact, are many different "ways of death," reflecting attitudes, beliefs, and customs of culturally diverse groups. In describing families from the United States, David Olson and John DeFrain (2006, p. 32) remind us that "tremendous diversity exists among people who are commonly grouped together."

The extent to which people identified as belonging to a specific cultural group maintain distinctive attitudes and practices varies widely, both between different subcultural or ethnic groups and among people who share a particular heritage. In a cosmopolitan world, individuals may find themselves wrestling with the dilemma of seeking to maintain their cultural distinctiveness while also taking steps to broaden the conventional terms of what it means to be a member of their culture. When a person's opinions or views differ markedly from those commonly held within his or her culture, this can lead to "cultural dissent" from majority views. For example, influenced by body disposition practices in a global context, an individual might opt for cremation instead of burial, despite the latter being the strongly held preference and conventional practice within his or her own cultural group. Such choices reflect the fact that today's societies are increasingly homogeneous (similar) *across* cultures and heterogeneous (diverse) *within* them (Sunder, 2001, pp. 497-498).

Nevertheless, ethnicity and other cultural factors often have an impact on such matters as methods of coping with life-threatening illness, the perception of pain, social support for the dying, behavioral manifestations of grief, mourning styles, and funeral customs. A comparison of bereavement customs among ethnic and other cultural groups in the United States shows that, "while adapting partly to Western patterns, these groups also adhere to the bereavement procedures of their own cultures" (Stroebe & Stroebe, 1993, p. 201; see also Eisenbruch, 1984; Goss & Klass, 2005, pp. 92, 188; Hayslip & Peveto, 2005; Howarth, 2007, pp. 227, 266; Sanders, 2002).

African American funerals and mourning practices illustrate how traditional customs can persist despite the passage of time and changed circumstance. Elements of traditional West African practices retain their importance for many African Americans (Barrett, 1995a; Barrett, 1995b). This is evident in customs such as gathering at the gravesite to bid godspeed to the deceased and referring to funerals as a "home-going" ceremony honoring the spirit of the deceased. David Roediger (1981) says such customs "grew from deep African roots, gained a paradoxical strength and resilience from the horrors of mid-passage, and flowered in the slave funeral—a value laden and unifying social event which the slave community in the United States was able to preserve from both physical and ideological onslaughts of the master class."

Similarly, Spanish-speaking people in northern New Mexico continue to practice traditional forms of *recuerdo*, or remembrance, which memorialize the dead and comfort the bereaved. Presented as a written narrative or ballad, the *recuerdo* tells the story of a person's life in an epic, lyrical, and heroic manner. This memorialization is a kind of farewell, a leave-taking or *la despedida*, on behalf of a deceased person. Such memorials frequently contain reminders of the transitory nature of life and express the notion that life is on loan from God for only a short time, that we are only shadows. The poignant beauty of the *recuerdo*, given to the bereaved family and often published in local newspapers, suggests that life has meaning because there is death. Alvin Korte (1995-1996) says, "The wisdom of the culture has provided many termini [points on the journey] where family, friends, and community may take their leave and depart from a deceased person." He adds, "It is critical that persons become involved in the process so that the final letting go or *despedida* can be accomplished with ease and lack of guilt."

When children grow up participating in the *recuerdo* they learn how to respond to a death. Another source of learning is children's literature. Many classic children's stories and fairy tales depict death, near deaths, or the threat of death (Tatar, 2002). There are "tales of children abandoned in woods; of daughters poisoned by their mothers' hands; of sons forced to betray their siblings; of men and women struck down by wolves, or imprisoned in windowless towers" (Windling, 2001, p. 227). Death has often had a place in children's stories, and is especially true of the earliest versions of familiar stories that parents and other adults share with children. Children in the United States are taught to read with textbooks such as *McGuffe's Eclectic Readers* found that death was presented as tragic, but inevitable, and many of the death-related stories conveyed a moral lesson (Lamers, 1995). In the 19th century, the violence in children's stories was usually graphic and gory so that it would make the desired moral impression (Marvin, 2000). The manner in which death is presented in children's stories communicates cultural values. Consider, for example, the contrasts between the European and Chinese versions of the tale of Little Red Riding Hood.

In the Western version, Little Red Riding Hood goes by herself to visit her grandmother, encounters the wolf, and is tricked into believing the wolf is her grandmother (Orenstein, 2002). In the traditional version of the story, the wolf eats Little Red Riding Hood, but she is saved by a woodsman who kills the wolf and slits its stomach, allowing Little Red Riding Hood to emerge unharmed. In more recent versions, Little Red Riding Hood's screams alert the woodsman, who chases the wolf and then returns to announce that she will be bothered no more (the killing of the wolf occurs offstage and is not mentioned) (Morel, 1970, pp. 11-13).

The Chinese tale of *Lon Po Po* (Granny Wolf) comes from an oral tradition thought to be over a thousand years old. In this version of the story, three young children are left by themselves while their mother goes away to visit their grandmother. The wolf, disguised as Po Po (Grandmother), persuades the children to open the locked door of their house. When they do, he quickly blows out the light. By making perceptive inquiries, however, the oldest child cleverly discovers the wolf's true identity and, with her younger siblings, escapes to the top of a ginkgo tree. Through trickery, the children convince the wolf to step into a basket so they can haul him up to enjoy the ginkgo nuts. Joining together, the children start hauling up the basket. But, just as it nearly reaches the top of the tree, they let the basket drop to the ground. The story says, "Not only did the wolf bump his head, but he broke his heart to pieces" (Young, 1989). Climbing down to the branches just above the wolf, the children discover that he is "truly dead." Unlike the European version, which has a solitary child facing the threat of the wolf by herself and ultimately being saved by someone else, the Chinese folk tale emphasizes the value of being part of a group effort to do away with the wolf.

Although death is fundamentally a biological fact, socially shaped ideas and assumptions create its meaning. Consider the experiences of the Hmong who emigrated from Southeast Asia to North America (Hayes & Kalish, 1987-1988). In the mountains of northern Laos, their traditional funeral customs included firing mortars to alert the village that a death had occurred and slaughtering oxen and buffalo for the funeral ceremony. In the significantly different social setting of their new homeland, mostly urban settings in the United States, the traditional elements of Hmong funeral ritual cannot be readily accommodated and have been dramatically changed. In a predominantly Caucasian Northern Wisconsin area around Lake Winnebago, there is only one funeral home available for Hmong rituals. When asked about this exclusivity, it was explained that even the scaled-down, somewhat accommodated rituals involve family gatherings lasting extended periods of time that take over the entire establishment for the duration of the funeral (personal communication, staff, Edwin S. Shneidman Program in Thanatology, Fond du Lac, Wisconsin, September 30, 2006).

Similarly, migrant Muslims in Germany are pressured to adapt their funeral ceremonies to European cultural norms and practices. Religious leaders "carry out a balancing act in order to adapt to the new situation without violating the ritual which holds their community together," a cultural dilemma that has been characterized as "the knife's edge" (Jonker, 1996).

Hindus who live in England encounter similar cultural imperatives related to death rituals. In India, where there are few undertakers or funeral directors, funeral arrangements are usually made by the deceased's family. Cremation is a public event, and a principal mourner lights the sacred flame of the funeral pyre. In Britain, the body is placed inside a coffin and concealed from view inside the cremator, which is operated by employees of the crematorium. "For the mourners there is neither the smoke to sting their eyes, nor the fire to singe their hair, nor the smell of burning flesh to bring the poignant immediacy and reality of the experience to their consciousness" (Laungani, 1996). Living in a very different cultural environment, some Hindus in England feel that they are socially constrained to give up a communal and spiritual ceremony and, in its stead, are left with an anonymous, individualistic, materialistic, and bureaucratic procedure.

The Hmong in North America, Muslims in Germany, and Hindus in Britain illustrate the multicultural nature of modern societies and the resulting challenges to traditional cultural identities. Such challenges apply not only to members of immigrant populations, but to people generally. Social scientists point out that diversity of identity is growing along with increasing globalization, such that most people worldwide now develop a bicultural or "hybrid" identity that "combines their local cultural identity with an identity linked to elements of the global culture" (Arnett, 2002).

This change in how people think about themselves in relation to their social environment is especially evident in the lives of children and young adults, as "where a child grows up now matters less than in the past in determining what the child knows and experiences" (Arnett, 2002, p. 782 ; see also Buchholtz, 2002).

Just as society has a natural interest in the way its educational systems are organized to provide services to individuals, it also has an intrinsic interest in such matters of public policy as procedures for legally defining and making a determination of death, rules governing organ donation and transplantation, ways of classifying different modes of death into socially useful categories, the manner in which investigative duties are carried out by coroners and medical examiners, and the criteria that apply to performing autopsies. These various aspects of public policy are sometimes interrelated, mutually affecting one another and differing between nations. For example, in recent decades, new legal and administrative procedures for defining death had to be created when modern medical technologies led to organ transplantation. These matters of public interest are all aspects of what Robert Kastenbaum (2007, pp. 74-97; see also Doka, 2003; Hayslip, 2003, p. 35; Kastenbaum, 1989; Kastenbaum, 1996, p. 113) calls the "death system"—that is, the elements of a society that have an impact on how people deal with dying and death. Kastenbaum says: "We may think of the death system as the interpersonal, sociophysical, and symbolic network through which an individual's relationship to mortality is mediated by his or her society" (2007, p. 102).

According to Kastenbaum, the components of a death system include *people* (for example, funeral directors, life insurance agents, weapons designers, people who operate slaughterhouses, as well as people who care for the dying), *places* (for example, cemeteries, funeral homes, battlefields, war memorials, disaster sites), *times* (for example, memorial days and religious commemorations such as Good Friday, anniversaries of important battles, Halloween), *objects* (for example, obituaries, tombstones, hearses, the electric chair), and *symbols* (for example, black armbands, funeral music, skull and crossbones symbols, language used to talk about death).

How the death system functions varies among different societies and at different times in the same society. The functions of a death system include:

1. Warnings and predictions about potentially life-threatening events (for example, storms, tornadoes, and other disasters, as well as advice to specific individuals, such as doctors' reports of laboratory results or mechanics' warnings about faulty brakes)

2. Preventing death (for example, emergency and acute medical care, public health initiatives, antismoking campaigns)

3. Caring for the dying (for example, hospice, home health aides, trauma workers, family caregivers)

4. Disposing of the dead (for example, funerals and memorial services, cemetery plots, memorialization processes, identification of bodies in disasters)
5. Social consolidation after death (for example, coping with grief, maintaining community bonds, settling estates)
6. Making sense of death (for example, religious or scientific explanations, support groups, poetry and consolation literature, last words)
7. Killing (for example, capital punishment, war, hunting, raising and marketing of animals)

In practice, there are many interconnections and mutual influences among these functions. It should be clear from this brief listing, however, that the elements composing the death system touch on virtually every aspect of social and individual life.

Diversity in death attitudes, customs, and death systems can benefit society as a whole by making available a wealth of resources for coping with death. Yet it also presents challenges in pluralistic societies. When everyone in a society shares the same beliefs and customs, there are known and socially accepted ways of dealing with death and grief. Cultural diversity may jeopardize this comforting situation because there is less agreement among the members of a society about which practices are socially sanctioned for managing death and minimizing "existential dread" (Mellor, 1993, pp. 12-13, 18-19; see also Littlewood, 1993; Mellor & Schilling, 1993). Such uncertainty about the social norms for dealing with death is apparent when people at modern funerals are anxious about how they should act or what they should say to the bereaved. In modern societies, people find themselves in situations where socially sanctioned rites for dealing with dying and death are in flux.

On the other hand, becoming culturally competent, that is, able to relate to rites that are not socially sanctioned in one's own culture, can give greater understanding and connection to those people and customs unfamiliar to us. Rather than making a judgment that a funeral is "serious" as our TV reporter did, we might understand that socialization, culture, and death systems produce different actions and reactions to dying, death, and bereavement. Becoming culturally competent allow each of us to better serve diverse populations.

LEARNING Objective: (40/40)
Describe the influence of Socialization and Culture on the provision of death education.

Chapter 32

Religion, Spirituality, and Death Education

Robert G. Stevenson

This chapter examines the connections among death education, religion, and spirituality. Death education has been defined as, "instruction that deals with death, dying, grief and loss and their impact on the individual and on humankind" (Stevenson, 1984). It has also been defined as:

> "education about death that focuses on the human and emotional aspects of death. Though it may include teaching on the biological aspects of death, teaching about coping with grief is a primary focus. Death education is sometimes part of the training of those who encounter dying or bereaved people in their professions, for example those who work in nursing homes. It can also involve education aimed at the public, where it is often intended to correct misconceptions surround death and dying and encourage more openness about the subject" (Wikipedia, 2006).

Such instruction can be *formal*, through texts, courses, conferences, workshops, and/or lectures/sermons. It can also be *informal*, through life experience, observation, or something as simple as a parent's use of a teachable moment. Formal death education may contain components dealing with religion and spiritual beliefs as they relate to death, to life after death, or to the grief process. These units and their effects can be studied and evaluated. In contrast, informal death education can vary widely from incident to incident. By its nature, it may include religious beliefs, rituals, statements, or spiritual exercises. Religious or spiritual beliefs and traditions are often used at such moments in an attempt to soften the blow of a loss. However, it is also possible that in individual situations none of these things will be present.

Death education takes place on many levels and in many contexts. It can be found in secondary schools, colleges, graduate school programs, professional development programs, and in religious teachings. When the students are adolescents, or younger children, the place of death education has been a cause of active debate. It might be assumed that, when the students are adults there would be less difficulty merging the topics of religion and spirituality with death education because these students are able to choose whether they wish to pursue this avenue of investigation.

In formal death education courses, the connection shared by death education, religion, and spirituality can appear obvious because the common areas of interest are numerous. However, recognizing this connection is not always the case. When teaching a community college course on death, grief, and loss to sociology and psychology majors and student nurses, one instructor was denied permission to select for the students any text on death and/or grief that referred to religion. His supervisor stated that the study of religion and spirituality had no place in an objective examination of death, loss, or grief. For that reason, the supervisor rejected two texts that were being used in many death education classes at that time. Each of the texts had a chapter that mentioned "religion" (Vernon, 1970; Bender, 1974). Students often brought up issues linked to religion, but found no references within the approved course texts. The course was intentionally limited in its ability to address the needs of the "whole" person.

How can the needs of the whole person be addressed if religion and spirituality are excluded even though people have "spiritual needs"? Hospital chaplain Carole Smith-Torres examined this question when she addressed Spiritual Care of Patients at a Columbia-Presbyterian Symposium in New York City. She spoke of the need to work with the whole person. She expressed agreement with the earlier work of Fish & Shelly (1978) who said that, "Man is a physical, psychosocial, and spiritually integrated being, created to live in harmony with God, himself, and others" (p. 33). If people are meant to life this way, issues related to the end of life impact each of these aspects of humanity as well. One need not personally hold such beliefs to understand that there are many people who do. It is possible to see that there will be many students who will be unable to fully grasp the meaning of death, dying, and grief if the issues related to religion and spirituality are never addressed.

Mwalimu Imara is a hospital chaplain who worked with Elisabeth Kubler-Ross in Chicago, during the time when she was engaged in developing her five-stage model of dying. In a 1980 interview concerning death education, he described a concept known as "authentic religion." His research found that belief in a particular religion did not, by itself, necessarily influence the way in which a person dealt with death or with grief. He stated that it was "authentic religion" that described what it takes to be a "real" person. Imara defined authentic religion as one that provides answers to the following three questions:

- *Who are you?* This question is answered by relationships, not through a single title or job description. "Authentic religion" helps the individual form his/her self-identity.
- *What are your priorities in life?* Every religion requires its members to set and follow priorities. Those who believe in "authentic religion" take their life priorities from that faith.
- *What is it that makes sense out of life/death?* To be a whole person one must make choices and be willing to face the consequences of those choices.

Spirituality has been defined as the name given to issues related to the "non-material" aspects of life (Morgan, 1993). It involves a quest for answers to the questions posed by life and by death. If that is the case, then Imara's concept of "authentic religion" describes the quest that is part of spirituality. People who are able to use religion to answer the three questions identified by Imara were said to have "authentic religion." People with this "authentic religion" have found a way to answer the questions that life and death pose to everyone. As a group, they had less anxiety about, and less fear of, death. These people were better able to cope with loss and to move through the grief process to recovery. If religion can offer such a seemingly effective way of coping with death and grief, how does one justify omitting it from any curriculum that addresses those topics?

Before examining the relationship that exists between religion/spirituality and death education, it is important to remember the many forms of death education and the variety of contexts in which education about death occurs. To discuss the connections of death education, religion, and spirituality, it is necessary to start with an operational definition of each. In this reading, religion is defined as codified belief in the transcendent in an integrated system that is oriented toward helping people find meaning and purpose in life (Gladding, 2001). Spirituality is defined as a unique, personally meaningful experience of a transcendent dimension that is associated with wholeness and wellness. (Gladding, 2001). The chief difference between the two terms is that religion is defined as a *set of beliefs*, and related practices, which can provide meaning, while spirituality is defined as an ongoing *quest to find meaning*. The two concepts are not precisely the same but they are interwoven. In simple terms, one can say that religion is *external*, while spirituality is *internal* (Gamino, *et. al.*, 2003). Religion addresses the group while spirituality is individual. Richard Gilbert (2002a) says, "the function of religion is to build the person spiritually."

Religious orientation can be further described as either *intrinsic* or *extrinsic*. Those people with an intrinsic orientation tend to see religion as an end in itself, while those with an external religious orientation use religion as a means to an end (Allport and Ross, 1967). Either orientation can influence the behavior and feelings of those facing death, or the coping of survivors after a death. This insight would appear to make religious orientation an integral part of any examination of attitudes toward death.

Religion and spirituality can influence the content and organization of death education courses, programs, and workshops. In terms of content, religious beliefs and practices are often included in:

- Definition of the "moment of death"
- Views of the afterlife
- Funeral rituals
- The role of ritual
- The grief process
- Ethical issues (such as euthanasia, suicide, or abortion)

Religion has been one of the means used to examine these topics. It has also provided some people with answers to the questions that the study of these topics can raise (Stevenson, 1993). Sigmund Freud linked death and religion by claiming that, for early man, death was "natural, undeniable, and unavoidable" (Freud, 1915/1959) and that the basis of religion is an attempt by man to lessen his terror of death (Hardt, 1979).

Young people have at least as many questions as adults about these issues. Religion has provided many with answers to these questions, but how should the different teachings of different religions be included in a death education course? How can death educators avoid offending the beliefs of some while describing the beliefs of others?

Religion in a Pluralistic Society

Religious institutions have always provided a type of death education, even if it was not, as yet, labeled such. Diversity of religious belief, or the lack of such belief, in our pluralistic society makes it difficult to generalize about the impact of religion in the education of young people about death. Christians may view death as a transition to eternal reward but they can also see it as punishment for sin. Some Christians have attributed their feelings of guilt to a traditional religious portrayal of death. On the other hand, their faith can also offer comfort in times of grief. Jesus said, "Blessed are those who mourn for they shall be comforted" (Matthew 5:4). The comfort is said to come through the belief that Jesus is the resurrection and the life and that one who believes in him "will live, even when he dies" (John 11:25). The reaction to any of these individual statements can vary among individuals — becoming a source of comfort, suffering, or a combination of both.

Eastern religion speaks of death as a "transition" in which the life force moves on to a new plane of existence or another life in this world. Eastern faiths, such as Hinduism, Buddhism, or Taoism do not speak of "personal" salvation. There is common ground with Western faiths, however, in religious teachings about death. In general, religious belief offers explanation for events that may otherwise seem incomprehensible, such as, "Why did he have to die?" Religion offers belief that can calm fears regarding the fate of the deceased (Heaven, reunion with Brahma, movement to a new physical form through reincarnation) and through ritual (wakes, shiva, cremation, graveside services) can be a source of communal strength. In addition, when one feels hopeless, religion can be a source of hope...hope that the deceased in now beyond this "vale of tears" and that those who mourn may one day be reunited with their loved one. Religion generally offers the belief that life continues in some form after the event of physical death and may help the bereaved to move on with their lives.

The roles of family and religion must both be taken into account when working with bereaved individuals. When death education is offered in schools, it is not done in isolation. Teachers must try to be conscious of the many influences in the lives of their students. Cultural, regional, and religious differences must all be acknowledged if death education is to be truly responsive to the needs of students (Stevenson, 1993).

In a secular environment, even in American secondary schools where it is required to preserve the separation between church and state, there is clearly a difference between teaching religion and teaching about religion. There are numerous courses that traditionally teach about religion. Social studies include information about deities of the ancient world (Egypt, Greece, and Rome), the beliefs of the Hebrews, the rise of Christianity in the Roman Empire, the teachings of Mohammed and the rise of Islam, the Renaissance, the Reformation, and the beliefs of Europeans who emigrated to the New World seeking religious freedom. World Cultures classes describe the teachings of Hinduism, Buddhism, and Islam in order to understand their role in the cultures they have helped to create and to shape. In humanities classes, the Bible, the Torah, the Koran, and other religious texts are studied as keys to understanding human values and beliefs (Stevenson, 1993).

Death education courses in schools present religious information related to death and grief in much the same way. Patricia Zalaznik (1979) created a curriculum that used student writings, guest speakers, and/or group discussion to cover the beliefs of a variety of religions. An earlier high school curriculum, started in 1972, used religious sources, along with secular sources, to address student questions in units entitled "Death and Beyond," "Death and Ritual" and "Why Do People Die?" (Stevenson, 1972) The inclusion of religion in these courses is consistent with the use that young people have made of religion since long before death education courses existed. It has been shown that students use religion to:

- Provide a framework to discuss death (Mills et. al., 1976)
- Confront and cope with the fear of death (Hardt, 1979; McHugh, 1980)
- Answer questions about death and what happens "after we die" (Grollman, 1967; Mills, 1976; Stevenson, 1993)
- Understand the religious origins and role of many death-related rituals (Grollman, 1967; Vernon, 1970)

These uses of religion are not relegated to young people alone. One study of the elderly in rural communities showed that they used religion to "render the world intelligible"(Tellis-Nayak, 1982). If these uses of religion to understand death-related issues continue throughout the life span, surely religion should be included in any course attempting to discuss the topics in which religion plays such an important role.

Treatment of Controversial Issues

Even if religion is used by individuals to help them understand the world in which they live and to cope with the crises they face in that world, the inclusion of religion in death education is still seen by many as controversial. It should be noted that death education itself is still seen by many as controversial. In an amazing piece of writing, combining partially correct information (selectively chosen) and personal opinion, Samuel L. Blumenfeld stated that death education was being used "in virtually every public school in America for at least the last 15 years" (Blumenfeld, 1999). The reason for such gross overstatement is to raise concern in parents and to create a split between parents and educators. Blumenfeld particularly attacked the inclusion in death education of the topic of reincarnation — implying that such teaching was the reason for the mass murder at Columbine High. Blumenfeld's article first appeared on the Internet in 1999. It is still being circulated as if it were written only yesterday. The Internet gives such articles a life of their own, with little or no way for an individual to check their validity.

 There is yet another reason why teaching about religion and spirituality belong in a death education curriculum. It has been pointed out that the modern denial of death may be a result of the decline in the belief in personal immortality (Kovacs, 1982). It has also been stated that religious belief in an afterlife can provide support to the bereaved and that the secularization and deritualization of grief deprives individuals of the solace such rituals may provide (Brennan, 1983). Denial of death has been shown to be ineffective for adolescents in dealing with death-related issues and/or the grief process (Stevenson, 1984). In attempting to prolong their use of denial in dealing with death and bereavement, some adolescents engage in "risk-taking" behavior to prove to themselves the validity of their belief in their own personal immortality. It is this sort of affirmation of personal belief that is taking the place of traditional belief concerning an afterlife. Both Hostler (1978) and Yalom (1980) attribute increased "risk-taking" behavior to adolescent attempts to preserve the coping mechanism of denial. The belief that adolescents should "learn to deal with bereavement and grief on their own" when developing coping skills is not borne out by the facts and may be itself a contributing factor to the increase in potentially self-destructive adolescent behavior (Stevenson, 1993).

Religion and Spirituality as Controversial Issues

If educators are to avoid damaging pressure being brought to bear on their courses when religion or spirituality are discussed, it may be helpful to have a procedure in place in advance for dealing with these issues as "controversial issues." There is a variety of policies and practices in schools for dealing with controversial issues when one looks beyond the United States and Canada to other countries and cultures. However, it seems that in the United States there has been the greatest need for a policy that allows controversial issues, such as religion or spirituality, to be included in death education. One school district's approach will be used as an illustration of what can be done.

There is an existing policy that has been in place for more than 30 years in one school district in New Jersey. It is a policy that can be used to fit this situation. This policy, approved by the Regional Board of Education, defines a controversial issue as a question in which,

> ...one or more proposed answers...arouse strong reaction in a section of the citizenry...The immediate cause of this reaction may be personal belief or interest, or allegiance to an interested group. The most critically controversial questions are those characterized by current importance and by group opinions and interest" (River Dell, 1970).

Religion and spirituality each fit this definition. "Personal beliefs" will be addressed if religion and spirituality are addressed. "Interested groups" can include all organized faiths, as well as persons who do not believe in a higher power, or those who do not want any mention of religion in public schools.

The decision whether a particular question should be a matter for school study is made by the board of education, through approval of the course of study. When a potentially controversial issue arises unexpectedly, the educator is guided by five key questions.

1. Is this a question of "timeless importance? Questions related to death, suffering, life after death and the quality of life have been asked by people since the beginning of recorded history. Religion and spirituality have played a key role in providing answers to these questions.

2. *Are the students "mature" enough to deal with this question?* With religion and spirituality, as with any other topic in education, it is important that the topic be addressed in a way that is age appropriate.

3. *Do answers to this question help meet student needs?* A balanced presentation of religious values and teachings that can have an impact on the lives of students can be beneficial to the students involved.

4. *Is consideration of this question compatible with the purposes of the school?* Public schools in the United States are charged with educating the "whole child." With the importance of religious and spiritual belief in the developing lives of children (as described most significantly by C. G. Jung and by other contemporary researchers), it would be difficult to meet this charge if the major role of religion and spirituality in the life of each child were to be ignored.

5. *Is the teacher prepared for the responsibility of dealing with this question?* The question of "adequate" preparation is a tricky one. Rather than state specific characteristics of such preparation, the policy states the following, "The wise teacher avoids going into a controversial topic which is beyond his/her own depth (of understanding). A student would be better uninformed about a question than misinformed about it" (Stevenson, 1993).

The following list of suggestions can serve as a basis for procedures to apply with courses that include religion in a death education curriculum. It is based on a similar list of points related to teaching about religion in public schools developed by the Public Education Religious Studies Center (PERSC) of Wright State University, Dayton, Ohio (Smith, 1981). In any procedure for including religion and spirituality in death education courses/programs in secular institutions, it is suggested that:

- A public institution may sponsor the *study* of religion, but not the *practice* of religion.
- A school may *expose* students to all religious views, but may not *impose* any particular view.
- The approach to religion is one of *instruction*, not one of *indoctrination*.
- The function of instruction is to *educate* about religions, not to *proselytize* any one religion.
- The approach of death education to religion is *academic*, not *devotional*.

- Death education courses/programs in a secular context should study what *people do believe*. These courses/programs should not teach students what *people should believe*.
- Death education courses/programs should strive to increase student *awareness* of the beliefs and the role(s) of religion, but should not press for *acceptance* of any one religion, or even religion is general.
- Death education courses/programs seek to *inform* students about a variety of beliefs, but should not seek to *conform* to any one belief (Smith, 1981).

Policies and procedures, such as those cited above, may assist death educators to avoid unnecessary controversy if they decide to include religion and spirituality in a curriculum. To not include religion or spirituality because these are potentially controversial issues implies that these topics are either not important, or that they are important, but schools and educators are unable to discuss them in an objective manner. As a consequence, students may believe that:

1. *such topics are not important* enough to be considered by students, or
2. *such topics are too difficult* for educators and schools and are therefore beyond the ability of students to comprehend.

The existence of a policy on the treatment of controversial issues, by itself, shows there are educators and boards of education that believe some questions lack one correct answer and that these questions are of such importance that they still deserve to be addressed throughout society, including schools.

Death Education in Religious Schools

Death and grief should already be in every religious school. The worry that a discussion of religion, or religious values, in public school may undermine the influence of religious advisors should not be an issue in this environment. In most religious schools, there would be a clear central focus and students would not necessarily have to confront beliefs that might be contrary to their own. However, there can be concerns here as well. In one parochial high school, for over a year after a teenage student had died in a completed suicide attempt, the faculty members were prohibited from speaking about the death with any students. The principal believed that this discussion would increase the likelihood of other suicides. What resulted was emotional chaos as everyone tried to cope with the death, without the ability to actually speak about it. It was only when an outside speaker was brought in to address the faculty on a professional development day that the silence was finally broken.

In a nearby parochial elementary school, a father had a psychological break-down. He killed his children and his wife. He then stabbed himself multiple times. The principal visited every class and spoke about the deaths of their friends and classmates. However, she then cautioned the students not to speak about this to "the little ones." The principal then went to grades 1 through 3 and told those students that the family had moved away. This principal's approach created a situation where children in the same family could not speak to each other. Some of the children asked their parents, "Why did Sister lie?"

It was in this same school that the pastor had visited the classes to discuss the dangers of death education. He stated that students in these classes were told there was no life after death and that caused them to kill themselves. A fifth grade student asked the priest why, if they believed there was no place to go, people would want to hurry their arrival there? The priest ignored the question.

Each of these cases could be viewed as an exception that had no connection to death education. However, the point to be made is that it cannot be assumed that all religious schools address issues related to death and grief. In these schools there is a place for prayer. The faith of these students allows prayer to be used as a way of coping with a loss and in most religious schools the underlying theology of the sponsoring religion allows comments, such as, "They have gone to be with God" to be made in all sincerity.

The main point here is that is religious schools, as in any other institution, death education needs to be offered in an age-appropriate, planned manner. The presence of religious faith, by itself, does not guarantee that the topic will be dealt with in a helpful or professional, caring manner.

Death Education in Clergy Education

It was stated above that, "It might be assumed that, when the students are adults there would be less difficulty merging the topics of religion and spirituality with death education because these students are able to choose whether they wish to pursue this avenue of investigation." Religion offers many definitions for, or explanations of, death. It has been identified in ways that range from death as "the wages of sin" to death as the "ultimate step in reunion with God." These broad differences in meaning must be understood by clergy if they are to be able to assist their followers in ways that take personal spirituality and religious differences into account. An issue for clergy, especially those serving as chaplains in a medical or military setting, is the ability to help individuals deal with the need to cope on some level with the problems posed by loss and by suffering. When the death education is offered in the context of a particular faith system, there is not as great a concern about offending the beliefs of others as might exist in a secular context. Pastoral counseling typically includes discussion of helping others to deal with loss and/or suffering and death education is a part of such preparation.

While pastoral counseling in general may be more attuned to psychological responses to loss and suffering than was the case some years ago, there are clergy/spiritual advisors who receive a broader preparation that acknowledges differences in belief and tries to prepare the clergy to assist individuals whose religious practices or spiritual beliefs they may not share. That group consists of military and hospital chaplains. For chaplains, the possibility of death and the reality of suffering and grief are constantly present. These possibilities affect the individuals whom they are trying to assist. These affected individuals hold a wide variety of beliefs that may come from different religious traditions. They may also have very different ways of relating to the spiritual dimension in their lives. In this context death education takes a different approach.

In a study of practicing chaplains, Sakurai (2006) examined the themes the chaplains themselves found to be important in their pastoral roles. The responses showed that 84% saw "attending to suffering" as the major theme in their work. They then saw inviting the individual to share his/her story or dialogue as the next most important theme (59%). Any professional death education programs aimed at assisting chaplains, with the very diverse beliefs of this client base, would do well to share personal stories as a starting point.

Reverend Richard Gilbert, a director of chaplaincy services, has studied the role of spirituality in helping individuals to face illness and loss. He offers the following common threads that chaplains can use to carry on in the face of suffering and grief. His points seem to parallel the questions identified earlier by Mwalimu Imara (and listed above). Gilbert sees these common threads as:

- The person's understanding of God/his or her beliefs (creed)
- The person's sense of the transcendent in his or her life
- The role of the religious leader/spiritual advisor
- The symbols identified as important by the individual
- How this set of beliefs/practices engages the individual
- The way(s) in which this religion/set of beliefs helps the individual to determine the meaning of life, suffering, and death
- The ritual(s) that may be beneficial to individuals coping with personal loss and suffering (R. Gilbert, 2002a)

These common threads shared by most religions should be a component of any professional death education program for clergy. Some of these points may also be included in death education programs in the context of schools where, too often, the spiritual dimension is omitted. When such omission happens, the rituals and coping styles of grieving individuals can become more difficult for young people to comprehend (Cox, Bendiksen, & Stevenson, 2002; R. Gilbert, 2002b, R. Gilbert, 2006).

Religious Values and Society

Traditionally, religion has fulfilled several functions in society. It has been a kind of "social glue" that provided people with a common set of values and beliefs that helped to develop a sense of community. It can give people a sense that life and death have some larger meaning or purpose. Religion reinforces most of the norms of a society. In addition, religion can provide help during major life events or periods of change by assisting people to face, and to deal with, these events and the stress that accompanies them (Robertson, 1977).

Religious values can provide a sense of belonging to those who share those values. They have provided some with a feeling of security when one is confronted with the reality of personal mortality or the death of loved ones. Finally, religious values have been shown to give to some a sense that life has meaning…even a life of suffering. This last function of religious values in society is of increasing interest to educators and parents at a time when schools are being asked to take a more active role in stemming a rising tide of adolescent suicide. Schools are being asked to take on "values education" to place greater emphasis on life and its relationships. Death education can assist in meeting this challenge.

A simple goal of all education is, or should be, to have students accept as fact the belief that each of us is responsible for the consequences of his/her actions (Stevenson, 1983). A decision about an act being "right/wrong" or "good/evil" is essentially a value judgment. Gordon and Klass (1979) saw such value judgments as one of the major goals of death education. They saw this death education goal as "defining value judgments raised by issues related to death." They cautioned that educators would need to be aware of their own values and personal beliefs, and to understand the complexity of the issues involved to be able to present all sides in a clear, straightforward manner (Gordon & Klass, 1979). Even if we were to decide that religion, religious values and spirituality had no place in death education, how can anyone be sure of the personal values (religious and otherwise) that educators may be using to create and implement lesson plans? If we first set guidelines for discussion of values, including religious values, and discussion of religion as these apply to death education, there is a greater chance to approach such values in a conscious manner.

A conscious understanding of our values and those of others can give us a greater feeling of "control" over our lives. Such an understanding, to be complete, must include religious values and the spiritual questions asked about the meaning of life and death. In some cases, discussion of values is said to be limited to "humanistic values." However, since humanism is seen by some as becoming more and more like a religion in its own right, adopting humanistic values may not solve the situation. It may merely add a new dimension to it.

Summary

Death education, defined earlier as "instruction that deals with death, dying, grief, and loss and their impact on the individual and on humankind" exists to provide individuals with information. Those who take such courses/programs typically want such information to 1) better understand themselves and others and 2) to make informed decisions related to loss and grief. Religion and spirituality, as well as the lack of any formal religious belief, can play a role in the majority of people's lives. Since no decision can be better than the information upon which that decision is based, it is necessary to include all relevant areas in any course/program that seeks to educate students about death, loss, and/or grief and their impact on a person's life. To try to have meaningful curriculum about death and grief without examining the role played by religion/spirituality means that such a curriculum is consciously omitting a section of important information on this topic. Anthropological interpretations of religion have generally held that the supportive effects on a culture outweigh disruptive consequences (Barra, *et. al.*, 1983). The possible pitfalls in adding religion and spirituality to a death education can be addressed in advance of their inclusion in a curriculum. By creating appropriate policies and procedures for the inclusion of this important information, death education students will be better equipped to examine death, loss, and grief in the context of the impact on the "whole person."

LEARNING Objective! (30/40) (25/40)
Recognize the Special Issues in death
education that religious + Spiritual
Concerns present.

Chapter 33

Historical and Contemporary Perspectives on Death Education

Illene C. Noppe

It could be easily said that death education began as soon as human beings realized the boundaries of their own life spans. Death education, or the formal and informal study of issues pertaining to dying, death, and grief, has been a significant part of folklore, oral traditions, rituals, literature, art, and, of course, religion, throughout history. How death was understood paralleled the historical and social institutions of a particular culture anchored into a specific time. Greek mythology, the changing nature of the understanding of the universe in relation to human's place within, the black plague of Europe in the 14th century, and world wars may serve as organizing frameworks for understanding how both life and death was known. Generally speaking, individuals learned early on in life that people died, what behaviors and ideas were expected in the face of death, and derived a concept of the afterlife from religious teachings and secular responses.

According to the social historian Philippe Aries (1981), Western concepts of death approximated sociohistorical events. Thus, the cultural view of death prior to the Middle Ages was shaped by the attitudes of knights and monks, into a "tamed death." This was simple death, orchestrated by the dying person him or herself, publicly acknowledged and ritualized as a known aspect of life on this earth. Death was viewed not as much about personal loss, but more as a part of the natural order of things. "Death education" during this period most likely took the form of learning, via observation, the appropriate rituals and behaviors accompanying the death bed scenario. This form of death changed during the Middle Ages, when self awareness and religion's emphasis on a judgment day led to a focus on "death of the self." The focus of death education reflected the emphasis on living life in preparation of the afterlife and eternal salvation.

Another change in death attitudes occurred during the 18th century. In tandem with the Industrial Revolution and trends toward social secularism, romantism and spiritualism, the mourning and memorialization of the death of significant others became central to the concept of death. Proper mourning behavior, typically different for males and females, was an important aspect of learning about death and dying.

Whereas Aries (1981) concedes that these past themes reflect an acceptance of death, he notes that significant demographic trends and historical events in the 20th century changed how people relate to death. People lived longer, became increasing mobile, and were more easily distanced from immediate contact with death. Death, dubbed by Aries (1981) as denied and forbidden, became wrapped in a conspiracy of silence, at least in Western society.

Perhaps the most significant death education lesson learned in the 20th century was that death is a topic not to be acknowledged nor studied. Although Freud wrote of death and grief in *Mourning and Melancholia*, (1917), death as a topic of teaching and learning was largely nonexistent. A culturally toxic topic, death was not formally discussed until individuals were directly confronted with the death of their loved ones or the impending death of themselves. Uneducated, fearful, and poorly socialized into the multifaceted aspects of issues such as dying, grieving and legal aspects of death, stress from dying and death was compounded by cultural ignorance.

Perhaps then, it was inevitable that the need for education about death would emerge during the latter half of the 20th century. Death education as an articulated focus of study, is traditionally dated to Herman Fiefel's (1959) landmark publication, *The Meaning of Death*, an edited set of articles that sought to remove the taboo of honest discussion about death. It was from such humble beginnings that the multidisciplinary field of thanatology arose (the study of death and dying) evolving into books, journals, courses, workshops, and Internet offerings throughout the world. Because the field of thanatology is so new, death education has undergone significant transformation in a relatively short period time, approximately 45 years. This chapter will provide a brief "road map" of death education, with a focus on the formal aspects of death education in higher and professional educational contexts (where the "movement" began). How death education for children and adolescents has evolved will be discussed in the section on "Life Span Issues."

There are three main themes that will be used as the overarching conceptual framework for understanding death education: 1) the definition and articulation of the field, 2) pedagogy and death education, and 3) the current and future concerns of death education.

The Definition and Articulation of Death Education

Even in its earliest days, death education was recognized as occurring both in formal and informal settings. At the informal level, death education occurs whenever there is a "teachable moment" that spurs conversation and discussion about death. Unless a family's communication is completely closed, children are exposed to such talks when a pet or grandparent dies, when there is a death affecting a classroom, or when newsworthy events make such discussion unavoidable, such as when the tragic events of 9/11 saturated our lives. However, many adults profit from these informal discussions as well, stimulated by a movie, current events (e.g., Iraq, the Terry Schaivo case), family crises, or an issue arising in a professional setting. Such spontaneous discussions rely on attitudes and knowledge arising from religious teachings and past exposure to death and dying. Unfortunately, with little education, misconceptions and misinformation could be the end result of such conversations.

The formal aspects of death education center around educational goals and objectives, a curriculum, and assessment and evaluation. Its history has been traced back to the first few college courses that were created in the 1960s, such as Robert Fulton's course at the University of Minnesota, and Robert Kastenbaum's course at Wayne Statue University, with new course offerings subsequently appearing in departments of psychology, religion, and sociology (Pine, 1977). Their number has mushroomed to the point that virtually every college campus now offers some form of thanatological coursework (Doka, 2003). Death education also can be found at primary and secondary grade levels, although the extent to which younger students are exposed to information is difficult to gauge, as it typically does not appear as a stand-alone subject, but rather is integrated into other course content as a module (Doka, 2003). The work of Kubler-Ross (1969) highlighted the need for death education for the medical profession, and was of particular interest to nurses, who thirsted for guidance in the care of patients who were dying of chronic degenerative diseases.

Although the goals of the early death education courses varied, their major focus was to create an environment where it was safe for participants to discuss a culturally taboo topic. Additionally, they were designed to promote values clarification, reflect on the experience of death as structured by cultural and social forces, promote understanding of the processes of grieving and dying, prepare citizens for politically informed decisions, and to promote professional development (Corr & Corr, 2003; Leviton, 1977; Pine, 1977). Leviton (1977) aptly noted that the thematic "glue" of the goals of death education were to improve the quality of life and living as well as dying, an emphasis that remains central to the field today. Thus, thanatology can be defined as "the study of life with death left in" (Kastenbaum, 2004, p. xviii).

According to Leviton, the value of education about death and dying would be to improve communication amongst those whose death is imminent and their loved ones, help students to become more aware of measures that could be taken to prolong life with quality, and to be able to recognize and cope with the symptoms of grief. Leviton's (1977) perceptive and prescient writing also called for measurable and testable means for death education's learning outcomes. The most apparent of these has been in the assessment of death education as a means toward the reduction of death anxiety through increased knowledge (Durlak, 1994). Although research does suggest that students gain increased knowledge about topics in thanatology, such as funeral rituals, theories of grief and mourning, the process of dying, and life span issues in death and dying, research also indicates that the goal of lowering anxiety about death and dying is only partially successful (Durlak, 1994; Maglio & Robinson, 1994).

As a testimony to the farsighted vision of the "pioneers" (dubbed by Pine in 1977) of death education, the goals and learning outcomes of contemporary courses in death education have not changed significantly from those of the recent past. Rather, what has changed is the virtual explosion of materials available to students and scholars. Scholarly and trade books on topics of death and dying regularly appear, instructors have an increased array of textbooks from which to choose, including several now in their fifth, seventh and eighth editions (e.g., Corr, Nabe, & Corr, 2006; DeSpelder & Strickland, 2005; Kastenbaum, 2004, respectively). Journals and newsletters (e.g, *Omega: The Journal of Death and Dying; Death Studies; Mortality; The Forum: Newsletter of the Association for Death Education and Counseling*) provide recent theoretical and empirical work in thanatology, and of course, the Internet abounds with Web sites related to a cornucopia of topics in the field. Professional organizations such as the International Work Group on Death, Dying, and Bereavement, the Association for Death Education and Counseling, and the Hospice Foundation of America were formed during the 1970s and 1980s and currently enjoy respect as major contributors to knowledge in the field. Included in their missions is the promotion of education about death and dying. As the recognition (and sensationalism) of the importance of knowledge of death has grown, informal death education now regularly occurs from information provided in newspapers, television, and the movies. Death, still a taboo topic, has nonetheless become the quirky darling of the media (as in witnessed in the popular television show, *Six Feet Under*).

Pedagogy and Death Education

Cognitive and Affective Components of Death Education

One of the unique features of death education is the inescapable fact that it offers students opportunities to explore the subject both on intellectual and affective planes. The two major teaching methodologies are didactic, involving the dissemination of knowledge, and experiential, providing a focus on affective factors. While the didactic method, emphasizing lecture, reading, and discussion of content-driven material promotes increased cognitive awareness, Durlak 's (1994) and Maglio & Robinson's (1994) metaanalysis of death anxiety indicated that it is the experiential method, with a focus on personal reflection, or a combination of didactic and experiential methods, that aids in reduction of death anxiety. Students' knowledge, behavioral, and affective changes with respect to death-related issues is tied to the type of education received.

Death Education as Interdisciplinary and Multidisciplinary

The first contemporary death educators recognized the need to draw knowledge and approaches from a number of different perspectives, a multidisciplinary approach that involved fields as diverse as philosophy, religion, anthropology, history, psychology, and sociology (Corr & Corr, 2003). The early courses frequently drew upon guest speakers from a number of disciplines as a way of ensuring the inclusion of differing perspectives (Morgan, 1987). That tradition continues today (Wass, 2004) and ensures creative collaboration across disciplinary units. However, as thanatology has evolved into its own specific field of study, it has also developed a scholarly and pedagogical tradition that is inherently interdisciplinary in nature, an orientation that integrates the wisdom and approaches of many traditional fields into its own framework. Once considered experimental or "renegade," courses in death education now are viewed as legitimate on most college campuses and may even be part of the requirements for general education or for a major.

The "New" Pedagogy of Higher Education and Death Education

The teaching of death and dying has always demanded a certain degree of creativity from instructors. However, as undergraduate education has recently enjoyed an upsurge in interest in enhancing the effectiveness of teaching and learning via new classroom experience, many ideas have been adapted in death education courses. Recently, service learning, wherein students perform volunteer work relevant to the course topic and simultaneously engage in related academic activities, offers many rich experiential opportunities for thanatology students, and has been demonstrated by Basu & Heuser (2003) as an effective learning tool in death education. Perhaps the most significant pedagogical change in thanatology courses has been increased involvement of the computer as a tool for teaching and learning. Fifty years ago, the early thanatologists could not have possibly envisioned the information age of the new millennium. Today, thanatology courses are offered online, sources of material are studied from a variety of web sites, and students have access to materials from sites physically remote but readily accessible in their virtual state. In addition, communication barriers between student and scholar have fallen as e-mail and Internet discussion sites offer a level playing field for intellectual interchange. Indeed, the World Wide Web might be the single most influential source of death education today at all levels.

Current Issues and Future Concerns of Death Education

The early years of death education primarily saw survey courses that were part of a liberal arts curriculum. Professional fields such as medicine, social work and mental health saw little in terms of formal course work; rather death education occurred in workshops and extracurricular events that largely were one-shot affairs. Many of these modules of death education were driven by nursing educators, who as frontline caregivers felt the a great need to learn how to help the dying, although palliative care issues are still inadequately covered in undergraduate nursing curricula (Mallory, 2003). The inadequacies of the health care system to care for the dying, the "right to die" movement, and other public policy concerns has led to increased demand for such education. Hospice has been at the forefront in trying to expand death education. For example, the National Hospice Foundation offers a yearly satellite conference, geared to professionals (but open to anyone), that has foci on topics such as children's grief, loss and public tragedy, and ethical dilemmas at the end of life. However, most of the material is integrated within the basic curriculum and in workshops with few full courses offered (Dickinson, 2002; Wass, 2004). In addition, medical textbooks offer limited coverage of material pertaining to end-of-life care (Rabow, Hardie, Fair & McPhee, 2000). Some specialties, such as emergency medical services, do not for the most part offer death education, and for those that do, the units are taught by instructors with no formal training (Smith & Walz, 1998).

Today, death education has expanded into professional and graduate education. Graduate-level programs, such as the master's level programs at Brooklyn College, Hood College in Frederick Maryland, and Madonna University in Livonia, Michigan, and certification programs, as offered by the Association for Death Education and Counseling, are valuable in helping to develop death educators for medical and mental health professionals. Clinical psychologists are also recognizing that they may play a significant role in treating individuals facing end-of-life issues, although opportunities for training in death and dying content, clinical assessment, the understanding of evidence-based practice, and supervised practica is sparse (Haley, Larson, Kasl-Godley & Neimeyer, 2003). Adult and continuing education courses have also reached out to professionals and the general public.

A second issue that has received more extensive discussion among death educators involves recognition of the need to understand the influence of culture and race on the dying process (Crase, 1987; Doorenbos et al., 2003). In death education, such recognition means going beyond treating varying cultural practices and beliefs towards death as interesting "oddities." Rather, it involves examining how culture and diversity permeate the social construction of the dying process, the meaning of death, spirituality and religiosity, and moral and ethical issues at the end of life (Doorenbos et al., 2003). In addition, global studies has become increasingly important in higher education in the United States and death education has responded to such international trends. Learning about how death education is taught in other countries can lead to an important cross-fertilization of ideas in the teaching of multicultural content and teaching techniques. Faculty from American universities who have the opportunity to teach death and dying abroad learn a greater appreciation for the role of culture in end-of-life issues and may be more effective in imparting that approach in their death education courses in the United States (Shatz, 2002). As the United States becomes increasingly diverse, understanding the impact of culture on values and cognitions about death and dying will do much to diminish miscommunication and disenfranchisement (Noppe, 2004).

Kastenbaum (1977), in an early examination of death education, raised a number of important questions regarding educational techniques, the qualifications and motivations of the death educators themselves, expectations of and by students, and the dangers and benefits of such courses. We should not become complacent about such issues just because three decades have passed and death education is legitimized on most campuses. Death education must include carefully conducted research on student learning outcomes (including but not limited to death anxiety and basic content knowledge), and on the effectiveness of teaching practices and methods (including use of electronic-based education). This research, referred to as the scholarship of teaching and learning (Boyer, 1880; Glassick, Huber, & Maeroff, 1997), must be an integral component of any death education program (Noppe, 2004). It is incumbent on professional death educators, then, that they have the tools for proper assessment and evaluation of their programs. In all fields of higher education, and for death educators who train in more informal settings, the same tenants apply: death education involves knowing the research, understanding its usefulness, and translating it into "educational action" (Wass, 1995).

Conclusion

In a relatively short period of time, death education has changed in terms of its number of course offerings, its broadening beyond traditional liberal arts curriculum into graduate and professional education, recognition of the significance of a multicultural perspective, and increased reliance on electronic media for teaching, learning, and scholarship. Yet, the central motivation behind the creation of such educational experiences remain the same—the belief that as more is learned about dying, death, and loss, the greater the potential for enhancement in the quality of living.

Learning Objective: (40/40)
   Explicate the various historical +
   contemporary perspectives on D.E.

Chapter 34

Life Span Issues and Death Education

Illene C. Noppe

As with any educational endeavor, death education occurs in a number of formats and venues with variable content and emphases. Death education, for example, may occur in an informal way, such as when a conversation spontaneously develops in the home or gym when a news event puts death in the forefront (e.g., the Terry Schiavo case). Formal approaches to death education appear as courses in school settings, as community-based workshops, or as presentations in professional conferences. Regardless of the format of death education, death educators agree that its goals are the acquisition of knowledge, as well as reflection on and understanding of attitudes, values, and emotions about death and dying (Wass, 2004). In addition, the articulation of a philosophy of life and death, and behaviors for the self and towards others that are consistent with that philosophy are significant to death education (Corr & Corr, 2003).

No matter how death is "taught," it is undeniable that the ways in which humans understand, perceive, and interpret death and dying are influenced by factors such as gender, social and cultural context, life experiences, and religious orientation. Most significantly, where individuals are situated within their life spans, their associated normative developmental tasks will be of great consequence to the efficacy of any educational experience in death and dying. Thus, the study and design of death education is enhanced when it is examined as an intersection with issues imbued in developmental phases or stages.

Death Education and the Normative Death Issues of the Life Span

Erikson (1968) presented the life span as a series of psychosocial issues and tasks that confront individuals from birth until death. These issues (or "crises") appear throughout the life span, but one issue takes on a particular salience, for example trust during infancy, at each stage of the life span. Thus, the awareness and meanings of death are intimately intertwined with the major developmental tasks of each stage. As Erikson (1968) insightfully noted, these developmental tasks are embedded within cultural context, so that the entry into adulthood and the tasks associated with childhood and adult life will vary with social structure. In addition to developmental tasks, conceptual understandings of death framed by overall cognitive development and individual experiences, such as the death of a parent or a sibling, greatly influence the meaning of death throughout the lifespan.

The continuum of formality in death education may be most effective as a U-shaped function across the life span. Thus, during the early childhood years, death education typically and appropriately is taught in informal ways. However it is taught, death education for children must consider how death concepts evolve from early to later childhood. Maria Nagy (1948) suggested that children initially perceive death to be a transitory, reversible phase where the dead exhibit limited life functions. During a second phase, death is perceived as a person such as a "bogeyman," who may be outsmarted by a fast and clever child. Finally, toward childhood's end, a "mature" concept of death evolves, incorporating the principles of universality, inevitability, nonfunctionality, and noncorporeal continuation (separation of body and soul, with the soul continuing on). During the developing conceptualizations of death, a major source of education, which may be spontaneous, comes from the behaviors of adults, both verbal and nonverbal, and from the real and fantastic deaths portrayed in the media (Wass, 2003). Aside from their modeling of behaviors, parents and teachers in the early grades are a major source of information about death in the ability (or inability) to answer spontaneous questions and offer reassurance to their children about their fears and anxieties. These are known as "teachable moments" (Corr & Corr, 2003). Many adults are uncomfortable with such discussions, unaware of the developmental differences in death conceptions, and are at a loss as to what words to use to explain death to young children. Stammering through or avoiding such a conversation teaches children much about the taboo nature of death. In such cases, books specifically designed to guide children through the concept of death, paying mind to how death concepts differ from adults' concepts, have been helpful in breaking the ice. Parenthetically, one aspect of adult death education is how to explain death to young children. A key feature of such explanations is providing adults with the developmentally appropriate words to use with young children. Schaefer (1988) suggests that adults can tell children that it is a sad time, that death refers to the time when "a person's body stops working and will not work any more" (p. 132). Referring to death as sleep, going on vacation, or passing away are misleading, confusing, and ultimately frightening to young children.

Of course, one of the most potent death educators during the early childhood years is experience. Recent work has suggested that an early acquisition of a mature understanding of death occurs when the child has experienced a death of a loved one (Silverman, 2000), experienced a life-threatening illness (Bluebond-Langner, 1978), or has lived in an environment rife with death and violence (Barrett & DeSpelder, 1997).

Few formal death education programs exist for young and elementary school children because teachers may be unprepared for such lessons, because of the concern that it may do more harm than good, and because of the belief that this topic is better taught in the home (Wass, 1985; Shackford, 2003). However, mental health professionals who work with children in the schools have been increasing their calls for more formal school-based death education for children (Aspinall, 1996; Shackford, 2003).

Formal types of death education may be seen in middle school and high schools, although such coursework is relatively uncommon. The material may be integrated as units within other subjects (health education is a favorite) or may appear as independent courses in the curriculum (Corr & Corr, 2003). In the presentation of such materials, educators need to consider the fact that whereas adolescents clearly have a mature concept of death, the developmental tasks of this period of the life span influence their death awareness. Issues of identity development, increasing independence from their family, and increasing reliance on peers for support and socialization, sophisticated use of technology and the media, biological maturation, and the demands of a complex, global society frequently move death to the foreground in interesting ways such as risk-taking behavior, and a fascination with death in music, Web sites, and television (Noppe & Noppe, 1997). This developmental period is associated with life-affirming activities and with "mature" understandings of death, and coping with death is often unanticipated, unsupported, and disenfranchised. Unfortunately, many adolescents actively avoid seeking help from adults, particularly those whom they do not know; they may seek isolation, or may receive faulty advice and misinformation from their peers.

For many adolescents and young adults, death frequently occurs in a sudden and tragic way through suicide, vehicular accidents, and violence (Hayslip & Hansson, 2003; Noppe & Noppe, 1997). As a result, death education frequently may be framed by crisis and occur within the context of peer grief support groups or counseling sessions run by school psychologists or guidance counselors. Aside from work on suicide prevention, attending to the acute grief needs often are primary goals of those running of such groups (Corr & Corr, 2003) and as such, are not a part of continuing instruction (Wass, 2003). In addition, educators frequently are at a loss as how to handle information during public tragedies such as

September 11, 2001—they may even be required by administrative personnel to minimize exposure of the news to their students (Noppe, Noppe & Bartell, 2006).

Formal courses in death and dying are found on virtually every college and university campus in the United States (Doka, 2003) and are well received by students. These courses are taught in a variety of different departments by faculty from a number of disciplinary perspectives (e.g., psychology, sociology, religious studies). Although the content of these courses may vary, they usually cover material on dying, bereavement and grief, funeral customs, and medical issues. In addition to being intellectually engaging, students may find such courses helpful in their coping with personal crises. College death educators must respond to the fact that approximately 22-30% of traditionally aged college students are in their first year of suffering the loss of a significant other (Balk, 2001). As in the adolescent years, young adults encounter death most often through sudden and traumatic ways. In addition, the very real prospect of going to war or seeing friends sent to life-threatening political hotspots and "normative" deaths of grandparents and pets make such courses popular and valued. However, instructors of such courses frequently have to walk the tightrope of balancing such interest with reality that the college years are a time of increasing independence from one's family of origin, career preparation and formulation of intimate relationships—the antithesis of death and loss. Thus, students who are death anxious may not find relief from their thanatology courses (Durlak, 1994), find coursework not personally relevant to their career goals or immediate lives, or have a difficult time responding to significant end-of-life issues (such as writing advance directives).

Adults seek out both formal and informal ways of learning about death. For those interested or involved in work in the medical field, formal instruction in death, once notably lacking in the professional curricula, is increasing in number (Dickinson & Field, 2002; Wass, 2004). Material on death and dying typically does not appear in stand-alone courses, but rather are integrated as modules in larger courses or as a part of a clinical internship (Dickinson & Field, 2002). Course modules and professional development workshops, often associated with conferences such as the annual conference of the Association for Death Education and Counseling, are also offered for individuals who see themselves encountering death issues in the workplace, such as nurses, social workers, educators, hospice workers, funeral directors, and clergy.

As the adult years involve increasing responsibilities in family and work, many adults seek out information about death and loss in order to be more informed about how to provide for their families in the case of an untimely accident or terminal illness. In their parenting role, adults may desire to learn something about how to discuss death with their children. The market has certainly responded to such demand, witnessed by a surge in the number of publications about death intended for children and adults. Moreover, some adults may face the tragic loss of a child (Hayslip & Hansson, 2003), and support groups, such as Compassionate Friends, frequently have speakers who offer education as well as comfort.

These issues will continue on into the middle adulthood years, but as parents die and as the possibilities for life-threatening illnesses such as heart disease and cancer increase, the awareness of one's own mortality moves to the forefront (Hayslip & Hansson, 2003). Aside from the career-related workshops and seminars, middle, aged adults rely upon informal death education such as from the media, books, and the Internet to enhance their understanding about death. Most "baby boomers" fit this demographic, encouraging the media to respond to concerns about their increasing encounters with dying and death with articles in newspapers and magazines, discussion groups in book clubs and churches, and television shows that explore these issues in serious and comedic venues. Recognizing that not all of these sources provide accurate information in a sensitive, effective manner, they nonetheless open possibilities for dialogue and exposure to issues that were considered taboo not so long ago.

That elderly persons must frequently confront death is a given as they increasingly experience the loss of their friends and spouses (Hayslip & Hansson, 2003). Thus, encountering death, to the point of bereavement overload, can lead to a framework of life wherein death and loss predominate. Despite the obvious association between aging and death, the elderly are given few opportunities for education about end-of-life issues and death other than the popular modalities discussed above. The literature on death anxiety (Fortner & Neimeyer, 1999) suggests that relatively speaking, the elderly do not necessarily manifest high levels of death anxiety. Yet, as Wass (2004) notes, many elderly do express concerns and fears about dying and death. Fortner and Neimeyer's (1999) meta-analytic study of the aged and death anxiety found higher levels of death anxiety in older adults who were in relatively poor physical and mental health. Death educational content specifically geared to the developmental issues of the aged, such as coping with pain and negotiating the medical system, aspects of widowhood, or the dying process may help to alleviate some of these worries (Wass, 2004). Furthermore, many elderly are genuinely interested in the topics covered in death education. Learning about various funeral customs, differing religious beliefs about death, and perspectives on grief and loss can be favored topics in community workshops, and university outreach programs for retirees. In addition, hospice nurses and volunteers may be particularly effective in providing one-on-one educational experiences for the elderly. Wass (2004) suggests that nursing home personnel and family members be taught how to more effectively communicate about death-related issues to the elderly.

Grief in an aged population may also involve the loss of an adult child or a grand-child (Hayslip & Hansson (2003) and should be addressed in death education pro-grams for those who work with the elderly.

The Efficacy of a Life Span Approach to Death Education

Teaching and learning implies change and development, and death education is no exception. Given that the goals and content of death education vary as a function of the developmental needs of its recipients, it is not surprising that a clear and consistent picture of the efficacy of the pedagogy of death has not emerged. Relevant to the developmental needs of the intended audience, death educators face the decision of how to measure the effectiveness of their educational program. How do you know, for example, if preschoolers have benefited from a teachable moment when a class pet dies? Is it enough to report anecdotally that the children are more considerate of one another subsequent to the discussion (Hopkins, 2002), or should they have advanced toward a more "mature" concept of death?

Most of the research on the effectiveness of death education assesses content and death anxiety, especially in college courses. For younger age groups, few sys-tematic assessments using psychometrically sound instruments exist. For the adult courses, those that emphasize content in a lecture-style format are more likely to encourage cognitive changes, whereas those that focus on experiential dimensions that provide opportunities for learners to process their own personal understand-ings show modest success in modifying feelings and attitudes (Durlak, 1994).

Assessment of death education for professional development tends to focus on the adequacy of preparation of materials for medical and mental health personnel (Dickinson & Field, 2002). Given the inadequacy of intervention efforts in communi-cation among physicians and patients (SUPPORT, 1995), longitudinal research needs to be continued on the relationship between education and intervention efficacy.

Wass (2004) points out that data needs to be obtained about the preparation received by death educators, as well as standards and guidelines that would serve to improve the quality of death education for grief counselors, many of whom work with children and adolescents. Given that death education occurs across the life span in a variety of formats, systematic assessment on the interaction of pedagog-ical techniques and age-related needs of learners, known as the "scholarship of teaching and learning" would further advance the field (Noppe, 2004).

Life Span Death Education: Present and Future Needs

Age-related concerns about death and dying are normative but also reverberate to the rhythms of a rapidly changing world. In order to maximize its humanistic potential, death education and death educators must be responsive to contempo-rary issues and how these affect youth, adults and the elderly. For example, death educators should consider how to teach about death to youngsters who are coming of age in a world of increased globalization, terror, and violence that confront them daily on television, the Internet, and in their personal lives. Death educators must learn how to effectively use the Internet and electronic technology, particularly for those populations (e.g., adolescents and young adults) who rely on such technology as primary sources of information. The development of educational programs responsive to the needs of middle-aged and older adults, many of whom are living longer, healthier lives in age-segregated communities away from families of origin will become of increasing importance in the future. And finally, a pressing issue will consider who are to be the next generation of death educators and how are they to be trained, as the field of thanatology itself matures.

Regardless of how the many questions of death education evolves in the future, there is consensus that death education is needed and important for all ages—an important component of life-long learning in all senses of the term.

LeARNing ObJective: (25/40)
Explain the role of D.E. Across the
Life Span.

Chapter 35

The Family, Larger Systems, and Death Education

Kathleen R. Gilbert & Colleen I. Murray

The intent of this chapter is to provide information on the ways in which families educate their members about death and orient them to ways to behave in situations associated with death. In addition, ways in which larger systems, exemplified here primarily by the media, also serve to educate individuals about death will be addressed.

The development of an understanding of death is a meaning-making process (K. Gilbert, 1996; Nadeau, 2001; Neimeyer, Prigerson, & Davies, 2002), and this process of making meaning begins early in life. We come to an understanding of death and how we should respond to it through what is an essentially collaborative meaning making process with others. Through interaction with others, our subjective interpretations of death are confirmed by others and given an objective reality (Berger & Luckman, 1966) that we come to view as "real" because significant others reinforce its reality. The family and larger systems are integral parts of this social construction of reality (K. Gilbert, 1996), and we will explore their role in death education.

The Family as a Death Education System

Our family is the first source of death education we encounter in our lives, and its influence continues on throughout our lives. It serves as a — many would say "the" — primary force in initially shaping our world view and then contributes to the way in which we encounter and comprehend new information throughout life. This shaping occurs in many ways: formally and informally; directly and indirectly; in concert with other sources of death education. It occurs obviously through such socially recognized rituals as funerals and memorials, but less obviously through small rituals like bed time prayers or, in the old days, watching one's father remove his hat when a funeral cortege passed. Everyday activities within the family also contribute to the family's education of its members. A family that easily deals with issues of death likely will produce individuals who are less fearful of death than a family in which death is only spoken of in hushed and fearful tones, if discussion is permitted at all (Weber & Fournier, 1985). In every case, though, an essential role of the family is to convey, both verbally and nonverbally, information about death—that is, to serve as sources of death education.

The Family an Agent of Death Education

The family contributes to each member's acquisition of cultural norms and expectations while also leading them to adapt their behavior to fit those norms. Typically, we think of this influence in terms of values, standards, beliefs, and appropriate behaviors associated with those values, standards, and beliefs (Day, 2002). Acquiring such socialization allows family members to function within society.

An example of this informal education is the way in which children often are socialized along gender lines toward different male and female roles. According to Doka and Martin (2001), boys and girls are informed in different ways, leading them toward approaching death and grief differently. Boys engage in team play, with interactions centered around activities. They are encouraged to view relationships in a hierarchical rather than collaborative way and focus on control of their emotions. Girls, on the other hand, are encouraged to be more cooperative, have more empathy for others, to share confidences, and to be more supportive of others. The end result is different, resulting in complementary approaches to life and death and to grief that generally follow along lines fitting each gender role.

This educational process occurs most obviously in children's early years. Less obvious, and less studied, is death education that takes place across time as family forms shift and change when members join, leave, and create new families. Yet, this process continues throughout life, as members respond to the needs to fulfill new roles within their family as it evolves over time. One of the authors of this chapter (KG), having grown up in a family whose death-related behavior was heavily influenced by its Eastern European heritage, was shocked when attending the funeral of her grandmother in-law, to see, among other alien sights and experiences, "Mammaw" dressed in a negligee in the casket. She was not "waked" for long hours, with coffee provided in the basement of the funeral home. Instead, the family held a "viewing" that lasted two hours, in the evening. Although there were similarities, many aspects of the funeral and its aftermath were different, requiring that she (KG) be quickly tutored on role appropriate behavior.

Talking about death in the family. Family members attempt to anticipate questions, concerns, and needs when they prepare for an impending death-related event, such as a funeral. This preparation is most obvious with children, but, as noted above, continues through the life of the family. In terms of children, and depending on the family, parents might talk with their child about what to expect and how to behave, they may provide coaching, or they might simply tell the child to behave, not ask questions, and not act out. Some parents might choose not to involve the child or refuse to answer questions. In adulthood, couples might rehearse appropriate ways to respond. The film *The Funeral* (Hosogoe & Itami, 1984), demonstrates such rehearsal clearly as a bereaved daughter and her husband watch instructional films to prepare for their roles as bereaved family members in her father's Buddhist funeral.

Children's books about death and loss along with other media may be used as a resource by parents who wish to supplement their own knowledge base as they address their child's questions (Carney, 2003-2004). This type of information exchange may be planned, possibly in response to a death or in anticipation of a death in the family. It may also happen spontaneously, in response to some sort of triggering agent or event. Losing a pet (Kaufman & Kaufman, 2006) or hearing someone discussing a death can be such an event or agent. The death of a pet can be a particularly difficult loss for a child, and parents must be sure not to trivialize the death (Kaufman & Kaufman, 2006) as they discuss it with their child.

In addition to children's books on death, family members may refer to informational books on death, dying, loss, and grief for their own use or as a resource to help other family members. Increasingly, Web sites and other Internet resources serve as informational resources (Cook & Oltjenbruns, 1998). In addition, other media, like television programs (Charkow, 1998) or films (Cox, Garrett, & Graham, 2004-2005) might be used as a planned or spontaneous triggering agent for discussion.

Families also may be involved indirectly in formal death education. In a study of a combined school instruction and family discussions, Waldrop and her colleagues (Waldrop, Tamburlin, Thompson, & Simon, 2004), found the discussions increased students' comfort level with the idea of organ donation. Although the study looked only at students' response to the discussions and did not look at family changes, it would be interesting to learn about effects of the discussions on the larger family, that is changes in comfort level in discussing death, the effects on the discussions, or any end-of-life decisions that were made by others in the family.

Modeling of death-related behavior. Another way in which families teach their members about how to behave when they are confronted with death is through the modeling of appropriate behavior associated with death, essentially serving as role models for family-approved behavior. Young children, in particular, learn by example, and significant others in the family become role models for how to behave in situations associated with death. In this modeling, the family members serve as examples of the norms and behaviors associated with death.

Families Making Meaning:
Collaborative Death Narratives in the Family

From the family systems perspective, the critical process that underlies all interaction in the family is the process of meaning making (Nadeau, 2001). It is important to note that the family's involvement in the attribution of meaning is embedded in the broader culture and society (K. Gilbert, 1996) and is a process that is ongoing throughout the existence of the family. As family members encounter new information in their environment, or are faced by situations when old meanings no longer "fit," they test their theories and use other family members as a "reality check" on what things mean and how one should respond. If family members find their own views confirmed by others in the family, these views are given objective reality—what they perceive comes to be seen as reality because significant others also see it that way (Berger & Luckman, 1966; Thomas & Thomas, 1928). If their views are challenged, they may question their views, that of their family members, or both (K. Gilbert, 1996). The death of a child in the family, for example, may result in radically different perspective on the meaning of the loss and the implication for family members. Parents may feel a need to protect the surviving children, may feel overwhelmed by their own grief, or may perceive the other children as unaffected by the loss. The children may end up with a distorted view of their sibling's death, its meaning for them, their culpability in the death, and the legitimacy of their own rights as a griever (Schwab, 1997).

Mutually validated views facilitate communication, provide structure and meaning to family interactions, and serve as the basis for familial coping behavior (Reiss, 1981). However, the various family systems and larger systems in which we live may result in family members holding contradictory or competing views on appropriate beliefs and behaviors associated with death. This discrepancy in views can be seen most clearly with children of divorce, who may face contradictory views from their parents, in each of their households. An example would be when religious beliefs are a key source of disagreement and conflict in the divorce. These children could then find themselves pulled between two different and conflicting belief systems about death and the afterlife, and might find the views and expectations of their parents, now untethered from each other, changing and evolving away from each other over time.

Decision making in the family. The same potential for conflict or collaboration on attributed meaning may be found in families dealing with a variety of decisions that are made in the family: choices made about end-of-life care, advance care planning discussions, wakes, funerals, and periods of mourning. These decisions come with significant transitions in the family's life course and these are associated with high stress (White & Klein, 2002). In her study of end-of-life decisions, Gauthier (2005) found that family concerns were an important factor in the decision making of terminally ill patients. Increased dependence, the need to relocate to be near family, decisions made to accommodate the needs of family caregivers, the economic burden on family, concerns about a lack of communication were all social concerns that were associated with family function. Interestingly, the study did not identify family factors that positively affected end-of-life decision making, but it may be that the participants saw the focus of the study on impediments to easy decision making.

Rituals as a tool for dealing with death. Rituals often become more valuable to the family during times of loss. Rituals are composed by metaphors, symbols and actions that are "packaged" in a highly condensed, time and space-bounded, dramatic form to establish and maintain family identity (Imber-Black, 2004). Family rituals serve five functions within families: relating, issues of expressing and maintaining relationships; changing, transitions for self and others; healing, recovery from relationship betrayal, trauma or loss; believing, voicing beliefs and making meaning; and celebrating, affirming deep joy and honoring life with festivity (Imber-Black & Roberts, 1992).

In their overview of cultural variations in approaches to end-of-life decisions as well as associated rituals, Searight and Gafford (2005) described a wide range of approaches to decision making in the family, even to the extent of whether or not the dying person should be involved in the decision making process or even if they should be informed that a decision needed to be made. In a world that allows greater mixing of culturally diverse individuals and the blending of cultures in families, issues of meaning may become intense at these times (Klessig, 1992).

Death Education in Larger Systems

Just as the family plays a role as a source of death education, so too do the larger systems. From our general society and our personal communities, we are exposed to information and beliefs about death though formal and informal means, as well as responses and practices surrounding death-related events. The process of meaning making, on the other hand, becomes less interactive and far more unidirectional, the larger the system becomes.

Although they are a key source of death education, and the principal venue for formalized death education, the role of schools and religious organizations will not be addressed in this chapter. The way in which death education plays out in these more common sources of death education are addressed in greater depth in other chapters on death education in this text. Instead, we have explored the role of media as a source of death education, including the ways in which death is treated in the media in general and responses by the media to specific events such as deaths of important individuals in a community, coverage of murders, large-scale death such as the attacks of 9/11 or the tsunami of 2004. In addition, more creative approaches will be explored.

Books and Other Printed Materials

Books and other printed materials are readily available resources for death education. As noted earlier in this chapter, these resources can be used either directly, as a tool for discussion of death or as a source for detailed information on death, dying, and bereavement. The difficulty is in selecting high-quality resources that meet the specific needs of the reader. Schuurman (2003-2004) has identified a selection of high-quality texts that can be used for a variety of audiences so they may talk with children. Other resources, like pamphlets and circulars, also require that the reader be attentive to the source and credentials of the author or source.

Internet

As noted earlier, various Internet-based media are now available and, as Cook and Oltjenbruns (1998) have noted, they range in quality and should likely not serve as the only resource used. These media include a variety of resources that contribute to death education: static Web pages; chat rooms; bulletin board systems that may include moderated and unmoderated support groups; Web logs, or "blogs," which are personal web pages established by individuals to tell their personal story or to address concerns of personal interest; and podcasts, short videos that can are designed to be downloaded and played on personal computers or on such personal video players as iPods.

Television and Formalized Death Education

Public television has had a long history of developing and presenting content that addresses death and dying. A recent example is the PBS program, *Dealing with Death* presented under the "In the Mix" banner. This program, directed at teens and with its own Web site, has a companion discussion guide, for use in formal death education. The Frontline series on PBS has presented richly textured documentaries addressing thanatology issues; four examples include *Abortion Clinic, The Death of Nancy Cruzan, The Last Abortion Clinic,* and *Living Old* (www.pbs.org/wgbh/pages/frontline.view/).

In addition to its national mandate, public television has a local one. Continuing education courses as well as for-credit courses focusing on death and dying have been set within the local mandate for community education. Studies have been conducted on the effects of death-related content in educational service programs. In the case of Sharapan's (1977) study of death content on *Mr. Roger's Neighborhood,* for example, letters from families indicated that they engaged in discussions of death related themes after viewing the show.

Journalistic Media—Print and Electronic

Death education takes place in a wide variety of ways in print and electronic media. One form, obituaries, memorializes common people as well as public figures (Field & Walter, 1997-1998). In addition to obituaries, newspapers and magazines publish stories of individuals who have been diagnosed with a life-threatening or terminal condition or have coped with the death of loved ones. These articles typically present a model for coping with dying in a "quiet but 'heroic' way and in so doing offer models of 'good dying' for their readers" (Field and Walter, 2003, pg. 2). In addition, the narratives of these stories are selective and serve a social purpose. The story that devoloped in the news media following the Oklahoma City bombing was one of brave, highly resilient Midwesterners. This story line made it difficult for personal narratives that contrasted with that image. In addition, any personal story that was different from the "normal" stage model of grief was treated as somehow abnormal (Levine, 1996).

Similar to the media stories of extraordinary deaths of common people, the death of a public figure often takes on more significance in the media than the simple recognition and memorializing of an individual. These "celebrity deaths" often become media events (Merrin, 1999), providing opportunities to present a culturally approved role for the deceased along with implied rules for ways in which the bereaved should behave (Furedi, 1998, Merrin, 1999), in an exaggerated version of the process described by Levine (1996). Such a death can also become a political event (Furedi, 1998), one intended to shape the view that society holds of itself and of the world. The impact of these deaths can extend over decades. We, the authors of the chapter, still can remember childhood images of President Kennedy's funeral in 1963 and the admiring observations of television commentators as they talked about Jackie Kennedy's behavior. The message was that contained, reserved, tear-free mourning was socially desirable while any overt display of grief was, by implication, wrong.

Television and, to a lesser extent, radio news can have a uniquely intense emotional impact and concern has been raised about the coverage of death and grieving in the news media (Gamino, 2005). Of particular concern are images of violence as news content and the coverage of personal details. The phrase "If it bleeds, it leads" is said to describe and define the guiding rule of television news. Graphic images sell programs and sensationalistic stories have a longer "shelf life." Violent images are used in news coverage to portray consequences of events and, as education about death and that which is valued in the society, the portrayal of those who should receive sympathy and support, those who deserve to die, who should receive our attention if missing, are all part of a possibly unintended educational process.

Saylor and his colleagues (Saylor, Cowart, Lipovsky, Jackson, & Finch, 2003) studied elementary students' media exposure to images of the 9/11 terrorist attacks. Even though the children in their study were in South Carolina and did not know anyone directly affected by the attacks, evidence of effect of television viewing of both positive and negative images resulted in higher levels of symptoms of post-traumatic stress disorder (PTSD). Thus, the exposure to trauma-related media images appeared to have been the trigger for higher symptoms, regardless of valence of the images. They did note that the children who developed symptoms may have been predisposed toward developing them. Saylor and his colleagues also found that the media balanced positive and negative images, so it was not that the children were exposed to primarily negative images. Therefore, the situation may be more complex than simply searching for a simple solution to negative effects.

TV & Film (Fictional)

Fictional death scenes in film and on television can trigger strong emotion, can emotionally engage the viewer, and can serve as a tool for discussion of death and dying. Schiappa and her colleagues (Schiappa, Gregg, & Hewes, 2004) examined the effect that college students' viewing of a television show, Six Feet Under (Ball, 2001-2005), had on the death attitudes. They found that viewing the program adversely affected death attitudes among students, a finding consistent with earlier studies. On the other hand, concerns among students about what happens to the body after death seemed to have lessened. As discussed earlier, television viewing is a common tool for parents to use as they address their children's questions about death. Perhaps the goal, then, should not be to desensitize people to death through the use of television but to help them explore their attitudes and beliefs.

Criticisms of fictional depictions of death, dying, and grief in the media include the fact that images presented of death are unrealistic. Meyer (2005, p. 3) looked at major films and identified several distortions: narrative short-cuts that advance the story of the revenging hero, often after the death of an innocent; a primary focus on the violent act itself; consequences that are commonly abbreviated and edited to include only glimpses, or are verbally or visually implied; in some films, violent consequences are shown in graphic and gory detail; on television, where the Federal Communications Commission, viewer complaints, and advertisers' concerns limit the range of options, images of death may be sanitized.

Cox, Garret, and Graham (2004-2005) examined the depiction of death in Disney films and found the depictions of death were also unrealistic and often accompanied by some sort of moral message. Because of this moral message, they recommend that children should view these films under parental supervision, as the children may need to process, among other things, the idea of someone "deserving" to die.

Popular Music

The final medium that will be addressed will be popular music. Over the years, parents of adolescents have expressed concern about the influence of popular music on their children. Certainly, popular musicians appear to have enjoyed their portrayal as "living on the edge" Plopper and Ness (1993) examined the messages about death that were communicated in Top 40 songs. Overall themes were death of common people, death of celebrities or public figures, and novelty death songs. Death of common people represented the largest number while the other two categories were far smaller. Death themes were consistent with those in other media: violent, tragic, the deceased more often male. Death by natural causes was rare. Death commonly is seen as the ultimate payment for a reckless or evil life, punishment for having done evil. Suicide is seen as a way to deal with pain and loss. Death is sometimes seen as heroic, as when the hero dies saving lives. The focus of these songs is on the act of death, less so on the effects of the death, providing few models for ways of dealing with death.

Conclusion

Both the family and larger systems contribute to the education of family members with regards to death and behavior related to it. They make this contribution through the sharing of information, and in maintaining a structure in which collaborative meaning about death can come to be known. The larger system also contributes to the knowledge of individuals about death and related behaviors. Images of death, dying, and grief presented in the media are only partially realistic, intended to move a storyline forward, and to serve a larger purpose. Thus, caution should be taken in using these as resources for death education, in formal settings or in the family.

Learning Objective: (40/40)
Understand how the family and the media provide a forum for death education.

Chapter 36

Death Education: Ethical and Legal Issues

Carla J. Sofka

Perceptions of ethical and legal issues related to death education are quite polarized. This chapter will summarize ethical and legal issues related to death education from a range of perspectives. Literature can be categorized into contributions from two "camps" of authors: "the advocates or believers" (widely published thanatology scholars, death educators, and experienced clinicians affiliated with hospice or thanatology-oriented areas of practice) and "the critics" (stories published in the mass media or by conservative columnists). It was surprising not to find more literature representing a third camp — "the skeptics."

Death education, once called a "nasty little secret" by vocal critic Phyllis Schlafly (1988), has been in the public eye for many years since Schlafly's scathing exposé and the video she assisted in producing with the Eagle Forum of Colorado that aired on 20/20 on September 21, 1990. Death education has also been described as an "edufad" (McKeever, 1999). Patrick Vernon Dean (1995), a death educator and advocate, was grateful to the critics for breaking the alleged silence about death education.

Ethical Issues

Merriam-Webster Online (2006) defines ethics as "a set of moral principles or values, or a guiding philosophy", and 'ethical' as "involving or expressing moral approval or disapproval as well as conforming to accepted professional standards of conduct." Ethics and ethical issues are relevant to death education from personal and professional points of view. Significant differences exist in personal and professional perceptions of the appropriateness and value of death education

One must be mindful that remarkable variations in personal values about these topics are influenced by factors including, but not limited to, individual differences in age, life experience, cultural and religious/spiritual background, and differences in political perspectives and other societal factors. Corr (1984) notes the importance of the valuational dimension of death education — the role of death education in identifying, articulating, and affirming basic values that influence human lives and death-related issues in society. While some persons assume that fundamental values can be separated from everyday interactions with life and death (Corr, 1984), death educators must respect that "individuals bring to their educational programs experiences that have emerged from a diversity of social, cultural, and religious backgrounds" and "provide for an appreciation and utilization of individual differences" (International Work Group on Death, Dying, and Bereavement, 1992, p. 63).

There are legitimate concerns about death education that focus on how death education is taught, to whom, by whom, where, what content is covered, and potential outcomes of death education. These factors will be used to structure the current examination of ethical issues related to death education.

When Death Education Occurs

What event might prompt an individual to seek out an opportunity for death education? Why might death education efforts be initiated to reach a specific audience? Corr, Nabe, and Corr (2006) note that death education can occur in three ways: formal education, informal education, and "teachable moments."

Opportunities for formal education are affiliated with organized instruction at levels ranging from K-12, college courses, professional and postgraduate education, in-service trainings, or workshops for clients or the general public (Corr, Nabe, & Corr, 2006). Significant concerns arise when participants are minors. If a death education opportunity is sought out by an adult capable of informed consent to participate, ethical issues may arise if the teacher is not competent or if there is a negative reaction to the course by a participant. Materials for use in death education exist for individuals of all ages, including children's books that can be used in an informal way (Berns, 2003/2004).

Informal education is described as beginning "in the arms of a parent or guardian and through interactions within a family or similar social group" (Corr, Nabe, & Corr, 2006, p. 7). Informal education is a lifelong process of lessons learned as a result of personal experiences, the experiences of others, or exposure to thanatology-related issues through the media or travel.

Opportunities for informal education arise as a result of teachable moments, defined as "unanticipated events in life that offer important occasions for developing useful educational insights and lessons as well as for personal growth (Corr, Nabe, & Corr, 2006, p. 7). These moments combine a need for support with opportunities for education about life and death. Silverman (2000) also advocates for wisely using teachable moments in the lives of children to promote competence in dealing with loss and grief.

To Whom and Under What Obligations?

Who is the intended audience and what are the obligations of death educators vis-à-vis an intended audience? The answer to these questions varies tremendously depending on the setting and the intended goals and content. Ethical issues often come into play when the target audience includes minors, when parents have not been involved in the planning, or when parental consent has not been secured prior to their children's participation.

Death education efforts for children may be a necessity in light of the situations involving loss and grief that are commonly experienced by children in our society. At what age is it appropriate for children to participate? Developmental levels of children and the "readiness" for children and adolescents to deal with death education topics should be carefully assessed (Gibson, Roberts, & Buttery, 1982). A child may be involved in death education at an early age due to a "teachable moment" combined with the presence of an adult who is comfortable discussing relevant topics and skilled at communication using age-appropriate language (e.g., Brent, 1977-78). Death education efforts for children with special needs and adults with developmental disabilities must also be tailored to account for developmental and cognitive challenges (Hoover, Markell & Wagner, 2004/2005; Kauffman, 2005).

Participants of any age may have negative reactions to a death education effort. Kubler-Ross and Worden (1977-78) reported that adults attending death education workshops were people who, for professional or personal reasons, wanted to come to grips with death. Studying the relationship between personal experience with loss and death education merits future research.

What information about students should be considered prior to their participation (Gibson, Roberts, & Buttery, 1982)? Are there contraindications for participation? It is the responsibility of the instructor to 1) anticipate and be sensitive to the death-related experiences of their students and 2) be skilled in counseling and crisis intervention techniques or identify skilled professionals to be available for follow-up with participants for whom the experience triggers a need for support and/or access to community resources (Doka, 1981-82; International Work Group on Death, Dying, and Bereavement, 1992; Leviton, 1977).

Cook, Oltjenbruns, & Lagoni (1984) explored a fascinating issue: Do death education programs have a "ripple effect" on individuals who do not even attend? These authors noted that "death education programs appear to serve as stimuli for death-related thoughts and conversations that extend beyond the boundaries of the instructional setting" (p. 189). Identification of these types of "ripple effects" and the mechanisms by which they operate is an important topic for future research.

Where and By Whom?

The answers to the questions "Who is the teacher?" and "Where does death education occur?" have a significant impact on whether ethical issues are present. Key issues of debate include the implications of the setting, how the teacher is related to the student, and the qualifications and characteristics of the death educator.

Some believe that death education should not occur in schools but in the home (Noonan, 1999). Some advocate for death education within the context of religious education, health education, or family life education (Crase, 1981; Moore, 1989; Somerville, 1971). One's views about the appropriate setting for death education are largely influenced by the valuational component of death education previously defined (Corr, 1984). At the center of this debate is the following question: Does instruction that instills "critical thinking" (instead of values clarification) undermine parental authority? This important question remains to be empirically explored.

Dean (1995) found that parents and teachers, with very few exceptions, share the goal of acting in the best interests of the children. Family life educators have been noting the importance of death education for many years, and it should be noted that "life education," of which content on loss, death, and grief is included, is commonly occurring in schools in Japan (Yomiuri, 1998) and Taiwan (Wong, 2003). The view held by Dean (1995) of the parent-teacher relationship as a "meeting of the minds" rather than the battleground envisioned by Schlafly (1988) can guide the development of effective death education partnerships in the schools.

These partnerships can be facilitated by: 1) considering the readiness of the community and the compatibility with community value systems when selecting and/or developing appropriate curriculum materials and 2) identifying strategies to deal with moral, ethical, cultural, and religious/spiritual considerations based upon the societal and family context of students (Gibson, Roberts, and Buttery, 1982; Leaman, 1995). Common concerns raised by parents and community members about death education initiatives can be effectively managed by proactively involving them in the planning stages and monitoring for reactions once the initiative has been completed (Gibson, Roberts, & Buttery, 1982; Leaman, 1995; Silverman, 2000). Death education be viewed as an ongoing process throughout the life cycle, with responsibility shared by the home, church, other community agencies, and the schools.

The most common forums for death education on a daily basis are the print, electronic (radio, television, and online), and entertainment media. Most death professionals can readily give examples of times when the media proved a great resource, but also recall situations where individuals impacted by tragedy have been revictimized by the media during the time that they or their situation was "newsworthy."

Informational support is a valuable resource that is often eagerly sought out during times of crisis or tragedy (Sofka, 1997), and the media provide timely information of importance to the public. Stories involving thanatology issues that are sensitively and accurately written 1) can validate and normalize an experience or reaction, 2) provide valuable information about resources designed to address unmet needs, and 3) educate the public about ways to support those impacted by these events. Stevenson (1990) also notes that the media can inform the public about the benefits of death education.

The role of the entertainment media must also be recognized. We are all recipients of death education when we begin to watch cartoons or Disney movies. While the accuracy of the information gained in some cartoons is questionable (e.g., Wile E. Coyote's ability to cheat death), wonderful vehicles for death education have evolved (e.g., Mr. Roger's Neighborhood, Sesame Street). According to Bader (2001), the entertainment media can also put death in the public eye, potentially influencing the way that the general public perceives death professionals.

Death education in the media can have benefits, but at whose expense? It is not difficult to find horrific examples of the insensitivity and unethical behavior by reporters and the media outlets that disseminate the stories. The media can skirt dangerously close to or cross the line of appropriateness in the process of educating the public. Books about media ethics note the fundamental conflict between the public's right to know and an individual's right to privacy (Kieran, 1997) and the challenges inherent in accountability of the media to members of the public (Pritchard, 2000).

Additional concerns involve the impact on people who are contacted by the media and the impact on viewers who are exposed to the images and content of a media report. What is the impact of media contact and the subsequent coverage that occurs on survivors of the deceased? How does exposure to crisis, tragedy, and death in the media impact individuals who have a similar experience in their past? Does repeated exposure to this content desensitize individuals to thanatology issues over time? Death educators should remain mindful of these concerns.

Numerous community death education opportunities also occur through local health care organizations (particularly hospice programs), senior centers, adult education programs, or through community education offerings of local department stores. Another significant ethical issue involves the qualifications and characteristics of the death educator. Who is motivated to promote and teach death education? Some may join the field due to its popularity (Pine, 1977). Leviton and Kastenbaum (1975) wondered what kind of person is "tapped" to teach death.

Since some death educators may "self-select" into this role, it is important to note that the experience of a significant loss in one's life may result in the desire to become a death educator.

There may be times when the personal lives of death educators have an impact on their professional roles and responsibilities. Noppe (2004) poignantly describes having a pedagogical "out of body" experience (described as "being the recipient of her own death education", p. 4) while dealing with her mother's illness, death, and coping with her grief. She notes that death educators are "ultimately the survivors of our own lessons" (p. 4). Manis and Bodenhorn (2006) recognize the importance of examining the meaning-making of life and death on a personal and professional level to maintain personal well-being, and Stillion (as quoted in Bordewich, 1988) believes that death educators must have training in handling their own feelings about death, dying, and loss. One's personal experience must be used without negative consequences to the students or the course, such as becoming upset or over-involved or imposing one's own values and style (Engel, 1980-81). Wass (1995) wisely notes that personal experiences are helpful, but "they do not transform us into death educators" (p. 334).

The literature has also identified characteristics that are important for death educators to possess: 1) thorough knowledge about thanatology and the willingness to be a lifelong learner in light of a constantly changing knowledge base; 2) basic knowledge about scientific study to the extent that the educator becomes an educated consumer of the research, determines its usefulness, and translates research into educational action; 3) appropriate training as a death educator to acquire competencies and techniques that are necessary for effective teaching; 4) the ability to integrate knowledge about loss with a student's developmental level; 5) sensitivity and availability to the individual needs of trainees who are intellectually challenged and/or emotionally affected by the content of the training; 6) basic communication skills and the specialized group facilitation skills required to lead discussions, raise appropriate questions, involve participants by establishing an atmosphere of trust and respect, and handle group dynamics when highly emotional or controversial topics are discussed; 7) the skill to help individuals with death-related problems and the ability to guide them to professional helpers should the need arise; and 8) responsibility and integrity, including the courage to admit when there are no clear answers or when one is ignorant (Stillion, as quoted in Bordewich, 1988; Crase, 1989; Wass, 1995; Papadatou, 1997). This author believes that "I don't know" are, in some cases, the three most important words to be able to say to students.

The absence of adequate death education among the curriculum offerings of teachers and health professionals also remains a concern. These professionals need increased access to death education during their initial training as well as opportunities for continuing education throughout their professional careers. Wass (1995) notes the need for systematic training and screening of death educators at all levels, but expresses concern that there is no mechanism in place to stop the individuals who enter the field (most often at the continuing education level) possessing none of the requisite knowledge, skills, and characteristics. Theoretically, anyone can teach a workshop or course to a group of unsuspecting adults as long as the participants don't ask for educational credits or want proof of the instructor's credentials (Wass, 1995). Therefore, settings offering death education opportunities have a responsibility to the students/participants to make sure that the educator is experienced and competent.

What Content Should Be Included?

Gibson, Roberts, and Buttery (1982) noted that one of the goals of death education is "to assist individuals in the process of clarifying values related to social and ethical issues" (p. 17). The list of value-laden issues published in the early 80s is still relevant in the 21st century: euthanasia, abortion, capital punishment, and prolonging life by artificial or extraordinary means. In 1982, the following value-laden question was significant: "Am I doing things that may cause me or others to die unnecessarily and prematurely?" (p. 17). At the present time, this statement would need to be modified: "Am I being exposed to things that are out of my control that might cause me or others to die unnecessarily and prematurely?" If one lives in an urban area, the news often includes descriptions of children and youth who were killed by stray bullets or murdered by a parent or abuser. Do we as a society have an obligation to provide these murdered victims' siblings and friends with information and resources for coping with these tragic deaths and the fear that these tragedies might instill?

Three current textbooks commonly used in death education courses note in some manner a variety of value-laden issues such as suicide, euthanasia, abortion, capital punishment, quandaries posed by modern medicine and its complex technologies at the end of life as well as throughout the life span (reproductive technology, assistive technology during times of physical trauma), and other societal and global issues such as terrorism, disasters, nuclear warfare, epidemics, famine, malnutrition, genocide, and dislocation of populations (Corr, Nabe, & Corr, 2006; DeSpelder & Strickland, 2005; Kastenbaum, 2007). The appropriateness of including these topics in the curricula of students at various levels of education must be carefully considered. It is crucial to develop strategies to monitor the well-being and safety of students and to guarantee access to appropriate resources for assistance should suicidal ideation be experienced by participants in death education.

Regardless of the topics being included, the material must be current, accurate, and based on sound empirical research when the content merits a scientific focus.

Death educators have an ethical obligation to stay current on new developments, even though this can be a daunting and time-consuming challenge. Dennett (1998) states: "Information technology has multiplied our opportunities to know, and our traditional ethical doctrines overwhelm us by turning these opportunities to know into newfound obligations to know" (p. 87).

How Death Education is Taught

Ethical issues can also arise based on how death education is taught. Literature describing the impact of experiential learning vs. didactic teaching methods raises an interesting issue for debate: Is it ethical to use pedagogical strategies that increase anxiety about death? The answer to this question seems to depend upon whether the participants are capable of managing the resultant anxiety, if resources are available to help participants deal with any negative consequences (Leviton, 1977), or if the educator can skillfully process role plays without turning a class discussion into a therapy session (Barton & Crowder, 1975).

In her pioneering work with computer-assisted resources for death education, Lambrecht (1991) provided death educators with innovative resources. The changing face of educational technology, particularly the prevalence of online opportunities for death education, is creating new ethical issues. A wide range of courses for students, professionals, or consumers is offered by colleges, universities, and Web-based training companies. While it is wonderful to see death education becoming so accessible, numerous questions need to be asked and examined through sound empirical research.

How does a death educator prepare to offer a death education opportunity online? What competencies are required to successfully implement death education opportunities that use educational technology? Death educators are encouraged to consult the growing body of literature about e-learning and Web-based pedagogy for guidance (e.g., Cole, 2001; Salmon, 2003). Continuing education opportunities about e-learning and Web-based pedagogical workshops should be included at thanatology conferences and should be available online. Death educators can gain insight about online learning and distinguish between effective and ineffective strategies for web-based teaching by participating in an online course.

One must carefully consider how existing online resources are used in death education efforts since there is no guarantee that information on a Web-based resource is accurate or reliable (Sofka, 1997). Consumers of online information need to become educated consumers of electronic resources (K. Gilbert, 1997; Lozano-Nieto, Guijarro, & Berjano, 2006). Instructors have a responsibility to make sure that content is reliable and valid and that students also gain information literacy skills.

There are also significant differences between "classroom dynamics" and the dynamics of interactions in a virtual classroom. How does the absence of face-to-face interactions (between the instructor and students as well as between fellow students) influence the experiences of the students as well as the desired educational outcomes? Drawing on this author's experiences, the absence of non-verbal cues in a virtual classroom provides a simple but powerful illustration. In death education courses, it is not uncommon for students to disclose personal experiences, an act that involves some degree of emotional risk-taking. Moderators are responsible for creating and maintaining a safe environment in which this type of disclosure can take place (Salmon, 2000).

How does a moderator create and maintain this safety in a virtual classroom, where it is not possible to gauge the immediate reactions of classmates to the information that has been shared? Misperceptions can and will take place in online discussions, particularly during "conversations" that are asynchronous (e.g., do not occur in "real time"). Moderators must carefully monitor all postings for content that could be misinterpreted or content that may startle, shock, or upset other students in the class. While it is important to try to anticipate issues or situations that may create discomfort for the author of a posting or among fellow students when they read a posting, it is impossible to predict them all. Another situation that can prove to be awkward is the inevitable posting to which few students (or no students) respond. The moderator has the ultimate responsibility to make sure that at least they post a response and that efforts to facilitate discussion are consistently made in a timely manner.

Bates (1999) reminds us that cultural and ethical issues can arise during distance education efforts when international students are enrolled in the course. Language barriers may impact the degree of active participation of a student expected to communicate using a second language. Do the participation grades of students for whom English is not their native language suffer as a result of cultural differences in teaching and learning? It is important to make sure that international students are not unfairly penalized for being a stranger in a strange online land.

Due to changes in the teaching process online, one must consider the possibility that outcomes of the educational process may also change. Is online death education effective? Death educators need to consider how to best evaluate their courses using valid and reliable measurement strategies (e.g., Winn, 2002). It is also crucial for death educators to work collaboratively on empirical tools and share results as quickly as possible to facilitate comparison of outcomes. Web-based resources provide opportunities for expedient dissemination of information, provided that intellectual property rights that guide online publications are respected.

Ethical issues can relate to the timeframe and timing of a death education offering. For traditional courses, it is important to schedule the course in a time slot that provides access to the instructor in a timely manner after the class ends. Opportunities for follow-up once the course is completed may also need to be considered. Time-limited death education opportunities, such as brief workshops or those provided via distance education, may present special challenges. If an instructor does not live nearby, have arrangements for contact via phone or e-mail been made? Who does the follow-up if a student experiences difficulties after a workshop or course is completed? Has the instructor made arrangements with local resources to be available? Is each distance-education student aware of local resources that can assist should the need arise? Dunn (2005) notes professional and ethical considerations and challenges related to the provision of counseling services to distance students. Administrators responsible for the scheduling and oversight of these courses and workshops must be aware of these special considerations.

The evaluation of death education efforts has always presented challenges to death educators. Scholarly literature provides guidance with this task (Durlak, 1978-79; Durlak & Reisenberg, 1991; Papadatou, 1997), including guidelines for ethical issues related to thanatology research (Cook, 1995). Research about the impact and effectiveness of death education must be conducted, particularly for courses involving students who have personal experience with loss (Balk, 1995). Alternative educational programs such as large-scale symposiums involving a variety of events and media coverage are generally not evaluated (Waldman & Davidshofer, 1983-84). Longitudinal outcome studies must also be considered since a significant limitation involves the absence of information about the long-term impact of death education on participants' professional roles (Durlak, 1978-79).

The evaluation of educational outcomes through distance learning presents some new challenges (Winn, 2002). Death educators must consider the following questions: How does an instructor evaluate skill-based competencies when the student has not been involved in face-to-face opportunities for direct observation and assessment? In addition to the ethical issues of academic integrity and honesty when written work and exams are submitted online, do written responses on an exam accurately reflect one's ability to effectively apply knowledge and skills in a real-world situation?

Death educators have an obligation to consider these issues and to conduct research that will either confirm that the use of technology does not compromise the desired educational outcomes or challenge death educators to consider whether online education is an appropriate method to gain skill-based competencies. The use of both online and traditional strategies may be required. Research comparing perceptions of the quality of online and traditional learning and the reasons why students prefer one type of learning environment over the other suggests that there is reason for offering more "hybrid" courses, that is, courses combining face-to-face and Internet interaction (Hannay & Newvine, 2006).

Legal Issues

The distinction between ethical and legal issues related to death education appears to be a subtle one. The remainder of this chapter will focus on the following legal issues regarding death education: intellectual property rights and copyright issues, liability issues related to a negative outcome resulting from a death education opportunity, and the certification of death educators.

Intellectual property rights and copyright issues are relevant to all educators. These already complex issues have been further complicated by rapid change, much of which is due to new technology and its use in distance education (American Association of University Professors, 2004). Death educators have a responsibility to be familiar with not only the laws that govern these issues but also the policies and procedures governing these issues at his or her host institution. Useful summaries of matters to address in distance education policy and contract language are also available (AAUP, 2004). Faculty are advised to clarify with administrators whether a faculty member retains copyright ownership of works that are created or if those works become the property of the institution and to get any agreements about ownership in writing. The development and use of new technologies always leads to uncertainty about these issues, so a wise educator with an institutional affiliation should take note of these suggestions in a proactive manner (AAUP, 2004).

Death educators must also be mindful of intellectual property rights in relation to pre-existing materials that are utilized in death education courses. Death educators who taught before the advent of Blackboard, WebCT, and other online course support resources will recall that concerns about a visit from the "copyright police" could be avoided by honoring fair use policies through library reserve or preparing readings packets after securing permissions through one's institution or the staff at the local copy shop. Blanke (2002) has created a useful introduction to copyright law as it relates to print, video, music, Web sites, and other expressive content that has provided educators with opportunities to liven up in-class and online teaching. Being vigilant about citing sources on course materials, PowerPoint™ slides, or any materials disseminated to students not only keeps you in good standing with the "copyright police" but demonstrates academic integrity and provides good role modeling for students.

In our litigious society, it is possible for death educators and the institutions in which death education occurs to be held accountable for a negative outcome that could be connected with involvement in a death education opportunity (e.g., an attempted or completed suicide after participating in a suicide prevention program; exacerbated symptoms of mental illness — depression, anxiety, post-traumatic stress — following involvement in a death education opportunity). It is important to possess the requisite knowledge and skills, ensure parental involvement of minors in the planning process, and identify strategies for being aware of the loss histories of participants in death education opportunities (which can be particularly challenging for community-based workshops or professional trainings). At a minimum, reactions to the content and process of the death education experience should be monitored. Mechanisms for follow-up or a process for referrals to resources for support that participants may need following completion of the death education opportunity should be in place in advance. Evaluation of all death education efforts should occur to asssseé the effectiveness of the death education opportunity and to assist in identifying potentially problematic situations. Legal counsel should be involved in the review of informed consent documents that describe potential risks/potential for harm and in the creation of any relevant disclaimers. Creating a process to document the accountability of death educators has occurred in the form of certification efforts for over 30 years.

Wass (2004) noted the topic of teacher competence as particularly relevant to discussions of legal issues and death education. Do death educators have the knowledge and skills required to facilitate death education efforts that are effective? Do they understand basic group dynamics, and are they able to create psychologically "safe" environments within the classroom? Is there a need to develop competencies for death educators in general or within various disciplines involved in death education? There is also a need to obtain data on death educators regarding their preparation, their competencies, continuing education that has been completed throughout their careers, and to whom they are accountable.

One strategy for assessing competencies of death educators is the process of certification (Zinner, 1992). While thanatology-related certification is becoming more common, most certificates represent the completion of training designed to enhance knowledge and/or to indicate competence in the provision of services or support to those in crisis, the dying, or bereaved. Certificates allow individuals to label themselves as being certified in relation to a particular competency or skill area, but are not equivalent to being licensed with the affiliated legal powers and liabilities. At present, three certification opportunities related to death education are available through the Education in Palliative and End-of-life Care Project, the Family Life Education Institute, and the Association for Death Education and Counseling.

While it is encouraging to note that several avenues for certification of death educators are available, certification processes may not adequately evaluate the pedagogical skills of death educators. How do death educators gain pedagogical skills? What is the best way to assess the competencies and effectiveness of death educators once they are certified? These questions merit attention.

Conclusion

Implementing effective opportunities for death education that adequately and respectfully address the ethical and legal issues outlined in this chapter is a task that would present challenges for even the most experienced death educators and the organizations in which death education opportunities are delivered. Wass (1995), a respected death educator and scholar, stated: "I have tried for the past 14 years to become a good death educator. I am still trying" (p. 334). May we all, with humility and grace, accept the fact that the knowledge base for thanatology is constantly growing and willingly adopt Wass's philosophy of lifelong learning as we strive to become the best death educators that we can be.

LARNING Objective: (30/35)
Identify the ethical + legal issues
facing death educators.

Two Overarching Indicators: Professional Issues and Resources

Introduction to Part 7, Chapters 37-38

Chapters 37 and 38 focus on two overarching indicators: professional issues and resources. The Body of Knowledge defines Professional Issues this way: **factors that affect professionals' training, abilities, and responsibilities in providing care.** *Resources* **involve materials, organizations, and groups of individuals who facilitate knowledge acquisition. Ideas and materials are based upon the findings of empirical research and theoretical synthesis that add to the knowledge base.**

The authors of these two chapters have synthesized information that cut across the six major categories of dying, end-of-life decision making, loss, grief, and mourning, assessment and intervention, traumatic death, and death education.

Chapter 37

Professional Issues and Thanatology

Carol Wogrin

The field of thanatology has changed dramatically over the past few decades. Medical advances that enable us to keep people alive in the face of life-threatening illnesses create a vast array of challenges and responsibilities for the professionals providing care. Models of care for the dying have developed significantly since the start of the first hospice in the United States in the early 1970s, as discussed in detail in chapters 3 and 5. Development of the theoretical understanding of the grief process, as described in chapters 15 and 21, has brought about a fundamental paradigm shift that consequently alters clinical practice. Such rapid change in the field over such a relatively short time span places significant responsibility on the caregiver to keep his or her knowledge base up to date, including general knowledge of the field of thanatology and the body of knowledge specific to his or her own discipline and area of practice with in the field.

When providing end-of-life and bereavement care, professional caregivers need to possess in-depth knowledge, experience, and skills in order to be able to attend to a wide variety of specific and often complicated circumstances (International Work Group on Death, Dying, and Bereavement, 2006). In a report by the Institute of Medicine (Field & Cassel, 1997), the authors identify the requirements of professionals who provide care at the end of life. These requirements include strong interpersonal skills, along with clinical knowledge and technical proficiency that is informed by scientific evidence, values, and personal and professional experience. This report stresses the responsibility that health care professionals have for educating themselves and the larger community regarding good care for the dying and their families. However, they also recognize that there are many deficiencies in the education of health care professionals to date. The education of professionals often fails to provide them with the attitudes, knowledge and skills that are required to provide optimal care. Areas identified that are important to professional preparation across disciplines include the following.

Interpersonal skills and attitudes, including:
- Listening to patients, families, and other members of the health care team
- Conveying difficult news
- Understanding and managing patient and family responses to illness
- Providing information and guidance on prognosis and options
- Sharing decision making and resolving conflicts
- Recognizing and understanding one's own feelings and anxieties about dying and death
- Cultivating empathy
- Developing sensitivity to religious, ethnic, and other differences

Ethical and professional principles, including:
- Doing good and avoiding harm
- Determining and respecting patient and family preferences
- Being alert to personal and organizations conflicts of interests
- Understanding societal/population interests and resources
- Weighing competing objectives or principles
- Acting as a role model of clinical proficiency, integrity, and compassion

Organizational skills, including:
- Developing and sustaining effective professional teamwork
- Understanding relevant rules and procedures set by health plans, hospitals, and others
- Learning how to protect patients from harmful rules and procedures
- Assessing and managing care options, settings, and transitions
- Mobilizing supportive resources (e.g., palliative care consultants, community-based assistance)
- Making effective use of existing financial resources and cultivating new funding sources

(Fields & Cassel, p.11)

It is critical that clinicians stay current in their knowledge base in the rapidly growing field of thanatology. Models of care for the dying have evolved over the past few decades, as has the field's understanding of the grief process and needs of the bereaved. Chapter 15 discusses the shift in the theoretical framework from understanding grief as a process oriented towards disconnecting from the deceased to one that recognizes the importance of continuing bonds with the deceased. This shift in thinking subsequently alters the ways in which we approach intervention with the bereaved. We are only beginning to understand the ways in which the professional community can support the bereaved, including identifying who benefits from what kind of intervention as discussed in chapter 21. To date there are as many questions as there are answers.

While important, keeping up to date on current understanding and empirically based recommendations for practice can be very challenging. There presently exists a significant gap between research and clinical practice (Bridging Work Group, 2005; Devilly, Gist & Cotton, 2006). Many practitioners regard much of the available research as holding little relevance for their work. Likewise, many researchers believe that clinical practice has little to contribute to the scientific study of bereavement (Bridging Work Group, 2005). Given the expanding field, including issues such as the evolving empirical evidence that challenge assumptions about effective strategies for caring for the bereaved, as discussed in chapter 21, this gap is particularly problematic.

An example of an area where both practice and research have been developing along somewhat parallel and non-intersecting tracks is that of community crisis response to traumatic death. Hospices and bereavement professionals are often called to support organizations and larger communities when traumatic deaths occur. The bereavement needs of people in the immediate aftermath of public tragedy have aspects that are unique to this sort of event. Those who will respond to these requests have a responsibility to have appropriate training in crisis response as well as the knowledge and experience to adapt the intervention to the type of trauma being addressed (Homan, 2005). Training in crisis response can be obtained from several different organizations including the International Critical Incident Stress Foundation (www.icisf.org), the American Red Cross (www.red-cross.org), the National Organization for Victims Assistance (www.nova.org) (Homan, 2005).

There is a gap separating clinical practices and the growing body of empirical data that challenge beliefs and assumptions surrounding intervention strategies. Devilly, Gist & Cotton (2006) examined the literature involving psychological debriefing. They identify significant disagreement between clinicians who employ models of crisis management and the research data regarding the effectiveness of these models. They conclude that while the serious literature of psychology and related disciplines has increasing evidence that brings into question the effectiveness of traditional debriefing practices, information flowing to consumers about debriefing has been almost solely in the domain and control of intervention proponents. As a result, there are conflicting bodies of information, one presenting objective, refereed, independent assessments of measured efficacy, and another, dominated by a social movement attempting to argue away those accumulating empirical data. The fact that the discrepancy is intensifying over time is a troubling indicator of a schism between research and practice, with academic psychologists becoming detached from the realities of application and practice, and many practitioners becoming progressively more estranged from the empirical underpinnings of their discipline (Devilly, Gist, & Cotton, 2006).

Crisis response in communities is merely one example of the prevalent gap between research and practice in the field of thanatology. In the time to come, it is the responsibility of both researchers and practitioners to close this gap. Efforts will need to include recognition of how much each group has to learn from the other, as well as the development of collaborative models for sharing information, increasing theoretical understanding, and investigating the effectiveness of various interventions (Bridging Work Group, 2005).

In addition to maintaining an up to date knowledge base, good communication skills are fundamental to the role and responsibility of the professional caregiver. These skills include the ability to use active listening and empathic understanding of an individual's internal and social world (International Work Group on Death, Dying, and Bereavement, 2006). In order to communicate effectively and responsibly, as discussed in chapter 7, the caregiver must have a solid understanding of and pay close attention to issues of culture. Culture informs a person's beliefs and values surrounding illness and death, the experience of pain, beliefs about sharing information about dying, the interpretation of the ethical imperative for truth telling, and practices around care and disposal of the body (Koenig and Gates-Williams, 1995). It is extremely important that professionals working with death and grief have an awareness of the influence of culture on their own beliefs, values, and biases as well as maintaining an awareness of cultural beliefs and values in the people to whom they are providing care. As medical advances result in increasingly more options for treatment, and therefore choices to be made, it is important for caregivers to have an understanding of the interplay between culture and the ethics of caring when working with the dying, their families, and the bereaved.

Practitioners working in the field of thanatology also have responsibility to develop expertise in understanding the dynamics of the caregiver/client relationship. Throughout the remainder of this chapter, the term "caregiver" is used exclusively to refer to professional caregivers.

People elect to work with the dying and bereaved for a variety of personal and professional reasons, but generally their motives stem from believing that the work is meaningful and rewarding. Professionals who work in the field know what a gift it is for people to allow them into their worlds at such difficult and important times, allowing caregivers to share in some of the most meaningful and intimate moments of their lives. Every day, professional caregivers to the dying and the bereaved are reminded of the transient nature of life, and consequently the importance of appreciating and making use of the life we have while we have it. However, with the rewards come some significant challenges and responsibilities. Caregivers have a responsibility to their patients, clients, and to themselves to understand and attend to the dynamics of the caregiving relationship, and the impact this relationship has on the patient as well as on him or herself. While many professional issues for caregivers are common to most service professions, some issues take on particular importance when working with matters surrounding death, and others are unique to the field of thanatology. The remainder of this chapter will explore the concepts involved and their application to practice.

The challenge to the professional is to be aware of a number of factors that comprise a helping relationship. These include the inherent power and authority of the caregiver, the vulnerability of the client, the opportunity to help, the potential to harm, the feelings, behavior, and perceptions of the client, the professional's own feelings and behavior and the impact these can have on the client (Sheets, 1999). Daily, thousands of nurses, social workers, psychologists, physicians, counselors, clergy, nursing assistants, physical therapists, volunteers, and many others provide care to those who are suffering and in need. These professionals must negotiate a delicate interplay between the needs and expectations of the patients with their own unspoken needs and expectations (Arbore, Katz, & Johnson, 2006).

An understanding of the therapeutic relationship relies, in part, on the professional caregiver having an understanding of him or herself and what he or she brings to the relationship. When working with death and grief, it is important that the professional be aware of their own relationship to death, their personal values and belief system about death, grief, and mourning. These values and beliefs will be influenced by personal experience of death and significant loss. It is helpful to spend some time thinking about one's own experiences. Professionals should ask themselves the following questions.

- What are the significant losses that I've experienced?
- How did I react?
- How did those around me react?
- What have I learned about death and grief from my experiences?
- What are my religious and/or spiritual beliefs about death?
- What are my cultural beliefs and assumptions about the expressions of grief, e.g., that it is respectful and "strong" to stay contained and keep a "stiff upper lip," or that it is respectful to the deceased and healthy to emote intense emotion?

- Based on my experiences, what do I believe and what assumptions do I make about what people need from others as they cope with grief and loss?

When working with issues surrounding death, the professional caregiver is working with people during some of the most emotionally charged and vulnerable times their lives. In order to offer the kind of support, understanding, and empathy needed when someone is dying or coping with the death of a loved one, a professional needs to be emotionally open and willing to get very close to intense and difficult emotions. Because death and grief are universal, caregivers likely have experienced the death of people they love and/or have had other significant losses, as well as knowing they will face the death of people they love. They could easily find themselves in the position of the person they are working with. For example, if a counselor who is also a parent is working with a bereaved parent, on some level the counselor will know that their child, like that of this parent, could die. Their child, too, could be killed in an accident, diagnosed with cancer, etc. The personal feelings of the professional will easily be tapped into when coming up against the feelings of the other person. Tapping into one's own feelings can serve as the basis for empathy, but can also run the risk of confusing one's own emotions with those of the client. Because of this, it is imperative that caregivers work diligently to be aware of their own feelings so that they don't confuse their own needs with those of the client or patient.

Being aware of one's own feelings can help caregivers make appropriate and responsible choices in interactions with clients. Personal feelings of the caregiver, referred to as countertransference in the mental health fields, may manifest in many ways, including feelings of nervousness, anxiety, or anger, and can help a person connect with those who suffer. By viewing countertransference as a tool for understanding the patient, the dynamic in the relationship and oneself, rather than as an obstacle, a professional can become a better helper to those for whom he or she provides care (Arbore et al., 2006). At times it can be very difficult to remain truly present with a person who is suffering or in intense levels of emotional pain. In an attempt to feel emotionally safe, or cope with their own feelings of helplessness, helpers may retreat from the pain of their clients, by becoming "professional" or "objective." This retreat often manifests as distancing or aloofness. By remembering that simply our presence and caring can be a healing experience for our patients, we can often sustain ourselves during those emotionally challenging situations (Arbore, et. al., 2006).

It is helpful to those in the caring professions to recognize countertranference responses to suffering. Abore et al. (2006) offer a list of responses that are common but unhelpful.

- Helplessness (may distance by becoming over or under-involved)
- Shame and embarrassment ("look the other way" and not "see" the suffering)
- Denial and the wish for it to go away (helpers convincing themselves that talking about it, seeing it, will contribute to or increase the pain or suffering)
- Anger and hostility (if unaware of their own anger at the disease or the inability to change things, helpers can displace anger into the helping situation.)
- Sorrow (deep sorrow can make it hard for the helper to maintain a connection because of being too involved in one's own suffering.)
- Restlessness (impose own agenda, take precedence over the needs of the client's)

Professional Boundaries

In addition to understanding one's own experiences, feelings and reactions, a professional caregiver must develop an understanding of the dynamics of a professional-client/patient relationship. First and foremost is the importance of understanding the concept of professional boundaries. The concept of boundaries is important to anyone in any kind of professional caregiving situation or position, but never more so than when working with death and grief. Boundaries can be defined simply as "the edge of appropriate behavior" (Gutheil & Gabbard, 1998), or as the lines we draw to help us define our roles and interactions in relationships (Leurquin-Hallett, 1999). The establishment of clear boundaries is designed to create an atmosphere of safety and predictability and allow for a therapeutic connection between the practitioner and the client (Gutheil & Gabbard, 1998; Sheets, 1999). Stated another way, boundaries protect the space between our power, gained from our professional position and the access we have to private information, and the client's vulnerability (Leurquin-Hallett, 1999). These boundaries can be expressed in physical, social, or psychological terms (Martsolf, 2002).

Ethical guidelines for practice help establish the line around appropriate behavior that one should not step over. Where this line is drawn is defined by many different factors, including the discipline within which a person practices, the setting a person practices in, e.g., a facility versus home care, or a city versus a small rural area. It is the responsibility of the professional to establish the boundaries at the outset of the relationship and to maintain them for the duration of the relationship. The rules for appropriate behavior usually include guidelines for contact, including how much, how often, and method, types of information to be shared, physical closeness and the setting in which the interactions may occur (Martsolf, 2002). For example, it may be appropriate for a nurse or a home health aide to give a patient a back rub, but it would be inappropriate for a social worker or bereavement counselor to engage with a patient in a similar fashion.

There is an inherent power dynamic in caregiving relationships that makes issues of ethical practice and clear boundaries particularly important. Simon (1995) offers five principles regarding the establishment of boundaries.

Principle One. First is the rule of abstinence — a professional must abstain from personal gratification at the client's expense. This principle is the foundation on which the other principles rest. Working with the dying and the bereaved is often personally gratifying to the professional as he or she is in the role of offering support at a time when it is needed acutely, and in a position of helping diminish or alleviate suffering. However, in keeping with this principle, any gratification for the caregiver should come from accurately understanding and then appropriately meeting the needs of another person. It is imperative that the action and communication always be oriented toward the client's needs, and that the client is never asked, in any way, to attend to the emotional needs of the professional caregiver.

Principle Two. Second is the duty to neutrality — not to interfere in a client's personal relationships. When working with the dying, in hospice or other settings, caregivers may work with people over long periods of time, and frequently in times of crisis, or other emotionally demanding times. While crisis can bring people closer together, it can also exacerbate the differences in coping styles, or perhaps longstanding conflicts in families. When caregivers offer a listening ear and the therapeutic relationship grows it can be seductive for the caregiver to be in the position of the "chosen one," the confidant, the one who understands. While it is important to offer a listening ear and emotional support, the caregiver must also keep an eye not to encourage the patient to lean on him or her as a way to avoid working things out between family members; further, the caregiver must not step into a position that should be occupied by available family members or other social supports. Adherence to the first principle helps in maintaining the second.

Principle Three. Third is the promotion of client autonomy and self-determination. It is important for the professional to recognize and support a patient's strength and competence, regardless of physical decline from illness and the consequent losses, and not encourage dependence because it makes the caregiver feel important.

Principle Four. Fourth is the fiduciary relationship, the contract with the client that the professional will serve to protect. There is a contract between the patient and caregivers that mandates the professional to uphold recognized standards of care. Also, the fact that the client/patient is paying for services, directly or through insurance, helps create a power dynamic in the caregiving relationship. Payment for services means that there is a skill or expertise around which the relationship is oriented. Those who provide the expertise are in the position of power and authority, and that position that must be treated with care and respect.

Principle Five. Fifth and finally is the respect for human dignity. In order to respect the human dignity of a person who is dying or bereaved professionals must do their best to understand a client's cultural view, their values and belief system, and base interactions on this understanding.

Whether due to blatant disregard for ethical principles on the part of the caregiver, carelessness or lack of understanding, inevitably there will, at times, be problems with maintaining professional boundaries. Boundary transgressions can be understood in two important ways, as boundary crossing and boundary violations (Gutheil & Gabbard, 1998; Sheets, 1999). Boundary crossings are "brief excursions across boundaries that are often inadvertent or thoughtless." When recognized, the boundary crossing must be pulled back from and the implications and consequences evaluated (Sheets, 1999, 2000). Boundary violations occur when there is confusion between the needs of the professional and the needs of the client. These violations can be in the form of excessive personal disclosure on the part of the professional, reversal of roles, accepting personal favors, or sexual misconduct. Boundary violations make up the highest number of complaints to the Ethics Committee of the APA (Knapp & Slattery, 2004). Boundary violations and boundary crossings may not be recognized by the client or the professional until the development of harmful consequences (Sheets, 1999, 2000). Most practitioners understand the more obvious and clear boundary violations, such as engaging in sexual relations with a client. However, there are other more subtle boundary violations and crossings that are not always as clear such as sharing personal information that shifts the focus from the needs of the client to the needs of the caregiver, or visiting clients outside of work hours. With these violations it is more common or easier for practitioners to justify their actions as being in the interest of the client.

One of the important methods that help maintain clear boundaries is to have clearly spelled out goals for care and a care plan for the achievement of those goals. When the delivery of care stays directed towards the goals and care plan, boundary violations are less likely to occur (Martsolf, 2002). For example, when professionals are working for hospice as a member of an interdisciplinary team, focusing on the benefits and strength of a team and the role the different team members have in meeting the physical, emotional, and spiritual goals of care will help avoid the risk of one person slipping into a "special" position and functioning as if only they can meet the needs of an individual or family.

Sheets (1999) identifies a "zone of helpfulness" when discussing the concept of boundaries. There is a continuum of professional behavior with over-involvement on one end, which can include boundary crossings and boundary violations, and under involvement on the other, which includes distancing, disinterest, and neglect. The middle of this continuum, the "zone of helpfulness," is where most professional/client interactions should occur. Where on the continuum the line would be drawn that separates "helpful" from under or over-involvement shifts from situation to situation based on a number of factors. Appropriate professional behavior is, in part, determined by professional discipline, specific professional role, situation and context. An example given by Sheets (1999) is when working in a prison the zone of safety would most likely shift towards the more distant end of the continuum, as the practitioner guards against potentially manipulative behavior, and when working in a hospice environment, the zone of safety would more likely shift towards the over-involvement end of the spectrum, as the patient and family tend to be more vulnerable and coping with crises and intense need. The determination of the appropriateness of shifting toward one end of the continuum or another should be based on the needs of the client, the goals of care, and the therapeutic purpose the shift serves.

There are a number of reasons to guard against boundary crossings, some of which may be less obvious and others that are easier to justify as being in the best interest of the client. When working with people with life-threatening illnesses, professional relationships can get very close. Long-term illnesses and the treatment protocols for many conditions, whether in a clinic, hospital, nursing home, inpatient hospice, or home care, result in professionals and patients spending a lot of time together over long periods of time. As the relationships develop and difficult, as well as pleasurable life experiences are shared, familiarity and potentially deep connection develops. In a study conducted at Dana Farber Cancer Institute, Peteet, Ross, Medeiros, Walsh-Burke, & Rieker (1992) looked at relational issues between staff and oncology patients. An important distinction was made between social friendships and professional-patient relationships that shared some qualities of friendships. The distinction was that in a social friendship there is a reciprocity in the sharing and support. In a close professional relationship, where appropriate attention is given to professional boundaries, there is a type of loyalty and interest that feels similar to that of a friendship, but there is not the sharing of the professional's concerns and problems, which would burden the patient. This same study identified problems that can arise in the relationship when a shift towards a friendship is allowed. These included decreased objectivity, greater difficulty in delivering bad news, and greater difficulty managing one's own feelings on the part of the professional. Another problem inherent in shifting to the role of that of a friend can lead to making promises you can't keep (Taylor, 1998). For example, if boundaries are crossed and a friendship develops in a relationship with someone who is ill and receiving treatment that will end, or with a family member of a terminally ill person, the implication or expectation is that the friendship will continue after the professional role ends. However, the work demands on the caregiver continue, new patients will need attention and the caregiver may find himself or herself less inclined to make the time for an on-going relationship. Or, the patient who is used to the relationship revolving around their needs may feel burdened, betrayed, or violated when the professions begins to expect the reciprocity of support for their own problems that is typical of a friendship.

Often times, professionals who cross the appropriate boundary and enter into a social relationship rationalize their choice, maintaining that the situation is unique and that, for one reason or another, it is in the best interest of the client/patient, or what the client wants. However, these relationships tend to be exploitive; they cross the boundaries of ethical practice, serve the needs of the practitioner, and impair his/her judgment. The practitioner's power and client's vulnerability carry over from the professional to the personal relationship. When the shift occurs, a practitioner's power remains but is no longer checked by professional rules of conduct (Kagle & Giebelhausen, 1994).

An important issue in caregiving relationship that is often very challenging for professionals is that of self-disclosure. In end-of-life care, where relationships may be long term, very close in nature, and often take place in homes, there may be an inclination on the part of the caregiver to share details of their own lives as part of the sharing themselves in their work. The problem with self-disclosure, regardless of how insignificant it seems or whether it is information specifically requested by the patient, is that it shifts the attention from the patient to the caregiver, and in the long run, does not serve the patient.

With the changes in the health care delivery system over the past couple decades, health care is more often provided in community settings and homes, which increases the possibility of blurring boundaries between patient and professional caregiver and between professional and social activities (Martsolf, 2002). Knapp and Slattery (2004) identified three specific concerns for professionals who deliver services in client's homes. First is that boundary crossings are more likely to occur when services are provided in homes rather than institutions. Second is that the nature of home-based services provides a professional with more opportunities to act out or step outside professional boundaries, and third is that people working with clients in their homes are more likely to drift into a more social relationship rather than maintaining a strictly defined professional one. Because of these challenges, the importance of professional training and ongoing supervision cannot be overestimated.

It is important to highlight that the type of community a person practices in warrants attention, as it has a bearing on the way in which a person must think about boundaries. The theory and understanding of professional boundaries has, to some degree, been developed with an eye to urban and more densely populated suburban areas. The idea that a professional's personal life can be kept completely separate from professional-client relationships assumes a level of anonymity and control on the part of the professional that does not exist in rural or geographically isolated areas. In rural areas where the professional will see clients in the grocery story, attend the same church, have children in the same class at school, and serve on the same community committees as a client, the practitioner has less control over what's known about his or her own life (Helbok, Marinelli, & Walls, 2006). In sparsely populated areas there is not the luxury of referring a client to another professional whose personal life does not overlap with that of the client. In these settings, the importance of addressing boundary issues with clients takes on a new form. Informed consent is of importance in a new way, with the professional discussing with the client the implications and limits of meeting in social settings, and finding a way to keep the professional relationship separate, establishing clearly with a client at the beginning of the relationship the rules for "in office" and "out of office" boundaries (Helbok et al., 2006). Issues of confidentiality and dual relationships all need to be carefully addressed.

It is imperative that a professional always engage in conscious self-monitoring, to be sure that he/she doesn't inadvertently cross boundaries, or fail to notice if they begin shifting from giving good compassionate care based on the needs of a client, to a relationship in which their own needs and personal gratification are moving to the fore. There are red flags or warning signs in a caregiver's behavior that are easy to spot when paying attention (Sheets, 1999; Taylor, 1998). These include:

- excessive self-disclosure on the part of the professional caregiver, including discussing personal problems or aspects of intimate life
- beliefs on the part of the professional that s/he is the only one who can meet the client's needs
- giving out a home phone number and encouraging patients to depend on him or her instead of working with other members of the health care team
- repeated or lengthy calls to patients outside of working hours
- inviting patients or families to join him or her in activities outside work
- giving special treatment to a specific client, or giving excessive attention to one client to the detriment of others
- selective communications, where the professional reports selectively on a client's behavior, gives double messages, and/or provides care with a level of secrecy
- the professional taking on a "you and me against the world" position, becoming overly protective of a client
- buying gifts for or accepting gifts from patients or families
- lending money or personal belongings
- flirtatious behavior

- failure on the part of the professional to seek supervision when the professional is aware of a risk or occurrence of a boundary crossing or violation

Burnout

Good boundaries not only protect the patient in the therapeutic relationship, they serve to protect the professional as well, albeit in different ways. While the work is very rewarding, it can also take its toll, particularly when the professional is dealing with high levels of stress in their personal life, or when their work environments are not supportive. Over time, without proper support or attention, two different conditions may develop. The professional may experience compassion fatigue or burnout. While these terms are sometimes used synonymously, they are actually somewhat different and it is helpful to be aware of the risks of both.

In her work on stress of professional caregivers, Vachon (2004, p. 992) states, "Not only do patients and their families suffer distress when confronting terminal illness, but so do those who care for them. The professional who cares and empathizes with patients and their families can experience significant stress in response to working with dying persons as well as in response to the death of particular patients." She goes on to note that the stress may be due to a variety of internal factors, such as previous or current life experiences, personal death experience, too much emotional investment in patients without sufficient replenishment over too long a time, or from feelings of powerlessness and lack of control in the health care system.

Systems issues in the work place can place a person at risk of high levels of stress, resulting in burnout. These stressors include high demands placed on individuals, unrealistic expectations of workload, limited or inadequate resources, or limited professional support. Burnout can be defined as a state of physical, emotional, and mental exhaustion, depersonalization, and reduced personal accomplishment caused by long-term involvement in emotionally demanding situations (Maslach, 1982). The emotional demands are usually caused by high expectations combined with chronic situational stress (Pines & Aronson, 1988).

Burnout tends to be high when professionals perceive a low level of control over the care they provide, whether that's due to authoritarian supervisors, lack of input into policies that govern a person's job, or being given more responsibility or higher work volume than a person feels it is possible to handle (Maslach, 1982). Hospice and palliative care staff, specifically, have been found to experience increased stress when work loads were unrealistic, level of involvement in decision making was low, and social support was not available (Vachon, 2004). In her study on occupational stress in caregivers for the terminally ill, Vachon (1987) noted that despite her expectations that much of the stress experienced by caregivers would be related to their interactions with patients, she found that this was not the case. Most of the stress experienced was attributed to the work environment and occupational role rather than the direct work with dying patients and their families.

Welsh (1999) offers strategies for managing stress and decreasing burnout. The strategies include:

1. Practice responsible selfishness, recognizing one's own needs as important as the needs of others. The external demands imposed on the professional helper coupled with the internal belief that one's own needs are secondary to those of others can significantly drain a person's emotional energy.

2. Separate work from home. Use the transition time between work and home to "emotionally decompress," or "shift gears." Techniques such as mental imagery, e.g., visualizing the pressures of work evaporating; distraction, e.g., listening to music during drive home; or getting physical exercise, can be helpful.

3. Develop positive support groups, either formal self-help groups or informal empathic supports.

4. Remember to laugh. Laughter offers tremendous benefit and can provide a powerful antidote to the toxicity of chronic stress.

5. Redefine "success." For professionals who are passionately dedicated to their work and have a strong drive to be successful, a sense of personal failure is a tremendous source of stress and burnout. When working with terminal illness or bereavement, it is of utmost importance to pay careful attention to what is defined as success. If cure or significant physical improvement is the measure of success, the experience of failure will be high. When success can be redefined to helping someone's journey be easier, final days more comfortable, feelings of isolation and fear decreased, a sense of failure will be low.

Supporting the idea that self-care is an important factor in diminishing burnout, Holland and Neimeyer (2005) found that engaging regularly in spiritual practices significantly helped reduce burnout, including physical fatigue, cognitive weariness, and emotional exhaustion.

Compassion Fatigue

Elements of burnout can be seen in all professional settings. A unique form of it, labeled compassion fatigue, is directly linked to people in caregiving professions. (Joinson, 1992). Compassion fatigue can be defined as a pattern of tiredness, emotional depletion, from too much caring and too little self-caring (Ochberg, 1998). Other terms for the concept include compassion stress, secondary traumatic stress, or vicarious traumatization. Figley (1995, p. 7) defines the concept of secondary traumatic stress as "the natural consequent behaviors and emotions resulting from knowing about a traumatizing event experienced by a significant other — the stress resulting from helping or wanting to help a traumatized or suffering person."

Working with the dying and the bereaved is emotionally demanding work. Hospice workers, palliative care professionals, and others who provide care for people with life-threatening conditions frequently come up against high levels of suffering in the people they care for. Those who have enormous capacity for feeling and expressing empathy are the ones who tend to be at highest risk of compassion stress (Figley, 1995). Ironically, it is the most effective therapists who are most the most vulnerable to this mirroring or contagion effect. Professional work that is centered on the emotional suffering of clients includes absorbing information that is about suffering. Absorbing the information about suffering often includes absorbing that suffering itself as well (Figley, 1995).

Joinson (1992) identified three core issues in compassion fatigue:

1. Caregivers may perform a number of functions, but the essential product they deliver is themselves. This can be very taxing. If they don't have ways to regularly renew themselves, they will be in trouble.
2. Human need is infinite. Caregivers tend to feel "I can always give a little more," but sometimes they hit their limit.
3. Caregivers fill multiple roles that can be psychologically conflicting. For instance, nurses may move from patient care to administrative tasks to planning and delegation, then to a crisis. Shifting between roles can be emotionally draining. The trick is to be conscious of each change and ease into it gracefully, without fighting the new role.

Additionally, a person may also feel as though they are working two full-time jobs — giving of themselves all day at work, then going home to nurture some more. Unfortunately, a caregiver can sometimes completely forget how to turn off that nurturing mindset.

It is important that professional caregivers learn about limits and boundaries. A significant red flag that people can guard against is contradictions between what they say and what they do. For example, someone who says, "I'm not a workaholic,' yet works 7 to 7, six days a week, says "My family is my first priority," yet spends every waking moment away from them, or most important says, "I'm a caring, giving person," yet finds it impossible to nurture him or herself is at high risk of developing compassion fatigue (Joinson, 1992).

Signs and symptoms of compassion fatigue follow classic stress patterns. A person may find that they forget or lose things more frequently, or have a shorter attention span. They may be exhausted and have frequent headaches or stomachaches. Resistance can be low resulting in more frequent illnesses. One particular sign to watch for is anger, especially when it's too frequent and too intense for the situation (Joinson, 1992). Additionally, signs of compassion fatigue can include increasing countertransference issues with certain individuals, difficulty separating work from personal life, diminished sense of purpose and enjoyment with career, lowered functioning in nonprofessional settings, loss of hope, and depression (Becvar, 2003).

Suggestions for avoiding compassion fatigue or managing it if it develops are oriented around activities and behaviors that support physical, emotional, and spiritual health (Becvar, 2003; Joinson, 1992). Regular exercise, good nutrition, and adequate rest help support physical health. Emotional health may be promoted through meditation, journaling, personal psychotherapy, and developing good social support systems. It is also important that caregivers are able to set appropriate limits, organize workloads, and maintain boundaries in both their professional and personal lives. Spiritual well-being may be enhanced through spending time in nature, either alone or with others, or through engaging in the religious or spiritual practices of one's choice. Other ways, such as taking mini vacations, including regular massages, personal retreats, relaxing activities such as going to the movies, as well as indulging in childlike behavior (e.g., taking risks, being open to experience, dreaming, and just enjoying life) also may be useful (Becvar, 2003).

Finally, adhering to the principles of good professional boundaries help mitigate against the development of compassion fatigue as well. Learning how to not take on a patient's needs and suffering as one's own is an important and necessary skill in order to do the work well over long periods of time. Keeping a clear line between work and home so that the needs and distress of clients don't spill over, and time away from work is truly time off is of extreme importance. Additionally, knowing you're not "in it alone," but rather, have other team members and colleagues with whom to share the work can make a big difference. When boundaries are maintained and good self-care is engaged in regularly, caregivers are much more likely to feel, over time, ongoing passion about their work and enjoy the rewards that come from it.

Learning Objective: (35/35)
Understand the Many Professional issues that impact thanatology.

Chapter 38

Resources in Thanatology

Gordon Thornton, Scarlett Jett & Mary Lou Zanich

It is vital for certified thanatology professionals of all kinds to keep abreast of current research and to be familiar with important organizational resources in the field as well. For clinicians, such resources may be an adjunct to counseling. For instance, a self-help group experience might add to individual therapy; written materials can provide the foundation for psycho-educational aspects of therapy. For educators, resources may aid in teaching about dying, death and bereavement. Moreover, access to resources to recommend might be helpful, as educators are often sought out by individuals who are facing a crisis in dying, or bereavement. For researchers, these resources may provide an inspiration for ideas and even suggest sources of research participants.

A few provisos must be noted. First, the purpose of this chapter is to identify organizational resources expected for professionals who have a basic foundational knowledge about thanatology. These resources will be organized around the basic competency areas that structure this handbook. Also, the emphasis will be on organizational resources on the national level in the United States; of course, professionals need to be familiar with local resources. Lastly, a non-exhaustive list of text resources is provided at the end of the chapter; the works identified might be thought of as modern "classics" in the field.

Organizational Resources: Dying

The **National Hospice and Palliative Care Organization (NHPCO)** (www.nhpco.org) is dedicated to increasing the availability of hospice care and improving end-of-life care for terminally ill patients and their families. Their philosophy is to provide health care, pain management, and emotional support to patients along with their families. Members of NHPCO include hospices, palliative care programs, bereavement programs, researchers, home health agencies, and health care consultants. The NHPCO Web site allows individuals to find local hospice programs, palliative care programs, bereavement programs, and grief therapy.

Hospice Foundation of America (HFA) (www.hospicefoundation.org) offers "leadership in the development and application of hospice." This organization provides programs for professionals (who are dealing with dying and grief on a personal or professional basis), disseminates information to the public, and publishes work on dying and grief. An annual teleconference, *Living With Grief*, educates professionals on a variety of topics in thanatology and may provide continuing education credits. The organization's Web site also has a listing of the *Living with Grief* books and videos published by HFA. A monthly newsletter, *Journeys*, is distributed to those experiencing grief as a way to offer support and guidance. HFA's Web site provides information on subjects such as: myths about dying; what to expect before and after death, pain, and hospice. Information designed specifically to assist caregivers is also provided.

Make Today Count (national office 800-432-2273) is a national support organization committed to helping patients with life-threatening illnesses, their families, friends, and health care professionals. Self-help support groups, seminars, and retreats are offered to these individuals through local chapters in approximately 200 locations in the United States These support groups are led by health care professionals and allow members to share their thoughts, emotions, and fears with others who are having similar experiences.

The Candlelighters Childhood Cancer Foundation (www.candlelighters.org) is an international organization established in 1970 by parents of children suffering from cancer. This organization offers information and support to children with cancer, childhood cancer survivors, their families, and health care providers. Links to medical sites specializing in answering children's questions about cancer are displayed on the organization's Web site. Also, free books on cancer are provided to children coping with cancer. A directory of locations and contact information is offered for the Children's Oncology Group (COG), the Pediatric Brain Tumor Consortium (PBTC), follow up clinics, kid's cancer camps, and local affiliates,. Additionally, e-mail support groups for parents of children coping with cancer or who have lost children to cancer are offered. An online community for children suffering from cancer is also available. This organization also produces a quarterly journal which offers information on childhood cancer.

Make-A-Wish Foundation® of America (www.wish.org) mission is to make wishes come true for children between the ages of 2 1/2 and 18 who have life-threatening illnesses. The foundation's goal is to instill hope and bring happiness to these children. Examples of the wishes that this foundation has brought to life include: attending a movie premiere, cycling with Lance Armstrong, attending a hockey game, meeting Donald Trump, and going to Disney World. Approximately 144,000 children's wishes have been turned into a reality by Make-A-Wish Foundation of America and the 25,000 volunteers that serve it. Professionals in the medical field, parents, and the children themselves may refer a child for his/her wish to be granted. Also, the foundation's Web site allows a search for local chapters.

Alzheimer's Association (www.alz.org) supports research and advocacy to find prevention methods, new treatments, and, ultimately, a cure for Alzheimer's disease. The association provides referrals, online network for caregivers, and support groups.

HIV/AIDS has multiple Web sites. The CDC National Prevention Information Network (www.chcnpin.org) provides references, referrals and information. The Elton John Aids Foundation (www.ejaf.org) funds research and education. The Gay Men's Health Crisis (gmhc.org) offers a variety of programs for men, women and children that include education and outreach programs, a hotline, and counseling services.

Organizational Resources: End-of-Life Issues

The **National Donor Family Council (NDFC)** (www.donorfamily.org) provides support and advocacy to families of deceased organ/tissue donors and assistance to health care professionals working with these individuals. NDFC publishes a newsletter called *For Those Who Give and Grieve*, which provides information on organ/tissue donation and offers grieving families the chance to memorialize a donor through stories, poetry, and pictures. The newsletter also has a Donor Family Friends column which utilizes a pen pal system that allows grieving families to offer support to other families having a similar experience. NDFC also has the National Donor Family Quilt that allows a donor's relatives to be memorialized in a unique way. Another program offered by NDFC is Giving, Grieving, Growing (GGG). The GGG program provides information on organ/tissue donation and grief, allows families to share their experiences with others, and conducts a Quilt Pinning ceremony in which families memorialize their donor relative through pinning a patch on the National Donor Family Quilt. NDFC also offers the Butterfly Garden and Written Tributes to honor a loved one who was a donor on the NDFC's

Web site. Furthermore, the Web site offers the Message Board and the Comfort Café, which allows families to connect and share their experiences with one another. Families may ask questions concerning bereavement and organ/tissue donation of Ask the NDFC. Finally, the Web site provides a listing of books as well as links to bereavement Web sites.

Five Wishes (www.agingwithdignity.org/5wishes.html) is a booklet that serves as a Living Will that documents how individuals wish to be treated if they are not able to make their own end-of-life decisions due to a serious illness. It takes into account an individual's medical wishes, while also attending to his/her personal, emotional, and spiritual needs. Additionally, it encourages preplanning for funerals. Five Wishes is written in layman's terms and may be signed at home. Approximately 6 million copies of *Five Wishes* may be found in the United States and 10,000 organizations offer it, such as churches, hospices, hospitals, and law offices. This Web site allows access to an non-downloadable copy of *Five Wishes;* the booklet may be ordered online. The Web site also allows individuals to search for states that recognize *Five Wishes* as a legal document.

Donate Life: Make Organ and Tissue Donation Your Way of Life, the United States government's Web site for organ donation, www.organdonor.gov, gives valuable information about organ donation. The Web site notes that about 19 people die each day waiting for an organ transplantation. Sections on frequently asked question and myths and facts about donation dispel common misconceptions. The site provides organ donor cards and special information for minority donations.

Compassion and Choices (www.compassionandchoices.org) works to improve end-of-life care including issues regarding pain control, advance directives, and physician assistance in dying. This nonprofit organization has more than 60 chapters. In addition to education so that the dying and their families understand options and rights, the group is actively involved in the legal and legislation arena. Compassion and Choices' vision: a society where everyone receives state-of-the-art care at the end of life, and a full range of choices for dying in comfort, dignity, and control.

Organizational Resources: Loss, Grief, and Mourning

The Compassionate Friends (TCF) (www.compassionatefriends.org) has 600 support groups across the United States with the mission of helping bereaved families following the death of a child. These local chapters have monthly meetings to offer support and the opportunity to work on grief issues. TCF's Web site provides

chatrooms where the bereaved can offer support to each other and help each other
to conquer their grief and provides resources and information on grief. TCF also
has a penpal program for grieving siblings of children who died. A monthly
newsletter, phone calls, and home visits are used by the local chapters to reach out
to people grieving over the death of a child. *We Need Not Walk Alone* is TCF's
bimonthly magazine that discusses grief issues. There is also a national conference,
which includes workshops, siblings' program, and a two-mile "Walk to Remember."
During TCF's Worldwide Candle Lighting program, candles are lit around the world
for one hour on the second Sunday in December in remembrance of children who
have died.

Bereaved Parents of the USA (BP/USA) (www.bereavedparentsusa.org) is a
self-help group for bereaved parents, grandparents, and siblings who are suffering
after the death of a child. The organization's Web site provides information on the
grief process and produces a newsletter called *A Journey Together*, which discusses bereavement. Local chapters hold monthly meetings, and these meeting times
and locations may be found on the Web site. BP/USA also offers those grieving over
the loss of a child the opportunity to attend workshops on grief and rebuilding life.
Finally, a special page is dedicated to links to helpful resources.

**Widowed Persons Service (WPS), American Association of Retired Persons
(AARP)** (www.aarp.org) is national organization that offers information and
resources on the grief process, coping with grief, and grief support organizations
to the widowed.

Tragedy Assistance Program for Survivors (TAPS) (www.taps.org) is a
national organization that provides information and support for bereaved individuals that have lost a loved one serving in the armed services. TAPS has a toll-free
hotline (800-959-8277) staffed with trained crisis intervention professionals to help
these individuals with their grief. Additionally, TAPS has a survivor network which
connects people who have experienced the death of a loved one while in the armed
services. The Annual National Military Survivor Seminar and Good Grief Camp for
Young Survivors were established by TAPS in order to "remember the love, celebrate the life, and share the journey" through workshops and support groups.
TAPS' Web site offers a chatroom for bereaved individuals where they can share
experiences with one another. Finally, TAPS publishes *A Kids Journey of Grief*,
TAPS Edition as well as *TAPS Quarterly Magazine*.

RTS Bereavement Services (www.bereavementprograms.com) is a support
group for bereaved parents following a miscarriage, ectopic pregnancy, stillbirth,

or infant death. This support group offers grieving parents the opportunity to share their experiences with other parents in the same situation. Described as a national group that is based in local hospitals, RTS Bereavement Services also provides information to bereaved parents.

SHARE — Pregnancy and Infant Loss Support, Inc. (www.nationalshareoffice.com) is a national organization committed to helping individuals who have experienced the death of a baby through miscarriage, stillbirth, or infant fatality. The organization's Web site provides a directory for local SHARE support groups, as well as information on the grief process, funeral services, and on how to honor and remember a baby. This Web site also offers a chatroom and message board. There is also a page that displays current research on miscarriage, stillbirth, and support to parents after losing a baby as well as upcoming research on these topics asking for participants. For professionals, a listing of resources is offered and training is provided. Finally, SHARE publishes a bi-monthly newsletter called *Sharing* for bereaved parents.

Organizational Resources: Traumatic Death

American Association of Suicidology (AAS) (www.suicidology.org) is dedicated to research, information dissemination, and prevention of suicide. Members of AAS include mental health care providers, researchers, crisis intervention centers, school employees, and suicide survivors. AAS provides certification to crisis intervention centers and crisis workers. A directory of local survivor support groups is offered; AAS also sponsors a Healing After Suicide Conference. The organization's Web site offers pages on how to identify and assist a suicidal individual, as well as links providing more in depth information on suicide and prevention resources. Many publications are offered by AAS including, *Suicide and Life-Threatening Behavior* (bimonthly journal), *Newslink* (members' newsletter), *Surviving Suicide* (survivors' newsletter), and a *Directory of Suicide Prevention and Crisis Intervention Agencies in the U.S.*

Concerns of Police Survivors (COPS) (www.nationalcops.org) is a national organization that provides assistance to families of police officers that have been killed in the line of duty. COPS communicates with the surviving family members six times during a year; peer support is available. Membership is extended to the spouses, children, parents, siblings, significant others, and co-workers affected by the death of a police officer while on duty. The National Police Survivors' Conference takes place each May, which allows law enforcement survivors to work on grief and share information. Also, the COPS Kids/Teens Program and Summer

Camp are offered to children who are grieving over the loss of a parent. During these programs, the children receive support and guidance from professionals. COPS' Annual Wilderness Experience is designed for surviving children between the ages of 15 to 21; this program is designed to increase self-esteem. Among COPS' many programs are: annual retreats, which include activities and grief counseling, offered for surviving parents, spouses, siblings, adult children, and in-laws; supplying volunteers who will attend the trial of the accused and provide support to the victim's family; and financial assistance to the victims' children for therapy to work on grief issues surrounding the death of a parent. COPS' publications include a quarterly newsletter and a handbook entitled *Support Services to Surviving Families of Line-of-Duty Death.*

National Fallen Firefighters Foundation (www.firehero.org) is dedicated to honoring and remembering firefighters who died in the line of duty and to provide support for survivors. Activities include a memorial weekend for families, coworkers and the public to honor firefighters who died in the line of duty during the year and a surviviors weekend for families to interact with trained grief counselors. The foundation provides support programs for survivors including a lending library, grief brochures and a Fire Service Survivors Network.

Mothers against Drunk Driving (MADD) (www.madd.org) is an organization dedicated to ending drunk driving, providing support to victims of drunk drivers, and. educating the public about drunk driving. There are approximately 600 local chapters of MADD. Extensive information may be located on the Web site concerning the grief process after losing a loved one in a drunk driving accident, posttraumatic stress disorder due to witnessing the traumatic event, and physiological consequences of the accident and how to cope. Also online discussion forums are provided on MADD's Web site to allow victims to have a space to talk to others who are experiencing similar situations. Local chapters offer support groups. Victims may be provided with a victim advocate that assists with the legal and court issues by providing information (e.g., on steps to execute in order to receive a crash report, victim's rights, attorneys, and the legal system, etc.), working on the impact statement with the victim, and accompanying the victim to court. Victim advocates are also a source of emotional support and may also help victims seeking financial services from the Crime Victims Compensation Fund. MADD publishes *MADDvocate*, a magazine designed for victims of drunk driving and for victims' advocates.

National Organization for Victim Assistance (NOVA) (www.try-nova.org) offers information, support, and advocacy for victims of violent crimes and their survivors. NOVA offers a 24-hour toll-free hotline called the National Crime Victim Information and Referral Hotline which provides crisis counseling, advocacy, referrals to local programs, and information for violent crime victims and survivors. NOVA's Web site operated offers victims and survivors essential information on crime, the steps to take following a crime, and possible trauma caused by a violent crime. NOVA has also created the National Community Crisis Response Team, a "multi-disciplinary team" that goes to sites affected by a catastrophic event, and the Hostage Family Project, designed to help meet the needs of families of Americans who have been taken hostage.

The membership of NOVA includes violent crime victims and survivors, mental health professionals, researchers, and legal professionals. To assist victim advocates in helping victims and survivors, NOVA publishes the Directory of Victim Assistance Programs and Resources in the United States, the Directory of National Programs Serving Survivors of Crime, Crisis and Trauma, and the Directory of International Programs Serving Survivors of Crime, Crisis and Trauma. NOVA offers an annual conference, training seminars, and workshops.

Parents of Murdered Children (POMC) (www.pomc.com) is a national organization providing assistance, crisis intervention, and referrals to local chapters for those grieving due to the murder of a child. Members include those who are grieving as well as the professionals that support them. POMC local chapters provide monthly meetings, connect members through telephone contact, discuss grief, and arrange for murder survivors to be accompanied to court. POMC's Web site offers a "Forum of Hope," which allows members to share thoughts, emotions, and experiences with other individuals also grieving the loss of a loved one to murder. Also, the Web site provides individuals the opportunity to ask questions of various experts, such as a forensic pathologist, bereavement specialist, homicide detective, judge, funeral director, chief counsel, forensic scientist, or criminal profiler. Helpful information is also offered on the Web site about writing a victim's impact statement, and information is provided for professionals about the problems facing murder survivors. POMC offers other programs including: a self-help weekend developed to help murder survivors grieve and rebuild a new life; the National Murder Response Team, established in order to help and support communities following a violent murder; *Survivors*, a tri-annual newsletter offering important information to murder survivors; and training for mental health professionals, social workers, doctors, nurses, ministers, teachers, lawyers, and law enforcement personnel on murder survivors and the consequences of murder.

Crisis intervention training is available from the Red Cross (www.redcross.org) for mental health disaster training, International Critical Incident Stress Foundation (www.icisf.org), and National Organization for Victims Assistance (www.trynova.org). There is some controversy about the effectiveness of crisis interventions; however, many professionals have provided those services.

Organizational Resources: Death Education

The Association for Death Education and Counseling (www.adec.org) is an international, multidisciplinary professional organization. Its purpose is to promote excellence in research, theory and clinical practice in the area of death education, care of the dying, and bereavement counseling.

The Centers for Disease Control and Prevention (www.cdc.gov/index.htm) provides information on many health related issues including suicide. In particular, the CDC's National Center for Health Statistics (www.cdc.gov/nchs) summarizes overall death and mortality rates for the United States.

CMI Educational Institute (www.cmieducation.org) conducts seminars across the United States as the nonprofit American Academy of Bereavement (AAB). AAB is dedicated to providing education for professionals and general public on topics concerned related to thanatology, especially bereavement.

The **International Work Group on Death, Dying and Bereavement (IWG)** consists of professionals from around the world. IWG develops and publishes policy statements regarding thanatology issues.

Online courses and programs are available from many sources (such as National Center for Death Education at www.mountida.edu). It is important to note that the quality of these educational programs may vary greatly and that the qualification of the faculty and the objectives of the program should be investigated before enrollment.

Organizational Resources: Assessment and Intervention

The **Center for the Advancement of Health** (www.cfah.org) has the goal of "translating health research into effective policy and practice." The Grief Research: Gaps, Needs, and Action Project was designed to observe and report on bereavement and grief research with the goal of improving research and care. Of focus was the use of research to guide intervention strategies. One report from the project looks at the field of bereavement research (Center for the Advancement of Health,

2004), and a report from the project's Bridging Work Group (2005) examines the gap separating bereavement practitioners and researchers.

Many of the organizations listed above provide intervention and educational programs. Grief and death anxiety measures are other resources for assessment. **The Grief Experience Inventory** by Sanders, Mauger, and Strong (1985) is a 135-item selfreport questionnaire. It is designed to measure 17 dimensions of grief and also has a social desirability rating. The inventory is available from Department of Psychology, Hood College, Frederick, MD. The **Hogan Grief Reaction Checklist** (Hogan, Greenfield, & Schmidt, 2001) is a 61-item questionnaire designed to measure grief reactions after the death of a child. Six dimensions of grief are delineated in the checklist. **The Death Anxiety Scale** by Templar (Templar, 1970) is a 15-item true or false scale with scores from 0 to 15. **The Threat Index: Provided Forms** (Tip) (Epting & Neimeyer, 1984) has 40 bipolar dimensions. Examinees choose from the poles to identify their present self and their attitudes toward death. The difference between the selections for self and death indicates death anxiety. The **Collett-Lester Fear of Death Scale** (Collett & Lester, 1969) consists of ratings of disagreement/agreement on 36 statements. The measure provides scores for four dimensions of fear: death of self, death of others, dying of self, and dying of others.

A Brief Annotated List of Text Resources

In addition to the organizational resources listed above, it is important for certified thanatologists to be aware of and use the resources provided in texts/journals published in the areas of death and dying. The chapters in the *Handbook* cite a wealth of books and articles. In the section below is a non-exhaustive list of books/journals with brief annotations; among these books are those which may be considered modern "classics" in the field.

- *On Death and Dying* is the classical work by Elizabeth Kubler-Ross (1969). Reporting transcript data from dying patients, the book describes stages of the dying process: denial and isolation, anger, bargaining, depression, and acceptance.
- Barney Glaser and Anselm Strauss (1965) in *Awareness of Dying* provided the foundation for four types of communication patterns (closed awareness, suspected awareness, mutual pretense, and open awareness) common in those confronting death.
- In *Living with Life Threatening Illness: A guide for Patients, Families, and Caregivers*, Kenneth Doka (1993) considers the dynamics that affect

people living with a life-shortening illness. He proposes five distinct phases: prediagnositic, acute, chronic, recovery, and terminal.

- *Grief Counseling and Grief Therapy* by J. William Worden (2002) provides a wide range of information on clinical intervention and assessment of bereavement. Besides arguing for a distinction between counseling and therapy for the bereavement, Worden describes four basic tasks for coping with the mourning process, i.e., accept the reality of death, experience the anguish of grief, adjust to the environment without the deceased, and emotionally relocate the deceased and move on.

- In *Meaning Reconstruction and the Experience of Loss*, Robert Neimeyer (2001) outlines the challenges to the bereaved in finding meaning after a death. The griever's assumptive world as well as self and relationship/ attachments to the deceased will often need to be reconfigured.

- Lulu Redmond, a past president of the Association for Death Education and Counseling, has a practical and informative book, *Surviving: When Someone You Love Was Murdered* (1989). The book has sections on the grief associated with a death by homicide and assessment and therapy guidelines and suggestions for professionals.

- Lynne DeSpelder and Al Strickland's *The Last Dance: Encountering Death and Dying* (2005) is a popular college text for courses on death and dying. The text provides a board range of topics in thanatology and gives rich cultural information. From 2002 through 2007 the book was one of the required readings for the ADEC certification examination.

- Charles Corr, Cyde Nabe, and Donna Corr's *Death and Dying, Life and Living* (2006) is a comprehensive coverage of the field of thanatology. A popular textbook in thanatology, the authors' analyses of statistical data to illustrate trends, providing a wealth of resources, and including thoughtful synthesis of research and practice are strengths of the book. Based on the hospice philosophy, the book also has a good description of four tasks (physical, psychological, social, and spiritual) of the dying person. From 2002 through 2007 the book was one of the required readings for the ADEC certification examination.

- Herman Feifel's *The Meaning of Death* (1959) is considered the pioneer book of modern thanatology.

- In *The Private Worlds of Dying Children*, Myra Bluebond-Langner (1978) describes children with leukemia and their understanding of their illness. Changes in self-concept and recognition of the seriousness of the illness for these children are outlined.

- In *Disenfranchised Grief: Recognizing Hidden Sorrow* (1989), editor Kenneth Doka coined the term disenfranchised grief as grief that is not recognized or sanctioned.

- In *Explaining Death to Children* (1967) and other books such as *Talking About Death: A Dialogue between Parent and Child* (1990) and *Living When a Loved One Has Died* (1977), Earl Grollman has encouraged professionals and laypersons to recognize and to educate children about death, dying and bereavement.

- There are numerous resources for children who have experienced loss. In two books, *Life & Loss* (2000) and *Breaking the Silence* (2002), Linda Goldman provides a wealth of information about bereaved children. *Breaking the Silence* focuses on violent deaths and is a guide to helping children with complicated grief. *The Grieving Child* (2003) by Helen Fitzgerald is written as a guide for parents. Based on her experiences with bereaved children the book has practical advice appropriate for parents and professionals. *Growing through Grief: A K-12 Curriculum to Help Young People though All Kinds of Loss* (O'Toole, 1989) is a manual in age appropriate sections with over 120 handouts for educators or professionals working with bereaved children.

- In the *Handbook of Bereavement Research* (2001) Stroebe, Hansson, Stroebe, and Schut provide a theoretical and empirical base to understanding various facets of bereavement including the methodology and ethics, bereavement consequences, coping with bereavement and intervening in the coping process.

- *The Psychology of Death* by Robert Kastenbaum and Ruth Aisenberg (1992) was the first broad comprehensive book on thanatology.

- Therese A. Rando in a variety of books such as *Treatment of Complicated Mourning* (1993) and *Grief, Dying, and Death: Clinical Interventions for Caregivers* (1984) describes theoretical and clinical approaches to issues in bereavement including her theory about coping with loss by: recognizing the loss, reacting to the separation, recollecting and experiencing the deceased and the relationship, relinquishing the old, readjusting to move adaptively, and reinvesting.

- *Omega — Journal of Death and Dying* provides articles on terminal illnesses, dying, and the grief process. Among the contributors are professors, medical doctors, and funeral directors. Along with the journal *Death Studies*, this journal is recognized for scholarship on issues related to death and dying and serves to assist mental health professionals in working in crisis management.

- *Death Studies* is a professional journal that publishes articles on bereavement counseling, research, education, care of the dying, and ethics. Contributors include professors, clinicians, nurses, and medical doctors. Book Reviews and News & Notes are special sections in each issue.
- *Suicide and Life — Threatening Behavior* publishes articles on research, theory and clinical practice that are concerned with self-inflected deaths.
- *Living with Loss* magazine (www.bereavementmag.com) is characterized as "a support group in print" for bereaved individuals. Grief professionals and individuals experiencing grief contribute articles, poetry, and stories to the magazine.

LeARNiNg OBJEctive:
List the VARioUS Resources involved in thanatology
As well As the maJOR ReseARch publicAtions in the
thanatology field.

References

Abrams, D., Albury, S., Doka, K., Crandall L., & Harris, R. (2005). The Florida clergy end-of-life education enhancement project: A description and evaluation. *American Journal of Hospice & Palliative Medicine*, 22(3), 181-187.

Adams, David W. (2002). The consequences of sudden traumatic death: The vulnerability of bereaved children and adolescents and ways professionals can help. In Gerry R. Cox, Robert A. Bendiksen, and Robert G. Stevenson (Eds.), *Complicated grieving and bereavement: Understanding and treating people experiencing loss*. Amityville, NY: Baywood.

Adams, D.W., & Deveau, E.J. (1987). When a brother or sister is dying of cancer: The vulnerability of the adolescent sibling. *Death Studies*, 11, 279-295.

Adams, R.E., Boscarino, J.A., & Figley, C.R. (2006). Compassion fatigue and psychological distress among social workers: A validation study. *American Journal of Orthopsychiatry*. 76, 103-108.

Aden, LeRoy H. (2005). *In life and death: The shaping of faith*. Minneapolis: Augsburg Books.

Aitchison, Stewart. (1992) *Red Rock Sacred Mountain: The canyons & peaks from Sedona to Flagstaff*. Stillwater, MN: Voyageur Press.

Alexander, Jeffrey (2004). Towards a theory of cultural trauma. In J. Alexander, R. Eyerman, B. Giesen, N. Smelser, P. Szompka (Eds.). *Cultural trauma and collective identity*. Berkeley: University of California Press.

Alexander, I.E., & Alderstein, A.M. (1958). Affective responses to the concept of death in a population of children and early adolescents. *Journal of Genetic Psychology*, 93, 167-177.

Allport, G.W., & Ross, J.M. (1967). Personal religious orientation, and prejudice. *Journal of Personality and Social Psychology*, 5, 432–4 43.

Amella, E.J., Lawrence, J.F., & Gresle, S.O. (2005). Tube feeding: Prolonging life or death in vulnerable populations? *Mortality*, 10(1), 69-81.

American Association of University Professors (2004). Distance education and intellectual property issues. Retrieved on December 15, 2006, at http://www.aaup.org/AAUP/issuesed/DE/.

American Psychiatric Association (2000). *Diagnostic and Statistical Manual of Mental Disorders DSM-IV-TR*. Washington, DC author.

Anderson, S.A., & Sabatelli, R.M. (2007). *Family interaction: A multigenerational developmental perspective*. Boston: Allyn and Bacon.

Aneshensel, C.S., Botticello, A.L., Yamamoto-Mitani, N. (2004). When caregiving ends: The course of depressive symptoms after bereavement. *Journal of Health and Social Behavior*, 45, 422-440.

Antonovsky, A. (1990). Pathways leading to successful coping and health. In M. Rosenbaum (Ed), *Learned resourcefulness: On coping skills, self control, and adaptive behavior* (pp. 31-63). New York: Springer-Verlag.

Applegate, J K. (1997). *Ambivalence toward the spouse as related to the grief of widows in the second year of bereavement*. Unpublished doctoral dissertation, University of Kansas.

Arbore, P., Katz, R.S., & Johnson, T.A. (2006). Suffering and the caring professional. In R.S. Katz & T.A. Johnson, *When professionals weep* (pp.13-26). New York: Taylor & Francis.

Aries, P. (1981). *The hour of our death* (H. Weaver, Trans.). New York: Knopf.

Arlow, J.A. (2004). Psychoanalysis. In R. Corsini & D. Wedding (Eds.), *Current Psychotherapies* (7th Ed.) (pp.15-51). Belmont, CA: Thompson/Brooks/Cole.

Arnett, J.J. (2002). The psychology of globalization. *American Psychologist, 57,* 774-783.

Aspinall, S.Y. (1996). Educating children to cope with death: A preventive model. *Psychology in the Schools, 33,* 341-349.

Atkinson, M.J. 1935. *Indians of the Southwest.* San Antonio: Naylor.

Attig. T. (1979). Death respect and vulnerability. In A. DeVries & A. Carmi (Eds.) *The dying human* (pp. 3-15). Tel Aviv: Turtledov.

Attig, T. (1996). *How we grieve: Relearning the world.* New York: Oxford University Press.

Attig, T. (2000). *The heart of grief: Death and the search for lasting love.* New York: Oxford University Press.

Attig, T. (2001). Relearning the world: Making and finding meanings. In R. A. Neimeyer (Ed.) *Meaning reconstruction and the experience of loss* (pp. 33-53). Washington, DC: American Psychological Association.

Attig, T. (2002). Questionable assumptions about assumptive worlds. In Jeffery Kauffman (Ed). *Loss of the assumptive world: A theory of traumatic loss* (pp. 55-68). New York: Brunner-Routledge.

Azarian, A.G., & Skriptchenko-Gregorian, V.G. (1998). Traumatization and stress in children and adolescents of natural disasters. In T. W. Miller (Ed.). *Children of trauma.* Madison, CT: International Universities Press.

Bader, J.L. (2001, June 10). Death be not bad for ratings. *The New York Times,* Section 4, Column 5, p. 2.

Baker, J.E., & Sedney, M.A. (1996). How bereaved children cope with loss: An overview. In C.A. Corr & D. Corr (Eds.) *Handbook of childhood death and bereavement* (pp. 109-129). New York: Springer Publishing Co.

Balaswamy, S., Richardson, V., & Price, C.A. (2004). Investigating patterns of socialsupport use by widowers during bereavement. *The Journal of Men's Studies,* **13,** 7-84.

Baldwin, S.A., Williams, D.C., & Houts, A.C. (2004). The creation, expansion, and embodiment of post-traumatic stress disorder. A case study in historical critical psychopathology. *Scientific Review of Mental Health Practice, 3.* Retrieved 2006 at http://www.srmhp.org/0301/hcp.html.

Balk, D.E. (1995). Bereavement research using control groups: Ethical obligations and questions. *Death Studies,* 19(2), 123-138.

Balk, D.E. (2001). College student bereavement, scholarship, and the university: A call for university engagement. *Death Studies,* 25, 67-84.

Balk, D.E. (2007). Working with children and adolescents. In K.J. Doka (Ed.), *Living with grief: Before and after the death* (pp. 209-227). Washington, DC. Hospice Foundation of America.

Ball, A. (Executive producer). (2001-2005). *Six feet under.* [Television series]. Home Box Office.

Baltes, P.B., Reese, H.W., & Nesselroade, J. R. (1977). *Life-span developmental psychology: Introduction to research methods.* Monterey, CA: Brooks/Cole.

Barra, D.M., E.S. Carlson, M. Maize, W.I. Murphy, B.W. O'Neal, R.E. Sarver, & E.S. Zinner (1993). "The dark night of the spirit: Grief following a loss in religious identity." In K.J. Doka and J.D. Morgan, (eds). *Death and Spirituality* Amityville. NY: Baywood Publishing.

Barrett, R.K. (1995a). Contemporary African-American funeral rites and traditions. In L.A. DeSpelder & A.L. Strickland (Eds.) *The path ahead: Readings in death and dying* (pp. 80-92). Mountain View, CA: Mayfield.

Barrett, R.K. (1995b). Psychocultural influences on African-American attitudes toward death, dying, and funeral rites. In J. D. Morgan (Ed.) *Personal care in an impersonal world: A multidimensional look at bereavement* (pp. 213-230). Amityville, NY: Baywood.

Barrett, R.K. (1998). Sociocultural considerations for working with blacks experiencing loss and grief. In K.J. Doka & J.D. Davidson (Eds.), *Living with grief: Who we are, how we grieve* (pp. 83-96). Philadelphia: Brunner/Mazel.

Barrett, R. (2001). Recommendations for culturally competent end-of-life care giving. Virtual Mentor, American Medical Association, published online. http://www.ama-assn.org/ama/pub/category/6824.html (Retrieved on January 18, 2007)

Barrett, R.K. & DeSpelder, L.A. (1997, June). *Ways people die: The influence of environment on a child's view of death.* Paper presented at the annual meeting of the Association for Death Education and Counseling, Washington, DC.

Barrett, T.W., & Scott, T.B. (1989). Development of the grief experience questionnaire. *Suicide and Life-Threatening Behavior, 19*, 201-215.

Barton, D. & Crowder, M.K. (1975). The use of role playing techniques as an instructional aid in teaching about dying, death, and bereavement. *Omega, The Journal of Death and Dying, 6*(3), 243-250.

Basu, S. & Heuser, L. (2003). Using service learning in death education. *Death Studies, 27*, 901-927.

Bates, T. (1999, September). Cultural and ethical issues in international distance education. Paper presented at the UBC/CREAD conference, Vancouver, Canada.

Beauchamp, T.L. & Childress, J.F. (2001). *Principles of biomedical ethics* (5th ed.). New York: Oxford University Press.

Beavers, W.R., & Hampson, R. (2003). Measuring family competence: The Beavers Systems Model. In F. Walsh (Ed.) *Normal family processes: Growing diversity and complexity* (3rd Ed.) (pp. 549-580). New York: Guilford Press.

Becker, E. (1971). *The birth and death of meaning* (2nd Ed.). New York: Free Press.

Becker, E. (1973). *The denial of death.* New York: Free Press.

Beckwith, S. (2005). When families disagree: family conflict and decisions. In K. Doka, B. Jennings, & C. Corr (Eds.) *Ethical dilemmas at the end of life.* Washington, DC: Hospice Foundation of America.

Becvar, D.S. (2003). The impact on the family therapist of a focus on death, dying, and bereavement. *Journal of Marital and Family Therapy, 29*, 469-477.

Becvar, D. & Becvar, R. (2006). *Family therapy: A systemic integration.* Boston.

Bender, D.L. (Editor) (1974). *Problems of death: Opposing viewpoints.* Anoka, MN: Greenhaven Press.

Benight,C.C., Flores, J., & Tashiro, T. (2001) Bereavement coping self-efficacy in cancer widows. *Death Studies*, 25, 97-125.

Bennett, S.M., Litz, B.T., Lee, B.S., & Maguen, S. (2005). The scope and impact of perinatal loss: Current status and future directions. *Professsional Psychology: Research and Practice*, 36, 180-187.

Benoliel, J.Q. & Degner, L.F. (1995). Institutional dying: A convergence of cultural values, technology, and social organization. In H. Wass & R.A. Neimeyer (Eds.), *Dying: Facing the facts* (pp. 117-141). Philadelphia: Taylor & Francis.

Berger, P. & Luckman, T. (1966). *The social construction of reality.* New York: Doubleday.

Bernat, J. (1992). How much of the brain must die in brain death? *Journal of Clinical Ethics, 3*, 21-26.

Berns, C.F. (2003/2004). Bibliotherapy: Using books to help bereaved children. *Omega, The Journal of Death and Dying*, 48(4), 321-336.

Bell, L.V. (1970). Death in the technocracy. *Journal of Human Relations*, 18, 833-839.

Bellah, R.N., Madsen, R., Sullivan, A.S., & Tipton, S.M. (1985). *Habits of the heart; Individualism and commitment in American life.* Berkeley: University of California Press.

Berg, S. (2006). In their own voices: Families discuss end-of-life decision making — part 2. *Pediatric Nursing*, 32, 238-242.

Bernal, G. & Saez-Santiago, E. (2006). Culturally centered psychosocial interventions. *Journal of Community Psychology*, 34(2), 121-132.

Binswanger, L. (1963). *Being in the world.* New York: Harper & Row.

Birenbaum, L.K. (2000). Assessing children's and teenagers' bereavement when a sibling dies from cancer: A secondary analysis. *Child: Care, Health and Development*, 26(5), 381-400.

Biziou, B. (1999). *The joys of everyday ritual: Spiritual recipes to celebrate milestones, ease transitions, and make every day sacred.* New York: St. Martin's Griffin.

Blackhall, L.J., Murphy, S.T., Frank, G., Michel, V., & Azen, S. (1995). Ethnicity and attitudes toward patient autonomy. *Journal of the American Medical Association*, 274, 820-825.

Blanchot, Maurice (2000). *The instant of my death.* (tr.) F. Morgana. Stanford: Stanford University Press.

Blanke, J.M. (2002, June). To copy, or not to copy, that is the quandary: An introduction to copying under the copyright law. Paper published in the proceedings of the ASCUE Conference, Myrtle Beach, SC. Retrieved online on April 4, 2006. at http://fits.depauw.edu/ascue/Proceedings/2002/index.asp#

Blazer, D.G. (1982). The epidemiology of late life depression. *Journal of the American Geriatrics Society*, 30, 587-592.

Blevins, D. & Papadatou, D. (2006). The effects of culture in end-of-life situations. In J.L. Werth, Jr. & D. Blevins (Eds.), *Psychosocial issues near the end of life: A resource for professional care providers* (pp. 27-55). Washington, DC: American Psychological Association.

Bluebond-Langner, M. (1978). *The private worlds of dying children.* Princeton, NJ: Princeton University Press.

Blumenfeld, S.L. (1999). *Death Education at Columbine High.* Western Journalism Center: WorldNetDaily.com.

Bookwala, J., Coppola, K.M., Fagerlin, A., Ditto, P.H., Danks, J.H., & Smucker, W.D. (2001). Gender differences in older adults' preferences for life-sustaining medical treatments and end-of-life values. *Death Studies,* 25, 127-149.

Bonanno, G.A. (2004) Loss, trauma, and human resilience: Have we underestimated the human capacity to thrive after extremely aversive events? *American Psychologist,* 59, 20-28.

Bonanno, G.A. (2006). Research that matters – 2006: New findings on loss and human resilience. A symposium presented at the Annual Conference of the Association for Death Education and Counseling, Tampa, FL.

Bonanno, G.A., Wortman, C.B., Lehman, D.R., Tweed, R.G., Haring, M., Sonnega, J., Carr, D., & Neese, R.M. (2002). Resilience to loss and chronic grief: A prospective study from preloss to 18-months postloss. *Journal of Personality and Social Psychology,* 83, 1150-1164.

Bonanno, G.A., Wortman, C.B., & Neese, R.M. (2004). Prospective patterns of resilience and maladjustment during widowhood. *Psychology and Aging,* 19, 260-271.

Bordewich, F.M. (1988). Education: Mortal fears. *The Atlantic,* 262(2), 30-32, 34.

Bosley, G.M. & Cook, A.S. (1993). Therapeutic aspects of funeral ritual: A thematic analysis. *Journal of Family Psychotherapy,* 4(4), 69-83.

Boss, P. (1991). Ambiguous loss. In F. Walsh & M. McGoldrick (Eds.) *Living beyond loss* (pp. 164-175). New York: W.W. Norton.

Boss, P. (1999). *Ambiguous loss: Learning to live with unresolved grief.* Cambridge, MA: Harvard University Press.

Boszormenyi-Nagy, I. (1987). *Foundations of contextual therapy: Collected papers of Ivan Boszormenyi-Nagy, M.D.* New York: Brunner/Mazel, Publishers.

Boszormenyi-Nagy, I., Grunebaum, J. & Ulrich, D. (1991). Contextual therapy. In A.S. Gurman & D.P. Kniskern (Eds.). *Handbook of family therapy,* Volume II. New York: Brunner/Mazel.

Bowen, M. (1985). *Family therapy in clinical practice.* Northwale, NJ: Jason Aronson.

Bowlby, J. (1961). Processes of mourning. *The International Journal of Psychoanalysis,* 42, 317-340.

Bowlby, J. (1969-1980). *Attachment and loss.* New York: Basic Books. [Vol. 1, *Attachment;* Vol. 2, *Separation: Anxiety and anger;* Vol. 3, *Loss: Sadness and depression.*]

Bowman, K.W. & P.A. Singer (2001). Chinese seniors' perspectives on end-of-life decisions. *Social Science & Medicine,* 53, 455-464.

Boyd-Franklin, N. (2003). *Black families in therapy: Understanding the African American experience* (2nd edition). New York: Guilford Press.

Boyer, E.L. (1990). *Scholarship reconsidered: Priorities of the professoriate.* New York: The Carnegie Foundation for the Advancement of Teaching.

Brabant, S., Forsyth, C.J., & McFarlain, G. (1997). The impact of the death of a child on meaning and purpose in life. *Journal of Personal and Interpersonal Loss,* 2(3), 255-266.

Bracken, Patrick (2002). *Trauma: culture, meaning and philosophy.* London: Whurr Publishers.

Bradach, K.M. & Jordan, J.R. (1995). Long-term effects of a family history of traumatic death on adolescent individuation. *Death Studies*, 19, 315-336.

Brave Heart, M.Y. (2003). The historical trauma response among natives and its relationship with substance abuse: A Lakota illustration. *Journal of Psychoactive Drugs*, 35, 7-13.

Braun, K.L. & Nichols, R. (1996). Cultural issues in death and dying. *Hawaii Medical Journal*, 55, 260-264.

Bregman, L. (2006). Spirituality: A glowing and useful term in search of a meaning. *Omega: The Journal of Death and Dying*, 53, 5 - 26

Bregman, L. & Thiermann, S. (1995) *First person mortal: Personal narratives of illness*. New York: Paragon.

Brennan, A.J. (1983) Paper presented at the Children and Death conference, Columbia-Presbyterian Medical Center.

Brenneis, D. (2002). Some cases for culture. *Human Development*, 45, 264-269.

Brent, S.B. (1977-78). Puns, metaphors, and misunderstanding in a two-year-old's conception of death. *Omega, The Journal of Death and Dying*, 8(4), 285-293.

Bridging Work Group (2005). Bridging the gap between research and practice in bereavement: Report from the Center for the Advancement of Health. *Death Studies*, 29, 93–122.

Brier, N. (2004). Anxiety after miscarriage: A review of the empirical literature and implications for clinical practice. *Birth: Issues in Perinatal Care*, 31, 138-142.

Brison, K. J. (1992). *Just talk: Gossip, meetings, and power in a Papua New Guinea village*. Berkeley, CA: University of California Press.

Brosius, J.P. (1995-1996). Father dead, mother dead: Bereavement and fictive death in Penan Geng society. *Omega, The Journal of Death and Dying*, 32, 197-226.

Brown, E.J. & Goodman, R.F. (2005). An exploration of the construct in children bereaved on September 11. *Journal of Clinical Child and Adolescent Psychology*, 34, 248-259.

Brown, E.J., Pearlman, M.Y., & Goodman, R.F. (2004). Facing fears and sadness: Cognitive-behavioral therapy for childhood traumatic grief. *Harvard Review of Psychiatry*, 12, 187-198.

Brown University, Center for Gerontology and Health Care Research (2006). *Facts on Dying*. (n.d.). Retrieved November 12, 2006, from http://www.chcr.brown.edu/dying/factsondying.htm.

Buchholtz, M. (2002). Youth and cultural practice. *Annual Review of Anthropology*, 31 525-552.

Bugental, J.F. & Bugental E.K. (1984). A fate worse than death: the fear of changing. *Psychotherapy*, 21, 543-549.

Bullock, K. (2006). Promoting advance directives among African Americans: A faith-based model. *Journal of Palliative Medicine*, 9, 183-195.

Burroughs T.E., Hong B.A., Kappel D.F., & Freedman B.K. (1998). The stability of family decisions to consent or refuse organ donation: would you do it again? *Psychosomatic Medicine*, 60, 56-162.

Burt, R.A. (2005). The end of autonomy. Improving end of life care: Why has it been so difficult? *Hastings Center Report Special Report*, *35*(6), S9-S13.

Butler, R.N. (1963). The life review: An interpretation of reminiscence in the aged. *Psychiatry*, 26, 65-70.

Butler, R. & Lewis, M. (1982). *Aging and mental health*. St. Louis: Mosby.

Byock, I. (1997). *Dying well: The prospect for growth at the end-of-life*. New York: Putnam.

Byock, I. (2004). *The four things that matter most: A book about living*. New York: Free Press.

Calhoun, L.G., & Tedeschi, R.G. (1990). Positive aspects of critical life problems: Recollections of grief. *Omega, The Journal of Death and Dying, 20*(4), 265-272.

Callahan, D. (1987). *Setting limits: Medical goals in an aging society*. Washington, DC: Georgetown University Press.

Callahan, D. (1990). *What kind of life: The limits of medical progress*. New York: Simon & Schuster.

Callahan, D. (1993). *The troubled dream of life: In search of a peaceful death*. New York: Simon & Schuster.

Callahan, D. (1998). *False hopes*. New York: Simon & Schuster.

Campbell, S., & Silverman, P.R. (1987). *Widower: When men are left alone*. New York: Prentice-Hall.

Campione, F. (2005). *Manifesto della Tanatologia* [Manifesto of Thanatology]. Bologna: Cooperativa Libraria Universitaria Editrice Bologna.

Caralis, P.V., Davis, B., Wright, K., & Marcial, E. (1993). The influence of ethnicity and race on attitudes toward advance directives, life-prolonging treatments, and euthanasia. *Journal of Clinical Ethics, 4*(2), 155-165.

Carnelley, K.B., Wortman, C.B., Bolger, N., & Burke, C.T. (2006). The time course of grief reactions to spousal loss: Evidence from a national probability sample. *Journal of Personality and Social Psychology, 91*, 476-492.

Carney, K.L. (2003-2004). Barklay and Eve: The role of activity books for bereaved children, *Omega, The Journal of Death and Dying, 48*, 307-319.

Carrillo, E., Green, A., & Betancourt, J. (1999). Cross-cultural primary care: A patient-based approach. *Annals of Internal Medicine, 130*, 829-834. Retrieved January 18, 2007 from http://www.annals.org/cgi/reprint/130/10/829.pdf

Carter, B.S., & Sandling, J. (1992). Decision making in the NICU: The question of medical futility. *Journal of Clinical Ethics, 3*(2), 142-145.

Carter, J. (1998). *The virtues of aging*. New York: Ballantine Publishing Group.

Caruth, C. (1995). *Trauma exploration in memory*. Baltimore Johns Hopkins University Press.

Casarett, D. (2006). Understanding and improving hospice enrollment. *LDI Issue Brief* 11(3),1-4. Retrieved June 26, 2006, from http://www.upenn.edu/ldi/issuebrief11_3.pdf

Cassel, E.J. (1982) The nature of suffering and the goals of medicine. *New England Journal of Medicine, 306*(11), 639-645.

Cecil, R. (1994). Miscarriage: Women's views of care. *Journal of Reproductive and Infant Psychology, 12*, 21-29.

Center for the Advancement of Health (2004). Report on bereavement and grief research. *Death Studies, 28*, 489-575.

Center to Advance Palliative Care (2006). Hospital palliative care programs continue rapid growth. Retrieved January 22, 2007, from http://www.capc.org/news-and-events/releases/december-2006-release.

Centers for Disease Control. (2006). Deaths: Final Data for 2003. Retrieved November 12, 2006, from http://www.cdc.gov/nchs/data/hestat/finaldeaths03_tables.pdf .

Centers for Medicaid and Medicare Services (2006). Hospice conditions of participation. Retrieved January 22, 2007, from http://www.access.gpo.gov/nara/cfr/waisidx_04/42cfr418_04.html.

Charkow, W. B. (1998). Inviting children to grieve. *Professional School Counseling*, 2(2), 117-122.

Chen, I., Kurz, J., Pasanen, M., Faselis, C., Panda, M., Staton, L.J., O'Rorke, J., et al. (2005). Racial differences in opioid use for chronic nonmalignant pain. *Journal of General Internal Medicine*, 20, 593-598.

Cheung, Peter Ka Hing, Chan, C.L.W., Fu, W., Li, Y., & Cheung, G.Y.K. P. (2006). "Letting go" and "holding on": Grieving and traditional death rituals in Hong Kong. In Cecilia Lai Wan Chan & Amy Yin Man Chow (editors), *Death, dying, and bereavement: A Hong Kong Chinese Experience*. Hong Kong: Hong Kong University Press.

Chibbaro, J.S. & Jackson, C.M. (2006). Helping students cope in an age of terrorism: Strategies for school counselors *Professional School Counseling*, 9, 314-321.

Chidester, D. (2002). *Patterns of transcendence: Religion, death, and dying*, 2nd Edition. Belmont, CA: Wadsworth.

Children's Rights Task Force of the Midwest Bioethics Center. (1995). Health care treatment decision making guidelines for minors. *Bioethics Forum* 11, A1-A16.

Christakis, N.A. & Iwashyna, T.J. (2003). The health impact of health care on families: A matched cohort study of hospice use by decedents and mortality outcomes in surviving, widowed spouses. *Social Science & Medicine*, 57, 465-475.

Chochinov, H.M. & Cann, B.J. (2005). Interventions to enhance the spiritual aspects of dying. *Journal of Palliative Medicine*, 8 Suppl 1:S103-115.

Cicirelli, V.G. (1997). Relationship of psychosocial and background variables to older adults' end-of-life decisions. *Psychology and Aging*, 12(1), 71-83.

Cicirelli, V.G., MacLean, A.P., & Cox, L.S. (2000). Hastening death: A comparison of two end-of-life decisions. *Death Studies*, 24, 401-419.

Cimete, G., & Kuguoglu, S. (2006). Grief responses of Turkish families after the death of their children from cancer. *Journal of Loss and Trauma*, 11, 31-51.

Cleiren, M. & VanZoelen, A.J. (2002). Post-mortem organ donation and grief: A study of consent, refusal, and well-being in bereavement. *Death Studies*, 26, 837-849.

Cohen, J. (2005). Treating traumatized children: Current status and future directions. *Journal of Trauma and Dissociation*, 6, 109-121.

Cohen, J.A., Goodman, R.F., Brown, E.J. & Mannarino, A. 2004. Treatment of childhood traumatic grief: Contributing to a newly emerging condition in the wake of community trauma. *Harvard Review of Psychiatry*, 12, 213-216.

Cohen, J.A. & Mannarino, A.P. (2004a). Treating childhood traumatic grief: A pilot study. *Journal of the American Academy of Child & Adolescent Psychiatry*, 43, 1225-1233.

Cohen, J.A. & Mannarino, A.P. (2004b). Treatment of childhood traumatic grief. *Journal of Clinical Child and Adolescent Psychology*, 33, 819-831.

Cohen, J.A., Mannarino, A.P. & Deblinger, E. (2006). *Treating trauma and traumatic grief in children and adolescents*. New York: Guilford Press.

Cole, R.A. (2001). *Issues in web-based pedagogy: A critical primer*. Westport, CT: Greenwood Publishing Group.

Collett, L.J., & Lester, D. (1969). The fear of death and the fear of dying. *Journal of Psychology*, 72, 179-181.

Connor, S.R. (1992). Denial in terminal illness: To intervene or not to intervene. *The Hospice Journal*, 8, 1-15.

Connor, S. (1998). *Hospice: Practice, pitfalls and promise*. Washington, DC: Taylor and Francis.

Connor, S.R. (1999). New initiatives transforming hospice care. *The Hospice Journal*, 14, 193-203.

Connor, S.R., Lycan, J., & Schumacher, J.D. (2006). Involvement of psychologists in psychosocial aspects of hospice and end-of-life care. In J.L. Werth, Jr. & D. Blevins (Eds.), *Psychosocial issues near the end of life: A resource for professional care providers* (pp. 203-217). Washington, DC: American Psychological Association.

Connor, S.R. & McMaster, J.K. (1996). Hospice, bereavement intervention and use of health care services by surviving spouses, *HMO Practice*, 10, 20-23.

Conway, K. & Russell, G. (2000). Couples' griefs and experience of support in the aftermath of miscarriage. *British Journal of Medical Psychology*, 73, 531-545.

Cook, A.S. (1995). Ethical issues in bereavement research: An overview. *Death Studies*, 19(2), 103-122.

Cook, A.S. (2001). The dynamics of ethical decision making in bereavement research. In M.S. Stroebe, R.O. Hansson, W. Stroebe & H. Schut (Eds.), *Handbook of bereavement research: Consequences, coping, and care*. (pp. 19-142). Washington, D.C.: American Psychological Association.

Cook, A.S. & Dworkin, D.S. (1992). *Helping the bereaved: Therapeutic interventions for children, adolescents, and adults*. New York: Basic Books.

Cook, A.S., & Oltjenbruns, K.A. (1998). *Dying and grieving: Lifespan and family perspectives* (2nd Ed.) Fort Worth, TX: Harcourt Brace.

Cook, A.S., Oltjenbruns, K.A., & Lagoni, L. (1984). The "ripple effects" of a university sponsored death and dying symposium. *Omega, The Journal of Death and Dying*, 15(2), 185-190.

Cook, J. A. (1988). Dad's double binds: Rethinking fathers' bereavement from a men's studies perspective. *Journal of Contemporary Ethnography*, 17(3), 285-308.

Cook-Cottone, C.P. (2004). Childhood posttraumatic stress disorder: Diagnosis, treatment, and school. *The School Psychology Review*, 33, 127-39.

Corr, C. (1984). Helping with death education. In H. Wass and C.A. Corr (Eds.), *Helping children cope with death: Guidelines and resources* (pp. 49-73). Washington: Hemisphere Publishing Corporation.

Corr, C.A. (1992). A task-based approach to coping with dying. *Omega, The Journal of Death and Dying*, 24, 81-94.

Corr, C.A. (1993). Coping with dying: Lessons that we should and should not learn from the work of Elisabeth Kübler-Ross. *Death Studies*, 17, 69-83.

Corr, C.A. (1996). Children, development, and encounters with death and bereavement. In C.A. Corr & D. Corr (Eds.) *Handbook of childhood death and bereavement* (pp. 3-28). New York: Springer Publishing Co.

Corr, C.A. (1998). Enhancing the concept of disenfranchised grief. *Omega, The Journal of Death and Dying*, 38, 1-20.

Corr, C. (1999). Children, adolescents, and death: Myths, realities, and challenges. *Death Studies*, 23(5), 443-464.

Corr, C.A. (2002). Revisiting the concept of disenfranchised. In K.J. Doka (Ed.), *Disenfranchised grief: New directions, strategies, and challenges for practice* (pp. 39-60). Champaign, IL: Research Press.

Corr, C.A. (2005). Coping with challenges to assumptive worlds. In J. Kauffman (Ed.), *Loss of the assumptive world: A theory of traumatic loss* (pp. 127-138). New York: Brunner-Routledge.

Corr, C.A. & Corr, D.M. (2000). Anticipatory mourning and coping with dying: Similarities, differences, and suggested guidelines for helpers. In T.A. Rando (Ed.), *Clinical dimensions of anticipatory mourning: Theory and practice in working with the dying, their loved ones, and their caregivers* (pp. 223-251). Champaign, IL: Research Press.

Corr, C.A. & Corr, D.M. (2003). Death education. In C.D. Bryant (Ed.), *Handbook of death & dying* (Vol. 1, pp. 292-301). Thousand Oaks, CA: Sage Publications.

Corr, C.A., Doka, K.J., & Kastenbaum, R. (1999). Dying and its interpreters: A review of selected literature and some comments on the state of the field. *Omega: The Journal of Death and Dying*, 39, 239-259.

Corr, C.A., Nabe, C.M., & Corr, D.M. (2003). *Death and dying, life and living* (4th Edition). Belmont, CA: Wadsworth.

Council on Ethical and Judicial Affairs. (2006). *Code of Medical Ethics 2006-2007 edition*. Chicago, IL: American Medical Association.

Courtois, C.A. (2004). Complex trauma, complex reactions: Assessment and treatment. *Psychotherapy: Theory, Research, Practice, Training*, 41, 412-425.

Cox, C., & Monk, A. (1993). Hispanic culture and family care of Alzheimer's patients. *Health and Social Work*, 18(2), 92-100.

Cox, G.R., Bendiksen, R.A., & Stevenson, R.G. (2002). (Editors). *Complicated grieving and bereavement: Understanding and treating people experiencing loss*. Amityville, NY: Baywood Publishing.

Cox, M., Garrett, E., & Graham, J. A. (2004-2005). Death in Disney films: Implications for children's understanding of death. *Omega, The Journal of Death and Dying*, 50, 267-280.

Craig, E.L. & Craig, R.E. (1999). Prison hospice: an unlikely success. *The American Journal of Hospice and Palliative Care*, 16, 725-729.

Crase, D. (1981). Death education within health education: Current status, future directions. *Journal of School Health*, 51, 646-650.

Crase, D. (1987). Black people do die, don't they? *Death Studies*, 11, 221-228.

Crase, D. (1989). Development opportunities for teachers of death education. *The Clearing House*, 62(9), 387-390.

Crawley, L., Payne, R., Bolden, J., Payne, T., Washington, P., & Williams, S. (2000). Palliative and end-of-life care in African American communities. *JAMA*, 284, 2518-2529.

Crenshaw, D.A. (2002). *Bereavement: Counseling the grieving throughout the life cycle*. Eugene, OR: Wipf & Stock Publishers.

Crenshaw, D.A. (2004). *Engaging resistant children in therapy: Projective drawing and storytelling strategies*. Rhinebeck, NY: Rhinebeck Child and Family Therapy Publications.

Crenshaw, D.A. (2005). Clinical tools to facilitate treatment of childhood traumatic grief. *Omega: The Journal of Death and Dying*, 51, 239-255.

Crenshaw, D.A. (2006). *Evocative strategies in child and adolescent psychotherapy*. Lanham, MD: Jason Aronson.

Crenshaw, D.A. & Mordock, J.M. (2005). *A handbook of play therapy with aggressive children*. Lanham, MD: Jason Aronson.

Cronen, V.E., Pearce, W.B., & Changsheng, X. (1989). The meaning of 'meaning' in the CMM analysis of communication: A comparison of two traditions. *Research on Language and Social Interaction*, 23, 1-40.

Cruzan v. Director, Missouri Dept. of Health. 497 US 261 (1990).

Csikai, E.L. & Chaitin, E. (2006). *Ethics in end-of-life decisions in social work practice*. Chicago, IL: Lyceum Books, Inc.

Cunningham, A. (2003). Principles and guidelines for research with vulnerable individuals and families. *Research from the Centre for Children & Families in the Justice System*: 1-8.

Currier, J.M., Holland, J.M., Neimeyer, R.A. (2006). Sense-making, grief, and the experience of violent loss: Toward a mediational model. *Death Studies*, 30(5), 403-428.

Currier, J.M., Holland, J.M., & Neimeyer, R.A. (2007). The effectiveness of bereavement interventions with children: A meta-analytic review of controlled outcome research. *Journal of Clinical Child and Adolescent Psychology*, in press.

Daaleman, T.P. & VandeCreek, L. (2000). Placing religion and spirituality in end-of-life care. *JAMA*, 284(19), 2514-2517)

Daly, M. & Wilson, M. (1996). Violence against stepchildren. *Current Directions in Psychological Science*, **5**, 77-81.

Dane, B. (2000). Thai women: Mediation as a way to cope with AIDS. *Journal of Religion and Health*, 38, 5-21.

Danish, S.J. (1977). Human development and human services: A marriage proposal. In I. Iscoe, B.L. Bloom, & C.C. Spielberger (Eds.), *Community psychology in transition*. New York: Halsted.

Danish, S.J. & D'Augelli, A.R. (1980). Promoting competence and enhancing development through life development intervention. In L.A. Bond C.J. Rosen (Eds.), *Primary prevention of psychopathology* (vol. 4). Hanover, NH: University Press of New England.

Davies, B. (1991). Long-term outcomes of adolescent sibling bereavement. *Journal of Adolescent Research*, 6(1), 83-96.

Davies, B., Reimer, J.C., Brown, P., & Martens, N. (1995). *The experience of transition in families with terminal illness.* Amityville, NY: Baywood Publishing, Inc.

Davis, J.A. (1998). Providing critical incident stress debriefing to individual and communities in situation crisis. *American Academy of Experts in Traumatic Stress, Inc.* Retrieved 2006 from http://www.aaets.org/arts/art54.htm

Davoine, Françoise and Gaudilliè Jean-Max (2004). *History beyond trauma: Whereof one cannot speak. thereof one cannot stay silent.* (tr.) S. Fairfield. New York: Other Press.

Day, R. (2002). *Introduction to family processes (4th ed.).* Mahwah, NJ: Lawrence Erlbaum Assoc., Pub.

Dean, P.V. (1995). Is death education a "nasty little secret"? A call to break the alleged silence. In L.A. DeSpelder and A.L. Strickland (Eds.), *The path ahead* (pp. 322-326). Mountain View, CA: Mayfield Publishing Co.

Deeken, A. (1999). Evolving Japanese perspectives on death and dying. *Budhi*, 215-232. Published by Office of Research and Publications School of Arts and Sciences, Ateneo de Manila University, Philippines.

Defining death. (1991). In B. Furrow, S. Johnson, S. Jost, & R. Schwartz, (Eds.), *Health law: cases, materials, problems* (pp. 1034-1055). St. Paul, MN: West Publishing.

DeFrain, J.D., Jakub, J.K., & Mendoza, B.L. (1991-1992). The psychological effects of sudden infant death on grandmothers and grandfathers. *Omega The Journal of Death and Dying*, 24, 165-182.

Deitsch, M. (1992). Work and families: What are companies doing. *Financial Executive*, 8, 60-62.

Delgado, M., & Tennstedt, S. (1997). Puerto Rican sons as primary caregivers of elderly patients. *Social Work*, 42(2), 125-134.

Dennett (1998). Information, technology, and the virtues of ignorance. In R.N. Stichler and R. Hauptman (Eds.), *Ethics, information, and technology readings* (pp. 79-94). Jefferson, NC: McFarland & Company, Inc.

Da Pena, E. (2002). *Subjective experiences of daughters as caregivers of their frail elderly parent(s): An exploratory study.* Unpublished doctoral dissertation, Alliant International University.

Deri-Bowen, A. (2001). Cot death. In G. Howarth & O. Leamann (Eds.), *Encyclopedia of death and dying* (pp. 121-123). New York: Routledge.

DeSpelder, L.A. (1998). Developing cultural competency. In K.J. Doka & J.D. Davidson (Eds.), *Living with grief: Who we are, how we grieve* (pp. 97-106). Philadelphia: Brunner/Mazel.

DeSpelder, L.A. (2006). The mission of death education (K. Takeuchi, Trans.). In S. Hinohara, A. Deeken, & J. Mizuno (Eds.), *The death education for adults.* Tokyo: Kawadeshobo Shinsha.

DeSpelder, L.A., & Barrett, R.K. (1997, December). Developing multicultural competence. *The Director*, 64, 66-68.

DeSpelder, L.A., & Strickland, A.L. (2004, January/February/March). The life of a death textbook and its authors. *The Forum*, 30, 8-9.

DeSpelder, L. A. & Strickland, A. L. (2005). *The last dance: Encountering death and dying* (7th edition). Boston: McGraw-Hill.

Devilly, G.J., Gist, R. & Cotton, P. (2006) Ready! Fire! Aim! The status of psychological debriefing and therapeutic interventions: In the workplace and after disasters. *Review of General Psychology*, 10, 318-345.

Dickinson, G.E. (2002). A quarter century of end-of-life issues in U.S. medical schools. *Death Studies*, 26, 635-646.

Dickinson, G.E. & Field, D. (2002). Teaching end-of-life issues: Current status in United Kingdom and United States medical schools. *American Journal of Hospice & Palliative Care*, 19, 181-186.

Dinhofer, L. (2003). The differences in grief responses and outcomes between organ and tissue donor families. Unpublished masters' thesis, Brooklyn College of the City University of New York.

Ditto, P.H. (2006). What would Terri want? On the psychological challenges of surrogate decision making. *Death Studies*, 30, 135-148.

Ditto, P.H., Druley, J.A., Moore, K.A., & Danks, J.H. (1996). Fates worse than death: The role of valued life activities in health-state evaluations. *Health Psychology*, 15, 332-343.

Diwan, S., Hougham, G.W., & Sachs, G.A. (2004). Strain experienced by caregivers of dementia patients receiving palliative care: Findings from the Palliative Excellence in Alzheimer Care Efforts (PEACE) Program. *Journal of Palliative Medicine*, 7, 797-807.

Doka, K.A. & Martin T. (2001). Take it like a man: Masculine response to loss. In D.A. Lund, (Ed.), *Men coping with grief* (pp. 37-47). Amityville, NY: Baywood Publishing Co.

Doka, K.J. (1981-82). Recent bereavement and registration for death studies courses. *Omega The Journal of Death and Dying*, 12(1), 51-59.

Doka, K.J. (1989). (Editor). *Disenfranchised grief: Recognizing hidden sorrow*. Lexington, MA: Lexington Books.

Doka, K.J. (1993a). (Editor). *Death and spirituality*. Amityville, NY: Baywood Press.
Doka, K. (1993b). *Living with life-threatening illness: A guide for patients, their families, and caregivers*. Lexington, MA: Lexington Books.

Doka, K.J. (1995). Coping with life threatening illness: A task based approach. *Omega: The Journal of Death and Dying*, 32, 111-122.

Doka, K.J. (1996). The cruel paradox: Children who are living with life-threatening illnesses. In Corr, C.A., & Corr, D.M. (Eds.), *Handbook of childhood death and bereavement*. New York: Springer Publishing Co.

Doka, K.J. (1997).The effect of parental illness and loss on adult children. In I. Deitch & C.W. Howell (Eds.), *Counseling the aging and their families* (pp. 147-155). Alexandria, VA: American Counseling Association.

Doka, K.J. (1998). (Editor). *Living with grief: Who we are, how we grieve*. New York: Brunner/Mazel.

Doka, K.J. (2002). (Editor). *Disenfranchised grief: New directions, strategies, and challenges for practice*. Champaign, IL: Research Press.

Doka, K.J. (2003). The death awareness movement. Description, history, and analysis. In C.D. Bryant (Ed.), *Handbook of death & dying* (Vol. 1, pp. 50-56). Thousand Oaks, CA.

Doka, K.J. (2003). Death system. In R. Kastenbaum, (Ed.), *Macmillan encyclopedia of death and dying* (pp. 222-223). New York: Macmillan.

Doka, K.J. (2005). Ethics, end-of-life decisions and grief. *Mortality*, **10**(1), 83-90.

Doka, K. (2006). Social, cultural, spiritual, and psychological barriers to pain management. In K. Doka (Ed.) *Pain management at the end of life: Bridging the gap between knowledge and practice*. Washington, DC: The Hospice Foundation of America.

Doka, K.J. & Morgan, J.D. (1993). (Editors). *Death and spirituality*. Amityville, NY: Baywood Publishing Co.

Dominguez, M.E. (1999). The treatment of complicated mourning in childhood. *Dissertation Abstracts International: Section B: The Sciences and Engineering*, 60 (6-B), 2938.

Donaldson, T. (1988). *24th century medicine*. Worcester, MA: Davis PublicationsEurotransplant International Foundation (2004). Retrieved July 10, 2006, from http://www.eurotransplant.nl/?id= statistics.

Douglas, C. (1992). For all the saints. *BMJ*, 304, 579.

Douglas, J.D. (1990). Patterns of change following parent death in midlife adults. *Omega, The Journal of Death and Dying*, 22, 123-137,

Doukas, D.J., & McCullough, L.B. (1991). The values history: The evaluation of the patient's values and advance directives. *Journal of Family Practice*, **32**, 145-153.

Dowdney, L. (2000). Annotation: Childhood bereavement following parental death. *Journal of Child Psychology and Psychiatry*, 41, 819-830.

Drolet, J.L. (1990). Transcending death during early adulthood: Symbolic immortality, death anxiety, and purpose in life. *Journal of Clinical Psychology*, 46(2), 148-60.

Dula, A. (1994). African American suspicion of the health care system is justified: What do we do now? *Cambridge Quarterly of Health care Ethics*, 3, 347-357.

Dunn, H. (2001). *Hard choices for loving people*. Herndon, VA: A & A Publishing,

Dunn, S.T.M. (2005). A place of transition: Directors' experiences of providing counseling and advising to distance students. *Journal of Distance Education*, 20(2), 40-57.

Durlak, J.A. (1978-79). Comparison between experiential and didactic methods of death education. *Omega, The Journal of Death and Dying*, 9(1), 57-66.

Durlak, J.A. (1994). Changing death attitudes through death education. In R.A. Neimeyer (Ed.). *Death anxiety handbook. Research, instrumentation, and application*. (pp. 243-260). Washington, DC: Taylor & Francis.

Durlak, J.A., & Reisenberg, L.A. (1991). The impact of death education. *Death Studies*, 15(1), 39-58.

Dyregrov, K. (2004). Strategies of professional assistance after traumatic deaths: Empowerment or dis-empowerment? *Scandinavian Journal of Psychology*, 45, 181-189.

Dyregrov, K. & Mitchell, J.T. (1992). Work with traumatized children: Psychological effects and coping strategies. *Journal of Traumatic Stress*, 5, 5-17.

Eckersley, R. (1993). Failing a generation. *Journal of Paediatrics & Child Health*, 29, S16-S19.

Eckersley, R., & Dear, K. (2002). Cultural correlates of youth suicide. *Social Science & Medicine*, 55, 1891-1904.

Eisenbruch, M. (1984). Cross-cultural aspects of bereavement: Ethnic and cultural variations in the development of bereavement practices. *Culture, medicine, and psychiatry*, 8, 315-347.

Eliot, T.S. (1936). *Selected writings*. New York: Winggold Press.

Emanuel, E. (2006). Drug addiction. *The New Republic*.

Emanuel, E.J., Fairclough, D.L., & Emanuel, L.L. (2000). Attitudes and desires related to euthanasia and physician-assisted suicide among terminally ill patients and their caregivers. *JAMA* 284(19), 2460-2468.http://www.tnr.com/doc.mhtml?i=20060703&s=emanuel070306

Engel, G.L. (1980-1981). A group dynamic approach to teaching and learning about grief. *Omega, The Journal of Death and Dying*, 11(1), 45-59.

Engel, S.E., Keily, D.K., & Mitchell, S.L. (2006). Satisfaction with end-of-life care for nursing home residents with advanced dementia. *Journal of the American Geriatrics Society*, 54, 1567-1572.

Epting, F.R., & Neimeyer, R.A. (1984). *Personal meanings of death: Applications of personal construct theory to clinical practice*. Washington, DC: Francis and Taylor.

Erickson, F. (2002). Culture and human development. *Human Development*, 45, 299-306.

Erikson, E.H. (1959). *Identity and the life cycle*. New York: International Universities Press.

Erikson, E.H. (1963). *Childhood and society* (2nd ed.). New York: W. W. Norton.

Erikson, E.H. (1968). *Identity: Youth and crisis*. New York: W. W. Norton.

Erikson, E.H. (1982). *The life cycle completed: A review*. New York: W. W. Norton.

Erikson, E.H. (1997). *The life cycle completed. Extended version with new chapters on the ninth stage of development by Joan M. Erikson*. New York: W. W. Norton.

Erikson, K. (1976). *Everything in its path*. New York: Simon and Schuster.

Etzioni, A. (2000). Toward a theory of public ritual. *Sociological Theory*, 18, 44-59.

Everly, G.S., Jr. (Editor.) (1995). *Innovations in disaster and trauma psychology, Vol 1: Applications in emergency services and disaster response*. Ellicott City, MD: Chevron.

Everly, G.S., & Mitchell, J.T. (1999). *Critical Incident Stress Management (CISM): A new era and standard of care in crisis intervention* (2nd ed.). Ellicott City, MD: Chevron.

Eyetsemitan, F. (1998). Stifled grief in the workplace. *Death Studies*, 22, 470-480.

Faber-Langendoen, K., & Lanken, P.N. (2000). Dying patients in the intensive care unit: Forgoing treatment, maintaining care. *Annals of Internal Medicine*, 133, 886-893.

Fadiman, A. (1997). *The spirit catches you and you fall down*. Stanford, CA: Stanford University Press.

Fairbank, J.A., Schlenger, W.E., Saigh, P.A., and Davidson, J.R.T. (1995). An epidemiologic profile of post-traumatic stress disorder: prevalence, comorbidity, and risk factors. In M. Friedman, D. Charney, & A. Deutch (Eds.), *Neurobiological and clinical consequences of stress: from normal adaptation to post-traumatic stress disorder*. Philadelphia/New York: Lippincott-Raven.

Falicov, C. (1998). *Latino families in therapy: A guide to multicultural practice*. New York: Guilford Press.

Farrell, Kirby (1998). *Post-traumatic culture: injury and interpretation in the nineties*. Baltimore: Johns Hopkins University Press.

Faschingbauer, T.R. (1981). *Texas Revised Inventory of Grief Manual*. Houston, TX: Honeycomb Publishing.

Faust, J. & Katchen, L.B. (2004). Treatment of children with complicated posttraumatic stress reactions. *Psychotherapy: Theory, Research, Practice, Training*, 41, 426-437.

Federal Trade Commission (1994). *Funeral industry practices trade regulation rule: Final amended trade regulation rule*. Washington, DC: Bureau of Consumer Protection.

Feifel, H. (1959). *The meaning of death*. New York: McGraw-Hill.

Field, D. & Walter, T. (2003). Death and the media, *Mortality*, 8, 1-4.

Field, M. (in press). How people die in the United States. In J.L. Werth, Jr. & D. Blevins (Eds.), *decision making near the end of life: Recent developments and future directions*. Philadelphia: Routledge.

Field, M.J., & Cassel, C.K. (Eds.) (1997). *Approaching death: Improving care at the end of life*. Washington, DC: Institute of Medicine.

Field, N. P. & Friedrichs, M. (2004). Continuing bonds in coping with the death of a husband. *Death Studies*, 28, 597-620.

Field, N.P., Gao, B., & Paderna, L. (2005). Continuing bonds in bereavement: An attachment theory based perspective. *Death Studies*, 29, 277-299.

Figley, C.R. (1995). (Editor). *Compassion fatigue: Copying with secondary traumatic stress disorder in those who treat the traumatized*. New York: Brunner/Mazel.

Figley, C.R. and McCubbin, H.I. (1983). (Editors.) *Stress and the family, Volume II: Coping with catastrophe*. New York: Brunner/Mazel.

Fineberg, I.C. (2005). Preparing professionals for family conferences in palliative care: Evaluation results of an interdisciplinary approach. *Journal of Palliative Medicine*, 8(4), 857-865.

Finlay, I.G., Wheatley, V.J., & Izdebski, C. (2005). The House of Lords Select Committee on the Assisted Dying for the Terminally Ill Bill: Implications for specialist palliative care. *Palliative Medicine*, 19, 444-453.

Finucane, R.C. (1996). *Ghosts: Appearances of the dead and cultural transformation*. Amherst, NY: Prometheus Books.

Fish, S. & Shelly, J.A. (1978). *Spiritual Care: The nurse's role*. Downers Grove, IL: InterVarsity Press.

Fitzgerald, H. (2003). *The grieving child (2nd Edition)* NY: Simon & Schuster.

Fleming, S., & Adolph, R. (1986). Helping bereaved adolescents: Needs and responses. In C. Corr & J. McNeil (Eds.), *Children and death* (pp. 97-118). New York: Springer Publishing Co.

Fleming, S. & Balmer, L. (1996). Bereavement in adolescence. In C. Corr & D. Balk (Eds.), *Handbook of adolescent death and bereavement* (pp. 139-154). New York: Springer Publishing Company.

Foley, G.V. & Whittam, E.H. (1990). Care of the child dying of cancer: Part I. *CA: A Cancer Journal for Clinicians*, 40,327-354.

Folkman, S. (1991). Coping across the life span: Theoretical issues. In E. M. Cummings, A.L. Greene, & K.H. Karraker (Eds.), *Life-span developmental psychology: Perspectives on stress and coping* (pp. 3-19). Hillsdale, NJ: Lawrence Erlbaum.

Folkman, S. (1997). Positive psychological states and coping with severe stress. *Social Science & Medicine, 45,* 1207-1221.

Folkman, S. (2001). Revised coping theory and the process of bereavement. In M.S. Stroebe, R.O. Hansson, W. Stroebe, & H. Schut (Eds.), *Handbook of bereavement research: Consequences, coping, and care* (pp. 563-584). Washington, DC: American Psychological Association.

Ford, S.G. (2006). *The role of imagined interactions and self-efficacy in psychosocial adjustment to spousal bereavement: A communication perspective.* Unpublished doctoral dissertation, Louisiana State University.

Fulton, R. (2003). Anticipatory mourning: A critique of the concept. *Mortality, 8,* 342-351.

Forbat, L., & Service, K.P. (2005). Who cares? Contextual layers in end-of-life care for people with intellectual disability and dementia. *Dementia, 4,* 413-425.

Forbes, T.R. (1970). Life and death in Shakespeare's London. *American Scientist, 58,* 511-520.

Fortner, B.V., Neimeyer, R.A. (1999). Death anxiety in older adults: A quantitative review. *Death Studies, 23,* 387-411.

Foster, L.W., & McLellan, L.J. (2002). Translating psychosocial insight into ethical discussions supportive of families in end-of-life decision making. *Social Work in Health Care, 35*(3), 37-51.

Foti, M.E., Bartels, S.J., Van Citters, A.D., Merriman, M.P., & Fletcher, K.E. (2005). End-of-life treatment preferences of persons with serious mental illness. *Psychiatric Services, 56,* 585-591.

Fox, M. (1981). (Editor). *Western spirituality: Historical roots, ecumenical routes.* Santa Fe, NM: Bear & Company.

Fraiberg, S. (1959). *The magic years: Understanding and handling the problems of early childhood.* New York: Charles Scribner.

Frankl, V.E. (1959). *Man's search for meaning.* New York: Pocket Books.

Fremont, W.P. (2004) Childhood reactions to terrorism-induced trauma: A review of the past 10 years. *Journal of the American Academy of Child and Adolescent Psychiatry, 43,* 381-392.

Freud, S. (1959). Thoughts for the times on war and death. In *Sigmund Freud: Collected Papers Volume 4.* New York: Basic Books. (Originally published 1915).

Freud, S. (1959). *Mourning and melancholia.* In J. Strachey (Ed. & Trans.), *The standard edition of the complete psychological works of Sigmund Freud* (Vol. 14, pp. 237-258). London: Hogarth Press. (Original work published 1917).

Freud, S. (1961a). Totem and taboo. In J. Strachey (Ed. & Trans.), *The Standard Edition of the Complete Psychological Works of Sigmund Freud,* (Vol. 13, pp. 1-162.) London: Hogarth Press. (Original work published 1912-13.)

Freud, S. (1961b). Mourning and melancholia. In J. Strachey (Ed. & Trans.), *The Standard Edition of the Complete Psychological Works of Sigmund Freud,* (Vol. 14, pp. 243-258.) London: Hogarth Press. (Original work published 1917.)

Freud, S. (1975). *The standard edition of the complete psychological works of Sigmund Freud.* (J. Strachey, A. Freud, A. Strachey, & A. Tyson, translators). London: Hogarth Press.

Freudenberger, H.J. and Gallagher, K.M. (1995). Emotional consequences of loss for our adolescents. *Psychotherapy: Theory, Research, Practice, Training, 32,* 150-153.

Freyer, D.R. (2004). Care of the dying adolescent: Special considerations. *Pediatrics*, 113(2), 381-388.

Friedman, Matthew, J. & Marsella, Anthony, J. (2001). Posttraumatic stress disorders: an overview. In A. Marcalla, M. Friedman. E. Gerrity, & R. Scurfield (Eds.), *Ethnocultural aspects of posttraumatic stress disorder: Issues research and clinical application.* p. 107. Washington, DC: American Psychological Association.

Fritzsche, Peter (2004). *Stranded in the present: modern times and the melancholy of history.* Cambridge: Harvard University Press.

Fullerton, C.S., Ursano, R.J., Reeves, J., Shigemura, J. & Grieger, T. (2006). Perceived safety in disaster workers following 9/11. *Journal of Nervous and Mental Disease.* 194, 61-63.

Fulton, R. (1987). Unanticipated grief. In C.A. Corr & R.A. Pacholski (Eds.). *Death: Completion and discovery* (pp. 49-60). Lakewood, OH: The Association for Death Education and Counseling.

Fulton, R. (2003). Anticipatory mourning: A critique of the concept. *Mortality*, 8, 342-351.

Fulton, R. & Fulton, J. (1971). A psychosocial aspect of terminal care: Anticipatory grief. *Omega: The Journal of Death and Dying*, 2, 91-100.

Fulton, R. & Owen, G. (1987-1988). Death and society in twentieth century America. *Omega: The Journal of Death and Dying*, 18, 379-395.

Fulton, R., & Gottesman, D.J. (1980). Anticipatory grief: A psychosocial concept reconsidered. *British Journal of Psychiatry*, 137, 45-54.

Funeral Consumer Alliance (2006). What you should know about embalming. Retrieved November 20, 2006, from http://www.funerals.org/faq/embalm.htm.

Furedi, F. (1998). New Britain—a nation of victims. *Society*, 35(3), 80-84.

Fuse, T. (1980). To be or not to be. *Stress*, 1(3), 18-25.

Gabbay, B.B., Matsumura, S., Etzioni, S., Asch, S.M., Rosenfeld, K.E., Shiojiri, T., et al. (2005). Negotiating end-of-life decision making: A comparison of Japanese and U.S. residents' approaches. Academic medicine: *Journal of the Association of American Medical Colleges*, 80, 617-621.

Gallup International Institute. (1997). *Spiritual beliefs and the dying process: A report on a national survey.* Princeton, NJ: Nathan Cummings Foundation and Fetzer Institute, sponsors.

Galvin, K.M., Bylund, C.L., & Brommel, B.J. (2004). *Family communication, cohesion, and change (6th Edition).* Boston: Allyn and Bacon.

Gamble, V.N., & Stone, D. (2006). U.S. policy on health inequities: The interplay of politics and research. *Journal of Health Politics, Policy and Law*, 31, 93-126.

Gamino, L.A. (2003). Critical incident stress management and other crisis counseling approaches. In M. Lattanzi-Licht & K.J. Doka (Eds.), *Living with Grief: Coping with Public Tragedy* (pp. 123-138). New York: Brunner-Routledge.

Gamino, L.A. (April/May/June, 2005). Bereaved parents' reactions to media reporting: A case study. *The Forum*, 31(2), 9-10.

Gamino, L.A., Easterling, L.W. and Sewell, K.W. (2003) The role of spiritual experience in adapting to bereavement. In G.R. Cox, R.A. Bendiksen and R.G. Stevenson (Eds.), *Making sense of death: Spiritual, pastoral and personal aspects of dying, death and bereavement.* Amityville, NY: Baywood Publishing.

Garand, L., Mitchell, A.M., Dietrick, A., Hijjawi, S.P., &. Pan, D. (2006). Suicide in older adults: Nursing assessment of suicide risk. *Issues in Mental Health Nursing*, 27, 355-370.

Garbarino, J., & Kostelny, K. (1996). The effects of political violence on Palestinian children's behavior problems. *Child Development*, 67, 33-45.

Garces-Foley, K. (2006). Hospice and the politics of spirituality. *Omega: The Journal of Death and Dying*, 53, 117-136.

Gardner, J.E., Scherman, A., Efthimiadis, M.S., & Shultz, S.K. (2004). Panamanian grandmothers' family relationships and adjustment to having a grandchild with a disability. *International Journal of Aging & Human Development*, 59, 305-320.

Gaster, T.H. (1964). In J. Frazer, *The new golden bough*. New York: New American Library.

Gauthier, D.M. (2005). Decision making near the end of life. *Journal of Hospice & Palliative Nursing*, 2, 82-90.

Gauthier, D.M., & Swigart, V.A. (2003). The contextual nature of decision making near the end-of-life: Hospice patients' perspectives. *American Journal of Hospice & Palliative Care*, 20, 121-128.

Geis, H., Whittlesey, S., McDonald, N., Smith, K., & Pfefferbaum, B. (1998). Bereavement and loss in childhood. *Childhood and Adolescent Psychiatric Clinics of North America*, 7(1), 73-85.

Genevro, J.L., Marshall, T. & Miller, T. (2003). *Report on bereavement and grief research*. Washington, DC: Center for the Advancement of Health.

Gert, B., Culver, C., & Clouser, K.D. (1997). *Bioethics: A return to fundamentals*. Oxford, UK: Oxford University Press.

Gibbs, L. (2002). *Evidence-based practice for the helping professions: A practical guide*. Pacific Grove, CA: Thompson/Brooks Cole.

Gibson, A.B., Roberts, P.C., & Buttery, T.J. (1982). *Death education: A concern for the living*. Bloomington, IN: Phi Delta Kappa Educational Foundation.

Gibson, C.A., Breitbart, W., Tomarken, A., Kosinski, A., & Nelson, C.J. (2006). Mental health issues near the end of life. In J.L. Werth & D. Blevins (Eds.), *Psychosocial issues near the end of life: A resource for professional care providers* (pp. 137-162). Washington, DC: American Psychological Association.

Gil, E. (2006). *Helping abused and traumatized children: Integrating directive and nondirective approaches*. New York: Guilford Press.

Gilbert, K.R. (1989). Interactive grief and coping in the marital dyad. *Death Studies*, 13, 605-626.

Gilbert, K.R. (1996). "We've had the same loss, why don't we have the same grief?" Loss and differential grief in families, *Death Studies*, 20, 269-283.

Gilbert, K.R. (1997). Evaluating internet resources. Available online at http://www.indiana.edu/~hperf656/spring98/evaluate.html .

Gilbert, K.R., & Smart, L.S. (1992). *Coping with infant or fetal loss: The couple's healing process*. New York: Brunner/Mazel.

Gilbert, R. (1995) Protestant perspectives on grief and children. In E. Grollman (Ed.), *Bereaved children and teens: A support guide for parents and professionals*. Boston: Beacon.

Gilbert, R. (1996) *Spirituality: Course, journey, experience.* Unpublished workbook used at the International Bereavement Conference, London, Ontario.

Gilbert, R. (1999). *Finding your way after your parent dies.* Ave Maria Press: Notre Dame, Indiana.

Gilbert, R. (2002a). *Health care and spirituality: Listening, assessing, caring.* Amityville, NY: Baywood Publishing.

Gilbert, R. (2002b) Spirituality and religion: Risks for complicated mourning. In G.R. Cox, R.A. Bendiksen and R.G. Stevenson (Eds.), *Complicated grieving and bereavement: Understanding and treating people experiencing loss.* Amityville, NY: Baywood Publishing.

Gilbert, R. (2006). A pastoral reflective on the spiritual dimensions of loss. *Illness, Crisis and Loss,* 14(2), 89-199.

Gilliland, G. & Fleming, S. (1998). A comparison of spousal anticipatory grief and conventional grief. *Death Studies,* 22, 541-569.

Girard, C. (1993). Age, gender, and suicide. *American Sociological Review,* 58, 553-574.

Gist, R. & Lubin, B. (1999) *Response to disaster: Psychosocial, community, and ecological approaches.* Philadelphia, PA: Brunner/Mazel.

Gladding, S.T. (2001). *The counseling dictionary: Concise definitions of frequently used terms.* Upper Saddle River, NJ: Merrill Prentice Hall.

Glaser, B. & Strauss, A. (1965). *Awareness of dying.* Chicago: Aldine.

Glaser, B. & Strauss, A. (1968). *Time for dying.* Chicago: Aldine.

Glick, I.D., Weiss, R. S., & Parkes, C.M. (1974). *The first year of bereavement.* New York: Wiley.

Golden, T.R. (1996). *Swallowed by a snake: The gift of the masculine side of healing.* Kensington, Maryland: Golden Healing Publishing.

Goldman, L. (2000). *Life and loss: A guide to help grieving children* (2nd Edition). New York: Taylor and Francis.

Goldman, L. (2002). *Breaking the silence: A resource guide to help children with complicated grief - Suicide, Homicide, AIDS, Violence, and Abuse (2n ed.)* Washington, DC: Taylor & Francis.

Goldman, L. (2004). Counseling with children in contemporary society. *Journal of Mental Health Counseling,* 26(2), 168-187.

Gonzales, Alberto, Atty. Gen., et al. v. Oregon, et al., No. 04-623 (2006).

Goodkin, K.U., Baldewicz, T.T., & Blaney, N.T., Asthana, D., Kumar, M., Shapshak, P., Leeds, B., Burkhalter, J.E., Rigg, D., Tyll, M.D., Cohen, J., & Zheng, W.L. (2001). Physiological effects of bereavement and bereavement support group interventions. In M.S. Stroebe, R.O. Hansson, W. Stroebe, & H. Schut (Eds.), *Handbook of bereavement research: Consequences, coping, and care* (pp. 671-703). Washington, DC: American Psychological Association.

Goodkin, K., Blaney, N. T., Feaster, D. J., Baldewicz, T., Burkhalter, J., & Leeds, B. (1999). A randomized controlled clinical trial of a bereavement support group intervention in human immunodeficiency virus type 1-seropositive and seronegative homosexual men. *Archives of General Psychiatry,* 56, 52-59.

References 421

Goodkin, K. Lee, D. Molina, R., Zheng, W., Frasca, A., O'Mellan, S., Asthana, D., Shapshak, P. & Khamis, I. (2006). Complicated bereavement: Disease state or state of being? *Omega: The Journal of Death and Dying.* 52, 2005-2006, 21-36.

Goodman, N. (1992). *Introduction to sociology.* New York: HarperCollins.

Gordon, A. K. & Klass, D. (1979). *They need to know: How to teach children about death,* Englewood Cliffs, NJ: Prentice-Hall.

Goss, R. & Klass, D. (2005). *Dead but not lost: Grief narratives in religious traditions.* Walnut Creek, CA: AltaMira.

Goss, R. & Klass, D. (2006). Buddhisms and death. In K. Garces-Foley (Ed.), *Death and religion in a changing world.* Armonk, NY: M.E. Sharpe.

Grassman, E.J. & Whitaker, A. (2006) With or without faith. Spiritual care in the Church of Sweden at a time of transition. *Omega: The Journal of Death and Dying,* 53, 153-172.

Green, B.L. (2000). Traumatic loss: Conceptual and empirical links between trauma and bereavement. *Journal of Personal and Interpersonal Loss,* 5, 1-17.

Green, C.R., Anderson, K.O., Baker, T.A., Campbell, L.C. Decker, S., Fillingim, R.B., et al. (2003). The unequal burden of pain: Confronting racial and ethnic disparities in pain. *Pain Medicine,* 4, 277-294.

Green, C.R., Ndao-Brumblay, S.K., West, B., & Washington, T. (2005). Differences in prescription opioid analgesic availability: Comparing minority and White pharmacies across Michigan. *Journal of Pain,* 6, 689-699.

Greenberg, J., Solomon, S. & Pyszczynski, T. (1997). Terror management theory of self-esteem and cultural worldviews: Empirical assessments and conceptual refinements. In M. P. Zanna (Ed.), *Advances in experimental social psychology* (Vol. 29, pp. 61–139). Orlando, FL: Academic Press.

Greenberg, L.S., Watson, J.C., & Lietaer, G. (Eds.) (1998). *Handbook of experiential psychotherapy.* New York: Guilford Press.

Grollman, E.A. (1967). *Explaining death to children.* Boston: Beacon Press.

Grollman, E.A. (1977). *Living when a loved one has died.* Boston: Beacon Press.

Grollman, E.A. (1990). *Talking about death: A dialogue between parent and child* (3rd ed.). Boston: Beacon Press.

Grollman, E.A. (2000). *Living with loss, healing with hope: A Jewish perspective.* Boston: Beacon Press.

Grunfeld, E., Coyle, D., Whelan, T., Clinch, J., Reyno, L., Earle, C.C., Willon, A., Viola, R., Coristine, M., Janz, T. & Glossup, R. (2004). Family caregiver burden: results of a longitudinal study of breast cancer patients and their principal caregivers. *Canadian Medical Association Journal,* 170, 1795-1801.

Gunaratnam, Y. (1997). Culture is not enough: A critique of multi-culturalism in palliative care. In D. Field, J. Hockey, & N. Small (Eds.), *Death, gender and ethnicity* (pp. 166-186). New York: Routledge.

Gutheil, T.G. & Gabbard, G.O. (1998). Misuses and misunderstandings of boundary theory in clinical and regulatory settings. *American Journal of Psychiatry,* 155, 409-414.

Haine, R.A., Wolchik, S.A., Sandler, I.N., Millsap, R.E., Ayers, T.S. (2006). Positive parenting as a protective resource for parentally bereaved children. *Death Studies*, 30, 1-28.

Haley, A. & Brody, B. (1996). A multi-institutional collaborative policy on medical futility. *Journal of the American Medical Association*, 276, 571-574.

Haley, W.E., Larson, D.G., Kasl-Godley, J., Neimeyer, R.A., & Kwilosz, D.M. (2003). Roles for psychologists in end-of-life care: Emerging models of practice. *Professional Psychology: Research and Practice*, 34, 626-633.

Hall, M. & Irwin, M. (2001). Physiological indices of functioning in bereavement. In M.S. Stroebe, R.O. Hansson, W. Stroebe, & H. Schut (Eds.), *Handbook of bereavement research: Consequences, coping, and care* (pp. 473-492). Washington, DC: American Psychological Association.

Hallenbeck, J., Goldstein, M.K., & Mebane, E. (1996). Cultural considerations of death and dying in the United States. *Clinics in Geriatric Medicine*, 12, 393-406.

Handy, E.S.C., & Pukui, M.K. (1972). *The Polynesian family system in Ka'u, Hawai'i*. Rutland, VT. Tuttle.

Hannay, M. & Newvine, T. (2006). Perceptions of distance learning: A comparison of online and traditional learning. *MERLOT Journal of Online Learning and Teaching*, 2(1), 1-11. Retrieved on July 3, 2006 at http://jolt.merlot.org/Vol2_No1.htm.

Hansson, R.O., Berry, J.O., & Berry, M.E. (1999). The bereavement experience: Continuing commitment after the loss of a loved one. In J.M. Adams & W.H. Warren (Eds.), *Handbook of interpersonal commitment and relationship stability* (pp. 281-291). Dordrecht, Netherlands: Kluwer Academic Publishers.

Hanzlick, R. (1997). Death registration: History, methods, and legal issues. *Journal of Forensic Science*, 42(2), 265-269.

Hardt, D.V. (1979). *Death: The final frontier*. Englewood Cliffs, NJ: Prentice-Hall.

Hardwig, J. (1990). What about the family? *Hastings Center Report*, 20(2), 5-10.

Harris, C.E. & Alcorn, S.P. (2001). To solve a deadly shortage: Economic incentives for human organ donation. *Issues in Law & Medicine*, 16, 215-225.

Hawley, D.R. (2000). Clinical implications of family resilience. *The American Journal of Family Therapy*, 28, 101-116.

Hawley, D.R. & DeHaan, L. (1996). Toward a definition of family resilience: Integrating life-span and family perspectives. *Family Process*, 35, 283-298.

Hawton, K. & Harriss, L. (2006). Deliberate self-harm in people aged 60 years and over: Characteristics and outcome of a 20-year cohort. *International Journal of Geriatric Psychiatry*, 21, 572-581.

Hayes, C.L., & Kalish, R.A. (1987-1988). Death-related experiences and funerary practices of the Hmong refugee in the United States. *Omega: The Journal of Death and Dying*, 18, 63-70.

Hayslip, B. (2003). Death denial: Hiding and camouflaging death. In C. D. Bryant (Ed.), Handbook of death and dying (pp. 34-42). Thousand Oaks, CA: Sage.

Hayslip, B., Allen, S. E., & McCoy-Roberts, L. (2001). The role of gender in a three-year longitudinal study of bereavement: A test of the experienced competence model. In D.A. Lund (Ed.), *Men coping with grief* (pp. 121-146). Amityville, NY: Baywood Publishing Co.

Hayslip, B. & Hansson, R.O. (2003). Death awareness and adjustment across the life span. In C.D. Bryant (Ed.). *Handbook of death and dying* (Vol.1, pp.437-447). Thousand Oaks, CA: Sage.

Hayslip, B. & Peveto, C.A. (2005). *Cultural changes in attitudes toward death, dying, and bereavement.* New York: Springer.

Heins, J.K., Heins, A., Grammas, M., Costello, M., Huang, K., & Mishra, S. (2006). Disparities in analgesia and opioid prescribing practices for patients with musculoskeletal pain in the emergency department. *Journal of Emergency Nursing*, 32, 219-224.

Helbok, C.M., Marinelli, R.P., & Walls, R.T. (2006). National survey of ethical practices across rural and urban communities. *Professional Psychology: Research and Practice*, 37, 36-44.

Hemmings, P. (2005). The family perspective in bereavement. In B. Monroe & F. Kraus, *Brief interventions with bereaved children* (pp. 49-64). New York: Oxford University Press.

Henig, N.R., Faul, J.L., & Raffin, T.A. (2001). Biomedical ethics and the withdrawal of advanced life support. *Annual Review of Medicine*, 52, 79-92.

Henry, A.F., & Short, J.F. (1954). *Suicide and homicide.* New York: Free Press.

Henry, D.B., Tolan, P.H. & Gorman-Smith, D. (2004). Have there been lasting effects associated with the September 11, 2001, terrorist attacks among inner-city parents and children? *Professional Psychology: Research and Practice*, 35, 542-547.

Herman, J. (1992).*Trauma and recovery.* New York: Basic Books.

Hern, H.E., Jr., Koenig, B.A., Moore, L.J., & Marshall, P.A. (1998). The difference that culture can make in end-of-life decision making. *Cambridge Quarterly of Healthcare Ethics*, 7, 27-40.

Hickman, S.E., Hammes, B.J., Moss, A.H., & Tolle, S.W. (2005). Hope for the future: Achieving the original intent of advance directives. Improving end of life care: Why has it been so difficult? *Hastings Center Report Special Report* 35(6), S26-S30.

Hodge, D. (2005). Developing a spiritual assessment toolbox: A discussion of the strengths and limitations of five different assessment methods. *Health & Social Work*, **30**, 314-323.

Hogan, N., & De Santis, L. (1992). Adolescent sibling bereavement: An ongoing attachment. *Qualitative Health Research*, 2, 159-177.

Hogan, N. & DeSantis, L. (1996). Basic constructs of a theory of adolescent sibling bereavement. In D. Klass, P. Silverman, & S. Nickman (Eds.) *Continuing bonds: New understandings of grief* (pp. 235-254). Washington, DC: Taylor and Francis.

Hogan, N. S., Greenfield, D.B., & Schmidt, L.A. (2001). Development and validation of the Hogan Grief Reaction Checklist. *Death Studies*, 25, 1-32.

Hogan, N.S., Greenfield, D.B., & Schmidt, L.A. (2001). Development and validation of the Hogan Grief Reaction Checklist. *Death Studies*, 25, 1-32.

Hogan, N.S., Worden, J.W., & Schmidt, L.A. (2006). Considerations in conceptualizing complicated grief. *Omega, the Journal of Death and Dying*, 52, 81-85.

Holinger, P. C. (1987). *Violent deaths in the United States.* New York: Guilford.

Holland, J. M., Currier, J. M., & Neimeyer, R. A. (2006). Meaning reconstruction in the first two years of bereavement: The role of sense-making and benefit-finding. *Omega, The Journal of Death and Dying*, 53, 175-191.

Holland, J.M. & Neimeyer, R.A. (2005). Reducing the risk of burnout in end-of-life settings: The role of daily spiritual experiences and training. *Palliative and Supportive Care*, 3, 173-181.

Homan, P. (2005). Responding to crisis: A bereavement perspective. *NHPCO Newsline Quarterly Insights Edition*, 3, 35-37.

Hoover, J.H., Markell, M.A., & Wanger, P. (2004/2005). Death and grief as experienced by adults with developmental disabilities: Initial explorations. *Omega, The Journal of Death and Dying*, 50(3), 181-196.

Hopkins, A.R. (2002). Children and grief. The role of the early childhood educator. *Young Children*, 57, 40-46.

Hosogoe, S. (Producer), & Itami J. (Director). (1984). *The funeral.* [Motion picture]. Japan: Fox Lorber.

Hostler, L. (1978). The development of the child's concept of death. In O.J.Z. Sahler (Ed.), *The child and death.* St. Louis, MO: C.V. Mosby.

Howarth, G. (2007). *Death and dying: A sociological introduction.* Malden, MA: Polity, 2007.

Hoyert, D. (2001) The autopsy, medicine, and mortality statistics. National Center for Health Statistics. *Vital Health Statistics* 3, 32.

Hurd, R.C. (2004). A teenager revisits her father's death during childhood: A study in resilience and healthy mourning. *Adolescence*, 39, 337-354.

Hutchison, J. & Rupp, J. (1999) *May I walk you home? Courage and comfort for caregivers of the very ill.* Notre Dame, IN: Ave Maria Press.

Hutti, M.H. (1992). Parents' perceptions of the miscarriage experience. *Death Studies*, 16, 401-415.

Hwang, W. (2006). The psychotherapy adaptation and modification framework: Applications to Asian Americans. *American Psychologist*, 61(7), 702-715.

Hynes, A.M., & Hynes-Berry, M. (1986). *Bibliotherapy: The interactive process: A handbook.* Boulder, CO: Westview Press.

Imara, M. (1980) Director of the Center for Religion and Psychotherapy and the Psychological Counseling Center (Brandeis University), interview – Paramus, NJ.

Imber-Black, E. (2004). Rituals and the healing process. In F. Wash & M. McGoldrick (Eds.), *Living beyond loss: Death in the family* (2nd Edition) (pp. 341-3), New York: W.W. Norton.

Imber-Black, E. (2005). Creating meaningful rituals for new life cycle transitions. In B. Carter & M. McGoldrick (Eds.), *The expanded family life cycle: Individual, family, and social perspectives* (3rd Edition) (pp. 202-214). Boston: Allyn & Bacon.

Imber-Black, E. & Roberts, J. (1992). *Rituals for our times: Celebrating, healing, and changing our lives and our relationships.* New York: Harper Collins.

Impens, A. J. (2005). Bereavement related mortality among older adults. Unpublished doctoral dissertation, University of Michigan.

Institute of Medicine (2003). *Unequal treatment.* Washington, DC: National Academies Press.

International Work Group on Death, Dying and Bereavement(1994). *Statements on dying, death, and bereavement.* London, Ontario: King's College.

International Work Group on Death Dying and Bereavement (1999). Assumptions and Principles of Spiritual Care. In K.J. Doka & J.D. Morgan (Eds.), *Death and Spirituality*. Amityville, NY: Baywood Publishing Co.

International Work Group on Death, Dying, and Bereavement (2006). Caregivers in death, dying, and bereavement situations. *Death Studies*, 30, 649-663

In the matter of Karen Quinlan, an alleged incompetent (1976). Supreme Court of New Jersey. 70 NJ 10; 355 A.2d 647.

Irion P., (1999). Ritual responses to death. In J.D. Davidson & K.J. Doka, (Eds.), *Living with grief: At work, at school, at worship*. Littleton, PA: Brunner/Mazel.

Irish, D., Lundquist, K.F., & Nelsen, V.J. (1993). (Editors). *Ethnic variations in dying, death, and grief: Diversity in universality*. Washington, DC: Taylor & Francis.

Irwin, W.H. (2006). Feeding patients with advanced dementia: the role of the speech-language pathologist in making end-of-life decisions (Health care forum). *Journal of Medical Speech-Language Pathology*, 14(2), 3-6.

Iwashyna, T.J. & Christakis, N.A. (1998). Attitude and self-reported practice regarding hospice referral in a national sample of internists. *Journal of Palliative Medicine*, 1, 241-248.

Jackson, J.D. (2003). Justice for all: Putting victims at the heart of criminal justice? *Journal of Law and Society*, 30, 309-326.

Janet, P. (1978). *Mental state of hysteria*. New York: University Publishers of America.

Janoff-Bulman, R. (1992). *Shattered assumptions*. New York: Free Press.

Janoff-Bulman, R., & Berger, A.R. (2000). The other side of trauma, In J. H. Harvey & E. D. Miller (Eds.), *Loss and trauma*. Philadelphia: Brunner Mazel.

Jayasinghe, N., Spielman, L., Cancellare, D., Difede, J.A., Klausner, E.J., & Giosan, C. (2005). Predictors of treatment utilization in World Trade Center attack disaster workers: Role of race/ethnicity and symptom severity. *International Journal of Emergency Mental Health*, 7, 91-100.

Jezuit, D.L. (2000). Suffering of critical care nurses with end-of-life decisions. *Official Journal of the Academy of Medical-Surgical Nurses*, 9, 145-152.

Johnson, S.H. (2005). Making room for dying: End of life care in nursing homes. Improving end of life care: Why has it been so difficult? *Hastings Center Report Special Report* 35(6), S37-S41.

Joinson, C. (1992). Coping with compassion fatigue: Taking care of one's self while taking care of others. *Nursing*, 22, 116-121.

Jones, J.H. (1992). *Bad blood: The Tuskegee syphilis experiment*. New York: Simon & Schuster.

Jones, K. (2005). Diversities in approach to end-of-life: A view from Britain of the qualitative literature. *Journal of Research in Nursing*, 10(4), 431-454. Paper and annotated bibliography Retrieved January 18, 2007 from http://www2.warwick.ac.uk/fac/med/research/csri/ethnicityhealth/research/end_of_life/

Jonker, G. (1996). The knife's edge: Muslim burial in the diaspora. *Mortality*, 1, 27-43.

Jordan, J.R. (2000) Research that matters: Bridging the gap between research and practice in thanatology. *Death Studies* 24, 457-468.

Jordan, J.R. (2001). Is suicide bereavement different? A reassessment of the literature. *Suicide and Life-Threatening Behavior,* 31(1), 91-102.

Jordan, J.R. & Neimeyer, R.A. (2003) Does grief counseling work? *Death Studies,* 27(9), 765-786.

Jordan, J.R., Baker, J., Matteis, M., Rosenthal, S., & Ware, E.S. (2005). The Grief Evaluation Measure (GEM): An initial validation study. *Death Studies,* 29, 301-332.

Juckett, G. (2005). Cross-cultural medicine. *American Family Physician,* 72, 2267-2274.

Jung, C.G. (1933/1971). The stages of life (Translated by R.F.C. Hull). In J. Campbell (Ed.),*The portable Jung,* pp. 3–21. New York: Viking.

Jung, C.G. (1974). *The collected works of C.G. Jung.* Edited by H. Read, M. Fordham & G. Adler. London, UK: Routledge & Kegan Paul.

Kagawa-Singer, M. & Blackhall, L.J. (2001). Negotiating cross-cultural issues at the end of life: "You've got to go where he lives." *Journal of American Medical Association,* 286, 2993-3001.

Kagle, J.D. & Giebelhausen, P.H. (1994). Dual relationships and professional boundaries. *Social Work,* 39, 213-220.

Kahana, B., Dan, A., Kahana, E., & Kercher, K. (2004). The personal and social context of planning for end-of-life care. *Journal of the American Geriatric Society,* 52, 1163-1167.

Kalayjian, A.S. (1996). *Disaster and mass trauma: Global perspectives on post disaster mental health management.* Long Branch, NJ: Vista.

Kapust, L.R. (1982). Living with dementia: The ongoing funeral. *Social Work in Health Care,* 7(4), 79-91.

Kastenbaum, R. (1977). We covered death today. *Death Education,* 1, 85-92.

Kastenbaum, R. (1989). Death system. In R. Kastenbaum & B. Kastenbaum (Eds.), *Encyclopedia of death* (pp. 90-93). Phoenix: Oryx Press.

Kastenbaum, R. (1993). Reconstructing death in postmodern society. *Omega, The Journal of Death and Dying,* 27, 75-89.

Kastenbaum, R.J. (1995). *Death, society, and human experience* (5th Edition). Boston: Allyn & Bacon.

Kastenbaum, R. (1996). A world without death? First and second thoughts. *Mortality,* 1, 111-121.

Kastenbaum, R.J. (2001). *Death, society, and human experience* (7th Edition). Needham Heights, MA: Allyn & Bacon.

Kastenbaum, R. (2004). *Death, society, and human experience* (8th ed.). Boston: Allyn and Bacon.

Kastenbaum, R. (2004a). *On our way: The final passage through life and death.* Berkeley, CA: University of California Press.

Kastenbaum, R. (2004b). Death writ large. *Death Studies,* 28, 375-392.

Kastenbaum, R. (2007). *Death, society, and human experience* (9th ed.). Boston: Allyn & Bacon.

Kastenbaum, R. & Aisenberg, R. (1972). *The psychology of death.* New York: Springer.

Kauffman, J. (2005). *Guidebook on helping persons with mental retardation mourn.* Amityville, NY: Baywood Publishing Co.

Kaufman, K.R. & Kaufman, N.D. (2006). And then the dog died. *Death* Studies, 30, 61-76.

Kieran, M. (1997). *Media ethics: A philosophical approach.* Westport, CT: Praeger Publishers.

Kilier, C.M., Geller, P.A., & Ritsher, J.B. (2002). Affective disorders in the aftermath of miscarriage: A comprehensive review. *Archives of Women's Mental Health,* 5, 129-149.

Kilpatrick, D.G. (1986). Addressing the needs of traumatized victims. *The Practical Prosecutor.* 15-18. Houston, TX: The National College of District Attorneys, University of Houston Law Center.

Kilpatrick, D.G. & Resnick, H.S. (1993). PTSD associated with exposure to criminal victimization in clinical and community populations. In J. R. T. Davidson and E. B. Foa, (Eds.), *Posttraumatic stress disorder: DSM-IV and beyond* (pp. 113-143). Washington, DC: American Psychiatric Press.

King, P.A., & Wolf, L.E. (1998). Empowering and protecting patients: Lessons for physician-assisted suicide from the African-American experience. *Minnesota Law Review,* 82, 1015-1043.

Kingsbury, L.A. (2005). Person-centered planning and communication of end-of-life wishes with people who have developmental disabilities. *Journal of Religion, Disability, and Health,* 9(2), 81-90.

Kirkmayer, L.J. (2001) Confusion of the sense: Implications and ethnocultural variations in somatoform and dissociative disorders for PTSD. In A. Marcalla, M. Friedman. E. Gerrity, & R. Scurfield (Eds.), *Ethnocultural aspects of posttraumatic stress disorder: Issues research and clinical application.* Washington, DC: American Psychological Association.

Kirwin, K.M., & Hamrin, V. (2005). Decreasing the risk of complicated bereavement and future psychiatric disorders in children. *Journal of Child and Adolescent Psychiatric Nursing,* 18(1), 62-78.

Kissane, D. & Bloch, S. (2002). *Family focused grief therapy: A model for family-centered care during palliative care and bereavement.* Philadelphia: Open University Press.

Kissane, D.W., McKenzie, M., Block, S., Moskowitz, C., McKenzie, D.P., & O'Neill, I. (2006). Family focused grief therapy: A randomized, controlled trial in palliative care and bereavement. *American Journal of Psychiatry,* 163, 1208-1218.

Klaiman, M.H. (2005). Whose brain is it anyway? The comparative law of post-mortem organ retention. *Journal of Legal Medicine* 26, 475-490.

Klass, D. (1986). Marriage and divorce among bereaved parents in a self-help group. *Omega, The Journal of Death and Dying,* 17(3), 237-249.

Klass, D. (1988). *Parental grief: Solace and resolution.* New York: Springer.

Klass, D. (1999). Developing a cross-cultural model of grief: The state of the field. *Omega, The Journal of Death and Dying,* 39, 153-176.

Klass, D. (1999). *The spiritual lives of bereaved parents,* Philadelphia: Brunner/Mazel.

Klass, Dennis (2001). The inner representation of the dead child in the psychic and social narratives of bereaved parents. In Robert A. Neimeyer (Editor), *Meaning reconstruction & the experience of loss.* Washington, DC: American Psychological Association.

Klass, D. & Hutton, R.A. (1985.) Elisabeth Kübler-Ross as a religious leader. *Omega: The Journal of Death and Dying,* 16, 89-109.

Klass, D., Silverman, P.R., & Nickman, S.L. (Eds.). (1996). *Continuing bonds: New understandings of grief*. Washington, DC: Taylor & Francis.

Kleespies, P. (2004). *Life and death decisions: Psychological and ethical considerations in end-of-life care*. Washington, DC: American Psychological Association.

Klein, A.C. (1998). Buddhism. In C.J. Johnson & M.G. McGee (Editors), *How different religions view death and afterlife* (pp. 47-63). Philadelphia: The Charles Press.

Klein, H. (1974). Child victims of the holocaust. *Journal of Clinical Child Psychology*, 3, 44-47.

Klein, J., Stein, Z., & Susser, M. (1989). *Conception to birth: Epidemiology of prenatal development*. New York: Oxford University Press.

Kleinman, A. (1990). *The illness narratives: Suffering, healing and the human condition*. New York: Basic Books.

Klessig, J. (1992). The effects of values and culture on life-support decisions. *Western Journal of Medicine*, 157, 316-322.

Klopfenstein, K.J. (1999). Adolescents, cancer, and hospice. *Adolescent Medicine*, 10,436-43.

Knapp, S. & Slattery, J. (2004). Professional boundaries in nontraditional settings. *Professional Psychology: Research and Practice*, 35, 553-558.

Koenig, B. & Davies, B. (2003). Cultural dimensions in end-of-life care for children and their families. *When children die*. Institute of Medicine, Washington, DC: National Academies Press. Chapter pdf online retrieved January 18. 2007, from http://books.nap.edu/html/children_die/index.html

Koenig, B.A. & Gates-Williams, J. (1995). Understanding cultural difference in caring for dying patients. *Western Journal of Medicine*, 163, 244-249.

Koenig, H.G. (1997). *Is religion good for your health?* Binghamton: Haworth Press.

Koenig, H.G. (1998). Religious beliefs and practices of hospitalized medically ill older adults. *International Journal of Geriatric Psychiatry* 13, 213-224.

Koenig, H. (2004). Religion, spirituality, and medicine: Research findings and implications for clinical practice. *Southern Medical Journal*, 97, 1194-1200.

Koenig, H.G., McCullough, M.E., & Larson, D.B. (2001). *Handbook of religion and health*. New York: Oxford University Press.

Kogan, S.L., Blanchette, P.L., & Masaki, K. (2000). Talking to patients about death and dying: Improving communication across cultures. In K.L. Braun, J.H. Pietsch, & P.L. Blanchette (Eds). *Cultural Issues in End of Life Decision Making* (305-326). Thousand Oaks, CA: Sage.

Koocher, G. & O'Malley, (1981). *The Damocles syndrome: Psychological consequences of surviving childhood cancer*. New York: McGraw-Hill.

Korte, A. O. (1995-1996). *Despedidas* as reflections of death in Hispanic New Mexico. *Omega: The Journal of Death and Dying*, 32, 245-267.

Kovacs, G. (1982). Death and the question of immortality. *Death Education* 1, 15-24.

Kristjanson, L.J., & Aoun, S. (2004). Palliative care for families: Remembering the hidden patients. *Canadian Journal of Psychiatry*, 49, 359-365.

Krystal, H. (2002). What cannot be remembered or forgotten. In J. Kauffman (Ed.), *Loss of the assumptive world*. New York: Brunner-Routledge.

Kübler-Ross, E. (1969). *On death and dying*. New York: Macmillan.

Kübler-Ross, E. (1975). *Death: The final stage of growth*. Englewood Cliffs, NJ: Prentice-Hall.

Kubler-Ross, E. (1991) The dying child. In D. Papadatou & C. Papadatos (editors), *Children and death*. New York: Hemisphere Publishing Company.

Kubler-Ross, E., & Worden, J.W. (1977-78). Attitudes and experiences of death workshop attendees, *Omega, The Journal of Death and Dying*, 8(2), 91-106.

Kushner, H. (2001). *When bad things happen to good people*. 20th Anniversary edition. Schocken Books.

Kwak, J., & Haley, W.E. (2005). Current research findings on end-of-life decision making among racially or ethnically diverse groups. *The Gerontologist*, 45, 634-41.

Lacy, D. (2006). End-of-life decision making for nursing home residents with dementia: A survey of nursing home social services staff. *Health and Social Work*, 31(3), 189-199.

Lamb, V.L. (2003). Historical and epidemiological trends in mortality in the United States. In C.D. Bryant (Ed.) *Handbook of death and dying, Volume 1*, pp. 185-197. Thousand Oaks, CA: Sage.

Lambrecht, M. (1991). The value of computer-assisted instruction in death education. *Loss, Grief, and Care*, 4(1), 67-69.

Lamers, E.P. (1995). Children, death, and fairy tales. *Omega: The Journal of Death and Dying*, 31, 151-167.

Lamers, W. (2005). Autonomy, consent, and advance directives. In K. Doka, B. Jennings, & C. Corr (Eds.), *Ethical dilemmas at the end of life*. Washington, DC: Hospice Foundation of America.

Landsman, I.S. (2002). Crises of meaning in trauma and loss. In Jeffery Kauffman (Ed.). *Loss of the assumptive world: A theory of traumatic loss* (pp. 13-30). New York: Brunner-Routledge.

Lang, A. & Gottlieb, L. (1993). Parental grief reactions and marital intimacy following infant death. *Death Studies*, 17, 233-255,

Larman, J.S. (2004). Conjugal bereavement in younger and older widows and widowers: Influences of health and social support. Unpublished doctoral dissertation, Fielding Graduate Institute.

Lattanzi-Licht, M., & Doka, K.J. (2003). Coping with public tragedy. In M. Lattanzi-Licht & K.J. Doka (Eds.), *Living with Grief: Coping with Public Tragedy* (pp. 119-121). New York: Brunner-Routledge.

Lattanzi-Licht, M. Mahoney, J.J., & Miller, G.W. (1998). *The hospice choice*. New York: Simon & Schuster/Fireside.

Laungani, P. (1992). Cultural variations in the understanding and treatment of psychiatric disorders: India and England. *Counselling Psychology Quarterly*, 5(3), 231-244.

Laungani, P. (1996). Death and bereavement in India and England: A comparative analysis. *Mortality*, 1, 191-212.

Leaman, O. (1995). *Death and loss: Compassionate approaches in the classroom*. London: Cassell.

Ledger, S. (2005). The duty of nurses to meet patients' spiritual and/or religious needs. *British Journal of Nursing*, 14, 220-225.

Leenaars, A.A. (1989). Suicide across the adult life-span. *Crisis*, 10, 132-151.

Leenaars, A.A. (1996). Justin. In A. Leenaars & D. Lester (Ed.) *Suicide and the unconscious*, 139-174. Northvale, NJ: Jason Aronson.

Lehman, D.R., Lang, E.L., Wortman, C.B., & Sorenson, S.B. (1989). Long-term effects of sudden bereavement: Marital and parent-child relationships and children's reactions.*Journal of Family Psychology*, 2, 344-367.

Leichtentritt, R.D. (2004). The meaning that young Israeli adults ascribe to the least undesirable death. *Death Studies*, 28, 733-759.

Leming, M.R., & Dickinson, G.E. (2007). *Understanding dying, death, & bereavement* (6th ed.). Belmont, CA: Thomson/Wadsworth.

Lenhart, A.M. & McCourt, C. Adolescent unresolved grief in response to the death of a mother. *Professional School Counseling*, **3**(3), 189-196.

Leong, F.T. & Lopez, S. (2006). Guest editors' introduction. *Psychotherapy: Research, Practice and Training*, 4, 378-379.

LeShan, L. (1964). The world of the patient in severe pain of long duration. *Journal of Chronic Diseases*, 17, 119-126.

Lester, D. (1982). The distribution of sex and age among completed suicides. *International Journal of Social Psychiatry*, 28, 256-260.

Lester, D. (1986). The distribution of sex and age among victims of homicide. *International Journal of Social Psychiatry*, 32(2), 47-50.

Lester, D. (1990). Suicide prevention in the schools. *High School Journal*, **73**, 161-163.

Lester, D. (1994a). Are there unique features of suicide in adults of different ages and developmental stages? *Omega, The Journal of Death and Dying*, 29, 337-348.

Lester, D. (1994b). A comparison of fifteen theories of suicide. *Suicide & Life-Threatening Behavior*, 24, 80-88.

Lester, D. (1996). Psychological issues in euthanasia, suicide, and assisted suicide. *Journal of Social Issues*, 52, 51-62.

Lester, D. (1998). *Suicide in African Americans*. Commack, NY: Nova Science.

Lester, D. & Frank, M.L. (1987). When are babies perceived as male or female? *Perceptual & Motor Skills*, 65, 698.

Leurquin-Hallett, L. (1999). Professional boundaries in nephrology nursing practice. *ANNA Journal*, 26, 80-82.

Levine, J.E. (1996). Oklahoma City: The storying of a disaster. *Smith College Studies in Social Work*, 67, 21-38.

Leviton, D. (1977). The scope of death education. *Death Education*, 1, 41-56.

Leviton, D. & Kastenbaum, R.J. (1975). Death education. *Death Education*, 6 (3), 179-181.

Lichtenstein, R.L., Alcser, K.H., Corning, A.D., Bachman, J.G., & Doukas, D.J. (1997). African-Caucasian differences in attitudes toward physician-assisted suicide. *Journal of the National Medical Association*, 89, 125-133.

Lieberman, A.F., Compton, N.C., Horn, P.V. and Ippen, C.G. (2003). *Losing a parent to death in the early years: Guidelines for the treatment of traumatic bereavement in infancy and early childhood.* Washington, DC: Zero to Three Press.

Lifton, R.J. (1979). *The broken connection.* New York: Simon & Schuster.

Lifton, R. & Olsen, G. (1974). *Living and dying.* New York: Bantam Books.

Lin, H. & Bauer-Wu, S. (2003). Psycho-spiritual well being in patients with advanced cancer: An integrative review of the literature. *Journal of Advanced Nursing,* 44, 69-90.

Lin, K.K., Sandler, I. N., Ayers, T.S., Wolchik, S. A., Luecken, L. J. (2004). Resilience in parentally bereaved children and adolescents seeking preventive services. *Journal of Clinical Child and Adolescent Psychology,* 33(4), 673-683.

Lindemann, E. (1944) The symptomatology and management of acute grief. *American Journal of Psychiatry,* 6, 193-199.

Littlewood, J. (1993). The denial of death and rites of passage in contemporary societies. In D. Clark (Ed.), *The sociology of death: Theory, culture, practice* (pp. 69-84). Cambridge, MA: Blackwell.

Litz, B.T. (2004) *Early intervention for trauma and traumatic loss.* New York: Guilford Press.

Lo, B. (2000). *Resolving ethical dilemmas: A guide for clinicians.* Philadelphia: Lippincott, Williams, & Wilkins.

Lo, B. et al. (2002). Discussing religious and spiritual issues at the end of life. *JAMA,* 287 (6), 749-754.

Lomnitz, C. (2005). *Death and the idea of Mexico.* Cambridge, MA.: MIT Press.

Lozano-Nieto, A., Guijarro, E., & Berjano, E.J. (2006). Critical assessment of the World Wide Web as an information resource in higher education: Benefits, threats, and recommendations. *MERLOT Journal of Online Learning and Teaching,* 2(1), 22-29. Retrieved on July 3, 2006 at http://jolt.merlot.org/Vol2_No1.htm .

Lubetkin, E.I., Jia, H., Franks, P., & Gold, M.R. (2005). Relationship among sociodemographic factors, clinical conditions, and health-related quality of life: Examining the EQ-5D in the U.S. general population. *Quality of Life Research,* 14, 2187-2196.

Lund, D.A. (1989). Conclusions about bereavement in later life and implications for interventions and future research. In D.A. Lund (Ed.), *Older bereaved spouses* (pp. 217-231). New York: Hemisphere.

Lund, D.A. Caserta, M.S., & Dimond, M.R. (1993). The course of spousal bereavement. In M.S. Stroebe, W. Stroebe, & R.O. Hansson (Eds.), *Handbook of bereavement: Theory, research, and intervention* (pp. 240-254). Cambridge, UK: Cambridge University Press.

Lunney, J.R., Lynn, J., Foley, D.J., Lipson, S., & Guralnik, J.M. (2003). Patterns of functional decline at the end of life. *JAMA,* 289, 2387-2392.

Luthar, S. (2006). Resilience in development: A synthesis of research across five   decades. In D. Cicchetti & D. Cohen (Eds.). *Developmental psychopathology: Risk, disorder and adaptation,* pp. 739-795. New York: Wiley.

Lyness, J.M. (2004). Treatment of depressive conditions in later life real-world light for dark (or dim) tunnels. *Journal of the American Medical Association,* 291, 1626-1628.

Lynn, J. (2000). Rethinking fundamental assumptions: SUPPORT's implications for future reform. *Journal of the American Geriatric Society*, 48, S214-S221.

Lynn, J. (2005). Living long in fragile health: The new demographics shape end of life care. Improving end of life care: Why has it been so difficult? *Hastings Center Report Special Report* 35(6), S14-S18.

Lyon, M.E., McCabe, M.A., Patel, K.M., and D'Angelo, L.J. (2004). What do adolescents want? An exploratory study regarding end-of-life decision making. *The Journal of Adolescent Health: Official Publication of the Society for Adolescent Medicine*, 35, 529-535.

Macconville, U. (2006). Mapping religion and spirituality in an Irish palliative care setting. *Omega: The Journal of Death and Dying*, 53, 137–152.

MacDorman, M.F. & Atkinson, J.O. (1999). Infant mortality statistics from the 1997 period linked birth/infant death set. *National Vital Statistics Reports*, 47(23). Hyattsville, MD: National Center for Health Statistics.

Machado, N. (2005). Discretionary death: Conditions, dilemmas, and normative regulation. *Death Studies*, 29, 791-809.

Maglio, C.J. & Robinson, S.E. (1994). The effects of death education on death anxiety: A meta-analysis. *Omega, The Journal of Death and Dying*, 29, 319-335.

Maguire, T.V. (1997). *A recovery bill of rights for trauma survivors.* Retrieved 2006 at http://www.sidran.org/recovery.html

Mallory, J.L. (2003). The impact of a palliative care educational component on attitudes toward care of the dying in undergraduate nursing students. *Journal of Professional Nursing*, 19, 305-312.

Manis, A.A., & Bodenhorn, N. (2006). Preparation for counseling adults with terminal illness: Personal and professional parallels. *Counseling and Values*, 50(3), 197-207.

Maris, R. (1985). The adolescent suicide problem. *Suicide & Life-Threatening Behavior*, 15, 91-109.

Marotta, S.A. (2000). Best practices for counselors who treat posttraumatic stress disorder. *Journal of Counseling and Development*, 78, 492-495.

Marrone, R. (1997). *Death, mourning, and caring.* Pacific Grove, CA: Brooks/Cole.

Marsella, Anthony, J., Friedman, Matthew, J. & Spain, Huland. (2001) Ethnocultural aspects of PTSD: overview of issues and research directions. In A. Marcalla, M. Friedman. E. Gerrity, and R. Scurfield (Eds.), *Ethnocultural Aspects of Posttraumatic stress disorder: issues research and clinical application*, p. 107. Washington, DC: American Psychological Association.

Marshall, G. (Ed.). (1994). *The concise Oxford dictionary of sociology.* New York: Oxford University Press.

Martin, T.L., & Doka, K.J. (2000). *Men don't cry, women do: Transcending gender stereotypes of grief.* Philadelphia: Bruner/Mazel.

Marvin, C. (2000). On violence in media. *Journal of communication*, 50, 142-149.

Maslach, C. (1982). *Burnout— the cost of caring.* Englewood Cliffs, NJ: Prentice-Hall.

Materstvedt, L.J., Clark, D., Ellershaw, J., Forde, R., Gravgaard, A.-M.B., Mueller-Busch, H.C., et al. (2003). Euthanasia and physician assisted suicide: A view from an EAPC Ethics Task Force. *Palliative Medicine*, 17, 97-101.

Martsolf, D.S. (2002). Codependency, boundaries, and the professional nurse caring: Understanding similarities and differences. *Orthopedic Nursing*, 21, 61-67.

May, R., Angel, E., & Ellenberger, H. (Eds.), (1958). *Existence: A new dimension in psychiatry and psychology.* New York: Basic Books.

May, R., & Yalom, I. (2005). Existential psychotherapy. In R. Corsini & D. Wedding (Eds.), *Current psychotherapies* (7th Ed.). Belmont, CA: Thompson/Brooks/Cole.

Mayo Clinic Health Letter (2005). *Meditation.* 23(3), 3-4.

Mayo, D.J., & Gunderson, M. (2002). Vitalism revitalized: Vulnerable populations, prejudice, and physician-assisted death. *The Hastings Center Report*, 32, 14-21.

McAliley, L.G., Hudson-Barr, D. C., Gunning, R. S., & Rowbottom, L. A. (2000). The use of advance directives with adolescents. *Pediatric Nursing*, 26, 471-80.

McCabe, M. (1994). Patient Self-Determination Act: A Native American (Navajo) perspective. *Cambridge Quarterly of Healthcare Ethics*, 3, 419-421.

McClain, C.S., Rosenfeld, B., Breitbart, W. (2003). Effect of spiritual well-being on end-of-life despair in terminally-ill cancer patients. *Lancet*, 361(9369), 1063-1067.

McClatchey, R.S., & Vonk, E.M. (2005). An exploratory study of post-traumatic stress disorder symptoms among bereaved children. *Omega, The Journal of Death and Dying*, 51, 285-300.

McConnell, Y., Frager, G., & Levetown, M. (2004). Decision making in pediatric palliative care. In B. S. Carter & M. Lovetown (Eds.), *Palliative care for infants, children, and adolescents: A practical handbook* (pp. 69-111). Baltimore, MD: John Hopkins University Press.

McDaniel, S., Lusterman, D., & Philpot, C. (2001). *Casebook for integrating family therapy: An ecosystemic approach.* Washington, DC: American Psychological Association.

McDannell, C. & Lang, B. (1988). *Heaven: A history.* New Haven, Yale University Press.

McGoldrick, M., & Walsh, F. (2005). Death and the family life cycle. In B. Carter & M. McGoldrick (Eds.), *The expanded family life cycle: Individual, family, and social perspectives* (3rd ed.) (pp. 185-201). Boston: Allyn & Bacon.

McHugh, M. (1980). *Young people talk about death.* New York: Franklin Watts.

McKeever, A. (1999, December). Psychobabble and edufads invade the church. *Education Reporter*, 167. Retrieved online 6/20/06 from http://www.eagleforum.org/educate/1999/dec99/focus_church.html.

McKinley, E.D., Garrett, J.M., Evans, A.T., & Danis, M. (1996). Differences in end-of-life decision making among black and white ambulatory cancer patients. *Official Journal of the Society for Research and Education in Primary Care Internal Medicine*, 11, 651-656.

McKissock, Dianne (1998). *The grief of our children.* Australian Broadcasting Company: Sydney, Australia.

McMaster, G. & Trafzer, C.E. (2004). (Eds). *Native universe: Voices of Indian America.* Washington, DC: Smithsonian.

Medical futility in end-of-life care. (1997). http://www.ama-assn.org/ama/pub/category/8390.html.

Meisel, A. (1995). *The right to die* (2nd Ed.). New York: John Wiley and Sons.

Meisel, A. (2005). The role of litigation in end of life care: A reappraisal. Improving end of life care: Why has it been so difficult? *Hastings Center Report Special Report* 35(6), S47-S51.

Melhem, N.M., Day, N., Shear, M.K., Day, R., Reynolds, C.F., & Brent, D. (2004). Traumatic grief among adolescents exposed to a peer's suicide. American Journal of Psychiatry, 161, 1411-1416.

Mellor, P.A. (1993). Death in high modernity: The contemporary presence and absence of death. In D. Clark (Ed.), *The sociology of death: Theory, culture, practice* (pp. 11-30). Cambridge, MA: Blackwell.

Mellor, P.A., & Schilling, C. (1993). Modernity, self-identity and the sequestration of death. *Sociology*, 27, 411-431.

Merriam-Webster Online (2006). Definition retrieved 6/11/06 from www.m-w.com.

Merrick, J.C. (2005). Death and dying: The American experience. In R.H. Blank & J.C. Merrick (Eds). *End-of-life Decision Making: A Cross-National Study (219-241)*. Cambridge, MA: MIT Press.

Merrin, W. (1999). Crash, bang, wallop! What a picture! The death of Diana and the media. *Mortality*, 4, 41 – 62.

Meshot, C. & Leitner, L. (1993). Adolescent mourning and parental death. *Omega, The Journal of Death and Dying*, 26(4), 287-299.

Mesler, M.A. (1995). Negotiating life for the dying: Hospice and the strategy of tactical socialization. *Death Studies*, 19, 235-255.

Meyer, T.P. (April/May/June, 2005). Media portrayals of death and dying. *The Forum*, 31(2), 3-4.

Middleton, W., Burnett, P., Raphael, B., & Martinek, N. (1996). The bereavement response: A cluster analysis. *British Journal of Psychiatry*, 169, 167-171.

Miller, G.R., & Steinberg, M. (1975). *Between people: A new analysis of interpersonal communication*. Chicago: Science Research Associates.

Miller, J. (1994). The transforming power of spirituality. Presentation to a conference on transformative grief. Burnsville, NC, November.

Miller S., Gozalo P., & Mor V. Outcomes and utilization for hospice and non-hospice nursing facility decedents. Retrieved January 18, 2007, from http://aspe.hhs.gov/daltcp/reports/oututil.htm.

Miller, W. & Thoresen, C. (2003). Spirituality, religion, and health: An emerging research field. *American Psychologist*, 58, 1-19.

Mills, G. et al. (1976). *Discussing death: A guide to death education*. Palm Springs, CA: ETC Publications.

Minino, A.M. (2005, March 29). Personal communication. National Center for Health Statistics (2005). National Vital Statistics System. Unpublished tabulations.

Mishell, D.W. (1993). Recurrent abortion. *Journal of Reproductive Medicine*, 38, 250-259.

Moberg, D. (2001) *Aging and spirituality: Spiritual dimensions of aging theory, research, practice and social policy*. Binghamton: Haworth.

Moore, C.M. (1989). Teaching about loss and death to junior high school students. *Family Relations*, 38(1), 3-7.

Moos, R.H. & Schaefer, J. (1986). Life transitions and crises: A conceptual overview. In R.H. Moos (Ed.), *Coping with life crises: An integrated approach* (pp. 3-28). New York: Plenum.

Morel, E. (Ed.). (1970). *Fairy tales and fables.* New York: Grosset & Dunlap.

Morgan, J. D. (1993). The existential quest for meaning. In K.J. Doka & J.D. Morgan, (Eds.), *Death and spirituality.* Amityville, NY: Baywood Publishing Co.

Morgan, J.D., & Laungani, P. (Eds.). (2002-2005). *Death and bereavement around the world,* vols. 1-4. Amityville, NY: Baywood Publishing Co.

Morgan, M.A. (1987). Learner-centered learning in an undergraduate interdisciplinary course about death. *Death Studies,* 11, 183-192.

Morrison, R.S. (2005). Health care system factors affecting end-of-life care. *Journal of Palliative Medicine,* 8(S1), S79-S87.

Morrison, R.S., Maroney-Galin, C., Kralovec, P.D., & Meier, D.E. (2005). The growth of palliative care programs in United States Hospitals. *Journal of Palliative Medicine,* 8(6), 1127-1134.

Morrison, R.S., & Meier, D. E. (2004). High rates of advance care planning in New York City's elderly population. *Archives of Internal Medicine,* 164, 2421-2426.

Morrison, R.S., Wallenstein, S., Natale, D.K., Senzel, R.S., & Huang, L.-L. (2000). "We don't carry that"—failure of pharmacies in predominantly non-White neighborhoods to stock opioid analgesics. *New England Journal of Medicine,* 342, 1023-1026.

Moss, M.S. (2001). End of life in nursing homes. In M. P. Lawton (Ed.), *Annual review of gerontology and geriatrics, Vol. 20, The end of life: Scientific and social issues* (pp. 224-258). New York: Springer Publishing Co.

Moss. M.S., Moss, S.Z., & Hansson, R.O. (2001). Bereavement and old age. In M.S. Stroebe, R.O. Hansson, W. Stroebe, & H. Schut (Eds.), *Handbook of bereavement research: Consequences, coping, and care* (pp. 241-260). Washington, DC: American Psychological Association.

Mowery, R.L. (2005). *Family decision making about end-of-life care: A case study and commentary.* In B. Schragg (Ed.). Graduate Research Ethics Education Conference Proceedings. Indiana University, Bloomington, IN.

Muller, J., & Desmond, B. (1992). Ethical dilemmas in a cross-cultural context: A Chinese example. *Western Journal of Medicine,* 157, 323-327.

Muller, W. (1997). *Touching the divine.* Boulder, CO: Sounds True.

Murray, H. (1981). Endeavors in psychology. In E.S. Shneidman (Editor), *Comprehending suicide: Landmarks in 20th-century suicide.* New York: Harper & Row.

Murray, T.H., & Jennings, B. (2005). The quest to reform end of life care: Rethinking assumptions and setting new directions. Improving end of life care: Why has it been so difficult? *Hastings Center Report Special Report* 35(6), S52-S57.

Mutran, E.J., Danis, M., Bratton, K.A., Sudha, S., & Hanson, L. (1997). Attitudes of the critically ill toward prolonging life: The role of social support. *Gerontologist,* 37, 192-199.

Myers, S.S. & Lynn, J. (2001). Patients with eventually fatal chronic illness: Their importance within a national research agenda on improving patient safety and reducing medical error. *Journal of Palliative Medicine,* 4, 325-332.

Nagayama-Hall, G. (2001). Psychotherapy research with ethnic minorities: Empirical, ethical and conceptual issues. *Journal of Consulting and Clinical Psychology,* 69, 502-510.

Nadeau, J.W. (1997). *Families making sense of death.* Newbury Park, CA: Sage.

Nadeau, J.W. (2001). Meaning making in family bereavement: A family systems approach. In M. S. Stroebe, R.O. Hansson, W. Stroebe, & H. Schut, Eds.), *Handbook of bereavement research: Consequences, coping, and care.* Washington, DC: American Psychological Association.

Nagy, M.A. (1948). The child's theories concerning death. *Journal of Genetic Psychology, 73,* 3-27

Nahm, E. & Resnick, B. (2001). End-of-life treatment preferences among older adults. *Nursing Ethics,* 8, 533-543.

Nannis, E.D., Susman, E.J., Strope, B.E. (1978, June). *The adolescent with a life-threatening illness: Cultural myths and social realities.* Paper presented at the 13th Annual Conference of the Association of the Care of Children in Hospital, Washington, DC

National Center for Health Statistics (2000, July 24). Gun deaths among children and teens drop sharply. *HHS News.* Washington, DC: U.S. Department of Health and Human Services New Release.

National Center for Health Statistics. Health Data for All Ages: 2000-2003. Retrieved January 15, 2007 from http://www.cdc.gov/nchs/health_data_for_all_ages.htm.

National Center for Health Statistics, Centers for Disease Control and Prevention (2005). *Health, United States, 2005.* Hyattsville, MD: Author. Retrieved February 26, 2006, from http://www.cdc.gov/nchs/data/hus/hus05.pdf#summary

National Consensus Project for Quality Palliative Care (2004). *Clinical practice guidelines for quality palliative care.* Available at www.nationalconsensusproject.org.

National Hospice and Palliative Care Organization. (n.d.). *NHPCO's 2004 facts and figures.* Alexandria, VA: Author. Retrieved June 26, 2006, from http://www.nhpco.org/files/public/Facts_Figures_for2004data.pdf

National Hospice and Palliative Care Organization (2000). *Standards of practice for hospice programs.* Alexandria, VA: National Hospice and Palliative Care Organization.

National Hospice and Palliative Care Organization (2006). *NHPCO's facts and figures – 2005 findings.* Retrieved November 12, 2006, from the National Hospice and Palliative Care Organization Web site: http://www.nhpco.org/files/public/2005-facts-and-figures.pdf.

National Institutes of Health. (1997). *Symptoms in terminal illness: A research workshop.* Rockville, MD: Author.

National Institutes of Health Technology Assessment Conference Statement (1995). *Integration of behavioral and relaxation approaches into the treatment of chronic pain and insomnia.* Rockville, MD: Author.

National Kidney Foundation (2002). Bill of Rights for Donor Families: A revised document originally prepared by C.A. Corr, L.G. Nile and members of the 1994 Executive Committee of the National Donor Family Council. Retrieved February 20, 2006, from http://www.kidney.org/transplantation/donorFamilies/infoBooksDFBR.cfm

Neimeyer, R.A. (Ed.) (1994). *Death anxiety handbook: Research, instrumentation, and application.* Washington, DC: Taylor & Francis.

Neimeyer, R.A. (1998). *Lessons of loss: A guide to coping.* New York: McGraw-Hill.

Neimeyer, R. A. (2000). Searching for the meaning of meaning: Grief therapy and the process of reconstruction. *Death Studies, 24,* 541-558.

Neimeyer, R.A. (Ed.). (2001). *Meaning reconstruction and the experience of loss.* Washington, DC: American Psychological Association.

Neimeyer, R.A. (2002). *Lessons of loss: A guide to coping* (2nd Ed.). Memphis: Center for the Study of Loss and Transition.

Neimeyer, R.A. (2002) Traumatic loss and the reconstruction of meaning. *Journal of Palliative Medicine*, 5, 935-942.

Neimeyer, R.A. (2006a). Complicated grief and the quest for meaning: A constructivist contribution. *Omega, The Journal of Death and Dying*, 52, 37-52.

Neimeyer, R.A. (2006b). Widowhood, grief and the quest for meaning: A narrative perspective on resilience. In D. Carr, R.M. Nesse & C.B. Wortman (Eds.), *Late life widowhood in the United States* (pp. 227-252). New York: Springer Publishing Company.

Neimeyer, R.A. Baldwin, S.A., & Gillies, J. (2006). Continuing bonds and reconstructing meaning: Mitigating complications in bereavement. *Death Studies*, 30, 715-738.

Neimeyer, R.A., & Hogan, N. (2001). Quantitative or qualitative? Measurement issues in the study of grief. In H.S.M. Stroebe, R. Hansson, & W. Stoebe (Eds.), *Handbook of bereavement research* (pp. 89-118). Washington, DC: American Psychological Association.

Neimeyer, R.A., & Jordan, J.R. (2002). Disenfranchisement as empathic failure. In K. Doka (Ed.), *Disenfranchised grief* (pp. 97-117). Champaign, IL: Research Press.

Neimeyer, R.A. Prigerson, H.G., & Davies, B. (2002). Mourning and meaning. *American Behavioral Scientist*, 46, 235-251.

Neimeyer, R.A., Wittkowski, J., & Moser, R.P. (2004). Psychological research on death attitudes: An overview and evaluation. *Death Studies*, 28, 309-340.

Nelson, H.L., & Nelson, J.L. (1995). *The patient in the family: An ethics of medicine and families.* New York: Routledge.

Neria, Y. & Litz, B.T. (2003). Bereavement by traumatic means: The complex synergy of trauma and grief. *Journal of Loss and Trauma*, 9, 73-87.

Neugebauer, R., Kline, J., O'Connor, P., Shrout, P., Johnson, J., Skodol, A., Wicks, J., & Susser, M. (1992). Depressive symptoms in women in the six months after miscarriage. *American Journal of Obstetrics & Gynecology*, 166(1Pt1), 104-109.

Neugarten, B. L., & Datan, N. (1973). Sociological perspectives on the life cycle. In P. B. Baltes & K. W. Schaie (Eds.), *Life-span developmental psychology: Personality and socialization.* New York: Academic Press.

Newman, B. M. & Newman, Pr. R. (1999). *Development through life: A psychosocial approach.* New York: Brooks/Cole-Wadsworth.

Nichols, M.P., & Schwartz, R.C. (1998). *Family therapy: Concepts and methods* (4th Ed.). Boston: Allyn and Bacon.

Nolan, M.T., Sood, J.R., Kub, J., & Sulmasy, D.P. (2005). When patients lack capacity: The roles that patients with terminal diagnoses would choose for their physicians and loved ones in making medical decisions. *Journal of Pain and Symptom Management*, 30(4), 342-353.

Noonan, P. (1999, April 22). The culture of death. *The Wall Street Journal*, p. 1.

Noppe, I.C. (2004). Death education and the scholarship of teaching: A meta-educational experience. *The Forum*, 30, 1, 3-4.

Noppe, I.C., & Noppe, L.D. (1996). Ambiguity in adolescent understandings of death. In C. A. Corr & D. E. Balk (Eds.), *Handbook of adolescent death and bereavement*. New York: Springer Publishing Co.

Noppe, I.C. & Noppe, L.D. (1997). Evolving meanings of death during early, middle and later adolescence. *Death Studies*, 21, 253-275.

Noppe, I.C. & Noppe, L.D. (2004). Adolescent experiences with death: Letting go of immortality. *Journal of Mental Health Counseling*, 26, 146-67.

Noppe, I.C., Noppe, L.D., & Bartell, D. (2006). Terrorism and resilience: Adolescents' and teachers' responses to September 11, 2001. *Death Studies*, 30, 41-60.

Noyes, R. & Clancy, J. (1977). The dying role: Its relevance to improved patient care. *Psychiatry*, 40, 41-47.

Ochberg, F. (1998). *When helping hurts*. Retrieved August 7, 2006, from http://www.giftfromwithin.org/html/helping.html

Olive, K. (2004). Religion and spirituality: Important psychosocial variables frequently ignored in clinical research. *Southern Medical Journal*, 97, 1152-1153.

Olson, D.H. (2000). Circumplex model of marital and family systems. *Journal of Family Therapy*, 22, 144-167.

Olson, D.H., & DeFrain, J. (2006). *Marriages and families: Intimacy, diversity and strengths* (5th Ed.). New York: McGraw-Hill.

Oltjenbruns, K.A. (2001). Developmental context of childhood: Grief and regrief phenomena.. In M.S. Stroebe, R.O. Hansson, W. Stroebe, & H. Schut (Eds.), *Handbook of bereavement research: Consequences, coping, and caring* (pp. 169-197). Washington, DC: American Psychological Association.

Oregon Department of Human Services. (2005, March 9). *Eighth annual report on Oregon's death with dignity act*. Portland, OR: Office of Disease Prevention and Epidemiology. http://www.oregon.gov/DHS/ph/pas/docs/year8.pdf.

Orona, C., Koenig, B., & Davis, A. (1994). Cultural aspects of nondisclosure. *Cambridge Quarterly of Healthcare Ethics*, 3, 338-346.

Orenstein, C. (2002). *Little Red Riding Hood uncloaked: Sex, morality, and the evolution of a fairy tale*. New York: Basic Books.

Osterweis, M., Solomon, F., & Green, M. (1984). (Editors). *Bereavement: Reactions, consequences, and care*. Washington, DC: National Academy Press.

Osvath, P., Kovacs, A., Voros, V., & Fekete, S. (2005). Risk factors of attempted suicide in the elderly: The role of cognitive impairment. *International Journal of Psychiatry in Clinical Practice*, 9, 221-225.

O'Toole, D. (1989). *Growing through grief: A K-12 curriculum to help young people though all kinds of loss*. Burnsville, NC: Mountain Rainbow Publications. (available from Compassion Books, 477 Hannah Branch Road, Burnsville, NC, 28714).

O'Toole, D. (1995) *Facing change: Falling apart and coming together again in the teen years*. Burnsville, NC: Compassion Books.

Ott, C.H. (2003). The impact of complicated grief on mental and physical health at various points in the bereavement process. *Death Studies*, 27, 249-272.

Palmer, L.I. (2000). *Endings and beginnings: Law, medicine, and society in assisted life and death.* Westport, CT: Praeger Publishers.

Panke, J.T.,& Ferrell, B.R. (2005). Emotional problems in the family. In D. Doyle, G. Hanks, N.I. Cherny, & K. Calman (Eds.). *Oxford textbook of palliative medicine* (3rd Ed.), 985-992. Oxford, UK: Oxford University Press.

Papadatou, D. (1997). Training health professionals in caring for dying children and grieving families. *Death Studies*, 21(6), 575-600.

Pare, D. & Larner, G. (2004). (Eds.). *Collaborative practice in psychology and therapy.* New York: Haworth Clinical Practice Press.

Pargament, K., Koenig, H., Tarakeshwar, N., & Hahn, J. (2004). Religious coping methods as predictors of psychological, physical, and spiritual outcomes among medically ill elderly patients: A two-year longitudinal study. *Journal of Health Psychology*, 9, 713-730.

Park, H.L., O'Connell, J.E., & Thompson, R. G. (2003). A systematic review of cognitive decline in the general elderly population. *International Journal of Geriatric Psychiatry*, 18, 1121-1134.

Parkes, C.M. (1972). *Bereavement: Studies of grief in adult life* (2nd Ed., 1986; 3rd Ed., 1996). London: Tavistock.

Parkes, C.M. (1975). Determinants of outcome following bereavement. *Omega, The Journal of Death and Dying*, 6, *303-323.*

Parkes, C.M. (1987). *Bereavement: Studies of grief in adult life* (2nd Ed.). Madison, CT: International Universities Press.

Parkes, C.M. (1990). Risk factors in bereavement: Implications for the prevention and treatment of pathologic grief. *Psychiatric Annals* 20(6), June 1990, 308-313.

Parkes, C.M. (1997). *Death and bereavement across cultures.* London: Routledge.

Parkes, C.M. (2004). *Love & loss: The roots of grief & its complications.* NY: Routledge.

Parkes, C.M. (Editor.). (2006a). Symposium on complicated grief [Special issue]. *Omega, The Journal of Death and Dying*, 52(1).

Parkes, C.M. (2006b). Part I. Introduction to a symposium. *Omega, The Journal of Death and Dying*, 52, 1-7.

Parkes, C.M. & Brown, R.J. (1972). Health after bereavement: A controlled study of young Boston widows and widowers. *Psychosomatic Medicine*, 34, 449-461.

Parkes, C.M., & Weiss, R.S. (1983). *Recovery from bereavement.* New York: Basic Books.

Parkes, C.M. & Weiss, R.S. (1995). *Recovery following bereavement* (2nd Ed.). New York: Basic Books.

Pattison, E.M. (1977). *The experience of dying.* New York: Simon & Schuster.

Pattison, E.M. (1978). The living-dying interval. In C. Garfield, (Ed.), *Psychological care of the dying patient.* (pp. 163-168). New York: McGraw-Hill.

Penson, R.T., Rauch, P.K., McAfee, S.L., Cashavelly, B.J., Clair-Hayes, K. Dahlin, C., et al. (2002). Between parent and child: Negotiating cancer treatment in adolescents. *The Oncologist*, 7, 154-162.

Perkins, H.S., Supik, J.D., & Hazuda, H.P. (1993). Autopsy decisions: The possibility of conflicting cultural attitudes. *Journal of Clinical Ethics*, 4, 145-154.

Peteet, J.R., Ross, D.M., Medeiros, C., Walsh-Burke, K., & Rieker, P. (1992). Relationships with patients in oncology: Can a patient be a friend. *Psychiatry*, 55, 223-229.

Pfeffer, C. (1986). *The suicidal child.* New York: Guilford.

Pfefferbaum, B., North, C.S., Doughty, D.E., Pfefferbaum, R L., Dumont, C.E., Pynoos, R.S., Gurwitch, R.H., & Ndetei, D. (2006). Trauma, grief and depression in Nairobi children after the 1998 bombing of the American embassy. *Death Studies*, 30, 561-577.

Pfefferbaum, B. Tucker, P. North, C.S., Jeon-Slaughter, H., Kent, A.T. Schorr, J.K., Wilson, T.G., & Bunch, K. (2006). Persistent physiological reactivity in a pilot study of partners of firefighters after a terrorist attack. *Journal of Nervous and Mental Disease*, 194, 128-131.

Phillips, B.J. (2005). Determining brain death: A summary. *The Internet Journal of Law, Healthcare and Ethics*, 2: Retrieved August 15, 2006 from http://www.ispub.com/ostia/index.php?xmlFilePath=journals/ijlhe/vol1n1/ethics2.xml

Phillips, S.B. (2005). The role of the bereavement group in the face of 9/11: A self-psychology perspective. *International Journal of Group Psychotherapy*, 55, 507-525.

Pine, V. (1977). A socio-historical portrait of death education. *Death Education*, 1, 57-84.

Pine, V. (1986). The age of maturity for death education: A socio-historical portrait of the era 1976-1985. *Death Studies*, 10, 209-231.

Pines, A. & Aronson, E. (1988). *Career burnout: Causes and cures.* New York: Free Press.

Pinquart, M. (2003). Loneliness in married, widowed, divorced, and never-married older adults. *Journal of Social and Personal Relationships*, 20, 31-53.

Pitman, R.K. & Sparr, L.F. (1998). PTSD and the law. *PTSD Research Quarterly*, 9(2), 1-8.

Plopper, B.L., & Ness, M.E. (1993). Death as portrayed in adolescence through top 40 rock and roll music, *Adolescence*, 28, 793-807.

Ponzetti, J.J. (1992). Bereaved families: A comparison of parents' and grandparents' reactions to the death of a child. *Omega, The Journal of Death and Dying*, 25, 63-71.

President's Commission for the Study of Ethical Problems in Medicine and Behavioral Research (1981). *Defining death: A report on the medical, legal and ethical issues in the determination of death.* Washington, DC: Government Printing Office.

Preston, T. & Kelly, M. (2006). A medical ethics assessment of the case of Terri Shiavo. *Death Studies*, 30, 121-133.

Prigerson, H. (2005). Complicated grief when the path of adjustment leads to a dead end. *Counseling and Psychotherapy Journal*, 5 (3), 10-14.

Prigerson, H.G., & Jacobs, S.C. (2001). Diagnostic criteria for traumatic grief. In M.S. Stroebe, R.O. Hansson, W. Stroebe & H. Schut (Eds.), *Handbook of bereavement research* (pp. 614-646). Washington, DC: American Psychological Association.

Prigerson, H.G., & Maciejewski, P.K. (2006). A call for sound empirical testing and evaluation of criteria for complicated grief proposed by the DSM V. *Omega, The Journal of Death and Dying*, 52, 9-19.

Prigerson, H.G., Shear, M.K., Bierhals, A.J., Pilkonis, P.A., Wolfson, L., Hall. M., Zonarich, D.L., & Reynolds, C.F. (1997). Case histories of traumatic grief. *Omega, The Journal of Death and Dying*, 35, 9-24.

Pritchard, D. (2000). The future of media accountability. In D. Pritchard (Ed.), *Holding the media accountable: Citizens, ethics, and the law* (pp. 186-193). Bloomington, IN: Indiana University Press.

Prochaska, J.O. & DiClemente, C.C. (2005). The transtheoretical approach. In J.C. Norcross & M.R. Goldfried (Eds.), *Handbook of psychotherapy integration* (2nd Ed.), pp. 147-171. New York: Oxford University Press.

Prochaska, J. & Norcross, J. (2003). *Systems of psychotherapy: A transtheoretical analysis*. Pacific Grove, CA: Thompson/Brooks Cole.

Psychological Work Group of the International Work Group on Death, Dying, and Bereavement (1993). A statement of assumptions and principles concerning psychological care of dying persons and their families. *Journal of Palliative Care*, 9, 29-32.

Pynoos, R.S., Goenjian, A.K. & Steinberg, A.M. (1998). A public mental health approach to the postdisaster treatment of children and adolescents. *Child and Adolescent Psychiatric Clinics of North America*, 7, 195-210.

Pynoos, R.S. & Nader, K. (1990). Children's exposure to violence and traumatic death. *Psychiatric Annals*, 20, 334-344.

Pyszczynski, T., Solomon, S., & Greenberg, J. (2003). *In the wake of 9/11: The psychology of terror*. Washington, DC: American Psychological Association.

Puchalski, C.M. (2001). The role of spirituality in health care. *Baylor University Medical Center Proceedings*, 14(4), 352–357.

Rabow, M.W., Hardie, G.E., Fair, J.M., & McPhee, S.J. (2000). End-of-life care content in 50 textbooks from multiple specialties. *JAMA*, 283, 771-778.

Racanelli, C. (2005). Attachment and compassion fatigue among American and Israeli mental health clinicians working with traumatized victims of terrorism. *International Journal of Emergency Mental Health*, 7, 115-124.

Rai, R., Backos, M., Rushworth, F., & Regan, L. (2000). Polycystic ovaries and recurrent miscarriage – a reappraisal. *Human Reproduction*, 15, 612-615.

Rainer, J. & McMurry, P. (2002). Caregiving at the end of life. *Journal of Clinical Psychology: In Session*, 58(11), 1421-1431.

Randall, B. (2003). *Songman: The story of an Aboriginal elder*. Sydney: Australian Broadcasting Corporation.

Randell, T.T. (2004). Medical and legal considerations of brain death. *Acta Anaesthesiologica Scandinavica*, 48, 139-144.

Rando, T.A. (1984). *Grief, dying, and death: Clinical interventions for caregivers*. Champaign, IL: Research Press.

Rando, T.A. (Ed.) (1986). *Loss and anticipatory grief*. Lexington, MA: Lexington Books.

Rando, T.A. (1988). Anticipatory grief: The term is a misnomer but the phenomenon exists. *Journal of Palliative Care*, 4(1/2), 70-73.

Rando, T.A. (1993). *Treatment of complicated mourning*. Champaign, IL: Research Press.

Rando, T.A. (1995). Grief and mourning: Accomodating to loss. In H. Wass & R.A. Neimeyer (Eds.), *Dying: Facing the facts* (pp. 211-241). Washington, DC: Taylor and Francis.

Rando, T.A. (Ed.). (2000). *Clinical dimensions of anticipatory mourning: Theory and practice in working with the dying, their loved ones, and their caregivers.* Champaign, IL: Research Press.

Rando, T.A. (2000a).Anticipatory mourning: A review and critique of the literature. In T.A. Rando (Ed.), *Clinical dimensions of anticipatory mourning: Theory and practice in working with the dying, their loved ones, and their caregivers* (pp. 17-50.). Champaign, IL: Research Press.

Rando, T.A. (2000b). The six dimensions of anticipatory mourning. In T.A. Rando (Ed.), *Clinical dimensions of anticipatory mourning: Theory and practice in working with the dying, their loved ones, and their caregivers* (pp. 51-101.). Champaign, IL: Research Press.

Rank, O. (1958). *Beyond psychology.* New York: Dover reprint.

Raphael, B. (1983). *The anatomy of bereavement.* New York: Basic Books.

Raphael, B. (1994). *The anatomy of bereavement.* New York: Jason Aronson.

Redmond, L.M. (1989). *Surviving: When someone you love was murdered.* Clearwater, FL: Psychological Consultation and Educational Services, Inc.

Reed, P.G. (1987). Spirituality and well-being in terminally ill hospitalized adults. *Res Nurs Health,* 10, 335-344.

Reiss, D. (1981). *The family's construction of reality.* Cambridge, MA: Harvard University Press.

Ribbentrop, E., Altmaier, E., Chen, J., Found, E. & Keffala,V. (2005). The relationship between religion/spirituality and physical health, mental health, and pain in a chronic pain population. *Pain,* 116, 311-321.

Rich, D.E. (2000). The relationship between type and timing of post pregnancy loss services and grief outcome. (Doctoral dissertation, University of Minnesota, 2000). *Dissertation Abstracts International,* 60(7-B), 3614.

Richards, T.A. (2002). The spiritual self and meaning. In Robert A. Neimeyer (editor), *Meaning reconstruction & the experience of loss.* Washington, DC: American Psychological Association.

River Dell Regional Schools Board of Education, 700 Series – Instruction adopted September 8, 1970, p. 4 (mimeographed).

Robertson, I. (1977). *Sociology.* New York: Worth Publishers.

Rodriguez, K.L., & Young, A.J. (2006). Patients' and health care providers' understandings of life-sustaining treatment: Are perceptions of goals shared or divergent? *Social Science & Medicine,* 62, 125-133.

Roediger, D.R. (1981, Spring). And die in Dixie: Funerals, death & heaven in the slave community, 1700-1865. *The Massachusetts review,* 22, 163-183.

Rogers, J.E. (2007). *The art of grief.* New York: Routledge.

Rogers, L.S. (2004). Meaning of bereavement among older African American widows. *Geriatric Nursing,* 25, 10-16.

Rosenblatt, P.C. (1993). Cross-cultural variation in the experience, expression, and understanding of grief. In D.P. Irish, K.F. Lundy, & V.J. Nelson (Eds.), *Ethnic variations in dying, death, and grief: Diversity in universality* (pp. 13-19). Washington, DC: Taylor & Francis.

Rosenblatt, P.C. (1997). Grief in small scale societies. In C. M. Parkes, P. Laungani, & B.Young (Eds.), *Death and bereavement across cultures* (pp. 27-51). London: Routledge.

Rosenblatt, P.C. (2001). A social constructionist perspective on cultural differences in grief. In M.S. Stroebe, R.O. Hansson, W. Stroebe, & H. Schut (Eds.), *Handbook of bereavement research: Consequences, coping and care* (pp. 285-300). Washington, DC: American Psychological Association Press.

Rosenblatt, P.C. & Elde, C. (1990). Shared reminiscence about a deceased parent: Implication for grief education and grief counseling. *Family Relations, 39,* 206-210.

Rosenblatt, P.C., & Nkosi, B.C. (2007). South African Zulu widows in a time of poverty and social change. *Death Studies,* 31, 67-85.

Rosenblatt, P.C., & Wallace, B.R. (2005a). Narratives of grieving African-Americans about racism in the lives of deceased family members. *Death Studies,* 29, 217-235.

Rosenblatt, P.C. & Wallace, B.R. (2005b). *African American grief.* New York: Routledge.

Rosenblatt, P.C., Walsh, R.P., & Jackson, D.A. (1976). *Grief and mourning in crosscultural perspective.* New Haven, CT: Human Relations Area Files Press.

Rosenblatt, P.C., & Yang, S. (2004). Love, debt, and filial piety: Hee Gyung Noh's view of Korean intergenerational relations when a mother is terminally ill. *Journal of Loss and Trauma, 9,* 167-180.

Rothera, I.C., Jones, R., Harwood, R., Avery, A.J., & Waite, J. (2002). Survival in a cohort of social services placements in nursing and residential homes: Factors associated with life expectancy and mortality. *Public Health,* 116, 160-165.

Rowling, L. (2005). Loss and grief in school communities. In B. Monroe & F. Kraus, *Brief Interventions with Bereaved Children* (pp. 159-173). New York: Oxford University Press.

Rubin, R.J. (1978). *Using bibliotherapy: A guide to theory and practice.* Phoenix, AZ: Oryx Press.

Rubin, S. (1999). The two-track model of bereavement: Overview, retrospect and prospect. *Death Studies,* 23, 681-714.

Rubin, S.S., Malkinson, R., & Witzum, E. (2003). Trauma and bereavement: Conceptual and clinical issues revolving around relationships. *Death Studies,* 27, 677-690.

Rurup, M.L., Onwuteaka-Philipsen, B.D., Roeline, H., Pasman, W., Ribbe, M.W., & van der Wal, G. (2006). Attitudes of physicians, nurses, and relatives toward end-of-life decisions concerning nursing home patients with dementia. *Patient Education and Counseling,* 61, 372-380.

Rynearson, E.K. (2005). The narrative labyrinth of violent dying. *Death Studies,* 29, 351-360.

Sagar, R.R. (Editor) (1997). *Bowen theory and practice: Feature articles from the Family Center Report, 1979-1996.* Washington, DC: Georgetown Family Center.

Sakurai, M.L. (2006). Chaplains' view of role covers a wide range. *Vision,* April, 6-7.

Salmon, G. (2003). *E-moderating: The key to online teaching and learning.* London: Taylor & Francis.

Sanders, C.M., Mauger, P.A., & Strong, P.N. (1985). *A Manual for the Grief Experience Inventory.* Blowing Rock, NC: Center for the Study of Separation and Loss.

Sanders, J.M. (2002). Ethnic boundaries and identity in plural societies. *Annual review of sociology,* 28, 327-357.

Sandler, I. (2001). Quality and ecology of adversity as common mechanisms of risk and resilience. *American Journal of Community Psychology,* 29, 19-61.

Sandler, I. & Ayers, T. (2001). Fostering resilience in families in which a parent has died. In *Innovations in end of life care*, **3**(6). [Special Issue, Coping with loss]. Includes detailed program description, online at http://www2.edc.org/lastacts/archives/archivesNov01/default.asp

Sandler, I.N., Ayers, T.S., Wolchik, S.A., Tein, J.-Y., Kwok, O.-M., Haine, R.A.Twohey-Jacobs, J., Suter, J., Lin, K., Padgett-Jones, S., Weyer, J.L., Cole, E., Kriege, G., & Griffin, W.A. (2003). The Family Bereavement Program: Efficacy evaluation of a theory-based prevention program for parentally bereaved children and adolescents. *Journal of Consulting and Clinical Psychology*, 71, 587-600.

Satcher, D., & Pamies, R.J. (Eds.) (2006). *Multicultural medicine and health disparities*. New York: McGraw-Hill.

Saunders, C. (1959). The problem of euthanasia ... When a patient is dying (A series of articles). *Nursing Times*, October 9 –November 13, pp. 960-961, 994-995, 1031, 1091-1092, 1129-1130.

Saunders, C. & Kastenbaum, R. (1997). *Hospice care on the international scene*. Beverly Hills, CA: Sage.

Saunders, C.M. (1967). *The management of terminal illness*. London: Hospital Medicine Publications.

Saylor, C.F., Cowart, B.L., Lipovsky, J.A., Jackson, C., & Finsh, A.J., Jr. (2003). Media exposure to September 11: Elementary school students' experiences and posttraumatic symptoms, *American Behavioral Scientist*, 12, 1622-1642.

Schaefer, J.A., & Moos, R.H. (2001). Bereavement experiences and personal growth. In M.S. Stroebe, R.O. Hansson, W. Stroebe, & H. Schut (Eds.), *Handbook of bereavement research: Consequences, coping, and caring* (pp. 145 - 167). Washington, DC: American Psychological Association.

Scharlach, A.E. (1991). Factors associated with filial grief following the death of an elderly parent. *American Journal of Orthopsychiatry*, 6, 307-313.

Scharlach, A.E. & Fredriksen, K.I. (1993). Reactions to the death of a parent during midlife. *Omega, The Journal of Death and Dying*, 27, 307-317.

Schiappa, E., Gregg, P. B., & Hewes, D. E. (2004). Can a television series change attitudes about death? A study of college students and Six Feet Under. *Death Studies*, 28, 459-474.

Schindler v. Schiavo (In re Guardianship of Schiavo) 851 So. 2d 182 (Fla.DCA 2003); review denied, 855 So. 2d 621 (Fla. 2003) (table decision).

Schiffman, D.D. (2004). *Coping with sudden infant death: An integrated approach to understanding family grief and recovery*. Unpublished doctoral dissertation, Alliant International University.

Schlafly, P. (1988, April 13). Death comes into the open. *Brooklyn Spectator*.

Schneiderman, G., Winders, P., Tallett, S. & Feldman, W. (1994). Do child and/or parent bereavement programs work? *Canadian Journal of Psychiatry*, 39, 215-218.

Schoeman, F. (1980). Rights of children, rights of parents, and the moral basis of the family. *Ethics*, 91, 6-19.

Schrag, D., Gelfand, S.E., Bach, P.B., Guillem, J., Minsky, B.D., & Begg, C.B. (2001). Who gets adjuvant treatment for Stage II and III rectal cancer? Insight from surveillance, epidemiology, and end results-Medicare. *Journal of Clinical Oncology*, 19, 3712-3718.

Schroeder-Sheker, T. (1994) Music for the dying: A personal account of the new field of Music-Thanatology — History, theory and clinical narratives. *Journal of Holistic Nursing*, 12, 83-99.

Schulz R., Beach S.R., Lind B., Martire L.M., Zdaniuk B., Hirsch C., Jackson S., & Burton L. (2001). Involvement in caregiving and adjustment to death of a spouse: Findings from the caregiver health effects study. *JAMA*, 285, 3123-3129.

Schulz, R. & Aderman, D. (1974). Clinical research and the stages of dying. *Omega: The Journal of Death and Dying*, 5, 137-143.

Schuurman, D.L. (2003-2004). Literature for adults to assist them in helping bereaved children. *Omega: The Journal of Death and Dying*, 48, 415-424.

Schwab, R. (1997). Parental mourning and children's behavior. *Journal of Counseling & Development*, 75, 258-265.

Seale, C. (1998). *Constructing death: The sociology of dying and bereavement*. New York: Cambridge University Press.

Seale, C. (2000). Changing patterns of death and dying. *Social Science and Medicine*, 51, 917-930.

Searight, H. & Gafford, J. (2005). Cultural diversity at the end of life: Issues and guidelines for family physicians. *American Family Physician*, 71(3), and retrived January 18, 2007, from online http://www.aafp.org/afp/20050201/515.html

Searle, J.R. (1995). The *construction of social reality*. New York: Free Press.

Sehgal, A., Galbraith, A., Chesney, M., Schoefield, P., & Lo, B. (1992). How strictly do dialysis patients want their advance directives followed? *JAMA*, 267(1), 59-63.

Sekaer, C. & Katz, S. (1986). On the concept of mourning in childhood. *The Psychiatric Study of the Child*, 41, 287-314.

Sephton, S., Koopman, C., Shaal, M., Thoresen, C. & Spiegel, D. (2001). Spiritual expression and immune status in women with metastatic cancer: An exploratory study. *Breast Journal*, 7, 345-353.

Shackford, S. (2003). School violence: A stimulus for death education—A critical analysis. *Journal of Loss and Trauma*, 8, 35-40.

Schaefer, D.J. (1988). Communication among children, parents, and funeral directors. In H.M. Dick, D.P. Roye, Jr., P.R. Buschman, A.H. Kutscher, B. Rubinstein, & F.K. Forstenzer (Eds.), *Loss, grief and care* (Vol. 2, Nos. 3/4, pp. 131-142). New York: Haworth Press.

Shalev, A.Y., Tuval-Mashiach, R., & Hadar, H. (2004). Posttraumatic stress disorder as a result of mass trauma. *Journal of Clinical Psychiatry*, 65, 2004, 4-10.

Shapiro, E. (1994). *Grief as a family process*, New York: Guilford Press. (2nd Ed. in preparation).

Shapiro, E. R. (1996). Family bereavement and cultural diversity: a social developmental perspective. *Family Process*, 35, 313-332.

Shapiro, S. (1988). *Infertility and pregnancy loss*. San Francisco: Jossey-Bass.

Sharapan, H. (1977). "Mister Rogers' Neighborhood:" Dealing with death on a children's television series. *Death Education*, 1, 131-136.

Shatz, M.A. (2002). Teaching thanatology in a foreign country: Implications for death educators. *Death Studies*, 26, 425-430.

Shavers, V. L., & & Shavers, B. S. (2006). Racism and health inequity among Americans. *Journal of the National Medical Association*, 98, 386-396.

Shea J. (2000). *Spirituality and health care: Reaching toward a holistic future.* Chicago: The Park Ridge Center.

Shear, K., Frank, E., Houch, P.R., & Reynolds, C.F. (2005). Treatment of complicated grief: A randomized controlled trial. *Journal of the American Medical Association,* 293, 2601-2608.

Sheets, V. (1999). Professional interpersonal boundaries: A commentary. *Pediatric Nursing,* 25, 657.

Sheets, V. (2000). Staying in the lines. *Nurse Management,* 31, 28-34.

Sherell, K., Buckwalter, K.C., & Morhardt, D. (2001). Negotiating family relationships: Dementia care as a midlife developmental task. *Families in Society,* 82, 383-392.

Shneidman, E. (1982). Reflections on contemporary death. Keynote presentation to the Forum for Death Education and Counseling, San Diego, CA. September.

Siegel, D.J. (1999). *The developing mind.* New York: Guilford Press.

Siegel, K. & Schrimshaw, E. (2002). The perceived benefits of religious and spiritual coping among older adults living with HIV/AIDS. *Journal for the Scientific Study of Religion,* 41, 91-102.

Siggins, L. (1966). Mourning: A critical survey of the literature. *The International Journal of Psychoanalysis,* 47, 14-25.

Silverman, P. (2000). *Never too young to know.* New York: Oxford.

Silverman, P.R. (2004). *Widow to widow: How the bereaved help one another* (2nd Ed.). New York: Routledge.

Silverman, P. & Worden, W. (1992). Children's reactions in the early months after the death of a parent. *American Journal of Orthopsychiatry,* 62 (1), 93-104.

Silverman, P.R. & Worden, J.W. (1993). Children's reactions to the death of a parent. In. M.S Stroebe, W. Stroebe, & R.O. Hansson (Eds.), *Handbook of bereavement: Theory, research, and intervention* (pp. 300-316). Cambridge, UK: Cambridge University Press.

Silverstein, O. (1995). Inclusion/Exclusion. A presentation at the Ackerman Institute for the Family. New York: Ackerman Institute.

Simon, R. (1995). The natural history of therapist sexual misconduct: Identification and prevention. *Psychiatric Annals,* 25, 90-94.

Simon, R.I. (1995). *Posttraumatic stress disorder in litigation: Guidelines for forensic assessment.* Washington, D.C.: American Psychiatric Association Press.

Slovenko, R. (1994). Legal aspects of post-traumatic stress disorder. *Psychiatric Clinics North America,* 17, 439-446.

Smart, N. (1996). *Worldviews: Crosscultural exploration of human beliefs* (2nd Ed.). Englewood Cliffs, NJ: Prentice Hall.

Smart, N. (1977). *The long search.* Boston: Little, Brown.

Smith, H. (1994). *The illustrated world's religions: A guide to our wisdom traditions.* New York: Harper San Francisco.

Smith, L.H. (1981). Honk! If your school's got religion. *Today's Education,* Sept.-Oct. 64-71.

Smith, S.H. (2005). Anticipatory grief and psychological adjustment to grieving in middle-aged children. *American Journal of Hospice & Palliative Medicine,* 22, 283-286.

Smith, T.L. & Walz, B.J. (1998). The cadre of death education instructors in paramedic programs. *Prehospital and Disaster Medicine*, 13, 55-58.

Smith-Torres, C. (1985). Lecture at Columbia-Presbyterian Medical Center, NYC March Conference of the Foundation of Thanatology.

Smolinsky, K.M., & Colon, Y. (2006). Silent voices and invisible walls: Exploring end-of-life issues with lesbians and gay men. *Psychosocial Oncology*, 24, 51-64.

Sofka, C.J. (1997). Social support "internetworks," caskets for sale, and more: Thanatology and the information superhighway. *Death Studies*, 21(6), 553-574.

Solomon, P. & Draine, J. (1995). Adaptive coping among family members of persons with serious illness. *Psychiatric Services*, 46, 1156-1160.

Somerville, R.M. (1971). Death education as part of family life education: Using imaginative literature for insights into family crises. *Family Coordinator*, 20(3), 209-224.

Sosa, N., Lin, C., Barrett, T., Johns, J., Phillips, R., & Yuille, J. (2005, March 18). *Schiavo's feeding tube removed.* http://www.cnn.com/2005/LAW/03/18/schiavo.brain-damaged/

Speece, M.W. & Brent, S.B. (1992). The acquisition of a mature understanding of three components of a death concept. *Child Development*, 55, 1671-1686.

Speece, M.W. & Brent, S.B. (1996). The development of children's understanding of death. In C.A. Corr and D. Corr (Eds.), *Handbook of childhood death and bereavement* (pp. 29-50). New York: Springer Publishing Co.

Sperling, D. (2004). Maternal brain death. *American Journal of Law & Medicine*, 30, 453- 501.

Spiro, J.D. (1967). *A time to mourn: Judaism and the psychology of bereavement.* New York: Bloch Publishing Co.

Sprung, C.L., Cohen, S.L., Sjokvist, P., Baras, M., Bulow, H.H., Hovilehto, S. et al. (2003). End-of-life practices in European intensive care units: The Ethicus Study. *Journal of the American Medical Association*, 290, 790-797.

Sque, M., Long, T., & Payne, S. (2005). Organ donation: Key factors influencing families' decision making. *Transplant Procedures*, 37, 543-546.

Stahlman, S.D. (1996). Children and death of a sibling. In C.A. Corr and D. Corr (Eds.), *Handbook of childhood death and bereavement* (pp. 149-164). New York: Springer Publishing Co.

Stanworth, R. (2004) *Recognizing spiritual needs in people who are dying.* New York: Oxford University Press.

Steen, K. (1998). A comprehensive approach to bereavement. *The Nurse Practitioner*, 23(3), 54-68.

Steeves, R.H. (2002). The rhythms of bereavement. *Family Community Health*, 25, 1-10.

Stefanek, M., McDonald, P., & Hess, S. (2005). Religion, spirituality and cancer: Current status and methodological challenges. *Psycho-Oncology*, 14, 450-463.

Stevens, M.M. & Dunsmore, J.C. (1996). Adolescents who are living with a life-threatening illness. In C.A. Corr & D.E. Balk (Eds.), *Handbook of adolescent death and bereavement* (pp. 107-13). New York: Springer Publishing Co.

Stevenson, R.G. (1972). *Issues of life and death.* Oradell, NJ. (unpublished school curriculum).

Stevenson, R.G. (1984). *A death education course for secondary schools: Curing death ignorance.* Unpublished doctoral dissertation, Fairleigh Dickinson University.

Stevenson, R.G. (1990). The eye of the beholder: The media look at death education. *Death Studies,* 14(2), 161-170.

Stevenson, R.G. (1993). Religious values in death education. In K.J. Doka and J.D. Morgan (Eds.) *Death and spirituality.* Amityville, NY: Baywood Publishing.

Stillion, J.M. (2006). Understanding the end of life: An overview. In J.L. Werth, Jr. & D. Blevins (Eds.) *Psychosocial issues near the end of life: A resource for professional care providers* (pp. 11-26). Washington, DC: American Psychological Association.

Stoddard, S. (1978). *The hospice movement: A better way of caring for the dying.* New York: Vintage Books.

Stoddard, S. (1992). *The hospice movement: A better way of caring for the dying* (Rev Ed.). New York: Vintage Books.

Stokes, J. (2005). Family assessment. In B. Monroe & F. Kraus, *Brief Interventions with Bereaved Children* (pp. 29-47). New York: Oxford University Press.

Storey, P. & Knight, C. (1997) *Unipac Two: Alleviating psychological and spiritual pain in the terminally ill.* Gainesville, FL: The American Academy of Hospice and Palliative Care.

Street. E. & Sibert, J. (1998). Post-traumatic stress reactions in children. *Clinical Child Psychology and Psychiatry,* 3, 553-560.

Stroebe, M. & Schut, H. (1998). Culture and grief. *Bereavement Care,* 17(1), 7-11.

Stroebe, M. & Schut, H. (1999). The dual process model of coping with bereavement: Rationale and description. *Death Studies,* 23, 197-224.

Stroebe, M. & Schut, H. (2005). To continue or relinquish bonds: A review of consequences for the bereaved. *Death Studies,* 29, 477-494.

Stroebe, M.S. (2001). Gender differences in adjustment to bereavement: An empirical and theoretical review. *Review of General Psychology,* 5(1), 62-83.

Stroebe, M.S., Gergen, M., Gergen, K., & Stroebe, W. (1992). Broken hearts or broken bonds: Love and death in historical perspective. *American Psychologist,* 47, 1205-1212.

Stroebe, M.S., Hansson, R.O., Stroebe, W. & Schut, H. (2001) (Eds.). *Handbook of bereavement research: Consequences, coping, and care.* Washington, DC: American Psychological Association.

Stroebe, M.S. & Stroebe, W. (1993). The mortality of bereavement: A review. In M. S. Stroebe, W. Stroebe, & R.O. Hansson (Eds.). *Handbook of bereavement: Theory, research, and intervention* (pp. 175-195). Cambridge, UK: Cambridge University Press.

Stroebe, W. & Schut, H. (2001). Risk factors in bereavement outcome: A methodological and empirical review. In M. Stroebe, R.O. Hansson, W. Stroebe, and H. Schut (Eds.) *Handbook of bereavement research.* (pp. 349-372). Washington, DC: American Psychological Association Press.

Stroebe, W., & Stroebe, M. (1993). Is grief universal? Cultural variations in the emotional reaction to loss. In R. Fulton & R. Bendiksen (Eds.). *Death and identity* (3rd Ed.) (pp. 177-209). Philadelphia: Charles Press.

Stroebe, W., Stroebe, M.S., & Abakoumkin, G. (1999). Does differential social support cause sex differences in bereavement outcome? *Journal of Community & Applied Social Psychology*, 9, 1-12.

Stroebe, W., Stroebe, M.S., Abakoumkin, G., & Schut, H. (1996). The role of loneliness and social support in adjustment to loss: A test of attachment versus stress theory. *Journal of Personality and Social Psychology*, 70, 1241-1249.

Stroebe, W., Zech, E., Stroebe, M.S., & Abakoumkin, G. (2005). Does social support help in bereavement? *Journal of Social & Clinical Psychology*, 24, 1030-1050.

Stubbs, D. (2005). Shrinking the space between people. In B. Monroe & F. Kraus. *Brief Interventions with Bereaved Children* (pp. 97-112). New York: Oxford University Press.

Suárez-Orozco, M.M. & Robben, Antonius, C.M.G. (2000). The management of collective trauma. In C. Antonius & M. Suárez-Orozco (Eds.), *Culture under siege: collective violence and trauma.* Cambridge, UK: Cambridge University Press.

Sudnow, D. (1967). *Passing on: The social organization of dying.* Englewood Cliffs, NJ: Prentice-Hall.

Sullivan, H.S. (1956). In H. Perry, M. Gawell, & M. Gibben (Editors), *The collected works of Harry Stack Sullivan.* New York: W. W. Norton.

Sunder, M. (2001). Cultural dissent. *Stanford law review*, 54, 495-567.

The SUPPORT Principal Investigators (1995). A controlled trial to improve care for seriously ill hospitalized patients. The Study to Understand Prognoses and Preferences for Outcomes and Risks of Treatments (SUPPORT). *Journal of the American Medical Association*, 274, 1591-1598.

Swanson, K.M. (1999). Effects of caring, measurement, and time on miscarriage impact and women's well-being. *Nursing Research*, 48, 288-298.

Sweasey, P. (1997) *From queer to eternity: Spirituality in the lives of lesbian, gay & bisexual people.* London & Washington: Cassell.

Tanner, J.G. (1995). Death, dying, and grief in the Chinese-American culture. In J. K. Parry & A.S. Ryan (Eds.) *A cross-cultural look at death, dying, and religion* (pp. 183-192). Chicago: Nelson-Hall.

Tatar, M. (Editor) (2002). *The annotated classic fairy tales.* New York: W.W. Norton.

Taylor, P.B. (1998). Setting your boundaries. *Nursing*, 28, 56-67.

Tedeschi, R.G., & Calhoun, L.G. (2006). Time of change? The spiritual challenges of bereavement and loss. *Omega: The Journal of Death and Dying*, 53, 105-116

Tein, J-Y., Sandler, I.N., Ayers, T.S., & Wolchik, S.A. (2006). Mediation of the effects of the Family Bereavement Program on mental health problems of bereaved children and adolescents. *Prevention Science*, 7, 179-195.

Tellis-Nayak, V. (1982). The transcendent standard: The religious ethos of the rural elderly. *Gerontologist*, 22, 359-363.

Templer, D.I. (1970). The construction and validation of a death anxiety scale. *Journal of General Psychology*, 82, 165-177.

Terr, L. (2003). *Lessons learned from 9/11 and Columbine.* Invited address at the New York Association for Play Therapy Annual Conference, June, 1st, 2003, Melville, Long Island.

Thomas, N. (2001). The importance of culture throughout all of life and beyond. *Holistic Nursing Practice*, 15(2), 40-46.

Thomas, W.I., & Thomas, D.S. (1928). *The child in America*. New York: Johnson Reprint.

Toedter, L.J., Lasker, J.N., & Alhadeff, J.M. (1988). The perinatal grief scale: Development and initial validation. *American Journal of Orthopsychiatry*, 58, 435-449.

Tomer, A. & Eliason, G. (1996). Toward a comprehensive model of death anxiety. *Death Studies*, 20, 343-366.

Tong, K.L., & Spicer, B.J. (1994). The Chinese palliative patient and family in North America: A cultural perspective. *Journal of Palliative Care*, 10(1), 26-28.

Townsend, M., Kladder, V. & Mulligan, T. (2002). Systematic review of clinical trials examining the effects of religion on health. *Southern Medical Journal*, 95, 1429-1434.

Transaction Council of the National Kidney Foundation (1999-2000). Transplantrecipients' bill of rights and responsibilities. Retrieved November 20, 2006 from http://www.kidney.org/atoz/pdf/txBillofRights.pdf.

Traylor, E.S., Hayslip, B., Kaminski, P.L., & York, C. (2003). Relationship between grief and family system characteristics: A cross lagged longitudinal analysis. *Death Studies*, 27(7), 575-601.

True, G., Phipps, E.J., Braitman, L.E., Harralson, T., Harris, D., & Tester, W. (2005). Treatment preferences and advance care planning at end of life: The role of ethnicity and spiritual coping in cancer patients. *Annals of behavioral medicine: a publication of the Society of Behavioral Medicine*, 30, 174-179.

Tschann, J., Kaufmann, S., & Micco, G. (2003). Family involvement in end-of-life hospital care. *Journal of the American Geriatrics Society*, 51, 835-840.

Tulsky, J.A. (2005). Interventions to enhance communication among patients, providers, and families. *Journal of Palliative Medicine*, 8(S1), S95-S102.

Turner, L. (2005). From the local to the global: Bioethics and the concept of culture. *Journal of Medicine and Philosophy*, 30, 305-320.

Twycross, R.G. (1976). Long-term use of diamorphine in advanced cancer. In J.J. Bonica & D. Albe-Fessard (Eds.) *Advances in pain research and therapy* (Vol. 1, pp. 653-661). New York: Raven Press.

Umberson, D., Wortman, C.B., & Kessler, R.C. (1992). Widowhood and depression: Explaining long-term gender differences in vulnerability. *Journal of Health and Social Behavior*, 33, 10-24.

United States Department of Justice, Bureau of Justice Statistics. (2003). *Census of State and Federal Correctional Facilities, 2000*. Washington DC: Bulletin NCJ 198272.

Unruh, A., Versnel, J., and Kerr, N. (2002). Spirituality Unplugged: A review of commonalities and contentions, and a resolution. *Canadian Journal of Occupational Therapy*, Feb., 5-19.

Utz, R.L. (2006). Economic and practical adjustments to late life spousal loss. In D. Carr, R.M. Nesse, & C.B. Wortman (Eds.) *Spousal bereavement in late life* (pp. 167-192). New York: Springer Publishing Co.

Vachon, M.L.S. (1987). *Occupational stress in the care of the critically ill, the dying, and the bereaved*. Washington: Hemisphere Publishing Corporation.

Vachon, M.L.S. (2004). The stress of professional caregivers. In D. Doyle, G. Hanks, N. Cherny & K. Calman (Eds.). *Oxford Textbook of Palliative Care, 3rd edition* (pp. 992-1004). New York: Oxford University Press.

Vaillant, G.E. (1985). Loss as a metaphor for attachment. *American Journal of Psychoanalysis*, 45, 59-67.

Valent, P. (1998). *From survival to fulfillment*. Philadelphia, PA: Brunner/Mazel.

Valsiner, J. (2000). *Culture and human development*. Thousand Oaks, CA: Sage Publications.

van Baarsen, B. & van Groenou, M.I. (2001). Partner loss in later life: Gender differences in coping shortly after bereavement. *Journal of Loss & Trauma*, 6, 243-262.

Vance, J.C., Najman, J.M., Thearle, M.J., Embelton, G., Foster, W.J., & Boyle, F.M. (1995). Psychological changes in parents eight months after the loss of an infant from stillbirth, neonatal death, or sudden infant death syndrome—a longitudinal study. *Pediatrics*, 96(5 Pt 1), 933-8.

van der Kolk, Bessel (1987). *Psychological trauma*. Washington, DC: American Psychiatric Press.

van der Kolk, B. (2003). *The frontier of trauma treatment*. Invited address at the Psychotherapy Networker Symposium, March 22, 2003. Washington, DC.

Vanderwerker, L.C. & Prigerson, H.G. (2004). Social support and technological connectedness as protective factors in bereavement. *Journal of Loss & Trauma*, 9, 45-57.

Van Gennep, A. (1960). *Rites of passage*. (M . Vizedom & G. Caffee, Trans.). Chicago: University of Chicago Press.

Vernon, G.M. (1970). *Sociology of death: An analysis of death-related behavior*. New York: Ronald Press.

Vess, J.S., Moreland, J.R., & Schwebel, A.I. (1985). A follow-up study of role functioning and the psychological environment of families of cancer patients. *Journal of Psychosocial Oncology*, 3(2), 1-14.

Voigt, A. & Drury, N. (1998) *Wisdom from the earth: The living legacy of the Aboriginal dreamtime*. Boston: Shambbala.

Wachter, R. & Lo, B. (1993). Advance directives for patients with human immunodeficiency virus infection. *Critical Care Clinics*, 9, 125-136.

Waechter E.H. (1971). Children's awareness of fatal illness. *American Journal of Nursing* 71, 1168-1172.

Wagner, B., Knaevelsrud, C., & Maercker, A. (2006). Internet-based cognitive-behavioral therapy for complicated grief: A randomized controlled trial. *Death Studies*, 30, 429-453.

Waldman, D.A., & Davidshofer, D.A. (1983). Death anxiety reduction as the result of exposure to a death and dying symposium. *Omega, The Journal of Death and Dying*, 14(4), 323-328.

Waldrop, D.P., Tamburlin, J.A., Thompson, S., & Simon, M. (2004). Life and death decisions: Using school-based health education to facilitate family discussion about organ and tissue donation. *Death Studies*, 28, 643-657.

Walker, C. (1993). Sibling bereavement and grief responses. *Journal of Pediatric Nursing*, 8(5), 325-334.

Walker, G. & Maiden, R. (1987, April). Lifespan attitudes toward death. Paper presented at the Annual Meeting of the Eastern Psychological Association, Arlington, VA.

Walker, Phillip L. (2001). A bioarchaeological perspective on the history of violence. *Annual Review of Anthropology*, 30, 573-596.

Walsh, F. & McGoldrick, M. (2004). *Living beyond loss: Death in the family* (2nd Ed.). New York: Norton.

Walter, T. (1999). *On bereavement: The culture of grief.* Philadelphia: Open University Press.

Walter, T. (1994). *The revival of death.* London: Routledge.

Warren, C. (1993, September). Disrupted death ceremonies: Popular culture and the ethnography of Bali. *Oceania,* 64, 36-56.

Wass, H. (1985). *Visions in death education.* Keynote address presented at the annual meeting of the Association for Death Education and Counseling, Philadelphia, PA.

Wass, H. (1995). Visions in death education. In L.A. DeSpelder and A.L. Strickland (Eds.). *The path ahead. Readings in death and dying* (pp. 327-334). Mountain View, CA: Mayfield Publishing.

Wass, H. (2003). Death education for children. In I. B. Corless, B. B. Germino, and M. A. Pittman (Eds.). *Dying, death, and bereavement: A challenge for living* (2nd ed.) (pp. 25-41). New York: Springer.

Wass, H. (2004). A perspective on the current state of death education. *Death Studies,* 28(4), 289-308.

Way, P. & Bremner, I. (2005). Therapeutic interventions. In B. Monroe & F. Kraus, *Brief Interventions with Bereaved Children* (pp. 65-80). New York: Oxford University Press.

Webb, N.B. (2002). *Helping bereaved children: A handbook for practitioners (2nd Ed.).* New York: Guilford Press.

Webb, N.B. (Editor) (2004). *Mass trauma and violence: Helping families and children cope.* New York: Guilford Press.

Weber, J.A., & Fournier, D.G. (1985). Family support and a child's adjustment to death. *Family Relations,* 34, 43-49.

Weisman, A. (1972). *On dying and denying. A psychiatric study of terminality.* New York: Behavioral Publications.

Weisman, A. (1980). Thanatology. In O. Kaplan (Ed.) *Comprehensive textbook of psychiatry.* Baltimore: Williams and Williams.

Weisman, A. & Hackett, T. (1962). *The dying patient: Special treatment situations.* Des Plaines, IL: Forest Hospital Publications.

Welsh, D. (1999). Caregiving for the caregiver: Strategies for avoiding "compassion fatigue." *Journal of Clinical Oncology,* 3, 183-184.

Werth, J. (2006). The implications of the Theresa Schiavo case for end-of-life care and decisions. *Death Studies,* 30(2), 99-100.

Werth, J.L., & Blevins, D. (2002). Public policy and end-of-life care. *American Behavioral Scientist,* 46(3), 401-417.

Werth, J.L., Blevins, D., Toussaint, K.L., & Durham, M.R. (2002). The influence of cultural diversity on end-of-life care and decisions. *The American Behavioral Scientist,* 46, 204-223.

Westbrook, L.A. (2002). *The experience of mid-life women in the years after the deaths of their parents.* Unpublished doctoral dissertation, Institute for Clinical Social Work.

Whetstine, L., Streat, S., Darwin, M., & Crippen, D. (2005). Pro/con ethics debate: When is dead really dead? *Critical Care Forum,* 9, 538-542.

White, J.M., & Klein, D.M. (2001). *Family theories* (2nd Ed.). Thousand Oaks, CA: Sage.

Wikan, U. (1988). Bereavement and loss in two Muslim communities: Egypt and Bali compared. *Social Science and Medicine*, 27, 451-460.

Wikipedia® (2006). entry updated January 10, 2006. Wikimedia Foundation, Inc.

Wikipedia Encyclopedia (2006). Organ transplant. Retrieved August 14, 2006, from http://en.wikipedia.org/wiki/Organ_transplant#demographics.

Wilcox, A.J., Weinberg, C.R., O'Connor, J.F., Baird, D.D., Schlatterer, J.P., Canfield, R.E., Armstrong, E.G., & Nisula, B.C. (1988). Incidence of early loss of pregnancy. *New England Journal of Medicine*, 319, 189-194.

Williams, M.B., Zinner, E.S., & Ellis, R.R. (1999). The connection between grief and trauma: An overview. In E.S. Zinner & M.B. Williams (Eds.). *When a Community weeps: Case studies in group survivorship* (pp. 3-17). Philadelphia: Brunner/Mazel.

Wilson, G.T. (2005). Behavior therapy. In R.J. Corsini & D. Wedding (Eds.). *Current psychotherapies* (pp. 202-237). Toronto, Ontario, Canada: Brooks/Cole.

Windling, T. (2001). On Tolkien and fairy-tales. In K. Haber (Ed.). *Meditations on Middle-Earth* (pp. 215-229). New York: St. Martin's.

Wing, D.G. Burge-Calkaway, K., Rose, P.C., & Armistead. L. (2001). Understanding gender differences in bereavement following the death of an infant: Implications for treatment. *Psychotherapy: Theory, Research, Practice, Training*, 38, 60-73.

Winn, W.D. (2002). Current trends in educational technology research: The study of learning environments. *Educational Psychology Review*, 14(3), 331-351.

Winston, C.A. (2006). African American grandmothers parenting AIDS orphans: Grieving and coping. *Qualitative Social Work: Research and Practice*, 5, 33-43.

Winzelberg, G.S., Hanson, L.C., & J.A. Tulsky. (2005). Beyond autonomy: Diversifying end-of-life decision making approaches to serve patients and families. *Ethics, Public Policy, and Medical Economics*, 53, 1046-1050.

Wolfelt, A.D. (2002). *Resource for mourners*. Fort Collins, CO: The Center for Loss and Life Transition.

Wolfson, J. (May-June, 2005). Erring on the side of Theresa Schiavo: reflections of the special guardian *ad litem*. *Hastings Center Report*, 35, 16-19.

Wong, P.T.P. (2003, April 1). Death education flourishes in Taiwan. *Science and Theology News* (online edition). Article retrieved June 9, 2006 from http://www.stnews.org/rlr-1328.htm.

Worden, J.W. (1982, 1991, 2002). *Grief counseling and grief therapy: A handbook for the mental health practitioner* (Eds. 1, 2, 3). New York: Springer Publishing Co.

Worden, J.W. (1996). *Children and grief: When a parent dies*. New York: Guilford Press.

Worden, J.W., & Silverman, P. (1996). Parental death and the adjustment of school-age children. *Omega, The Journal of Death and Dying*, 33, 91-102.

World Health Organization (2006). Cancer Fact Sheet No. 297. Retrieved January 14, 2007, from the World Health Organization Web site: http://www.who.int/mediacentre/factsheets/fs297/en/index.html

Wright, M., Wood, J., Lynch, T., & Clark, D. for the International Observatory on End of-Life Care (2006). Mapping levels of palliative care development: A global view. Retrieved January 13, 2007, from the National Hospice and Palliative Care Web site: http://www.nhpco.org/files/public/palliativecare/World_map_report_final-0107.pdf

Yalom, I.D. (1980). *Existential psychotherapy.* New York: Basic Books.

Yampolskaya, S. & Winston, N. (2003). Hospice care in prison: general principles and outcomes. *American Journal of Hospice & Palliative Care,* 20, 290-296.

Yeo, G. (1995). Ethical considerations in Asian and Pacific Island elders. *Clinics in Geriatric Medicine,* 11, 139-151.

Yomiuri, S. (1998). Teaching about death to learn about life. *The Daily Yomiuri,* p. 16. Retrieved online [LexisNexis Academic] on June 26, 2006.

Young, Allan (1995). *The harmony of illusions: inventing post-traumatic stress disorder.* Princeton: Princeton University Press.

Young, E. (1989). (Trans.). *Lon Po Po: A Red-Riding Hood story from China.* New York: Philomel.

Young, E.W.D. & Jex, S.A. (1992). The Patient Self-Determination Act: Potential ethical quandaries and benefits. *Cambridge Quarterly of Healthcare Ethics,* 2, 107-115.

Young, M. & Erickson C. (1989). Cultural impediments to recovery: PTSD in contemporary America. *Journal of Traumatic Stress,* 14, 431-443.

Young, M. (1997) Victim rights and services: A modern saga. In R.C. Davis, W.G. Skogan, & A.J. Lurigio (Eds.), *Victims of crime: second edition.* (pp. 194-210). Thousand Oaks, CA: Sage Publications.

Zalaznik, P. (1979). *Dimensions of loss and death education.* Minneapolis: Ed-Pac Publishing.

Zerzan, J., Stearns, S., & Hanson, L. (2000). Access to palliative care and hospice in nursing homes. *JAMA* 284(19), 2489-2494.

Zhang, B., Maciejewski, P.K., Block, S.D., Vanderwerker, L.C., & Prigerson, H. (2007). An empirical examination of the stage theory of grief resolution. *Journal of Palliative Medicine, in press.*

Zisook, S., Schuchter, S.R., Sledge, P., & Mulvihill, M. (1993). Aging and bereavement. *Journal of Geriatric Psychiatry and Neurology,* 6, 137-143.

Zinner, E.S. (1992). Setting standards: Certification efforts and considerations in the field of death and dying. *Death Studies,* 16(1), 67-77.

Zucker, A. (1980). Terminal and safe. *Journal of Health Politics, Policy and Law,* 6(1), 6-9.

Native American spirituality 267
religious and spiritual perspectives 205
religious and spiritual practices and beliefs 205
spiritual concerns 12
spiritual crisis 203
spiritual needs 11, 12
spiritual neglect and abuse 68
spiritual quadrant 265
spiritual tasks 29, 206
transcendent meaning 11
Suicide 61, 271, 272, 279
assisted suicide (see also Euthanasia) 75
contributing factors to suicide 279
distressing life circumstances 279
level of economic development 279
impact of suicide on survivors 280, 287
physician assisted suicide
(see also Euthanasia) 46, 87, 108, 109
suicide, gender, and age 279
suicide rates by age 279
suicide and 15-24 year olds 279
suicide and age differences 280
suicide and young children 280
theories of suicide 280
Support 147
bereavement support (see also Assessment and Intervention) 231
Bramley Story Series 231
caregivers, bereaved children and adolescents 147
consistent parenting (see also Bereavement) 147, 166
crisis support teams 231
Critical Incident Stress Debriefing 221
Dougy Center 222
parenting following bereavement
(see also Bereavement) 156
schools 241, 242
self-help groups 231
social support 161, 216
spiritual support 211
support group model 222
support systems 167, 168
trauma support services 287
Trauma
annihilation anxiety 269
attachment theory 133, 270, 283
behavioral theory 271
cognitive/behavioral theory 271
collective trauma 258
continuous stress syndrome 296
crisis response 373
cultural protection against trauma 261
definition of traumatization 255
disasters 235

disaster planning and intervention 289
disaster workers/rescue workers 289
compassion fatigue (see also Professional Caregiver Issues) 290, 383, 384
hyperarousal 289
intrusion 289
secondary trauma 290
disruption of memory in trauma 255
disruption of the temporal continuity of experience 256
disruption of self 255
distant trauma 286
ethical intervention issues 295
executive functioning 286
existentialism 272
family strategies for coping with trauma
(see also Coping) 285
family systems approach 283
relational framework 284
relational questions 284
homicide 271, 278
homicide and age differences 278
homicide and gender 278
incidence of homicide 278
perpetrators of homicide 278
victims of homicide
infants as homicide victims 278
impact on the family system 283
impact of trauma on survivors 280, 284
impact of traumatic death on survivors 280
kinds of forgetting 257
major disasters 234
mass violence 288
modernity/postmodernity 256
sociocultural reaction of modernity 258
mortality statistics and traumatic death 151, 162, 277
natural disaster 287
negative religious outcomes
(see also Religion) 263
personal experience of death 277
perspective of the culture 298
plastopatholic 255
positive religious outcomes (see also Religion) 263
post-traumatic stress disorder (PTSD) 217, 232, 255, 259, 260, 284, 288, 292, 293
complex post-traumatic stress disorder 294
disorders of extreme stress not otherwise specified 294
PTSD diagnoses errors 294
pre-modern post-traumatic sociocultural practices 259
psychodynamic theory 269
psychological debriefing 373
public tragedy 373

License Plate Q vs. Q

http://www.adec.org/source/onlineexam/welcome

P. 330 — why to teach this topic.
331   "
332

334 Schools w/ DYD programs

P340

p.343